The Structure
and Design of
Programming
Languages

The Structure and Design of Programming Languages

JOHN E. NICHOLLS
IBM (UK) Laboratories Ltd.

 ADDISON-WESLEY PUBLISHING COMPANY
Reading, Massachusetts • Menlo Park, California
London • Amsterdam • Don Mills, Ontario • Sydney

ISBN 0-201-14454-9
FGHIJKLMNO-HA-89876543210

To Sheila

THE SYSTEMS PROGRAMMING SERIES

*The Program Development Process
Part I—The Individual Programmer   Joel D. Aron

The Program Development Process
Part II—The Programming Team   Joel D. Aron

*The Design and Structure of
Programming Languages   John E. Nicholls

Mathematical Background of
Programming   Frank Beckman

Structured Programming   Harlan D. Mills
Richard C. Linger

*An Introduction to Database Systems   C. J. Date

Compiler Engineering   Patricia Goldberg

Interactive Computer Graphics   Andries Van Dam

Sorting and Sort Systems   Harold Lorin

Compiler Design Theory   Philip M. Lewis
Daniel J. Rosenkrantz
Richard E. Stearns

Recursive Programming Techniques   William Burge

Compilers and Programming
Languages   J. T. Schwartz
John Cocke

*Published

IBM EDITORIAL BOARD

Joel D. Aron, Chairman
Edgar F. Codd
Robert H. Glaser*
Charles L. Gold
James Griesmer*
Paul S. Herwitz

James P. Morrissey
Ascher Opler*
George Radin
David Sayre
Norman A. Stanton (Addison-Wesley)
Heinz Zemanek

*Past Chairman

Foreword

The field of systems programming primarily grew out of the efforts of many programmers and managers whose creative energy went into producing practical, utilitarian systems programs needed by the rapidly growing computer industry. Programming was practiced as an art where each programmer invented his own solutions to problems with little guidance beyond that provided by his immediate associates. In 1968, the late Ascher Opler, then at IBM, recognized that it was necessary to bring programming knowledge together in a form that would be accessible to all systems programmers. Surveying the state of the art, he decided that enough useful material existed to justify a significant codification effort. On his recommendation, IBM decided to sponsor The Systems Programming Series as a long term project to collect, organize, and publish those principles and techniques that would have lasting value throughout the industry.

The Series consists of an open-ended collection of text-reference books. The contents of each book represent the individual author's view of the subject area and do not necessarily reflect the views of the IBM Corporation. Each is organized for course use but is detailed enough for reference. Further, the Series is organized in three levels: broad introductory material in the foundation volumes, more specialized material in the software volumes, and very specialized theory in the computer science volumes. As such, the Series meets the needs of the novice, the experienced programmer, and the computer scientist.

Taken together, the Series is a record of the state of the art in systems programming that can form the technological base for the systems programming discipline.

The Editorial Board

Preface

This book is concerned with the design of programming languages, or to be more precise, the design of high-level procedural programming languages. In spite of its title, it is not primarily intended as a manual for language designers, but rather for applications and systems programmers who use high-level languages in their day-to-day work. The programming languages now in widespread use contain many common facilities, although these are made available to the user in a variety of different ways. The approach taken in the book is to present, in turn, those features that form an essential part of any high-level language—such as: scalar and aggregate variables, arithmetic and logical expressions, and iteration elements. For each of these, a summary of underlying requirements is stated, followed by a description of how the feature is represented in various high-level languages.

This comparative view is valuable in placing languages in their context, so that decisions made by language designers are not seen in isolation. Such a view can help give a wider perspective to those who move between different languages in their work or who have to select a language for a particular purpose. It should also give insight into some of the principles of language design which apply equally to the design of application programs. For example, the designer of an application program may be concerned with binding, scope of names, complex data structures, and functional application; all of these are problems which have been addressed in the design of programming languages.

In writing the book, I am of course indebted to the work of previous writers on languages, compilers, and related topics; these works are ac-

knowledged in the bibliographies that follow each chapter. Other ideas have
come from the many people with whom I have worked on various aspects
of language design, especially those acknowledged below. My own experience of language design has been for the most part with the PL/I language,
though I have tried not to let an undue bias towards PL/I appear in the
book. Its prominence in the text is at least partly explained by the fact that
it is a language with many facilities, touching on most of the topics presented in the book.

My first acknowledgement is to my colleagues on the design and
development of PL/I: especially to George Radin, Paul Rogoway, Jim
Cox, and Ray Larner of the original PL/I project, and to David Beech,
Roger Rowe, and David Allen of the PL/I language department in Hursley.
During development of PL/I, and particularly in the establishment of a
formal definition, we had many stimulating discussions with members of
the IBM Vienna Laboratory, especially with Peter Lucas, Kurt Walk, Kurt
Bandat, and Hans Bekic. I should also like to acknowledge discussions on
language matters with members of the Computer Science department of
IBM Yorktown Heights, notably Bill Burge, Patricia Goldberg, Richard
Goldberg, Martin Hopkins, Burt Leavenworth, and David Lomet.

I have had useful discussions on the nature of current "scientific" and
"commercial" programming with Professor Roger Hockney of the University of Reading and Mr. Ewart Willey of the Prudential Assurance
Company respectively and am grateful for the insights gained from these
discussions.

As the book was being written I received much encouragement from
the Editorial Board of the series. I am particularly grateful to Joel Aron for
many suggestions which have materially improved the form and content of
the book. My thanks are due to David Sayre and Paul Herwitz for help
and encouragement.

I have also received comments and suggestions on parts of the book
from Professor Brian Randell of the University of Newcastle and Mr. Mike
Woodger of the National Physical Laboratory. Sections of the book were
reviewed by a number of people in the IBM language departments in
Time/Life and Palo Alto. These reviewers helped on many aspects of the
book, especially those connected with FORTRAN and COBOL. For their
aid, I am grateful to the following: J. Ascoly, Maurice Ackroyd, J. Cherny,
Bob Friedman, J. H. Green, Bill Heising, Arno Krakauer, Lucille Lee, Matt
Schein, Ron Sherman, and Phil Shaw.

An early draft of the book was read by a number of students then
undergoing training at Hursley and I received helpful comments from Sally
Owens, Pat Speers and Guy Wilson. I am also grateful for careful reviews

and many helpful suggestions from Ian Brackenbury and Charles Wilson, both of the Hursley Laboratories.

The original manuscript of the book was prepared on the ATS system and my thanks are due to Anne Sansome, Margaret Whittaker, and Rosemary Cowan for their work in typing and editing the manuscript.

Winchester, England   J.E.N.
March 1975

Contents

PART 2
ELEMENTS OF PROCEDURAL PROGRAMMING LANGUAGES

CHAPTER 6
PROGRAM STRUCTURE AND REPRESENTATION

CHAPTER 7
DATA ELEMENTS, VARIABLES, AND DECLARATIONS

CHAPTER 8
DATA STRUCTURES

CHAPTER 9
EXPRESSIONS AND ASSIGNMENT

CHAPTER 10
SEQUENCING AND CONTROL STRUCTURES

CHAPTER 11
BASIC INPUT-OUTPUT

CHAPTER 12
SUBROUTINES, PROCEDURES, AND PROGRAMS

Part 1

Introduction: Background and Technical Foundations

1
Introduction

Everyone making direct use of a computer employs some form of computer language, and language study is therefore essential for an understanding of computer systems. There are a great number of different kinds of computer languages, ranging in scope from the simplest operator commands to complete systems for special applications. In spite of this diversity, all computer languages share a number of similar concepts.

This book is concerned with a special class of languages—the high-level procedural programming languages which have dominated the field of computer languages in the past decade. These are now the main working tools of a majority of programmers and sustained growth in their use is leading to the gradual disappearance of the "engineering view" of computers embodied in machine languages. The machine-language user's view of a computer, composed of registers, binary words, numerical addresses, etc., is being replaced by higher-level concepts of variables, blocks, iterative elements, files, etc. As programmers increase their use of high-level languages, it is as if hardware machines are replaced by FORTRAN, COBOL, or PL/I "machines," with properties quite different from the hardware on which the programs will run. One of the objectives of this book is to clarify the high-level view of computer systems, the view as seen by a high-level language user.

Each programming language has two important parts. First, there is a set of rules which enable us to say whether or not a given text is well formed, that is, whether it can be considered a valid program. The other is a set of interpretation rules, which relate the execution of a program to the behavior of a computing machine. These, known as syntax and semantics,

1

completely specify a programming language. Its implementation is quite another aspect, and many different implementations of the same language are possible.

To begin, let us consider some of the properties by which high-level languages differ from machine or assembler languages. The following list includes some of the most important properties possessed by such high-level languages.

1. They do not require the user to be aware of such specific machine features as registers, internal representation of data, I/O channels, etc.

2. They offer the possibility of transferring programs from one machine to another. That is, they provide a degree of independence from a particular machine or system.

3. They allow programs to be written more concisely than is possible in machine language.

4. They allow programs to be written in problem-oriented terms. Examples include the ability to give symbolic names to data and the inclusion of mathematical operators and expressions in programming languages.

The development of languages with such properties is one of the most interesting topics in computer history. The impetus for such development has been partly economic, but has also been supported by technical, theoretical, and aesthetic forces. Computers could not have been accepted as widely as they have been, if the tools for programming them had not radically changed from the simple tools available in the form of early machine languages. These languages were concerned with the most minute details of registers and machine instructions. However, more advanced languages could not be developed until means for translating them had become available. The development of programming languages has been in step with a surge of interest in linguistics and the formal structure of languages, including natural languages. The development of practicable compilers has relied on advances in programming techniques, including the facility for constructing and manipulating complex data structures.

The aim of this book is to illustrate the main principles of language design, using existing languages as models. Illustrations are mostly taken from FORTRAN, ALGOL 60,† COBOL, and PL/I, which provide a field of study with sufficient breadth to illustrate most of the critical issues in

---

† Throughout the book, and following the usual custom, "ALGOL" refers to ALGOL 60. The newer and different language is always referred to as ALGOL 68.

language design. Several special-purpose languages are also discussed, especially those which have suggested or inspired advances in language design—examples include LISP, SNOBOL, POP-2, and APL.

The book thus emphasizes current languages rather than the many new languages that continue to be developed. One reason for this is that these are the languages most users of the book are likely to encounter in their work. Although they might well prefer to use more recently developed languages, most systems and applications programmers will encounter, and may well have to use exclusively, the standard languages discussed here. As it turns out, the study of these languages allows many of the essential principles of language design to be explored. By approaching the important concepts in language design from the point of view of the major, standard languages, it is easier to appreciate where advances have been made in more recent proposals.

Many people feel that the continued support and teaching of the programming languages developed so early in computing history may have a damaging effect on the thinking and programming habits of programmers. Whorf's widely-quoted view (Whorf, 1941) that a language may limit its users' powers of thought is a compelling one and must concern those who are responsible for introducing new programmers to their first programming language. At some stage, however, in order to get work done on a computer, most programmers must come to grips with one or more of the established languages. (There is a parallel with other fields; for example, most western musicians find it useful to master the established system of musical notation, in spite of its obvious imperfections.)

The book is informal in nature and does not deal with the formal or mathematical structure of language, although a summary of work in this area is given in Chapter 5. So far, the formal theory of language has mostly influenced the design of language syntax; much less is known of the semantic principles on which programming-language design might be based. Most languages, including recent ones, have therefore been developed by largely informal and pragmatic methods.

The book is not intended for language designers, who need a more complete and rigorous treatment than is given here, but for users and implementors of languages. For such, it is hoped that by better understanding the objectives and choices available to language designers, they will better understand the languages themselves.

In developing large programs, the ideas that are discussed in this book —the properties of data elements and structures, the techniques for constructing and linking program modules, the design of iteration elements, the treatment of input-output—are all relevant, and raise similar problems to those that arise in the design of languages. Indeed, the design of a large programming system of any kind has much in common with language design.

The importance of programming languages as a means of communication has led to considerable efforts to develop *standard* languages. This tends to emphasize the stability and permanence of language design. However, most languages in widespread use have shown considerable change. It therefore seems appropriate to regard languages not as fixed entities but as organic systems and to consider the factors which tend to influence their growth and change.

A fascinating discussion of system growth is given in the book, *On Growth and Form* by the 19th century biologist and mathematician D'Arcy Thompson. This book is one of the foundation texts for "systems science." Thompson applied mathematics to the study of the growth of living organisms. Some of his most graphic illustrations came from a study of the shape of fishes and crustaceans in various parts of the world and under different living conditions. He showed that these shapes and sizes were determined by the conditions in which the organisms found themselves and that their current shapes represented a "diagram of forces" similar to that of elementary mechanics.

Suppose we apply this hypothesis to the growth of programming languages and ask: What are the forces that have acted on our current programming languages? In other words what is the diagram of forces acting on a programming language? A suggested answer is that these forces come from three directions:

- applications,
- users,
- implementation techniques.

Each of these exerts its own influence on language design, creating a state of tension from which the design for a language emerges. For example, with current techniques, "ease of use," a quality sought by many users, can often only be obtained by sacrificing computing speed. However, for certain applications, the resulting efficiency loss may be intolerable. The act of design consists of reconciling these opposites. This theme is developed in the first part of the book, in which the different influences are examined.

The comparative study of language design provides a base for the study of many fundamental topics in programming. A list of the most important inventions in programming might include:

symbolic references,

variables,

arrays and techniques of subscript access,

list processing,

subroutines,

iterative control structures.

These all find their place in high-level languages, and the ways in which they have been included in languages provide valuable insight into their properties.

In spite of many superficial differences, certain basic principles are common to many languages. There are many small differences: some almost accidental and arising from a lack of uniform concepts; others more basic and stemming from profound differences in design. During the late 1950's, the variety of languages being developed led several people to attempt (in the UNCOL project) a unification in language design, to be expressed in the form of a common processor of many programming languages. The approach in this book essentially favors the UNCOL spirit, in which it is assumed there is an underlying set of concepts in language design; that languages are more alike than they are different; and that, by study and experimentation, a set of unified design principles for language can be agreed upon which can form the basis both of improved understanding of languages and systems, and better implementation techniques.

The need for unity in language design has not noticeably lessened since UNCOL was proposed. The failure of earlier efforts to unify language design and implementation need not deter us. We now have available a far greater knowledge of language topics resulting from studies of such topics as data and storage structures, control structures, formal models of syntax and semantics, empirical studies of language use, etc.

The Tower of Babel, often used as a paradigm of programming languages, suggests an unduly pessimistic outlook for the future. An alternative is the Rosetta Stone, the tablet on which the same information was inscribed in three different languages, enabling scholars to decipher a language which would otherwise have been lost. The comparative study of languages can lead to unity where there is apparent diversity and help users and language designers to understand and appreciate the lasting merits of the languages available to them.

To conclude this introduction, I should mention some of the sources of information for the study of programming languages.

There are possibly more papers and books on programming languages than on any other subject in computing and I have looked on the provision of a bibliography as an important part of this book. For each chapter, I have collected a representative selection of references, for many of which short notes have been included. Sometimes these papers are directly referenced in the text; in other cases I hope they will suggest to the reader further ideas related to the main theme of the chapter.

Except in one or two cases, I have not referenced complete language specifications in the individual chapters; instead, an appendix provides references to specifications and an outline of the structure of the major languages discussed.

As will be apparent, the main sources of papers are the published journals of the Association of Computing Machinery—namely the Communications (referenced as *CACM*), the Journal (referenced as *JACM*), and *Computing Surveys;* and the journals of the British Computer Society—the *Computer Journal* and the *Computer Bulletin.* Another journal, also published by the ACM, which is of interest to all concerned with language design and structure is *SIGPLAN Notices,* the journal of the Special Interest Group on Programming Languages. In addition to general papers and symposium reports, this group publishes certain individual language bulletins, such as the ALGOL Bulletin, the SNOBOL Bulletin, and the APL Quote-Quad, which are often of considerable general interest. The ALGOL Bulletin in particular has for many years been a source of extremely interesting papers on language design.

BIBLIOGRAPHY

Bemer, R. W., "A checklist of intelligence for programming systems," *CACM,* Vol. 2, No. 3, Mar. 1959, pp. 8–13.

An early paper which retains much of its topicality, since even some of the latest systems do not meet some of the objectives in Bemer's list.

Chao, Y. R. *Language and Symbolic Systems,* Cambridge, England: Cambridge University Press, 1968.

An excellent introduction to linguistics which also considers the "wider" view of language as including symbolic systems. The final chapter includes a list of ten "requirements for good symbols," which could well be studied by language designers.

Cheatham, T. E., Jr., "The recent evolution of programming languages," *Proceedings IFIP Congress,* 1971, Amsterdam: North Holland, 1972.

The author advocates the "cleansing" of current programming languages—the removal of *ad hoc* properties and the inclusion of powerful general facilities known to be useful. Among the proposed additions are facilities to allow users to extend programming languages, a field in which Cheatham has made important contributions.

Cherry, C., *On Human Communication,* Cambridge, Mass.: MIT Press, 1957.

A wide-ranging study of the entire field of human communication written by an eminent engineer with a rare breadth of scholarship and vision.

Higman, B., *A Comparative Study of Programming Languages,* London: Macdonald and New York: American Elsevier, 1967.

This was one of the first books to compare and evaluate a number of programming languages. The earlier and more general chapters are interesting and well worth reading. In the later part of the book, however, where specific languages are discussed in detail, the author allows a number of personal prejudices to affect the style of presentation.

Ledgard, H. F., "Ten mini-languages: a study of topical issues in programming languages," *Computing Surveys*, Vol. 3, No. 3, Sept. 1971, pp. 115–146.

A mini-language is one which embodies a single language feature and can be studied within a simple framework. The paper discusses block structure, assignment, flow of control, type checking, parameter passing, string handling, and similar topics and provides a valuable introduction to the comparative study of programming languages.

Minnis, N. (ed), *Linguistics at Large*, London: Victor Gollancz, 1971.

This book contains fourteen lectures on linguistics presented at the Institute of Contemporary Arts in London in the winter of 1969. It provides a picture of the breadth of scope of modern linguistic studies.

Mock, O., J. Olsztyn, T. Steel, J. Strong, A. Tritter, J. Wegstein, "The problem of programming communication with changing machines: a proposed solution," Part I, *CACM*, Vol. 1, No. 8, Aug. 1958, pp. 12–18. Part II, *CACM*, Vol. 1, No. 9, Sept. 1958, pp. 9–15.

This is the famous UNCOL proposal which has remained topical in spirit, although the many attempts to implement it have so far all come to grief. One factor discussed, which was important in the 1950's and is not so critical now, is the variety of machine designs that were then growing up.

Sammet, J. E., *Programming Languages: History and Fundamentals*, Englewood Cliffs, N.J.: Prentice-Hall, 1969.

An invaluable book on the history and development of programming languages up to 1967. Languages are dealt with in groups—Numerical Scientific, Business Data Processing, String and List Processing, etc. Nearly a hundred languages are listed in the table of contents, and many more in the text and bibliography. For each of these, a history and list of important features is given. Only those languages designed in the United States or by international groups containing U.S. participants are discussed.

Thompson, D'Arcy W., *On Growth and Form*, Abridged edition edited by J. T. Bonner, Cambridge, England: Cambridge University Press, 1961.

Whorf, B., "The Relation of Habitual Thought and Behaviour to Language," reprinted in, P. Adams (ed.), *Language in Thinking*, Harmandsworth, England: Penguin Books, 1973.

Whorf is perhaps the best known exponent of the view that language determines our patterns of thought. This book, a collection of papers on the relationship of language and thought, contains both Whorf's point of view and other, contrary opinions.

2

User
Aspects

2.1 INTRODUCTION

In this chapter we discuss the three "forces" on language design outlined
in Chapter 1, considering first the effect of the user.

The languages used for programming are artificial creations, constructed
by humans for use by humans. However, the designer is not free to create
a language of any kind—if this were possible, natural language would be
considered by some to be an ideal. However, many in the field (the author
included) feel that natural language is not appropriate for *programming* and
that we should look more towards a stylized form of nonprocedural language. This is because the precision needed for communicating programs
is far greater than that needed for everyday communication. Natural languages, as normally used, are much too ambiguous for the exacting requirements of a computer. Whatever the merits of "natural" languages on the
one hand or "stylized" languages on the other, the current state of our skill
in language processing ultimately restricts our capabilities for natural expression of programs. However, there remain many ways in which languages
can come closer to meeting the wishes of their users for more easily understandable programs.

Considerable progress can be seen, if we compare today's languages
with those designed for early machines. In the early days of computing there
were so few machines that all programmers were to some extent systems
programmers. Since the system lacked even the simplest tools, they were
forced to help in constructing their own. Early users were tolerant of shortcomings in the design of languages and compilers and aware of the techni-

9

calities of systems programming. Today's users expect compilers and operating systems to be provided with the hardware. The users themselves, unlike the specialized and skilled programmers who made use of the first compilers, now come from a great diversity of backgrounds. Some are professional programmers with a vocational training in computer science or data processing, but there are many who have much less expertise in computing. Programming is now carried out by accountants, engineers, librarians, meteorologists, and school-children—the needs of this increasingly diverse population must be considered by the language designer.

Users can directly influence the design of languages by joining user groups or standards committees. PL/I exemplifies user influence on language design. Originally sponsored by a user group, this language has gained considerably from the continued participation of active users during its development.

2.2 OBJECTIVES FOR LANGUAGE DESIGN

A programming language is an interface between machines and users providing a new "machine" with properties more suited to the users' needs. Among the most important objectives in language design are the following:

2.2.1 Ease-of-Use

The expression of a problem is made easier if the mode of expression is familiar to the programmer. However mathematics, the most obvious source of suitable symbolism, has relatively little notation for expressing algorithmic processes and complex data structures which lie at the heart of computing problems. Secondly, "naturalness" is not a well-defined concept; what is natural to one user may be strange and bizarre to another. Current languages are primarily suited to English-speaking, mathematically sophisticated users. The effects of "natural" languages, such as Hebrew, Chinese, Urdu, etc., remain largely unexplored.

2.2.2 High-Level Design

An intuitive, if not easily measurable, concept is that of the *power* of a language—the amount of computing that can be done for a given size of program. For many, this *power* is the essence of high-level languages. It allows complex algorithms to be expressed in compact notation, simplifying their construction and checkout. Most importantly, use of such a high-level language transfers the need for concern about the details of a computation from the human to the machine.

2.2.3 Transferability

Transferability allows a program written in a high-level language to be run on two or more dissimilar computers. Current languages have not been particularly successful in achieving this objective. A survey of the difficulties and suggestions for remedies are included in the report on program transferability compiled for the Rome Air Development Center (Mealy, *et al.,* 1968). These include: greater control over the behavior of programmers, better models for the specification of programming languages, and the development of extensible languages.

2.2.4 Ease-of-Debugging

Some languages such as PL/I and recent versions of COBOL, incorporate special features to allow debugging in source-language terms. This is not the only way of simplifying debugging and other factors such as ease-of-use and high-level design also contribute to ease-of-debugging.

2.2.5 Ease-of-Documentation

A programming language should be successful in communicating to other users as well as to machines. Problems of maintenance and extension of systems, which consume so much of our resource today (Boehm, 1973), can be reduced by effective, accurate documentation. A programming language can have a considerable effect on documentation—ideally, the program itself with interspersed comments can serve as its own documentation.

While the above are characteristics of programming languages in general, some languages have more specialized objectives. For example, in the case of the major languages discussed in this book:

- FORTRAN emphasizes numerical computation and the evaluation of mathematical formulae. It also allows the user to add library routines for facilities not directly available in the language. (This facility was not in the very first FORTRAN system, but was included in the widely used FORTRAN II compiler.)

- ALGOL also emphasizes computational processes but unlike FORTRAN (originally designed for a particular machine) was developed from the start as a machine-independent language. The ALGOL specifications set a new standard in clarity of definition. The notation used for the syntax description in the ALGOL report (known as BNF) has been adopted for many other languages.

- COBOL was developed primarily for "business-type" applications, and for the expression of programs and results in natural (close to English language) terms. COBOL was developed by a committee representing users of several different types of machine. Ease of transfer from one machine to another was an important objective.

- PL/I combined a variety of facilities needed for scientific, commercial and other applications. It was designed to allow the user access to the full range of facilities of a modern machine (including its operating system).

2.3   USERS AND THEIR CHARACTERISTICS

It is only necessary to compare machine language with the simplest of programming languages to see that considerable progress has been made in making computers more accessible and natural to human users. In spite of this, programming languages have a long way to go before they provide as convenient and usable an interface to humans as other complex artifacts such as the telephone, the television, the motor car, or the camera.

To design attractive, easily used systems, it is not enough to construct efficient systems programs—one must also have a good grasp of human characteristics and limitations. A designer must assess the legibility, the ease of learning, the proneness to errors, and the complexity of various designs. Some of these topics have been investigated by psychologists, although so far psychological principles have not been systematically used in the design of programming languages.

The first limitation to be considered is that of size or, as Dijkstra (1972) puts it, of our "inability to do much." This topic is discussed by G. A. Miller (1956) in his paper "On the Magic Number Seven Plus or Minus Two," in which he shows that, for a wide range of human capabilities, the power to discriminate levels of intensity falls off rapidly as the number of levels exceeds a number close to seven. Although the experiments quoted by Miller were based on senses such as sight, hearing, and taste, the result also relates to other problems of discrimination such as those in writing a program. This effect is due to an inherent characteristic of the human brain, namely its limited capacity for storing information in short-term memory. It can be observed that many highly useable systems control the number of choices and options open to a user at any point of time. It can also be observed that when complicated subjects are being presented by skillful teachers, they (perhaps unconsciously) restrict the choices available to something like the "magic number."

One of the most powerful aids for the control of systems complexity is the use of *hierarchies* or tree structures for structuring and presenting complex information. A central paper on this theme is "The Architecture of Complexity" by H. A. Simon (reprinted in Simon, 1969) which illustrates how the structure of many man-made objects can be organized more simply by using hierarchies. Pager (1973) has illustrated the use of this technique in presenting complex information (in this case, mathematical proofs) and has shown how hierarchies, indentation, and other techniques can be utilized to make such information appear simpler.

As an example of experimental work in this area, Sime, Green, and Guest (1973) evaluated differences in ease-of-use and accuracy of two designs of the conditional IF statement in a programming language. By giving nonprogramming subjects a simple logical task to perform in one of two mini-languages, they were able to compare the ease-of-use of a nested IF statement similar to that provided in ALGOL, COBOL and PL/I, with a multiway branch similar to that in FORTRAN. Their conclusion showed significant superiority of the nested IF, a somewhat surprising result to those who have felt that nested constructions in languages offer some difficulty in comprehension.

A difficulty is raised by the dual nature of data as represented in many programming languages. To a user, data may appear as a collection of items, perhaps ordered for convenient access as in an array or matrix. In a conventional machine, arrays of data are usually stored in a linearly addressable store which has additional properties to that of the original data. The importance of separating these two views of data in programming languages is discussed in Chapter 8.

Another difficulty faced by programmers is that of designing and specifying flow of control in a program. Most humans find it difficult to conceive highly parallel activities and the simplest control structure to deal with is a sequential flow of control from one statement to the next. However many applications require complex branching based on the computed values of data. In the machine itself, it may be more efficient to have several activities going on in parallel, without the programmer necessarily being aware that this is occurring. Methods of specifying flow of control are discussed in Chapter 10.

In the next section we will examine some observational data on the use of programming languages. Considering the extent of such use, this data is remarkably sparse, but it obviously must form the basis for any quantitative study of language usage.

2.4   STUDIES OF THE USE OF PROGRAMMING LANGUAGES

Studies of the use of languages are of two kinds: statistical studies of the frequency of use of different parts of the language (statements, operators, built-in functions, etc.), and more searching studies of the quality of programming involving a knowledge or estimate of the programmer's intentions in writing the program.

Most available evidence suggests that the frequency distribution in the use of language features is very skew, a small selection of statements, operators, etc., being used a large proportion of the time.

The most extensively studied language is probably FORTRAN. Three different samples of FORTRAN programs gave the following percentages.

STANFORD UNIVERSITY (KNUTH, 1971)

Feature	Percentage
Assignment	51
IF	8.5
GO TO	8
DO	5
WRITE	5
CALL	4
	81.5 percent

LOCKHEED (KNUTH, 1971)

Feature	Percentage
Assignment	41
IF	14.5
GO TO	13
CALL	8
CONTINUE	5
WRITE	4
	85.5 percent

WISCONSIN UNIVERSITY (MOULTON AND MULLER, 1967)

Feature	Percentage
Assignment	45.6
WRITE	9.1
DO	8.5
IF	7.4
GO TO	4.9
FORMAT	4.8
	80.3 percent

In all examples, the six most frequently used FORTRAN statements represented over 80 percent of the use of all statements in the sample.

In studying ALGOL usage, the relative frequency of statement use does not have the same significance as in FORTRAN because there are so few

ALGOL statements. Wichmann (1970) carried out measurements on a set of ALGOL programs at the National Physical Laboratory. He gathered statistics on the use of basic ALGOL symbols, among which are the statement keywords. Excluding letters, digits, and the characters space, tab and newline, the most frequently used basic characters in the sample were:

Symbol	Percentage
:	15.5
.	15.0
:=	7.6
(	6.4
)	6.4
[	5.6
]	5.6

If we adjust Wichmann's figures, taking out the bracketed and multiple constructions (parentheses, **begin** ... **end, if** ... **then, for** ... **do,** etc.), we have the following:

Symbol	Percentage
;	20.4
,	19.7
:=	9.9
( )	8.3
[ ]	7.4
−	3.6
×	3.4
+	3.4
Cf. the symbol:/	1.2

Approximate figures of the basic symbols related to statements are as follows:

Symbol	Number
:=	21,000
if	4,000
for	3.500
go to	1,500

It is not possible to relate the : = symbol directly to the assignment statement, since it is also used in the **for** statement and (less commonly) in the **switch** declaration. The figures therefore do not give an exact measure of the frequency of the assignment statement, but a rough estimate suggests that over half the statements in the sample are assignments.

The studies discussed above simply involve a count of the frequency of appearance of statements in a program. Even though such simple information is difficult and expensive to obtain, it obviously represents only one small aspect of the use of programming languages.

Knuth and others at Stanford carried out a deeper analysis of language use, the static part of which has been quoted above. One purpose of this study was to examine new ways of optimizing FORTRAN programs, hence there was strong emphasis on looping programs, since the efficiency of many scientific programs depends on the speed of an inner program loop. In most of the programs analyzed a large proportion of the execution time was spent in a small part of the program. This shows the value of specialized forms of optimization and, more important, of means of informing the programmer about which parts of a program are most frequently used. A presentation to the user of execution frequency can considerably affect the programming quality, often outweighing the most elaborate schemes of automatic optimization. (See Knuth, 1971.)

2.5   THE PROGRAMMING PROCESS

Much of today's programming is carried out in a manner which can be traced to the earliest days of computing, coming originally from the work of Goldstine and von Neumann (1947). A computing problem is often first expressed in *flowchart* form, from which detailed coding is prepared at a later stage. The Goldstine and von Neumann papers employ a surprisingly close approximation to the flowchart notation now widely used for describing algorithms. Flowcharts are so extensively used that it has been suggested that they be used for entering programs directly into a computing system. (See, for example, Ellis, Heafner, and Sibley, 1969).

Early computing machines were small and limited in power, and considerable ingenuity had to be used to overcome these limitations. The introduction of the flowchart as an explicit phase in the programming process was justified by the fine level of detail and the difficulty of coding in machine language.

Another programming practice whose origin can be traced to the first days of computing is program testing by means of test cases. The early computer designers recognized that it was easy to make errors in coding and that systematic testing of programs was necessary. Later, the provision of automatic *tracing* routines was developed, however even in this phase the procedure remained the same—programs were written, then tested.

The sequence—planning, flowcharting, coding, test case running, . . . etc., has provided the pattern for many projects. It has led to practices and conventions in programming which, though now regarded as natural, come from the particular way in which programming was originally carried out.

2.6 STRUCTURED PROGRAMMING

The existing methodology of programming has frequently been shown to be inadequate. A succession of failures in large programming projects—not simply failures to complete projects on time, but failure to produce programs that meet their specifications—has led to a search for improved methods of developing programs. The aim has been to find ways of developing correct programs, rather than to expend effort in debugging incorrect ones. This is an objective of the technique known as "structured programming." Dijkstra's (1972) paper contains a description of programming by "stepwise composition" and emphasizes the importance of making timely decisions, often delaying them to a much later stage than would seem natural to many programmers.

Another good description of the construction of a non-trivial program (i.e., one whose solution is not known at the outset) is a paper by Wirth (1971) entitled "Program development by stepwise refinement." The problem discussed in this paper is the eight-Queens problem in chess, which requires finding arrangements of eight queens such that no queen may be taken by any other. The method of solution is not immediately obvious. Enumeration of all configurations is not feasible because of the extremely large number of combinations to be tested (about 2 to the power 32). Hence the method of approach is, as indicated by the title of the paper, one of searching for solutions, continuously refining and adjusting the method until an acceptable technique has been found. The paper emphasizes both the notion of *levels* of solution and the need to express the problem broadly but completely in terms of subroutines which can later be expanded to a finer level of detail. As the steps in the program are refined, the programmer develops more precise ideas on the structure of data needed for the problem. As Wirth points out, the development of program structure and data structure are in parallel, both working toward greater detail and precision.

Tools for structured programming will allow the user to follow this pattern of refinement and abstraction. A crucial problem, to be decided at the outset of any programming task, is the design of the most satisfactory data structures. In this choice the question of scale may dominate the decision. For example, the problem of printing the first N prime numbers differs radically if we consider N taking the values 10, 100 and 1,000,000. For the first, it is feasible to construct an array of all positive integers and remove the nonprimes. This approach becomes less attractive and may finally be impossible as N approaches 1,000,000. For structured programs the user therefore needs a variety of types of data aggregate in which he need not initially (and possibly need never) make the final decisions about internal storage and data representation.

It is important to be able to postpone the details of a computation so that the top level design can be constructed and examined first. This can be achieved by defining functions and subroutines, which correspond to the postponed decisions. Hence the ability to define and use functions conveniently is an important requirement for structured programming. A related property is the ability to limit the scope of names to a selected portion of the program, so that name clashes can be avoided as the program becomes more explicit.

Finally, as Dijkstra points out, one of the most difficult choices facing a program designer is the appropriate sequence of operations. If our objective is the ability not only to construct programs easily but also to ascertain their correctness, it is essential to keep the program's control structures as simple as possible. Many advocates of structured programming now accept the need to restrict control mechanisms to a fairly simple group of three or four, each with a single entrance and a single exit. These mechanisms correspond to the **if, do while, do until,** and **case** statements, which if used in a disciplined way can lead to programs whose correctness is more easily determined than those with unconstrained **go to** statements.

Finally, to ensure legibility and documentation the program should, at each level of refinement, be read and checked by the user and if possible by others. For this to be accomplished, the programming language should be such that prose-like statements can be written, suitably indented to show the static structure of the program, and then expanded to represent more detailed stages of the program.

Of languages now available for structured programming, the nested scope, free-format languages of the style of ALGOL or PL/I seem to be most appropriate. Both FORTRAN and COBOL offer too little in the way of program structure (particularly nested structure) to be ideal. APL has too little in the way of sequence control statements to be suitable, although its treatment of data is appropriately high level for the top levels of program construction. The ease of defining and using APL functions helps considerably in structuring the programming process since the functions can be made to correspond to the levels in a program.

2.7   THE DIALOGUE BETWEEN USER AND SYSTEM

The first users of experimental computers communicated directly with machines, feeding in data by setting switches on the machine console and obtaining output by reading directly from a cathode-ray tube. This direct contact with machines continued through the first generation of commercial machines, although the means of input and output became more convenient. As machines became larger and the average number of users of a single computer rose from a handful to perhaps many hundreds, it was no longer possible to allow each person direct access to the system, and the so-called "batch" systems came into being. These required users to submit large, self-contained units of work and to receive their results in correspondingly large units.

The high point of batch computing coincided with a period of great activity in programming language design. During the late 1950's and early 1960's the standard forms of language which now dominate the computing field were first developed. Most current standard languages, including FORTRAN, ALGOL, COBOL and PL/I, originated in this period and are constructed in such a way as to exploit and make use of batch methods. Characteristics of batch systems which relate to language design include:

- the use of large units of program text, which are translated and executed as single entities;

- the fixing of data types and program structure in these units, allowing techniques of compilation and optimization to be applied.

With the introduction of *time sharing* during the 1960's, it was possible to allow many independent input-output (I/O) units to be connected to the same CPU, allowing the user to conduct a dialogue with the system. There is effectively a partnership between the user and system, in which each party can carry out the tasks for which it is most suited. This point is well illustrated in the paper by Michie *et al.* (1968), which contrasts the behavior of an individual with that of an individual-plus-computer in solving a complex problem. The human user can provide objectives and judgment, the system supplying computing power and large accurate memory. This partnership between user and machine is compared by Licklider (1962) to a *symbiosis* in nature.

When users and system work in such a partnership, there is invariably some form of dialogue between the two, with the system issuing information which prompts the user to reply and possibly requesting confirmation for or correcting data which appears to be incorrect. Such dialogues are not part of established language systems as currently understood although they do point the way to likely future systems.

2.8   ERRORS IN PROGRAMMING

One type of dialogue which arises in nearly all systems consists of user input followed by a system response in the form of error messages. The design of error messages, an important part of any compiler project, is discussed briefly in Chapter 4. From the language designer's point of view, it is important to know what kind of errors occur in programs, and how these may be reduced by suitable choices in the language design.

The work of Sime and his colleagues has been mentioned above (Sime, Green, and Guest 1973). Other work on this subject has been carried out by Pyle (1971) and by Boies and Gould (1972). The debugging process, a systematic procedure by which errors are removed from programs, has been studied and measured by Gould and Drongowski (1972). Their findings include the observation that errors in assignment statements are harder to detect than errors in looping and array subscripting.

BIBLIOGRAPHY

Baker, F. T., "Chief programmer team management of production programming," *IBM Systems Journal,* Vol. 11, No. 1, 1972, pp. 56–73.

Describes a project developed by a small team, using top-down, structured programming and a set of aids to documentation and library maintenance. The project was led by a "Chief Programmer"—a manager-cum-programmer who had direct knowledge and control of the entire project.

BCS Conference (D. Simpson, ed.) "High-level programming languages—the way ahead" NCC Publications, 1973.

This report contains the proceedings of a BCS conference at York University in October 1972. There are reviews of the status and likely futures of FORTRAN, PL/I, ALGOL 68, SIMULA and other languages, and some discussion of the objectives for language design. One of these, by Professor Hoare, paints a picture of unrelieved gloom—in his opinion things have become steadily worse since the inception of FORTRAN and ALGOL 60.

Boies, S. J., J. D. Gould, "A behavioral analysis of programming: on the frequency of syntactical errors," IBM Research Report RC 3907, June 1972.

All transactions on a large, time-sharing system (using TSS/360) over a period of 18 months were logged and analyzed. The results showed a rather low incidence of syntactic errors and, for this particular system, a low use of the interactive facilities provided by the system.

Boehm, B. W., "Software and its impact: a quantitative assessment," Datamation Vol. 19, No. 5, May 1973, pp. 48–59.

Describes a U.S. Air Force study (CCIP-85) of future computer requirements. The study concluded that, of all the problems facing the future users of computing systems, software would continue to be the most daunting. The author points out the difficulty of giving precise measure to software problems and presents a number of interesting statistics on errors, proportion of time spent in various parts of systems, relative costs of production and maintenance, and the productivity of programmers.

Cross, E. M., "Behavioral styles of computer programmers—revisited," (Willoughby, ·T. C., ed.) *Proceedings of 9th Annual Computer Personnel Research Conference,* SIGPR ACM, 1971.

Emphasizes the behavioral aspects of programming work. The picture that emerges is of introverted behavior and of individuals who are prepared to work with a low degree of social interaction.

Dahl, Ole-Johan, "Programming languages as tools for the formulation of concepts" *Lecture Notes in Mathematics 118*, pp. 18–29 (proceedings of the 15th Scandinavian Congress, Oslo, 1968) Springer-Verlag, 1970.

Daniels, E., D. Yeates, (eds.) *Basic Training in Systems Analysis*, London: Pitman, 1969.

Prepared for the National Computing Center, and based on their Systems Analysis Package, this book emphasizes the systems' analyst's role in contrast with that of the programmer.

Dijkstra, E. W., "Notes on structured programming," *Structured Programming*, APIC Studies in Data Processing, No. 8, London, New York: Academic Press, 1972.

Originally published in 1969, this is one of the earliest and best expositions of programming in a structured manner, that is, by stepwise composition. The author illustrates, with discursive anecdote and interesting game-like examples, the process of composing a non-trivial program. In doing so, he provides by implication a feeling for the kind of framework in which this activity can best succeed.

Ellis, T. O., J. F. Heafner, W. L. Sibley, "The GRAIL language and operations," Technical Report RM-6001-ARPA, RAND Corporation, Santa Monica, California, Sept. 1969.

Evershed, D. G., G. E. Rippon, "High-level languages for low-level users," *Computer Journal*, Vol. 14, No. 1, Feb. 1971, pp. 87–90.

Discusses the usefulness of conventional programming languages to those who only use computers occasionally and who are not dedicated to the more esoteric aspects of computer lore. The paper is highly critical of the design of current languages and includes illustrations from ALGOL and FORTRAN. It discusses some aspects of the design of I/O, the use of reserved words, and the various kinds of **go to** statements.

Gould, J. D., P. Drongowski, "A controlled psychological study of computer program debugging," IBM Research Report, RC 4083, Oct. 1972.

This paper describes an experiment in which 30 experienced programmers debugged one-page FORTRAN programs that were syntactically correct, but contained various nonsyntactic bugs. It was discovered that bugs in assignment statements were harder to detect than those in arrays and iterations. Suggestions for a debugging "strategy" are made.

Goldstine, H. H., J. von Neumann, "Planning and coding problems for an electronic computing instrument," Part II, Vol. 1.

Report prepared for U.S. Army Ordnance Dept., 1947, (in) John von Neumann, Collected Works (ed. A. H. Taub) Vol. V, Oxford: Pergamon Press, 1963, pp. 80–151.

Gold, M. M., "Time sharing and batch processing: an experimental comparison of their values in a problem-solving situation," *CACM*, Vol. 12, No. 5, May 1969, pp. 249–259.

Hare, van Court, *Systems Analysis: A Diagnostic Approach,* New York: Harcourt, Brace, and World, Inc., 1967.

Many of the subjects treated here are closely related to language design, although the main importance of the book is in placing a language system in perspective and relating it to the world at large.

Henderson, P., R. Snowdon, "An experiment in structured programming," BIT, Vol. 12, No. 1, 1972, pp. 38–53.

This paper describes an experiment in structured programming. An error was made in the process of program development. The authors are frank in discussing the shortcomings, as well as the advantages, of the methods.

Knuth, D. E., "An empirical study of FORTRAN programs," IBM Research Report RC 3276, March 1971.

Describes analyses (both static and dynamic) of some 40 to 50 FORTRAN programs covering a wide variety of applications. The analysis was carried out by a group of about a dozen people, using mechanical and manual methods, who examined the loop structures of the programs in some detail. The paper throws interesting light on the styles of different programs used within the same installation.

Licklider, J. C. R., W. E. Clark, "On-line man-computer communication," *Proc. SJCC,* AFIPS, 1962, pp. 113–128.

Discusses the complementary capabilities of man and computer and the need for establishing a *symbiosis* between the two. The human can set goals, formulate hypotheses, select approaches, detect relevance, and recognize patterns. The computer can store and retrieve information, calculate rapidly, and build up a repertoire of procedures.

Miller, G. A., *Language and Communication,* New York: McGraw-Hill (revised edition) 1963.

A collection of papers by a distinguished psychologist who has studied human communication from a scientific point of view and has also addressed problems of man-machine communication.

Miller, L. A., "Programming by non-programmers," IBM Research report RC 4280, IBM Research, Yorktown Heights, Mar. 1973.

Describes work whose objective is to lead to the design of systems with improved programmer performance and better understanding of problem-solving behavior. An experimental laboratory programming language consisting of 19 commands was developed and used by nonprogramming subjects to carry out tasks involving simple card-sorting problems. Factors influencing their performance were conjunctive *vs* disjunctive problems, positive *vs* negative expressions, control structures.

Miller, R. B., *Response Time in Man-Computer Conversational Transactions, Proc. FJCC* (1968) pp. 267–277 Thompson Book Company, 1968.

Michie, D., J. G. Fleming, J. V. Oldfield, *A Comparison of Heuristic, Interactive and Unaided Methods of Solving a Shortest-Route Problem in Machine Intelligence 3,* (D. Michie, ed.) Edinburgh: Edinburgh University Press, 1968, pp. 245–255.

Describes an experiment to compare the performance of a human with that of a human-plus-a-computer on the Travelling-Salesman problem. The results are given in the form of notional costs of solution. The problem turned out to be less exacting than was originally expected, a particularly skilled solver being able to achieve surprisingly good results without any aid. However, "average" solvers were able to achieve a six percent improvement with the assistance of an on-line system.

Moulton, P. G., M. E. Muller, "DITRAN—A compiler emphasizing diagnostic," *CACM,* Vol. 10, No. 1, Jan. 1967, pp. 45–52.

A FORTRAN compiler with more extensive error checking than usual, both at compile time and at execution time. The technique used is based on "storage unit vectors," which monitor accesses to storage during execution of the program.

Meadow, C. T., *Man-Machine Communication,* New York: Wiley-Interscience, 1970.

Mealy, G. H., T. E. Cheatham, D. J. Farber, E. Morenoff, Sattley, K. "Program transferability study," Technical Report of Project 5581, Task 558102, Rome Air Development Center, 1968.

Points out that the transfer of programs from one environment to another has generally been unsuccessful. Lists some of the reasons, such as the difficulty of expressing data in a machine-independent manner and implicit assumptions by compilers. Included in the list of possible remedies are greater control over the behavior of programmers, better models for the specification of programming languages, and extensible programming languages.

Naur, P., B. Randell, (eds.) "Software engineering," Report on a Conference Sponsored by the NATO Science Committee NATO, 1969.

Nicholls, J. E., "Complexity and duplicity in programming languages," Technical report TR. 12.101 IBM United Kingdom Laboratories, Mar. 1972.

Advocates principles of simplicity in the design of programming languages. Illustrations from COBOL and PL/I.

Pager, D., "On the problem of communicating complex information," *CACM,* Vol. 16, No. 5, May 1973, pp. 275–281.

Discusses the difficulty of communicating information such as mathematical proofs and suggests ways in which improvements can be made. These include methods of display, notations and linguistic devices, and the use of an interactive system.

Pyle, I. C., "A second-order bug with delayed effect," *Software-Practice and Experience,* Vol. 1, No. 3, 1971, pp. 231–233.

Analysis of a single bug—the erroneous over-writing of a critical piece of data due to an unknown side-effect.

Roberts, K. V., "The publication of scientific FORTRAN programs," *Computer Physics Communications,* Amsterdam: North-Holland, Vol. 1, 1969, pp. 1–9.

The author points out that many computer programs constructed at great expense by individual scientists are not usable by the scientific community at large because of their limited range of application or difficulty of understanding. Suggestions are made for conventions of coding and use of automatic documentation tools.

Russell, E. C., G. Estrin, Measurement based automatic analysis of FORTRAN programs," Proc. AFIPS, Vol. 34, SJCC AFIPS Press, 1969, pp. 723–733.

Sackman, H., *Man-Computer Problem Solving: Experimental Evaluation of Time-Sharing and Batch Processing,* Auerbach, 1970.

Sharpe, W. F., *The Economics of Computers,* Columbia University Press, 1969.

Sime, M. E., T. R. G. Green, D. J. Guest, "Psychological evaluation of two conditional constructions used in computer languages," *Int. J. Man-Machine Studies,* Vol. 5, No. 1, Jan. 1973, pp. 105–113.

The authors, concerned with the psychological aspects of computers in industry, point out the advantages of an empirical approach to the study of programming languages. Rather than carrying out an overall evaluation of languages, they try to extract features of language design and subject them to experimental evaluation. This report describes a controlled experiment, using unskilled subjects, in which two approaches to conditional branching were evaluated. The two languages forms were the nested **if** statement, as used in ALGOL **(NEST),** and the branch-to-label construction similar to that of FORTRAN (JUMP). The results showed that in many ways **NEST** was better, in the sense of leading to fewer errors, than JUMP.

Simon, H. A., "The architecture of complexity," *Proc. American Philosophical Society,* Vol. 106, No. 6, Dec. 1962, pp. 467–482.

Simon, H. A., "The sciences of the artificial" MIT Press, 1969.

This contains the previous paper (Simon, 1962), expanded to give a fuller account of the control of complexity in artificial structures. This book is highly recommended to all language and system designers. Although its scope is much wider than just that of programming languages, it touches on many subjects that are, or should be, of concern to language designers.

Simmons, D. B., "The art of writing large programs," IEEE Computer, Vol. 5, No. 2, Mar./Apr., 1972 pp. 43–49.

Discusses the difference in productivity between programmers in large and small groups. A good review article.

Streeter, D. N., "Cost/benefits of computing services in a scientific environment," Technical Report RC 3453 IBM Research, July 1971.

An attempt to develop measures of the benefits of computing services in terms of the *value* of the service provided.

Thompson, D. A., "Man-computer system: toward balanced cooperation in intellectual activities," *Proceedings International Symposium on Man-Machine Systems,* IEEE Conference Record No. 69C 58-MMS, Sept. 1969.

General survey and discussion of the use of decision trees in man-machine communication.

Weinberg, G. M., *The Psychology of Computer Programming,* Van Nostrand Reinhold, 1971.

A stimulating and readable book, ranging over many subjects from the management of programming projects to the principles of design of programming languages.

Wichmann, B. A., "Some statistics from ALGOL programs," Technical report CCU 11, Aug. 1970, National Physical Laboratory.

A static and dynamic ALGOL analysis whose aim was to help compiler writers to know which features to optimize. From the figures an ALGOL mix which allowed comparisons of different compilers was devised.

Willoughby, T. C., (ed.) *Proceedings of Ninth Annual Computer Personnel Research Conference*, SIGPR, ACM, 1971.

Papers on selection and training of computer personnel. These give, by implication, a picture of some of the characteristics of programmers. See the paper by Cross.

Wirth, Niklaus, "Program development by stepwise refinement," *CACM*, Vol. 14, No. 4, Apr. 1971, pp. 221–227.

3
Applications

3.1 INTRODUCTION

It has become usual to classify programming languages into various categories such as "scientific," "commercial," "systems," and others. The effects of this classification extend far beyond the applications themselves and are felt throughout computing, influencing the design of machines and programming systems and even the job descriptions applied to programmers and systems analysts. It is not surprising, therefore, that these influences should also be felt by the designers of programming languages, leading to designs which differ quite markedly in content and structure. Although some recently developed languages contain a broader collection of facilities and can be considered as "general purpose," the differences between scientific, commercial, systems, and other applications are important, if for no other reason than the effect they have had on the design of present languages.

The two main influences on languages have undoubtedly been those from "scientific" and "commercial" applications. To see how some of the differences came about, we must look into the early history of computing. The first scientific users came from branches of physical science which had reached a stage where mathematical solutions of their problems could be stated. Such users saw the computer as providing a dramatic increase in power over the hand or electric calculator which until then had been their most powerful tool. Their main emphasis was in extending the range and power of algorithmic solutions to numerical problems—computing became a welcome assistant in the science of numerical analysis.

Commercial users, coming into computing with experience of business machines, were already accustomed to processing data stored on punched cards with sorters, collators and tabulators. Though simple in principle, some of these could carry out powerful operations. These users were not so interested in the numerical capabilities of computers, as in their capacity for storing, rearranging, and printing large volumes of highly structured data— with what came to be known as "data processing."

For both scientific and commercial users, computers introduced faster, cheaper ways of doing work which they were already doing by other means. Hence the early influence of applications on computing systems design was to reinforce existing practices, rather than to stimulate alternative approaches to information handling. "Scientific" users were primarily interested in the expression of numerical algorithms and looked for ways in which to communicate these algorithms to other members of the scientific community. "Commercial" users were concerned with storing and retrieving data, and in particular with problems of input and output of large files.

In determining the influence of applications on language design, it is useful to consider two important factors which, as we shall see in later chapters, embody the most critical features of a language. These two factors are:

Data structures—These include the types of data elements, the relation between the elements, and the methods of access.

Program structures—These include methods of constructing programs, of controlling program sequencing, and of segmenting programs.

In the following sections, applications are considered in the light of their needs for data structures and program structures.

3.2 SCIENTIFIC COMPUTING

Most of what is usually regarded as scientific computing involves finding numerical solutions to an equation or set of equations which represent a model of a physical system. The elements of data are for the most part numbers, often in a floating-point system of representation. Scientific programs are often characterized by a large amount of computation and relatively little input/output.

Over the past several decades, there has been continuous development and improvement in *matrix* methods of solution for numerical problems. This has been reinforced by the advent of computers because of the close affinity of matrices to the usual method of storing and accessing data structures in digital computers. Hence the most common data structure used in scientific computing is the *array* which contains an ordered set of elements of the same type accessed by subscript.

Corresponding to the array as the predominant data structure, the most common control structure is the loop. Many numerical methods involve scanning arrays in some regular pattern, row by row, column by column, or along one of the diagonals. The looping construction represented by the FORTRAN DO, the ALGOL **for** and the PL/I DO, allow such scans to be conveniently expressed and efficiently executed. Iterative methods of solving equations generally require many accesses to the same elements of data before a result is achieved. Hence arrays are often held in high-speed storage and often the input and output for a numeric application only occurs at the beginning and end of a program.

It is impossible to define all the properties that make up either a scientific or commercial program, but the examples given below illustrate some of the different features of these classes of application. We first illustrate a scientific application.

The *potential problem,* as described in a paper by Hockney (1970), arises in several contexts.

- In astrophysics—in calculating the gravitational potential of a distribution of stars
- in plasma, semi-conductor, or solid-state physics—in calculating the electrostatic potential over a region, from a given distribution of charges
- in hydrodynamics, in calculating the stream function from a given distribution of vorticities

The mathematical requirement is to find solutions to Poisson's equation† under certain constraints. The equation is an elliptic partial differential equation of the form:

$$\frac{\partial^2 f}{\partial x^2} + \frac{\partial^2 f}{\partial y^2} = g(x,y)$$

In its original form, Poisson's equation applies to continuous variables. Digital techniques of solution are based on transforming the continuous differential equation into a difference equation. This involves splitting up the region of solution into a grid or mesh of points. The fineness of the mesh strongly influences the accuracy of the solution.

Hockney describes a direct method of solution involving the use of the Fourier transform which may be used on general problems in potential theory; the details given relate to its use in star simulation. Each run of the program is a simulation of the life of a star system or galaxy. For each

---

† The two-dimensional form of Poisson's equation is shown. Ideally, many problems call for a three-dimensional form, but the time and space requirements for three-dimensional analysis have until recently been considered prohibitive. However, calculations on $64 \times 64 \times 64$ meshes are now possible on large mega-byte machines.

time interval, the program computes the forces acting on each individual star and the resulting accelerations. The positions and velocities at the end of the time step are then calculated, providing a new configuration to serve as input for the next time interval.

In typical runs, the number of stars in the model is 50,000, and the mesh consists of 64 × 64 points. With a model of this size, an IBM System/360 Model 195 can compute about 1,000 time steps per hour. A single run may last about 1 to 2 hours, representing about 5 rotations of a typical galaxy. A complete experimental run may consist of about 10 rotations; however, this may depend on the results obtained. A run may be cut short if the configuration does not prove interesting. Rather than execute a single experimental simulation in one run, it is usual to break it up into several runs, to allow the results obtained to be evaluated during the course of the experiment.

Input data for the program may consist simply of the parameters needed to define the initial conditions. For example, a uniform random distribution of the stars may be established by invoking a random number generator in the initialization phase of the program. Output is on a tape suitable for subsequent processing on a microfilm recorder. For normal runs, output of the current configuration is only once every 50 or so steps. Special runs are made to generate movie films, and in this case there is output after each time step. In this mode, the program is output bound, and the speed of simulation is reduced from 1,000 to about 400 steps per hour of computer time.

The *data structures* used in the potential problem are large arrays of numbers. The method of solution makes use of a five-point difference equation—as each point in the potential mesh is processed, the effects of the four neighboring points are computed. (See Fig. 3.1.)

The *program structure* of this application is as follows: there is a main program, together with a number of subprograms, some of which are carefully written in machine code. The *control structure* is comparatively simple. It consists of a main loop with several conditional branches where intermediate results are tested and stored. Large numerical problems may run for many hours on even the largest machines. To avoid waste of machine time it is often necessary to monitor critical results to discover when a size goes out of bounds or a tolerance is exceeded. These tests can be coded by means of conditional branching statements, or may be more conveniently handled by means of condition-handling statements such as the ON statement of PL/I.

Although the similarity between the facilities provided by FORTRAN and ALGOL might suggest that these languages contain all the essential facilities for scientific computing, this is misleading. These languages match

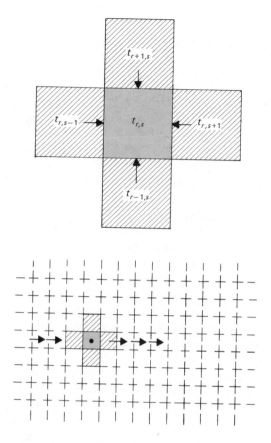

Fig. 3.1   Access to local points in the solution to Poisson's equation.

well with the traditional view of numerical analysis, but the impact of new kinds of data and control structure are likely to have a greater impact on numerical analysis than is currently apparent (for an amplification of this view, see Rice 1972).

3.3 COMMERCIAL COMPUTING

Turning now to commercial computing, we find that a main objective of many commercial applications is to record, update, and retrieve information used in the day-to-day work of a business enterprise. It is hard to illustrate a representative commercial program in detail; actual programs tend to be larger and more complex than scientific programs, since they relate closely to social and human organizations rather than to mathematical structures.

The elements of commercial data typically have a wide variety of types —numbers, strings of letters, and special characters. These correspond to: names, addresses, part numbers, quantitites, prices, discounts, etc. Compared with scientific applications, there is both a greater diversity of types and a less homogeneous structuring of the data. Many data structures in commercial programs correspond to documents used in business, such as checks, invoices, bills of lading, and various types of reports. In some cases, before installing a computer, a firm may have already converted part of its operations to work with punched cards; in such cases the recorded data will already have the imprint of punched card format.

Consider the policy records of an insurance company—a well-established field of application for commercial data processing. The policy master file is a critical set of data, governing the daily activities of the firm. There might typically be a record for each policy containing: policy number, name and address, sum assured, premium, and perhaps details of claims. In a large company, this file may be very large—for example, one major company in the United Kingdom has over 20 million policies in its main file. Clearly, the space occupied by each record becomes of critical importance in such a file, and several different techniques for storage sharing and overlaying are used. Often, each record consists of a fixed part of constant length, followed by several fields of variable length (such as the "record of claims" in our example).

The basic data structure used in this type of application is the record, a collection of diverse elements packed as closely as possible consistent with convenient access. The nature of this file determines the type of processing carried out on it. As we shall see in Chapter 11, the pattern is similar to programs for sequential file processing; a typical program consists of a main loop in which each record is accessed in turn while various operations are carried out. New information is collected on an auxiliary file, which must be sorted in the same order as the master file.

In the future, this type of application will be influenced by the advent of large on-line storage and by the possibility of using "data-base" systems rather than current filing systems. This will affect the languages used for commercial programming which will move away from sequential I/O (still the cornerstone of commercial data processing) towards greater use of special-access languages, query languages, reporting systems, etc. Data-base systems are discussed in a volume in this series (Date, 1975).

3.4 SYSTEMS PROGRAMMING

There is as much difference between a compiler and a supervisor as between many scientific and commercial programs. However, some factors are common to all systems programs:

- greater intensity of use

  Systems programs are usually more heavily used than applications programs. A supervisor is used by all programs on a system, a compiler by all programs written in a certain language. This factor imposes special requirements for the performance and reliability of systems programs.

- special access to hardware

  Systems programs, the programs closest to the hardware of a computer, often need to access special addresses in storage or special machine instructions.

Apart from these requirements, it is possible to consider, as Peter Naur (1966) has done, that the tasks associated with systems programming—compiler writing, scheduling, buffer management, etc.—are best seen as general data-processing problems, with slightly more demanding requirements for data structuring, sequencing, etc. This view is strengthened by reading articles reviewing systems programming as a "special" problem (see, for example, Sammet, 1971). The listed requirements for systems programming in such articles are remarkably like those for other programming tasks.

As an example of the needs of a particular branch of systems programming, we consider some of the data and program structures applicable to *compiler* design. Two kinds of data structure are important in compilers:

- the structure of the *text* either in its original form as a string or in its parsed form as a tree structure. In either case, the data structuring has to be very flexible to allow for the variety of input programs that will be encountered.

- the structure of the *symbol table*. This may be in the form of a list structure to allow for easy insertion and deletion of items. In the process of compilation, the structure and efficiency of the symbol table is of the greatest importance for efficient processing.

Program structures for compilers include:

- one-pass load-and-go compilers in which the compiler and text remain in high-speed store until the compilation is complete.

- n-phase compilers (small n) in which there are a small number of phases (say, 2 to 8), the program text being scanned each phase.

- n-phase compilers (large n) in which the program text remains in high-speed store while many (say 10 to 100) program phases are successively brought in to process the text.

Surveys of the needs of systems programming have been published by Bergeron *et al.* (1971), Sammet (1971) and Lyle (1971). Several languages have been designed specifically for systems programming—for example, BCPL (Richards, 1969) and BLISS (Wulf *et al.*, 1971).

3.5 COMBINATORIAL PROGRAMMING

Combinatorial analysis is a branch of mathematics which is concerned with partitions, permutations, and other structured arrangements of elementary objects. There is a corresponding branch of programming known as *combinatorial programming* which is important to systems programmers and applications programmers working on certain types of large problems. Combinatorial programming has interesting requirements for data and program structures.

Applications of combinatorial programming include:

- the generation of partitions,
- the generation of permutations,
- finding the minimum spanning tree of a graph,
- finding the shortest path through a network (the Travelling-Salesman problem).

Although such problems may appear primarily mathematical, combinatorial algorithms have uses in network and circuit theory, in file searching and sorting, and in several branches of systems programming. One of the problems which has become almost a testpiece for "structured programming" is the eight-queens problem referred to in Chapter 2. This is a combinatorial problem with a long ancestry (Ginsburg, 1939).

Two references describing the mathematical basis of combinatorial analysis and several of its applications are those by Riordan (1958) and Beckenbach (1964).

Combinatorial problems often require systematic enumeration of all members of a given class satisfying a given property. These may be graphs, permutations, latin squares, etc. If the field of search is very wide, and the conditions so stringent that there are only a few solutions, the enumeration becomes a *search*.

The *data structures* used in combinatorial analysis include structures such as arrays, trees, graphs, and sets. Only a few of these structures can be directly represented in most languages. Among the techniques developed to overcome this lack of means of direct representation are: use of vectors of bits to represent sets, use of incidence arrays to represent graphs, and use of a *signature* (a vector of indices) to represent a permutation.

One of the techniques used for systematically searching a large number of possible combinations goes under the name of *backtrack programming*.

Other terms are "tree programming" (Wells, 1971) and "nondeterministic algorithms" (Floyd, 1967).

A typical backtrack program is a sophisticated (and in some cases optimized) form of exhaustive search, but the type of program it represents is sufficiently distinctive and widely used to make it typical of combinatorial problems.

We consider a problem organized in such a way that its solution can be expressed in the form of a *search tree* of the form shown in Fig. 3.2.

The problem is to construct an efficient way of traversing this tree so that as soon as a solution is found, the search is stopped. The backtrack

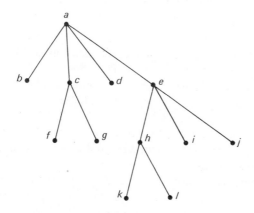

Fig. 3.2 A search tree

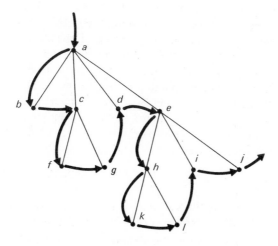

Fig. 3.3 Pattern of search in a tree

solution of such problems involves a path through the tree of the form shown in Fig. 3.3.

In order to program a search through such a tree, we need a form of looping in which the depth of nesting of the loops is not known beforehand. This form of program can be written using a combination of iteration and recursion, but ideally would use a form of variable depth iteration.

The needs of combinatorial computing are somewhat greater than can be directly provided by most current languages and seem likely to provide a challenge to language designers for some time to come. The nature of combinatorial programming and its programming-language requirements are discussed by Wells (1971).

3.6 SUMMARY

The needs of various kinds of application have influenced the design of programming languages in many ways. The effects can be seen in the considerable differences between scientific languages like FORTRAN and ALGOL and commercial languages like COBOL (and the earlier FACT, FLOWMATIC and COMMERCIAL TRANSLATOR). Some of these differences have come about for historical reasons, while some arise from genuine differences in the data structures and processing methods adopted in the different disciplines.

The development of *general-purpose* languages such as PL/I and others is an affirmation of unity in language design—their existence implies that it is both possible and useful to combine the facilities needed for several classes of application in one framework.

The historical differences between scientific and commercial languages now seem likely to diminish in future designs—general-purpose languages have been particularly successful in merging the FORTRAN/COBOL concepts and in showing how unnecessary some of the divergences between these languages are. However, the attainment of a *universal* language for all applications seems as remote as ever. Two other classes of applications, systems programming and combinatorial programming, have been used to illustrate special needs not fully met by current general-purpose languages. Other areas, such as real-time, graphics, and query/update, all have special requirements and impose special constraints on space or speed and on data structures or control structures.

BIBLIOGRAPHY

ACM, "Proceedings of a SIGPLAN symposium on languages for systems implementation," *ACM SIGPLAN Notices*, Vol. 6, No. 9 Oct. 1971.

Beckenbach, E. F. (ed.), *Applied Combinatorial Mathematics*, New York: John Wiley, 1964.

Bergeron, R. D., J. D. Gannon, F. W. Tompa, D. P. Shecter, A. van Dam, "Systems Programming Languages" (in) *Advances in Computers, Vol. 12,* New York: Academic Press, 1972.

Date, C. J., *An Introduction to Database Systems,* Reading, Mass.: Addison-Wesley, 1975.

Floyd, R. F., "Nondeterministic algorithms," *JACM,* Vol. 14, No. 4, Oct. 1967, pp. 636–644.

A short description of backtracking methods with examples of algorithms for the eight-Queens problem and an algorithm for finding the cycles in a graph.

Ginsburg, J. "Gauss's arithmetization of the problem of 8-queens," *Scripta Mathematica,* Vol. 5, 1939, pp. 63–66.

Golumb, S. W., L. D. Baumert, "Backtrack programming," *JACM,* Vol. 12, No. 4, Oct. 1965, pp. 516–524.

This paper describes a technique useful for combinatorial problems. Backtrack programming is a method of exhaustive search requiring much less than the maximum possible number of tests of possible combinations.

Hockney, R. W., "The potential calculation and some applications," *Methods of Computational Physics,* Vol. 9, 1970, pp. 136–211.

Hohl, F., R. W. Hockney, "A computer model of disks of stars," *Journal of Computational Physics,* Vol. 4, No. 3, Oct. 1969, pp. 306–323.

Lyle, Don M., "A hierarchy of high order languages for systems programming," *ACM SIGPLAN Notices,* Vol. 6, No. 9, Oct. 1971, pp. 73–78.

A summary of some of the ideas behind Burrough's use of high-level languages for systems programming.

McGee, W., "The formulation of data processing problems for computers", *Advances in Computers,* Vol. 4, New York: Academic Press, 1963, pp. 1–52.

This is a review of computing problems from the point of view of programming languages, especially languages designed for "data processing." The languages discussed are FACT, COMTRAN, COBOL and 9PAC, a general report-writing language. There is also one of the few published discussions of the famous report on "Information Algebra," by the CODASYL committee. There is a good bibliography of early works on data processing.

Naur, P., "Program translation viewed as a general data processing problem," *CACM,* Vol. 9, No. 3, Mar. 1966, pp. 176–179.

Emphasizes the need for reliability in translation and includes a proposal for a "reliability factor." Criticizes some aspects of language design, especially what he calls "empty options" and "the default mechanism."

Ord-Smith, R. J., "Generation of permutation sequences," *Computer Journal* Part 1: Vol. 13, No. 2, May 1970, pp. 152–155; Part 2: Vol. 14, No. 2, May 1971, pp. 136–139.

The author describes some of the uses of permutation-generating algorithms. In Part 2 he compares the efficiency and ease of use of six published algorithms.

Rice, J. R., "On the present and future of scientific computation," *CACM,* Vol. 15, No. 7, Jul. 1972, pp. 637–639.

An outspoken criticism of the current situation in scientific computing and some predictions for the future. Rice condemns the conservatism of much of today's numerical analysis, and points out that the impact of current knowledge of such topics as data structures and pattern recognition have yet to make their full impact on scientific computing.

Richards, M., "BCPL: a tool for compiler writing and system programming," *Proc. AFIPS,* Vol. 34 (SJCC), New Jersey: AFIPS Press, 1969, pp. 557–566.

BCPL was developed specifically for systems programming and although its structure is similar to that of other high-level languages, it has only one data type, the binary bit pattern. This gives it the simplicity and efficiency needed for systems programming.

Riordan, J., *An Introduction to Combinatorial Analysis,* New York: John Wiley, 1958.

Sammet, J. E., "Brief survey of languages used in systems implementation," *ACM SIGPLAN Notices,* Vol. 6, No. 9, Oct. 1971, pp. 1–19.

Wells, Mark B., *Elements of Combinatorial Computing,* Elmsford, N.Y.: Pergamon Press, 1971.

An excellent survey. There is an informal proposal for a language for combinatorial computing and an extended discussion of techniques of backtrack programming and other methods of enumeration.

Wulf, W. A., D. B. Russell, A. N. Haberman, "BLISS: a language for systems programming," *CACM,* Vol. 14, No. 12, Dec. 1971, pp. 780–790.

BLISS was designed as an implementation language for a specific machine, the PDP-10. It is an "expression language" in which every executable construct, even those which effect control of sequencing, computes a value. The GO TO statement has been eliminated and in its place is a wide range of looping and branching operations.

4

The Implementation of Languages

4.1 INTRODUCTION

In Chapters 2 and 3 we have considered the influence of users and applications on language design. Now we look at the problem of implementation, which produces yet another type of influence on language design. Users have always been reluctant to employ languages which, however conceptually excellent, are not implemented with acceptable standards of efficiency. In comparing one system with another, the effects of the language design and its implementation must be carefully distinguished.

In implementing a language, two kinds of machine are involved. One is the hardware machine, a collection of circuitry, control boxes, terminals, etc. The other is the high-level "machine" seen by the user, accessed by means of programming languages, command languages and operating-system facilities. The two machines have always differed, sometimes radically; the problem of implementing languages is essentially that of bridging the gap between them. The gap creates a form of tension which is relieved:

- by leanings in the design of languages toward the design of machines;
- by the evolution of machines which incorporate facilities found in programming languages.

Whatever may eventually happen as languages and machines come closer together, the implementor of today has to construct a program which translates programs from one language to the other. There are two approaches to this—compilation and interpretation.

A *compiler* is usually taken to mean a translator whose primary objective is to produce efficient programs in machine language. In a compiler, attention is given to the performance of the object program by careful use of the most appropriate machine language instructions, by efficient register allocation, and by carrying out optimizing transformations of the program.

An *interpreter* is a form of implementation in which, although there may be some translation, the source language is altered as little as possible. An interpreter requires a set of subroutines to be present when the program is executed.

Compiling and interpreting are at two ends of a spectrum, emphasizing different types of performance during translation and execution. The distinction between the two can best be considered in terms of the concept of *binding*, which is discussed in Chapter 7. In terms of binding, a compiler is a processor which closely binds the source program, fixing the types of variables if optimization is carried out and also fixing the forms of expression and program structure in the source program. An interpreter leaves variables unbound until execution time so that type-testing and similar actions are carried out by a set of routines which must be present at run time.

Very few implementations are "pure" compilers or interpreters. Even those compilers which carry out the most ambitious forms of optimization have some part of their object code executed by general-purpose subroutines such as those of an operating system. Similarly, few interpreters execute source programs exactly as written and there is usually some form of translation before the code is executed.

Compilation, the most common form of implementation, exerts a stronger influence on language design than interpretation. A knowledge of compiler construction is therefore important to the study of programming languages.

Another major influence on compiler design is that of the source language. Perhaps the biggest influence is the approach to type-fixing in the language, either demanding interpretive code or allowing the development of compiled code. Thus an APL implementation (such as that of Breed and Lathwell, 1968) differs from that of most other languages in being essentially interpretive. The development of a compiler for APL is made difficult, if not impossible, by the treatment of type in the language.

4.2 TYPES OF COMPILERS

The form of a compiler shows many variations. The design is influenced by:

- the purpose for which the compiler is intended,

- the nature of the language being compiled,
- the target machine and operating system.

One choice facing the designer of a compiler is that between fast compilation and fast execution of object programs. Historically, several early compilers for scientific languages were designed to produce as efficient a code as possible. Early compiler designers were sensitive to the need for efficient execution. A classic example is that of the first FORTRAN compiler (Backus, 1957) which used methods of flow analysis of a sophistication rarely exceeded since then. (The most highly optimizing compilers have always been those for FORTRAN, a language which lends itself particularly well to this approach.)

Other types of compiler, emphasizing fast compilation, have been developed primarily for use in universities and colleges. A computing center in a teaching establishment has to compile many hundreds of short programs. Most of these student problems contain errors and are generally not intended to produce results on a regular basis. Fast compilation and good error messages are therefore more important than fast execution. Examples of this type of compiler are the WATFOR compiler for FORTRAN produced at the University of Waterloo (Cowan and Graham, 1970) and the PL/C compiler for PL/I at Cornell University (Conway and Wilcox, 1971).

The two forms of compiler give different kinds of assistance to the user—the first for developing and testing programs, the other for routine production. It is impossible to reconcile these two objectives in a single compiler, and the designer has to select a compromise. Since both objectives are important, one solution is to produce two compilers—a high-speed interpreter-compiler and an optimizer. A pair of ALGOL compilers was provided for the English Electric KDF9 compiler: the Whetstone compiler (Randell and Russell, 1964), a fast compiler producing semi-interpretive code, and the Kidsgrove optimizing compiler (Hawkins and Huxtable, 1963).

The first *compatible* pair of compilers for a single language was the PL/I "pair," the Checkout and Optimizing Compilers for System/360. These produce modules of code which use the same storage and linkage conventions and share the same library for operating system functions. Hence modules from either compiler can be linked together within the same program. The Checkout compiler has a number of additional diagnostic features which help in program development (see Cuff 1972).

Another form of compiler, specially developed for interactive programming, is the *incremental* compiler. In this form of implementation, the user is able to modify parts of a program without having to recompile the complete program. The translated text is kept in small segments typically corresponding to a single statement or declaration, and interpretive methods generally have to be used. Incremental compilers have not yet become widely available; techniques for their construction are described in Rishel (1970) and in Berthaud and Griffiths (1973).

In later chapters, it is shown how language designers have made various compromises in favor of implementation efficiency. These include factors in the design of loops, data structuring and storage, and parameter mechanisms.

4.3 OUTLINE OF COMPILER DESIGN

We can best study implementation problems by considering the structure of a typical compiler, as shown in Fig. 4.1.

In the early phases of a compiler, the main task is to discover the logical structure of the source program. It is usual to subdivide the input phases into two separate parts, a *lexical* scan and a *syntactic* scan.

The purpose of the lexical scan is to separate the *tokens* of the text—the individual units which make up the distinguishing symbols of the language.

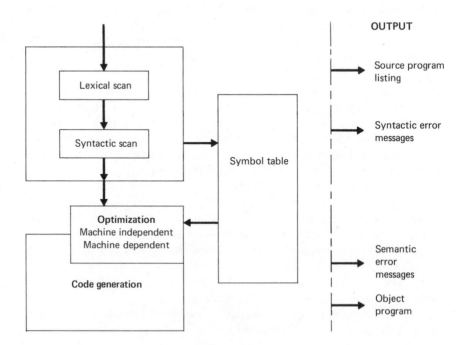

Fig. 4.1 Compiler structural outline

Examples of tokens include:

- identifiers used as names of variables;
- keywords used for statements, attributes, etc.;
- operators such as: $+$, $-$, $*$, etc.

The purpose of the syntactic scan is to discover the structure of the source program and to display the blocks, statements, expressions, and other units of the language to serve as a basis for the subsequent phases of the compiler. Conceptually, the task of a syntax analyzer is to recognize and correctly label the components of a program. The result of a syntactic scan can be expressed in the form of a tree structure, as shown in Fig. 4.2.

Source program statement (COBOL):

```
MOVE NAME TO EMPLOYEE, ADD 1 TO TOTAL OF TRANSACTIONS
```

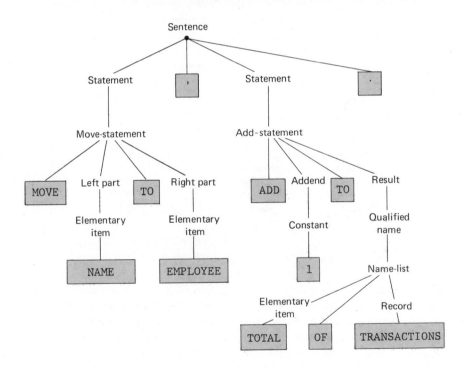

Fig. 4.2 Tree structure obtained by syntactic analysis

The *symbol table* or *dictionary* is central to any implementation of a symbolic language. Techniques for constructing symbol tables have led to the development of many new ideas in systems programming (hash addressing, binary searching, list processing). The main purpose of a symbol table is to provide a correspondence or mapping between the names of the variables in a program and their properties. Information for the symbol table is built up during the early stages of compilation and is collected from declarations in the source text.

The symbol table is referenced at almost all stages of compilation and its design is an important factor in determining the performance of a compiler. At various stages of compilation there are different requirements for the symbol table; in the early stages it is used primarily for assembling and checking information, in later stages as a source of information for code generation.

A complete symbol table contains *names, attributes* and *addresses.* One of the simplest designs is therefore an array containing these quantities.

Consider the following ALGOL program fragment.

$$\textbf{integer } x,y; \quad \textbf{Boolean } t;$$
$$\cdots$$
$$L1: x := x + 17;$$
$$\textbf{if } x > y \textbf{ then go to } L1;$$
$$t := \textbf{false};$$
$$\cdots$$

A simple symbol table for this might be:

name	attribute	address
x	**integer**	101
y	**integer**	102
t	**Boolean**	103
$L1$	**label**	354
..	..	..

The first two columns of the table can be built up during a syntactic scan of the program. At this stage, entries may be inserted in order of their appearance in the program since there can be no prior knowledge of the number of variables to be used or of their distribution. At a later stage, when statements are being scanned to prepare them for code generation the problem is altered—it is then important to search the table rapidly to find the attributes and addresses that go with each variable name. A major concern in symbol table design is therefore to devise efficient techniques of searching. Some compilers sort all names and use a *binary search* to locate an entry from a given name. Another approach is to use a *hashing* method, in which the names are transformed into an integer to provide an entry to a small table from which short chains of search may be used to locate the entry required. (An early paper referring to the use of this technique is by Williams (1959).)

When all names and attributes have been collected, a valuable saving of space can be made by replacing the variable names in the program text by the relative location of the corresponding entries in the symbol table. The statement

$$L1: x := x + 17;$$

in the above program effectively becomes

$$(4) : (1) := (1) + 17;$$

This shortens the text and speeds the search for names in the table. It also allows part of the symbol table (the part containing names) to be discarded during later stages of compilation when space may become critically short.

Block structure languages (see Chapter 6) allow the same identifier to be used in different blocks but with different meanings. To deal with block structure, the symbol table must be suitably segmented (see Busam, 1971).

Finally, there is the question of storage space for the symbol table. In commercial data-processing applications, there may be a thousand or more identifiers in a single program, many having long names. It may be necessary to have a means of storing and retrieving the symbol table on backing storage.

The design of *internal text* is an important part of compiler construction, since it provides the bridge between syntax analysis and code generation. In the case of interpreters, the text formed after syntactic analysis and construction of the symbol table can be directly executed. A convenient form for direct interpretation is the so-called "Polish" form, a string of symbols in which operators and operands (references to the symbol table) are intermingled. Polish notation is discussed in Chapter 9 as it applies to expressions, for which it was first developed.

Example

The assignment statement:

```
x := a * (b + c)
```

may be expressed in Polish notation as:

```
x a b c + * :=
```

Polish notation provides a compact form for program representation but is hard to scan. Compilers often use a tabular representation such as the following:

Example

In the form known as "quadruples" the above expression is:

operation	op1	op2	result
+	b	c	T1
*	a	T1	T2
:=	T2	—	x

In this, *T1* and *T2* are "temporary" locations needed for storage of intermediate results.

The quadruple form of internal text is convenient for compilation since it resembles the machine instruction format of some computers.

The final stages of a compiler are concerned with *code generation*. This is the remotest point from the source program and the one with the closest connection with the machine. Methods of code generation are discussed in several of the works listed in the bibliography, but the following two topics —optimization and compiler output—are of special interest in the design of programming languages.

4.4 OPTIMIZATION

The term "optimization" refers to a set of techniques for producing more efficient code—generally, the aim is to produce faster-running programs. The best optimization techniques now available can produce programs comparable with hand-coded programs. The implications on language design are twofold.

- Special language forms have been introduced to indicate where optimization can be applied.

- Some methods of optimization require a certain latitude in programming language design, to allow for rearrangement of the text.

It is usual to classify optimization into machine-dependent and machine-independent techniques.

Machine-dependent optimization is concerned with:

- selection of the best instructions. For example, it is sometimes advantageous to repeat an instruction a small number of times, rather than generate a short loop.

- effective use of high-speed registers. Many machines have a small number of registers used for arithmetic and indexing. The allocation of these presents a complex problem in resource allocation (see Horwitz, *et al.,* 1966).

- efficient allocation of variables to storage, taking into account machine storage boundaries (words, double words, etc.).

On the whole, machine-dependent techniques are mainly of interest to the compiler writer and do not effect users of high-level languages. On the other hand, machine-independent optimization can be looked upon as equivalent to transformations of the source program. To give an idea of the type of transformation that is carried out, we give a list of commonly applied techniques with examples of their use.

- **Redundant-expression elimination**

This saves repeated evaluation of the same expression when no new result would be computed. For example, in the program

```
DO I = 1 TO 100;
    A(I*4) = B(I*4) + C(I*4);
    ...
```

the expression $I*4$ produces the same result for each subscript. It is more efficient to compute the expression once and assign it to a temporary variable than to carry out the three multiplications implied by the source program.

- **Code motion**

This involves moving code from regions of high execution frequency to those of lower frequency. For example, in the loop

```
DO I = 1 TO 100;
    A(I) = B(I);
      X = 1;
   END;
```

the assignment to X is executed 100 times, although the same effect would be achieved if this statement were moved outside the loop.

- **Dead-code elimination**

Programs which have been subject to extensive updating and editing often contain sections which cannot be reached by normal program flow.

This "dead code" is located and removed. For example, in the code

```
IF P>R
        THEN GO TO LAB4;
        ELSE GO TO LAB5;
    X = 5;
LAB4:    R = P*4.5;
    . . .
```

the assignment statement after the IF statement cannot be reached and can therefore be removed.

- **Strength reduction**

This involves replacing certain operations by equivalent, but more efficient, operations. For example, instead of writing

```
T = X ** 4;
```

it is sometimes more efficient to write

```
T = X * X;
T = T * T;
```

Each of these four types of transformation is such that it might be carried out by an experienced programmer, although certain types of code movement can only be discovered by rather extensive analysis of the source program.

One of the problems of constructing highly optimizing compilers is that in certain languages it is not always easy to detect whether certain variables or functions can be transformed by moving or replacing them. In the case of data, there is an "alias" problem in some languages, in which the same stored data may be referred to by several different names. Another barrier to the optimization of functions is the presence of side-effects (see Chapter 12). It has been proposed that attributes be introduced for data or functions which make it plain whether these properties apply to the variables. Discussion of the problem, and a partially developed solution, is contained in the paper by A. H. Rogers (1972).

4.5 COMPILER OUTPUT

The main output of a compilation is, of course, a translated program ready for execution. The exact form of this output does not concern us here, since it depends on the operating system of the target machine. However, in addition to a translated program, other output is important to users—the set of listings and messages returned to a programmer after compilation. These provide the basic information for debugging programs. The analysis of a source program carried out by a compiler, particularly an optimizing compiler, reveals more about a program than its author can reasonably be expected to know, much as literary critics discover unconscious meanings in the works of great writers. In this case, the knowledge is factual, not interpretive, and includes, for example, details of the loop structure of the program, areas of the program where certain variables are referenced, storage requirements, and similar information useful for optimizing the program. This information can help the user to understand the program better and to remove those errors which may lie on the surface and yet are not apparent from simple reading of the program text.

Compiler listings and messages are not now regarded as part of language standards, in most of which the whole question of listings, errors, error messages, etc. is relegated to a subsidiary role. There is much to be said for establishing a more consistent framework for compiler listings and messages, which in current compilers often display a capricious variety. A more uniform treatment would allow systematic methods of error diagnosis to be established and taught as part of a programmer's training.

Among the listings produced by many current compilers are the following:

- **Source program listing**—the program as submitted to the compiler.

For editing purposes, it is essential to produce an exact copy of the source program, but statement or line numbers may be added to help in referencing the individual statements.

- **Error messages**

Errors detected by the compiler may be listed either individually within the text or together at the end. Errors may be classified according to severity. The messages may refer to statement or line numbers to help the programmer pinpoint the error.

- **List of variables and their attributes**—(particularly important in languages which allow implicit or default declarations).

External variables, that is variables to be linked outside the scope of the program unit, should also be noted. A particularly useful feature is a *cross-reference* list, indicating where each variable is *declared* and when it is *used*.

- **Program statistics**

These indicate program size (source program and object program), number of variables, statements, and a list of the library modules needed.

■   **Object program listing**

It is also common to include a list of the code generated by the compiler. Strictly speaking, this form of listing should not be necessary, and some systems deliberately make such listings unavailable to the general user. (Early compilers were often so slow and unreliable that often the quickest way to develop a working program was to patch and correct the generated code. Many users of today do not feel happy unless they can see this code and perhaps adjust their programming style to achieve the most efficient code.)

The set of listings described above makes up a substantial amount of information, even for a small program. The output of these listings are sometimes optional and controllable by means of parameters on the compiler control card.

4.6   FORMAL METHODS OF COMPILER CONSTRUCTION

Since writing a compiler involves a substantial programming task, it is natural for systems programmers to have looked for efficient methods of construction. An early approach to universal compiler writing was that of Glennie (1960), which was used in some early compilers for large machines. A more ambitious project was that put forward in the UNCOL proposal, developed by a SHARE committee (see references in Chapter 1). Although several attempts have been made to implement the UNCOL idea, no attempt at a full implementation has produced a viable production compiler.

One of the most sustained and successful efforts in automatic compiler-writing has been the "compiler-compiler" of Brooker and Morris (1960, 1962, 1963). This is a system for constructing a compiler from a specialized, formal description of a programming language and has been used to produce compilers for several machines and several languages. A summary of the Brooker and Morris work is given in the paper by Rosen (1964) and it is also discussed in the monograph on compiler writing by Hopgood (1969).

Since the formalization of syntax has been the most successful and longstanding part of language formalization, it might be expected that the syntax phases of a compiler-compiler would be the most successful part of the effort. Indeed, if we look at compiler designs which stop short of the generality of the compiler-compiler principal, we see several that embody the idea of a formal syntax recognizer. See, for example, Cheatham and Sattley (1964) and McKeeman, Horning and Wortman (1970).

It is in code generation that the real test of compiler writing arises. This is also the most crucial part of the design of formal compiler generators.

One technique is to associate a "semantic routine" containing the generated code with each statement type. The effectiveness of such a routine depends on the extent to which it uses information about the surrounding environment of the statement in the source program. It is on such information that the best, indeed sometimes the only, correct object code can be generated. The Brooker and Morris technique uses the parsed text in performing a tree-searching routine, which identifies the environment of the source statement. A somewhat similar scheme is that described in the paper by Elson and Rake (1970), a tree-searching technique which is potentially suitable for the automatic writing of compilers.

To date, compiler-compilers have been successful in relatively few circumstances, those mainly in research environments. So far, they have provided neither the high quality of object code nor the quality of diagnostic information that is possible with handmade compilers. Compiler-compilers are of practical importance in the rapid and economical construction of compilers for special-purpose languages. In such cases, it is feasible to consider designing the programming language specifically for easy compiler writing.

4.7 PROGRAMMING LANGUAGES AND MACHINE DESIGN

For many years, the design of digital computers has been overshadowed by what has come to be known as a "von Neumann" machine. The papers of Goldstine and von Neumann (1946) constituted the original designs for the JOHNNIAC machine and provided both an inspiration and a design pattern for the entire computing industry in its early formative years. Some of the implicit design principles in early machines were as follows:

- numerically coded instructions and addresses,
- a uniformly addressed linear store,
- a single accumulator,
- data stored in binary form,
- programs and data treated in the same way.

The last point, allowing the creation and modification of programs, is one of the most significant features of the von Neumann design and has been considerably exploited in the construction of systems programs.

It is clear, from reading the Goldstine-von Neumann papers, that they were written with the assumption that most programming would be done in machine language. Although they anticipated (or initiated) many of the techniques of programming which were to follow, they did not allow for the general use of high-level language.

Now, two or three decades later, the situation has completely changed and a majority of the programming population uses high-level languages for much of their programming work. One might expect that this would have influenced machine design, but the majority of machines now in use show remarkably little effect from the change in their patterns of use. An exception is the Burroughs machines, which from an early stage adopted a "high-level language approach," both to machine and operating system design. (See Burroughs (1961) and also the reference to the paper by Hauck and Dent (1968) in Chapter 8.)

Among the papers showing how programming languages can influence machine design, the work of Iliffe (1972, also referenced in Chapter 8) and Rice (Mullery, Schauer and Rice, 1963, Rice and Smith 1971) are especially interesting. See also symposium proceedings on this subject (ACM, 1973).

BIBLIOGRAPHY

ACM "Proceedings of a symposium on high-level-language computer architecture," *ACM SIGPLAN Notices,* Vol. 8, No. 11, Nov. 1973.

Abrams, P. S., "An APL machine" Tech. Report STAN-CS-70-158 Stanford University Compiler Science Dept., 1970.

Allard, R. W., K. A. Wolf, R. A. Zemlin, "Some effects of the 6600 Computer on language structures," *CACM,* Vol. 7, No. 2, Feb. 1974, pp. 112–127.

Allen, F. E., "Program optimization" (in) *Annual Review in Automatic Programming,* Vol. 5, Elmford, N.Y.: Pergamon Press, 1969.

Allen, F. E., "Control flow analysis," *ACM SIGPLAN Notices,* Vol. 5, No. 7, Jul. 1970, pp. 1–19.

Allen, F. E., J. Cocke, "A catalogue of optimizing transformations," Research report RC 3548, IBM, Yorktown Heights (Sept. 1971).

The transformations discussed in this review paper include: procedure integration, loop transformation, redundant-expression elimination, code motion, constant folding, dead-code elimination, strength reduction, linear-function-test replacement, instruction scheduling, register allocation, storage mapping, anchor pointing, special-case code generation.

Backus, V. W. *et al.,* "The FORTRAN automatic coding system," *Proc. WJCC,* Vol. 11, Feb. 1957, pp. 188–198.

Barron, D. W., *Assemblers and Loaders,* Macdonald, American Elsevier, 1970.

Most of this short volume is concerned with assemblers and macroassemblers. It will be found useful as an introduction to compiler writing since many of the techniques used apply to symbolic programming in general. A chapter on loaders and linkage editors includes topics related to the static linking of programs.

Batson, A., "The organization of symbol tables," *CACM,* Vol. 8, No. 2, Feb. 1965, pp. 111–112.

Berthaud, M., M. Griffiths, "Incremental compilation and conversational interpretation," *Annual Review in Automatic Programming,* Vol. 7, Oxford: Pergamon Press, 1973, pp. 95–114.

Breed, L. M., R. H. Lathwell, "The implementation of APL/360", *Interactive Systems for Applied Mathematics,* New York: Academic Press, 1968, pp. 390–399.

Brooker, R. A., D. Morris, "An assembly program for a phrase structure language," *Computer Journal,* Vol. 3, No. 3, 1960, pp. 168–174.

Brooker, R. A., D. Morris, "Some proposals for the realization of a certain assembler program," *Computer Journal,* Vol. 3, No. 4, 1960, pp. 220–231.

Brooker, R. A., D. Morris, "A general translation program for phrase structure languages," *JACM,* Vol. 9, No. 1, Jan. 1962, pp. 1–10.

Brooker, R. A., R. R. MacCallum, D. Morris, J. S. Rohl, "The compiler-compiler," *Annual Review in Automatic Programming,* Vol. 3, Elmsford, N.Y.: Pergamon Press, 1963, pp. 229–275.

Brooker, R. A., "Influence of high-level languages on computer design," *Proc. IEEE,* Vol. 117, No. 7, Jul. 1970, pp. 1219–1224.

The author considers the contribution made by languages to the design of instruction sets, the representation of data, referencing or arrays, stack administration, and dynamic storage allocation. A discussion of Burroughs and Manchester University machines is included.

Burgess, C. J., "Compile-time error diagnostics in syntax-directed compilers," *Computer Journal,* Vol. 15, No. 4, Nov. 1972, pp. 302–307.

Discusses the feasibility of specifying diagnostic error messages as part of the grammar of a programming language. This can be done for left-factored languages, and may be extended to other kinds of grammar.

Burroughs Corporation, "The Descriptor—a definition of the B5000 information processing system," Burroughs Corporation, 1961.

Cheatham, T. E., K. Sattley, "Syntax directed compiling," *Proc. SJCC,* AFIPS, 1964, pp. 31–57.

Cocke, J., "Global common subexpression elimination," *ACM SIGPLAN Notices,* Vol. 5, No. 7, Jul. 1970, pp. 20–24.

Cocke, J., "On certain graph-theoretic properties of programs," Research report RC 3391, IBM, Yorktown Heights, June 1971.

In considering the control structure of a program, the *interval* is an important concept, since certain techniques of optimization depend on reducing an entire program to a single interval. This paper shows that any program can be transformed into a single interval, given certain node-copying operations.

Conway, M. E., "Design of a separable transition-diagram compiler," *CACM,* Vol. 6, No. 7, Jul. 1963, pp. 396–408.

An early reference to the construction of a COBOL compiler. Apart from the technical interest of the design, the paper is important in giving one of the first published references to co-routines.

Conway, R. W., T. R. Wilcox, "Design and implementation of a diagnostic compiler for PL/I," Report 71–107, Sept. 1971, Dept. of Computer Science, Cornell University, Ithaca, New York.

Cowan, D. D., J. W. Graham, "Design characteristics of the WATFOR compiler," *ACM SIGPLAN Notices,* Vol. 5, No. 7, Jul. 1970, pp. 25–36.

Cuff, R. N., "A conversational compiler for full PL/I," *Computer Journal,* Vol. 15, No. 2, May 1972, pp. 99–104.

Dijkstra, E. W., "An ALGOL 60 translator for the XI" *Annual Review in Automatic Programming Vol. 3,* Pergamon Press, 1963, pp. 329–345.

   An account of the first ALGOL compiler which became available in 1960.

Earnest, C., "Some topics in code optimization," *JACM,* Vol. 21, No. 1, Jan. 1974, pp. 76–102.

   A tutorial presentation of some optimization techniques of Cocke and Schwartz, together with some extensions by the author.

Elson, M., S. T. Rake, "Code generation technique for large-language compilers," *IBM Systems Journal,* Vol. 9, No. 3, 1970, pp. 166–188.

Feldman, J., D. Gries, "Translator writing systems," *CACM,* Vol. 11, No. 2, Feb. 1968, pp. 77–113.

   A large amount of material is presented concisely with valuable and constructive comments.

Freeman, D. N., "Error correction in CORC, the Cornell computing language," *Proc. FJCC,* Vol. 26, AFIPS press, 1964, pp. 15–34.

   Describes a compiler with both emphasis on error treatment and some error correction.

Glennie, A. E., "On the syntax machine and the construction of a universal compiler," Tech Report No. 2, Computation Center, Carnegie Inst. of Tech., Pittsburgh, Pa., 1960.

Goldberg, P. C., "A comparison of certain optimization techniques," Technical Report RC 3347, IBM, Yorktown Heights, May 1971.

Grau, A. A., U. Hill, H. Langmaack, *Translation of ALGOL 60,* New York: Springer-Verlag, 1967.

   This is a complete description of how to write a compiler for a subset of ALGOL 60 for a single-address machine. There are interesting discussions of the language and of some of the difficulties of compiling certain features.

Gries, D., "Compiler construction for digital computers," New York, John Wiley, 1971.

   A treatise on compiler writing, which covers all aspects in sufficient detail to form a practical handbook for systems programmers.

Griffiths, T. C., S. R. Petrick, "On the relative efficiencies of context-free grammar recognizers," *CACM,* Vol. 9 No. 5, May 1968, pp. 289–299.

Haines, L. H., "Serial compilation and the 1401 FORTRAN compiler," *IBM Systems Journal,* Vol. 4, No. 1, 1965, pp. 73–80.

Compilation of a high-level language on the IBM 1401 machine presented many problems because of the small core size (8k bytes) and the lack of a backing store of the machine. The strategy used was to load the program into core store, and then to pass the compiler through, phase by phase, altering the program *in situ.* There were 63 phases, with an average of 150 instructions per phase. The techniques developed in this compiler were later used as a basis for the design of the PL/I F-level compiler.

Hansen, P. B., R. House, "The COBOL compiler for the Siemens 3003," *BIT,* Vol. 6, No. 1, 1966, pp. 1–23.

A 10-pass compiler, based on a design of P. Naur and J. Jensen. The size of the compiler is 39,000 words (24 bits) (Cf. the Gier ALGOL compiler of 5,800 words of 42 bits). The difference in size between the two compilers is attributed to the complicated structure of COBOL, with its large number of unrelated clauses.

Hawkins, E. N., D. H. R. Huxtable, "A multi-pass translation scheme for ALGOL 60," *Annual Review in Automatic Programming Vol. 3,* Elmsford, N.Y.: Pergamon Press, 1963, p. 163.

Hopgood, F. R. A., *Compiling techniques,* Macdonald, New York: American Elsevier, 1969.

An introduction to compiler technology. The book considers important data structures in the compiling process (strings, arrays, lists, etc.) and separately treats lexical analysis, syntax analysis, code generation, and storage allocation. It also includes a section on compiler-compiler techniques.

Horwitz, L. P., R. M. Karp, R. E. Miller, S. Winograd, "Index register allocation," *JACM,* Vol. 13, No. 1, Jan. 1966, pp. 43–61.

Iliffe, J. K., *Basic Machine Principles* (second ed.), Macdonald, New York: American Elsevier, 1972.

A key work on the design of higher-level machines. The "Basic Machine" has data and control structures much closer to problem solvers' needs than the conventional von Neumann machine. The book contains many insights into language and system design.

Irons, E. T., "An error-correcting parse algorithm," *CACM,* Vol. 6, No. 11, Nov. 1963, pp. 669–673.

Lee, J. A. N., "The anatomy of a compiler," New York: Reinhold, 1967.

A tutorial on compiler writing, based on the FORTRAN language.

Lowry, E., C. W. Medlock, "Object code optimization," *CACM,* Vol. 12, No. 1, Jan. 1969, pp. 13–22.

A systematic technique for global optimization, first used in a Fortran compiler, and subsequently adapted for the IBM System/360 optimizing compiler.

McKeeman, W. M., J. J. Horning, D. B. Wortman, *A compiler generator,* Englewood Cliffs, N.J.: Prentice-Hall, 1970.

A treatise on compiler writing using a particular technique and language, XPL. It contains much interesting material on the design of languages and operating systems.

Moulton, P. G., M. E. Muller, "DITRAN—a compiler emphasising diagnostics," *CACM*, Vol. 10, No. 1, Jan. 1967, pp. 45–52.

Mullery, A. P., R. F. Schauer, R. Rice, "ADAM: a problem-oriented symbol processor," *AFIPS Conference Proceeding, Vol. 23 (SJCC)*, New York: Spartan Books, 1963, pp. 367–380.
The paper describes an experimental processor which directly executes a problem-oriented language with a structure similar to English. There is a strong emphasis on variable-length data, stored hierarchically with embedded markers.

Naur, P., "The design of the GEIR ALGOL compiler," *BIT*, Vol. 3, 1963, pp. 124–140, 145–166.

Nicholls, J. E., "PL/I—a status report," *Software 71*, London: Transcripta Books, 1971, pp. 120–126.
Describes the objectives of the PL/I Optimizer-Checker compilers and illustrates the use of the language extensions introduced with these compilers.

Noble, A. S., R. B. Talmadge, "Design of an integrated programming and operating system," *IBM Systems Journal*, Vol. 2, June 1963, pp. 152–181.

Prosser, R. T., "Applications of Boolean Matrices to the analysis of flow diagrams," *Proc. EJCC*, 1969, pp. 133–138.

Randell, B., D. J. Russell, *ALGOL 60 Implementation*, New York: Academic Press, 1964.
A complete description of an ALGOL implementation for the English KDF9 computer. This book is so well written that several other groups were able to utilize it as a basis for constructing similar compilers for other machines—an impressive and unusual achievement.

Rice, R., W. R. Smith, "SYMBOL: A major departure from class software-dominated von Neumann computing systems," *AFIPS Conference Proceedings*, Vol. 38, AFIPS Press, 1971, pp. 575–587.

Rishel, W. J., "Incremental compilers," *Datamation*, Vol. 16, No. 1, Jan., 1970, pp. 129–136.

Rogers, A. H., Optimization in PL/I and its effect on language development, *IBM Technical Report*, TR 12.112, June 1973, Hursley: IBM United Kingdom Laboratories Ltd.
Discusses the problems of optimizing PL/I, particularly the effects of "aliasing" data and the interrupt-handling facilities. Discusses how the user can help by informing the compiler about his program and also proposes language for indicating the usage of variables.

Rosen, S., "A compiler-building system developed by Brooker and Morris," *CACM*, Vol. 7, No. 7, Jul. 1964, pp. 403–414.

Russell, E. C., G. Estrin, Measurement-based automatic analysis of FORTRAN programs, Proc. AFIPS Conference, Vol. 34 (SJCC), AFIPS Press, New Jersey, 1969, pp. 723–732.

Shows how a translator can be constructed to produce frequency counts of program execution, useful both for studies of program optimization and for computer design.

Wattenburg, W. H., "Design automation for computer software," *IEEE Trans. on Electronic Computers,* Vol. EC-15, No. 3, June 1966, pp. 378–380.

A description of bootstrapping procedures used in producing software by compiler-compiler techniques.

Wichmann, B. A., "ALGOL 60 compilation and assessment," *APIC Studies in Data Processing, No. 10,* New York: Academic Press, 1973.

One of the few books to give precise statistics on efficiency of implementation. Over twenty ALGOL compilers were studied, six of them in depth. The author includes comments both on the design of languages and on the design of computer architecture for high-level languages.

Williams, F. A., "Handling identifiers as internal symbols in language processors," *CACM,* Vol. 2, No. 6, June 1959, pp. 21–24.

An early account of a technique for transforming identifiers (names) into an internal form by means of "hash coding."

Wirth, N., "A basic course on compiler principles," *BIT,* Vol. 9, 1969, pp. 362–386.

This paper deals with two basic aspects of compiler construction: syntactic analysis and output generation. Wirth outlines a set of "work rules" for constructing simple compilers. He emphasizes the properties of reliability and precise documentation.

Yershov, A. P., "The ALPHA automatic programming system," *APIC Studies in Data Processing, No. 7,* New York: Academic Press, 1971.

ALPHA is a variant of ALGOL 60. This book contains papers by members of the group led by Yershov which, around 1964, produced an ALPHA system (including a translator and a debugging system) for the M-20 computer at Novosibirsk. The book provides an unusually balanced view of the technical and organizational problems of systems programming. In an appendix, a set of "problems" is discussed which would provide valuable insight to anyone interested in the practical problems of compiler construction.

5

Theoretical Foundations

5.1 INTRODUCTION

From the time of the Greeks, the systematic study of language has been regarded as an essential part of an educated person's background. Its importance in education can be seen from the name "grammar school," given to the type of school which for centuries formed the main stream of education in England. (Sadly, the name is now passing away with the change in the British system of schooling.)

Programming languages play a central role in the field of computing and their study is essential to an understanding of programming. The languages we deal with in this book such as FORTRAN, COBOL, ALGOL and PL/I differ from natural languages in many ways. Many workers in linguistics would not dignify them with the name *language* at all. In linguistics, a language is usually defined as a means of human communication involving speech, while programming languages, as currently understood, are essentially written notations.

In this chapter, a summary of some of the underlying theory of programming languages is given. Such a theory helps in understanding the structure of programs and languages to facilitate:

- writing syntactically correct programs;
- in compiler writing—constructing both a scanner which correctly determines the program structure and a code generator which correctly represents its meaning;
- in language extension—designing additions which blend harmoniously with the existing structure.

The simplicity and regularity of the structure of programming languages have encouraged the use of mathematical methods of description. Some of the most powerful tools originally came from the analysis of natural languages, notably from the work of Noam Chomsky (Chomsky, 1956, 1959).

This work is mathematical in flavor because mathematics, alone of the sciences, provides effective tools for the study of structure. The relevant mathematical topics such as set theory, graph theory, and the theory of formal systems, have become increasingly important in the study of programming problems. Many concepts originally derived for the formal study of languages have come into general use. This chapter is intended to give a general understanding of these concepts.

One approach to this study originated in the writings of Charles Morris. In his work on *semiotics* or the Theory of Signs (Morris, 1938), he distinguished three aspects of language study, *syntax, semantics,* and *pragmatics.* The meaning of these terms is indicated by the following approximate definitions.

Syntax: the study of language *structure*
Semantics: the study of language *meaning*
Pragmatics: all other aspects of language

These terms, particularly the first two, are frequently used in discussing programming languages. Perhaps the best way of distinguishing between them is to consider the types of question each is concerned with.

Syntactic questions:
What is the *type* of the variable X in program P?
How many arguments does the procedure Y expect? Is

```
DO1J=DO1J,DO1J
```

a valid DO statement in FORTRAN?

Such questions can be answered by considering only the *form* of program text and not its execution.

Semantic questions
What is the value of X after procedure P has been executed?
How many times is the loop $L2$ executed if, at the start of the loop, the variable T has the value 20?

To answer such questions, one must consider program execution. It may also be necessary to know the values of the data used in the calculation.

Pragmatic questions
How does program P compare in efficiency with program O?
How much space does it occupy?
How many errors are likely to be made in the program?

Such questions, although of great importance to language designers, cannot be answered by appeal to the syntactic or semantic descriptions of a language.

Morris's classification of language topics is widely used. However, it must not be imagined that the divisions are clear-cut or that it is always possible to decide whether a particular issue is syntactic, semantic, or pragmatic. The following example of a hazy borderline between syntax and semantics comes from the description of ALGOL 60. The *syntax* of ALGOL is defined by the rules of the ALGOL report (Naur, 1963). Following these rules exactly, we can construct the following program:

> **begin**   **integer** *a,b;*
>
> .   .   .   .
>
> .   .   .   .
>
> **go to** *a;*
> **end**

This program is obviously wrong, since it does not make sense to "go to" an integer variable. This can be seen without executing the program. However, it is not strictly a syntactic error in ALGOL, since the program could be constructed by following the syntax rules. In fact, the method of syntax description used for ALGOL (context-free production rules) are not able to exclude such forms—to do so would require more of the context to be included in the rules.

Much of this chapter is concerned with syntax and semantics, especially with techniques of precise description. In Section 5.8 (the analysis of algorithms) the pragmatic question of the *efficiency* of programs is discussed. Much of the rest of the book is also concerned with pragmatic questions, such as ease of use, machine independence, and the aesthetics of language design. These often provide the severest difficulties to the designer and the majority of controversial issues in language design arise from pragmatic rather than syntactic or semantic questions.

5.2 ALGORITHMS

An idea basic to all computing is that of an *algorithm,* the term used in mathematics for a systematic computational procedure. Programming languages provide, in essence, a means of representing algorithms. (The word algorithm is not related, as one might suspect, to logarithm, but owes its origin to a 9th-century Persian mathematician whose name was shortened to al-Khowarzami—"from the town of Khowarazm." The town is now known as Khiva and is in Uzbekistan.)

An algorithm consists of a well-defined, finite sequence of operations which produces a desired result. The algorithmic process is fundamental to computing—the basic operations of an algorithm corresponding to the instructions carried out by a digital computer. The essential properties of a computing algorithm are as follows.

- It must carry out the required process, i.e., it must be *effective.*
- It must be precisely described so that a machine can be programmed to carry it out.
- It must complete its task in a finite number of steps.

Programming languages, the primary tool for all programmers, are essentially means for describing algorithms.

5.3   BASIC MATHEMATICS

The following section describes some basic mathematical ideas used in language theory. No attempt is made to include a complete or mathematically rigorous account of these topics. A more complete description can be obtained from the works cited in the bibliography.

A dominant concept is that of a *set,* a collection of distinguishable objects or elements. The elements of a set may themselves be sets. Examples of sets arising in programming languages are:

- the set of *characters,* used for representing a language;
- the set of *values,* corresponding to a data type;
- the set of *states,* representing a computation.

There are several ways of defining a set:

- listing the elements,
- stating the properties possessed by members of the set,
- giving rules for generating members of the set.

Each of these is used in language descriptions, the third being the usual method for describing complete languages.

In constructing languages from sets, various set operations are used. The basic set operators are:

union	A ∪ B	the set of objects which are either in set *A* or set *B* or both.
intersection	A ∩ B	the set of objects in both set *A* and set *B.*

Another important set operation is:

complement	∼A	the set of objects which are *not* in *A.*

The following set relations are commonly used:

membership	a ∈ A	the element *a* is a member of the set *A.*
identity	A ≡ B	*A* and *B* are identical sets.

| *subset* | A ⊆ B | All members of the set A are also members of B. |
| *proper subset* | A ⊂ B | A is a subset of B and is not equal to B. |

We next come to ideas leading to the important concepts of *relation* and *function*. The first is that of an *ordered pair,* a pair of elements chosen from two sets. The set of all possible ordered pairs chosen from two sets A and B is called the *cartesian product* of the two sets (after the French mathematician Descartes), and is written $A \times B$. A *relation* between A and B is any subset of the cartesian product $A \times B$.

Example

- If A is the set of positive integers: $\{1,2,3,...\}$ and B is the set: $\{1,4,9,16,...\}$ then (1,1),(2,4),(3,9),... is a relation between A and B corresponding to the *square* of an integer.
- The set: (1,1),(2,16),(3,81),... is another relation between A and B corresponding to the *fourth power* of an integer.

As we see, a relation provides a means of obtaining a member of a set B, given a member of set A. The relation is said to be "from A to B." As we see in the example, A and B may contain common elements, or may in fact be the same set.

A *function* from A to B is a relation such that, if an element of A is given, there is only one element of B to which it corresponds. The *domain* of such a function is the set of values of A for which there is a corresponding value B. If the domain of a function from A to B is the whole of A, then the function is said to be a *mapping*.

Examples

symbol table   a relation between names and locations (Chapter 5)
translate table   a relation between two character sets (Chapter 8)

It is often convenient to name a function and to treat it as an entity in its own right. Thus we can speak of a function "f," whose pairs of corresponding elements are denoted by, for example, x and $f(x)$.

Expressed in terms of ordered pairs, the function f represents the set

$$(x_1, f(x_1)), (x_2, f(x_2)), (x_3, f(x_3)),...$$

Example

In the previous example, the first function or relation can be represented by the name "square," so that the pairs of elements are: (1, square(1)), (2, square(2)), . . . etc.

Another way of representing the function "square" is by means of the *expression,* x^2. In representing a function, however, we must be careful to distinguish between a function and a *form.* The function, "the square of," is mathematically the mapping from a certain set of numbers to another set of numbers, the squares of the first set. The form, "x^2," additionally indicates a method of computing the function. From this form we know that, given a value x, its square can be computed by multiplying it by itself. This illustrates an aspect of the term function which differs slightly from the previous view as a set of ordered pairs of values. It also provides a method by which, given one member of an ordered pair, the other can be computed. An expression used in this way is a means of representing the algorithm for computing the function.

The concepts of sets, functions, and mappings are fundamental to the mathematical theory of language and appear in many guises in descriptions and discussions of programming languages.

5.4 FORMAL SYSTEMS

The tools of mathematics and logic may be used to construct what is known as a *formal system.* By this means, what would otherwise be intractable problems can be converted to a form in which they can be studied and manipulated with precision and rigor. The elements of a formal system are:

- a set of formal *symbols*—including identifiers, logical symbols, predicate symbols, etc.

- a set of *formation rules*—analogous to the syntax rules of language—defining a set of valid *formulas,* constructed from finite sequences of the formal symbols.

- a set of *deductive rules* by which results, including *proofs,* can be obtained.

The use of the term "formal" indicates that in manipulating symbols or constructing proofs the symbols of the system are to be regarded simply as abstract entities, characters, or marks on paper, without any regard to what they correspond to in the "outside" world. It is simply the *form* of sentences that is of interest, not their significance. To relate the symbols of a formal system to some external object requires an act of *interpretation.*

Formal methods have been used for the study of mathematics itself to determine a basis for mathematical symbols and their laws of combination. It is on this foundation that the formal theory used for programming languages is based. The history and an outline of the basis of formalism are given in Chapter 3 of Kleene's "Introduction to Metamathematics" (Kleene, 1964).

5.4.1   Applications of Formal Theory

We next describe how formal methods have been applied to the two following problems:

- the formal definition of languages;
- the development of formal proofs of program correctness.

5.4.1.1   Formal definition of languages

The size and complexity of modern programming languages are noticeable to their users, but are matters of everyday concern to language designers and compiler writers. One saving fact for users is that they do not necessarily have to understand an entire language, but only those parts which help in solving their problem. At worst, they can try out a doubtful point on a compiler and see what happens—many users acquire their language knowledge this way, by experiment and interaction with a compiler.

This experimental approach is not open to language designers or compiler writers. For one thing, a compiler may not be available; this is certainly the case when a new language is first implemented. More important, the answers obtained by submitting programs to a compiler are specific, whereas the answers needed by designers and implementors must be consistent with the general principles on which a language is constructed.

The set of valid programs in a given programming language is effectively infinite and the rules of grammar of the language—its syntax—must be framed to allow all the different combinations and orderings that correspond to valid programs. The full complexity of languages can be seen by considering the execution of programs. Here we have not only the large number of operations in a typical program, but also the possibility of a different set of operations for each set of input data.

It is not enough to have "approximate" rules for language construction, as in natural language. Many people communicate adequately in natural language without consciously knowing the rules of grammar and in spite of making many "mistakes." This is not possible with computer languages; most compilers require strict observance of syntactic rules. The fact that a program is a set of instructions to a machine, rather than a question or an expression of opinion or emotion, places a more severe requirement on accuracy of expression.

Given a need for precision and completeness in language specifications, there remains the question of what form these should take. Many people feel that an *informal* description, in natural language, is adequate for the definition of languages. There would be many advantages if this was the case, but natural languages such as English are normally used so imprecisely that informal descriptions frequently contain many ambiguities. Even when

English is used very carefully and precisely, as in most programming-language specifications, there are inevitably a number of undecidable points which cannot be resolved from an informal description.

To overcome these difficulties, the mathematical apparatus of a formal system may be set up to define language systems and semantics.

5.4.1.2   Formal models of syntax

The greatest attention has been given to formal methods of syntax. A *syntax* or *grammar* is a set of rules for specifying valid sentences of a language. The word "sentence" is commonly used to denote a complete utterance or message; in the case of programming languages, it is usually taken to mean a *program.*

The usual means of specifying syntax is by a set of *production rules.* Starting with basic elements such as characters, the rules give ways of stringing elements together to make intermediate constructions called *phrases,* and for assembling these to form sentences. Note that a "phrase" is not used in its usual sense of a group of words expressing some notion or concept; it is simply a convenient unit for expressing the structure of a programming language. (Languages defined in this form are sometimes called *phrase-structure-languages*). A phrase is defined in the production rules in terms of symbols, or other phrases.

For example, a *digit* may be defined as:

the character zero (0), *or*

the character one (1), *or*

the character two (2)

     .   .   .

etc.

The rules are not concerned with how the choice is to be made; this is assumed to be determined by the objectives of the programmer.

The number of syntax rules must be finite, although the number of sentences in a language is infinite. To allow the generation of infinite sets of strings from a finite set of rules, we need something more than simply offering alternative choices of phrase or symbol. In addition to the primary operation of concatenating ("stringing together") symbols and phrases, most production systems involve the use of *recursive definitions*. We recall that a phrase may be expressed in terms of symbols or phrases, and that in any definition, alternative choices may be offered. A recursive definition is one in which one or more of the alternative choices in the definition of a phrase involves the use of the phrase itself.

For example, if the set of strings we wish to define is the set of unsigned integer numbers (called simply "numbers") we may use the rules:

a number is a *digit, or*
a number is a *digit* followed by a *number*

This simple syntax defines an infinite set of numbers, because the recursion in the second rule can be applied any number of times, each application resulting in the addition of an extra digit. In this case, recursion is used simply to express the stringing together of an arbitrary number of digits. We could as well say:

a number is a string composed of an arbitrary number of digits.

This is a perfectly adequate and precise definition, equivalent to the recursive definition given above. A commonly used notation for this is the use of three dots (...) to denote arbitrary repetition of the preceding element. Thus *number* would defined as *digit*.... This notation is used in the COBOL and PL/I language specifications.

In the description above, we have shown the process of building up successively larger phrases from smaller units. Another way of looking at the production rules is as a way of *analyzing* a "sentence" (i.e., a program) into progressively smaller units, until finally it is seen to be made up from single characters or symbols. In this process, a production rule can be regarded equally as a "substitution" rule.

The components of a formal system for language syntax are as follows:

- a finite set of *terminal symbols, T*

These symbols are the *characters* of the language; they are called "terminal" because they represent the final stage in the substitutions implied by the rules for constructing languages.

- a finite set of variables, *V*

These are the intermediate constructions of the language, such as "expression," "do-list," etc., introduced to provide the internal structure of the language needed for analysis and processing.

- a specially distinguished variable, *S*

S is a member of the set *V*, and is the object to be constructed in the rules for the language. Often, the word used for *S* is "sentence"; the rules show how to construct all sentences of the language.

- a finite set of production rules, *P*

This is the most critical part of the system. The production rules are rules of substitution of the form

$$A \rightarrow B$$

where *A* and *B* may contain symbols from the sets *T* and *V*. Such a rule means: "Replace *A* by *B*." When this is done, a partly formed string consisting of terminals and variables is replaced by a more complete string, until finally an instance of *S* is created, consisting only of terminal symbols from the set *T*.

These four components together make up the formal language system. They are rather an uneven collection, since *T* and *V* are sets of simple objects, *S* is a single object which is a member of *V*, and *P* is a set of *rules*, a different kind of object from those in the other sets. A *formal language* (see, for example, Hopcroft and Ullman, 1969) is often defined as consisting simply of these four components. Hence we meet the rather enigmatic phrase at the beginning of papers on the mathematical theory of languages

"A language *L* is a 4-ple, $\{T, V, S, P\}$ ...."

The form of the production rules *P* has a strong bearing on the properties of the language generated by these rules. Chomsky (1959) classified languages into four types: recursively enumerable sets (type 0), context-sensitive languages (type 1), context-free languages (type 2), and regular sets (type 3). Of these, context-free languages are the most useful and have been widely used as a model for programming languages. Since Chomsky's paper, many other types of languages have been identified and studied:- LR(k) languages, precedence languages, and bounded context languages. Many of these are members of the class of context-free languages. Some have properties which allow bounds to be put on the size of storage needed for processing them. For descriptions of these and other formal languages, see Ginsburg (1966) and Hopcroft and Ullman (1969).

In a context-free language, the substitution of strings described above is carried out without regard to the neighboring strings (or "context"); this considerably simplifies the formal study of this kind of grammar. The most commonly used formal notation for describing the syntax of programming languages is that known as BNF (Backus Naur Form)†.

BNF is a notation for context-free languages which allows the compact representation of grammars, using certain special symbols and conventions. Essentially, it follows the pattern of the production rules outlined above, which have long been used in linguistics for describing the construction of languages from elementary symbols. To express the rules more compactly

---

†This is also known as "Backus Normal Form," and was presented in a paper by John Backus (1959). Knuth (1964) pointed out that it is not a "normal" form in the mathematical sense, and suggested the change in name to recognize the contribution of Peter Naur, the editor of the ALGOL report.

and to simplify their printing in commonly available character sets, a number of notational improvements were made. Among the conventions used in BNF are the following:

the use of special brackets < and >, to indicate "metasyntactic variables" or intermediate phrases;

the use of the vertical bar | to separate alternatives in the substitution rules;

the use of the symbol :: = instead of a right arrow.

BNF was used to define the syntax of ALGOL and since then either BNF itself, or some closely similar notation, has dominated all formal methods of syntax description. Because of this, languages definable by BNF (i.e., context-free languages) are sometimes known as "ALGOL-like languages." Actually, there are certain aspects of ALGOL which are not definable by means of the BNF notation—for example, the point noted above that a **go to** statement must refer to an identifier which is used as a label. The crucial factor which cannot be handled by BNF is the relationship between the declaration of a variable and its use. This relationship is, in fact, "context-sensitive" and properly belongs to a language of Chomsky's type-1 category. Proposals for extending BNF to accommodate context sensitivity have been made (for example, see Whitney (1969), Lee and Dorocak (1973), Hanford and Jones (1973), and Ledgard (1974)). Meanwhile, we are left with a situation that Lewis Carroll might have enjoyed, namely that ALGOL itself is not an "ALGOL-like" language.

5.5   ABSTRACT SYNTAX

The BNF notation used in the ALGOL report is a syntax for generating *strings* of characters—any language it defines is essentially a linear text of symbols. Following an idea originally put forward by McCarthy (1967), it has become more usual to define languages in terms of an *abstract syntax*. This has the valuable result that the essential features of a language—for example its structure and component parts—can be described without defining what characters or symbols are to be used to represent it, or even in what order they will appear.

For example, consider an assignment statement. The definition of this in BNF might be written as follows:

<assignment statement> :: =

<variable>|<procedure identifier> : =

<arithmetic expression>|<Boolean expression>

Each of the quantities in the brackets < and > is a phrase which will be defined in subsequent rules and eventually replaced by a concrete symbol. Even at this level, the rule has permitted the representation to include the symbol : = and to put the source and target of the assignment on the right and left of the symbol respectively.

In an abstract syntax, the definition of an assignment statement would simply list the two parts of the statement, name them, and specify the properties they may have. For example, in the notation used for describing the abstract syntax of PL/I during development of the language (Beech *et al.,* 1967), an assignment statement was defined as shown in Fig. 5.1.

The notation used in the Vienna definition of PL/I (Lucas and Walk, 1969), uses predicates to define "composite objects," whose components may

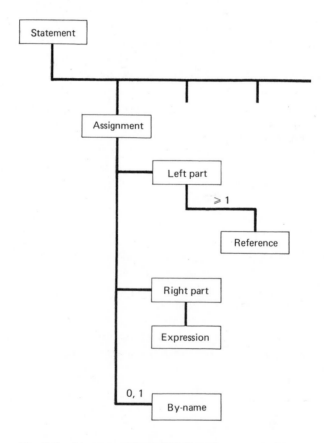

Fig. 5.1 Abstract syntax of PL/I assignment statement

be represented in any form. In this notation, an assignment statement is
written as follows:

$$\text{is--assign--st} =$$

$$(<\text{s--st:is--ASSIGN}>,$$

$$<\text{s--lp:is--ref--list--1}>,$$

$$<\text{s--rp:is--expr}>,$$

$$<\text{s--byname:is--opt}>)$$

In the notation, the names beginning with "is–" are *predicates,* while
those beginning with "s–" are *selectors,* a general form of reference to
composite objects.

The use of abstract syntax allows any of the following forms of an
assignment to be treated as equivalent:

```
X  := X+1
X   = X+1
X + 1 → X
SET X = X+1
```

5.5.1   Formal Models of Semantics

The formal description of language syntax has a relatively long history,
partly because of experience with the grammars of natural languages, but
also because of previous studies of the formal syntax of expressions in
mathematics and logic. When we come to descriptions of semantics, however, there is much less available experience of formal methods. The problem is to associate meanings with programs, or rather (in defining the semantics of a *language*) with all programs which can be written in the
language.

Among the approaches used there are three broadly different techniques:

- **translation**

An algorithm is given which translates a given program into an equivalent program written in a simpler language. Either the semantics of this language are assumed to be known or one of the other techniques is used for
its definition.

This technique is illustrated in a paper by Bekic (1965). It is essentially
the method advocated by the "definition by compiler" school of thinking,
in which the primitive language is machine language.

■ **interpretation**

Rules are given for interpreting the given program on a hypothetical abstract machine. This machine is completely defined by means of a *state;* the execution of a program is determined by a set of functions which transform the state.

This is the most common method of definition and is adopted by Landin (1965), Elgot and Robinson (1964) and the IBM Vienna Group (Lucas and Walk, 1969).

■ **axiomatic definition**

This differs from the other techniques in that a computation is not defined. Instead, a set of axioms is defined which must be satisfied by all programs written in a particular language. Provided these axioms are satisfied, any method of implementation is permitted. Hoare (1969) has advocated this method of definition.

A combination of the first and second methods is used in the Vienna definition of PL/I, one of the first complete formal definitions of any programming language, and certainly the first of an operational language of the size and complexity of PL/I.

The basis of the method is to express semantics by the behavior of a "PL/I machine" in executing programs written in an idealized version of PL/I. The definition of the meaning of a program is in two parts—the first deals with the *translation* of the PL/I program text into an abstract form (an *abstract program*), the second with the *interpretation* of the abstract program.

The structure of an abstract program is defined by the abstract syntax of PL/I, and this syntax plays a central role in the definitional method. Compared with the syntax of text strings in PL/I (called the *concrete syntax*), the abstract syntax has the following properties.

■ It is free from details of representation (i.e., character sets used, spelling of keywords, punctuation, etc.).

■ It is free from unnecessary ordering (for example, the ordering of declarative statements is not relevant; only the block in which they appear is).

■ It is "complete," in that there are no unresolved default or implicit attributes (see Chapter 7).

After translation, an abstract program is conceived of as one which is directly executed by an interpreter. The detailed actions of the interpreter define the semantics of the language. Clearly the structure of this interpreter forms a vital part of the definition. Care must be taken that, while the interpreter allows precise definition of all parts of the language, it does not prevent the use of certain implementation techniques (such as, for example, the optimization techniques described in Chapter 4).

At any point during execution of a program, the interpreter is represented by its *state*. The notion of a machine being completely characterized by its state is used in automata theory (see Tou, 1968), but will also be familiar to programmers in an analogous form, as a memory dump or checkpoint. The contents of a state contain the current values of all variables and values "saved" for later use (such as return addresses for subroutine calls, partially evaluated expressions, etc.).

In a block structured language like PL/I, the structure of the state—which may also mirror the execution-time store in a real implementation—may conveniently be expressed in the form of a *stack* or *push-down* store.

This stack is the heart of the abstract PL/I machine. In the Vienna definition, it is subdivided into five parts: environment, epilogue information, text part, statement counter, and control, each of which carries out special functions during program execution. As a PL/I program is executed, each semantically important element of the language may be defined as a function acting on the state which produces a new version of the state. Arithmetic operators act on values producing new values, branching statements may produce new values of the control, assignment affects the storage representations of variables, and so on.

Figure 5.2 shows an outline of the semantics of block entry and exit—this outline can be looked upon as the semantics of the composite text corresponding to the characters between a BEGIN statement and its matching END statement.

There are two sets of actions corresponding to block entry (the prologue) and block exit (the epilogue). These are defined in terms of the following components of the state.

AT	Attribute directory
BA	Block activation name
CI	Control information
CS	Condition status
D	Dump
DN	Denotation directory
EI	Epilogue information

In the definition, each of the boxes 1–6 and 8–10 is expanded to show the precise behavior of these components; in effect, an algorithm is presented which transforms the initial value of the state to its final value.

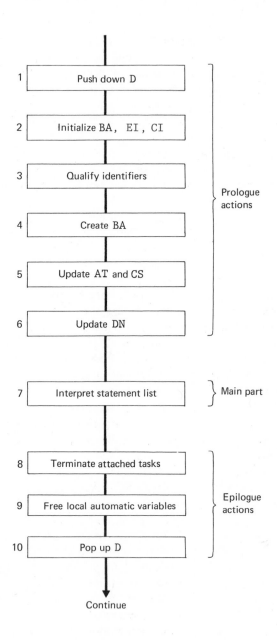

Fig. 5.2 Interpretation of a PL/I begin block

The flowchart in Fig. 5.2 shows how a "general" BEGIN–END block is interpreted. Each block in an actual program will differ according to the statements within it. The contents of the block are treated independently, as implied by box 7. For each statement type, there is a corresponding algorithm, again defined in terms of the system state.

The complete definition of PL/I, together with explanatory and supporting material, occupies several large reports; introductions are given by Bandat (1968) and by Lucas and Walk (1969). A survey paper by Wegner (1972) also provides a useful introduction and a commentary on various techniques for language definition. The main components of the semantic definition, the abstract syntax, and the formal semantics, are contained in the Technical Report, TR 25:098 (Walk *et al.*, 1969).

The completion of the "ULD" (Universal Language Definition), the complete formal definition of PL/I, was a landmark in the history of programming languages and has set a standard for extreme precision and completeness in definition. After publication of the first draft, the ULD was carefully validated against the informal documentation and, where this was not sufficiently precise, with the designers' and compiler writers' understanding of the language. The ULD was then used in "language control," the clarification of doubtful points of syntax or semantics.

Since the ULD definition was not available during the first implementations of PL/I, it was not possible to use it as a basis for compiler writing. However, there is some doubt if this particular definition would have been suitable for this purpose. First, those who were not regularly using formal methods found the notation used in the ULD extremely difficult to understand and to use. Second, the model of the PL/I machine adopted for the semantic definition was too general and abstract for those familiar with the actual code used in a PL/I implementation.

When the choice of a method of definition for the PL/I standard was discussed, the standardization committees felt unable to use the ULD. A new definition was developed, which retained the essential rigor of the ULD, but was more accessible to programmers.

The definition used in the PL/I standard is, like the ULD, based on a PL/I machine executing programs structured according to an abstract syntax. The relationship between concrete and abstract syntax is, as before, expressed by means of a "translator." The structure of the PL/I machine in this definition is precisely defined, but the functions corresponding to the statements and operators of the language are expressed more informally than in the ULD, in a form of disciplined English prose.

A description of the method used in the PL/I standard is given by Beech (1973).

5.6   PROVING PROGRAM CORRECTNESS

In addition to providing precise models of programming languages, the other major contribution of formal methods is in the field of program correctness.

To introduce this subject, let us consider the usual method of developing a program. First, an outline specification is drawn up, from which a more detailed logic diagram or flow chart is constructed. The programmer works from this, producing detailed code expressed in some programming language. This program is translated into machine code and after removal of syntax errors detected by the translator is ready for execution. Before using the program, it is *tested* by running it with trial data to confirm that it produces the expected results. In complex system programs, such as compilers or operating systems, the effort of writing and running test cases may consume a considerable proportion of the total manpower of a project.

Even after a program has been extensively tested in this way, it is far from being completely tested. We only have to think of a single procedure, with two or three parameters, and consider the number of combinations that would arise if *all* cases were tested. Expand this to a medium or large program and we can see that test cases can only exercise an infinitesimal number of the possible combinations of data for a typical program. Although considerable skill is required in laying out a pattern of test cases for a major program, the fact remains that, even with the best techniques, this is an imperfect method of assuring the correctness of a program.

An alternative does exist, the original proposals for which come from some of the earliest work on programming by Goldstine and von Neumann (1963), expanded and made more precise by J. McCarthy. In several papers discussing a basis for computer science (e.g., McCarthy, 1962, 1963), McCarthy put forward the possibility of *proving* that a program solves a problem.

The difference between proof and test-case techniques can be seen by considering how the techniques apply to a mathematical result, say the theorem of Pythagoras. Suppose we are told the result of the theorem, and asked to confirm it, using only test cases. We might duly examine a number of right-angled triangles, measure the sides and compare the results. As this work proceeded, several questions might occur to the testers. How many triangles should be examined? What about very large, or very small, triangles? How should we know when we had measured enough triangles to confirm the result?

The beauty of a *proof* of such a theorem is that these questions and doubts need not arise. Given certain entities (points, lines), with known properties (the axioms and theorems needed for the proof), and applying certain deductive rules, we can be certain of the truth of a theorem, for *all* cases.

Practical application of such a technique was not feasible in 1962, when many of the studies needed to support this approach were still relatively immature. However, McCarthy's objective—that of eliminating the need for test cases—has attracted increasing support and attention. It is now at least feasible to consider *proof* as a means for assuming the correctness of small and critically important programs. An idea of the scope and variety of the work in progress in this area can be obtained from ACM proceedings (ACM, 1972) and from a bibliography by London (1970).

There are two somewhat different techniques for formally establishing the correctness of a program. In the first, the programmer must express the problem to be solved as an *algorithm*. This algorithm must be written in a formal notation—that is, a notation whose properties are precisely known and can be formally manipulated. (Examples of such formal notations include the lambda calculus and recursive functions.) The task of proving a *program* correct resolves to a test of proving the *equivalence* of the program and the algorithm. The programming language in which the program is written must be formally described in order that a proof of equivalence can be carried out.

The second technique has been more widely applied and seems to offer more promise for practical use in programming projects. It derives from ideas expressed in a paper by Floyd (1967). The program to be proved is accompanied by *predicates* (expressions yielding the values *true* or *false*) referring to the variables in the program. The most important predicates are those referring to the ultimate results of the program—the relationship of the output data to the input data. The programmer may also insert predicates at intermediate points of the program to express other relationships that must exist during the course of program execution.

A *proof* of the correctness of a program or, as Floyd calls it, a *verification* of the program, is a proof that the predicates written with the program are indeed true.

Floyd further suggested incorporating predicates with the statements of each program and developing a compiler which would both translate the program and carry out mechanical verification of the predicates. A "verifying compiler" for a simple language was constructed by King (King, 1969), but this approach has not yet been found feasible for full-scale languages, or indeed for other than quite small programs.

The discipline of formally proving programs correct presents severe problems for large, complex programs. The objective, expressed by some workers in this field, that all programs should be accompanied by a proof of their correctness, seems a long way in the future, if we look at current techniques and skills. However it appears likely that formal proof methods will be applied to critical parts of systems programs and that the discipline of specifying predicates about the relationships between variables in a program will prove useful, even if a complete and formal program proof is not always developed.

Currently, much of the work in this area remains inaccessible to many programmers because of the difficulty of the notation and the mathematical background assumed by the writers of most papers. A tutorial introduction to correctness proofs and the *formal development* of programs is given by Date, McMorran, and Sharman (1974).

5.7 ANALYSIS OF ALGORITHMS

As we have seen, the algorithm is the basis of all programming. The *analysis of algorithms* is concerned with the study of existing algorithms, the development of improved solutions, and the selection of the "best" algorithm for a given set of circumstances. This analysis can be carried out systematically, independently of the language in which the algorithms are expressed.

This topic has only recently received the attention it deserves, perhaps because the discovery (or in many cases re-discovery) of algorithms has seemed a relatively unimportant part of a programmer's work. There has long been a prevailing emphasis on methods of developing new programs and relatively little attention to the analysis, selection and use of existing program material.

The total costs of developing an application include design, programming development (coding and testing), maintenance, and running. In many cases running cost is dominant and considerable efforts are made to minimize this, including the use of machine language rather than high-level language and the use of optimizing compilers. However, the improvements obtained by such means are often less than the differences between "average" and "best" algorithms. Furthermore, the steps taken to achieve such improvements in efficiency often lead to less reliable and less easily maintainable programs. If we optimistically assume that most programmers will produce an average algorithm, then we may expect at least as good a return in the form of efficiency and reliability from the selection of superior algorithms as from attempts to make poor algorithms run faster.

The analysis of algorithms is concerned with the establishment of "best" solutions to problems with some degree of generality and universality. Algorithms of sufficient importance to be systematically analyzed and studied are similar to operations included in high-level languages. Examples of high-level functions which appear as functions or statements in programming languages include the mathematical and trigonometrical functions included in most scientific languages, the SORT and SEARCH statements in COBOL, the built-in function POLY in PL/I. The topic is therefore related in an important way to the design of higher-level programming languages.

5.8   SOME RESULTS FROM THE ANALYSIS OF ALGORITHMS

The types of problem on which most emphasis has been placed are those which have arisen from mathematics or mathematical approaches to systems programming:

- **Combinational problems**

  sorting,
  searching,
  permutations;

- **Linear algebra**

  matrix arithmetic,
  matrix inversion;

- **Other problems**

  arithmetic (multiplication, division, LCM, etc.),
  polynomial evaluation.

The elements of an analysis include the following steps.

- establishing that each algorithm is correct, (i.e. that it carries out its intended purpose).

- determination of a figure of merit (generally the speed of execution, but perhaps the space occupied during running of the algorithm). Machine independent expression of this is difficult and often leads to simplified figures of merit such as number of multiplications (in polynomial evaluation) or number of compares (in sorting).

- evaluation of each algorithm in terms of the figure of merit.

  This may be done by analysis or in difficult cases by simulation. In some cases, the performance is strongly affected by the input data (e.g., searching problems are affected by the degree of randomness of the data).

- comparing each algorithm and recommending a specific algorithm for each set of circumstances.

This may sometimes be expressed in the form: "Algorithm A is best," although it is usually expressed in a form such as:

"Algorithm A is fastest for $N < 100$
Algorithm B is fastest for $N > 100$, . . . etc."

5.8.1 The Evaluation of Polynomials

Polynominals are commonly used as approximations to functions. They are also used, together with techniques of curve fitting, for the compact representation of experimental data.

The most efficient general method of evaluating an arbitrary polynomial is the nested method of multiplication due to Horner. In this, the expression $ax^3 + bx^2 + cx + d$ is evaluated as: $((ax + b)x + c)x + d$. Horner's method requires n multiplications and n additions for a polynomial of order n, and Borodin (1971) has shown that, for an arbitrary polynomial, it is optimal.

Suppose however that we have a table of values to compute with a given polynomial. It is then possible to devise a better method than Horner's.

For example, the 6th order polynomial

$$P = x^6 + ax^5 + bx^4 + cx^3 + dx^2 + ex + f$$

can be computed by first computing a series of auxiliary coefficients A to F, then calculating the auxiliary results, P_1 and P_2

$$P_1 = x(x + A)$$

$$P_2 = (P_1 + x + B)(P_1 + C)$$

P is finally given by the equation

$$P = (P_2 + D)(P_1 + E) + F$$

The values of A, B, C, . . F are computed by equating the coefficients of x in both equations and solving the fairly simple sets of equations that result. This calculation need only be done once for any given polynomial.

By means of this transformation and the preconditioning of the equations, the evaluation of P for a given value of x needs only 3 multiplications and 7 additions, a significant saving on most machines.

This technique was originated by Motzkin (1955). A general result due to Belaga (1958) is that the *minimum* number of operations needed for evaluating a polynomial, even with the use of precalculated polynomials, is:[†]

$$\text{floor}((n + 1)/2 + 1) \quad \text{multiplications}$$
$$n + 1 \quad\quad\quad\quad\quad \text{additions}$$

This theorem gives a lower bound for an arbitrary polynomial, without indicating how the auxiliary polynomials are to be computed. Another Russian author, Pan (1966) has given general methods of computing the coefficients of auxiliary polynomials. (The works of Belaga and Pan are published in Russian. See Reingold (1972) for references.)

So far, the discussion has ignored another important factor in polynomial evaluation, the *conditioning* of the results (i.e., their sensitivity to small errors in the coefficients or in the techniques of computation). For a further discussion of this, see Hart, *et al.* (1968) Chapter 4.

To sum up, although the widely used method of Horner is an excellent general purpose algorithm, it is by no means optimal if many values of a specific polynomial are to be computed. For constructing large tables of values of a given polynomial, it is almost always worthwhile to use the Motzkin type of technique.

The analysis of algorithms is an important and growing field of computer science. Its relevance to programming languages is twofold. Firstly, programming languages increasingly incorporate functions whose performance is being studied—these include mathematical functions, combinatorial algorithms, searching, and sorting. Secondly, programming languages must make available to the user the right sort of primitives to allow these algorithms to be coded.

Survey papers on the analysis of algorithms include those of Reingold (1972) and Frazer (1972). The standard work on the study of algorithms is undoubtedly the series of volumes on *The Art of Computer Programming* by D. E. Knuth.

BIBLIOGRAPHY

ACM, "Towards better documentation of programming languages," *CACM*, Vol. 6, No. 3, Mar. 1963, pp. 76–92.

A series of short papers describing the problems of adequately documenting a programming language. The languages covered are: ALGOL 60 (Naur), COBOL

[†] floor(n) is the largest integer less than or equal to n.

(Cunningham), COMIT (Yngve), FORTRAN (Heising), IPL-V (Newell), JOVIAL (Shaw), NELIAC (Halstead). The papers contain interesting comments on the earlier history of programming languages. The remarks by Naur on documenting a programming language are particularly interesting and worth reading.

ACM, "Proceedings of an ACM conference on proving assertions about programs," *ACM SIGPLAN Notices,* Vol. 7, No. 1, Jan. 1972.

Allen, C. D., "The application of formal logic to programs and programming," *IBM Systems Journal,* Vol. 10, No. 2, 1971, pp. 2–38.

Ashcroft, E. A., "Program correctness methods and language definition," *SIGPLAN Notices,* Vol. 7, No. 1, Jan. 1972, pp. 51–57.

This paper summarizes several ways of proving program correctness and relates them to current approaches to language design and definition.

Backus, J. W., "The syntax and semantics of the proposed international algebraic language of the Zurich ACM-GAMM Conference," *Proc. International Conf. on Information Processing,* UNESCO, 1959, pp. 124–132.

Bandat, K., "On the formal definition of PL/I," *Proc. AFIPS,* Vol. 32, Washington: Thompson Book Company, 1968, pp. 363–373.

Beech, D., R. A. Larner, J. E. Nicholls, R. Rowe, "Abstract syntax of PL/I," TN 3002 (version 2) Hursley, England: IBM, 1967.

The first published abstract syntax of PL/I derived during the development of the language and issued as part of a "semiformal" definition.

Beech, D., "On the definitional method of standard PL/I," *ACM Symposium on the Principles of Computing,* ACM, 1973.

Bekic, H., "Mechanical transformation rules for the reduction of ALGOL to a primitive language *M* and their use in defining the compiler function," Technical Report TR 25.051 Vienna: IBM, Feb. 1965.

Bekic, H., "Defining a language in its own terms," Technical Note TN 25.3.106 Vienna: IBM Laboratory, Dec. 1964.

Discusses the possibility of using a language to define itself, a technique used in LISP. The discussion is limited to a simple form of expression language.

Berman, R., J. Sharp, L. Sturges, "Syntactical charts of COBOL 61," *CACM,* Vol. 5, No. 5, May 1962, p. 260.

Borodin, A., "Horner's rule is uniquely optimal," *Theory of Machines and Computations,* (Z. Kohavi and A. Paz eds.), New York: Academic Press, 1971, pp. 45–58.

Cheatham, T. E., K. Sattley, "Syntax-directed compiling," *Proc. AFIPS,* Vol. 25, Baltimore: Spartan Books, 1964, pp. 31–57.

Chomsky, N., "Three models for the description of language," *IEEE Trans. Inform. Theory,* Vol. IT2, 1956, pp. 113–124.

Chomsky, N., "On certain formal properties of grammars," *Information and Control,* Vol. 2, 1959, pp. 137–167.

This is the primary reference for the important classification of grammars originated by Chomsky. In this paper he specifies the differences between grammars of types 0, 1, 2, and 3 and discusses which types are most useful for the study of natural languages. This work has had a profound influence on the formal study of programming languages.

Church, A., "The calculi of lambda-conversion," (in) *Annals of Mathematic Studies, No. 6*, Princeton, N.J.: Princeton University Press, 1941.

Church, A., *Introduction to Mathematical Logic*, Princeton, N.J.: Princeton University Press, 1956.

Date, C. J., M. A. McMorran, G. C. H. Sharman, "Program proving and formal development: a tutorial introduction," IBM Technical Report, Hursley: TR.12.127, May 1974.

An introduction to methods of proving programs correct using assertions. The paper is intended for those without extensive mathematical background.

Davis, M., *Computability and Unsolvability*, New York: McGraw-Hill, 1958.

Elspas, B., K. N. Levitt, R. J. Waldinger, A. Waksman, "An assessment of techniques for proving program correctness," *Computing Surveys*, Vol. 4, No. 2, June 1972, pp. 97–147.

A useful survey and analysis of methods of proving programs correct. After a section summarizing the mathematical background on abstract programs and schemata, the authors illustrate both formal and informal methods of proof and verification, and recommend subjects for further study. There is a selected bibliography.

Florentin, J. J., "Language definition and compiler validation," (in) *Machine Intelligence Vol. 3*, Edinburgh: Edinburgh University Press, 1968, pp. 33–41.

Floyd, R. W., "Syntactic analysis and operator precedence," *JACM*, Vol. 10, No. 3, Jul. 1963, pp. 316–333.

Floyd, R. W., "The syntax of programming languages—a survey," *IEEE Trans. on Electronic Computers*, EC13, Vol. 4, Aug. 1964, pp. 346–353.

Describes various types of phrase-structure grammars and their use in constructing syntax analyzers.

Floyd, R. W., "Assigning meanings to programs," *Proceedings of Symposia in Applied Mathematics*, American Mathematical Society, Vol. 19, 1967, pp. 19–32.

Most of the practical applications of correctness proving are based on the approach described in this paper. Correctness of a program is determined by associating predicates referring to variables in the program with various points in the program. To verify the program is correct is to confirm that the predicates are true.

Frazer, W. D., "Analysis of combinatory algorithms: a sampler of current methodology," *AFIPS Conference Proceedings*, Vol. 40, AFIPS Press, 1972, pp. 483–491.

This paper discusses the kind of measurements that might be applied in evaluating nonnumerical algorithms. These include extreme and mean performances as well as variance.

Galler, B. A., A. J. Perlis, *A View of Programming Languages*, Reading, Mass.: Addison-Wesley, 1970.

An introduction to the basic theories of programming and programming languages, based on Markov algorithms.

Ginsburg, S., *The Mathematical Theory of Context-Free Languages*, New York: McGraw-Hill, 1966.

Ginsburg, with several collaborators, is the author of many papers on language and automata theory. This book collects major results from this field of study, It is heavily mathematical and for the specialist reader only.

Goldstine, H. H., J. von Neumann, "Planning and coding problems for an electronic computer instrument," (in) *Collected works of John von Neumann, Vol. 5,* Elmsford, N.Y.: Pergamon Press, 1963.

Hanford, K. V., C. B. Jones, "Dynamic Syntax: a concept for the definition of the syntax of programming language," *Annual Review in Automatic Programming, Vol. 7,* Oxford: Pergamon Press, 1973, pp. 115–142.

This paper first explains the difficulties of expressing the effect of declarations in the conventional notation for context-free grammars. The technique described is to use declarations to form additional (context-free) rules which are added to the base rules of the language.

Hoare, C. A. R., "An axiomatic basis for computer programming," *CACM,* Vol. 12, No. 10, Oct. 1969, pp. 576–583.

In this paper, Hoare advocates the use of axioms rather than the more usual translational and interpretive methods for defining programs and languages. One advantage of axioms in language definition is that their use allows part of a language to remain undefined.

Hopcroft, J. E., J. D. Ullman, *Formal Languages and Their Relation to Automata,* Reading, Mass.: Addison-Wesley, 1969.

This book provides a comprehensive review of formal language theory. The authors discuss grammars, including the classification into types of grammar introduced by Chomsky. These are related to various types of automata and Turing machines. Basic theorems on decidability are reviewed in a final chapter.

King, J. C., *A Program Verifier,* Ph.D. Thesis, Carnegie-Mellon University, 1969.

Describes a "verifying compiler," based on the ideas of correctness-proving of Floyd (1967), which provides mechanical checks of the consistency of the predicates applied to a program.

Kleene, S. C., *Introduction to Metamathematics,* New York: Van Nostrand, 1952.

A standard work, including sections on mathematical logic (formal systems, formal deduction, propositional and predicate calculi), recursive functions, Gödel's theorem.

Knuth, D. E., "Backus Normal Form vs. Backus Naur Form," (letter to the editor) *CACM,* Vol. 7, No. 12, Dec. 1964, pp. 735–736.

Knuth, D. E., *The Art of Computer Programming Volumes 1, 2, 3,* Reading, Mass.: Addison-Wesley.

This magnificent series of volumes, part of a giant work in progress, contains an extensive analysis of algorithms commonly used in programming, together with their mathematical background, history, and related material.

Landin, P. J., "A correspondence between ALGOL 60 and Church's Lambda-notation," *CACM,* Vol. 8, Part I: No. 2, Feb. 1965, pp. 89–101, Part II: No. 3, Mar. 1965, pp. 158–165.

Although Landin was not the first to point out the connection between ALGOL and the lambda-calculus, he developed and discussed the correspondence in this and other papers. His main motivation was to develop an understanding, and eventually a precise definition, of advanced programming languages. The "SECD machine" is developed to deal with ALGOL features. It forms an "interpreter" similar to that later used in the definition of PL/I (Lucas & Walk, 1969).

Landin, P. J., "A lambda-calculus approach," in (ed) L. Fox. *Advances in Programming and Nonnumerical Computation,* Elmsford, N.Y.: Pergamon Press, 1966.

A slightly expanded version of Landin's 1964 paper "The mechanical evaluation of expressions."

Landin, P. J., "The next 700 programming languages," *CACM,* Vol. 9, No. 3, Mar. 1966, pp. 157–164.

This presents the author's point of view on programming languages—very much of the lambda-calculus school—expressed here with cogency and wit. The paper provides a good introduction to the abstract formulation of language problems. Landin refers to his system with the acronym ISWIM (If you See What I Mean) a useful phrase for designers who occasionally find themselves at a loss for precise words.

Ledgard, H. F., "Production systems: or Can we do better than BNF?" *CACM,* Vol. 17, No. 2, Feb. 1974, pp. 94–102.

Lee, J. A. N., J. Dorocak, "Conditional syntactic specification," *Proceedings ACM 73,* ACM, 1973, pp. 101–105.

A proposal for defining context sensitivity within the framework of BNF notation.

London, R. L., "Bibliography on proving the correctness of computer programs," (in) *Machine Intelligence, Vol. 5,* Edinburgh: Edinburgh University Press, 1970, pp. 569–580.

Lucas, P., K. Walk, "On the formal description of PL/I," (in) *Annual Review in Automatic Programming,* Vol. 6, Part 3, Elmsford, N.Y.: Pergamon Press, 1969, pp. 105–181.

The best introduction to the objectives and techniques used in the formal definition of PL/I. This major endeavor was the first application of formal methods to a programming language during the development and implementation of the language.

Manna, Z., "The correctness of programs," *Journal of Computing Systems Science,* Vol. 3, 1969, pp. 114–127.

McCarthy, J., "Towards a mathematical science of computation," (in) *Information Processing 1962, Proc. IFIP Congress,* 1962, North Holland, Amsterdam, 1963, pp. 21–28.

Discusses the prospect for a science of computation. The primary goal for such a science would be the proof that given procedures solve given problems—McCarthy suggests subsidiary goals that would help in achieving this end.

McCarthy, J., "A basis for a mathematical theory of computation," (in) *Computer Programming and Formal Systems,* P. Braffort & D. Hirshberg (eds), North-Holland, Amsterdam, 1963.

McCarthy, J., J. Painter, "Correctness of a compiler for arithmetic expressions," *Proceedings, Symposium on Applied Mathematics,* American Mathematical Society, Vol. 19, 1967.

    One of the first applications of correctness-proving techniques to a systems program.

Mendelson, E., *Introduction to Mathematical Logic,* Van Nostrand, 1964.

Morris, C., "Foundations of the theory of signs," (in) *International Encyclopaedia of Unified Science,* Vol. 1, No. 2, Chicago: University of Chicago Press, 1938.

Motzkin, T. S., "Evaluation of polynomials," *Bull. Amer. Math. Society,* Vol. 61, 1955, p. 163.

Munro, I., "Some results concerning efficient and optimal algorithms," *Proc 3rd Annual ACM Symposium on Theory of Computing,* 1971, pp. 40–44.

Naur, P., "Proof of algorithms by general snapshots," *BIT,* Vol. 6, No. 4, 1966, pp. 310–316.

    A "snapshot" is similar to the state vector of a computation as used in defining the semantics of programming languages. A "general snapshot" is however more like an assertion or predicate, in that it is represented as a mathematical expression in terms of the program variables.

Neuhold, E. J., "The formal description of programming languages," *IBM Systems Journal,* Vol. 10, No. 2, 1971, pp. 86–112.

Reingold, E. M., "Establishing lower bounds on algorithms—A survey," *AFIPS Conference Proceedings,* Vol. 40, AFIPS Press, 1972, pp. 471–481.

    A summary and history of a selection of best case algorithms including those for sorting, searching, selection, polynominal evaluation, matrix arithmetic, and scalar arithmetic. A useful bibliography is included.

Steel, T. B., Jr. (ed), "Formal language description languages," *Proc. IFIP Working Conference,* Vienna, 1964; North Holland, 1966.

    A collection of papers presenting the first consolidated picture of the formal definition of programming languages. The title is notoriously, and apparently deliberately, difficult to parse.

Strachey, C., *Towards a Formal Semantics: Formal Description Languages for Computer Programming,* (ed) T. B. Steel, Jr., Amsterdam: North Holland, 1965.

Tou, J. T. (ed), *Applied Automata Theory,* New York: Academic Press, 1968.

    A collection of papers; those by Hohn, McNaughton, and Ledley are especially relevant.

Walk, K., K. Alber, M. Fleck, H. Goldmann, P. Lauer, E. Moser, P. Oliva, H. Stigleitner, G. Zeisel, "Abstract syntax and interpretation of PL/I (ULD Version III)," *Technical Report TR 25:098,* Vienna: IBM, Apr. 1969.

The central part of the "ULD"—a complete formal definition of PL/I. This part of the definition contains an abstract syntax of PL/I and a formal model of an interpreter, an abstract machine whose execution of PL/I programs defines the semantics of the language.

Wegner, P., *Programming languages, information structures and machine organization,* New York: McGraw-Hill, 1968.

Wegner, P., "Operational semantics of programming languages," *ACM SIGPLAN Notices,* Vol. 7, No. 1, Jan 1972, pp. 128–141.

"Operational semantics" of a language are expressed by some form of implementation model. This paper summarizes some models that have been used in implementing languages and which might therefore serve as possible models for a semantic definition. For example, the ALGOL 60 "copy rule" has been implemented by various techniques, such as the static chain, the display, the procedure-activation record, etc. These are discussed as possible operational models.

Wegner, P., "The Vienna definition language," *Computing Surveys,* Vol. 4, No. 1, Mar. 1972, pp. 5–63.

This paper describes the techniques developed by the IBM Vienna Laboratory for the formal definition of PL/I. The technique is applied to a simple block structure language. The paper provides a good introduction to methods of formal definition.

Whitney, G. "An extended BNF for specifying the syntax of declarations," *AFIPS Conference Proceedings, SJCC,* Vol. 34, 1969, pp. 801–811.

Zemanek, H., "Semiotics and programming languages," *CACM,* Vol. 9, No. 3, Mar. 1966, pp. 139–143.

An introduction to the formal basis of language study, based on Morris's partition of language theory into syntax, semantics, and pragmatics.

Part 2
Elements of Procedural Programming Languages

In Part 1, some important influences on the structure of programming languages were indicated; in Part 2, the major part of this book, we shall see how these influences have shaped the design of some current languages. The languages chosen for most of the illustrations include FORTRAN, ALGOL 60, COBOL and PL/I; however, certain other languages which have more specialized objectives are also illustrated. It is expected that one or more of these languages will be familiar and easily accessible to the reader.

The topics in Part 2 are arranged as follows:

	Chapter
Program structure and representation	6
Data	
Data elements	7
Data structures	8
Data operators and expressions	9
Sequence control	10
Input and output	11
Procedures	12

Under these headings, the first section of each chapter indicates some of the problems being addressed, following which there is a comparative review of the relevant statements and other language forms.

The topics covered by each chapter correspond to specific language features or groups of features and it may be helpful to indicate some of the major themes appearing in the second part of the book.

One dominant and recurring topic is that of *structure*—the pattern on which languages are formed and which provides the underlying basis for their design and implementation. Several kinds of structure are discussed in the book: *program* structure in Chapter 6, *data* and *storage* structure in Chapter 8, *control* structure in Chapter 10. The important form known as *recursive* structure appears in many places in programming languages and is introduced in Chapter 6 and expanded upon in Chapters 8, 9, and 12.

Programming languages are deeply concerned with *data,* which is discussed in several chapters. One of the essential concepts in programming is that of a *variable*—introduced in Chapter 7 and reappearing in several other chapters. A closely related topic is that of *binding*—the association of certain properties with variables. One of the major concerns in language design is the degree of binding that should take place. If binding is too early or too rigid, a language may be difficult to use; if too late, efficient implementation may be impossible. This topic is also introduced in Chapter 7, but its influence extends throughout the book. Data in its external form is considered in Chapter 11, on Input-Output, although this chapter only covers some of the basic aspects of a very much larger subject.

Chapter 12 deals with the *procedure* and with methods of procedure invocation. This is the highest point in the hierarchy of language elements introduced in Chapter 6. The design of procedures, and of the argument/parameter relationship, represents one of the major achievements of programming language design.

6
Program Structures and Representation

6.1 INTRODUCTION

In this chapter we begin the detailed study of programming languages by looking at programs as complete structured entities, and considering how the different parts of a language are related to the whole. The statements, expressions, operators, and other elements that provide the basis of most programming languages are discussed in subsequent chapters.

Most programming languages are constructed from statements, which are themselves made up from smaller units. However, a program is not simply an arbitrary collection of statements, but has an internal structure, which is reflected in the types of statements used and the order in which they are written.

In studying the structure of programming languages, it is helpful to distinguish between the logical structure of a program and its means of representation. An important concept is that of an *abstract syntax* of a language, as outlined in Chapter 5. This allows us to consider program elements (tokens, statements, blocks, etc.), without making any commitment about how these are actually written by a programmer. Several languages share similar concepts, even though their spelling and punctuation may differ; by dealing with their abstract, rather than their concrete, syntax, the underlying similarities are more readily seen.

This is not to overlook the importance of the concrete form of program representation. The success of programming languages as means of communication depends on the availability of established character sets, with graphic symbols, recognized by a wide population of users, for which card

91

and tape punches, keyboards, printers, etc. are available. Ease of use and the incidence of minor errors are considerably affected by the concrete form of program representation.

6.2 THE IMPORTANCE OF STRUCTURE

Why is program structure so important in the study of programming languages? Firstly, it is important in *understanding* programming languages and programs written in them. The structure of a program, particularly of one written in a "free-format" language, can be obscured by the way it is written, as shown in Fig. 6.1.

```
TEST: PROC;          ON ERROR PUT ALL;
 PUT('TABLE OF X+LOG X :') SKIP(2); /* HEADING LINE 1*/
PUT('X','X+LOG X') SKIP(3);    /* HEADING LINE 2 */
    DO X=1 BY 1 TO 10;   /* COMPUTING LOOP*/
                  Y = X+LOG(X); PUT(X,Y)SKIP;END;
DCL X;
   END TEST;
```

Fig. 6.1   Program structure obscured by representation

On the other hand, program structure can be revealed by writing the program out in such a way that its inherent structure is displayed. Most programmers adopt some convention for laying out programs when using free-format languages; the listing in Figure 6.2 was, however, formatted automatically by an editing program. In this case, the editor is part of the compiler—the PL/I Checkout Compiler (Marks, 1973).

Program structure is also important in compilation. The logical structure of programs must be analyzed and checked by a compiler before code is

```
TEST:
  PROC;
  DCL
     X;
     ON ERROR
        PUT ALL;
     PUT('TABLE OF X+LOG X :') SKIP(2);/* HEADING LINE 1*/
     PUT('X','X+LOG X') SKIP(3);       /* HEADING LINE 2 */
     DO X=1 BY 1 TO 10;                /* COMPUTING LOOP*/
        Y = X+LOG(X);
        PUT(X,Y)SKIP;
     END;
  END TEST;
```

Fig. 6.2   Program structure revealed by editing

generated. Systems programmers therefore must have a close knowledge of the structure of those languages for which they are writing compilers.

6.3 FIXED- AND FREE-FORMAT LANGUAGES

Programming languages can be classified according to their format: languages with *fixed-format* (examples: FORTRAN, COBOL, RPG) and languages with *free-format* (examples: ALGOL, PL/I).

Fixed-format languages were the first to be developed and have been especially important in the U.S.A., where punched card equipment has been dominant. Many such languages are based on the 80-column card, although some of the more obvious dependencies on card size and format have gradually been reduced. In such languages, there is a built-in unit of the language, the *line,* typically consisting of 80 characters. Within each line, there are *fields* in which certain kinds of information may be written. For example, in FORTRAN the columns of a card are allocated as follows:

> col 1:   a letter C in column 1 indicates a comment line
> cols 1–5:   used for statement labels
> col 6:   denotes a continuation line
> cols 7–12:† contains statements

In early versions of COBOL, fields were also allocated to specific card columns. However, the COBOL standard is now less rigid and defines a "reference format" in which the exact allocation to character positions of a line can be decided by implementors. The basic positions defined by the standard are Margin L, the left-most character position, and Margin R, the right-most character position of a line. Relative to Margin L, the following special fields are defined:

> cols 1–6:   the sequence number area
> col 7:   the indicator area (used for continuation)
> cols 8–11:   Area A, used for the beginning of headings, procedure names, and level numbers
> col 12-col R: used for statements.

An extreme example of a fixed-format language is provided by Rapid-write (Humby, 1963), an early version of COBOL for small machines, in which the programmer used preprinted forms corresponding to the statements of the language. This approach obviously further reduces the need

---

†The statement field stops short at column 72 because of the structure of the IBM 704 machine, whose word length was 36 bits. This influenced the design of the card reader originally used for FORTRAN input.

to be concerned with layout and punctuation, at some considerable loss in flexibility. A similar idea is used in the various RPG languages.

Free-format languages have no fixed columns or other internal boundaries. Conceptually, a program written in free format consists of a stream of characters, whose structure is determined only by the delimiters of the language. In order to edit such programs for printing, it is necessary to introduce an additional nonrecording character, the character for *new-line* or *carriage return*. The development of free-format languages has been more extensive in countries outside the United States, particularly Europe, where paper-tape is commonly used for program input.

The advantages of free-format languages include:

- flexibility and economy;
- suitability for continuous media, e.g., paper tape;
- convenience for the mechanical processing of program text, e.g., "compile-time" processing, and automatic formatting.

On the other hand, there are several advantages of fixed format which offers:

- a standard appearance to programs, allowing easier reading and checking
- easier detection of some kinds of error
- easier scanning by a compiler.

6.4 COMMENTS

Comments are important in the use of high-level languages, although they do not affect the behavior of a program. The syntax of a language must be designed to allow comments to be written without ambiguity—this is largely a matter of choosing appropriate delimiters and possibly restricting the characters which may be written within a comment string.

Comment facilities should be designed to allow programmers flexibility in adding remarks and explanations to their programs, since these can be of great importance in modifying and extending programs. Apart from the need to be able to distinguish comments from program text, the convention for writing comments should not be sensitive to small errors on the part of the programmer, especially those which result in parts of the program text being treated as comments. Design criteria for comment conventions are outlined in a review paper by Scowen and Wichmann (1974).

FORTRAN has a special comment "card" or line, which is identified by a letter C in column 1. A similar convention is introduced in the 1973 revision of COBOL, where the symbols * and / in character position 7 denote a comment line. The symbol / also causes a page eject on the printer. This convention replaces the NOTE and REMARKS facilities in the 1968 standard. Neither FORTRAN nor COBOL allows comments to be written on the same line as a statement.

In free-format languages it is feasible to allow comments to be more freely interspersed with text. There may be problems with delimiters and it is generally necessary to restrict the contents of comment strings in some way.

ALGOL has a keyword, **comment,** which may be used, after any **begin** symbol or semicolon, to introduce an arbitrary string of 'comment text', which is delimited by a semicolon. It is also possible to write a comment appended to an **end** symbol—this string is also terminated by a semicolon.

Example

    begin comment in this block the array is transposed;
    statement-1;
    statement-2;

    . . .

    end end of transpose;

ALGOL also has an unusual convention, in which comments describing formal parameters may be interspersed with the names of the formal parameters in the procedure declaration. For example, if there is a procedure: LEAST, for calculating the least of a set of quantities, the beginning of the procedure declaration, without comments, might be written.

    procedure LEAST (A, N, E);

Using the ALGOL comment convention, this may be written

    procedure LEAST (A) ORDER: (N) TOLERANCE: (E);

In this form, the strings

) ORDER:(and   ) TOLERANCE:(

are used instead of commas in the procedure heading.

Similar rules apply in calling an ALGOL procedure. This particular procedure might be invoked by means of the statement

    LEAST(T) ORDER:(10) TOLERANCE: (0.002);

This has precisely the same effect as the statement

    LEAST(T, 10, 0.002);

In the paper referenced above, Scowen and Wichmann criticize the ALGOL comment convention as clumsy, both for users and implementors, and consider it one of "the worst features of the language."

In PL/I, comments are delimited by the two-character tokens, **/*** and ***/.** (These composite tokens are chosen since they do not naturally arise in expressions or other contexts.) A PL/I comment may appear in any place a blank may appear, that is, between any successive tokens. The use of the character pair ***/** as the "right-bracket" delimiter implies the restriction that this combination of consecutive characters must not appear in a comment string.

Example

The procedure heading for **LEAST** in PL/I would be written without comments as:

```
LEAST: PROCEDURE(A,N,E);
```

Comments may be added as follows:

```
LEAST: PROCEDURE(A, N /*ORDER*/, E /*TOLERANCE*/ );
```

and might be called as follows:

```
CALL LEAST(T, 10 /*ORDER*/, 0.002 /*TOLERANCE*/ );
```

6.5 A HIERARCHY OF PROGRAM ELEMENTS

In most programming languages, the elements from which a program is constructed form a hierarchic structure. Major units, such as procedures or blocks, contain smaller units such as statements, which in turn contain still

Name of Unit	Purpose
JOB	Unit of work in an operating system
PROGRAM	Unit of execution
PROCEDURE	Unit of compilation, modularity
BLOCK	Unit of name scope, interrupt handling
STATEMENT	Unit of sequencing
COMPOUND STATEMENT	
EXPRESSION	Value-producing unit
REFERENCE	Access function
TOKEN	Molecular unit of syntax
KEYWORD	
IDENTIFIER	
CHARACTER	Atomic unit of syntax

Fig. 6.3 A hierarchy of program elements

smaller units. In some languages, this structure is *recursive;* that is to say, elements of a certain kind may themselves contain elements of the same kind. Block-structured languages such as ALGOL and PL/I are good examples of recursively-structured languages—a *block* is defined as containing a sequence of statements or blocks. (Another example of a recursive structure is the arithmetic expression found in nearly all languages. See Chapter 9.)

The basic program elements are discussed in the following section. A hierarchy of these elements is shown in Figure 6.3.

6.5.1 Character

The *character* is the smallest unit of a language and is a single, distinguishable mark which can be impressed on one of the media used for programming (paper, card, tape, disk, etc). The design of character sets involves complex issues of hardware costs and efficiency. Many older languages suffer unduly because of the small size of their character sets. Smith (1960), shows how considerations about the size of character set may influence the internal structure of a machine.

FORTRAN and COBOL are both designed with small character sets of 48 and 50 characters respectively. PL/I has a slightly larger set of 58 characters; the extra characters are used primarily for operators and delimiters.

ALGOL 60, in its "reference" form, is defined in a larger character set of more than 100 characters. In addition to the usual letters, numbers and operators, the special signs used for statements and delimiters (**begin, end, if, for,** etc.) are each regarded as single symbols. However, implementors of ALGOL are allowed alternative forms of hardware representation, depending on the available machinery, and these will generally make use of the more usual forms of character.

Fig. 6.4 The APL/360 keyboard

APL is based on a newly designed character set, including a distinctive type face for letters and numerals. The importance attached to this aspect by the APL designers can be judged by the fact that they re-designed the conventional typewriter keyboard to accommodate the new character set. A discussion of the underlying principles behind the design of the APL character set is included in Iverson, 1964. The APL/360 keyboard is shown in Fig. 6.4.

6.5.2   Delimiters

Looked at simply, a computer program is a linear string of characters. To represent the structural elements of a language, it is necessary to delimit this string in some way, to mark out the blocks, sections, statements, expressions, tokens, and other syntactic elements. Certain symbols, called *delimiters,* are set aside for this. Two types of delimiter are commonly used: separators and brackets.

A *separator* is a symbol which marks a point in the program string, enabling the separated portions to be treated distinctively. The most common form of separator is the *blank,* which is used for this purpose in many linguistic systems. Its importance is sometimes overlooked, since it is represented as a space rather than a printed character, but it plays a vital part in language design and implementation.†

Other commonly used separators include the punctuation characters used in natural languages:

> .   period
>
> ,   comma
>
> ;   semicolon
>
> :   colon

Other separators used in programming languages include:

:=   (the assignment symbol in ALGOL)

BY   TO   FROM

OF   IN

step   until   while

Brackets are pairs of distinctive but related symbols (left bracket and right bracket) which delimit a region of a program, namely the contiguous string which lies to the right of a left bracket and to the left of a "matching"

---

† Theeffectofremovingspacesistomakeapieceoftextmuchhardertoread.

right bracket. The symbols used for brackets are assymetric, unlike separators, which have no directional properties.

Brackets involve the use of two characters instead of the single character needed for a separator. In the restricted character sets available in most computing systems, their introduction therefore has to be considered very carefully. The main advantage of brackets is in allowing the specification of nested structures. A bracketed structure can be completely contained within another, to an arbitrary depth of nesting. In this way, *recursive structures* can be built up; this is undoubtedly the most important way of creating complex structures from simple components.

The most commonly used brackets in programming languages are the parentheses: (and). ALGOL also uses square brackets: [and], to delimit the subscripts in array references, keeping round brackets for use in delimiting parameters. Thus the FORTRAN, COBOL or PL/I array reference: A(I) is written: *A[I]* in ALGOL. This convention has been followed by a few other languages, including APL, and POP2.

Some languages have statements which act as brackets. For example the statements: DO and END in PL/I act as brackets, allowing loops to be nested inside other loops.

PL/I has a special form of END statement, which may act as a multiple right bracket. If we have a PROCEDURE statement or a labeled BEGIN or DO statement, then the statement:

```
END label:
```

terminates this unit, and all others contained within it. (More precisely, a statement: END L; terminates the unclosed block or group labeled L that physically precedes and appears closest to the END statement.)

Example

```
MAINLOOP: DO I = 1 TO (N+R);
             DO WHILE(FLAG);
                X(I) = RESULT + F;
                IF RESULT<0 THEN
                   DO;
                      C = C + 1;
                      CALL EXEP;
         END MAINLOOP;
```

The last statement terminates all three DO groups and is therefore equivalent to three unlabeled END statements.

This form of END statement, providing what is called *multiple closure,* is a convenient form of short-hand, and is useful in terminal programming.

It requires special treatment in language specifications and in parsing, since a structure involving multiple closure is not "context-free" (see Chapter 5). A more serious objection is that multiple closure may cause program errors to be overlooked and it should therefore be used with caution.

6.5.3 Tokens

A token is a syntactic unit consisting of a character or group of characters; its inner structure is not significant, so long as it can be uniquely recognized.

In most languages, the following are regarded as tokens:

- *identifiers*—the names constructed by the programmer to reference his own data.
- *keywords*—names referring to elements of the system, or to special functions, statements, or other units of the language.
- *operators*—characters such as +,−,*,/, composite tokens such as ** (exponentiation), and >= (greater than or equal to)

We next discuss two of these types of token—the identifier and the keyword.

6.5.3.1 Identifiers

High-level languages allow programmers to define data, subroutines, and other entities and to give them identifiers, or names. The rules for constructing such names are a part of the language. Factors to be considered in the design of these rules include the following.

- It should be possible to achieve close correspondence between constructed names and the names of entities outside the program.
- User names must not be ambiguous with respect to other program elements.
- Efficiency of implementation must be considered.

The rules for constructing names establish what may be called a "name space" (Dennis, 1965). This is analogous to a geometric space, and consists of the very large set of possible names from which the programmer can make a choice. Although a name space may be very much larger than most computer stores, its occupancy by the names used in any given program is usually very sparse.

A frequently used rule for constructing names is the following: an *identifier* is a *letter* followed by a *letter* or a *digit*. This rule is used in ALGOL, FORTRAN and PL/I. In COBOL, it is not necessary for the *first* character to be a letter—it is sufficient simply that there should be at least one letter in the name.

An important factor in the implementation of languages is the maximum *length* of user names. In early machines, in which core and backing storage was extremely limited and techniques of compilation relatively crude, the size of symbol table needed during compilation was a critical factor. Several early languages restricted names to a small number of characters; FORTRAN to six characters, some languages to even less. Such restrictions severely limit the naturalness of programmer names.

The ALGOL specifications do not restrict the length of identifiers—the recursive definition given in the ALGOL 60 report:

$$\langle \text{identifier} \rangle ::= \langle \text{letter} \rangle \mid \langle \text{identifier} \rangle \langle \text{letter} \rangle \mid \langle \text{identifier} \rangle \langle \text{digit} \rangle$$

in principle, allows identifiers of infinite length. ALGOL compilers have generally not followed this rule strictly; some restrict identifier length, others accept long identifiers, but ignore all but the first 6 or 8 characters. Resulting incompatibilities between implementations were later dealt with by the ECMA and ISO standards for ALGOL (see Appendix).

COBOL designers took the commendable course of insisting on long identifiers—the COBOL standard is 30 characters—allowing much greater freedom in the choice of meaningful names.

Improved techniques of compilation and the availability of larger stores have now reduced the need for implementors' concern over identifier length, but there are still some reasons for restrictions. For example, difficulties may arise when identifiers have to be retained during linkage, loading, or execution of a program, where storage space for them may have to contend with space for data. The names in question may include those used in linkage ("external" names) and those used for dynamic tracing or other semi-interpretive code. An illustration of the concern for identifier length can be seen from the paper by Barrett and Grems (1960), proposing a systematic scheme for abbreviating names.

6.5.3.2   Keywords

Keywords are part of the built-in vocabulary of a programming language. Examples of keywords include:

statement keywords   which distinguish the types of statements

if, <code>GO TO</code>, <code>PERFORM</code>, etc.

descriptive words   used in data declarations

<code>FLOAT</code>, integer, <code>DISPLAY</code>

"noise" words   used to improve the readability of program text (these are called "optional words" in COBOL):

<code>IS, ON, WITH</code>.

In formulating the rules for constructing keywords, the language designer must decide whether to use the standard form for user-defined names or to adopt a special syntax, possibly involving the use of distinctive characters. Another decision to be made is whether keywords are to be *reserved* (i.e., prohibited from use as variable names)—this choice depends on the syntax of the language. PL/I was designed so that keywords, although syntactically like identifiers, need not be reserved. The COBOL syntax was not defined with this property and all COBOL keywords are reserved.

Because of problems in dealing with long names, some languages have adopted "official" abbreviations of keywords. Many of the longer PL/I keywords have official abbreviations, which are regarded as part of the language. For example, instead of the keywords: ALLOCATE, ALLOCATION, AUTOMATIC, . . . , the programmer may equally well write: ALLOC, ALLOCN, AUTO, . . . etc.

6.5.4 Reference

The reference is a means of access to an entity defined by the programmer. The reference is a key element in a symbolic system, and may range in form from a simple name to the most complex construction. Examples of more complex references include subscripted names, function references, qualified names, based-variable references, etc. The more powerful forms of reference are discussed in greater detail in Chapter 8.

6.5.5 Expression

In most programming languages, the form of expressions follows the traditional pattern of mathematics, and consists of variables and constants, linked by operators and possibly grouped together within brackets. Expressions are the simplest form of *recursive* structure in most languages, since one expression may be contained within another.

Example   The expression $(p+q)\ (ax^2+2bx+c)$ "contains" the two expressions: $p+q$ and $ax^2+2bx+c$.

The expression is one of the most important units in languages, both historically and conceptually, and is the subject of a separate chapter later in this book (Chapter 9).

6.5.6 STATEMENT

The statement is the starting-point for many people's study of programming languages. In the majority of languages, and particularly the languages we are concerned with in this book, a program consists of a sequence of statements.

There is an important distinction in many languages between *declarative* and *executable* statements. Declarative statements describe the data of a program and are normally not subject to rules of sequencing. Executable statements describe the actions in a program.

Simple statements, such as

```
GO TO L1
a := b+1
CALL PRINT2
```

specify single actions (even though, as in the case of the CALL statement, they may involve many complex sub-actions). There are also certain forms of statement which contain other statements; examples include the **if** statements of ALGOL, COBOL and PL/I and the ON statement of PL/I. See Fig. 6.5.

It is sometimes useful to collect a number of statements together to form a single unit equivalent to a single statement. Such a group is called a *compound statement,* and may be used for controlling the sequencing of actions in such statements as the **if** statement (see Chapter 10).

In ALGOL, a compound statement may be formed by enclosing a set of statements with **begin** and **end** brackets. In COBOL, a *sentence* can be formed by linking together a set of statements, optionally separating them

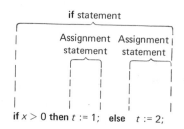

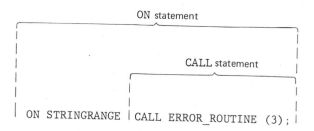

Fig. 6.5   Statements nested within other statements

ALGOL 60

> **begin** $a := a + 1$; $y := a \times t$;   print out;   **end**

COBOL

> ADD 1 to A, MULTIPLY A BY T GIVING Y,
>   PERFORM PRINTOUT.

PL/I

> DO; A=A+1; Y=A*T; CALL PRINT_OUT; END;

Fig. 6.6 Compound statements

by commas. In PL/I, the bracketing statements DO and END can be used to form a *group,* the PL/I equivalent of a compound statement. See Fig. 6.6 for examples of compound statements in ALGOL, PL/I and COBOL.

6.5.7 Blocks

It is important that the names introduced by a programmer to refer to data or subroutines should not necessarily apply, with the same meaning, over the complete system. Otherwise, it would be impossible, for example, to define a set of values and give it the name "TABLE," without first making sure that this name was not already in use in the system.

Some languages include means of delimiting the scope of names in a program. An important technique for achieving this is known as *block structure,* originally introduced with ALGOL 60. Block structure is used in a number of other languages, including variants and extensions to ALGOL 60 (JOVIAL, CPL, MAD, etc); it also appears in PL/I and ALGOL 68. The original ideas for block structure came from work on formal logic, which has a similar concern for the scope of variable names used in logical expressions.

The essential syntactic features of block structure include a system of brackets for delimiting regions or blocks of program text and a method of indicating the use of selected names within these blocks. Blocks are delimited by **begin**...**end** brackets in ALGOL, or by PROCEDURE...END or BEGIN...END statements in PL/I. The use of names is denoted by *declarations* associated with each block.

The rules for the scope of names in block-structured languages are as follows.

- The scope of a name includes the block in which it is declared but not any block surrounding it.

- The scope of a given name includes any block contained within its associated block. However, if the same name is used in a declaration within such a block, a new meaning for the name is thereby introduced. Refer to Fig. 6.7.

In addition to the syntactic importance of blocks, they also have considerable semantic implications, since in programming, variables are associated with *storage*. An advantage of block structure is that it leads to an efficient technique for storage handling. The fact that a variable is known inside a block, but not outside it, means that storage for variables in a block need

Notation

Block structure is indicated by brackets (e.g. **begin** . . . **end**) which must be properly nested.

Declarations are associated with a particular pair of brackets.

The brackets are denoted by *braces,* with declarations attached to the top: : A, B

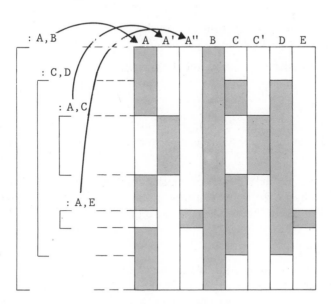

Fig. 6.7 The scope of names in block-structured languages

only be allocated when the block is entered and may be released when the block is left. This use of storage has been extremely valuable in implementing programming languages; the technique is known as *dynamic storage allocation.* Techniques for dynamic storage allocation at run time were originally developed for ALGOL and have been adapted for use with PL/I and other languages. The most commonly used techniques involve the use of a run-time *stack* or push-down store, a form of data structure with a close affinity to nested structures.

Some difficulties and disadvantages of block structure arise from those points where programming and logic differ. In programming, there is often a need to go outside the framework of the hierarchic structure implied by nested blocks. An example is the need to introduce a variable which will persist after the block in which it is declared has terminated. It is not always possible to achieve this effect by declaring the variable in a surrounding block. In ALGOL, this need was recognized and was to be handled by the introduction of **own** variables. However, these cause additional difficulties, especially when used in conjunction with arrays of dynamic size (**own** variables are discussed further in Chapter 8).

The advantages of block structure include the following.

- The rules for name scope allow the composition of large programs from small fragments without fear of name clashes.
- It is possible to design efficient run-time schemes for dynamic storage allocation, based on the scope rules of block structure.

On the other hand, there are some drawbacks.

- The hierarchy of scope implied by block structure does not suit all applications.
- Separate treatment of name scope and storage allocation, which are linked together in most implementations of block structure, is sometimes desirable.

Warnings about the *use* of block structure—particularly about the dangers in the indiscriminate use of global variables—are indicated in a paper by Wulf and Shaw (1973). See also the paper by Krutar (1973).

6.5.8 Procedure

The procedure or subroutine is the most important structural unit which can be created by the programmer. The invention of procedures and the design of the parameter mechanism which allows a single procedure to be used for a wide variety of purposes are among the most important developments in all programming.

In some languages (e.g. FORTRAN) a procedure is a separate structural unit; in others (ALGOL, PL/I) it is part of the recursive structure of the language and may be nested within other procedures.

The procedure forms an important unit for implementation purposes. In FORTRAN and PL/I, it is the smallest unit which can be independently compiled, and it is therefore a primary unit of programming modularity.

Note that in COBOL, the term "procedure" is used to denote a labeled sequence of statements, not a procedure with parameters. Early versions of COBOL did not have procedures in the same sense as ALGOL, FORTRAN and PL/I, although the PERFORM statement provided some of the functions of procedures in these other languages. COBOL now has a CALL statement, which may be used to invoke a separate program.

6.5.9   Program

We finally come to the highest point in the hierarchy of program units, the *program*. A program is a unit capable of *execution*; in most languages considered here, we need to construct a program before it is possible to execute any piece of text, however small.

The program is not necessarily the highest unit in all computing systems. In many cases an operating system will define a higher unit such as a *job*, which may comprise a single program or a set of programs, to be executed in sequence or in parallel.

Languages for specifying, invoking and controlling jobs are called job-control languages and have affinities with programming languages. At this point in time, job-control languages are strongly oriented to the design of particular machines and operating systems, although in principle there is no reason why certain aspects of these languages should not be standardized to allow easier transfer of programs from one system to another. The possibility of developing "standard" job control languages was discussed in a BCS Symposium in 1974 (Simpson, 1974).

6.6   PROGRAM STRUCTURES OF SOME CURRENT LANGUAGES

The following sections show how elements of the hierarchy described above are combined in forming the structure of four widely used languages.

6.6.1   The Structure of FORTRAN

A FORTRAN *program* consists of one *main program* and any number of *subprograms*. Main programs and subprograms are examples of *program units*; these are the modules of FORTRAN text which can be separately compiled. Subprograms are further classified as *subroutine, function,* and *block data* program units. A main program is defined as a program unit which is not a subroutine, function, or block data unit. (See Fig. 6.8.)

FORTRAN is a card-based language and programs are constructed from *lines*—these correspond to the cards of the original FORTRAN system. The following types of line are defined:

- initial line (in which a statement begins),
- continuation line (for continuing statements),
- comment line,
- end line.

Program units are defined as sequences of lines, terminated by end lines. They are headed by one of the statements—SUBROUTINE, FUNCTION, or BLOCK DATA, or, in the case of main programs, are unheaded. One unit cannot be nested inside another.

As with most languages, FORTRAN programs are composed of statements. Generally, one statement is written per line. It is possible to extend a statement over several lines by means of continuation lines—up to 19 continuation lines may be used.

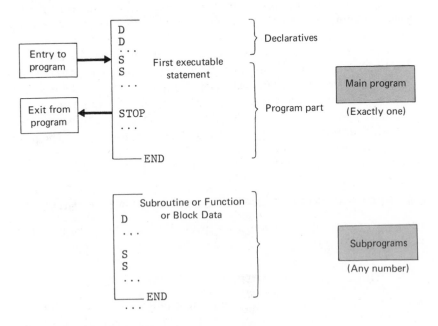

Fig. 6.8 FORTRAN program structure

Within a program unit, there is a *program body* consisting of specification statements, followed by a *program part* containing at least one executable statement. In general, declarative statements must precede executable statements. However, FORMAT statements which are clearly declarative in nature may be intermingled with executable statements. In the ANSI FORTRAN standard, there are 16 executable statements and 15 nonexecutable statements, including the five type statements REAL, INTEGER, etc.

The general form of a FORTRAN statement is:

{statement-number}   statement-keyword   statement-body

This rule is followed by all except the assignment statement, which has the form:

$a = e$

where a is a variable and e is an expression.

The keywords used in FORTRAN statements are not reserved and may be freely used for variables. Blanks may be freely added or omitted between tokens, provided the tokens are not merged together so that they can no longer be separately distinguished.

6.6.2   The Structure of COBOL

COBOL structure differs considerably from that of the other languages considered here. It was intended to provide a standard pattern for documenting business programs; it is intentionally redundant from a programming point of view since it is meant to record the relevant details needed for reference to and control of a program, as well as the program text itself.

A COBOL program consists of a number of *divisions,* each constructed according to a formal pattern and serving a specialized purpose. The major divisions, as shown in Fig. 6.9, are:

- **Identification division**

This contains descriptive information regarding the program—its author, the date it was written, etc. This information is purely documentary and does not affect the working of the program.

- **Environment division**

This specifies the "environment" expected by the program, including the machine and system specifications. COBOL was one of the first languages expressly designed to work on many different kinds of machine. The Environment Division provides a place in which factors critical to machine dependence can be specified.

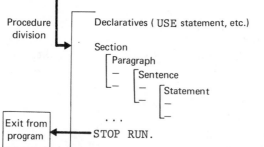

Fig. 6.9 COBOL program structure

- **Data division**

Specifications of the data and file structures used in a program are gathered together in the Data Division. This ensures that all data is declared prior to its use, an important factor in implementing a language.

- **Procedure division**

This includes the executable part of the program and has a rich structure of its own (described below).

Each of these divisions must be present in the order shown. COBOL programs therefore have a very stylized appearance, further accentuated by the fixed format and rigid structure of the statements.

The first three divisions all contain declarative information. There is also a short section called "Declaratives" at the head of the Procedure

Division which contains the USE statement, a means of specifying the actions to be taken when certain input/output and other conditions arise (see Chapter 10).

Within the Procedure Division, there is a hierarchy of program units.

Section
Paragraph
Sentence
Statement

The *section* is the largest unit within the Procedure Division and is a named block of coding which may be referenced in other statements. It is introduced by writing the section name, followed by the word SECTION, and is terminated by the beginning of the next section.

Example

```
PROCEDURE DIVISION.
PART-1 SECTION.
    ...

    ...
READIN SECTION.
    ...

    ...
ADJUSTMENT SECTION.
    ...
```

The absence of brackets to delimit sections and paragraphs means that sections within sections and paragraphs within paragraphs cannot be defined.

A COBOL *paragraph* is defined in a similar way, but without the keyword SECTION.

Example

```
PROCEDURE DIVISION.
INITIAL.
    ...

    ...
READIN.

    ...
```

The identifiers associated with sections and paragraphs are called *procedure-names* in COBOL. By implication, sections and paragraphs are therefore "procedures," although they differ considerably from the procedures of ALGOL and PL/I. A COBOL procedure-name is similar to a *label* in other languages.

The basic unit of sequencing in COBOL is the *sentence*. This is constructed from a series of *statements* linked by one of the separators: semicolon, comma, or space, and terminated by a period.

Examples

```
MULTIPLY PAY-RATE BY HOURS-WORKED GIVING GROSS-PAY,
SUBTRACT DEDUCTIONS FROM GROSS-PAY, PERFORM TAX-CALC.

IF MARRIED; NEXT SENTENCE; ELSE ADD 1 TO P-COUNT,
SUBTRACT TAX-ALLOWANCE FROM TOTAL, GO TO ADJUSTMENT.
```

The second example shows the value of the COBOL sentence in grouping together a sequence of statements. The phrase indicated by NEXT SENTENCE may be several statements later, these being grouped together by being in the same sentence.

The *statements* of COBOL are the main units for computation. There are over 60 different "verbs" in the 1973 ANSI standard, each with a distinctive keyword. These are used as the basis for statements, which have the form:

statement-keyword   statement-body

Even *assignment,* which is often an exception to this rule in other languages, follows this form. Assignment is represented by the MOVE statement or one of the arithmetic statements such as COMPUTE, ADD, SUBTRACT, MULTIPLY, and DIVIDE. SET is a special form of assignment used for setting values of indexes.

COBOL keywords are reserved and may not be used for variables. There were over 200 reserved words in the 1968 COBOL standard and this number grew to nearly 300 in the 1973 standard. Since many of these would be useful as variable names, the COBOL programmer may have to construct compound names (such as: FILE-A, INPUT-RECORD, etc.), to avoid using one of the names in the reserved list. What is more important, the set of reserved words causes problems in the extension of COBOL. Each time a new feature requiring additional keywords is added to the language, existing programs may become obsolete.

In COBOL, the "blank" character is highly significant and one or more blanks must be put between each token. This applies to expressions, so that:

```
A+B-C
```

is incorrect COBOL and such an expression must be written:

```
A + B - C
```

The origin of this rule lies in the dual use of the same character (–) as a hyphen and as a minus sign. As we have seen, composite names (ELEMENT-RECORD, REPORT-HEADING, GROUP-A) often must be used, to avoid the COBOL set of reserved words. In order that each composite name may be recognized as a single token, they must be written without blanks. This means that the form: A-B, without blanks, is syntactically a composite name, and to represent an expression, it must be written: A - B. The need for blanks does not strictly apply in the case of operators other than the *minus,* but the rule is extended to these other characters for reasons of consistency.

Many users find that the rigid structure imposed by COBOL is helpful in achieving a more standard program appearance, making programs easier to understand and maintain. The discipline of separating declarations from the procedural parts of a program is often voluntarily adopted by users of languages which allow programs to be written in freer format. The main disadvantage of COBOL lies in the details of its syntax, particularly in the requirement for reserved words; this must be considered an unfortunate design error.

6.6.3   The Structure of ALGOL

ALGOL was the first language to distinguish between the form of a program suitable for communicating between humans, and that needed for input to a computer. There are three forms of ALGOL:

- **A reference language**

   This is the "defining" language and is the basis for other versions. It is designed to provide the easiest form of communication and not to be restricted by the limitations of available character sets.

- **A publication language**

   This is designed for printing and publishing ALGOL programs. The characters (and keywords) may appear differently in different countries.

- **A set of hardware representations**

   These are to be designed to suit particular forms of hardware, and the details will depend on the character sets available.

   The existence of a separate publication language has made it possible to publish ALGOL programs in a much more readable form than most languages. However, the absence of a standard hardware format made it difficult to exchange actual programs between different systems, until standard hardware forms were defined. Even now, many different representations of the ALGOL language occur, making program interchange difficult.

ALGOL has one of the simplest of program structures. On first reading the language specifications, one might even wonder if the term "program" is ever defined, but it is there, unobtrusively listed in paragraph 4.1.1 of the ALGOL report (Naur, 1963):

<program> ::= <block> | <compound statement>

In other words, an ALGOL program consists of a single **begin .... end** bracket, with or without local declarations. There is no special syntax for programs, and a piece of code that one day is used as a separate program may next be nested inside a block to form part of a program. The only requirement is that it must be contained within just one **begin .... end** bracket. (See Fig. 6.10.)

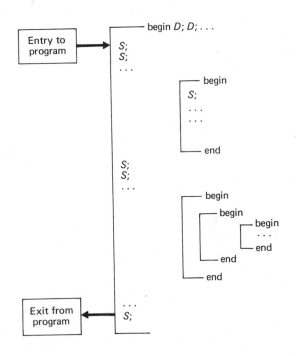

Fig. 6.10 ALGOL program structure

The difference between a block and a compound statement in ALGOL is that a block has local declarations, whereas a compound statement does not. If L represents a label, D a declaration and S a statement, then a compound statement has the form:

$L :$ **begin** $S;$ $S;$ $...$ $S;$ S **end**

while a block has the form:

$L :$ **begin** $D;$ $S;$ $S;$ $...$ $S;$ S **end**

Examples

Compound statements

begin $x : = 1;$ $y : = z : = 0$ **end**
$a5$: **begin** if FLAG **then begin** $range : = 100;$ $t : = 0$ **end**
                                            else $restart$

    end

Blocks
$section$ A: **begin real** $A, B;$
            $A : = leftside (x, 1);$
            $B : = xA2 + yA2;$
            $plot (A, B)$
            end

            begin integer $i,j;$
            for $i : = 1$ **step** 2 **until** 100 **do**
                $A : = table [i] + A;$
            for $j : = 1$ **step** 1 **until** F **do**
                $A : = A + t[j]$
            end

There are five types of ALGOL statement:

    assignment

    go to

    if

    for

    procedure

(ALGOL also has a **null** (dummy) statement to indicate "no action" on one arm of an **if** statement.)

Each statement is delimited by a semicolon.

ALGOL distinguishes the assignment statement by a special symbol $: =$, intended as a rough approximation to the left arrow, $\longleftarrow$. (The same symbol is also used in specifying the initial value of a loop index: **for** $i : = 1$ **step** n .....)

For all its simplicity, the program structure of ALGOL is very powerful, since it is highly recursive. Many constructions in ALGOL can be nested—

blocks may be written within blocks; **for** statements within **for** statements, etc. General expressions can be written in contexts where other languages may only allow simple variables or constants.

The main shortcoming of ALGOL program structure is the lack of provision for independently compiled subroutines or subprograms. The fact that each ALGOL program must consist of a single unit makes it difficult to provide such a scheme, although several implementations have overcome these difficulties by introducing new language rules for independently-compiled procedures.

6.6.4 The Structure of PL/I

PL/I has a recursively nested program structure like that of ALGOL. However, a PL/I *program* is not restricted to a single unit, but may be a set of units. Each of these must be a PL/I procedure block, and a program is defined as a set of these units, called *external procedures*. A PL/I external procedure is a single procedure block delimited by the statements PROCEDURE and END. Each external procedure may be compiled independently. See Fig. 6.11.

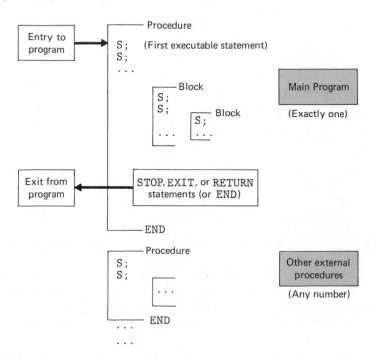

Fig. 6.11 PL/I program structure

The scope of PL/I names is determined by the bracketing statements BEGIN ... END and PROCEDURE ... END. There is an additional pair of bracketing statements, DO ... END, which is used simply to group statements together for sequencing control, as in IF statements. These differ from the other bracketing statements in that they do not introduce new scope boundaries. Compound statements are thus distinguished from blocks by the use of a special form of statement bracket, rather than by the absence of declarations, as in ALGOL. The DO statement is also used as a looping statement, as in FORTRAN.

There are 34 statements in the PL/I standard, which excludes the eleven "compile-time" statements in the IBM implementation of the language. Some of these statements are purely structural statements such as BEGIN, END, etc., which act as delimiters rather than commands. As in FORTRAN, there is a distinction between declarative statements (DECLARE, FORMAT, PROCEDURE, ..) and executable statements (assignment, GO TO, READ, CALL, ... etc.).

The keywords of PL/I are not reserved; an important characteristic which, however, has required considerable care in the design of the syntax of the language.

In its general form, a PL/I statement has an optional *condition-prefix* enclosed in parentheses, followed by an optional *label-prefix,* then a *keyword,* followed by the *statement body.* The assignment statement is an exception in not having a distinctive keyword.

Example

```
(SIZE,NOOVERFLOW):CALCULATION:Y=X+FUNC(T);
```

The condition-prefix specifies which conditions are to be enabled during execution of the statement; the label-prefix allows the statement to be named and referenced in other statements such as the GO TO statement.

The statement body may contain a simple reference or expression, although some statements, particularly the more complex input/output statements, contain a number of "options." These usually take the form of keywords followed by arguments or lists of arguments. Furthermore, the various "options" on statements can usually be written in any order, avoiding the need to memorize special versions of statements.

Examples

1. A DO statement may be written in either of the forms:

```
DO I = 0 BY 5 TO 50 WHILE (TEST > 0);
DO I = 0 TO 50 BY 5 WHILE (TEST > 0);
```

2. An OPEN statement may be written as:

```
OPEN FILE (J1) OUTPUT PRINT LINESIZE (40) PAGESIZE (50);
or
OPEN FILE (J1) PRINT OUTPUT PAGESIZE (50) LINESIZE (40);
etc.
```

Although there are some anomalies such as the absence of a keyword for the assignment statement, the syntactic structure of PL/I is for the most part uniform and regular, and has allowed the language to accommodate extensions and modifications without causing difficulties with existing programs or compilers. The free format allows convenient editing of programs during their development.

Example

Condition prefixes have been designed so that they can be readily inserted or deleted during debugging of a program.

```
(CHECK(A,B,C)):    /* REMOVE AFTER DEBUGGING */
CALC:
      PROCEDURE(R,S,T);
      DECLARE (A,B,C)...
      ...
      END:
```

These prefixes, which cause a trace of changes to the variables A, B and C to be printed out, can alternatively be written as follows:

```
(CHECK(A)):
(CHECK(B)):
(CHECK(C)):
CALC:
      PROCEDURE(R,S,T);
      etc.
```

Having each prefix on a separate line facilitates editing if the program is being prepared on an on-line terminal. Similarly, if the program is being prepared on cards, it is simple to add or delete a card.

6.7 EDITING AND PROCESSING PROGRAM TEXT

In this section, we consider how the concrete representation of a program can be automatically processed in various ways to assist the users of a language.

Although a programmer is mainly concerned with a program in terms of its execution, to a compiler it is *data*—a highly structured text, to be processed and transformed into another form, the object program. In any language in which string handling is allowed we may take a program and change its format, alter the names of variables, add or delete statements, etc. However, such processing often involves fairly difficult string-handling techniques. To simplify the programming of such transformations, some languages include facilities for manipulating program text. The provisions for program text handling within programming languages range from those which simply insert program text from a library to the elaborate forms of processing possible in macro-processing systems.

Two other techniques for editing programs should be mentioned. Although these techniques do not form part of a language, they have been incorporated in some language compilers. The first is an automatic formating technique, which produces an indented program print-out which displays the structure of a program. ALGOL procedures to edit programs have been published, including one by McKeeman (1965), and a more powerful one by Scowen at the National Physical Laboratory (Scowen, *et al.,* 1971). The second technique involves the use of an algorithm for detecting and correcting spelling mistakes in the keywords of a language. This is mainly useful for interactive systems. Papers describing spelling correction algorithms include those by Glantz (1957), Davidson (1962), Damerau (1964), Alberga (1967), and Morgan (1970). Algorithms for automatic formating and for correcting spelling errors are included in the "Checkout" compiler for PL/I which was developed for the IBM System/360 System (see Marks, 1973).

6.8   TEXT-COPYING SYSTEMS

In designing programming languages, considerable attention is given to allowing the re-use of program material, by including structures such as loops and subroutines. However, one of the simplest ways of re-using programs or parts of programs is simply to copy them.

In complex programs, especially those which need to be written by large groups of programmers, one of the most difficult organizational problems is to establish conventions for communicating between different groups. The earliest schemes for sharing program material were directed more to the sharing of data than programs. One of the first of such schemes was the COMPOOL (communications pool) of JOVIAL, the command and control language based on ALGOL (Shaw, 1963). By the use of the JOVIAL COMPOOL, or its derivatives in other languages, common data need only be defined *once*: since a COMPOOL definition is available to all users, they are able to maintain an up-to-date version of the common data description in their program, with no more effort than is needed to access the declarations, which are held in a commonly accessible library.

6.9   THE COBOL LIBRARY MODULE

An extension of the COMPOOL idea is employed in the *Library* module of COBOL. A COBOL "library" is a collection of program text, available to the source program at compile time. The contents of a library are decided by the user, although the means of getting the pieces of text into the library are not a part of the standard COBOL language, but are decided by each implementation.

At certain points of a COBOL program the user may call upon the system to insert text from the library. The statement used for this is the COPY statement, which has the format shown in Fig. 6.12.

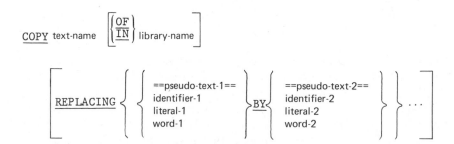

Fig. 6.12   Syntax of the COBOL COPY statement

The REPLACING option allows text to be modified during the insertion process. For example, identifiers can be replaced or qualified to avoid name clashes; constants or literals can be given new values; etc.

The COPY statement can be used in the Environment Division, the Data Division (where any item, at any level, can be copied), and the Procedure Division, for which the smallest unit of replacement is the paragraph.

Example

A COBOL program accesses several files which have standard characteristics. The file descriptions may be written:

```
FD FILE-A COPY S-FILE
...
FD FILE-B COPY S-FILE
...
FD FILE-C COPY S-FILE
...
```

where S-FILE is the standard file description in the library.

The first of these might finally appear in the source program, after copying has been carried out, as follows:

```
FD FILE-A BLOCK CONTAINS 10 RECORDS
RECORD CONTAINS 120 CHARACTERS
LABEL RECORDS ARE STANDARD.
```

The blocking factor of all files accessed by this program can be changed simply by changing the library description. Alternatively, the blocking factor for the first file can be altered by writing:

```
FD FILE-A COPY S-FILE REPLACING 10 BY 20.
```

In PL/I there are two text-copying facilities. The first, the LIKE attribute, is only used for record-structure declarations, and copies the names and logical structure of a record-structure declaration; there may also be a modification to the level-numbers of the declaration.

Example

With the use of the LIKE attribute, a record-structure declaration (or part of one) may be used at several points of a program:

```
DECLARE
     1 TEXTRECORD,
          2 FIRST,
               3 NAME CHAR(10),
               3 ADDRESS CHAR(30),
               ...
          2 SECOND LIKE FIRST,
          2 THIRD LIKE FIRST,
     ETC.
```

The declaration of FIRST is copied, using the same names, attributes, and structural relationships. The original declaration need not be in the same DECLARE statement as the LIKE attribute.

If necessary, the actual level numbers are modified to preserve the structuring. Thus if a level-3 structure is being specified:

```
3 RECORD4 LIKE FIRST
```

the level numbers would be adjusted as follows:

```
3 RECORD4,
     4 NAME CHAR(10),
     4 ADDRESS CHAR(30),
     ...
```

Although the LIKE attribute has a fairly limited range of application, it provides a convenient shorthand method for composing what are often the most time-consuming parts of a program. It does not require the user to go through the extra step of storing program text in a "library."

The second facility for text copying in PL/I is provided by the %INCLUDE statement, which is similar in action to the COPY statement of COBOL, and allows text to be copied from a "library" to the program being compiled. This statement forms part of the PL/I "preprocessor" facilities, a set of special statements for processing PL/I text prior to compilation. The preprocessor facilities of PL/I provide an example of a "text-macro" system, one of several types of language *macroprocessors.*

6.10   MACROPROCESSORS OF HIGH-LEVEL LANGUAGES

A macroprocessor has been defined as "a piece of software designed to allow the user to add new facilities of his own design to an existing piece of software" (Brown, 1969). This definition covers a broad class of systems, ranging from simple macro-assemblers to the most ambitious self-extending language systems. Here, we are mainly concerned with macroprocessing as applied to compiler languages and with the possibilities of incorporating macroprocessors with language systems.

As its name suggests, a macroprocessor expands text from small units to larger units; it is essentially a text-generating system. Some workers in this field have argued that all programming language processors should be constructed as macroprocessors rather than in the more usual form of compilers and interpreters (see, for example, Halpern (1968)). This point of view is a matter of implementation rather than language design and would present many problems, particularly those of efficiency. It must be admitted that a widespread adoption of this view would have considerable effect on the design of programming languages.

Macroprocessors have been mainly used for the following purposes:

- **Systematic text editing**

  This includes the replacement of identifiers, the insertion of omitted punctuation, translation of character sets, etc.

- **Text generation**

  This includes the expansion of short phrases into standard forms (as in the COPY or LIKE facilities), the replacement of program "parameters" by constants, and the expansion of loops into in-line code, etc.

- **Language extension**

When combined with a programming language, macroprocessors allow new "statements" to be defined. These are, in effect, calls to the macro system to generate code in the basic language of the system. To the user, the basic language appears to have been extended.

Cheatham (1966) has divided macro sytems into the following classes:

- **Text macros**

These are implemented by a preprocessor, a separate text-processing system, which generates code in some programming language.

- **Syntactic macros**

These are called during the syntactic analysis phases of a language processor.

- **Computation macros**

These are called during the code-generation phases of a language processor.

The second and third classes are beyond the scope of this book. However, the design of text macros, which provide means of preprocessing programs written in high-level languages, is important in the study of program representation.

In a text macro system, there is a base language, the target for text generation, a means of specifying the code to be generated, a notation for indicating at which point of the text generation is to take place, and for supplying the "arguments" for generation.

There are many choices in the design of text macro systems, reflecting different techniques of scanning and code generation. These are well described in the survey paper by Brown (1969), who has himself designed and implemented a text macro system, ML/I, which has been used on a variety of machines (Brown, 1967). Other key papers on this subject are those of McIlroy (1960) and Strachey (1965).

6.11   THE PL/I PREPROCESSOR FACILITIES

These provide one of the few examples of a macro system whose design has been integrated with that of a high-level language. As indicated by its name, the system recognizes a phase of program translation which takes place prior to compilation. During this phase, a set of PL/I-like statements, each identified by the prefix '%' and embedded in a PL/I program, is scanned and processed. The remainder of the text acts as data and may be edited and changed by the preprocessor. The meaning of preprocessor statements is defined in terms of the actions of the preprocessor; the statements control the movement of the scanner, the construction of a dictionary, etc. The final output of the preprocessor, the generated text, is a PL/I program, which can subsequently be compiled by a conventional PL/I compiler.

The preprocessor statements are:

```
%ACTIVATE
%assignment
%DEACTIVATE
%DECLARE
%DO
%END
%GO TO
%IF
%INCLUDE
%null
%PROCEDURE
```

A key concept is that of the *activation* of an identifier, initially achieved by means of its declaration in a %DECLARE statement. When activated, an identifier may be replaced by some other object, typically a string of characters.

Example

If the text of a program before processing is:

```
%DECLARE V CHARACTER;
%V='X+10';
...
A(V) = B(V) + C(V):
```

then the generated text will contain:

```
A(X+10) = B(X+10) + C(X+10):
```

The %DEACTIVATE and %ACTIVATE statements are included to control the replacement process—they act as commands to the preprocessor. Thus, if the statement %DEACTIVATE V; is met in the course of scanning, V will not be replaced until a subsequent statement of the form: %ACTIVATE V; is encountered.

Two types of variable are available during preprocessing: CHARACTER variables, as shown above, for text, and FIXED variables, to act as counters, etc. Three built-in functions, SUBSTR, LENGTH, and INDEX may be applied to preprocessor variables during processing. These string-handling functions are discussed in Chapter 8.

The following example shows how a preprocessor loop may be defined.

```
%DECLARE NAMES CHARACTER, I FIXED, SUBSTR BUILTIN;
%NAMES = 'ABCDEF';
%DO I = 1 TO 6;
    X(I) = SUM(SUBSTR(NAMES,I,1));
%END;
```

The generated code† from this will be:

```
X(1) = SUM(A);
X(2) = SUM(B);
X(3) = SUM(C);
...
X(6) = SUM(F);
```

The sequencing statements, %IF and %GO TO, can be used for conditional generation of text, and preprocessor procedures can be defined.

The PL/I preprocessor facilities provide useful capabilities for text editing and the design of special-purpose languages. The limitations placed on the scanning process mean that certain actions, such as the replacement of operators, cannot be accomplished. The design of languages which allow these more radical transformations falls under the heading of "Extensible Languages"—see Christensen and Shaw (1969) and Schuman (1971).

6.12 SEGMENTATION

It is a common experience, when programming large problems, to find there is insufficient high-speed storage to accommodate the program and its data. It becomes necessary to subdivide the program, data, or both, to allow execution in the available space. Of the two, it is often easier to subdivide the data. Many of the "input-output" statements in programming languages are used primarily for transferring sections of data to and from the backing store of a machine. Sometimes, however, the program itself may also have to be divided—this is known as program *segmentation*. Segmentation is one method of tackling resource allocation, a fundamental problem in the design of all computing systems.

---

†The generated code will also contain a number of blanks, introduced as part of the scanning and replacement process. However, the effect of the code will be as shown.

In virtually all computers, code must be in high-speed storage before it can be executed, and data must be in high-speed storage before it can be operated upon. Segmentation of code, as opposed to data, is made difficult by the complex and often unpredictable flow of control in many programs. Unlike data, however, programs are not usually altered during the execution of a program, and their structure can be analyzed during the process of compilation.

Storage allocation in computing systems has been extensively studied, and an ACM conference on the subject was held in 1961 (ACM, 1961). Many of the issues discussed at that time are still valid. This conference was concerned with storage allocation for programs and data—both of which are of concern in the design of programming languages. In this chapter, however, the main emphasis is on the effect of segmentation on program structure.

Two essentially different approaches to program segmentation have been taken, *preplanned* and *automatic.*

In preplanned segmentation, the programmer must construct the program in segments (these may be subroutines, blocks, sections, or statements), and may be required to state how these relate to each other—particularly their relative frequency of use and whether they are required at the same time as other segments.

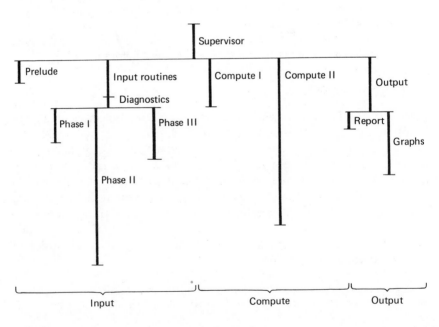

Fig. 6.13 The structure of a program in tree form

There is a common pattern to many computer programs. For example, there may be a supervisory section which must be in core storage all the time. Other segments may be called sequentially in a prescribed order, while others may only be used infrequently.

The structure of a typical program is shown in Fig 6.13. In such a program, the input, processing and output sections are distinct, and when one of these has been executed, its storage may be occupied by another phase. A natural structure to represent such a program is a *tree*, the root representing the most highly used part of the program.

Segmentation based on tree structure has been described in several papers (Heising and Larner, 1961; Holt, 1961) and forms the basis of the design for overlay segmentation in some loaders. An example of a tree-structured overlay scheme as part of an operating system is the linkage editor and loader for the IBM System/360 Operating System (See Presser and White, 1972).

In preplanned segmentation, the programmer must have a clear idea of the dynamic structure of the program, in order to be able to specify which segments may be overlaid.

In automatic segmentation, this analysis of the program is carried out by the system on the basis of the logical structure of the program. Among the arguments in favor of automatic, rather than manual, segmentation, are the following:

- the high cost of programming effort to undertake manual segmentation.
- the lack of flexibility of manually segmented programs. They are almost always oriented to a particular size of storage and it is difficult to adjust them for larger or smaller amounts of space.

The case for automatic segmentation (under the name: "folding") is given in a paper by Sayre (Sayre, 1969). The particular technique suggested in this paper should perhaps be called semi-automatic, since it works best with a technique known as "shadow folding." Based on tests carried out on a set of typical programs, results from the use of this technique indicated a loss of performance (about 20%), balanced by a reduction of programmer time (about 25%), compared with manual segmentation.

6.13   SEGMENTATION AND PROGRAMMING LANGUAGES

From the point of view of the designer of a programming language, automatic segmentation has obvious advantages, since no statements or operators are required specifically for the segmentation process. The process of segmentation is simpler in a language with a well-defined hierarchy of structural units (blocks, groups, compound statements, etc.), to serve as a basis for the analysis.

One of the pioneering efforts on automatic segmentation in operating systems was that developed for the Atlas computer (Fotheringham 1961). An early treatment of segmentation applied to a commercial data-processing language was the system associated with FACT (Greenfield, 1962).

Early versions of FORTRAN had a simple scheme for sequential overlay—the CHAIN facility. FORTRAN subprograms could be designated as "links" in a chain and segments were loaded and entered by executing a CALL CHAIN statement. This development is now mainly of historic interest, since although it formed part of the FORTRAN II system for the IBM 7090 machine, it was not included in later IBM versions of FORTRAN nor in the FORTRAN standard.

Another scheme for an implementation of ALGOL on a drum machine is described by Jensen, Mondrup, and Naur (1961). Here, the programmer may specify that segments are to be stored on the drum rather than in high-speed store. In contrast with the FORTRAN chaining technique, linking and loading of these segments are automatic. Again, this proposal does not form part of the standard ALGOL language.

6.13.1 COBOL Segmentation

For the most part, schemes for preplanned segmentation have been treated as being outside the scope of programming languages. Whatever language necessary has been introduced either as local, nonstandard extensions, or as part of the job-control language. An exception is the "Segmentation" module of COBOL, which forms part of the standard COBOL language, and provides preplanned, tree-structured, segmentation.

The basic unit of segmentation is known as a *section.* The Procedure Division of a COBOL program intended for segmentation must be divided by the user into sections. These fall into two parts, the *fixed portion,* and a group of *independent* segments. The fixed portion is that part of the program with the greatest need for high-speed storage, although it may itself be divided into *permanent* and *overlayable fixed* segments. The independent segments can overlay, or be overlaid by, other segments of the program.

In addition to dividing the program into two parts, the programmer can also specify the expected frequency of use of the different segments by assigning *priority* numbers to the sections. These are integers ranging from 0 to 99, the low priority numbers representing higher frequencies. The distinction between the two groups of segments is made on the basis of priority numbers; the priorities 0 to 49 being used for the fixed portion, 50 and above for the group of independent segments. There is a special clause in the Environment Division, the SEGMENT-LIMIT clause, which may be used to subdivide the fixed portion into a permanent part and an overlayable part.

Once the program is entered, the system will cause the segments to be loaded and entered automatically, provided the basic sequencing of the sections in the source program has been established in the source program.

The program illustrated in Fig. 6.14 may be segmented by assigning the supervisor to permanent storage, the basic input and compute sections to the fixed portion, and the prelude and output routines to independent segments.

Example

```
PROCEDURE DIVISION.
SUPERVISOR SECTION 1.
     code
     ...
PRELUDE SECTION 51.
     code
     ...
INPUT-BASIC SECTION 5.
     code
     ...
INPUT-PHASE-1 SECTION 10.
     code
     ...
COMPUTE-PHASE-1 SECTION 5.
     code
     ...
OUTPUT-PHASE-REPORT SECTION 51.
     code
     ...
```

The COBOL segmentation feature imposes certain constraints on the code that can be written in a program. Both the PERFORM and the ALTER statements must be used with care in a segmented program, so that program flow is not broken when they are executed. This is an example of difficulties that arise when manual, rather than automatic, segmentation is applied.

BIBLIOGRAPHY

ACM, "Papers presented at the ACM Storage Allocation Symposium," June 23–24, 1961, *CACM,* Vol. 4, No. 10, Oct. 1961.

A series of papers discussing "pre-planned" *vs* "dynamic" methods of storage allocation. The introductory discussion usefully summarizes the problem. Papers by Fotheringham, Heising and Larner, and Holt, are referenced below.

Bagley, Philip R., "Improving problem-oriented language by stratifying it," *Computer Journal,* Vol. 4, No. 3, Oct. 1961, pp. 217–222.

An early statement of a view which has now become much more widely accepted, namely that language design can be improved by separating the logic of programming ideas from their means of representation.

Barrett, J., M. Grems, "Abbreviating words systematically," *CACM,* Vol. 3, No. 5, May 1960, pp. 323–324.

Suggests a systematic method of abbreviating words for variable names, computer-language keywords, etc. The rules are roughly as follows: keep the left-most letter, drop letters from right to left, drop letters in order of frequency of use (i.e. E first, then T, A, O, . . . etc.).

Bemer, R. W., "Survey of coded character representation," *CACM,* Vol. 3, No. 12, Dec. 1960, pp. 639–642.

Bemer, R. W., W. Buchholz, "Character set," (in) W. Buchholz (ed.), *Planning a computer system: Project STRETCH,* New York: McGraw Hill, 1962.

Discusses the objectives of a character set containing 120 characters expressly designed for the Stretch machine. The set contains upper and lower case letters, relational operators, and additional brackets: ( ), { }, and [ ].

Blair, C. R., "A program for correcting spelling errors," *Information & Control,* Vol. 3, 1960, pp. 60–67.

Brown, P. J., "The ML/I macro processor," *CACM,* Vol. 10, No. 10, Oct. 1967, pp. 618–623.

Brown, P. J., "A survey of macro processors," *Annual Review in Automatic Programming,* Vol. 6, Elmsford, N.Y.: Pergamon Press, 1970.

Christensen, C., C. J. Shaw (eds), "Proceedings of the Extensible Languages Symposium," *SIGPLAN Notices,* Vol. 4, No. 8, Aug. 1969.

Dahl, Ole-Johan and C. A. R. Hoare, "Hierarchical program structures," (in) *Structured Programming, APIC Studies in Data Processing, No. 8,* New York: Academic Press, 1972.

Damerau, F. J., "A technique for computer detection and correction of spelling errors," *CACM,* Vol. 7, No. 3, Mar. 1964, pp. 171–176.

This method assumes that the erroneous word has at most one error, including a single transposition.

Dearnley, F. H., G. B. Newell, "Automatic segmentation of programs for a two-level store computer," *Computer Journal,* Vol. 7, No. 3, Oct. 1964, pp. 185–187.

This describes a one-pass algorithm for segmenting programs developed for the ICT 1301 computer.

Dennis, J. B., "Segmentation and the design of multiprogrammed computer systems," *JACM,* Vol. 12, No. 4, Oct. 1965, pp. 589–602.

A central paper on multiprogramming systems design which puts forward the idea of a *name space,* and contrasts it with the more usual idea of an *address space.* Discusses the problems of overlay and of program and data segmentation.

Fotheringham, J., "Dynamic storage allocation in the Atlas computer, including an automatic use of a backing store," *CACM,* Vol. 4, No. 10, Oct. 1961, pp. 435–436.

A report of the "virtual memory" concept, which was first implemented on the Atlas computer. The store of the machine, physically a core store with drum-backing store, is made to appear as a large randomly accessed store, requiring no special language for its access.

Greenfield, M. N., "FACT segmentation," *Proc. SJCC 1962,* AFIPS, 1962, pp. 307–315.

Discusses the dynamic allocation of program segments in the FACT compiler. Segments are constructed from program procedures, input edit procedures, report procedures, file areas, etc. Storage allocation is automatic and dynamic.

Halpern, M. I., "Towards a general processor for programming languages," *CACM,* Vol. 11, No. 1, Jan. 1963, pp. 15–25.

An argument in favor of macroprocessors rather than compilers for general-purpose implementation.

Hedberg, R., "Design of an integrated programming and operating system Part III: the expanded function of the loader," *IBM Systems Journal, Vol. 2,* Sept.–Dec. 1963, pp. 298–310.

Describes the function of the loader in the IBSYS/IBJOB system for the IBM 7090 system. This system incorporates a form of program segmentation, allowing modular program design.

Heising, W. P., R. A. Larner, "A semi-automatic storage allocation system at loading time," *CACM,* Vol. 4, No. 10, Oct. 1961, pp. 446–449.

A preplanned form of overlay segmentation, using tree structure.

Holt, A. W., "Program organization and record keeping for dynamic storage allocation," *CACM,* Vol. 4, No. 10, Oct. 1961, pp. 422–431.

Humby, E. "Rapidwrite," *Annual Review in Automatic Programming, Vol. 3,* Elmsford, N.Y.: Pergamon Press, 1963, pp. 299–309.

A simplified form of COBOL, using preprinted forms corresponding to the various COBOL statements, on which the keywords and linking words were already recorded.

Iverson, K. E., "Formalism in programming languages," *CACM,* Vol. 7, No. 2, Feb. 1964, pp. 80–87.

Iverson's views on notation and character sets, as developed for APL. See especially the report on the discussion which followed the first presentation of this report.

Jensen, J., P. Mondrup, P. Naur, "A storage allocation scheme for ALGOL 60," *CACM,* Vol. 4, No. 10, Oct. 1961, pp. 441–445.

In this scheme, for a 2K word machine with drum-backing store, ALGOL blocks may be specified as "drum programs"—these will only occupy space in high-speed store while they are in execution.

Krutar, R. A., "Restricted global variable in ALGOL 60," *SIGPLAN Notices,* Vol. 8, No. 12, Dec. 1973, pp. 15–17.

Lock, Kenneth, "Structuring programs for multiprogram time-sharing on-line applications," *Proc. AFIPS FJCC,* 1965, pp. 457–472.

A summary of the requirements for program structure for on-line computations. The basic unit for interaction is the statement, and the syntax of an extension to ALGOL 60 is described in which the system of a statement is augmented to include a statement number. The paper also discusses the need for incremental compilation and the technical problems this brings.

Marks, B. L., "Design of a checkout compiler," *IBM Systems Journal,* Vol. 12, No. 3, 1973, pp. 315–327.

Martin, E. and G. Estrin, "Models of computations and systems—evaluation of vertex probabilities in graph models of computations," *JACM,* Vol. 14, No. 2, Apr. 1967, pp. 281–299.

This paper, and the companion papers cited in its references, describe a school of work under Estrin at UCLA concerned with applications of graph theory to programs and computations. One of the motivations of this work is to improve the methods of storage allocation for data and programs, but the results also provide insights into the loop complexity of programs.

McCarthy, J., F. C. Corbato, M. M. Daggett, "The linking segment subprogram language and linking loader," *CACM,* Vol. 6, No. 7, Jul. 1963, pp. 391–395.

McIlroy, M. D., "Macro-instruction extensions of compiler languages," *CACM,* Vol. 3, No. 4, Apr. 1960, pp. 214–220.

A classic paper, showing how a macro system can be designed to extend the scope of a simple base language. The concepts are not limited to machine or assembly languages, but apply to high-level languages.

McKeeman, W. M., "Algorithm 268, ALGOL 60 reference language editor," *CACM,* Vol. 8, No. 11, Nov. 1965, pp. 667–668.

Menninger, K., *Number words and number symbols* (translated by Paul Broneer), Cambridge, Mass.: MIT Press, 1969.

The history of number systems, the origins of number symbols and words, and early examples of arithmetic methods. This book helps to see in perspective the slow and fitful evolution of the symbolism we often take for granted. Especially recommended: the section on Bede's finger-counting methods (which gave us, indirectly, the term "digit" for a unit of number), and the extracts from a book by al-Khwarizmi (whose name has been corrupted to give us the term "algorithm").

Morgan, H. L., "Spelling correction in systems programs," *CACM,* Vol. 13, No. 2, Feb. 1970, pp. 90–94.

Describes the use of a technique, based on Damerau's (1964) for use in compilers and operating systems. Has been used in compilers at Cornell and also in PL/I (IBM).

Pankhurst, R. J., "Program overlay techniques," *CACM,* Vol. 11, No. 2, Feb. 1968, pp. 119–125.

A general review of overlay systems and a description of a semi-automatic system developed for the CDC 6600.

Parmelee, R. P., T. I. Peterson, C. C. Tillman, D. J. Hatfield, "Virtual storage and virtual machine concepts," *IBM Systems Journal,* Vol. 11, No. 2, 1972, pp. 99–130.

A review of the concepts behind virtual systems, with illustrations from the IBM CP-67 System. There is an extensive, annotated bibliography.

Presser, L., J. R. White, "Linkers and loaders," *Computing Surveys,* Vol. 4, No. 3, Sept. 1972, pp. 149–167.

Raphael, B., "The structure of programming languages," *CACM,* Vol. 9, No. 2, Feb. 1966, pp. 67–71.

Ross, H. McG., "Considerations in choosing a character code for computers and punched tapes," *Computer Journal,* Vol. 3, No. 4, Jan. 1961, pp. 202–210.

Sayre, D., "Is automatic "folding" of programs efficient enough to replace manual?" *CACM,* Vol. 12, No. 12, Dec. 1969, pp. 656–660.

"Folding" is the arrangement of program or data to fit in a smaller space than would normally be required. "Manual" folding of programs includes the segmentation and overlaying of program segments. This paper describes an experiment in which the performance of five sample programs was compared when folded manually and automatically. The results showed a performance loss of about 20 percent with automatic folding but savings in programming-time cost of about 25 percent. Concluding remark: "... it is only a matter of time before a folding unit becomes a normal part of most computing systems."

Schuman, S. A. (ed), "Proceedings of the international symposium on extensible languages (Grenoble, September 1971)," *ACM SIGPLAN Notices,* Vol. 6, No. 12, Dec. 1971.

Scowen, R. S., D. Allin, A. L. Hillman, M. Shimmell, "SOAP—a program which documents and edits ALGOL 60 programs," *Computer Journal,* Vol. 14, No. 2, May 1971, pp. 133–135.

Scowen, R. S., B. A. Wichmann, "The Definition of Comments in Programming Languages," *Software Practice and Experience,* Vol. 4, No. 2, Apr. 1974, pp. 181–188.

The authors summarize the comment conventions in eleven programming languages and propose criteria for the design of comment facilities in new programming languages.

Shaw, C. J., "On declaring arbitrarily coded alphabets," *CACM,* Vol. 7, No. 5, May 1964, pp. 288–290.

Shaw, C. J., "A specification of JOVIAL," *CACM,* Vol. 6, No. 12, Dec. 1963, pp. 721–736.

Simpson, D. (ed), *Job Control Languages—Past, Present and Future,* Manchester, England: NCC Publications, 1974.

A report of a BCS Symposium which considered difficulties that users face with current job-control languages and prospects for the development of a standard language for job control.

Smith, H. J., "A short study of notation efficiency," *CACM,* Vol. 3, No. 8, Aug. 1960, pp. 468–473.

Given a need to express large character sets such as those needed for languages like ALGOL 60, this paper considers the relative merits of 6-bit and 8-bit codes for representation of a single byte. The conclusion:— 8 bits, with 4-bit decimal representation, has advantages over 6-bit representation.

Strachey, C., "A general-purpose macro-generator," *Computer Journal,* Vol. 8, No. 3, Oct. 1965, pp. 225–241.

This describes a simple but very general form of macroprocessor, suitable as a preprocessor for an assembler or general-purpose compiler. The power of this processor exceeds that of many systems available at the time of publication of the paper (and since); however, one of its disadvantages is its difficult notation.

Tonge, F. M., "Hierarchical aspects of computer languages," (in) Whyte, Wilson, Wilson, *Hierarchical Structures,* Elsevier, 1969, pp. 233–251.

A discussion of computer hierarchies, which have been developed to control and reduce complexity. Tonge points out that in some cases, for example in artificial intelligence, the imposition of a strict hierarchy may inhibit techniques of solution.

Ver Hoef, E. W., "Automatic program segmentation based on Boolean connectivity," *Proc. SJCC,* Vol. 38, AFIPS Press, 1971, pp. 491–495.

Gives an algorithm for segmenting a program. This operates in three phases: detection of loops; merging of program "units" until segment size is exceeded or the end of a path is encountered; and finally, merging of remaining units.

Wulf, W., M. Shaw, "Global variable considered harmful," *SIGPLAN Notices,* Vol. 8, No. 2, Feb. 1973, pp. 28–34.

Zemanek, H., *Alphabets and Codes for Information Processing,* Munchen: R. Oldenbourg Verlag, 1967.

A review of character sets used in computing, considering both their graphic and internal representations. Includes historical notes on the evolution of standard codes and a discussion of Japanese Katakana codes.

EXERCISES

6.1 Which of the following identifiers can be used in ALGOL, FORTRAN, COBOL, PL/I?

```
X
NUMBER4   No.4   No-4   #4
X1.5
PART#
END-OF-RUN
list
JOHN SMITH
```

6.2 The following programs have been written in a compressed form. Arrange the programs to show their structure.

ALGOL program:

procedure *matvec(m,n,a,x,y);*   **value**   *m,n;***integer**   *m,n;***array**   *a,x,y;***begin   real** *s;***integer** *i,k;***for** *i:* = 1**step** 1 **until** *m* **do begin** *s:* = 0;**for** *k:* = 1 **step** 1 **until** *n* **do** *s:* = *s* + *a*[*i,k*] × *x*[*k*];*y*[*i*]: = *s* **end** i;**end** matvec

PL/I program

```
ROMBERG:PROCEDURE(FCT,LGR,RGR,ORD) RECURSIVE RETURNS(FLOAT); DECLARE
FCT ENTRY(FLOAT(16)) RETURNS(FLOAT(16)),(LGR,RGR) FLOAT, ORD FIXED
BINARY, T(1:ORD+1)FLOAT, (L,M,N)(FIXED BINARY 31,0);
L=RGR-LGR;T(1)=(FCT(LGR)+FCT(RGR))/2;N=1;DO H=1BY1 TO ORD;U=0;
M=L/(2*N);DO J=1 BY 2 TO 2*N-1;U=U+FCT(LGR+J*M);END;
T(H+1)=(U/N+T(H))/2;F=1;DO J=H BY -1 TO
1;F=4*F;T(J) = (T(J+1)-T(J))/(F-1);END;N=2*N;END;RETURN(T(1)*L);END;
```

6.3 Write the flowchart of a program which will read in an arbitrary string of symbols assumed to be a computer program, and print out an edited and indented version of the program. Assume the language in which the program is assumed to be written is ALGOL, COBOL or PL/I.

6.4 List the tokens used in the following program fragments:

$$X = (A+1) * SIN(X+3);$$ (PL/I)
COMPUTE Y = A * RATE.   (COBOL)

go to (**if** B **then** $L1$ **else** $L2$);   (ALGOL)

6.5 List the punctuation characters normally used in natural language and indicate which of these characters are used in ALGOL, FORTRAN, COBOL, and PL/I. Which characters are not used in any of these languages? Suggest possible uses.

6.6 Consider the following section of PL/I code:

```
A: BEGIN;
   S1;
B: BEGIN;
   S2;
A: BEGIN;
   S3;
C: BEGIN;
   S4;
   END;
   END A;
```

Which block is terminated by the last statement?
Draw a flowchart of a program for: a) scanning a program involving multiple closure and b) determining its block structure.

6.7 Show how the example on the use of the COBOL COPY statement could be programmed in PL/I. Similarly, show how the replacement of identifiers in the PL/I examples could be programmed in COBOL.

6.8 "Self-reproducing programs" have been discussed by Bratley and Millo (*Software—Practice and Experience*, Vol. 2, 1972, pp. 397–400), who give examples written in SNOBOL, LISP, FORTRAN, and ALGOL. These programs produce copies of themselves, without relying on any knowledge of the internal representation of any item of data.
What properties of a programming language are useful in writing such programs? Write self-reproducing programs in COBOL and PL/I.

7
Data Elements, Variables, and Declarations

7.1 INTRODUCTION

One of the first and most important tasks to be accomplished before writing any program is to translate the data of the problem being solved into programming terms. In doing this, the programmer must rely on the data types and structures in the languages available to him. Generally, these are a fixed part of any programming language; the choice of a language implies the choice of a set of data elements and structures. The treatment of data is therefore one of the most important aspects of programming language design.

This chapter is the first of several concerned with data handling. In the first section of this chapter, the important concept of a *variable* is introduced, together with the attributes used in the specification of variables. The chapter also includes a description of data elements included in several programming languages. Later, in Chapter 8, this topic is continued and expanded to include a discussion of collections of data or data structures.

For scientific and technical problems, the choice of suitable data types and structures is relatively simple, and follows a long tradition of mathematical analysis and abstraction. Problems can readily be stated in terms of mathematical data (various classes of numbers) and data structures (vectors, matrices, etc.). Scientific languages such as FORTRAN and ALGOL have exploited this mathematical background—the necessary abstraction and analysis have preceded the development of programming ideas.

This experience is not available, however, for problems in other fields, particularly nonnumerical problems, for which the mechanical "processing" of data is a relatively new concept. For subjects with little tradition of mathematical abstraction, it is interesting to consider what types of data and data structure arise naturally from the problem field.

For example, in *text processing* we may have:

- *data elements:*
  characters, words, punctuation marks, etc.;

- *data structures:*
  lines, sentences, paragraphs, pages, etc.

The "operations" of text processing include scanning, insertion and deletion, the construction of dictionaries, etc.

As another example, in graph or image processing we may have:

- *data elements:*
  points, lines, planes;

- *data structures:*
  triangles, circles, graphs.

Operations include lateral and vertical movement, rotation, expansion, etc.

To obtain a better match with problems, some programming languages have been designed with special data structures and operations. Examples include:

- ICES—a language for civil and structural engineering (Roos, 1966);

- APT—a language for the control of machine tools (Brown, Drayton, and Mittman, 1963);

- SNOBOL—a language for string handling (see Chapter 8).

The importance of data and data structures was pointed out by A. J. Perlis in the first ACM Turing Lecture, "The Synthesis of Algorithmic Systems" (Perlis, 1967). This lecture is largely concerned with programming languages and discusses some proposed guidelines to be followed in designing new language systems. Perlis concludes that a natural starting point for this work should be a study of the organization and classification of data. He comments on the data types and structures now available in standard programming languages and, to overcome the limitations of a fixed set of data types, proposes methods for synthesizing data structures, in the same way that procedures can be synthesized in most languages. This theme is expanded in a joint paper with B. A. Galler (Galler and Perlis, 1967) in which the authors propose an extension to ALGOL which would allow new data types and structures to be defined by the programmer.

Chapters 7 and 8 present an elementary discussion of data in programming languages—elementary, since the ideas of data in the languages we discuss are not particularly well developed. Languages like FORTRAN, ALGOL, COBOL and PL/I were designed without a formal "theory" of data. It is only since these languages have been specified more precisely and, in particular, as extensions to them have been designed, that it has become necessary to develop a deeper understanding of their treatment of data and data structures.

7.2 ELEMENTS AND STRUCTURES

The first important distinction to make is between:

- basic units of data—*data elements;*
- organized collections of data elements—*data structures.*

It is difficult to frame a universal definition of *element* which would suit all languages. Such an approach would tend to suffer the fate of the various atomic theories in physics, which have repeatedly had to be abandoned as further elementary particles have been discovered. However, there is broad agreement on some of the elements found in programming languages—a widely acceptable list would include:

integers,

floating-point ("real") numbers,

logical variables,

labels.

There are operations corresponding to these elements in most high-level languages:

the arithmetic operations: $+ - \times \div$,

the logical operations: **and, or, not,**

go to.

There is also wide agreement on several standard forms of data structure. A representative list might include:

arrays,

structures (PL/I) or records (COBOL),

lists.

For these, there are corresponding operations, depending on the types of the elements in the structures. The components of data structures may be referenced by access functions:

subscript,

qualified name,

the list functions: **head, tail,** etc.

A data object which does not appear in either of these lists is the **string.** In some languages this is treated as an element, while in others it is treated as a data structure. Thus the distinction between elements and structures has to be established by study of the languages themselves, and in particular by the basic operations defined in each language.

7.3   THE CONCEPT OF A VARIABLE IN PROGRAMMING LANGUAGES

Here we introduce the concept of a variable, a topic of great importance in any study of programming. This is not always recognized, perhaps because (like Moliere's Monsieur Jourdain, who discovered he had spoken prose all his life without realizing it) most people use variables without much thought for the underlying concept.

Variables play a central part in mathematics, where they are used as "place-holders" in formulas and expressions. As Tarski has pointed out, the invention of variables constituted a "turning point" in the history of mathematics, paving a way for the advances of the past few centuries (Tarski, 1965).

Each of the programming languages we shall study has a different approach to variables, due to different *storage* treatments and *binding* strategies. Comparison of these approaches provides one of the most illuminating ways of comparing language designs.

In programming, variables have some of the same properties they have in mathematics. They allow the user to write programs in which the actual values of data items are not known until the program is executed. They differ in detail from mathematical variables in much the same way that programming differs from mathematics—by the implications of finite, rather than infinite, domains of values; by the requirements of "efficiency" in programs; and by the emphasis on algorithmic processes. In many ways, variables are to a programming language what a high-speed store is to a computing machine—a place to put and keep values, in which they may be saved for later stages of the computation. In fact, COBOL uses the term "Working Storage" for the collection of temporary data items that correspond to the variables of other languages.

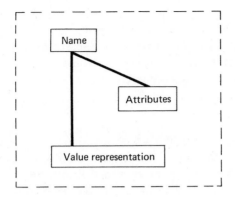

Fig. 7.1 A simplified picture of a variable

Figure 7.1 shows a simple model of a variable as used in a programming language. In later sections, this model will be expanded and elaborated to correspond more closely to the role of the variable in various programming languages.

The "attributes" of a variable shown in the figure are concerned with its treatment as a variable in a program. They determine, for example, its permitted range of values; how and when it is created; the scope of its name; etc. Below, the attribute *type,* the most important of these attributes, is discussed. Most languages discussed in this book allow the specification of type, though not all of them allow other attributes to be specified.

By means of attributes, we can load a variable with extra meaning, though it may still be referenced by a simple name. This is most clearly seen in the case of data structure variables. A reference to an array or record structure name may result in operations being carried out on all the contained elements. In such cases, the "expansion ratio" attained during compilation of a program (the ratio of the object-program units to source-language units) may reach several thousands.

In programming languages, variables are usually specified by means of special language forms known as *declarations.* A *declaration* provides the *name* and some or all of the *attributes* of a variable—additional attributes may be provided by other operations at a later stage. For example, in the case of dynamic arrays, the actual *extents* of the arrays (i.e., their upper and lower bounds) may not be known until the array is created.

Values may be given to variables by:

- initialization, when the variable is created;
- assignment;
- transmission to the variable by input operations.

In symbolic languages, an occurrence of the *name* of a variable is used to refer to the value associated with it. Some languages, for example PL/I and ALGOL 68, allow other methods of referencing and in these languages intermediate stages in the accessing mechanism (pointer or reference variables) may be manipulated separately.

7.4 BINDING

The act of associating attributes with a variable is known as *binding*. This term comes from mathematical logic, where a distinction is made between the "free" and "bound" variables of a logical formula. However, in programming, rather than considering variables as bound or free, we talk of variables with bound, or unbound, attributes. Another difference is that, in programming, there are specific transformations (translation, compilation, linking, etc.) which may contribute to the degree of binding of attributes. Thus, in comparison with mathematical logic, programming places more emphasis on the *act* of binding, a specific stage in the sequence of transformations carried out on a program before it is executed.

The most important feature of a language in determining the treatment of binding is the *declaration*. Languages with declarations, which include most widely used languages today, generally allow early binding of many attributes, particularly the important attribute, type. However, not all languages include declarations, as will be seen in a later section.

When an attribute is *bound* to a variable by means of a declaration, the association is usually firmly established and may not subsequently be changed. For example, when the variable A has been declared as an *integer,* it is usually impossible to treat it as other than an integer—noninteger values may be assigned to A, but they will be transformed or converted to appropriate integer values. In languages without declarations, attributes may be bound to a variable by means of an assignment statement.

The point at which attributes are associated with a variable is called the *binding time*. The choice of binding time is partly a matter of implementation. For example, it may be feasible for a compiler to allocate precise storage locations for all variables in a given program when the program is compiled. This was done in most early compilers, and may be the most efficient technique for small machines today. However, because of the more dynamic treatment of storage in most large systems today, this form of binding (binding to *location*) is now usually delayed until the program is loaded. In this case, where the binding time is moved to a *later* stage, no change in the design of the language is necessary. However, when the implementors of a language wish to move the binding time to an *earlier* point, the effect on the language design may be critical.

It can be seen that the concept of binding plays an important part both in the design of languages and in their implementation. Binding is obviously important in the treatment of variables, both for data elements and data structures. Binding also plays an important part in other aspects of language design—for example, in the degree of variability that may be allowed for program structure and control structures.

7.5 TYPE

The term "type" is used explicitly in FORTRAN, ALGOL, and several other languages (Fig. 7.2). In PL/I, type is simply one of the attributes of a variable, while in COBOL the type of most elements is determined by their PICTURE specification.

The *type* of a variable determines:

- the set of values it may assume;

- the set of operations to which it may be subjected.

For example, the type *integer* corresponds to the set of "representable" integers in a given language. Note that the set is finite, unlike the set of integers in mathematics. The designers of any language must make sure that this set is reasonable for the machines on which the language is to be implemented.

The set of valid operations on integers includes the arithmetic operators (addition, subtraction, multiplication, etc.). Because of the finite nature of the sets involved, the rules of arithmetic will sometimes differ from those of conventional mathematics—this point is further discussed in Chapter 9.

One sees that a data type can be treated as being in some sense equivalent to a set of values. This set-theoretic view of data types has been expounded by Reynolds (1970) and others, and is valuable in studies of the theory of programming languages. Type has also been related to a storage model by Goldberg and Oden (1973).

Although a type is often given a simple name such as *integer* or *real,* there is a proposal for specifying type declarations in the form of a *range* of values, as for example in the "constraint" of Wilkes (1964). This proposal, which contains a valuable idea related to the reliability of programs, has some similarity to the "assertions" discussed in Chapter 5.

A more familiar view of type is that which relates it to the actions of a compiler—this might be called the "syntactic" notion of type. For example, the association of *type* with variables allows checking of illegal operations to be carried out. This leads to a contrast between programming in machine

FORTRAN

```
    . . .
    . . .
    INTEGER A1, A2, A3

    . . .
```

ALGOL

```
    . . .
begin

    real a, b;

    Boolean s, t;

    . . .
end
    . . .
```

COBOL

```
    DATA DIVISION.
        . . .
        01  INPUT-RECORD.
        . . .
        . . .

        09   INDICATOR PICTURE 999   SYNCHRONIZED.

        . . .
        . . .
```

PL/I

```
                        ──── i.e. ENTRY

    MAIN: PROCEDURE;

        . . .
        . . .
    DECLARE   RATE FIXED   STATIC INITIAL(100);
        . . .
```

(Note the distinction between *type* and other attributes in COBOL and PL/I.)

Fig. 7.2 Examples of type declarations

language and in a high-level language. In most machines, instructions can be applied to any items in the store—any patterns of bits can be taken from a location in store, added together (or multiplied, shifted, inverted . . .) and stored in another location, however inappropriate this action might be. In contrast, the association of a type with each variable allows forms such as:

```
A + B
READ FILE(C)
```

to be checked by a compiler and the following kinds of question asked:

- are A and B numbers?
- is C a file?

In implementing a high-level language, the type of a variable is used for:

- storage allocation,
- code selection.

In *storage allocation,* the type of an elementary item of data determines the amount of storage needed. For each compiler there is a *storage mapping function,* which maps a sequence of data types, $t_1, t_2, \ldots t_n$ on to a set of relative addresses, $a_1, a_2, \ldots a_n$.

Code selection determines the sequence of machine instructions corresponding to a given expression, taking into account the types of the operands. To implement such statements as: ADD X,Y GIVING Z, when X, Y and Z are of differing types, a compiler must ensure that conversions are carried out before addition and assignment operations are carried out.

In most languages, the actual symbols used as names of variables do not influence the meaning of a program. In fact, any variable name can be systematically replaced by another, provided it retains the same separateness from other names in the program. This important property of symbolic systems, known as "referential transparency," helps in the composition of programs and in the design of the basic mechanisms of data declarations and access. This property is not satisfied by "implicit" declarations in FORTRAN and PL/I, in which the initial letter of an identifier may determine the attributes of a variable. Implicit declarations are discussed in Section 7.15 below.

7.6   OTHER ATTRIBUTES OF DATA ELEMENTS

In addition to type, programming languages may allow other properties of data to be specified in data declarations. As in PL/I, we use the term "attribute" in discussing these properties of variables.

We may classify attributes other than type by their effect on:

- the meaning of names,
- the creation and deletion of variables,
- storage.

This classification is summarized in Fig. 7.3, which also shows how the attributes of FORTRAN, ALGOL, COBOL, and PL/I fall into the various classes. We now consider these attribute classes in greater detail.

		FORTRAN	ALGOL	COBOL	PL/I
Meaning of names	Scope of names	COMMON	(Depends on block structure)	–	EXTERNAL (also depends on block structure)
	Selection of attributes	–	–	–	DEFAULT
	Selection of entry names	–	–	–	GENERIC BUILT-IN
Creation of variables	Time of creation	Start of program –no attribute	Entry to block (the **own** attribute may affect the values)	Start of program –no attribute	Depends on *storage class* attribute
	Initial values	DATA	–	VALUE	INITIAL
Storage	Storage sharing	EQUIV- ALENCE COMMON	–	REDEFINES	DEFINED
	Storage mapping	–	–	SYN- CHRO- NIZED	ALIGNED UNALIGNED CONNECTED

Fig. 7.3 Attributes of data elements other than type

7.6.1   Attributes Controlling the Meaning of Names

These attributes are of critical importance to the meaning of a program since they determine how to make the connection between a data *reference*—an appearance of a variable name in a program—and a data *value*.

One very important aspect of a variable is the *scope* over which its name is known. This assumes particular importance when the scope of a name depends on some structural property of the program, as in block structure languages (see Chapter 6). No explicit attribute is connected with the position of a name in a program, but we can think of each variable name being conceptually qualified by the block in which it is declared (Fig. 7.4).

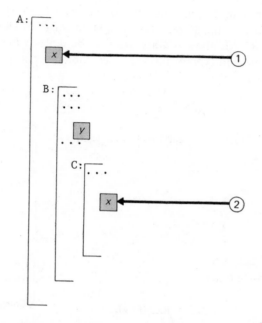

Fig. 7.4 Block-qualified names. The two identical names, *x*, have effectively been given unique identification by "qualifying" them with the names of their enclosing blocks. One way of referring to these names might be by the "block-qualified" names *A·x* or *A·B·C·x*.

This principle has, in fact, been used to identify variables in contexts where a simple name would be ambiguous.

Example

In COBOL, "qualified names" may be used to refer to locations in the program text. For example, in the statement:

```
GO TO FIRST-PART IN READ-IN
```

FIRST-PART refers to a paragraph, READ-IN to a section containing it.

Two attributes related to the scope of names are:

- FORTRAN COMMON,
- PL/I   EXTERNAL.

These allow data to be shared by independently compiled programs.

The EXTERNAL attribute (Fig. 7.5) provides the same kind of scope properties as COMMON in FORTRAN, but differs in being applied to *variables* rather than to segments of storage. The COMMON facility is closely involved with the storage representations of FORTRAN variables, whereas EXTERNAL allows data sharing to be done symbolically, based only on the name and type of the variables. Storage concepts in programming languages are discussed in Chapter 8.

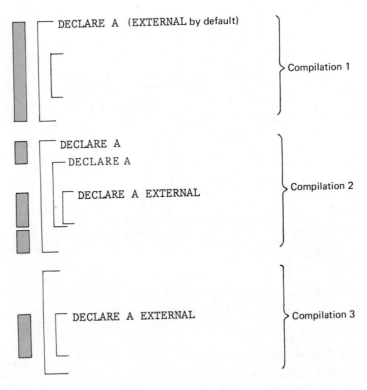

Fig. 7.5 The EXTERNAL attribute of PL/I. Shaded area at the left shows the scope of the variable *A*. References to *A*, at any point in the shaded area, are to the same variable.

7.6.2   Attributes controlling the creation of variables

Some languages include attributes which control the method of creation of variables and their initial values. These are not available in all languages; for example, in FORTRAN and COBOL, there is no such choice—all variables in these languages are created when execution of the program is begun.

However, in PL/I, there are four storage class attributes: STATIC, AUTOMATIC, CONTROLLED, and BASED, which control the creation of instances (or "generations") of variables. Briefly, these result in the following actions being taken.

STATIC variables are created at the beginning of a program.

AUTOMATIC variables are created automatically when a block is entered and are destroyed when the block is terminated.

CONTROLLED and BASED variables are only created when an ALLOCATE statement, referring explicitly to the variable, is executed.

The attributes are discussed further in Chapter 8.

7.6.2.1   The ALGOL attribute *own*

The **own** attribute in ALGOL has an effect similar to that of the STATIC storage class in PL/I, although it is not related to storage. When control leaves a block containing **own** variables, the values of variables local to the block are preserved and applied on re-entry. The behavior of **own** variables is more complex than that of PL/I STATIC variables for the following reasons:

- With PL/I STATIC variables, only one copy of a variable exists during the execution of a program. In ALGOL, multiple copies of **own** variables may be created if there are recursive calls of the same procedure.

- The upper and lower bounds of STATIC arrays in PL/I must be denoted by integer constants, while those of **own** arrays in ALGOL may be denoted by expressions.

One of the difficulties of dynamic **own** arrays is that the integrity of arrays may not be preserved, since the language defines the dimensions applied to an **own** array as the "most recent" dimension calculated, even though the values in the array may have been preserved from a previous invocation of a block. Strange errors may result from this.

Example

> **begin**
> **own array** a [1:m,1:n];
> . . .
> . . .
> **end**

When this block is first entered, the size of the array, a, is calculated from the current values of m and n, which must have been set in a surrounding block. When **end** is reached, the elements of the array are preserved, and will be restored if the block is re-entered.

However, if m and n are changed before reentry, then the new array may have new upper bounds, because the latest values of m and n will be used for recreating the array. This means, for example, that $a[1,1], a[1,2], a[2,1]$ may have their original values, but values like $a[1,n], a[m,1]$, etc., may either not exist or have an undefined value.

The difficulties of implementing dynamic **own** arrays has resulted in their omission from many implementations and from the IFIP subset of ALGOL (IFIP, 1964).

7.6.2.2   Initialization attributes

In most languages, the creation of a variable does not automatically result in its being given a value. The programmer must assign a value to a variable before using it and failure to do so may lead to unpredictable results. Access to a variable involves access to the storage allocated for it, and unless an assignment has been made, this may contain values from other computations.

This unsatisfactory situation is largely due to the prevailing emphasis on efficiency rather than reliability in current systems. One solution to problems caused by uninitialized variables is to require the automatic initialization of *all* variables in a program. This must be coupled with the introduction of a new "value" for all data types—the value *undefined*. This would have a profound effect on the reliability of programs—providing perhaps the simplest conceptual solution to many programming problems. However, there are many implications to such an approach, one being the need to introduce a means for denoting "undefined" values in storage. This may require an increase in the word or byte size of the machine (the 'nine-bit byte').

An alternative approach has been adopted in some languages—the inclusion of initialization attributes which may be applied by the programmer to selected variables. Examples of initialization attributes are:

- the DATA and BLOCK DATA statements in FORTRAN,
- the VALUE clause in COBOL,
- the INITIAL attribute in PL/I.

In FORTRAN, initial values of data (except data in blank COMMON) can be specified with the DATA statement. This consists of a sequence of pairs of lists separated by the character /.

$$k_1/d_1/k_2/d_2/ \ldots .$$

where $k_1, k_2, \ldots$ are lists of variable names or array element names, and $d_1, d_2, \ldots$ are lists of constants.

Example

```
DATA I,J,K/1,2,3
DATA A(1),A(2),A(3),A(4)/0,0,0,0/X/100
```

Note that a data list can only include data *elements,* and therefore array initialization must be specified by nominating each element in turn. The BLOCK DATA statement is used to head BLOCK DATA subprograms which are composed of sets of initial values only. They are used to define initial values in labeled COMMON blocks.

The VALUE clause in COBOL can be used to define the initial value of a *working storage* item. The VALUE clause may not be used in the File Section, for reasons which will be clear when we deal with the record formats associated with files. The restrictions placed on the use of the VALUE clause are, as in FORTRAN, rather severe; essentially, it may only be applied to scalar elements, and not to a REDEFINED item.

Example (initialization in COBOL)

```
WORKING-STORAGE SECTION.
...
02 REPORT-HEADING PICTURE A(18) VALUE 'REPORT FOR JANUARY'.
...
02 RATE-FACTOR PICTURE 999V9 VALUE 27.6.
```

The INITIAL attribute in PL/I specifies that data elements and structures are to be initialized. Initialization takes place when storage allocation occurs, in accordance with the storage class attribute of the variable. Two forms of the INITIAL attribute are provided, one in which the values are specified with the attribute itself, a restriction being that all such values must be constants and not variables. The other version specifies a named procedure to be called at the point of storage allocation for the variable and allows more complex initialization to be carried out. PL/I initialization can be applied to arrays and strings of adjustable bounds, in contrast with the restrictions noted above for FORTRAN and COBOL.

Examples   (Initialization in PL/I)

```
DECLARE(X,Y,Z) FIXED INITIAL(100);

DECLARE T (10,10) INITIAL ((100)(0));
```

Here, 100 is a "repetition factor" which determines the number of values to be applied.

If the array bounds are represented by variables, the same variables may be used to control the initialization:

```
DECLARE T (M,N) INITIAL ((M*N) (0));
```

7.6.2.3 Attributes relating to storage

In some programming languages, there is an underlying concept of *storage* which affects the treatment of data and particularly of data structures. This subject is treated in Chapter 8, in which the storage models in several languages are compared. Language forms for storage sharing include:

- the EQUIVALENCE statement in FORTRAN,
- the REDEFINES clause in COBOL,
- the DEFINED attribute in PL/I.

The pointer and based variable concepts in PL/I also allow certain types of storage sharing.

The language forms which control storage *mapping* are:

- the SYNCHRONIZED clause of COBOL,
- the ALIGNED and UNALIGNED attributes of PL/I.

7.7 LITERALS AND CONSTANTS

Up to this point, we have discussed the treatment of variables in programming languages. However, not all the data in a program needs to be changed and programming languages therefore have provisions for defining constants.

A *constant* is a data item whose value cannot be changed.

There is a special class of constant, commonly called a *literal*, whose name determines its associated value. Examples of literals include:

- the *numeric literal*, constructed from the digits 0–9 and special characters (decimal point, sign, exponent),
- the *string literal*, constructed from a character set determined by the language.

Example

Numeric literals:

```
10
3.14159
92E6
```

String literals:

```
'JOE BROWN'
'12.11.71'
'The value of X is:'
```

In addition to literals, there are also classes of constant which are given symbolic names, often suggestive of the value of the constant.

Examples

The *figurative constants* of COBOL

```
SPACE(S)
ZERO(S)
HIGH-VALUES
LOW-VALUES
```

The *logical constants*

> ***true, false*** in ALGOL
> `.TRUE.`, `.FALSE.` in FORTRAN

The *pointer constant,*

> `NULL`†, in PL/I.

From an implementation point of view, a constant can be regarded in much the same way as a variable, except that its value must be protected from change. In implementation, constants are often stored in a centrally accessible location (the "constant pool") so that multiple copies of the same value need not be stored. The protection of constants from changes by assignment does not generally present much problem in compiler writing, since illegal access can be detected syntactically. However, care is needed when a constant is passed as argument to a procedure which assigns to the corresponding parameter. In PL/I, constants are protected by the requirement that a "dummy variable" be created when they are passed as arguments to a procedure. (See Chapter 12.)

7.7.1 The "Type" of a Constant

As will be shown in Chapter 9, the type of each operand in an expression may determine which conversions, if any, are to be applied in evaluating

---

† For syntactic reasons, NULL is classified as a built-in function in the PL/I language specifications. However, since it always represents the same value, its behavior more closely resembles that of a constant.

the expression. This means that, when evaluating an expression, just as the types of all variables must be known, so must the types of constants.

Most languages include the numeric types *floating-point* and *integer* and have means of distinguishing between constants of these two types. The representation of integers is easier; integer constants are usually represented by digits, together with a plus or a minus sign.

Examples—integer constants:

$$100$$
$$+7936$$
$$-1$$

To distinguish a floating-point constant from an integer, most languages require an extra character. For fractional values a period may be used to indicate the position of the decimal point. Although the period is not needed for integer values, it is retained in FORTRAN as a type indicator. In PL/I, the letter E is used to signify a floating-point constant, to avoid confusion with the *fixed-decimal-point* type. In ALGOL, a suffix 10 may be used to indicate a floating-point constant.

Examples—floating-point constants:

ALGOL

$$\cdot 5384$$
$$+93.78$$
$$21.78_{10}-3$$

FORTRAN

$$3.14159$$
$$760153.$$
$$21.6E10$$

PL/I

$$3.14159E0$$
$$7.60153E-5$$

There is no floating-point type in standard COBOL.

7.7.2 String Literals

A string literal is represented by the characters themselves. However, when the string may contain *any* character, there is a syntactic difficulty in delimiting a literal. Since the character **space** is itself a member of the character set, it is obviously impossible to use a space or spaces for delimiting the string.

Two approaches are described for dealing with this problem. The first is the technique used in FORTRAN, in which a "Hollerith literal" is specified by means of the form:

$$n \; H\{the \; literal \; string\}$$

Example

The Hollerith literal: `15HNEXT QUESTION-`
represents the literal string: `NEXT QUESTION-`
or, with blanks represented by the letter b: `NEXTbQUESTION-b`

In other words, the programmer has to specify the number of characters making up the literal string. The length of the literal is n characters from the letter H; great care must be taken that this is accurately worked out, and especially that it does not include any part of the program. This single feature has apparently caused more errors in FORTRAN programs than any other in the FORTRAN language—programmers, whatever their abilities in logic and mathematics, are poor at counting. In more recently designed languages, this form of representation has been abandoned in favor of the approach described below.

The other approach is to select, from the character set, a suitable character as a string literal delimiter. The character usually chosen is the quote mark, (`'`), which is used in a rather similar way in natural language. This gives rise to another problem—that of representing a string which includes instances of the delimiting character. For example, we may wish to represent the string: ROSEMARY'S BABY as a literal. Earlier versions of COBOL avoided this problem by not allowing the quote mark to appear in a string literal. However, this is technically too cautious. A technique adopted by several languages, and by the 1973 ANSI version of COBOL, is to allow *two* instances of the quote sign to represent a single instance in the literal. With this convention, the literal form of ROSEMARY'S BABY is:

<code>'ROSEMARY''S BABY'</code>

These and other techniques for representing character string constants are discussed in a survey paper by Chroust (1970).

7.8   A SURVEY OF DATA ELEMENT TYPES

The types of data elements available in programming languages may be divided into two classes. The first is a class of *representable data,* for which the values correspond to data in the outside world. It includes:

numbers,

strings,

logical values.

The second is a class of data related only to a program, and includes:

labels,

procedures,

files.

7.9   NUMERIC DATA

All programming languages include numeric data. Even in nonnumeric data processing, there is a need for numbers to act as counters, field widths, scaling factors, and control values in a computation. An important distinction between the numbers in programming languages and those in mathematics is that the classes of numbers encountered in computing are all *finite*, as opposed to the infinite classes of numbers usually discussed in mathematics. Even in the most elementary calculations, carried out with pencil and paper, we can work as if the numbers are infinite. We simply know that, as values in the calculation grow larger, the sums take longer and we may have to carry out the computation on a larger size of paper.

As soon as any form of simple, manually operated calculator is used, we immediately become aware of the finite sizes of the machine's registers and the need to consider these in the calculations. However, the intimate connection with each stage of a calculation carried out on such machines obscures many of the decisions made by the user. With a stored-program machine, however, the inability to make minor, almost involuntary, adjustments during the course of a calculation means that our first experiences with computer arithmetic are often filled with surprises. This is especially true in using many high-level languages. We shall discuss this matter further in Chapter 9, but we emphasize here that many of the "problems" of computer arithmetic are primarily due to the finite nature of representable numbers in hardware systems.

7.9.1   Integers

As we have seen, the type *integer* used in programming languages does not exactly correspond to the integers or "natural numbers" of mathematics. In programming languages, the integer type describes a *finite* set of values, the largest of which has to be determined by the implementors of the language. Integers can be exactly represented in all digital computer systems, which essentially work in integers, although they may be programmed so as to appear to work with fractional data.

7.9.2 "Real" numbers

In mathematics, integers are a sub-class of the so-called "real" numbers, which form an infinite and infinitely densely packed continuum, including both very large negative and very large positive numbers.† The *real* numbers include as sub-classes the fractions (rational numbers), the roots of polynomial equations (the irrational numbers), and the transcendental numbers, a class which includes such numbers as π, the exponential number, e, etc.

The term "real" is also used in programming languages (for example, in FORTRAN and ALGOL), but in programming the term has quite a different meaning from that in mathematics. In FORTRAN and ALGOL, "real" denotes non-integral data. There is no conceivable digital computer in which it might be possible to represent the infinite class of values corresponding to the real numbers in mathematics.

In most implementations the term "real" in FORTRAN and ALGOL implies *floating point;* the most widely used representation of fractional numbers in most machines. A floating-point number has two parts, a *fraction* or *mantissa* which represents the significant digits of the number, and an *exponent* which indicates a scaling factor to be applied to the fraction. It is usual to express floating-point numbers in *normalized* form, in which the most significant digit is non-zero (this is always possible to achieve by suitable adjustment of the exponent).

We have previously seen how floating-point constants are represented—when an exponent is given, it is usual for this to be signed and to represent a power of ten. This is not always the case within a machine, where the fraction may be binary, decimal, or (as in the case of the IBM System/360) hexadecimal. Internally, the exponent may be unsigned and represented as an "excess" number (e.g., the range −49 to 50 might be represented internally by an exponent in the range 0 to 99).

The history of floating-point representation in computing systems goes back to the earliest designs of machines. (See Campbell, 1962; Wilkes, Wheeler, and Gill, 1951. Also see Knuth, 1969, Chapter 4.)

---

† The infinite nature of the real number class is not only a matter of an infinite *range* of values. Even within a small finite range of values, say in the range 0 to 10, there are infinitely many *real* values in the mathematical sense.

From our point of view, the most notable features of floating point numbers are:

- they are a *finite* class of numbers,
- they do not include the integers as a sub-class, as do the real numbers in mathematics,
- they are not uniformly distributed.

The second point in particular leads to many anomalies in the arithmetic of high-level languages. It results in a need for "conversion" routines for translating from one numeric data type to another, even for data which may be essentially integral. These conversions contribute to the complexity and, indeed, the inaccuracy of some arithmetic operations in computers.

The range of values expressible in floating-point representations depends primarily on the magnitude of the exponent. The field width of the fraction or mantissa primarily affects the *accuracy* of the representation. Virtually no machines with floating-point hardware allow separate specifications for the length of exponent and fraction. If extra precision is required, it is usually achieved by extending the length of the fraction, leaving the exponent size unchanged. Hence the introduction of "double-precision" floating-point representations may not increase the range of values which may be represented, but only the number of significant digits in the representation.

The distribution of numbers expressed in floating-point representation has been examined by Hamming (1970). If we look at the set of distinct values representable in floating-point format, it is clear that these values are nonuniformly distributed—for example, consecutive values are closest for smallest values of the exponent. Hamming investigated the effect of normalization on repeated arithmetic operations in floating-point, and developed a terminating distribution for the resulting values.

7.9.3 Fixed-point numbers

Fixed-point numbers can represent noninteger values, but in comparison with floating-point numbers, the programmer must take greater care in predicting the expected range of values of the data. Two key parameters are used in specifying fixed-point data, the total field width and the position of the decimal point. When arithmetic operations are to be performed, the compiler must generate code for appropriate scaling and alignment of the decimal point, based on the declared types of the data.

Fixed-point arithmetic in programming languages originated in commercial languages developed for early accounting machines and found its way into simple Assembler and "Autocoder" languages for "character" machines. At a later stage, fixed-point arithmetic was included in high-level languages, such as FLOWMATIC, COMMERCIAL TRANSLATOR, FACT, and COBOL. Fixed-point data was included in PL/I, partly to satisfy the requirements for commercial applications, but also providing a useful facility for engineering and mathematical calculations, for which the automatic normalization carried out in floating-point arithmetic may be insufficiently controllable.

7.9.4 Complex numbers

In mathematics, complex numbers are a generalization of real numbers, introduced so that all polynomial equations with real coefficients can have solutions. The absence of real-valued roots for such simple equations as

$$x^2 + 5 = 9$$
$$x^2 - 3x + 3 = 0$$

led mathematicians to extend the concept of real numbers, visualized as a continuum of values along a single line, and to introduce the concept of number-values disposed on a *plane*. A complex value is represented by a pair of values, the *real* part and the *imaginary* part, which can be visualized as the *(x,y)* coordinates of Cartesian geometry.

The importance of complex numbers is that they allow solutions to be found, not only for all quadratic equations, but for *all* polynomial equations of the general form:

$$a_0x^n + a_1x^{n-1} + a_2x^{n-2} + \ldots + a_n = 0$$

The arithmetic operations $(+, -, \times, \div,$ etc.) applying to real numbers have counterparts with complex numbers and these operations are extended to complex variables in FORTRAN and PL/I.

7.10 LOGICAL DATA

Logical data has the most limited range of values of the types we consider—it can take only two values, *true* and *false*.

Logical data is sometimes (e.g., in ALGOL) called *Boolean* after the mathematician and logician George Boole (1815–1864). In his book, *An Investigation of the Laws of Thought,* published in 1854, Boole outlined an algebraic approach to logic, and this work has had a strong effect on the development of symbolic logic.

In Boole's discussion of "Signs and their laws" we find the following passage:

Let us conceive, then, of an Algebra in which the symbols x, y, z, &c. admit indifferently of the values of 0 and 1, and of these values alone. The laws, the axioms, and the processes, of such an Algebra will be identical in their whole extent with the laws, the axioms, and the processes of an Algebra of Logic. Difference of interpretation will alone divide them. Upon this principle the method of the following work is based.

The two-valued quantities described in this passage are closely related to the logical variables in programming languages. Boole is concerned with *propositions* and with an algebra for evaluating complex combinations of propositions, something like the logical expressions discussed in Chapter 9. Boole's ideas have penetrated deeply into computer system design, both in hardware and in software.

In most programming languages, logical variables can be tested, assigned, passed as arguments, or subjected to input/output operations. In ALGOL and FORTRAN, the words "true" and "false" are used as representations of logical values. In some languages (e.g. PL/I, APL) a *characteristic function* is used to express logical values. The most obvious characteristic function is a quantity represented by a single bit, where the setting 1 represents *true* and 0 represents *false.* This is also a convenient internal representation of logical values.

Logical *values* are produced by:

- relational expressions such as

        (A > B)
        X IS EQUAL TO 2

- predicates, such as:

        the COBOL CLASS test,

        the PL/I ALLOCATION function.

Logical *variables* may be used to store the results of complex logical and relational expressions, whose calculation may have required considerable effort. They may also be used

- in simulating logical devices,
- to represent relationships between complex sets of data (e.g., as representations of graph and tree structures).

There are many computational techniques, particularly in combinatorial programming, in which two-valued data is useful. See, for example, Wunderlich (1967) for a sieving technique in which bit values are useful. Further examples may be found in the references on combinatorial programming in Chapter 3.

7.11 CONTROL VARIABLES

As noted earlier, there is a basic distinction between data types which have external meaning and representation ("problem data"), and data which exists only in the context of a computation ("control data"). This distinction becomes most important in discussing PL/I, in which the idea of control data is most advanced. However, two types of control data have appeared in many languages and can be considered separately.

7.11.1 Labels and Procedures

These two types of data may be considered together, for each represents a means of identifying and referencing program text. The evolution of these two types and the establishment of corresponding variables has been gradual and is still in progress. Their significance is related to the crucial discovery which opened the way to systems programming as we know it—*programs can be treated as data by a computing system.*

In most high-level languages, labels may be interspersed with program text, and their appearance establishes their values and meaning.

Although, in many respects, we can treat a label as a conceptual text-pointer, we must not regard labels as simple addresses. In the case of block structure languages, labels reflect the local environment in which they have obtained their initial values. For example, when a go to statement in ALGOL or PL/I causes a transfer out of a block, the effect is similar to that when the block is terminated by reaching the end (see Fig. 7.6). Local variables are destroyed and other activities may take place, making this kind of transfer quite different from a simple transfer instruction. This extra meaning implies that the *values* associated with labels in a program must contain information about the environment of the label.

```
L2:     if n1 > 1 then
        begin
          if A[n1, 2] = A[n1 − 1, 2] then
            begin
            n1 := n1 − 1;
            go to L2
            end
        end;
```

Fig. 7.6 A fragment of ALGOL defining the label, *L*2

The values assumed by label and procedure variables are limited to the values of the corresponding "constants" in a program. Thus, for these types of data, the range of allowable values is determined by the context in which they are used. In some cases this is an undesirable constraint on the power of such variables, particularly when dynamic operations are carried out on program text. For example, dynamic loading and unloading of procedure text, required by systems with unpredictable loads (e.g., message processing programs), is difficult when the values of procedure names are restricted to those known when a program is compiled.

Label and procedure variables are valuable for coding programs with complex sequencing. It is convenient to be able to write: "GO TO label-variable" or "CALL procedure-variable" and to adjust program flow simply by assigning different values to the variables. This form of sequencing logic is particularly useful in writing interpretive code.

7.12   DATA ELEMENTS IN CURRENT LANGUAGES

We next illustrate the treatment of data elements in programming languages—it is simplest to start with ALGOL and FORTRAN, each of which has fairly simple sets of data types. These are summarized in Fig. 7.7.

7.12.1   Data Elements in COBOL

COBOL relies almost entirely on the PICTURE clause as a means of data element description. The type of each data item has to be deduced from the form of its picture, rather than from a key-word attribute such as "real" or "integer". An exception to this is INDEX data, which cannot have a picture. However, the status of INDEX data in COBOL is not the same as that of a "pictured" item and it is doubtful whether it can be regarded as a true COBOL variable. COBOL pictures are also used for controlling the external representation of data—for inserting decimal points and commas, for removing leading zeros, for inserting currency signs, etc. However, the following discussion is primarily concerned with the use of pictures as type descriptors.

COBOL defines two terms, *class* and *category*, relating to data items. All items belong both to one of the classes and to one of the categories. We shall try to relate these terms to the idea of *type* as represented in other languages.

A COBOL picture clause has the form

PICTURE IS {string-of-picture-characters}

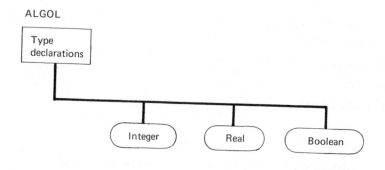

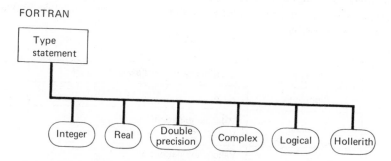

Fig. 7.7 Data elements in ALGOL and FORTRAN

The contents of the picture string must be characters of the allowable set of picture characters. These are:

$$\text{A B P S V X Z 9 0 , . + - CR DB * \$ /}$$

A syntactic device allows repetitions of the picture characters to be specified; thus A(9) is a shorthand form of AAAAAAAAA.

The picture characters may not be chosen in an arbitrary way, but must conform to certain restrictions.

- The maximum number of picture characters is 30 (this applies to the resulting string after expansion of repetitions).
- The following symbols may only appear once:

$$\text{S V . CR DB}$$

- There are several constraints on the ordering of picture characters within the string.

The contents of its picture determine the category of a data item. There are five categories:

alphabetic,

numeric,

numeric edited,

alphanumeric,

alphanumeric edited.

The distinctions between *numeric* and *numeric edited* and between *alphanumeric* and *alphanumeric edited* are made by the presence of editing characters in the pictures. Figure 7.8 shows the correspondence between picture and categories.

Category	Picture characters allowed
Alphabetic	A B
Numeric	Valid combinations of 9 V P S
Numeric edited	Valid combinations of B P V Z 0 9 , . / * + - CR DB $
Alphanumeric	Valid combinations of A X 9
Alphanumeric edited	Valid combinations of A X 9 B 0 /

Fig. 7.8 Categories and picture characters of COBOL items

We next discuss the range of values of the various categories of data; these are also indirectly determined by their pictures. First, a feature of the standard definition of COBOL should be noted. In contrast with FORTRAN, ALGOL, and PL/I, the COBOL standard places a finite upper bound on the size (and consequently the range of values) of data items. In other languages, it is recognized that an upper bound exists, but it is often left to an individual implementation to specify a particular upper bound.

Alphabetic items contain occurrences of the letters A to Z and the character "space." The maximum length of an alphabetic item is 30 characters.

Numeric items contain numbers (0 to 9) in their "digit positions." The *digit positions* of a COBOL numeric picture correspond to the picture characters 9 in the numeric category and 9 0 Z in the numeric edited category. The maximum number of digit positions in any COBOL number is 18.

In general, COBOL numbers are fixed point numbers, optionally signed, with an optional fractional part. Exact calculations, at least for addition and subtraction, can be carried out, subject to the size constraints of the field which is to receive the answer. The *numeric edited* category contains the most elaborate editing features in COBOL, allowing zero suppression, scaling, floating sign insertion, check protection, etc.

The *alphanumeric* categories contain strings of any characters in the computer's character set. They therefore correspond to the "general string" of other languages (e.g., the character string of PL/I).

The categories of COBOL data are introduced chiefly to distinguish between different kinds of external representations. (Refer to Fig. 7.9.) Another descriptive clause, the USAGE clause, is used to allow alternative forms of internal representation.

Level-number identifier

```
PICTURE IS   {Picture · character · string}

                      ⎧ COMPUTATIONAL
USAGE IS       ⎨ DISPLAY
                      ⎩ INDEX

VALUE IS     {Literal}
```

Fig. 7.9 Data element description in COBOL

INDEX data is used only for subscripting or indexing arrays. The two other terms, DISPLAY and COMPUTATIONAL, control the internal representation of data and may determine what operations may be carried out on the data. DISPLAY data is represented in character form, with a close correspondence between the characters stored and the characters displayed. COMPUTATIONAL data, which must be of the numeric class, may be stored in a form most suited to the computer. Some versions of COBOL (however, not the current ANSI standard) allow several versions of COMPUTATIONAL, e.g.,

COMPUTATIONAL-1 referring to floating-point

COMPUTATIONAL-2 referring to double-precision floating-point,
       etc.

The *classes* of COBOL data are related to the categories, as shown in Figure 7.10. The purpose of the classification of data into classes is to provide

Level of item	Category	Class
Elementary	Alphabetic	Alphabetic
	Numeric	Numeric
	Numeric edited Alphanumeric Alphanumeric edited	Alphanumeric
Group	All categories	Alphanumeric

Fig. 7.10 COBOL categories and classes

a basis for the *class-test,* a conditional test which may be used in IF statements. In effect, the class test is a *predicate* for testing the *contents* of a data field. There are two class tests, one for ALPHABETIC, the other for NUMERIC data—a typical use for them is in validating input data. Note that only data *elements* have one of the significant classes; a group item, even if composed entirely of elements of alphabetic or numeric class, will yield a *false* value if tested by one of the class tests. As can be seen by the interpretation of the MOVE statement in COBOL, group items are regarded as alphanumeric data.

Example

A given field in a record is defined as being of the Alphabetic category—for example it may contain the name of an area or district in which a product is being marketed.

After reading in a record, the field may be tested for valid data as follows:

```
    . . .
    IF LOCATION IS NOT ALPHABETIC THEN PERFORM
    ERROR-ROUTINE-1.
    . . .
```

The COBOL method of data element description has been described in some detail because it differs considerably from the methods employed in other languages. There are several advantages to be gained from the use of pictures in data specifications—their strong visual and mnemonic appeal simplifies the task of laying out records for printing forms and reports.

However, the lack of explicit types in COBOL leads to an unduly complex relationship between the picture characters and the range of values and operations applicable to the data items. The *categories* of COBOL data correspond most closely to the *types* of other languages, but they do not completely determine all the properties relating to type; the USAGE clause may also be needed to supplement this information.

7.12.2   Data Elements in PL/I

PL/I has the greatest variety of data types of the languages we are considering. Externally representable data, or *problem* data, is divided into two classes:

- the *numeric* class, in which integer and floating-point numbers are supplemented by a class of fixed-point scaled fractions;

- the *string* class, with sub-classifications *character* and *bit* string.

In addition there is a wide group of data types, collectively called *control data,* whose meaning is valid only during the course of a computation and which has no external representation. See Fig. 7.11.

		Real or complex	Fixed or float	Binary or decimal
Problem data	Arithmetic			
	String	Character		
		Bit		
Control data	Program referencing	Label		
		Entry		
	Data referencing	Pointer		
		Offset		
	Storage	Area		
	System control	File		
		Task		
		Event		

Fig. 7.11 PL/I data types

7.13   PL/I PROBLEM DATA

7.13.1   Arithmetic Data

There are four subdivisions of the arithmetic attributes of PL/I:

mode,

base,

scale,

precision.

These may be applied "orthogonally," so that all possible combinations of modes, bases, scales, and precisions are valid. Syntactically, the three attributes, mode, base, and scale, are specified by keywords; while precision and scaling factor are denoted by integer constants. Alternatively, a complete set of arithmetic attributes (Fig. 7.12) may be expressed by means of a PL/I picture.

- **Mode**—alternative attributes: REAL or COMPLEX

A complex number may be regarded as a simple data structure with two components, a real part and an imaginary part. PL/I includes two functions for accessing these components:

REAL(z)   for accessing the real part of z,

IMAG(z)   for accessing the imaginary part of z.

These may be used on the left-hand side of an assignment, providing examples of what are called *pseudo-variables* in PL/I.

Note that REAL numbers in PL/I differ from those in FORTRAN and ALGOL, which are normally floating-point numbers. In PL/I, the REAL and COMPLEX attributes can be applied to integers, fixed-point, and floating-point numbers.

- **Base**—alternative attributes: BINARY or DECIMAL

The base attribute is primarily of relevance in the case of FIXED data and has comparatively little relevance for floating-point data, since most machines do not have both binary and decimal floating-point representations.

- **Scale**—alternative attributes: FIXED or FLOAT

There is no separate "integer" attribute in PL/I and the FIXED attribute serves to specify both *integer* data, which is denoted by the FIXED attribute with a zero scale factor, and *fixed-point* data, in which the position

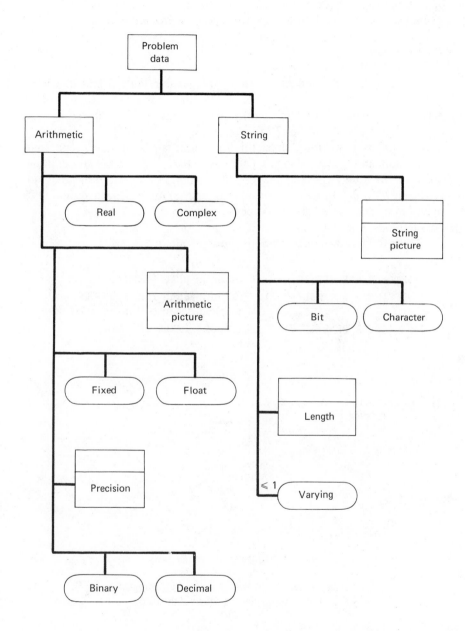

Fig. 7.12 PL/I problem data attributes: abstract syntax

of a decimal point (or in the case of BINARY data, a binary point) can be indicated. FLOAT indicates floating-point representation.

- **Precision**

Precision is expressed as a pair of integer constants p and q, which respectively denote the field width of a number and the position of its decimal or binary point. The significance of p and q are indicated in Fig. 7.13 and an example in Fig. 7.14.

The precision attribute takes the form of a pair of numbers separated by a comma and contained in brackets, thus: (10, 2). Since brackets denoting precision may not appear in an isolated position in a declaration (to avoid confusion with the dimension attribute for arrays) there is a convention that precision specifications can be appended to any of the keywords used to denote mode, scale, or base.

Thus, the following declarations are equivalent:

```
DECLARE A FIXED(10,2)      default: REAL DECIMAL
DECLARE A DECIMAL(10,2)    default: REAL FIXED (FIXED is
                           implied because of non-zero scale)
DECLARE A REAL(10,2)       default: FIXED DECIMAL
```

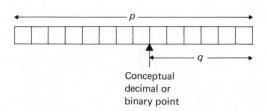

Precision (*p*,*q*)

   p   Specifies the total field width of the item

   q   Specifies the position of an implied decimal/binary point relative to the rightmost position of the field

Fig. 7.13 Representations of fixed-point numbers in PL/I

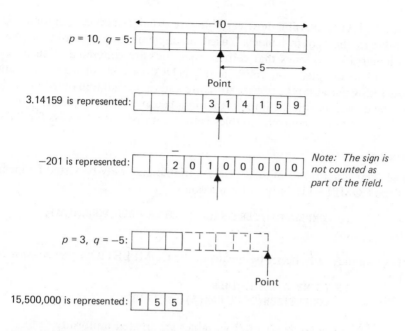

Fig. 7.14 Precision and scale factor in PL/I

7.14 PL/I CONTROL VARIABLES

A PL/I *control variable* denotes a quantity local to a program. This is in contrast with *problem variables* which correspond to the user's data. The uses of the various types of PL/I control variables are discussed in succeeding chapters—label variables in Chapter 10, entry variables in Chapter 12, etc. Here, we consider reasons for the introduction of such variables, and some aspects of their design.

One of the main objectives for introducing control variables is to increase the generality and flexibility of programs. At any point in a program where a value appears we may ask, "Does it help to have this value represented by a *variable* rather than by a *constant?*" If so, then this type of quantity may be considered as a possible control variable. The use of control variables allows later binding—the programmer no longer has to fix the corresponding values at the time the program is being written but may have them computed during program execution.

Control variables allow greater access to the facilities of the system on which a language is implemented. For example, consider the case of FILE, TASK, and ENTRY variables. In addition to their use in PL/I statements

(OPEN, CALL, WAIT), these variables are structured objects, in some ways similar to the "control blocks" used in implementing operating systems. Although PL/I implies that certain quantities are contained in such variables (for example, a bit value in an ENTRY variable or a priority value in a TASK variable) the precise structure and representation of the variables can be chosen to suit the implementation, because the only means of access to the contents of control variables is by means of special access functions.

Example

The *completion status* of an EVENT variable may only be tested by means of the COMPLETION built-in function:

```
IF COMPLETION(TERMINAL(8)) THEN CALL POLL(M,8);
...
```

Its value may only be *set* by means of the COMPLETION *pseudo-variable:*

```
IF (TIME & TERM) THEN
    COMPLETION(TERMINAL(8)) = '1'B;
```

As far as possible all PL/I variables are treated uniformly so that they have equal status and rights in the operations that can be carried out on them.

The "rights of a variable" for PL/I include:

assignment;

acting as an argument and returned value from procedures;

being a member of arrays and structures;

comparison (where appropriate);

initialization.

To establish these "rights," careful consideration must be given to the nature of the values that may be assumed by a variable. For example, the comparison of control variables is generally only possible for the relations *equal* and *not equal,* since in most cases the set of values of the variable is not ordered.†

The development of control variables has been one of the important advances in language design associated with PL/I. The concept has gradually been extended and developed during the evolution of the language since 1964.

---

† This is so, even for label values, although some people might argue that label values could be ordered by their position in a program.

This work has continued in the standards groups, where an additional control variable, the FORMAT variable, has been added. (In later stages of development of the standard, the TASK and EVENT variables were deleted, although they remain in the IBM version of PL/I).

7.15 DECLARATIONS

In the previous sections, we have considered the role of variables in high-level languages and the constituents of a variable—its name, attributes and value. We now come to the means for defining variables and giving them attributes—the language form known as a *declaration*.

The declaration is an essential feature of a compilable language. The process of compilation involves collecting information about variables and translating statements and expressions into machine code, depending on the types and location of each variable. The resulting *binding* of name and attributes carried out by a compiler is made possible by the existence of declarations in the source program.

The declaration is therefore a central point for information about variables in a program. When we read a program, we encounter many references to variables. To determine the meaning of each reference, we must look for its corresponding declaration, to discover the type, scope, initial value, etc. of the variable to which it refers. When *writing* a program, a similar process is carried out, but in reverse. Thus it is usual to start constructing a program by designing and declaring the data structures and files to be used, so that simple references in the procedural part of the code can be used to access the data.

In compilable languages such as ALGOL, COBOL, FORTRAN and PL/I, declarations are "non-executable" statements in contrast with statements such as: assignment, **if, go to,** etc. Declarations can be seen as instructions to the compiler, the information they contain being added to the compiler's symbol table, for use in storage allocation and code generation. In most cases, the symbol table can be dispensed with in the object program, this being one of the qualities which makes compilation such a successful technique for implementing languages.

7.15.1 The Syntax of Declarations

ALGOL and COBOL have a rather similar approach in the syntax of their declarations, requiring them to be fully specified in a standard position at the head of the block or program to which they refer.

ALGOL has a simpler form of declaration than COBOL because of its more limited range of data types and structures. Declarations of ALGOL variables may be written for any ALGOL *block,* in what is known as the *block head.* Declarations of elementary variables consist of the symbols **real,** **integer,** or **Boolean** followed by a list of variables. Array declarations follow the same pattern, the symbol **array** being added. Switch declarations have a more complicated form, consisting of the switch name followed by a list of *designational expressions* (ALGOL switches are discussed further in Chapter 10).

Examples

The following examples show ALGOL declarations:

1) **begin integer** x,y; **Boolean** $t1,t2$;

    . . . .

    end

2) **begin integer array** A $[1:m,10:n],E[1,X]$;
       switch $S: = S1,S2,S10$;
       $A[1,10] := 0; \ldots$
    end

All variables in an ALGOL program must be declared and, with one exception (the type of arrays), the declarations must be complete—all attributes being specified. This is achieved by an asymmetric attribute structure rather than by defaults, as in FORTRAN and PL/I. Thus, all variables are "local" unless they are declared **own;** all parameters are "name" unless they are in the **value** list. However, there are no symbols for "local" or "name" in the ALGOL language.

One of the notable features of COBOL is the elaborate formality of its declaration structure. Declarations must be complete and must precede the program, being placed in a separate division of the program known as the Data Division.

In the following section, we discuss two important kinds of COBOL declaration—the *file-declaration* (FD) and the *Working-Storage* section. The Data Division is also used to specify Sort Files and Reports, the other large-scale specifications needed for special features in the COBOL language.

The FD description in COBOL contains a specification of the expected layout of records on a COBOL file. At its head is the *file-name* and information relating to the file itself (the presence of standard tape labels, block and record sizes, etc.). If several record types are to be found on the same file, the descriptions of each type are given in the same FD. As we have seen, the PICTURE clause serves the purpose of a type attribute in other languages, as well as providing additional functions such as editing information.

The Working Storage section describes variables local to a COBOL program. These may be scalar variables, arrays or record structures. Scalar items in working storage which are not related to other data items and which can therefore be regarded as occupying independent storage, are given the special level-number, 77.

Other keywords used in COBOL declarations are as follows:

FILLER—a dummy name used for data "padding," which will not be referenced in the program. The use of FILLER relieves the programmer from making up fictitious names and also conserves space in the Symbol Table.

REDEFINES—a method of specifying storage sharing.

JUSTIFIED—indicates that alphabetic or alphanumeric data is to be justified to the *right* of a storage area. In the absence of this attribute, such data is normally justified to the left.

OCCURS—the COBOL array attribute.

ASCENDING/DESCENDING—for sorted arrays.

SYNCHRONIZED—storage alignment.

USAGE—to control the internal representation of data.

FORTRAN declarations are expressed by *statements*. Attributes are used as statement keywords, and are followed by a list of variables. Thus there are INTEGER, REAL, DOUBLE PRECISION, COMPLEX and LOGICAL statements for declaring these different types of variables. There are also statements for other attributes such as: DIMENSION, to declare arrays, COMMON and EQUIVALENCE, to express storage mapping and sharing, and EXTERNAL, to denote that a name is to be regarded as the name of an external function, rather than a variable.

FORTRAN and ALGOL both use the form:

{attribute}   {list of variables}

Example

ALGOL: **integer** *a,b;*

FORTRAN: `REAL X,Y`

In contrast, PL/I reverses this order:

{variable}   {list of attributes}

Example:

`X FIXED STATIC INITIAL(1)`

Explicit PL/I declarations are written as DECLARE statements, which may be written in any block. Corresponding to the "list-of-variables" in ALGOL and FORTRAN, there is a syntactic device known as *factoring* of attributes, to allow the same attribute to be given to one or more variables.

A declaration may be written:

(list of variables) list of attributes

and the attributes applied to all the variables inside the parentheses.

Example

```
DECLARE (A,B,C) LABEL;
DECLARE ((R,S) FLOAT,(T,U)FIXED)DECIMAL STATIC;
```

As the second example shows, factoring of attributes may be applied to several levels.

7.15.2   Partial Declarations

Before compilation can take place, it is necessary for all attributes of a variable to be known, since these affect the treatment of the variable in the compiled code. Some languages require full declaration of all variables, insisting on a strict correspondence between the outward form of a program and its meaning. Both ALGOL and COBOL follow this principle.

In contrast, FORTRAN allows variables to be used without declaration, and there are rules for associating attributes with undeclared variables. PL/I has adopted the FORTRAN principle, but also has additional capabilities for dealing with partial or omitted declarations.

The advantages of allowing partial declarations include the following:

- It is a help in program development, since complete programs can be compiled and checked for possible errors. If partial declarations are not allowed, compilation may have to terminate on the first undeclared variable.

- It allows simpler programming in languages with a large and complex attribute structure. In these languages, a "complete" set of attributes may be very extensive. It also allows growth and development of the language—new attributes can be added without invalidating existing "complete" declarations.

On the other hand, there are several disadvantages:

- Completion of declarations by the compiler rather than the user may encourage careless and undisciplined programming.

- It is difficult for designers of a programming language to choose appropriate rules for completing partial programs. This is particularly true for general-purpose languages, where the needs of one group (e.g., the "scientific" users), may differ from those of others (e.g., the "commercial").

- The completion of partial programs may introduce subtle logical errors, which may not be detected by a compiler.

Default and other types of treatment of partial programs are virtually essential in large language systems, although they should be used with care by the programmer to avoid the disadvantages noted above. For example, a suitable procedure for debugging would be to note down the default attributes supplied by the compiler, moving these into the source program. Default treatment would then be used simply during the period of developing a program.

As we have seen, FORTRAN included a number of techniques for completing partial programs. These were modified and extended in PL/I and the basic rules for completing attributes were put on a firmer footing.

We start with some definitions.

A *complete set of attributes* is a consistent set of all the attributes associated with a given type of variable.

A *partial* declaration is one in which the explicitly declared attributes do not form a complete set.

We distinguish three methods by which the attributes of a program may be completed.

- Default

- Implicit

- Contextual

When two or more attributes can be applied to a variable, one of them may be nominated as a *default*—this is the one to be applied in the absence of an explicit declaration.

Example

In PL/I, if no *storage class* attribute is specified, the default storage class is AUTOMATIC.

The treatment of default attributes in PL/I is extremely complex, because of the large number of attributes in the language. The "attribute structure" of PL/I, part of which is shown in Fig. 7.12, governs the treatment of defaults. The design of this structure has an important bearing on the treatment of partial programs.

Implicit attributes are determined by the form of the identifier used for a variable.

Example

In FORTRAN, if a variable has no explicit type declaration, then the type is implied by the first character of its name. Initial letters *I, J, K, L, M,* and *N* imply the type INTEGER, any other initial letter implies the type REAL.

A similar rule applies in the IBM version of PL/I.

This rule, introduced to help forgetful programmers in FORTRAN, has probably caused more difficulties in designing PL/I than any other rule of comparable complexity. The rule was taken over into the design of PL/I because it was felt that FORTRAN users would expect it; however, it fits very uneasily within the much more complex attribute mechanism of PL/I. See the notes below on the DEFAULT statement of PL/I.

Contextual attributes are applied to undeclared variables used in special contexts, for which only certain type attributes are appropriate.

Examples

PL/I recognizes seven "contexts" in which an undeclared variable may be given contextual attributes, such as

        GET FILE (X1)...
                    X1 is given the attribute: FILE
        DECLARE A BASED (X2)...
                    X2 is given the attribute: POINTER
        CALL P(A,B,C) TASK (X3)...
                    X3 is given the attribute: TASK

It is clear that the three methods of completing partial programs described above may give different results if applied individually to the same undeclared variable. If more than one such method is to be applied, it is necessary to define their order of application, since this affects the meaning of a program. The order of completion in PL/I is

    contextual,

    implicit,

    default.

7.16   THE CONTROL OF DEFAULTS

The rules for completing partial declarations in FORTRAN and PL/I form an essential part of these languages and must be known by their users. As we have mentioned above, the design of these rules presents tricky problems of balance between the needs of different classes of user, especially for a language like PL/I, intended to satisfy both scientific and commercial programmers.

For a long time it has been known that if defaults are to be allowed in a language, some users would like a means of controlling how they are to be applied. Several implementations of FORTRAN, for example, have included a form of IMPLICIT statement, which globally controls the attributes given to undeclared variables. This statement has not yet appeared in a FORTRAN standard, although it has been under consideration for the ANSI standard.

In PL/I, the need for controlling the partial program completion mechanism has been more acute as well as more difficult to solve. In the early "NPL" specifications (see Appendix), there was a sketch of an IMPLICIT statement based on FORTRAN experience. This statement vanished when PL/I, as it became, was first implemented—not because of a lack of need, but because of the difficulty of defining it in a satisfactory way. Work continued on the design of a suitable means of controlling defaults, but it was not until 1971, when the Optimizer/Checker compilers were released, that a default statement was implemented by IBM.

Meanwhile, the standards committees considering PL/I were not satisfied with the IBM solution, and further design work was undertaken. The DEFAULT statement in the proposed PL/I standard differs from the IBM statement in allowing wider control and in being able to reproduce completely the "system" defaults defined as part of the language.

The statement allows the control of attributes according to the "form" of the identifier. For example, in the statement:

```
DEFAULT (RANGE(A)) FLOAT AUTOMATIC;
```

RANGE (A) refers to identifiers beginning with letter A, RANGE(I:N) would mean identifiers beginning with letters I, J, K, L, M or N, while RANGE (*) would mean identifiers beginning with *any* letter.

Next consider the following example:

```
DEFAULT (FIXED & BINARY & CONSTANT) PRECISION(28);
```

In this statement, there is a Boolean expression involving attributes. If these attributes have already been "acquired" by a name, then the name is given the attribute that follows the parenthesis, PRECISION(28). Several default statements may be given, and "processing" of these must be in the order in which they appear in the program.

The "*I* to *N* rule" of PL/I can be expressed in the following sequence of statements:

```
DEFAULT (RETURNS & RANGE(I:N))
            RETURNS (FIXED BINARY REAL);
DEFAULT (RANGE(I:N) & ¬ (FIXED|FLOAT|BINARY|DECIMAL|
                                        REAL|COMPLEX))
            FIXED BINARY;
DEFAULT (¬CONSTANT) FLOAT, DECIMAL, REAL;
```

This new DEFAULT statement has emerged after 10 years work. From personal experience over part of this period, I know that as much effort has been expended on this single statement as on many complete languages. This may again raise doubts about the inclusion of defaults in programming languages (although there are strong arguments in their favor, as noted above). The PL/I DEFAULT statement has unduly suffered from inadequate integration with the language design at the outset, from having to relate to an over-complex attribute structure in the language, and from the need for compatibility with an existing feature of the language—notably the "*I* to *N* rule" taken over from FORTRAN.

7.17 FIXED AND VARIABLE TYPES

In the discussion of *type* earlier in this chapter, we did not state at what point in the sequence of operations, between writing a program and executing it on a machine, the type of a variable was to be established and fixed. The languages we are mostly concerned with, FORTRAN, ALGOL, COBOL and PL/I—in fact the majority of current programming languages—have the following feature in common: data types are effectively fixed when the program is compiled. They are not necessarily specified explicitly by the programmer—as we have seen from the rules for partial declarations. However they are fixed in the sense that once a program is compiled, there is no means of changing the type of a variable.†

Static type-fixing is widely used, mainly because of efficiency considerations. Even with such comparatively simple languages as FORTRAN and ALGOL it would require considerable extra space and time to include code to deal with all possible combinations of data types, plus the tests needed to "branch-on-type" at execution time. By making the programmer fix data types at the time of writing the program, it is possible to design a translator which selects the appropriate code in advance of execution. Static fixing

---

† There are some exceptions to this rule, even in the compilable languages listed above. For example, the type of an exponentiation operation in ALGOL 60 depends on the *value* of the exponent and can only be determined at execution time (see Chapter 9).

of data types distinguishes a *compilable language* from an interpretable language. The fixing of data types is one aspect of *binding*—in this case the object code is *bound* to the type of the data.

Static type-fixing will no doubt continue to play an important part in language design, at least while current techniques of machine design prevail. For example, in ALGOL 68 we have an explicit design principle such that no type checking at run time is necessary.

Next we consider the possibility of taking a more flexible approach to type fixing. As examples, we survey interpretive languages designed for terminal operation.

There are several terminal-based systems, in which a "desk-calculator" facility is provided for the occasional programmer. As their name suggests, these systems are most suited to relatively small programs such as scientific or engineering calculations. We may liken such a terminal to the traditional "back of an envelope," on which quick calculations are done by engineers. For informal calculations, it is customary to use symbolic names freely, with no scruples about redefinition. At one point in a calculation a symbol may represent a dimension of an aircraft wing; later on, the same symbol may represent an array of signal lights on an instrument panel. On pieces of paper, there is no confusion about what we mean, and it can be argued that we should also be allowed to work in this way at a terminal.

JOSS (Shaw, 1964; Smith, 1970) and APL/360 (Falkoff and Iverson, 1973—see Chapter 8) are two terminal systems which follow the principle of dynamic type-fixing. In these languages, type is established by assignment, not by declaration.

In JOSS, we may say:

$$a = 5$$

which establishes the variable, *a*, as an integer. However, we may then write:

$$a(5) = 7$$

and the variable *a* is transformed from an *integer* to an *array*—in this case, to a vector with at least 5 components.

APL is slightly less dynamic in its treatment of arrays, and unlike JOSS includes a means of checking array bounds. These bounds must be established when the original assignment of the type *array* is made. As in JOSS, there are no declarations of type in APL. Dynamic type-changing is shown in the following example:

$$A \leftarrow 5$$
$$A \leftarrow 1,2,3,8,10$$
$$A \leftarrow 'B'$$

In this sequence, the variable A successively takes the values of an integer, a vector with 5 elements, and a single character. Note that in the assignment of the array, the entire array must be assigned. After the second line, an assignment to the 5th element can be made: $A[5] \leftarrow 15$. However, an attempt to assign to the 6th element of A after line 2 would cause an *index error* in APL. In JOSS, however, the array would be enlarged to hold at least 6 elements.

There is little doubt of the value of such dynamic treatment of variables to the occasional user. Quick calculations such as formula evaluation, table building and interpolation, simple graph plotting, etc., can be very satisfactorily carried out without the elaborate type-fixing mechanisms found in more conventional languages.

There is an additional advantage to dynamic type in languages. When we specify and fix the type of an item of data, we constrain the values this data may assume. Programs written for data of a specific type will in general not work with data of another type. The capability for writing "general" algorithms (i.e., algorithms which work on any type of data) in compilable languages is therefore rather small. However, the capability for writing general algorithms is increasingly important in data-base systems, in which the operational data of an enterprise may frequently be changed, and in which it is desirable to avoid the need to change the programs accessing such data. Programs having this property are said to be *data independent*.

Dynamic type obviously has implications on the implementation of a language. In a typical compiler, as described in Chapter 4, we see how data attributes are used in forming a *symbol table* or *dictionary*. This information is collected and merged together from various sources in the program and may be expanded and elaborated during the compilation process. One of the merits of compilation as a technique of implementation is that this dictionary, which for a large program may itself be a very extensive data structure, can be discarded after compilation, since the information it contains has been embodied in the object code. The need for compilation depends not so much on a property of a language as on the relationship of the language to the object machine. This is seen by considering early mathematical languages, written for machines without floating-point hardware. In the translators for such languages, arithmetic operations were translated into code which called subroutines for floating-point addition, subtraction, etc. Today, with similar language but more advanced hardware, floating-point operations are compiled directly into machine language.

We have emphasized the relationship of compilation to type fixing in languages, and we can understand the distinction between compilation and interpretation if we relate it to the treatment of type in a typical machine.

Example

We can contrast the actions of compilation and interpretation (see also Fig. 7.15) by considering a language L, containing a binary function $F(A,B)$, in which the arguments may be of two types, t_1 and t_2. F might correspond, for example, to the operation of addition and might be represented in L as an infix operator $' + '$, but we will use a functional form here for convenience. In L, it may be specified that when A and B are both type t_1, the action represented by F_{11} is carried out; when A and B are both type t_2, the action F_{22} is carried out; and that it is an *error* to have mixed types—in other words no "mixed mode" operations are allowed. F_{11} and F_{22} may be likened to machine instructions for fixed-point addition and floating-point addition respectively.

Compilation

At compile-time: Compilation routine for F:

> **test** types of A,B
> **if** types both t_1 **then generate:** $F_{11}(A,B)$
>   **else**
>   **if** types both t_2 **then generate:** $F_{22}(A,B)$
>   **else**
>   **generate:** diagnostic ("types different")

At execution time: Execution routine for F:

> $F_{11}(A, B)$ or $F_{22}(A, B)$

Interpretation

At execution-time: Execution routine for F:

> **test** types of A,B
> **if** types both t_1 **then call** $F_{11}(A,B)$
>   **else**
>   **if** types both t_2 **then call** $F_{22}(A,B)$
>   **else**
>   **write:** error message ("types different")

> $F_{11}(A, B)$ and $F_{22}(A, B)$

Fig. 7.15 Comparison of compiled and interpreted code

In this example, we see the contrast between the direct code produced by a compiler and the branching and calling code typical of an interpreter. The other aspect which stands out here is the contrast between the error message produced *before* execution by the compiler, and the error message produced by the interpreter at execution time.

We now summarize the two approaches to type fixing and compare their relative advantages.

Static type fixing is the more common approach and is used by the majority of current programming languages. By requiring all data types to be fixed when the program is written, the selection of object code may be made prior to execution, according to the types of the variables. There are two principal advantages to the compilation process:

- more efficient code can be generated;
- better diagnostics can be given when the program is compiled.

With static type fixing, there is a certain lack of flexibility. A compiled program can only process data of the type for which it has been compiled, and compilation introduces a degree of data dependence. The association of fixed type with data does not always lead to the most efficient problem-solving method.

Dynamic types are available in some terminal language systems. There is an increasing tendency in more advanced work on language design to allow type fixing to be delayed to a later point in time. The main advantage of delaying such decisions ("delayed binding") is to secure greater flexibility in the design and development of applications. For some applications, it may be impossible to predict, when the program is being written and compiled, the ultimate form of the data.

A disadvantage of dynamic types is the lack of efficiency, at least by current methods of implementation. It can be argued that if a user knows that an entire file of invoices or sales orders has exactly the same record format, it is pointless for each record to be checked for type each time it is processed. This seems to point to a design in which, even if much of the code allows late binding, the user can retain the choice of *not* checking types at execution time, in other words of having selective compilation of programs.

7.18 FURTHER READING

First, we consider general works on data and its representation. Jolley (1968), in a wide-ranging study, includes many interesting examples from such diverse fields as biology and heraldry; he also discusses practical problems of representation on punched cards, etc. His work provides a good background for the topics discussed in this chapter.

A description of *variables,* as used in mathematics and logic, is included in Tarski (1965). A more extensive treatment is given in the long "Introduction" to Church's volume I (Church, 1956). This also deals with methods of naming and with the meaning of names, a subject which is treated more extensively in Quine, "Word and Object" (Quine, 1960).

The problems of data representation in computers, especially the representation of numbers, have been considered by Brown and Richman (1969), Buchholz (1959, 1962), Goldberg (1967), Grau (1962), McKeeman (1967), Knuth (1969). The special arithmetics of finite classes of numbers are included in Kemeny, Snell and Thompson (1966).

A theoretical treatment of type is given in Scott (1972) and in Ledgard (1972). Various static and dynamic treatments of type in programming languages are discussed in Ingerman (1961). A study of various languages will also yield different views on the treatment of type. JOSS has been mentioned in this chapter (Shaw 1964, Smith 1970), but also consider APL and ALGOL 68, for contrasting views on type fixing. The effects of a "typeless" language (meaning a language without type declarations) are discussed in a paper by Reynolds (1970).

BIBLIOGRAPHY

Boole, G., *An Investigation of the Laws of Thought* (1854 edition), New York: Dover Publications, 1961.

Brown, W. S., P. L. Richman, "The choice of base," *CACM,* Vol. 12, No. 10, Oct. 1969, pp. 560–561.
    Considers the choice of base for floating-point representations of numbers.

Brown, S. A., C. E. Drayton, E. Mittman, "A description of the APT language," *CACM,* Vol. 6, No. 11, Nov. 1963, pp. 649–658.

Buchholz, W., "Choosing a number base," (in) W. Buchholz, (ed.), *Planning a Computer System—Project STRETCH,* New York: McGraw Hill, 1962.

Buchholz, W., "Fingers or fists? (The choice of decimal or binary representations)," *CACM,* Vol. 2, No. 12, Dec. 1959, pp. 3–11.
    Describes the factors which led to the adoption of both decimal and binary radix representations in Project STRETCH.

Chroust, G., "A survey of the representation of character string constants," LN 25.3.069, IBM Laboratory Vienna, May 1970.

Church, A., *Introduction to Mathematical Logic, Vol. I,* Princeton, N.J.: Princeton University Press, 1956.

Fraser, A. G., "On the meaning of names in programming systems," *CACM*, Vol. 14, No. 6, June 1971, pp. 409–416.

Galler, B. A., A. J. Perlis, "A proposal for definitions in ALGOL," *CACM*, Vol. 10, No. 4, April 1967, pp. 204–219.

A proposal for an extension to ALGOL which would allow new data types and operators to be added to the language.

Goldberg, I. B., "27 bits are not enough for 8-digit accuracy," *CACM*, Vol. 10, No. 2, Feb. 1967, pp. 105–106.

Goldberg, R., P. Oden, "Data types and data type extensions in programming languages," *IBM Research Report*, RC 4651, Dec. 1973.

Presents a view of programming-language types based on sets, also related to an abstract storage model. The paper also includes a scheme for extending the system of primitive types in a language.

Grau, A. A., "On a floating-point number representation for use with algorithmic languages," *CACM*, Vol. 5, No. 3, Mar. 1962, pp. 160–161.

The author notes that, as usually implemented on computers, the set of fixed-point numbers is not a proper subset of the set of floating-point numbers, as they should be from a mathematical point of view. A normal form of representation is proposed which allows the mathematical relationship to be reestablished. It involves reducing the exponent to a value as close as possible to zero. It is claimed that the use of this representation eliminates the need for dynamic type checking in ALGOL for exponentiation and name parameters.

Hamming, R. W., W. L. Mammel, "A note on the location of the binary point in a computing machine," *IEEE Transactions on Electronic Computers EC-14*, No. 2, Apr. 1965, pp. 260–261.

Considers the placing of the binary point before and after the first digit in computer representations of numbers. With uniform distributions of numbers, there is an advantage in having it *after* the first digit. With more "realistic" (i.e., nonuniform) distributions, there is little on which to base a choice. The authors conclude that "for human reason" (i.e., close relationship with standard practice), it is better to have the point after the first digit.

Hamming, R. W., "On the distribution of numbers," *Bell System Technical Journal*, Vol. 49, No. 8, Oct. 1970, pp. 1609–1625.

Examines the distribution of the fractional parts of floating point numbers and shows how arithmetic operations of computers transform the distributions towards a limiting reciprocal distribution $r(x) = 1/(x \log b)$. The paper discusses the applications of this observation to hardware and software.

Hext, J. B., "Compile-time type-matching," *Computer Journal*, Vol. 9, No. 4, Feb. 1967, pp. 365–369.

Describes the set of types in a programming language in terms of a partially ordered sequence.

IFIP, "Report on Subset ALGOL 60," W. L. van der Poel (ed.), *CACM*, Vol. 7, 1964, pp. 626–628.

Iliffe, J. K., *Basic Machine Principles (2nd ed.)*, London: Macdonald, 1972.

Ingerman, P. Z., "Dynamic declarations," *CACM*, Vol. 4, No. 1, Jan. 1961, pp. 59–60.

Jolley, J. L., *Data Study*, Cincinnati: World University Library, 1968.

A good general review of data and data structures. The author is professionally concerned with classification and indexing and approaches data structures from a more general point of view than that adopted by most programmers. Topics include: data values and their representation in various media, data relations, rules of naming, searching, and retrieving.

Kemeny, J. G., J. L. Snell, G. L. Thompson, *Introduction to Finite Mathematics*, Second edition, Englewood Cliffs, N.J.: Prentice-Hall, 1966.

Ledgard, H. F., "A model for type checking—with an application to ALGOL 60," *CACM*, Vol. 15, No. 11, Nov. 1972, pp. 956–966.

In this paper, *type* is treated as one of a possible set of attributes, without considering its relationship to a value-set. The paper discusses various algorithms for type matching in current languages.

Mullin, J. P., "An introduction to a machine-independent data division," *CACM*, Vol. 5, No. 5, May 1962, pp. 277–278.

A brief note on the COBOL data division, stating that "Of all the problems facing COBOL in the future, perhaps the most challenging is establishing a machine-independent data division."

The paper points out that much of the material in the COBOL data division is concerned with how data is represented on a particular machine, while comparatively little deals with the logical structure of the data.

Perlis, A. J., "The synthesis of algorithmic systems (First ACM Turing Lecture)," *JACM*, Vol. 14, No. 1, Jan. 1967, pp. 1–9.

Quine, W. V. O., *Word and Object*, Cambridge, Mass.: M.I.T. Press, 1960.

Reynolds, J. C., "GEDANKEN—a simple typeless language based on the principle of completeness and the reference concept," *CACM*, Vol. 13, No. 5, May 1970, pp. 308–319.

Discusses a language with no type attributes or declarations. Type is associated with a variable only by assignment.

Roos, D., *ICES System Design*, Cambridge, Mass.: M.I.T. Press, 1966.

Scott, D., "Lattice theory, data types and semantics," (in) R. Rustin (ed.), *Formal Semantics of Programming Languages*, Englewood Cliffs, N.J.: Prentice-Hall, 1972, pp. 65–106.

Shaw, J. C., "JOSS: A designer's view of an experimental on-line computing service," *APIPS Conference Proceedings*, FJCC, Vol. 26, 1964, pp. 455–464.

Smith, J. W., "JOSS-II: Design Philosophy," (in) *Annual Review in Automatic Programming*, Vol. 6, Part 4, Elmsford, N.Y.: Pergamon Press, 1970, pp. 183–256.

Smith, R. V., "The literal and the variable in programming languages," *IBM Research Paper*, RC1444, 1965.

Tarski, A., *Introduction to Logic and to the Methodology of the Deductive Sciences*, (Paperback edition) New York: Oxford University Press, 1965.

Wilkes, M. V., "Constraint-type statements in programming languages," *CACM*, Vol. 7, No. 10, Oct. 1964, pp. 587–588.

"Constraints" are declarative statements which restrict the range of values which may be assumed by variables. They may be used in checking debugging programs.

Wunderlich, M. C., "Sieving procedures on a digital computer," *JACM*, Vol. 14, No. 1, Jan. 1967, pp. 10–19.

Discusses representation problems for sieving techniques pointing out the advantages of bit data for such problems.

EXERCISES

7.1 Consider the following "types" in a personnel data processing program. Indicate the range of values and the set of operators for each of these types:

    personnel number,   Max int.)

  / age,   Max. int.

    address,

    skill,

  ℓ, salary.

7.2 Design the syntax of a *type* specification which defines an integer as having the following values:

    a) from 1 to 99,

    b) from 13 to 157,

    c) even values from 0 to 5,000.

7.3 Some languages require declarations of variables to precede their use. Others allow declarations to appear in any position. Give examples of each language.

List the advantages and disadvantages of each approach.

7.4 An undeclared variable, *T*, appears in a given program in one statement only, where it is assigned the value 1. Write this assignment statement in ALGOL, FORTRAN, COBOL and PL/I.

Describe the action taken by a compiler for this statement in each of these languages.

7.5 Write a PL/I picture specification corresponding to the following PL/I data types:

- `FIXED`

- `FIXED(10.5)`

- `COMPLEX(5)`

7.6 In COBOL and PL/I, the picture specification corresponding to a given variable must be declared with the variable and is fixed when the program is compiled.

Discuss the possibility of introducing a PICTURE variable in high-level languages.

Design a simple picture variable for numeric data and outline an implementation scheme.

7.7 Design and give specifications of two or more internal and external representations of the following data:

```
1/2
five per cent
pi
WORD
 AAAAAABBBAA
```

7.8 There are no means of specifying the length of one of the COBOL figurative constants (SPACES, ZEROES, etc); their length is determined by the context in which they are used.

Give examples of the use of these figurative constants.

To what extent does the lack of a length specification limit the use of these constants?

7.9 In this chapter, the FORTRAN and PL/I treatment of partial or omitted declarations have been described, and limitations of this approach have been indicated.

Design a systematic procedure for use by programmers, in which these limitations are minimized. What extra information, other than that normally provided, might be helpful to the programmer, for example in compiler messages, listings, etc.

7.10 Outline an implementation method for ensuring that all variables are initialized when they are first created. Distinguish the following cases:

static storage allocation (FORTRAN, COBOL, PL/I STATIC),

dynamic storage allocation (ALGOL **local,** PL/I AUTOMATIC),

explicit allocation (PL/I CONTROLLED, BASED).

What value would be appropriate for each *type* of variable if the programmer does not specify one?

7.11 Express the following string literals:

26.73
NAME   ADDRESS   OCCUPATION
John Gielgud's production of "The Winter's Tale"
a) in FORTRAN notation
b) in PL/I notation

7.12 How many distinct values are there, corresponding to the following *type* declarations? *Note:* It may be necessary to relate the answer to a particular implementation.

COBOL:		PL/I:	
	PICTURE 999		BIT(8)
	PICTURE A(6)		BIT(8) VARYING
	PICTURE $ZZ.9		CHAR(6)
			FIXED(6,4)
FORTRAN:	INTEGER		

8
Data
Structures

8.1 INTRODUCTION

In the previous chapter, data was described in a simplified form—as isolated fragments of information, individually named, created, and accessed. However, in nearly all applications, we are concerned not so much with elements as with *collections* of data—the records in a file, the elements in an array, the words in a text. In this chapter we discuss a number of commonly occurring data structures, and consider how they are represented in programming languages.

The subject of data structures permeates the whole of computing, presenting many difficult problems to language and system designers. Data structures of a wide variety of size and shape are essential in allowing programmers to relate programs to the data of the outside world. For example, the user of a management-information system needs to be able to define structures which match, in some way, the enterprise it is serving. We have only to think of the complex web of formal and informal relationships, the shifts of influence and power, that arise in a large business enterprise to see how hard it is to provide in an automatic system a model of this kind of "real" world.

The data structures available in most programming languages are somewhat narrow and restrictive, compared with the richness of the structures in the outside world. Since data structures are usually at the heart of any program, the structures provided in a programming language determine its users' approach to all problems and influence their style and method of thinking about programming. It can be argued that many programmers suffer from "data-structure starvation"—their approach to programming being constrained by the poverty of the data structures available in the languages they use.

There is a strong, and in many ways unfortunate, separation in current languages between *internal* structures (arrays, lists, trees, etc.) and data in files (stored on tape, disk, etc.). It has become common to regard certain classes of operation as relating to "data structures" and others to "input-output"; there are different languages and conventions for each of these. Although an attempt is made in Chapter 11 to introduce I/O from the point of view of data structures, it is impossible to overlook the differences between the two points of view, as they have become embodied in current programming languages. Thus, although many of the problems being addressed by the language forms in this chapter and in Chapter 8 are similar, the resulting statements and operations will differ in many ways.

Definition   A data structure is an organized collection of data elements.

The building blocks from which data structures are formed are the elements discussed in the previous chapter. The programmer is concerned both with the components from which a data structure is composed and with the *relations* between these elements. The term "relation" is, strictly speaking, a mathematical one, but can be understood here in its informal sense. Examples of relations between structures A and B include the following:

- *A* contains *B*
- *A* is a successor of *B*
- *A* is equivalent to *B*

Containment is a relation between structures, or between structures and elements. For example, a record structure may itself *contain* a number of other structures. Ultimately, each record structure *contains* an ordered set of elements. This relation is important in considering operations on data structures.

The *successor* relationship defines an ordering of elements in a data structure. Important examples of ordering are:

- the ordering of elements in an array, which allows methods of subscripting to be used for accessing the elements;
- The ordering of records in a sequential data set.

There are several *equivalence* relations for data structures. One of these, the *conformity* relation, is necessary for the validity of certain data structure operations in APL and PL/I. Two arrays are conformable if they contain the same number of rows and the same number of columns. This is necessary for the correct treatment of element-by-element operations in APL and PL/I. Note that it is not enough for the arrays to have the same total number of elements, although this weaker relation would be sufficient to define some of the operations adequately. However, it is not necessary for the two arrays to have the same upper and lower bounds, but merely that the *difference* between upper and lower bounds should be the same for each dimension. Examples of these relations are shown in Fig. 8.1.

As might be expected, methods of constructing and accessing data structures are more complex than those for data elements. Following Mc-

Containment

Example: The record, {order}, *contains* {prefix}, {code-no}, {destination}

{prefix} *contains* {2 letters}
{code} *contains* {4 digits}
{destination} *contains* {10 letters}

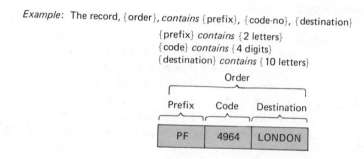

Successor

Example:

Table [$L : M$]

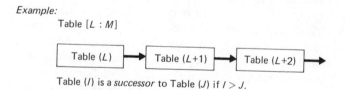

Table (I) is a *successor* to Table (J) if $I > J$.

Conformity

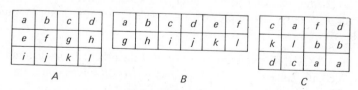

The arrays A & C are *conformable*; A & B, B & C are not.

Fig. 8.1 Three relations on data structures

Carthy (1960, 1963), operations on data structures are described in the form of *functions*. The following types of function are defined:

- constructors and destructors,
- access functions,
- predicates.

Constructors are functions which create data structures. A structure is composed of a set of elements, and there may be a choice of how it is to be created (simultaneously, row by row, etc.). Some current languages have only *implicit* constructors, for example the constructor implied by entry to a block in ALGOL. *Explicit* constructors are included in PL/I, APL and in the list processing language, LISP, from which many basic ideas on data structures originate.

Destructors are the inverse of constructors. Given a data structure, a destructor will break it down to a set of component elements. This, at least, is the sense of destructor as used in POP-2 (Burstall, *et al.,* 1971). There is also another type of destructor in which the *storage* for a data structure is returned to the system when the destructor function is applied. The FREE statement in PL/I acts as a destructor in this sense.

Access functions are included in all languages, both for data elements and data structures. The term covers a wide variety of referencing methods including the simplest method of referencing data by its *name,* also the *subscript* method of accessing arrays, and access to record structures by *qualified name.* As in the case of data elements, there are two senses in which a component of a data structure may be addressed, one involving access to its *value* (R-value), the other to its *location* (L-value). The terms "L-value" and "R-value" were coined by Strachey (1966) who showed that, in the usual form of assignment statement, variables on the left-hand and right-hand sides of the assignment symbol are treated in different ways. There is a special access function for the L-value of certain PL/I data structures—this is called a *pseudo-variable.*

Predicates are used to test whether or not an item or set of items has a certain property. Examples of predicates in programming languages include:

- the EXAMINE statement in COBOL (like others in this list, not a 'pure' predicate, since it also fulfils other functions such as counting instances of given characters and translation);
- the INDEX and VERIFY functions in PL/I;
- the set-membership (ε) operator in APL.

8.2   INVERSE-ACCESS FUNCTIONS

Access functions translate a *name* into a *value* or *location*. There is an inverse process—given the *value* of an item—to determine the item's *location*. A function which carries this out may be regarded as an *inverse*-access function; this mode of referencing is also called *content-addressing* or *associative addressing*.

Inverse-access functions are important for accessing large, complex data structures, especially those whose "structuring" is dynamic. With direct-access functions, it is hard to prevent the means of access to a data structure from becoming dependent on this structuring. However it can be avoided by using inverse functions, since they depend on the *values* of the data rather than on its organization. Examples of inverse-access functions include:

- the SEARCH statement in COBOL;
- the INDEX and VERIFY functions in PL/I;
- the index (ι) function in APL.

Inverse-access methods can be programmed in most languages with looping statements. They can also be programmed in APL and PL/I using bit-string arrays and search functions. Inverse-access functions for strings and arrays are described below; other developments in associative access to data structures are listed in the references at the end of the chapter. See especially the extensive bibliography by Minker (1971).

8.3   DATA STRUCTURES AND STORAGE STRUCTURES

Before describing the major types of data structure, we must recognize an important dividing line—the separation between ideal theoretical structures and the structures actually provided in most programming languages and systems.

It is important to recognize that in many languages—and in virtually all language implementations—we do not have *data* structures, but *storage* structures. The term "storage" here does not mean that programming languages are concerned with a particular engineering realization of storage, such as magnetic cores, thin-film memories, tapes, or disks. However, most widely used languages contain various subtle implications about the nature of storage which affect the behavior of programs in the languages.

An ideal data structure would consist of a collection of data elements, between which the only relationships would be those implied by the structure itself. As we shall see, the nature of storage introduces additional relationships between the elements, derived from the properties of the storage in which they are represented. Often, it is not easy to recognize these extra relationships; but it is important to be aware of their existence, since data handling may be distorted by the implications of storage.

The properties of the underlying storage model can be deduced by looking at certain features of the language, including the following:

- means of storage *sharing*
- concern with storage *mapping,* particularly with the alignment of data on word or byte boundaries
- treatment of initialization—in particular, whether it is possible to access the storage of a variable before it has been given a value
- input/output, especially of record structures
- storage ordering of elements in a data structure

In some cases, we may have to look beyond the language as defined in a standards document and consider its implementation on an actual system.

By studying the storage concepts in different programming languages, we can come to understand some of the deepest and most fundamental properties of different language designs.

8.4   STORAGE MODELS IN HIGH-LEVEL LANGUAGES

Consider the following science-fiction situation. Suppose you are a visitor to Earth from some distant planet and you see a number of humans engaged in the activity of "programming." You consult these programmers, inquiring about their work. They explain they are users of COBOL, PL/I, FORTRAN, etc. On asking for more details, you are given documents containing the standard specifications, which are said to "define" COBOL, PL/I, etc. On return to your planet, you send for your best technical people and tell them to make a "FORTRAN," a "COBOL," or a "PL/I" based only on the documents you have brought back. They will obviously make *machines;* for it will be clear on reading the specifications that each of these "languages" is, in effect, a computing machine. The question is: what kind of storage would each of these machines have? In other words, what kind of storage could be deduced from these language specifications alone without any preconceptions about the nature of computer hardware?

The following sections attempt to define the storage properties of a "FORTRAN machine," a "COBOL machine," and a "PL/I machine." The question can be asked of these three languages because each of these languages has an underlying storage concept. This is not necessarily the case with all languages. For example, ALGOL is free from storage implications, since all features related to storage concepts were skillfully avoided by the ALGOL designers. As a result, an ALGOL "machine" would have data structures more closely related to the "pure" structures discussed above. The same is true of APL, in which care was also taken to eliminate storage concepts.

8.4.1 A FORTRAN Storage Model

The storage concepts of FORTRAN clearly show the origins of the language on a binary machine with "words" of storage. In the FORTRAN specifications, data types are described in terms of their occupancy of "storage units"—in the first version of FORTRAN, these were the words of the 704 machine. INTEGER, REAL, and LOGICAL variables each occupy one storage unit, and DOUBLE PRECISION and COMPLEX occupy two units. These storage units form the basis of the storage model implied by the FORTRAN language.

Array handling in FORTRAN is also based on storage concepts. For each array element, a *successor-element* is defined based on the order in which FORTRAN arrays are stored. The sequential ordering of array elements in storage is a critical factor in the language design.

The COMMON and EQUIVALENCE statements may be used to specify storage allocation and sharing for FORTRAN variables. COMMON defines a *segment* of FORTRAN storage (i.e., a contiguous set of storage units). There are two forms—"blank" (that is, unnamed) COMMON and named COMMON. (See Fig. 8.2.) Variables in blank COMMON are allocated segments of storage according to a simple principle—variables appear in storage in the same order as they appear in the COMMON list in any program or subprogram. When a main program and a set of subprograms are linked together at execution time, there is no attempt to match the names or types of the variables. Therefore when a programmer wishes to define a set of variables in blank COMMON to be shared by several FORTRAN modules, care must be taken to obtain the correct storage layout for each separate module.

The amount of storage allocated for blank COMMON is that necessary to hold the largest number of variables declared in any program or subprogram. It is clear that anyone using COMMON must be aware of other programmers' use of COMMON. It may be necessary to include lists of variables not used in the current program to make sure the layout is correct.

Main Program

```
...
INTEGER I,J,K
COMMON I
...
REAL T1,T2
COMPLEX J1,J2
...
COMMON T1,J2,J1
...
```

Subprogram

```
...
REAL T1,T2,T3
COMPLEX J2,J9
COMMON I,T1
...
INTEGER I
COMMON J2,T2,J9
...
```

Layout of COMMON for main program: Layout of COMMON for subprogram:

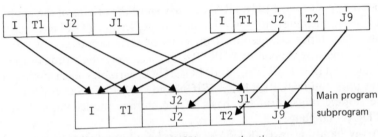

Actual layout of COMMON at execution time:

Fig. 8.2 Allocation of storage for blank COMMON

To overcome these and other difficulties, *named* COMMON was introduced. This allows the programmer to define named segments of storage. The main difference between named and blank COMMON is that for named COMMON the amount of storage occupied by the variables in each block with the same name must be identical. In a collection of separately compiled modules, care must be taken that all such blocks have the same length. This is made difficult by the interaction between COMMON and EQUIVALENCE—sometimes the use of EQUIVALENCE "induces" a variable into COMMON.

The EQUIVALENCE statement allows two or more variables to share the same storage. (See Fig. 8.3.) Once again, FORTRAN does not require a match between the types and sizes of variables in different programs and subprograms. Equivalencing of arrays is done simply on the storage occupancy of the contained elements. This makes it possible for one array to be equivalenced to parts (or all) of two other arrays.

Another effect of the FORTRAN treatment of storage is shown by the rules for transmitting an array argument to a subprogram—this is a critical part of the design of any language. Consider a subprogram, SUB, with a

Consider the following FORTRAN statements:

```
(1)   INTEGER A(3,2)
(2)   DIMENSION B(4)
(3)   COMMON /C1/ A,B
(4)   INTEGER T(8)
(5)   EQUIVALENCE (T(2),A(2,2))
```

(a) The first two statements specify a 3×2 array and a four-element vector. Statement (3) ensures that the array A and the vector B are stored in named COMMON block, C1.
The EQUIVALENCE statement (5), links A and T together, making sure that T is in COMMON and enlarging the size of the COMMON block C1.

(b) The allocation of storage units in COMMON block C1 is as shown.

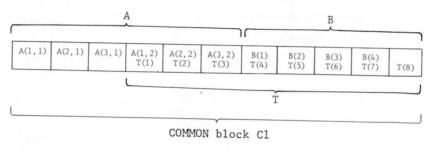

Fig. 8.3 The effect of the EQUIVALENCE statement

single array argument. If we call SUB, passing the array argument *A*, the questions arise:

- How much information is passed?

- What operations on the parameter corresponding to *A* are valid within the subprogram?

The FORTRAN treatment of array arguments is very simple. The information passed need only include the *address* of the first element of *A*. It is expressly defined in FORTRAN that an array parameter corresponds to the segment of *storage* appropriate to the argument. Hence, if we pass a 4 × 4 array as an argument, the subprogram may treat it as a 16-element vector or as a 2 × 8 array; the only requirement is that it must contain a total of 16 storage units. The argument and expected parameter may be of different types, different structuring, etc. The user of the subprogram may even obtain access to neighboring variables since there is no means of checking that the size of the array argument corresponds to the array expected as a parameter.

An illustration of FORTRAN storage is given in Fig. 8.4.

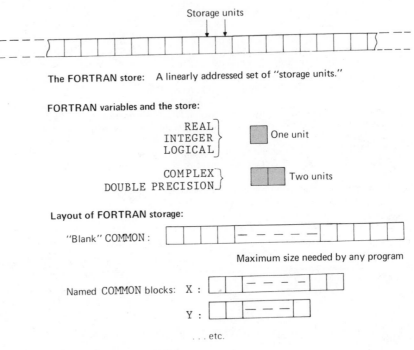

Fig. 8.4 FORTRAN storage model

8.4.2 A COBOL Storage Model

Just as the FORTRAN language strongly suggests a storage model based on machine *words,* the COBOL standard suggests, though perhaps not quite as strongly, a storage model based on *characters.* Several commercial machines of the late 1950's, on which COBOL was first implemented, had memories in which the basic addressable unit was a character rather than a binary word. The typical data element was a string of characters, and the user was free to choose various lengths of string to suit the needs of the application. The PICTURE technique of data description, the basic descriptive method in COBOL, fits well with this type of storage.

However, COBOL was also implemented on binary machines, on which it is difficult to process character data. This led to a need to develop ways in which data fields could be positioned, taking advantage of the natural boundaries and alignment of data in a word-oriented store. Hence the introduction of the SYNCHRONIZED clause for describing COBOL fields. The COBOL standard (USAS X3.23-1968, pages 1–85) describes the objectives of this feature:

> Some computer memories are organized in such a way that there are natural addressing boundaries in the computer memory (e.g., word

boundaries, half-word boundaries, and byte boundaries). The way in which data is stored is determined by the object program, and need not respect these natural boundaries.

However, certain uses of data (e.g., in arithmetic operations or in subscripting) may be facilitated if the data is stored so as to be aligned on these natural boundaries.

Data items which are aligned on these natural boundaries in such a way as to avoid such additional machine operations are defined to be synchronized.

Example

Geographical and population statistics on various towns are stored in a record called LOCATION.

```
01 LOCATION.
    02 PLACE-NAME PICTURE X(30).
    02 MAP-REF.
        03 LONGITUDE PICTURE 9(6).
        03 LATITUDE PICTURE 9(6).
    02 POPULATION PICTURE 9(6)
        SYNCHRONIZED RIGHT.
            . . .
```

This ensures that the population field, the most frequently accessed field in the record, is always kept in an efficiently accessible location. (Note that in some machines, the specification SYNCHRONIZED LEFT might be more efficient.)

A section of the COBOL Data Division is called the "Working Storage Section." Items in Working Storage are equivalent to *variables* in other languages. Each distinct entry, that is each separate element or record structure, occupies independent storage and it is not defined how the storage for any one of these items relates to that of any other item.

A central part of most COBOL programs is the specification of the files to be used in the program and the records associated with them. The language form for this is the FD (file description), the form of which is described below under *record structure*. It is important to note that a COBOL FD and its associated record description is not a specification of a variable but rather of the expected physical representation of data. It is a "template" for storage layout and serves a purpose similar to a BASED declaration in PL/I or a **record class** in ALGOL W, as discussed later in this chapter.

Control of the storage used by COBOL file data during I/O operations is not given to the user, who has no way of allocating, freeing, or accessing this storage. The space set aside for I/O buffer areas can be controlled, to some extent, by the RESERVE clause in the FILE-CONTROL paragraph of the INPUT-OUTPUT section.

Example

```
INPUT-OUTPUT SECTION.
FILE-CONTROL.
    SELECT PARTS-FILE ASSIGN TO DA-2311-I-MASTER
    RESERVE 2 AREAS
    ACCESS IS SEQUENTIAL
    . . .
```

This indicates that 2 buffer areas are to be allocated when PARTS-FILE is opened for processing.

8.4.3 A PL/I Storage Model

The storage concepts of PL/I have been more closely studied than those of other languages, particularly in the work leading to the formal definition of PL/I (Alber, *et al.,* 1969; Walk, 1971). There are several storage-oriented concepts in PL/I; a storage model is also needed to explain the working of *record* input-output, in which storage representations of data are transmitted. The PL/I methods of dynamic referencing with *pointers* and *based variables* and the PL/I *area* variable are also closely related to principles of storage.

The storage class attributes of PL/I (STATIC, AUTOMATIC, CONTROLLED and BASED) give considerable flexibility of control over the generation and creation of variables. The creation of variables in PL/I is in fact defined in terms of storage allocation, indicating the close correspondence between data and its storage occupancy in PL/I. (Refer to Fig. 8.5.)

The storage class attributes fall into two groups, implicit and explicit. STATIC and AUTOMATIC attributes result in implicit storage allocation, without action by the programmer; while CONTROLLED and BASED require execution of the ALLOCATE statement.

All STATIC data in a given PL/I program is allocated prior to entry to the program. AUTOMATIC data, on the other hand, is only allocated when the block in which it is declared is entered. This means that some AUTOMATIC variables may not be created in a given program run, if the procedure or block in which they appear is not executed. The PL/I STATIC storage class reproduces most of the properties of FORTRAN storage, while AUTOMATIC variables correspond closely to "local" variables in ALGOL.

Both CONTROLLED and BASED variables have to be explicitly created by the execution of ALLOCATE statements and may be destroyed by the execution of FREE statements. The difference between the two is that a CONTROLLED variable is a *stack* structure, in which the most

Storage class	Time of creation of variable	Time of destruction of variable
STATIC	Activation of main program	Termination of main program
AUTOMATIC	Activation of containing block (procedure or begin block)	Termination of containing block.
CONTROLLED	ALLOCATE statement	FREE statement *or* termination of task in which variable was allocated.
BASED	ALLOCATE statement system storage *or* named AREA	FREE statement *or* termination of task in which variable was allocated *or* freeing of AREA in which variable was allocated.

Fig. 8.5 PL/I storage classes and the creation of variables

recently allocated value is at the top of the stack. On the other hand, data with the BASED attribute has no automatic linking or stacking—if this is needed, it must be supplied by the programmer.

Explicit allocation, as provided by the CONTROLLED and BASED attributes, allows greater freedom than is possible with AUTOMATIC, since each variable may be individually created when it is needed. AUTOMATIC variables, and ALGOL **local** variables, are created in groups—all the variables from a block at one time. In order to write a program in which separate variables are created separately, it may be necessary to create artificial block boundaries or arrange for special patterns of procedure invocation.

In contrast with FORTRAN, there is no language-defined relationship between the storage occupied by one type of PL/I variable and that occupied by a different type. Conceptually, we may think of each distinct data type as occupying a different amount of space. The closest approach to the FORTRAN situation is in the case of strings, where it is specified that the storage occupied by each string element of the same *type* (CHARACTER or BIT) is identical. In other words, the storage for a string with attribute CHARACTER(10) comprises 10 of the elements of storage used for CHARACTER(1).

The PL/I DEFINED attribute may be used to specify storage sharing. The lack of a specific relationship between the storage requirements for different types of variables means that "mixed" defining is not allowed in PL/I, and any two variables which are to share the same storage by "defining" must be of the same data type.

There is a form of defining, called *string overlay defining,* in which the molecular nature of the storage allocated for PL/I strings can be exploited. In this form, the "base item" must be declared with the attribute UN-ALIGNED, so that the internal form of the data is densely packed. The defined item is overlaid on this, and may have some other form of structuring, provided it maps on to the same underlying string structure. The POSITION attribute can be used to locate the defined attribute on some intermediate position in the string.

Example

If the character string: ALPHABET is declared:

```
DECLARE ALPHABET CHARACTER(26) INITIAL('ABCDE...XYZ');
```

the defined variable:

```
DECLARE PAIR(13) CHARACTER(2) DEFINED ALPHABET;
```

consisits of a 13-element vector of 2-character strings whose values are:

```
'AB', 'CD', 'EF', etc.
```

8.4.4 A Summary of Storage Properties

The examples above illustrated the properties of storage in three languages. We now gather together these and other properties, to form a summary of storage properties in programming languages. The basic concept is that:

- values are contained in storage,
- values may be accessed by addresses.

The essential functions related to storage are:

- **the contents function**—given an address, this function retrieves the contents of storage;
- **the update function**—given an address and a value, this function replaces the contents of storage by the given value.

Each variable (or in PL/I each "generation" of each variable) requires storage. Some variables have their own *independent* storage, while some may share storage obtained for other variables. Examples of the latter include EQUIVALENCE, REDEFINED and DEFINED variables, in FORTRAN, COBOL and PL/I respectively.

Storage is composed of elementary particles, or *storage atoms*. There is a measure of storage, a numeric quantity, its *size*, which determines the number and type of elements that can be located in it. Some languages relate specific data types with the amount of storage needed for their representation—the FORTRAN rules for "storage units" are an example of such a relationship. The size of storage needed for a variable is dependent only on the *type* of the variable (for a data element) and on the types and number of elements, and their alignment properties, in the case of a structure. Two pieces of storage are *independent* if there are no atoms of storage common to both of them.

Addresses are quantities which may be used to access values in storage. Two modes of addressing are commonly used:

- **absolute addresses**—which access a unique element of storage,
- **relative addresses**—which, given the absolute address of a segment of storage, access a point within the segment.

The elements of a data structure may be storage-ordered. This ordering derives from the ordering of relative addresses of the elements. Examples of storage ordering are:

- **strings**—left-to-right,
- **arrays**—row-ordered (COBOL, PL/I),
  column-ordered (FORTRAN)
- **record-structures**—generally, the order of declaration of the elements.

Each program requires storage for the variables in it. For programs with dynamically created variables, there is an *allocation* function. Each application of this function yields a segment of storage, which is added to the addressable storage of a program. The *free* function decreases the addressable storage of a program.

The total storage resources of a system are finite. It is therefore possible that some programs cannot be executed because of storage limitations. This is one of the "pragmatic" aspects of programming languages, and is rarely discussed in standard descriptions of languages.

More extensive discussions of storage properties in programming languages are given in d'Imperio (1969), Henhapl (1969), and Walk (1971). Rosenberg (1971a, 1971b) discusses both absolute and relative addressing techniques from a mathematical point of view and relates this to the implementation of arrays.

8.5 THE PLACE OF STORAGE CONCEPTS IN PROGRAMMING LANGUAGES

The inclusion of explicit storage concepts has both good and bad effects on the behavior of a system. An important choice facing language designers is the extent to which storage concepts should be included in systems designs.

One of the reasons storage concepts found their way into FORTRAN and COBOL was to allow storage space to be shared by different variables. In many cases, sharing is useful in composing a program—for example, it is advantageous to be able to refer to the same *value* by different names in different sections of a program. However, storage sharing is mainly justified on grounds of economy. When a variable is no longer required in a computation, the space occupied by that variable can be made available for use by other data.

It is not essential to introduce storage concepts into high-level languages, as the design of languages such as ALGOL 60 and APL has shown. It might be argued that such languages have avoided storage concepts only by omitting important but difficult features such as nonhomogeneous structures, input-output, and so on. However, it has been demonstrated that there are storage-independent techniques of implementing data structures which have adequate flexibility and power. For example, by concentrating only on the relations inherent in the data itself and avoiding the additional relations introduced by storage, we are led to more abstract models of data structures, such as set-theoretic and relational models (Bosak, 1961; CODASYL, 1962; Childs, 1968; Codd, 1970; Schwartz, 1973).

The following factors favor the introduction of storage concepts in programming languages.

- Languages with storage concepts are adequate for many purposes. Many applications are based on simple, nondynamic data structures and do not require the flexibility and generality provided, for example, by relational structures.

- Data stored on tapes, cards, disks, etc. is conveniently accessed by a language which has a concept of physical storage.

- Explicit storage properties allow efficient implementation on current machines.

On the other hand:

- Storage concepts tend to restrict the users' ability to change data or data structures without affecting the procedural parts of a program.

- By introducing storage concepts, additional relationships between data elements are introduced. These may allow programmers to achieve "hidden access" to data—leading to less reliable programs.

8.6 DATA STRUCTURES IN PROGRAMMING LANGUAGES

Moving away from the basic principles of data structuring and data-representation techniques, we now consider the types of data structure available in current languages. These include:

- strings
- arrays
- lists
- stacks
- record structures.

These types of structure are represented in various degrees of generality in programming languages. In the following sections we discuss:

- methods for creating and destroying data structures (constructors and destructors);
- methods for gaining access to elements and groups of elements (access functions);
- operations on data structures.

8.6.1 Strings

A *string* is an ordered set of *elements,* chosen from a class of elementary objects. The number of elements in a given string is the *length* of the string. The class of objects from which the elements of a string are selected determines the *type* of a string. Thus we have *bit* strings composed of the binary digits (0 and 1), *numeric* strings composed of numbers, possibly with a sign (+ or −) and a decimal point, *alphanumeric* strings composed of alphabetic and numeric characters, and so on.

As we will see in Chapter 9, the operations on strings are not nearly so well established as the familiar arithmetic operations on numbers. The most important string operation is that of *concatenation,* or joining together. When two strings are concatenated, the length of the result is the sum of the lengths of its components. It is the concept of string *length* and its effect on implementation, particularly on storage management, which distinguishes string handling from other forms of data processing.

The importance of string handling was not widely appreciated during the period when high-level languages were first being developed. Thus languages such as FORTRAN and ALGOL have virtually no string processing capabilities. Commercial languages such as FACT, COMMERCIAL TRANSLATOR and COBOL had to be able to process character string data, but their needs were restricted to simple assignment and editing operations.

It was discovered that FORTRAN could be programmed to support character handling processes, although such techniques often worked only on particular machines or compilers (for examples, see Pyle, 1962; Poore, 1962). Over the past ten years or so, there have been several proposals that string-handling capabilities be added to FORTRAN (Ahl, *et al.*, 1971; Lambird, 1971) and to ALGOL (Wegstein and Youden, 1962; Shoffner and Brown, 1963).

However, most developments in string handling during this period have come from experience with specialized languages designed for string handling and symbol manipulation and from developments in list-processing languages. The list-processing languages IPL-V and LISP have been used for general string handling. TRAC, COMIT and SNOBOL are specialized developments in the area of string handling. Reviews of these and other languages are given in the proceedings of an IFIP Working Conference on Symbol Manipulation Languages (Bobrow, 1967).

In some languages, a string is treated as a vector or as a one-dimensional array. This simplifies language design, since the mechanisms used for arrays can then also be put to service for strings. Its effectiveness depends on the treatment of arrays in the language—in fact, there are very few languages which allow the dynamic treatment of array bounds needed for text processing. An exception is APL, which treats strings as character vectors. The APL treatment of array bounds is sufficiently flexible for many text-processing applications.

In another form of string treatment, the component characters are regarded as a *list structure*. The implementation of strings as list structures has a considerable effect on the operations which can be carried out on string data. Strings are represented as list structures in the string-handling language, SNOBOL (Griswold, Poage, Polonsky, 1968) (further discussed below).

In COBOL and PL/I, strings are related to the storage concepts in these languages and occupy contiguous segments of storage. This approach gives less flexibility in string operations than one using list structures; although, for simple operations, more efficient code can often be generated.

In recent general-purpose languages, it has been recognized that string-handling should be included as an integrated part of the design. In the following description, we include a discussion of string operations in PL/I and APL. Both of these treat strings in the general sense described above, with constructors, access functions, and predicates. As a contrast, we also include a brief discussion of SNOBOL, one of the most widely used specialized string-handling languages.

The manner of treatment in three languages which have string-handling capabilities is summarized below:

- APL—Strings are treated as *vectors* of characters, and are manipulated with the powerful APL array operators.
- PL/I—Strings are a distinct data type, with properties intermediate between those of scalars and vectors. The access functions for strings are strongly suggestive of an underlying storage structure.
- SNOBOL—Strings are treated as list structures, allowing operations which expand or contract the string. The SNOBOL language structure is specifically designed for scanning and replacement in strings.

8.6.1.1   String constructors

As with other forms of data structure, strings may be created either implicitly or explicitly. In the case of implicit construction, initiation of the procedure or block in which a string declaration occurs may be a signal for the creation of a string variable. In PL/I, it is also possible to create data structures of BASED or CONTROLLED storage class explicitly, by means of the ALLOCATE statement. This statement therefore acts as a *constructor* function for strings in PL/I. There is also a corresponding *destructor* function in the FREE statement. In APL, which has no declarations, strings are created when a string value is assigned to a variable name.

Examples

The following examples show the construction of strings in PL/I:

```
B: BEGIN;
   ...
   DECLARE S1 CHARACTER(100) INITIAL((100)'0');
   ...
   END
```

S1 is created implicitly, and is initialized with zero characters when block B is entered. In this example, there is also automatic destruction of S1, when block B terminates.

```
   DECLARE S2 CHARACTER(*) CONTROLLED;
   ...
   ALLOCATE S2 CHAR(LENGTH(TEXT));
   S2=TEXT;
   . . .
```

In this case, S2 is created by execution of a constructor, the ALLOCATE statement. In this case, no *value* is given to S2 by the constructor function.

Instead the value is set by the assignment statement that follows. The string may be destroyed by execution of the statement:

    FREE S2;

PL/I also has functions which act as string constructors:

    STRING (expr)

This function constructs a string by concatenating all the elements of expr into a single string element. The argument may be an array or structure or an expression including an array or structure.

    REPEAT (string,factor)†

This function constructs a string by concatenating $n + 1$ copies of the string represented by the first argument, where n is the value of the expression denoted by the second argument.

In APL, string variables like other data structures are created by evaluating expressions and assigning the results to variables:

    A ← 'APPLE'
    B ← 'FISH','AND','CHIPS' (in APL, the comma denotes concatenation)

Strings of arbitrary length can be created in this way. Since there are no declarations in APL, there is no way of specifying a maximum length for the string that is constructed, and new values of any length may be assigned to A and B.

There is no destructor function for strings in APL. However, a *null* string may be assigned, which has the effect of destroying the current value.

8.6.1.2 The substring access function

In string processing, a frequently occurring need is to be able to access a sequence of characters within a text. A set of consecutive elements of a string is called a *substring,* and this form of access is called *substring access.* As with other access techniques, there are two senses in which the substring access function may be required. One of these is used to retrieve values (R-value access), the other to access locations in order to set values (L-value access).

---

† In the proposed ECMA/ANSI standard for PL/I, the built-in function REPEAT is replaced by the built-in function COPY, which has a slightly different meaning.

In PL/I, substring access is by means of the SUBSTR built-in function. This has the form:

```
SUBSTR (string, i [,j])
```

The first argument, "string" is the string to be accessed. The arguments i and j, which are expressions convertible to integers, represent the first character *(i)* and the length *(j)* of the substring. The third argument, j, may be omitted, in which case the substring extends to the end of the string being accessed. (This is convenient if the length of "string" is not known.)

We can also use SUBSTR to construct the equivalent of the list-processing functions *head* and *tail*, as applied to strings. Thus SUBSTR(S,1,1) is equivalent to *head*, SUBSTR(S,2) to *tail*.

When SUBSTR is used on the right-hand side of an assignment statement, "string" may be any string-valued expression. When it is used on the left-hand side of an assignment, "string" may only be a string variable. In this position, the SUBSTR function is known as a *pseudo-variable*.

Example

If S1 is : `'AABBCC'`

   S2 is : `'PQRST'`

then `SUBSTR(S1,3,3)` has the value, `'BBC'`

               `SUBSTR(S1||S2,4,7)` has the value, `'BCCPQRS'`

The effect of the statement:

```
SUBSTR(S1,3) = 'XXXX';
```

is to change S1 so that its new value is: 'AAXXXX'. This shows the use of SUBSTR as a "pseudo-variable."

As noted above, PL/I strings have properties closely related to those of storage structures. Consequently there are restrictions on the means of access by the SUBSTR function. When SUBSTR is used as a pseudo-variable as in the third example above, the length of the resulting string after insertions have been made must not exceed its maximum length. The storage for the string being accessed does not grow or shrink when insertions are made, but remains at its initial-allocation length.

In APL, substring access is by means of:

- indexing
- the access function *take* (↑) and *drop* (↓)

Indexing a vector is primarily a means of accessing individual elements, but APL extends the indexing capabilities found in most languages by allowing the index itself to be a vector.

Example

If *AA* is the vector: `'ABCDEFGHIJKLMNOPQRSTUVWXYZ'` then we can select elements from it as follows:

> AA[3] has the value `'C'`
> AA[3 4 5] has the value `'CDE'`
> AA[20 8 5 27 3 1 20] has the value `'THE CAT'`
> AA[ι 10] has the value `'ABCDEFGHIJ'`

The APL functions *take* and *drop* may be used to select the first or last of a specified set of elements of an APL string.

The take operator (↑)

X↑Y means "take the first *X* elements of *Y*."

If *X* is negative, then the last *X* elements of *Y* are taken.

The drop operator (↓)

X↓Y means "drop the first *X* elements of *Y*," in other words, take all but the first *X* elements.

These two functions provide a generalized form of *head* and *tail* for vectors. They can also be combined to form a substring access function for strings. For example, a substring of S, starting at the $(i+1)$th element, j characters long, is:

$$j↑(i↓S)$$

8.6.1.3 Errors in access to strings

The access functions described above enable elements of strings to be accessed by their position or index, whose value may be represented by an expression. When such an expression is evaluated, the resulting integer must clearly not be allowed to lie outside the range of the string. Hence a check for validity must be made, and this must be carried out during execution of the program. In APL, an attempt to access outside the bounds of a string results in *INDEX ERROR,* which causes execution of the program to be halted. In PL/I, this error is detected by the STRINGRANGE condition, and in this case corrective action can be specified in an ON unit for this condition. (These errors are similar to subscript errors which may occur in access to arrays—discussed later.)

8.6.1.4   Inverse-access functions for strings

It is frequently necessary to *scan* a string for an occurrence of a character or pattern of characters. This is a basic process encountered in all except the simplest string processing. Scanning is an important activity in systems programming, text processing, message decoding, etc. and includes:

- searching for delimiters (spaces, punctuation marks) so that text can be broken up into sections, paragraphs, phrases, etc. and separately processed;

- searching for words in a text to construct indexes, concordances, etc.;

- searching for bit patterns in messages in order to recognize sections of the message.

Scanning can be programmed with the substring access function described above. Successive elements of a string can be retrieved and compared with a master pattern until a match is found. However, this method is slow and clumsy and does not compare with the direct provision of an operation for scanning.

In PL/I, the INDEX and VERIFY functions form a pair of scanning functions for strings. Their purpose is twofold. First, they may be used to detect the existence of an element or pattern in a given string; in this form, they act as string *predicates*. Second, they may be used to indicate the location of an element or pattern in a given string; in this mode, they act as inverse-access functions. The results of the functions may be interpreted either as truth-values, or as index positions. For example when these results are used as index positions in a substring function, the resulting index value may be used to extract or change the element or pattern.

For both functions, scanning takes place from left to right starting at the first element of the string. Only the first occurrence of the pattern is located, so a pointer must be reset if multiple copies of a pattern are to be searched for.

8.6.1.5   The INDEX function

The INDEX function has the form:

```
INDEX (string, pattern)
```

The two arguments are strings or string expressions: the first is the string to be searched; the second, the pattern being looked for. After execution, if there is no occurrence of the pattern in "string" the value of the function is zero, otherwise it denotes the index position of "pattern" in the string.

Examples

a) If the variable F has the value 'A + B*(T + 1)', then

INDEX(F,'(') has the value 5
INDEX(F,'*') has the value 4
INDEX(F,'-') has the value 0

b) If the bit string variable CODE has the value '1010010111110110'B, then

INDEX(CODE,'000'B) has the value 0
INDEX(CODE,'111'B) has the value 8

c) If the string variable REPORT has the value 'The rainfall was 2.1 inches. This is twice the average.'

INDEX(REPORT,'.') has the value 19—i.e. the decimal point.
INDEX(REPORT,'. ') has the value 28, locating the end of the first sentence.

To locate the end of the second sentence, having found the end of the first, we may write:

INDEX(SUBSTR(REPORT,29),'. '), which has the value 27.

8.6.1.6   The VERIFY function

The VERIFY function has the form:

VERIFY (string, test-set)

As before, the two arguments are strings, the first indicating the string to be searched, the second being used as the basis for the search. Instead of forming a pattern, as in INDEX, the second string provides a set of test characters. The action of the function is to verify that all elements of the first argument are members of the test set. If the elements of "string" are all in the test set, then the value of VERIFY is zero, otherwise its value is the left-most element of "string" that is *not* in the set.

Examples

If the string variable PART_NO has the value: 'XZ176',

VERIFY(PART_NO,'0123456789XYZ') has the value 0.

In other words, it is confirmed that the characters appearing in the part number are digits or one of the letters *X, Y* or *Z*. Similar tests can be applied to show that fields are numeric, alphanumeric, etc.

VERIFY(PART_NO,'XYZ') has the value 3.

In this case, the function is used to locate the numeric part of the part number.

The two functions, INDEX and VERIFY, form a related pair, one searching for the presence of certain characters, the other for their absence. They are not symmetric, however, for while INDEX looks for a pattern, VERIFY does not look for the absence of a pattern but for the absence of one of a designated set of characters. The two functions are best discussed in conjunction with another function, TRANSLATE, which is used for code conversion, another basic string-handling operation.

8.6.1.7   Operations on character codes

There are often several different ways of representing the same data as a character string; examples include:

- upper and lower case characters,
- alternative card or tape codes.

It is useful to have ways for translating data from one character set to another. In principle, all that is needed to specify such a transformation is a table indicating the correspondence between the two character sets. Such a table forms the basis of the PL/I TRANSLATE function.

A simple form of translation table would list the two character sets, pairing them off one against the other:

```
a1 → a2
b1 → b2
c1 → c2
... ...
```

A table of this form would require a listing of all the characters in the two character sets. However, there are cases when it is not required to translate all the characters of a string, and a shorter, more convenient form of table is desirable. This is allowed for in the TRANSLATE function.

The TRANSLATE function has the form:

```
TRANSLATE (string, replacement-string, position-string)
```

The first argument is the string to be replaced. The effective size of the translation table is determined by the length of the second argument, which specifies the characters to be inserted in the resulting string. The characters to be replaced are specified in the third argument. This argument may be omitted, in which case an implementation-defined string is used—the usual choice for this would be the full data-character set of the implementation.

During translation, the string represented by the first argument is scanned. Suppose the character currently being scanned is C; then if there is an occurrence of C in the position string, it is replaced by the corresponding element in the replacement string. If there is no occurrence of C in the position string, C is left unchanged in the translated string.

Examples

a) The character string, TEXT, can be changed from lower to upper case by writing:

```
TEXT = TRANSLATE(TEXT, U, L);
```

where U and L have been set to the values:

'ABCDEFGHIJKLMNOPQRSTUVWXYZ' and
'abcdefghijklmnopqrstuvwxyz' respectively.

b) The numeric digits in a formula F can be transformed into the letter N by writing:

```
F = TRANSLATE(F,'NNNNNNNNNN', '0123456789');
```

This second example shows how characters of a given set can be translated into a single character. For example, if we define "delimiter" as meaning one of the characters

```
+ − * / ( ) space
```

then by executing the statement

```
F = TRANSLATE(F,'ddddddd','+-*/() ');
```

the formula

```
(A+B)*(C−D)+E
```

is transformed into

```
dAdBdddCdDddE
```

Used in this way, the TRANSLATE function complements the INDEX and VERIFY functions to form a set of scanning and replacement functions.

In APL, there are similar functions, *code* and *decode*.

In COBOL, code translation and searching can be carried out with the INSPECT statement, but this does not allow the same flexibility as the use of functions. Each separate action must be programmed with a different statement and the result stored in temporary storage, contrasting with the use of nested functions in PL/I and APL.

8.6.1.8   String handling in SNOBOL

In the previous sections, it has been shown how string handling can be incorporated in a general-purpose language such as PL/I or APL. In such an approach, strings are regarded as data structures for which string operators and functions analogous to those of arithmetic can be defined.

It is interesting to compare this with the approach taken in SNOBOL, a system specially designed for string handling. SNOBOL is a family of languages, rather than a single language. The first version was developed around 1962 and derived in part from COMIT (Yngve, 1961), and from ideas inherent in the fundamental mathematical construction known as a Markov algorithm (Markov, 1954). Several versions of SNOBOL have been developed. SNOBOL4 provides the basis of the following discussion; this is described in the reference manual by Griswold, Poage and Polonsky (1968). Although recent versions have brought it closer to conventional languages, SNOBOL remains a distinctive development, with very different properties from most other languages.

A basic action in SNOBOL is to scan a string, looking for a *pattern*, a sequence of consecutive characters in the string. This is known as "pattern matching." Various actions may be defined to take place, depending on whether a match is or is not found. These include replacement of the pattern and assignment to variables in the program.

In early SNOBOL systems, there was only one data type, the string. In later versions, additional data types have been included for counting, for conditional branching, and for storing the results of intermediate operations. SNOBOL4 has eight "built-in" data types: *string, integer, real, name, array, pattern, table, expression.* New types of the programmers' own design may also be introduced.

Structurally, a SNOBOL4 program consists simply of a sequence of executable statements, terminated by an *end* statement. There are no declarations and the program has no block structure. A general form of a statement is:

```
label   rule  go to
```

Thus each statement may nominate its own successor, or rather successors, since the outcome of a statement may be used to determine the next statement. Any of the parts shown in the general form may be omitted, and if the "go to" is not present, the order of execution follows that of the program as written. There are three basic types of statement:

assignment,

pattern matching,

replacement.

Assignment statements are similar to those in other languages and may be used to set variables to the values of expressions or constants.

The pattern-matching statement is the most distinctive feature of SNOBOL. It takes the form:

```
subject pattern :S(label) F(label)
```

The action of the statement is to scan the subject string, searching for an occurrence of the pattern. If the pattern is found, the next statement to be executed is that with the S (success) label, otherwise it is that with the F (failure) label.

The replacement statement is the most powerful of all, and is a combination of pattern matching and assignment. It takes the form:

```
subject pattern = object :S(label) F(label)
```

In this case, when an occurrence of the pattern has been found, it is replaced by the object string.

The fact that scanning is an inherent part of a statement gives SNOBOL programs a style and appearance which is different from corresponding programs written in PL/I or APL, in which scanning must be introduced by means of functions and loops.

SNOBOL also differs from most other languages in its treatment of strings as data structures. Unlike PL/I and APL, SNOBOL strings are dynamic data structures. It is possible to search a string, replacing a given pattern by an alternative pattern of any length.

Example

The following statement scans the text, T, and causes all occurrences of the word MAN to be replaced by the word WOMAN.

```
T ' MAN ' = ' WOMAN '
```

Note that it is not necessary to create a new version of the text, as it would be in most languages; in SNOBOL, it will automatically *grow* to accommodate the extra characters.

As written above, the statement only replaces the first occurrence of MAN in the text. A statement to replace all occurrences of the word would be written:

```
LAB T ' MAN ' = ' WOMAN '  :S(LAB) F(NEXT)
NEXT
```

This statement will loop on itself while occurrences of MAN exist in the text *T*. When all such occurrences have been replaced, the program will branch to the next statement.

A SNOBOL pattern is not restricted to being a simple string and one of the most interesting and powerful features of the language is the facility for constructing patterns of complex form. Patterns can be constructed with the operators for alternation and concatenation.

Example

```
T 'A' | 'B'  searches for  A or B
T 'A' 'B'    searches for  A followed by B
```

Parentheses may be used to form expressions; and patterns of an arbitrary degree of complexity can be defined for use in constructing complex scanning algorithms.†

A variety of built-in functions and predicates are included. As with SNOBOL in general, these have been skillfully chosen for their convenience in programming string-handling applications.

Among the built-in functions which will be familiar to those who have performed string handling in other languages, are the following:

```
SIZE (string)
```

The value of this function is an integer giving the number of characters in the string.

```
TRIM (string)
```

This function returns the argument string with trailing blanks removed. It is helpful in input and output operations.

```
REPLACE(S,X,Y)
```

---

† To use complex patterns effectively, the scanning algorithm of the SNOBOL system must be known. This algorithm is defined in the reference manual by Griswold, *et al.*, 1968.

This returns the string S, in which characters in the string X are replaced by corresponding characters in Y. (This is similar to the PL/I function TRANSLATE.)

```
ANY (string)
NOTANY (string)
```

These are functions returning patterns that match (ANY) or do not match (NOTANY) any character in their arguments.

```
SPAN(string)
BREAK(string)
```

These functions return patterns that match (SPAN) or do not match (BREAK) runs of characters. They are used in searching for delimiters, digits, strings of blanks, etc.

In the built-in functions of SNOBOL, we can see a resemblance to the string-handling facilities of PL/I and APL. However, SNOBOL must be regarded as distinct from these languages, for two primary reasons—the scanning properties of its basic statement and the dynamic treatment given to string structures.

8.6.2 Arrays

Arrays are the most familiar kind of data structure in programming and are represented in virtually all high-level languages. They provide a natural representation for much of the data we meet in everyday life. We use arrays in the form of *tables* in technical reports, financial accounts, statistical observations, etc. Tabular data also occurs in technical and engineering problems, as:

- tables of physical constants,
- experimental data,
- sizes of standard components used in engineering (screwthreads, wire gauges, etc.).

Arrays are also important in computational methods based on matrix algebra, which has given us many powerful techniques for solving numeric problems.

Definitions

An *array* is an ordered set of elements of the same type.

The ordering of elements in an array is used to access the elements, by means of one or more *subscripts*. The number of subscripts used to access an element of an array is called the *dimensionality* of the array. There are two cases of particular interest:

- the *vector*, a one-dimensional array,
- the *matrix*, a two-dimensional array.

These are illustrated in Fig. 8.6, which also shows the commonly used mathematical notation for arrays. This notation and many of the fundamental theorems on arrays are due to A. Cayley (1821–1895).†

Vectors

$$V = \{v_1, v_2, v_3, \ldots, v_n\}$$

Arrays

$$A = \begin{bmatrix} a_{11} & a_{12} & a_{13} & \cdots & a_{1n} \\ a_{21} & a_{22} & a_{23} & \cdots & a_{2n} \\ \cdot & & & & \\ \cdot & & & & \\ \cdot & & & & \\ a_{m1} & a_{m2} & a_{m3} & \cdots & a_{mn} \end{bmatrix} \quad m \text{ rows}$$

$$\longleftarrow n \text{ columns} \longrightarrow$$

Fig. 8.6 The mathematical notation for arrays

One instance of the importance of matrices is illustrated by their use in representing the coefficients of a complete set of equations. For example, the x, y and z coefficients of the equations:

$$2x - 8y + 7z = 6$$
$$4x + y + z = 11$$
$$2x + 3y - 2z = 3$$

can be represented by the matrix

$$\begin{bmatrix} 2 & -8 & 7 \\ 4 & 1 & 1 \\ 2 & 3 & -2 \end{bmatrix}$$

---

† Cayley, a distinguished mathematician, who also practiced as a lawyer in London, did some of the earliest work on *trees*. He is thus responsible for fundamental work on the two most important structures used in computing and may be regarded as a founder of the theory of data structures.

and the equations themselves can be written in the form:

$$\begin{bmatrix} 2 & -8 & 7 \\ 4 & 1 & 1 \\ 2 & 3 & -2 \end{bmatrix} \begin{bmatrix} x \\ y \\ z \end{bmatrix} = \begin{bmatrix} 6 \\ 11 \\ 3 \end{bmatrix}$$

In this form, the coefficients have been separated from the variables and the 3×3 matrix on the left can be treated as a separate entity. It is this facility for extracting the essence of a set of equations that gives matrix methods their power in mathematics. The use of matrices is not restricted to linear equations but may be applied to polynomials, to ordinary and partial differential equations and to sets of equations which may arise in statistical analysis, nuclear physics, etc.

Matrix methods are so effective that a valuable tactical approach in solving many types of problem is to seek ways to express the problem in terms of matrices, so that one of the standard matrix algorithms can be used in its solution.

Example

Consider a problem which gives rise to a set of simultaneous first-order differential equations.

$$dy_1/dx = a_1 y_1 + b_1 y_2 + \dots$$
$$dy_2/dx = a_2 y_1 + b_2 y_2 + \dots$$
$$\dots \qquad \qquad \dots$$
$$dy_n/dx = a_n y_1 + b_n y_2 + \dots$$

We are given initial values of $y_1, y_2 \dots$ etc., and wish to know how the solutions behave for large values of x—for example whether they oscillate, and if so, whether they are stable, etc.

At first, this may seem to be a problem for one of the standard routines which carry out step-by-step integration, such as a Runge-Kutta method. However, step-by-step integration routines are frequently slow and may suffer from instability. Hence, it is often better to approach this as a matrix problem. It is known that the general solution to this problem is:

$$y = t_1 e^{\lambda_1 x} + t_2 e^{\lambda_2 x} + \dots$$

where $\lambda_1, \lambda_2, \dots$ etc. are *eigen-values* of the matrix:

$$a_1 \; b_1 \dots$$
$$a_2 \; b_2 \dots$$
$$a_3 \; b_3 \dots$$

Algorithms for finding eigen-values are generally faster and more accurate than those for step-by-step integration. By transforming this into a matrix problem, we have thus been able to achieve a more economical and reliable solution. For further illustrations, see Fox and Mayers (1968).

Matrices are used to represent complex, structured information in a wide variety of scientific disciplines. For example, they have been extensively used in the representation of chemical structures (Lynch, Harrison, and Town; 1971). (See Fig. 8.7.)

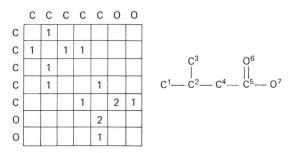

	C	C	C	C	C	O	O
C		1					
C	1		1	1			
C		1					
C		1			1		
C				1		2	1
O					2		
O					1		

(a) *Matrix representation of structure.*

Atom matrix

	1	2	3	4	5	6	7
C	0	1	0	0	1	0	0
Cl	1	0	1	0	0	0	0
N	0	0	0	1	0	0	0
O	0	0	0	0	0	1	1

Connection matrix

	1	2	3	4	5	6	7
1	0	1	0	0	0	0	0
2	1	0	1	1	0	0	0
3	0	1	0	0	0	0	0
4	0	1	0	0	1	0	0
5	0	0	0	1	0	1	1
6	0	0	0	0	1	0	0
7	0	0	0	0	1	0	0

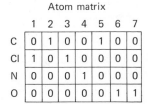

Bond matrix

	1	2	3	4	5	6	7
Single	1	1	1	1	1	0	1
Double	0	0	0	0	1	1	0

(b) *Alternative matrix representation of structure.*

Fig. 8.7 Matrix representation of chemical structure

Another illustration is provided by the "finite element" method, used in structural analysis and related fields. This technique is used for expressing continuous problems in structures in a form in which they can be solved by matrix methods. (See Zienkiewicz, 1967.)

Arrays not only provide a convenient way of representing naturally occurring data; they can also be efficiently implemented on digital computers. Some of the reasons for this are as follows:

- Since all elements of an array are of the same type, only a single type descriptor is needed. This is particularly valuable in interpretive systems, in which information about the types of variables must be kept available during execution of the program.

- The structure of an array is closely related to the addressing structure of many machines. Even in the case of multidimensional arrays, the mapping between subscripts and addresses is simple and can be efficiently computed.

- Given a sufficiently flexible approach to the size and structuring of arrays, it is possible to define elementary array functions which can replace many looping structures used in mathematical and data-processing programs.

In defining arrays, and in particular in compiling code to access and process them, the most important factors are:

- the type of the elements,
- the dimensionality,
- the number of elements in each dimension (a more precise measure is the highest and lowest value of the subscript for each dimension).

This information is used to calculate the storage needed for arrays and to generate code for operations on the elements of an array.

8.6.2.1 The type of array elements

The most widely occurring arrays are arrays of numbers; these appear in most languages. Many languages also allow arrays to be constructed from other data types; ALGOL, for example, allows Boolean arrays, and the ALGOL **switch** is a form of label array.

COBOL and PL/I allow arrays to be constructed from *record structures* (see Section 8.6.4), so that any type of data which may appear in a record may also appear in an array. In PL/I, any type of variable can be in an array, so there can be arrays of labels, pointers, events, files, entries, etc.

8.6.2.2   Dimensionality

The choice of an appropriate dimensionality for an array can strongly affect
the convenience of accessing its elements. For example, consider the problem of accessing the "neighbors" of a point in a two-dimensional plane,
a problem which arises in graphical processing, in heat flow problems, and
in many other applications.

The neighboring points of the *(I, J)* element of a two-dimensional array
are the points with subscripts $(I+1,J)$, $(I-1,J)$, $(I,J+1)$, $(I,J-1)$:

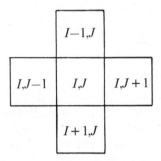

These neighbor addresses can be calculated simply by considering the
geometric properties of the grid of points, without knowing the size of the
array.

However, if the programming language we use does not have 2-dimen-
sional arrays, and we have to do what we can with 1-dimensional arrays
or vectors, we run into several complications. One approach is to arrange
the rows and columns of the array as follows:

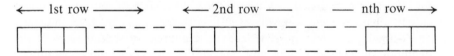

The subscripts for the neighbors of the *(I,J)* element now depend on the
size of the array, that is, its numbers of rows and/or columns.

Example

An 8 × 11 array, *A*, can be stored row-wise as a vector of 88 elements.
The element $A(3,4)$ corresponds to the element $V(26)$. Its neighbors, $A(2,4)$,
$A(4,4)$, $A(3,3)$, $A(3,5)$ correspond to the vector elements: $V(15)$, $V(37)$, $V(25)$,
$V(27)$ respectively.

The general rule is that the vector element corresponding to $A(I,J)$ is
$V(N*(I-1)+J)$, where N is the number of columns in *A*.

Ideally, the dimensionality of an array should be chosen to suit the needs of a problem, and it would be helpful to have no restrictions on the number of dimensions we could specify. However from an implementation point of view it is generally easier and more efficient to compile code for 1- or 2-dimensional arrays than for arrays of higher dimensionality. There are obvious uses for arrays of at least three dimensions and these are allowed by the standard versions of FORTRAN and COBOL. Although the language specifications of ALGOL and PL/I allow an arbitrary number of dimensions, compilers of these languages impose a limit. This is because, from a practical point of view, it is helpful for compiler writers to be able to allocate a fixed unit of storage to hold the integer which denotes the "dimensionality" of an array.

8.6.2.3   Dimension bounds

When deciding the *amount* of storage needed for an array, an important factor is the number of elements corresponding to each dimension. In accessing an array, the validity of a subscript depends on the *bounds* of the dimensions, these being defined as the smallest and largest values a subscript may assume for that dimension.

In some cases the value of the lower bound is fixed as the constant 1, so that, for example, an N-dimensional vector, T, contains the elements T_1, T_2, ... T_n. This approach is taken by several languages, including FORTRAN, COBOL, and BASIC.

In APL, it is possible to set the lower bounds of arrays in a given program as either 0 or 1, thus allowing both conventional mathematical numbering and the practice, more common in programming, of numbering from zero. The origin of arrays is set by a system command, and is effective for all arrays introduced in a user session. The effect of setting this origin clearly affects the meaning of several APL operations, such as indexing, index-finding and transpose. It leads to a number of special cases in the definition of such operations and, since it does not allow full generality of array bound specification, is a rather clumsy feature of APL.

As we shall now see, is convenient to be able to specify array bounds with greater freedom than is allowed in FORTRAN, COBOL, or APL.

Example

The statistics for rainfall in Hampshire may be expressed by a vector whose subscript takes values in the range from 1900 to 1980. It is helpful to the user to be able to write these as:

```
HANTS (1900), HANTS(1901),......, HANTS(1975), etc.
```

Both ALGOL and PL/I allow the upper and lower bounds of arrays to be arbitrary integers. In both languages, a colon (:) is used to separate the upper and lower bounds in the specification of an array.

Example

The vector described above may be declared as follows:

ALGOL

> **real array** *Hants* [*1900 : 1980*]

PL/I†

> ```
> DECLARE HANTS(1900:1980) FLOAT;
> ```

8.6.2.4　Ordering of elements in multidimensional arrays

The subscripts of an array are sets of consecutive integers; it is the ordering of these integers which determines the ordering of elements in the array.

Example

The elements

> ```
> V(23), V(17), V(3), V(12)
> ```

can be ordered by subscript:

> ```
> V(3), V(12), V(17), V(23)
> ```

The subscripts of elements in multidimensional arrays can also be used to order the elements in a particular row or column.

Examples

> ```
> X(2,5), X(2,6), X(2,7)
> RATE (3,5), RATE (8,5), RATE (9,5)
> t[1,1,3,−3], t[1,1,4,−3], t[1,1,7,−3]
> ```

From the subscripts alone it is not possible to give an ordering for all the elements of a multidimensional array, e.g., for ordering the elements $M(5,6)$ and $M(6,5)$.

---

† In PL/I, there is no keyword, ARRAY, and the array attribute is signified by the list of array bounds. To avoid confusion with other attributes, the array attribute must always be the first attribute, immediately following the name of a variable in a declaration.

There are several circumstances, however, in which it is necessary to specify a complete ordering of all the elements in 2-, 3-, or *n*-dimensional arrays. These include:

- the ordering of elements in an input-output "stream," in which the complete set of elements in an array is transmitted in a sequence;
- the order in which elements are selected for array operations, where these are carried out element by element, as in PL/I array operations.

An important ordering of array elements is that needed when a language is implemented on a machine with the conventional type of sequentially addressed memory. This *storage ordering* must be decided in any implementation; once decided, it is a dominant factor in determining the element ordering used for the other purposes noted above.

The two simplest ways in which arrays may be ordered in storage are:

- by rows
- by columns

Consider an array with 2 rows and 3 columns:

$$\begin{bmatrix} A(1,1) & A(1,2) & A(1,3) \\ A(2,1) & A(2,2) & A(2,3) \end{bmatrix}$$

The two ways in which this may be stored in a 6-element storage vector are as follows:

Row ordering:

A(1,1)	A(1,2)	A(1,3)	A(2,1)	A(2,2)	A(2,3)

Column ordering:

A(1,1)	A(2,1)	A(1,2)	A(2,2)	A(1,3)	A(2,3)

From a user's point of view, row ordering is generally to be preferred, since it corresponds more closely to the way we read arrays, line by line, from the printed page. Many languages have adopted row ordering, but there is a serious discrepancy between major programming languages, in that FORTRAN and a few closely related languages have adopted *column ordering* instead. The reason for this is connected with the addressing structure of the IBM 704 machine on which FORTRAN was first implemented.

There is, unfortunately, no question of this difference simply being an implementation-defined detail. Column ordering of arrays impinges on many aspects of program behavior, such as the treatment of COMMON and EQUIVALENCE and of array arguments to FORTRAN subprograms. It constitutes one of the more serious communication difficulties between FORTRAN programs and programs written in other languages.

8.6.2.5 The specification and creation of arrays

Quantities which must be known to a system for constructing an array include:

- the type of the elements,
- the dimensionality of the array,
- the upper and lower bounds of each dimension.

As in the case of strings, the ALLOCATE statement acts as an array constructor in PL/I, allowing the construction of arrays to be delayed until they are required.

Example

```
DECLARE TABLE(*) CONTROLLED FLOAT;
```

(A vector of floating-point numbers is declared. The number of elements in the vector is left unspecified.)
. . .

```
ALLOCATE TABLE (2*X);
```

(When this statement is executed, the vector is created—it has twice the number of elements as the current value of X.)
. . .

```
FREE TABLE;
```

(The table is destroyed and its storage is returned for re-use by the system.)

In APL there is a basic array constructor, the *reshape* function (ρ), which constructs an array of specified dimensions from a list of elements. The reshape function has two arguments. The first argument, written to the left of the operator, determines the dimensionality (or *valence*) and bounds of the result. This argument is in general a vector, with as many elements as dimensions in the result, the values of the elements giving the upper bounds of the corresponding dimensions. The second argument supplies the raw material for the array and is a set of values. This argument does not have to match the array specified by the first argument. There is a rule that if too much data is supplied, any surplus is ignored; if too little, array construction proceeds by taking another cycle through the supplied data.

Examples

a) $2\ 3\ \rho\ 1\ 4\ 7\ 9\ 6\ 2$

    result: 1 4 7
             9 6 2

b) $2\ 3\ \rho\ 1\ 4\ 7\ 9$

    result: 1 4 7
             9 1 4

c) $12\ \rho\ 6$

    result: 6 6 6 6 6 6 6 6 6 6 6 6

d) $3\ 2\ \rho\ 2\ 4\ 7\ 9\ 13\ 2\ 0\ 1$

    result: 2 4
             7 9
          13 2

There are several other functions which may be used to construct arrays from elements or from other arrays. For example:

$\iota\ X$ creates a vector of integers

$\uparrow V$ creates a vector whose values are indices of the vector V

$X\backslash[\ Z]\ Y$ expands X along the Zth dimension of Y.

More important, however, APL extends the meaning of operators so that, for example, the meaning of $A + B$ is an array formed by adding the elements of A and B. This approach, extended to other operators, allows APL arrays to be constructed dynamically for use in other expressions.

8.6.2.6 Adjustable dimensions

In some languages, it is necessary to specify the exact size of arrays when a program is written, so that the amount of storage and the details of address computation can be worked out by the compiler. In such programs, it is necessary to predict the sizes of tables in advance—failing this, the alternative is to recompile whenever a new array size is needed.

To allow for arrays with adjustable dimensions is as much a problem of implementation as of language design. It is relatively simple to extend a language to allow a variable or expression, rather than a constant, as the specifier of an array bound. However, there is more to the problem than this, and it is interesting to compare the approaches of FORTRAN, ALGOL and PL/I on the provision of this facility.

In early versions of FORTRAN, array sizes had to be specified as constants, and adjustable dimensions were only introduced later with FORTRAN IV. Adjustable dimensions may only be specified in subprograms or function subroutines, and the arrays in question, together with the array sizes, specified as parameters (or, in the FORTRAN terminology, "dummy arguments") of this subprogram or function.

An array with adjustable dimensions is declared in FORTRAN as follows:

```
DIMENSION A(N)
```

where A is the array name and N a variable name. Both A and N must be parameters of the procedure in which this declaration appears, so that their values are passed to the procedure when it is invoked. Thus when adjustable arrays are used in FORTRAN, their size must first be established in the program which calls the subprogram in which they are declared.

In ALGOL and PL/I array bounds may be specified as expressions. Obviously, the variables in such expressions must be initialized before the expression is evaluated. This means that:

- variables in any expression which denotes a bound of an array must be declared in a block whose scope is greater than, and includes that of, the block in which the array itself is declared;

- arrays in an outermost block (an *external* procedure in PL/I) cannot have adjustable dimensions.

Arrays with adjustable bounds may also, as in FORTRAN, be declared as parameters (in ALGOL, "formal parameters"). However, in this case there is no need to pass the array bounds as separate arguments, as in FORTRAN. Because of the different treatment of arrays in ALGOL and PL/I, this information must be made available when an array argument is passed.

8.6.2.7 Array access functions

In processing data in the form of an array, we may wish to access:

- a complete array,
- a subarray,
- a single component of an array.

There is an obvious notation which can be used for accessing a complete array—the use of the array name. In many languages, however, reference to a complete array is possible only in special circumstances; for example, when the array is passed as an argument. This is the case with FORTRAN. In COBOL, it is not legal to refer to the complete array at all, for the array name must always be subscripted when it is referenced. Full freedom of reference to complete arrays is possible in APL and PL/I, in which array references may appear in expressions or assignments.

8.6.2.8   The subscript access function

The most important access function for arrays is the *subscript*. Cayley's original notation used the typographic device of a subscript (subscriptus—that which is written underneath) for denoting array elements. In this notation, an array is written:

$$a_{11}\, a_{12}\, a_{13} \cdots$$

$$a_{21}\, a_{22}\, a_{23} \cdots$$

$$a_{31}\, a_{32}\, a_{33} \cdots$$

$$\cdots$$

This notation is not suitable for most computer printers or data-preparation equipment. Even in mathematical work, the notation becomes cumbersome when a large number of subscripts are used, or when complicated expressions are used for the values of subscripts. The form generally adopted in programming languages is similar to that used for function references, and consists of the array name, followed by a bracketed list of subscripts, e.g.,

```
A(1,1)
SLOPE(X1,Y1,Z1)
RATE(JAN,1970)
```

ALGOL, and some other languages, distinguish array references from function references by the use of different brackets.† A suitable convention, and the one adopted in ALGOL, is to use round brackets for functions, square brackets for arrays.

---

† Some writers, however, have argued for regarding array references as a special case of function references, and thus keeping the same notation for both. See, for example, the proposal for GEDANKEN (Reynolds, 1970), in which all compound data structures are accessed by functions.

Example

ALGOL function references

> *TOP (A,B)*
> **entier** $(5 \times x \uparrow 22 - 3 \times x)$

ALGOL array references

> $M[1, X]$
> *position*$[1, J + 1]$

FORTRAN, COBOL and PL/I, constructed with more modest-sized character sets than ALGOL, use the same form of brackets for arrays as for function references. It is therefore not clear from the form of the reference:

> `A(X,Y)`

in FORTRAN, COBOL or PL/I whether we are referring to the X, Y element of an array A, or to a function A with arguments X and Y.

We next discuss the form a subscript may take in various languages.

In standard FORTRAN, a subscript has to be of the form

> `C*V+K`

where C and K are integer constants and V is an integer variable reference. This form originated in the first FORTRAN implementation, and was related to the technique for compiling array references in this compiler. To minimize the time spent in computing array references, the "offset" to an array element was held in an index register of the 704 and used as a relative address to the origin of the array.

Although this form of expression is restrictive, it allows many of the more common forms of array reference to be directly expressed—including, for example, those for the "neighbor-points" of an array described above.

According to the strict interpretation of the FORTRAN standard the form of a subscript must exactly correspond to that shown, so that, for example, it is illegal to write a subscript as: A(3+4*K). However, many implementations do not require this pedantic adherence to the standard, and several have further extended the standard language to allow general expressions as subscripts.

ALGOL was the first language to allow general expressions for subscripts—this was a bold step at that time, when high-level programming languages were at an early stage of development. The general approach has since been adopted by many more recently developed languages, including PL/I, APL, ALGOL 68, etc. General subscript expressions often allow more direct expression of complex problems.

8.6.2.9   Access functions for subarrays

Certain subsets of the elements of an array are themselves arrays. For example, the rows and columns of a 2-dimensional array are vectors or 1-dimensional arrays and there are corresponding subarrays of higher-order arrays.

A useful type of subarray is that obtained by fixing one or more subscripts and allowing the remaining subscripts to extend over their full ranges from lower to upper bounds. In both APL and PL/I, any array of two or more dimensions may be accessed in this way—in PL/I it is called a *cross-section* of an array. The notation is similar to that for array elements, with fixed subscripts denoted by a value (i.e., an expression). The "free" dimension is indicated by an asterisk in PL/I and a null field in APL.

Examples

- If M is a matrix, the Ith row is denoted by:

$$M(I,*) \text{ in PL/I}$$

$$M[\ I,] \text{ in APL}$$

- If the three-dimensional array S, contains elements which denote the average shoe size of males of various ages, heights, and weights then, in PL/I, $S(*,66,*)$ is a matrix giving the shoe sizes of males of height 5 ft. 6 in.
  In APL, this matrix is represented by:

$$S[\ ,66,]$$

An array cross-section can be treated exactly like an array, and may, for example, form part of an array expression or be passed as an array argument.

8.6.2.10   Inverse access functions for arrays

Access to an array subscript may only be used when the location of an item is known. In some applications it is more important to base the access function on certain specific properties of the array elements. For example, it may be required to compute:

- the location of an element equal to a given value;

- the location of the largest or smallest element in an array;

- the number of elements in an array equal to (or less than or greater than) a given value.

Access of this kind is particularly important for arrays whose members are record structures containing several elementary items of data. Such arrays are commonly used in commercial data processing.

For example, a file of personnel information may be regarded as an array of records containing names, addresses, ages, and other information. In processing such a file, we may typically wish to locate and delete a record containing a certain name, print out the set of records with ages between certain limits, or calculate the number of records whose skill fields indicate a certain level of skill or experience. The fields whose contents are used for distinguishing these sets are called *keys*.

It is, of course, possible to write programs which access arrays in this manner using subscripts, by scanning through an array, using a looping statement to access and examine each record in turn. However, we now show two ways in which inverse access to arrays can be programmed without having to construct a loop. These are:

- the COBOL SEARCH statement,
- inverse access by array indexing.

8.6.2.11   The COBOL SEARCH statement

As we have mentioned, COBOL arrays are called *tables,* and facilities for handling arrays comprise the 'Table Handling' module in the COBOL standard. A COBOL table may be an array whose components are record structures (see below). The existence of an array or table is indicated by an OCCURS clause, which also specifies the number of components it contains.

Example

```
01 SKILL-TABLE.
   02 SKILL-ENTRY OCCURS 200 TIMES.
   03 NAME PIC X(30).
   03 AGE PIC 99.
   03 SKILL.
      04 SKILL-CODE PIC 99 OCCURS 10 TIMES.
      ...
```

Note that there is one name for the table, and a separate name for the records which make up its components. This is necessary here because the OCCURS clause cannot be written with a level-1 item.

In COBOL, the lower bound of an array need not be 1, although it must be positive. To have an array with bounds from 10 to 100, we write:

```
02 SKILL-ENTRY OCCURS 10 TO 100 TIMES.
```

The bounds of the array must, however, be specified as *constants*, not as variables.

In COBOL, a subscript used to access the components of an array may be an integer, a numeric data item or a special type of element called an *index*. An index is used only for accessing arrays and its value is set by special COBOL statements, SEARCH and SET. An index may be associated with an array as follows:

```
01 SKILL-TABLE.
   02 SKILL-ENTRY OCCURS 200 TIMES INDEXED BY S.
   03 NAME ...
   03 AGE ...
   03 SKILL ...
```

There are two forms of the SEARCH statement. One signifies a *sequential* search of the table, the other a more efficient type of nonsequential search to be defined by the implementors. The syntax for a sequential search is shown in Fig. 8.8.

```
SEARCH identifier-1   VARYING  [{identifier-2}]
                               [{index-name-1}]
   [; AT END imperative-statement-1]
    ; WHEN condition-1   {imperative-statement-2}
                         {NEXT SENTENCE           }
   [; WHEN condition-2   {imperative-statement-3}] ...
                         {NEXT SENTENCE           }
```

Fig. 8.8 The search statement: sequential search

A typical example of a sequential search follows:

```
SEARCH SKILL-ENTRY VARYING S
   AT END GO TO PHASE-2
   WHEN NAME (S) IS EQUAL TO KEY-NAME
      PERFORM OUTPUT-ROUTINE-1.
```

During this search, the index S is updated to point at successive records of the table, and its value may be used in the routine (OUTPUT-ROUTINE-1) entered when the condition in the WHEN clause becomes true.

The syntax for a nonsequential search is shown in Fig. 8.9. This results in a "nonserial" search of the table—the choice of method is open to the implementors, but a likely form is a *binary search*. For a binary search to be used, the table must be sorted on the *key* used for the search. This key

```
SEARCH ALL identifier-1  [; AT END imperative-statement-1]
```

$$; \text{ WHEN } \left\{ \begin{array}{l} \text{data-name-1} \left\{ \begin{array}{l} \text{IS EQUAL TO} \\ \text{IS} = \end{array} \right\} \left\{ \begin{array}{l} \text{identifier-3} \\ \text{literal-1} \\ \text{arithmetic-expression-1} \end{array} \right\} \\ \text{condition-name-1} \end{array} \right\}$$

$$\left[\text{AND} \left\{ \begin{array}{l} \text{data-name-2} \left\{ \begin{array}{l} \text{IS EQUAL TO} \\ \text{IS} = \end{array} \right\} \left\{ \begin{array}{l} \text{identifier-4} \\ \text{literal-2} \\ \text{arithmetic-expression-2} \end{array} \right\} \\ \text{condition-name-2} \end{array} \right\} \right]$$

$$\left\{ \begin{array}{l} \text{imperative-statement-2} \\ \text{NEXT SENTENCE} \end{array} \right\}$$

Fig. 8.9 The search statement: nonsequential search

must be specified in the declaration of the table. If the table is sorted on the NAME field, for example, the specification is expanded as follows:

```
01 SKILL-TABLE.
   02 SKILL-ENTRY OCCURS 200 TIMES
      ASCENDING KEY IS NAME
      INDEXED BY S.
   03 NAME ...
   03 AGE ...
   03 SKILL ...
```

The search can now be made by the following statement:

```
SEARCH ALL SKILL-ENTRY
   AT END GO TO PHASE-2
   WHEN NAME (S) IS EQUAL TO KEY-NAME
   PERFORM OUTPUT-ROUTINE-1.
```

8.6.2.12   Inverse access to arrays in PL/I

There is no search statement in PL/I, but, in addition to the use of conventional looping statements, array searches may be coded using array operators and built-in functions. The technique of searching illustrated below follows principles developed in APL. Although APL array operators are more flexible and powerful than those of PL/I, in this particular case the PL/I facilities are more useful because the arrays being accessed can include record structures, so that a variety of different types of element can be stored in the same table.

The search facilities make use of the following properties of PL/I arrays, derived from similar or identical properties in APL:

- the extension of scalar operators to form *array expressions* which are executed element by element. In searching, it is useful to be able to employ the *relational* operators: $<, >, =, ...$;
- the use of bit values as *characteristic values* of relational expressions. This allows logical and bit operators to be applied to the values returned by relational expressions.

The following examples show PL/I used in a functional way. This style of programming will be familiar to LISP users who carry out all programming by functional application and also to APL users who express complex sequences of processing by combining operators and functions. The functional style of programming contrasts markedly with COBOL programming, in which such facilities are generally expressed by statements rather than functions.

For the personnel-file example used above, the declaration of the table is a little slimmer in PL/I notation.

```
1 SKILL-TABLE (200),
    2 NAME CHAR(30),
    2 AGE PIC'99',
    2 SKILL-CODE (10)
            . . .
```

In PL/I terminology, this is an "array of structures." The components of the record, NAME, AGE, etc., each form an array of elements to which we can apply the array operators and built-in functions of PL/I.

Relational operators can be applied to these arrays, and, if we use a scalar as one operand, it is conceptually expanded to an array of the same size.

Thus the result of the array expression

$$(\text{AGE}>32)$$

is a *bit array,* of dimension 200, with a 1 bit ('1'B) in each location *I* where AGE(I) > 32, and a 0 bit elsewhere. Bit arrays of this form form the basis of the searching method.

Examples

Further examples of expressions resulting in bit arrays to be used for table searching are as follows:

NAME = 'JONES P.J.'	: an expression used to locate a particular name.
(AGE>17)&(AGE<25)	: an expression used in a composite search based on two relations

In order to compute the position of an item, the bit array resulting from a relational expression must first be converted to a bit-string, using the STRING function.

The result of the expression

```
STRING(NAME='JONES P.J.')
```

is a bit string of length 200, in which there is a 1 bit corresponding to the location or locations containing the name JONES P.J. in the array. To locate a 1 bit, the INDEX function can be applied to the expression:

```
INDEX (STRING(NAME='JONES P.J.'),'1'B)
```

This nested expression therefore computes the result of a sequential search through the array of structures, locating the index or position of an item in the table of values.

If we don't wish to preserve this index value, but simply to use it to access an item in the table, the expression can be used as it stands to form a subscript referring to one of the other arrays

```
AGE(INDEX(STRING(NAME='JONES P.J.'), '1'B))
```

The value of this array is the numeric value representing "the age of P.J.JONES."

This example has shown how repeated application of PL/I array and string functions can be used to provide a compact representation of complicated searches. This style of programming may be strange to programmers who are only familiar with ALGOL, FORTRAN, or COBOL, although it is a natural mode of working in APL. The object-time efficiency of expressions such as those shown above makes the techniques far from suitable for routine data processing, but their compactness and ease of expression make them attractive for interactive querying.

8.6.2.13   Arrays of special shape

We have stressed the advantages of the regularity of structuring in arrays and the help this gives in their implementation. In some applications, however, the data contained in an array variable may not completely fill the array. There are two types of such arrays:

- those in which the data fills some regular partition or partitions of the full array;
- those in which the data is thinly but more or less randomly scattered throughout the full array.

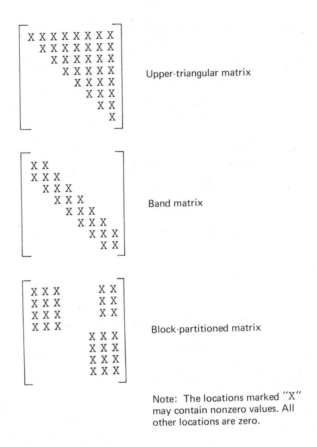

Upper-triangular matrix

Band matrix

Block-partitioned matrix

Note: The locations marked "X" may contain nonzero values. All other locations are zero.

Fig. 8.10 Some regular partitions of matrices

Examples of the first type of array are shown in Fig. 8.10. These regular partitions are comparatively common in numerical problems. Many matrix algorithms take advantage of such structures by mapping them on to more densely occupied matrices—this overcomes their main difficulty, that the storage in the full array is only partially utilized. An example of this approach is seen, for example, in the algorithm by Martin and Wilkinson (1965) in which a band matrix is mapped onto a smaller matrix as shown in Fig. 8.11.

Other approaches to this problem may be developed using the EQUIVALENCE statement of FORTRAN or the DEFINED attribute of PL/I, which allow a single "base" matrix to be shared by several smaller matrices.

X	X	X	X				
X	X	X	X	X			
X	X	X	X	X	X		
X	X	X	X	X	X	X	
	X	X	X	X	X	X	X
		X	X	X	X	X	X
			X	X	X	X	X
				X	X	X	X

An 8 × 8 band matrix
X indicates a nonzero element.

This is a symmetric matrix and only the following elements need to be stored:

X							
X	X						
X	X	X					
X	X	X	X				
	X	X	X	X			
		X	X	X	X		
			X	X	X	X	
				X	X	X	X

This lower diagonal part of the matrix is mapped into a smaller array as follows:

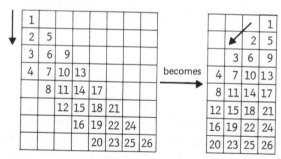

becomes

Fig. 8.11 Mapping of a symmetric band matrix (Martin and Wilkinson, 1965)

    The second form of matrix is called a *sparse matrix*. Such matrices arise in many large computational problems in which the need for economy of space is particularly acute. See Fig. 8.12 for a typical example of such a matrix.

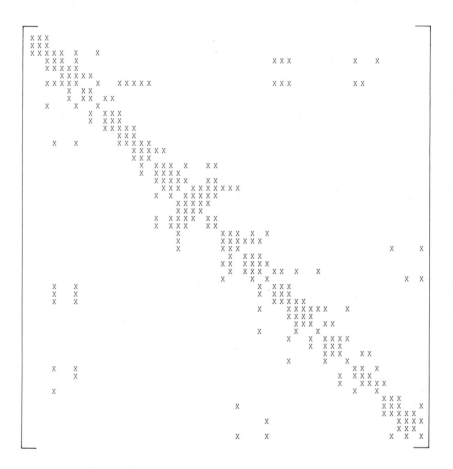

Fig. 8.12 A sparse matrix

Techniques for computing with sparse matrices using conventional languages are discussed in Willoughby, 1972. At least one programming language, JOSS (Smith, 1970), has a special provision for sparse matrices. The command:

`let A be sparse`

signals to the JOSS system that it should store the elements of A as a linked list, rather than in a block of contiguous storage.

Strings and arrays contain elements of uniform type. However, they are not adequate for all applications since much of the data arising from everyday applications does not fall into their regular pattern.

Accordingly, we need to consider structures in which:

- the types of the elements need not be uniform;
- there are other relationships between the elements than simple ordering and other means of access than indexing.

In the following sections, we first consider two forms of ordered structure, the *list* and the *stack*. We also consider the important structure known as a *tree*, an example of a *hierarchic* structure in which there may be several levels of structuring and naming. The *record structure* is an important form of hierarchic structure. Finally, we deal with referencing primitives (pointers or reference variables), which allow the user to define his own structures, which may be of any form whatsoever.

8.6.3   Lists

A *list* is an ordered set of components. These components may be atomic objects such as integers, single characters or bits, or composite objects such as strings, arrays or lists. It is not necessary for all components of a list to be of the same type.

Lists were first made widely available to programmers in two important languages, IPL-V (Newell and Tonge, 1960; Newell, *et al.*, 1965) and LISP (McCarthy, *et al.*, 1962; Weissman, 1967). These languages were developed for work on artificial intelligence and the mathematical basis of computing, and represent an important chapter in the history of computing.

The term *list processing* came to be associated with the use of these and similar languages. The research orientation of these languages tended at first to isolate them from other branches of programming, and list-processing ideas did not find their way into the general-purpose languages developed in the late 1950's and early 1960's.

List processing can be regarded as the processing of generalized dynamic data structures, a topic of central importance to many programming problems. The need for dynamic data structuring (i.e., data structures in which the "structuring" may alter during the course of a computation) is now widely recognized, and several recently developed languages contain facilities related to those of early list-processing languages. As an example of how these concepts have been found useful in other than research fields, the proposals for extensions to COBOL for Data Base (CODASYL 1971) are substantially based on list-processing ideas, and were in fact originally called the "list-processing" module.

We first describe some of the facilities provided in LISP which appear in a modified form in several other languages. It is not easy, in a short section, to give an adequate impression of the elegant nature of LISP—its

uniform treatment of data and programs, its method of representing programs by expressions, its deeply recursive structure. A more detailed study
of these must be left to the interested reader. LISP is historically important
because it illustrates, in the simplest way, the principles of data-structure
manipulation by means of *constructors, access functions,* and *predicates.* In
fact it was McCarthy (1962), the originator of LISP, who first proposed we
should consider data structures in these terms.†

In LISP, there are two types of object—elementary items known as *atoms*
and composite items known as *S-expressions.*

Atoms are indivisible objects, and may be numeric or nonnumeric. Examples are:

A,APPLE,LETTER (nonnumeric literals)

124, 17.6 (numeric atoms)

The simplest form of an S-expression is a *dotted pair,* consisting of two
atoms, the left part and the right part. In the representation usually adopted,
the symbols for the two atoms are enclosed in parentheses and separated
by a dot.

Examples

```
(A.B)
(APPLE.ORANGE)
```

We can also create dotted pairs whose left and right parts are themselves
dotted pairs,

Examples

```
(A.(APPLE.ORANGE))
((LEFT.RIGHT).(LEFT.RIGHT))
```

These are all examples of S-expressions—in LISP, programs, data, and
every other object that can be constructed by the programmer is an S-
expression.

An S-expression is defined as:

an atom,

or a dotted pair of atoms,

or a dotted pair of S-expressions.

---

† McCarthy used the term "selector" rather than access function.

Note how simple this definition is, and how it is based on *recursion*—an S-expression is defined in terms of an object which may itself be an S-expression.

By following this definition, we can recognize the following more complex objects as S-expressions.

```
(A.(B.(C.D)))
((L.M).((N.O).(P.Q)))
((THE.CAT).(SAT.(ON.(THE.MAT))))
```

It helps to visualize the structure of these if we illustrate them in two-dimensional diagrams—this form of diagram is frequently used in discussing other data structures such as trees and record structures. We represent the dotted pair: (A.B) by the diagram:

When one of the parts of a dotted pair is itself a dotted pair, we introduce another level in the diagram. Thus, the S-expression, (A.(B.(C.D))), is represented by the diagram:

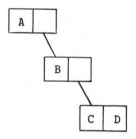

It is clear that we can make very general kinds of structures with dotted pairs, although the notation becomes cumbersome as we deal with large and complex structures.

A special LISP atom is defined, which can always be recognized and distinguished—this is the atom, NIL, which plays a special part in the definition of lists.†

Although dotted pairs are capable of representing general structures, they are notationally clumsy and a more concise and readable notation is needed for the structures most commonly encountered. A basic form used in all LISP data structures is the *list*.

---

† Uniquely distinguishable atoms play their part in other computational systems:*zero* in arithmetic, the *null string* in string processing.

A *list* may be written in the form:

(A,B,C,D)

which is equivalent to the S-expression:

(A.(B.(C.(D.NIL))))

The list form in LISP can always be transformed into dotted pairs; any right-hand part in the dotted pair representation is either a list or the atom, NIL. Note that the converse is not true—not all S-expressions can be represented as lists.

In LISP, any element of a list may itself be a list. A list of this general form, in which the elements may themselves be lists, is called a *list structure*. Some lists and their diagrammatic representations are illustrated below.

Examples

(P,Q,R)

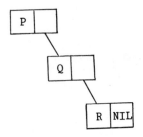

((R,S),T,U)

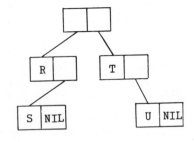

Diagrams of this kind will be seen in many papers on data structures. Techniques for representing data structures as trees and graphs are important, both in helping to visualize the shape of complex structures and in providing a model for possible techniques of implementation.

The basic functions of the programming language LISP all have a *functional* form—i.e., they consist of a function name, followed by a pair of parentheses enclosing the *arguments* of the function. Functional form is a hallmark of LISP; indeed, it is perhaps its most important and distinctive feature.

8.6.3.1   Constructing a data structure: the LISP function, CONS

The function CONS constructs an S-expression from its two arguments, which must themselves be S-expressions. Thus, CONS(A,B) constructs the dotted pair: (A.B).

If the two arguments are lists, then we have the following effect:

```
CONS((P,Q),(R,S))
```

produces:

```
((P,Q).(R,S)) or ((P,Q),R,S)
```

If we have a list (E,F,G), and wish to make a new list containing E, F, and G, but with the element D at its head, we apply CONS as follows:

```
CONS(D,(E,F,G))
```
which produces the result: (D,E,F,G)

8.6.3.2   Access functions

The LISP functions, CAR and CDR† (pronounced "car" and "cudder"), have a single argument, an S-expression, and produce atoms or S-expressions. They differ from the access functions for arrays and strings we have discussed earlier, in that they only produce *values,* not addresses.

The value of CAR(S) is the *left part* of the S-expression S. When applied to a list, its value is the first item in the list.

Examples

```
CAR(A.B)                  has the value: A
CAR(P,Q,R)                has the value: P
CAR((THE,BOX),IS,BIG)     has the value: (THE,BOX)
```

---

† The origin of the names for these functions is interesting. LISP was first implemented on an IBM 704 computer. The functions CAR and CDR referred to the layout of bits in the instructions for that machine—they stand for "contents of address register" and "contents of decrement register" respectively. It is ironic that LISP, conceptually one of the most machine-independent languages, should have basic operations named after a particular model of computer.

The value of CDR(S) is the *right part* of the S-expression S. When applied to a list, its value is the remainder of the list, when the first item has been deleted.

Examples

CDR(A.(B.C))	has the value: (B.C)
CDR((D,E),F,G,H)	has the value: (F,G,H)
CAR(CDR(L,M,N,O,P))	has the value: M

The last example shows how these functions may be used for accessing LISP structures. By repeated application of the functions it is possible to address any part of a structure. Since each S-expression has two parts, a left and a right part, we are in fact giving pointers to a path in a binary tree—CAR means "take the left branch," CDR means "take the right branch."

The application of a function to an argument which may itself be a function is a commonly used device in LISP. It is particularly useful for the access functions CAR and CDR, and to avoid the otherwise clumsy appearance of such constructions, there is a notation which allows "functions of a function" to be concisely represented.

Examples

CAR(CDR(S))	can be written: CADR(S)
CAR(CAR(CAR(CAR(S))))	can be written: CAAAAR(S)

8.6.3.3   Predicates

In LISP, computation is carried out by evaluating S-expressions. As in all programming languages, we need to be able to define alternative paths of the computation according to the nature of the data. This is achieved by means of *conditional expressions* (see Chapter 9).

In evaluating conditional expressions there is a need for functions to test data structures; these are the *predicates* of LISP. A predicate is a function which may be applied to one or more S-expressions to produce a value, *true* or *false*. Probably the most important LISP predicate is ATOM

8.6.3.4   Testing an S-expression: the LISP predicate ATOM

This function has a single argument, which must be an S expression. Application of the function gives the result *true* if this argument is an atom, otherwise it gives the result *false*.

Examples:

```
ATOM(A)            has the value true
ATOM(P,Q,R)        has the value false
ATOM(CAR(P,Q,R))   has the value true
```

There are other predicates in LISP, important ones being EQUAL, MEMBER, and GREATER. Unfortunately, the interpretation of some functions depends on the implementation of a particular LISP system.†

This concludes the description of the data structuring facilities in LISP. It will be noticed that there is no *destructor* function, only a constructor. At a remarkably early point in programming history, LISP took a radical position on this aspect of implementing data structure. In the LISP view, the release of data structures not needed by a program and the reuse of their storage are the responsibility of the *system* and not the programmer. Accordingly, there is no explicit means for the programmer to destroy unwanted data structures. Any structure which becomes inaccessible is destroyed and its storage returned to the system, following the execution of a search routine called the *garbage collector*. For details of this technique see Schorr and Waite (1967), Knuth (1968).

The four basic functions of LISP have been described in some detail because they appear in a similar form in many list-processing languages. In most systems, the names CAR and CDR have been replaced by more appropriate names such as: *head* and *tail*. Other constructors and predicates may also be included. However the four functions listed above represent essential primitive operations needed for all list processing, and the LISP design has provided a pattern for the development of list processing in other high-level languages.

8.6.3.5   Other forms of list structure

There are several forms of list structure which do not allow the full generality of structure and access provided in LISP. These can be classified according to the methods available for adding elements to, inserting elements in, or deleting elements from the list.

   stack—a list in which all insertions, deletions and accesses are made at one end of the list—this end is called the "top" of the stack.

   queue—a list in which additions can be made only at one end and deletions only at the other end.

   deque—"double-ended queue," a list in which insertions, accesses, and deletions may be made at either end of the list.

---

† See Weissman (1967), Chapter 12, for a discussion of this point.

Of these, *stacks* are the most common, because of their importance in systems programming. Queues are used in operating systems and in programs which simulate the behavior of resource-limited systems. Deques are generally not so widely used as stacks and queues, but have been employed in simulation and symbol manipulation.

8.6.4 Stacks

A *stack* is a data structure consisting of an ordered set of objects, only one of which can be accessed at a time. The point of access is called the *top* of the stack, and this is the only point at which objects can be added to or deleted from the stack. A stack is also known as a *push-down store*.

A stack may be illustrated as follows:

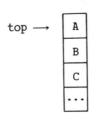

although it may in fact be implemented as a list structure:

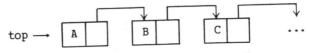

Stacks are widely used in systems programming and have a close affinity with techniques for processing nested structures, such as the bracketed expressions and block structures found in many programming languages. They are also used for storage management and other housekeeping functions needed for recursive programs (see Dijkstra, 1960; Samelson and Bauer, 1960; Yershov, 1959).

The advantages of stack structures are as follows:

- The methods of access are extremely simple. If there is only a single stack available in any program, it may be addressed implicitly, allowing very compact instruction codes to be designed.

- They allow data structures of unpredictable size to be built up. Stacks are the simplest structures with this property.

The method of adding and deleting the elements of a stack is referred to as "last-in, first-out" or LIFO. This term has a long-established use in accountancy and business practice as a method of replacing the items stored in a warehouse or stockroom. (*Queues* operate on a "first-in, first-out" or FIFO basis.)

The LIFO principle is suitable for many programming problems, particularly in systems programming. As a consequence, machine designs have been developed with built-in push-down stores (Burroughs, 1961; Iliffe, 1972; Haley, 1962) and stacks have also been included in programming languages such as CPL, PL/I, POP-2, etc. Considerable theoretical work on stack structures has also been carried out (Ginsburg, Greibach, and Harrison, 1967).

8.6.4.1   Access functions for stacks

Since only the top element of a stack is accessible, access functions for stacks can be simple in form. If there is only a single stack, we can define a language with simple operators (+,−,∗,etc.) such that

$$+ \; A$$

may be defined to mean: "add A to the top of the stack."

This form of programming is sometimes called "addressless" or "zero-address" programming. (See Wegner, 1968, Chapter 1.)

8.6.4.2   Constructor functions for stacks

A constructor function for stacks has the effect of adding new elements to the top of the stack. A commonly used stack constructor is the function: PUSH(V) which adds a new value V to the top of the stack.

Example

If a stack has the following initial state:

$$\longrightarrow \quad \boxed{\begin{array}{c} A \\ \hline B \\ \hline C \end{array}}$$

then execution of the function PUSH(X) transforms it to:

$$\longrightarrow \quad \boxed{\begin{array}{c} X \\ \hline A \\ \hline B \\ \hline C \end{array}}$$

8.6.4.3 Destructor functions for stacks

A commonly used destructor function for stacks is one which simply deletes the top element of the stack—this is often given the name "POP."

Example

If a stack has the following state:

then after executing the function POP the state of the stack will be as follows:

8.6.4.4 Predicates and other functions

Two types of predicate have been found useful in programming with stacks:

- a simple predicate, *empty* which has the value *true* if there is no component on the stack, otherwise it has the value *false.*
- an integer-valued function, *size,* which gives the number of elements currently on the stack.

8.6.4.5 The stack in POP-2

POP-2 (Burstall, Collins, Popplestone, 1971) is a conversational language designed for nonnumeric, as well as numeric, processing. An interesting feature of POP-2 is that the stack is an integral part of the language, much as the hardware stack forms a part of some machines. It is a permanent part of the operating environment of a POP-2 program, and since it is addressed implicitly, the user must be aware of its contents during execution of a program.

In POP-2 a *statement* may consist of a single expression, such as:

```
a + b;
```

The execution of this statement leaves the value of the expression on the stack. Any number of expressions can be written, separated by commas,

```
7, a+2*x+3*y, (16+4*t)/a, f(t,u)
```

These are put on the stack in the order in which they are executed from left to right.

Values are removed from the stack and assigned to a variable by the right arrow:

$$\longrightarrow \ v$$

This takes the top item from the stack and assigns it to the variable, v.

Example

```
∃,y,t+1;
  ⟶TEMP;
```

After executing these two statements, TEMP has been set to the value $t + 1$, and the values y and 3 remain on the stack, with y on top.

The POP-2 stack may also be used as a buffer for printing. The print arrow, ⇥, prints out the entire contents of the stack from top to bottom.

Perhaps the most interesting feature of the stack in POP-2 is the part it plays in user-defined function evaluation. The treatment of arguments and parameters and the method of returning function values are all defined in terms of stack operations.

Consider a simple function, which computes the root-mean-square of two numbers. The function may be specified as follows:

```
function rms x y;
sqrt ((x↑2 + y↑2)/2)
end
```

When this function is called, for example, by writing:

```
rms (5,12)
```

then the action is as follows:

The arguments 5, and then 12, are placed on the stack. When the function subroutine is entered, they are used in computing the result, sqrt((25 + 144)/2), but are removed from the stack as soon as their purpose has been served. Finally, the answer is placed back on the stack, and execution of the function is concluded.

This action is not unlike the work that goes on in the background when a function procedure is evaluated in any language. The difference is that in POP-2 the storage mechanism is made more explicit—in fact the POP-2 parameter mechanism is *defined* in terms of actions on the stack.

8.6.4.6 Stacks in PL/I

PL/I also has stack structures, in the form of CONTROLLED variables. Each distinct CONTROLLED variable can be considered as an individually named stack, for each of which there are constructors and destructors, access functions and predicates.

Since the attribute CONTROLLED may be given to any type of PL/I variable, it is possible to define stacks containing numbers, strings, labels, pointers, entries (the PL/I name for procedures), and tasks. However, each CONTROLLED stack can only be used for one type of data, unlike the POP-2 stack described above, which can accommodate a mixture of all kinds of data.

PL/I stacks can contain data structures such as arrays and record structures. When declaring a CONTROLLED variable containing a string or array, its size need not be specified. This means, for example, that each array stored in a PL/I stack may have a different number of elements, each string a different number of characters. The "structuring," however, must remain constant—there must be the same number of dimensions in all the separate versions of an array, the same hierarchy of names in the separate copies of a record structure that appear in the same stack.

A *constructor* function for CONTROLLED data is provided by the PL/I statement ALLOCATE. Execution of this statement creates a new variable as the top member of the stack, pushing down existing members. Normally, execution of an ALLOCATE statement does not provide a value for the new variable and such values must be set by assignment to the stack after allocation. However, values may be set automatically by giving the variable the INITIAL attribute.

There is also a *destructor* function for CONTROLLED variables, the FREE statement. This destroys the top member of the stack, bringing the next member to the top.

Access to a PL/I stack is by means of the name given to the CONTROLLED variable—the use of this name always accesses the top element of the stack. If the components of the stack are data structures, a reference to the stack may be in the form of an access function.

Examples

A stack of strings

```
DECLARE TEXTWORD CHARACTER(20) CONTROLLED;
```

Each member of this stack is a 20-character string. We can access the individual characters of the top word of this stack in various ways, as follows:

```
IF SUBSTR(TEXTWORD,10,1)='X' THEN...
SUBSTR(TEXTWORD,J) = PATTERN;
```

A stack of record structures

```
DECLARE 1 REPORT CONTROLLED,
             2 HEADING,
                 3 TITLE CHAR(20) VAR,
                 3 DATE CHAR(8),
             2 SUMMARY,
                   ...etc.
```

Each member of this stack is a record structure, containing a variety of types of element. Access to elements of the top member of the stack may be achieved by means of qualified names:

```
REPORT.HEADING.DATE = DATE.FUNCTION;
PUT FILE (DAILY) EDIT (HEADING,SUMMARY) (FORMAT1,FORMAT2);
```

The PL/I function ALLOCATION has a single argument, which must be a controlled variable. Its value is an integer, the number of current allocations on the stack. It may be used as a predicate:

```
IF(ALLOCATION(V)=0) THEN....
```

or to control the loading or unloading of a stack:

```
DO WHILE(ALLOCATION(V)>0);
    FREE V;
END;
```

8.6.5   Record Structures

We next come to an important form of data structure, whose individual elements need not all be of the same type. We give this the name, *record structure* (in PL/I terminology, it is simply called a "structure"). A record structure can be regarded as a collection of data, plus the set of names and relationships used for its access. As with other data structures, we discuss record structures in terms of constructors, access functions, etc.

Record structures were first developed in commercial assembly languages and autocodes. They were included in the early data-processing languages FACT (Clippinger, 1961) and COMMERCIAL TRANSLATOR, and from these came into COBOL, PL/I and other languages. The ability to process mixed collections of data is essential in commercial data processing, where record handling was first developed.

A *record* is an ordered set of data elements, which may contain a mixture of elements of different types. Here is an example:

floating-pt	binary	4 bits	7 characters

record structure

In COBOL and PL/I, record structures are closely associated with *storage structures* which were discussed earlier in this chapter. By exploiting this association, it is possible to make sure that:

- elements in record structures can be accessed by *relative* addresses;
- record structures can be used as the basis for input and output of "records."

The methods of specifying record structures in COBOL and PL/I provide a "naming tree", an example of a *recursive structure*. Such trees form the basis of the access methods which take the place of the indexing techniques used for arrays and strings.

A basic relationship in a record structure is that of *containment*.

Example

Consider the information in the name and address of a person:

MR. J. S. BEVAN, 14 HOLLY ROAD, DUNCHURCH, WESSEX.

In processing this record, we may sometimes wish to treat it as an entity, transmitting it to a data set to form part of an invoice, to address an envelope, etc. At other times, we may wish to access its parts, and will then be interested in its internal structure. The structure of the record may be described as follows:

record contains	name:	MR. J. S. BEVAN
	address:	14, HOLLY ROAD, DUNCHURCH, WESSEX
name contains	title:	MR.
	initials:	J. S.
	surname:	BEVAN

address contains   house number *or* name: 14
                            street name: HOLLY ROAD
                            town: DUNCHURCH
                            county: WESSEX

The programming language must make it possible to access elements, groups of elements, or the whole record structure.

As we see, the items of data in a record structure can be grouped together to form larger units, which in turn are contained in still larger groups, and so on. This illustrates the *recursive* nature of record structures, and shows their similarity to other recursive structures such as expressions and block structures. Recursive structures are often represented as graphs or trees, but in programming languages, because of the limitations of available character sets, a one-dimensional form must generally be used. Recursive structures are often represented as *bracketed* structures; however, in this case, there is a similar, though not quite equivalent notation using numeric values to denote the depth of nesting *(level)* of the contained items.

We now describe the method of record specification used in COBOL and PL/I. The principles used for the two languages are essentially the same, although there are differences in detail.

Example

For a simple record containing a name and an address, the first level can be declared as follows:

```
1   RECORD
      2 NAME
      2 ADDRESS
```

We can take this to a lower level by expanding each component as follows:

```
1 RECORD
    2 NAME
        3 TITLE
        3 INITIALS
        3 SURNAME
    2 ADDRESS
        3 STREET_NUMBER
        3 STREET_NAME
        3 TOWN
        3 COUNTY
        3 COUNTRY
```

The items at level 3 may represent the smallest units into which the elements of the record are subdivided. If so, they can be given type attributes, as in the following PL/I example:

```
1 RECORD,
   2 NAME,
      3 TITLE CHARACTER(6),
      3 INITIALS CHARACTER(4),
      3 SURNAME CHARACTER(20),
   2 ADDRESS
      3 STREET_NUMBER FIXED,
      3 STREET_NAME CHARACTER(15),
      . . .
```

Note that only the lowest levels are given type attributes. These lowest levels (called "elementary items" in COBOL) form the constituent fields of the physical record in storage.

As we have seen, the method of naming used in record-structure specifications allows the relationship of containment to be expressed; in the structure:

```
1X
   2Y
   2Z
```

Y and Z are contained in X. The names in a record-structure declaration are used to form *access functions*. In COBOL, we may say: "Y OF X" or "Y IN X" to access the element Y. In PL/I, the order is reversed and, instead of the keyword "OF" or "IN" a period (.) is used to form a composite name as follows: "$X.Y$."

This form of access is called a *qualified name*. Each component of a record structure may be accessed by a *list* of names, tracing the path between the top of the hierarchy (at level one) to the component being accessed. Figure 8.13 shows an outline structure definition, a diagram of the corresponding hierarchy, and a typical qualified name, with its path of access.

In the record structure of Fig. 8.13, the *elements* of the record are: B,D,F,G,H,J,L,M, the terminals of the tree shown in the diagram. As we shall see below, qualified names need not refer only to the elements of a structure—they may also access a substructure, that is, a nonelementary part of the record structure. Thus we can access substructure C, by means of the qualified name A.C (PL/I) or C IN A (COBOL).

In illustrating record structures, distinct names have been used for each component, and a full list of names starting at the root of the tree (a "fully

Structure declaration

```
1 A
   2 B
   2 C
      3 D
      3 E
         4 F
         4 G
      3 H
   2 J
   2 K
      3 L
      3 M
```

Tree structure

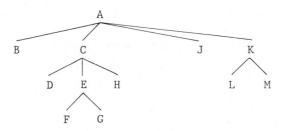

Record structure

Qualified names

The qualified name: A.C.E.F in PL/I
          or F IN E IN C IN A in COBOL
represents the element F, accessed by following the path:

```
  •A
  •C
  •E
•  F
```

Fig. 8.13 Structure declarations and qualified names

qualified name") is used for each reference. It helps to be able to relax these rules, as COBOL and PL/I have done, to allow more lenient methods of specification and reference. This is achieved by allowing

- the use of duplicate names in record-structure specifications,
- the use of "partly qualified" names.

Example

A record-structure may have the following names and structuring:

```
1A
  2B
  2C
    3X
    3Y
  2D
    3X
      4R
      4S
    3Y
```

Here, the names X and Y and repeated, but there is no ambiguity, since each fully qualified name is unique.

Valid references to components in the above structure (in Pl/I notation) are:

C.X   a partly qualified name, equivalent to   A.C.X
A.R.   a partly qualified name, equivalent to   A.D.X.R

However, the references

A.X   and   A.Y

are *ambiguous* references.

The rules for naming record structures in COBOL and PL/I are as follows:

Duplicate names for elements in record structures are allowed provided each "level-1" structure name and each fully qualified name in a COBOL program or a PL/I block is unique.

The similarity of names and structures within the same program led to the introduction of the LIKE attribute in PL/I described in Chapter 6. This allows a structure declaration, or part of one, to be copied and used in other declarations. The names, attributes and structuring remain the same, only the actual level numbers may be changed.

8.6.5.1   Access to substructures

We can refer to a collection of elements in a record structure by using a name that is not the name of an element, a substructure. In COBOL, a complete record structure is normally called a *record* and a substructure is called a *group item*. In PL/I, the complete structure is termed a *major structure* and the substructure, a *minor structure*.

In the previous example,

A

refers to a structure, while

A.C
D.X

refer to substructures.

Together with the rules for forming structures, the naming rules ensure that substructures to be referenced are in "connected" storage, so that relative addressing methods can be used.

There is an important difference between the treatment of substructures in COBOL and PL/I which demonstrates the different treatments of storage concepts in these languages.

Consider the structure in Fig. 8.13. In COBOL, if we refer to the substructure C, we gain access to the contents of *storage* occupied by C, that is, the contiguous segment containing D, F, G, and H. In PL/I, however, a reference to C accesses the components of C, namely the set of *elements* D, F, G, and H. The difference between COBOL and PL/I is most apparent in operations on structures, particularly the operation of assignment. In COBOL, the statement:

MOVE C1 TO C2.

where C1 and C2 are two substructures similar to C above, means: "transfer the storage contents of C1 to that of C2." In COBOL this is known as a group move. As the COBOL standard puts it:

"Any move that is not an elementary move is treated exactly as if it were an alphanumeric to alphanumeric elementary move, except that there is no conversion of data from one form of internal representation to another." (See USASI X3.23-1968 pages 2–91.)

In PL/I, the corresponding assignment statement:

C2 = C1;

moves all the elements of C1 to those of C2. All conversions and editing are carried out as they would be if the elements were moved individually.

8.6.5.2 Variable length records

In data-processing applications we frequently come across data sets whose individual records, though they have the same general structure, differ in size from one record to the next. Records which typically have this property are those which contain a history of events (personnel, medical), or differing numbers of items (reports, journals).

A valuable feature of record-structure handling in COBOL and PL/I is the ability to create and transmit such records to storage devices.

A "variable-length record" contains a field or fields which contain integer values which determine the record length. The record itself is defined as a record structure which contains one or more arrays. The number of elements corresponding to each dimension is used to represent the length of the record.

In COBOL, variable-length records are expressed by means of the DEPENDING ON clause, which defines the number of times a repeating group appears in a table. For example, in an account file containing invoices the record declaration may be given as follows:

```
01 ACCOUNT-RECEIVABLE.
    02 CUSTOMER-NUMBER PICTURE 9(10).
    02 CUSTOMER-NAME PICTURE A(25).
    02 NUMBER-OF-INVOICES PICTURE 99.
    02 INVOICE OCCURS 25 TIMES,
        DEPENDING ON NUMBER-OF-INVOICES.
      03 INV-DATE PICTURE 9(6).
      03 AMOUNT PICTURE 9(5)V99.
        . . .
        . . .
```

Note that, to establish addressability, the "number-of-invoices" field must precede the array and must be in a "fixed" part of the structure. The maximum number of invoices in the record shown is 25.

In PL/I, this principle is extended to other data structures whose size may be represented by an integer—this includes arrays and strings, also AREA's. The REFER option of PL/I, which may only be used in a BASED record structure, is used in a similar way to DEPENDING ON in COBOL; although, as with the use of based references in PL/I generally, the evaluation of size is carried out at the point of reference. An example of the use of the REFER option is given in the PL/I example below.

8.6.5.3 Dynamic data structures

In the previous sections, two kinds of directly addressable data structures have been defined.

- **strings** and **arrays**—referenced by numeric indices or subscripts

- **record structures**—referenced by qualified names

An index, as used for referencing strings and arrays, may be represented by an expression. Since the evaluation of such an expression can be delayed until object time, access by index can be very flexible and powerful. On the other hand, strings and arrays are a restricted form of structure, all of whose elements must be of the same type.

Record structures allow a greater measure of freedom in structuring and allow mixtures of data types. However, references to record structures in the form of qualified names must be constructed when the program is written, and it is not possible to delay the choice of element to be accessed until execution time of the program.

For some applications, we need data structures which combine the freedom of structuring of record structures with the flexibility of reference of strings and arrays. For such structures, we may postpone decisions on the size and shape of the structure until object time. We call these *dynamic data structures*. Examples of such applications include:

- **language processing**—In language processing, strings of characters are scanned and analyzed to find an underlying structure. Linguistic data processing has provided a stimulus for ideas in symbol manipulation languages such as COMIT and SNOBOL. (See Bobrow, 1968.)

- **graphic data processing**—The representation of graphic data structures in a computer requires extremely flexible data structuring, particularly when such structures can be dynamically updated.

One way to introduce dynamic data structures in a programming language is to include lists as built-in data structures. However, there are certain difficulties in introducing list structures in a general-purpose language. Some of these concern the representation of list structures. In many LISP systems, for example, each *character* of an S-expression is stored in a halfword of store, the other half of the word being used for an address linking the character to a next element. This leads to a very high ratio of address space to data space. Another difficulty is that the emphasis on the functional form in LISP does not always match well with the command-like statement structure of many programming languages.

In spite of such difficulties, some languages have included lists as built-in data structures and have successfully integrated list-processing and a general algorithmic language. Examples include: CPL (Barron, *et al.*, 1963), POP-2 (Burstall *et al.*, 1971).

There is another approach to dynamic data structuring, based on the introduction of *pointer* or *reference* variables. This approach follows similar principles to those of machine language programming, in which complex data structures may be represented by data fields linked together by addresses.

One of the earliest studies of pointers in high-level languages was undertaken by D. T. Ross in the AED system (Ross, 1969). This work goes back to the late 1950's, in which the APT system for the numerical control of machine tools was under development. In APT, techniques for addressing contiguous blocks of storage by means of pointers were designed; these were later adapted and included in the AED system.

8.6.5.4   Pointers and reference variables

The basic idea of *pointers* and *reference variables* is to introduce quantities whose values, instead of representing numbers, strings, Booleans, etc., are used to *refer* to other items of data.

A pointer value may be set to "point at" or "refer to" an item of data. We can then make reference to: "the data pointed at by P." Pointers can be stored along with other data, so that a linked structure can be built up, just as linked structures are implicitly built up in LISP systems. The difference is that, with pointer systems, the linkages are explicit and must be designed and created by the programmer, whereas in a LISP system they are automatically inserted by the system and cannot be separately manipulated by the programmer.

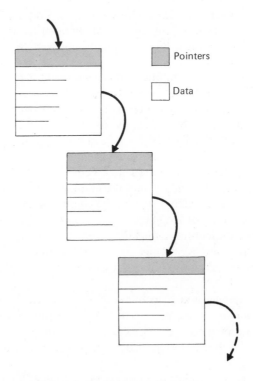

Fig. 8.14 List with multiword items

The introduction of pointers as items of data in a data structure gives the programmer greater control over the ratio of pointers to data. For example (see Fig. 8.14), if it is known that a certain data structure always contains a certain group of data items, these can be located together in contiguous storage.

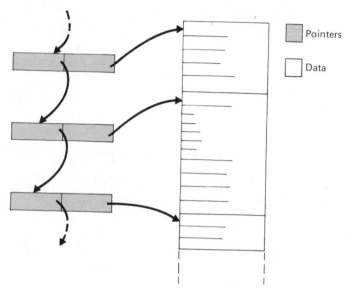

Fig. 8.15 Pointers and data stored separately

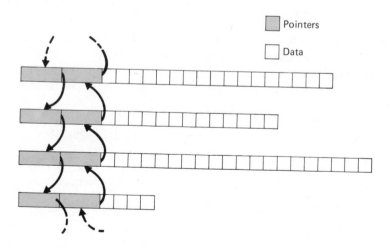

Fig. 8.16 Doubly linked list

It may be desirable to separate the data from the pointers, as shown in Fig. 8.15. By suitably placing and setting pointers, doubly linked lists (Fig. 8.16) and ring structures (Fig. 8.17) may be defined.

By having pointers or references as explicit data types, it is possible to define linked structures and to write procedures for processing them. The pointers embody the *relations* between the components of the data structures, and since they can be explicitly manipulated, the programmer has greater freedom than with the built-in relations of arrays, record structures, and lists.

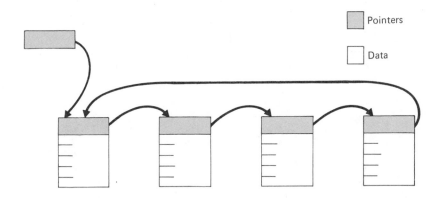

Fig. 8.17 Ring structure

In the following sections, two designs of language which include pointer or reference variables are described. The first is based on proposals for an extension to ALGOL 60 and has been adopted in several different languages with minor modifications and slightly different notations. The notation used here is that of ALGOL W. The other design is that of the pointer and based variables in PL/I, sometimes called the "list processing" facilities.

8.6.5.5   Record handling in ALGOL W

ALGOL W is an extended version of ALGOL, originally described by Wirth & Hoare (1966). The principles of record handling in ALGOL W have also been separately described by Hoare (1967, 1968)

Two important constructions in the ALGOL W scheme of record handling are the *record class* and the *reference variable.*

A record class is a description of a record, a set of elements not necessarily of the same type. A record class can be thought of as a template to be used in constructing and accessing records. A record-class declaration defines the fields within the associated records:

Example

record *person* (**string** *name;* **integer** *age;* **logical** *male;* **integer** *salary*)
This specifies a class of records called *person,* containing the four fields,
name, age, male, and *salary,* with types **string, integer, logical,** and **integer.**
　　We can introduce variables of type **reference,** which can be used for
accessing records of a given record class. In declaring reference variables,
the programmer must indicate the class of record that will be referenced.
For example, if we have the declaration:

　　reference *(person) fulltime, parttime;*

then the reference variables, *fulltime* and *parttime* can only be used to access
person records. This approach was deliberately designed so that the correspondence between references and data out could be checked by a compiler
before execution.
　　To access the salary field of a record referred to by the variable *fulltime,*
the following form is used:

　　salary (fulltime)

　　A reference to a record field is thus similar in form to a subscript reference to an array element.
　　We next come to the means of constructing records in ALGOL W. The
record-class name is used as a *constructor function* for creating records. To
construct a *person* record we use the function *person,* created by the declaration of the record-class name. The arguments of the function correspond
to the fields of the record being created. The result of applying this function
is twofold:

- A data structure is created.
- A reference value is returned, pointing at the created structure. This
  value can subsequently be used to refer to the record.

Example

The assignment statement:

　　r : = *person* ('A. B. JONES', 32, **true**, 1450);

creates a person record with the specified values, and assigns a reference
value which locates this record to the reference variable, *r.*
　　The fields of the *person* record can be accessed by:

　　age(*r*),

　　salary(*r*),

　　etc.

Note how the treatment of records in ALGOL W differs from the usual treatment of variables in ALGOL. Instead of variables being created automatically, a specific assignment command is required. The life of a record is not related to the block structure of the program; once created, a record persists until it is no longer needed.

There is no destructor function in ALGOL W and responsibility for retrieving unwanted storage is undertaken by the system itself, as in LISP. When available storage is used up, or at other times determined by the system, a "garbage collector" is invoked which searches for storage which can be released. To qualify for release, data must be such that it can no longer be accessed. In other words there must be no current reference which points at the data.

8.6.5.6   The PL/I list-processing facilities

The basic principle here, as in other pointer referencing schemes, is to have separate means of specifying the *attributes* and the *location* of an item of data.

To specify attributes, the notation used for declaring elements, strings, arrays, and record structures is used. The additional attribute BASED is used to denote that what is being specified is a description (or template); the data itself must be created by an explicit command.

Example

The description of the *person* record is as follows:

```
DECLARE  1 PERSON BASED,
             2 NAME CHARACTER(30),
             2 AGE FIXED,
             2 MALE BIT(1),
             2 SALARY FIXED;
```

A based item is referred to by a pointer, which specifies its location, and which may be declared as follows:

```
DECLARE  1 PERSON BASED(P),
             2 NAME . . .
             . . .
```

In this case, the pointer is *associated* with the description, which allows a shortened form of reference although it does not restrict the use of the pointer to this type of data. In the strict interpretation of the PL/I language, a pointer value is a pure location, unconnected with any attributes of data it may reference.

To access a based variable, the full form of reference is:

```
locator-reference — > based-reference
```

Such a reference may take on quite a complex form, but we first consider how it may be applied in a simple way to reference the fields of the person record.

```
P — > PERSON ... ... ... accesses the whole record
P — > NAME   ... ... ... accesses the name field
```

If the pointer P has been associated with the based record, then these references may be abbreviated to:

```
PERSON
NAME
```

To construct a based item of data, an ALLOCATE statement must be executed; this acts as a constructor function for based variables. To construct a *person* record we write:

```
ALLOCATE PERSON SET(P);
```

or simply,

```
ALLOCATE PERSON;
```

if P has been associated with PERSON.

PL/I does not have an automatic "garbage collector"; thus the programmer is responsible for releasing unwanted storage by means of the FREE statement which acts as a destructor function. To free the *person* record, we write:

```
FREE PERSON;
```

and the storage is returned for reuse by the system.

One disadvantage of this approach is that, since pointer variables have an independent life, pointers to a *person* record may be still around after the record itself has been destroyed. If they are used, they may illegally access storage used for some other purpose. This has been called a "dangling reference" by Wegner, who has written a useful survey of different strategies of data structuring and referencing (Wegner, 1971).

One of the difficulties of using pointer variables is that the pointer values set up during a computation are not necessarily valid for another execution of the same program. This is because the value of a pointer variable corresponds to an "absolute" machine address and may not be preserved from one run of a program to another. In general such values will differ according to any relocation of program or data.

This is a serious disadvantage for certain kinds of application, in which it may take many hours of computing time to build up a linked-data structure. In machine-language programming, problems of referencing relocatable data have been solved by using relative rather than absolute addresses. Much the same solution is followed in PL/I by introducing relative addressing in the form of OFFSET variables. These are associated with AREA variables, a form of variable whose value corresponds to a segment of connected storage.

By using lists, trees, rings, graphs, etc. formed from OFFSET rather than POINTER references, dynamic data structures can be built up which are independent of their location in storage, and can thus be stored on secondary storage devices between runs of a program.

The PL/I BASED attribute describes the type and structural properties of data, and indicates that such data is to be created dynamically. Strictly speaking, a BASED item of data is not a variable in the sense of Chapter 7, with name, attributes and representation. This is because the means of reference to BASED data is defined in the following way. We recall that a based reference has the form:

```
locator-reference - > based-reference
```

It is defined in PL/I that "locator-reference" is only evaluated at execution time. It may in fact be a complex expression, provided it ultimately yields a pointer value. The "based-reference" therefore has an undefined meaning until it is combined with the locator-reference, and it is the two combined that yield a value, and even then only when the program is executed.

The following example combines several of the concepts described in this chapter (see also Fig. 8.18). It shows how text strings can be held in a singly linked list, from which they can be accessed by writing a suitable search procedure. Successive items in the list may have different lengths, and the example shows how these are stored as "variable length records" using the PL/I REFER option. Finally, it is shown how the chain can be held in "relocatable" form, using OFFSETS rather than POINTERS, so that the AREA's in which the chains are held could be stored on a backing store using record I/O.

Example

```
CHAIN:
 PROCEDURE;
 /*  This procedure creates a data structure whose elements   */
 /* are character strings of varying length linked in a       */
 /* forward chain. The space allocated for each text record   */
```

```
/* depends on the length of the string. Text strings are    */
/* allocated in areas and each string is linked to the next  */
/* by offset. Successive areas are linked by pointers.       */
/*  The procedure uses an auxiliary procedure, MOVE, which    */
/* causes a new text string to be placed in an auxiliary     */
/* variable BUFFER, and sets the integer variable            */
/* L to the length of the string.                            */
/*  When the last record has been read in, the bit variable  */
/* T is set to zero.                                         */
/*  Declarations                                             */
   DECLARE
/*  Based variables                                          */

   1 HEADER BASED(HPOINTER),
      2 FIRSTEL OFFSET(A),
      2 LASTEL OFFSET(A),
      2 NEXTAREA POINTER,

   1 ELEMENT BASED(FLOFFSET),
      2 NEXTEL OFFSET(A),
      2 TEXTLENGTH FIXED BINARY,
      2 TEXT CHAR(L REFER(TEXTLENGTH)),
/*  Pointers and offsets                                     */

   FIRST POINTER,
   LAST POINTER,

   HPOINTER POINTER,
   ELPOINTER POINTER,

   APOINTER POINTER,  /* area pointer                         */
   ELOFFSET OFFSET(A),  /* link to next element               */
/*  Area for allocation of text records                      */

   A AREA BASED(APOINTER),
/*  Miscellaneous                                            */

   L FIXED BINARY INITIAL(0),
   BUFFER CHAR(1000) VARYING INITIAL(''),
   T BIT(1) INITIAL('1'B),
   NULL BUILTIN,
   MOVE ENTRY;
/*  End of declarations                                      */
/*  Initialization                                           */
/*  The first area is allocated and a header is allocated     */
/* within it. The pointer FIRST is set to point to this      */
/* header. An on-unit is established for the area condition   */
```

```
/* to allocate a new area and set up links for subsequent   */
/* allocations.                                              */
 ALLOCATE A;
 ALLOCATE HEADER IN(A);
 FIRST,LAST,FIRSTEL,LASTEL = HPOINTER;
 ON AREA
    BEGIN;
       NEXTEL = NULL;
       ALLOCATE A;
       ALLOCATE HEADER IN(A);
       FIRSTEL,LASTEL,LAST = HPOINTER;
    END;
/*  Main loop for creating the list                         */
LOOP:
 DO WHILE(T);
    CALL MOVE;
    ALLOCATE ELEMENT IN(A);
    TEXT = BUFFER;
    LASTEL — > NEXTEL,LASTEL = ELOFFSET;
 END;
/*  Termination                                             */
/*  The ends of the header and element lists are set null   */
TERMINATE:
 NEXTAREA,NEXTEL = NULL;

 END CHAIN;
```

8.6.5.7   Further developments

New techniques for constructing and accessing complex data structures will undoubtedly continue to be a dominant factor in programming language design.

A language which has extended the relatively simple and rigid record-defining capabilities described above, without departing from a conventional language framework, is SIMULA (Dahl *et al.,* 1970). The *class* concept in SIMULA provides a more powerful type of "template" than is available in COBOL or PL/I. It allows procedural as well as declarative information to be embodied in the class description, so that more simply structured programs can be written. Examples of the use of SIMULA in drafting are given by Kerr and Birtwistle (1971).

In data-base systems (which might be called "data structure systems"), the advantage of relational models of data (Codd 1970) contrast with the list-processing facilities embodied in the CODASYL proposals (CODASYL,

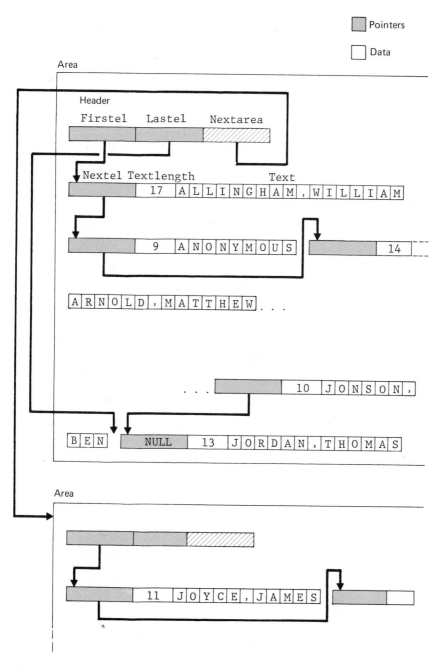

Fig. 8.18 List structure created by CHAIN

1971). The debate between these two approaches brings out many of the arguments which arise in programming language design, in which conflicting requirements of integrity, security, reliability, efficiency, and ease-of-use must be balanced in a final design.

8.7 FURTHER READING

8.7.1 General Reading

One of the most comprehensive books on data structures is that by Berztiss (1971). Knuth's Volume 1 (Knuth, 1968) has a large chapter on information structures, with detailed treatments of lists, trees, multilinked structures, and a section on techniques of storage allocation. Johnson's book (Johnson, 1970) emphasizes data structures and discusses several methods of searching, using APL notation.

Most books on programming include sections on data structures, indicating the important place they hold in the study of programming languages. Examples include the books by Wegner (1968), Hellerman (1967), and Galler and Perlis (1970). A complete issue of SIGPLAN Notices (Tou and Wegner, 1971) was devoted to data structures in programming languages, and contains several papers relevant to the topics of this chapter.

8.7.2 Storage Structures

Although a relationship between data and storage structures exists in most of the earliest programming language designs, the description of data structures in most language manuals tends to ignore this relationship. One of the first extensive discussions of data and storage structures was given in the paper by d'Imperio (1969).

The systematic study of the properties of storage from an abstract and mathematical point of view is even more recent. An early treatment of storage is contained in Elgot and Robinson (1964), a mathematical formalism for computing systems with the read-write property of real machines. This paper was aiming at a treatment of computability suitable for stored-program machines, rather than being primarily concerned with the abstract properties of storage. Formal treatments of storage were developed for the definition of PL/I (Alber, *et al.*, 1969; Henhapl, 1969; and Bekic and Walk, 1971). Another line of development has been followed by Rosenberg (1971(a) and (b)), who has developed a theory of storage which relates to the techniques of absolute and relative addressing.

8.7.3 Single-level Storage

At an early point in the history of computing, "backing stores" (generally in the form of drums) were attached to computers to augment the small high-speed stores then available. There were a number of attempts to make such two-level stores appear as single-level stores to the user. Pioneering work was done on the Atlas system (Kilburn, *et al.,* 1961; Kilburn, *et al.,* 1962; and Brooker, 1960). A good review of this work, with an extensive bibliography, is contained in the survey paper on "Virtual Memory," by Denning (1970).

8.7.4 The Implementation of Data Structures

In implementing data structures, there are two types of problem—the choice of storage allocation techniques, and efficiency of access, particularly in the translation of access function references to machine addresses. Data structure handling is an important part of compiler design and reference should be made to works cited in Chapter 5. However, there are discussions of methods of implementing strings in d'Imperio (1969) and of arrays in Hill (1962) and in Hellerman (1962).

Efficient and reliable implementation of data structures probably depends on assistance from hardware. A well-known early paper on this, from a hardware point of view, is by Blaauw (1959). From a programming-and-engineering point of view, some of the best work has been done by Iliffe (Iliffe, 1961; Iliffe and Jodeit, 1962; Iliffe, 1967). Another important landmark in this field was the design of the Burroughs machine (Burroughs, 1961), which included a hardware stack as part of the machine architecture. See also Haley (1962).

8.7.5 Strings

Some of the basic ideas of Markov, particularly the notion of a basic operation of scanning-and-replacing, were incorporated in the string-handling language COMIT, which was designed for linguistic research at M.I.T. (M.I.T. Press, 1962; Yngve, 1963). The ideas in COMIT were extended and improved in SNOBOL, which has become one of the most widely used specialist languages for string-handling. (See Griswold, *et al.,* 1968.)

There have been several good surveys of string manipulation and symbol manipulation languages, such as Bobrow (1968), Sammet (1966), Satterthwait (1966), and Madnick (1967). A good description of string-handling languages and a history of their development are included in Sammet (1969).

The relationship of string handling to general-purpose languages has been discussed from two points of view—the addition of string handling to languages which do not have it, and a description of the uses of string handling in various applications. In the first category, additions to ALGOL are discussed in Wegstein and Youden (1962), Shoffner and Brown (1963), and Milner (1968). Additions to FORTRAN are discussed in Poore (1962), Pyle (1962), and more recently by Ahl *et al.*, (1971) and Lambird (1971). The last two references are proposals for additions to standard FORTRAN, and contain a good deal of interesting explanatory information.

8.7.6 Arrays

Two-dimensional arrays, in the form of matrices, are familiar to mathematicians from their application in linear algebra and other branches of mathematics. For those without background an introductory description of matrix methods is given in Bickley and Thompson (1964) or Househoulder (1964).

Details of matrix interpretive schemes developed for early British machines are discussed by Robinson (1960). The design of matrix packages using essentially FORTRAN- or ALGOL-like notation is described by Branin *et al.*, (1965).

The design of languages for array processing has been influenced by the pioneering work of Iverson (1962), particularly his principle of extending simple scalar operators to work, element-by-element on arrays, and the development of a set of simple, but essential, array operators. A theory of arrays, drawing on APL concepts and notation, is given in a paper by More (1973). Extensions to the original APL concept of arrays are discussed in Ghandour and Mezei (1973). Another approach is discussed in Bayer and Witzgall (1970, 1972)—this is related to the work of Dantzig and others (Eisenstat *et al.*, 1970). Another approach to language design based on arrays using "natural" mathematical notation is represented by the work on AMTRAM (Reinfelds, 1971; Kratky, 1971). See also the papers on LYaPAS, a language for expressing logical and algorithmic problems which has some affinities with APL (Gavrilov and Zakrevskii, 1969).

Techniques of implementing arrays are discussed in most works on compiler construction (see Chapter 5). However, there are special papers on this topic by Sattley (1961), Galler and Perlis (1962), and Hellerman (1962). An interesting discussion of the implementation of arrays in APL, especially the treatment of the generalized array subscript, is given by Hassitt and Lyon (1972). See also Abrams (1970).

A language for processing regular partitions of arrays is described by Phillips and Adams (1972). Special problems of implementation which arise when matrices are very large and sparsely occupied are discussed in the papers given at a conference on sparse matrices (Willoughby, 1969). See also Curtis and Reid (1971).

8.7.7 Lists

There are a large number of good papers on list processing including a number of survey papers. Some of these (Bobrow, 1968; Sammet, 1966), relating to string handling, are referenced in the text. Classic papers in this field include those by McCarthy (1960, 1962) on LISP and Newell, Shaw, and Simon (1965) on IPL-V. These tend to be difficult reading but there are good expositions of list processing based on LISP by Woodward and Jenkins (1961) and in the tutorial primer by Weissman (1967). More general papers on the application of list processing are by Wilkes (1965) and Woodward (1966). The monograph by Foster (1967) is a good general introduction to the subject.

Methods of extending languages to include list processing include the techniques of "embedding" used for SLIP, a language related to FORTRAN (Weizenbaum, 1963; Bobrow and Weizenbaum, 1964).

8.7.8 Stacks

There are several papers on the theoretical basis of stack automata, for example, Schutzenberger (1963) and Ginsburg et al., (1967). For hardware representations of stacks see Hauck and Dent (1968). See also Baecker and Gibbens (1964).

8.7.9 Record Structures

Papers on record structures include Lawson (1962) on implementing COBOL records, and Ross (1969—references to earlier work are included in this report). Hoare (1967, 1968) has written a number of papers proposing a form of record structure less dependent on the addressing structure of physical storage; this work influenced the design for the nonhomogeneous record structures introduced in ALGOL 68 (van Wijngaarden et al., 1969). Maclaren (1970) has an interesting discussion of the implementation of record structures in PL/I, in which the impact of the storage properties of a machine are discussed. Knuth (1968) describes many of the techniques needed for implementing record structures, with a valuable discussion of alternative strategies of storage allocation.

8.7.10   Dynamic Data Structures

The first extensive publications on dynamic data structures using pointer-type data are by Ross in his descriptions of the AED project (Ross, 1969). The list-processing extensions to PL/I were first outlined by Lawson (1967).

BIBLIOGRAPHY

Abel, N.E., P. B. Budnik, D. J. Kuck, Y. Muraoka, R. S. Northcote, R. B. Wilhelmson, "TRANQUIL: A language for an array processing computer," *AFIPS Conference proceedings,* Vol. 34, (SJCC 1969) AFIPS press, 1969, pp. 57–73.

An algorithmic language (based on ALGOL) for the ILLIAC IV, in which the high degree of parallelism of the hardware can be exploited. The data types include arrays and sets. A mapping function specification must be included with each declaration of an array.

ACM, "1970 ACM SICFIDET workshop on data description and access," Second ed., Apr. 1971.

ACM, "Proceeding of the ACM symposium on symbolic and algebraic manipulation," *CACM,* Vol. 9, No. 8, Aug. 1966, (whole issue).

This collection of papers touches on many of the subjects of this chapter.

Alber, K., H. Goldmann, P. Lauer, P. Lucas, P. Oliva, H. Stigleitner, K. Walk, G. Zeisel, "Informal introduction to the abstract syntax and interpretation of PL/I," *Technical Report TR 25.099,* June 1969, IBM Laboratory, Vienna.

An introduction to the techniques used in the formal definition of PL/I (ULD). The important sections relating to data and storage structures are Chapter 4 (Storage and Data) and Chapter 5 (Identifiers and Their Significance). This report presents an extensively worked out theory of variables for a language with storage concepts.

Ahl, K.. J. Barrington, J. Hillier, E. Mack, W. Whipple, "Character and bit data types for FORTRAN—a proposal to ANSI subcommittee X3 J3," SIGPLAN Notices, Vol. 6, No. 10, Nov. 1971, pp. 22–40.

A summary of the problems of introducing bit and character data types in FORTRAN, including a discussion of the storage properties of the language. Contains a proposal, with examples, for new data types, BIT, and CHARACTER.

Arden, B. W., B. A. Galler, R. M. Graham, "An algorithm for equivalence declarations," *CACM,* Vol. 4, No. 7, July 1961, pp. 310–314.

Baecker, H. D., B. J. Gibbens, "A commercial use of stacks," *Annual Review in Automatic Programming,* R. Goodman (ed.), Vol. 4, Elmsford, N.Y.: Pergamon Press, 1964, pp. 183–191.

Describes the use of stacks in implementing TALK, a block-structured language with character string data. The technique involves the use of two stacks, a call stack and a work stack.

Balzer, R. M., "Dataless programming," *Proc. FJCC Vol. 31,* Nov. 1967, New York: Academic Press, 1967, pp. 535–544.

Describes an extension to PL/I which allows the programmer to ignore the details of data representations and express all accesses to data in a single canonical form.

Barron, D. W., J. N. Buxton, D. F. Hartley, F. Nixon, C. S. Strachey, "The main features of CPL," *Computer Journal,* Vol. 6, 1963, pp. 134–143.

Bayer, R., C. Witzgall, "Some complete calculi for matrices," *CACM,* Vol. 13, No. 4, Apr. 1970, pp. 223–237.

Considers a set of operations on matrices suitable for inclusion in a high-level language. The facilities are more advanced than those currently available, even in such languages as APL. They include concatenation of matrices (horizontal, vertical and diagonal), general extraction operators, and a wide range of other operators. This work contributed to the definition of MPL. (Eisenstat *et al.,* 1970)

Bayer, R., C. Witzgall, "Index ranges for matrix calculi," *CACM,* Vol. 15, No. 12, Dec. 1972, pp. 1033–1039.

A range is a sequence of positive integers, used as indices in a matrix. This paper considers range operators and expressions arising in a scheme for matrix arithmetic, and considers possible techniques for optimization.

Bekic, H., K. Walk, "Formalization of storage properties," (in) E. Engeler (ed.), *Symposium on Semantics of Algorithmic Languages, Vol. 188, Lecture Notes in Mathematics,* Berlin: Springer-Verlag, 1971, pp. 28–61.

Presents a general abstract-storage model, originally developed for ALGOL 68 but extended to deal with the storage properties of PL/I. Models for arrays, structures, and records are discussed. Conclusion: "ALGOL 68 and PL/I differ with respect to the balance between economy and security in programming."

Berztiss, A. J., *Data Structures: Theory and Practice,* New York: Academic Press, 1971.

The first part of this book is a presentation of subjects in discrete mathematics—set theory, function theory, and graph theory. The second part contains a more extended discussion of trees and graphs. Finally, there is a section on the computer representation of structures, dealing with arrays, stacks, and file structures.

Bobrow, D. G., J. Weizenbaum, "List processing and extension of language facility by embedding," *IEEE Transactions on Computers,* EC-13, No. 4, Aug. 1964, pp. 395–400.

Primarily a tutorial on list processing, indicating some of the elementary properties of lists and functions on lists. The languages discussed include LISP, IPL-V, COMIT, METEOR, and SLIP. The most important aspect of the paper is its discussion of "extensions" to programming languages and in particular of the techniques known as "embedding" as a method of extension.

Bobrow, D. G. (ed.), "Symbol manipulation languages and techniques," *Proceedings of the IFIP Working Conference on Symbol Manipulation Languages,* North-Holland, 1968.

A collection of 23 papers on string and symbol manipulation with a valuable annotated bibliography.

Bosak, R., "An information algebra," 16th National Meeting, *ACM,* Paper 6B-1, 1961.

Bovet, D. P., G. Estrin, "On static memory allocation in computer systems," *IEEE Transactions on Computers,* Vol. C-19, No. 6, June 1970, pp. 492–503.
Describes a method of analyzing a computer program, recognizing mutually exclusive sets of space-taking entities, and inserting instructions which allow the program to make use of secondary storage.

Branin, F. H., L. V. Hall, J. Suez, R. M. Carlitz, T. C. Chen, "An interpretive program for matrix arithmetic," *IBM Syst. Jour.,* Vol. 4, No. 1, 1965, pp. 2–24.
An interpretive matrix scheme for STRETCH. The technique of implementation uses *codewords,* similar to those proposed by Iliffe (Iliffe and Jodeit, 1962).

Brian, W. J., "A parts breakdown technique using list structures, *CACM,* Vol. 7, No. 6, June 1964, pp. 362–365.
The application is related to that known as "bill-of-material" processing, generally a fruitful field for the development of data structuring techniques. It is an example of the use of list processing outside the field of systems programming.

Brooker, R. A., "Some techniques for dealing with two-level storage," *Computer Journal,* Vol. 2, No. 4, Jan. 1960, pp. 189–194.
This describes techniques for using the drum for the matrices stored on a drum in Mercury Autocode. This is not the same as a "one-level store," but rather a simplified form of transfer instruction.

Burroughs Corporation, *The Descriptor—a definition of the B5000 information processing system,* Burroughs Corporation, 1961.

Burstall, R. M., J. S. Collins, B. J. Popplestone, *Programming in POP-2,* Edinburgh: Edinburgh University Press, 1971.
The data structures in POP-2 are derived *via* the work of Landin from LISP and the Lambda calculus. There are lists, arrays, records, strips, and a range of functions, including constructors, destructors, updaters, and closure functions.

Campbell, J. A., "LISP and its application to physical problems," *Computer Physics Communications,* Vol. 1, 1970, pp. 251–264.
Includes a tutorial on LISP and illustrates how list processing can be applied to problems in physics. These include problems in particle theory, quantum electrodynamics, network analysis and certain problems related to artificial intelligence.

Campbell, J. A., "A note on an optimal-fit method for dynamic allocation of storage," *Computer Journal,* Vol. 14, No. 1, Feb. 1971, pp. 7–9.
The problem of allocating storage on the basis of a free list of different-sized blocks is considered. Two classes of technique have been proposed—first-fit strategies and best-fit strategies. The former have been reported as giving good performance. This paper presents a proposal based on the theory of Markov process which it is claimed gives better performance than conventional first-fit methods.

Cayley, A., *Collected Mathematical Works,* Vols. 1–13 (1889–1897), Cambridge University, New York: Johnson Reprints (Subs. Academic Press).
A fundamental series of works including papers on matrices, trees, and graphs,

some emanating from work on the structure of algebraic formulas, some from the structure of chemical compounds.

Childs, D. L., "Description of a set-theoretic data structure," *Proc. FJCC.* (1968), Vol. 33, Part 1, pp. 557–564, Washington: Thompson Book Co., 1968.

Childs, D. L., "Feasibility of a set-theoretic data structure. A general structure based on a reconstituted definition of a relation," *Proc. IFIP Congress,* 1968, pp. 420–430, North-Holland, 1969.

Clippinger, R. F., "FACT—A Business Compiler: description and comparison with COBOL and Commercial Translator," R. Goodman (ed.), *Annual Review in Automatic Programming Vol. 2,* Elmsford, N.Y.: Pergamon Press, 1961, pp. 231–292.

CODASYL committee, "An information algebra," *CACM,* Vol. 5, No. 4, Apr. 1962, pp. 190–204.

CODASYL, *Data Base Task Group Report,* April 1971.

Proposals for a data-base language comprising a general language for data description and additions to COBOL to enable data-base access.

Codd, E. F., "A relational model of data for large shared data banks," *CACM,* Vol. 13, No. 6, June 1970, pp. 377–387.

Comfort, W. T., "Multiword list items," *CACM,* Vol. 7, No. 6, June 1964, pp. 357–362.

Recognizing the importance of list structures in programming, this paper points out the advantages of allowing each component of a list to contain more than one word or byte of data. Contains several illustrations of list-processing techniques, including the use of forward and backward pointers.

Curtis, A. R., J. K. Reid, "The solution of large sparse unsymmetric systems of linear equations," *Proc. IFIP Congress,* Aug. 1971, pp. TA-1-1 to 5.

Denning, P. J., "Virtual Memory," *Computing Surveys,* Vol. 2, No. 3, Sept. 1970, pp. 153–189.

The main topic of this paper is the description of hardware systems for making access to a large, segmented memory more convenient and efficient. The paper is valuable in presenting a conceptual view of storage and its properties, and a review of techniques that have been used for storage management both for conventional and for paging systems (84 references).

Dahl, O. J., B. Myhrhaug, K. Hygaard, "SIMULA Common Base Language" Publication S-22, Norsk Regnecentral, Oslo, 1970.

SIMULA is a derivative of ALGOL 60, originally intended for simulation problems. It contains powerful data-structuring facilities, including the concept of a *class.*

De Salvio, A. J., J. G. Purdy, J. Rau, "Creation and control of internal data bases under a FORTRAN programming environment," *CACM,* Vol. 13, No. 4, Apr. 1970, pp. 211–215.

This paper presents a technique for communicating information through the COMMON structure. Contains a discussion of FORTRAN storage concepts. The facility provided is similar to Jovial's COMPOOL (see Shaw, 1963).

Deuel, P., "On a storage-mapping function for data structures," *CACM,* Vol. 9, No. 5, May 1966, pp. 344–347.

Dijkstra, E. W., "Recursive programming," *Numerische Mathematik,* Vol. 2, No. 5, Oct. 1960, pp. 312–318.

Outlines the idea of a *stack* to be used in the execution of an ALGOL program.

Dodd, George G., "APL—a language for associative data handling in PL/I," *Proc. FJCC,* 1966, pp. 677–684.

A language embedded in PL/I to aid the user dealing with data structures in which complex relationships may be expressed. He allows N-dimensional data associations and the automatic extension of address area memory beyond the confines of high-speed store.

Dos, K. H. Otto, "Optimal dynamic use of memory of PL/I object programs in a real memory environment," *Computer Journal,* Vol. 15, No. 1, Feb. 1972, pp. 18–20.

Eisenstat, S., T. Magnanti, S. Maier, M. McGrath, V. Nicholson, C. Riedl, "MPL: Mathematical Programming Language," *Technical Report STAN-CS-70-187,* Nov. 1970, Computer Science Department, Stanford University.

Elcock, E. W., J. M. Foster, P. M. D. Gray, J. J. McGregor, A. M. Murray, "ABSET. A programming language based on sets: motivation and examples," (in) *Machine Intelligence, Vol. 6,* 1971, Edinburgh: Edinburgh University Press, 1971, pp. 467–490.

A good exposition of the reasons for using mathematical structures such as *sets* as a basis for the data structures in programming languages. ABSET is an experimental system for interactive programming.

Falkoff, A. D., K. E. Iverson, "The design of APL," *IBM Journal of Research and Development,* Vol. 17, No. 4, Jul. 1973, pp. 324–333.

An authoritative survey of the development of APL, emphasizing the principles underlying its design.

Farber, D. J., R. E. Griswold, I. P. Polonsky, "The SNOBOL3 programming language," *Bell System Technical Journal,* Vol. XLV, No. 6, 1966, pp. 895–943.

Feldman, J. A., P. D. Rovner, "An ALGOL-based associative language," *CACM,* Vol. 12, No. 8, Aug. 1969, pp. 439–449.

Describes LEAP, an extension of ALGOL for programming with complex associative-data structures. The simple elements of LEAP include *items* and *associations.* Data structures called *sets* may be defined and a range of set-handling functions are included.

Fleck, A. C., "Towards a theory of data structures," *J. Comput. Syst. Sc.,* Vol. 5, Oct. 1971, pp. 475–488.

Discusses the data structures found in list-processing languages, relating them to the set of context-free languages. The pattern-matching operations of SNOBOL are discussed in relation to the class of context-dependent languages.

Floyd, R. W., "A descriptive language for symbol manipulation, *JACM,* Vol. 8, No. 10, Oct. 1961, pp. 579–584.

Foster, J. M., *List Processing,* London: Macdonald, 1967; New York: American Elsevier.

A good short monograph on the essentials of list processing.

Fox, L., D. F. Mayers, *Computing Methods for Scientists and Engineers,* Oxford: Clarendon Press, 1968.

Galler, B. A., A. J. Perlis, "Compiling matrix operations," *CACM,* Vol. 5, No. 12, Dec. 1962, pp. 590–594.

Describes how vector and matrix types may be added to ALGOL together with the arithmetic operations $+$, $-$ and $\times$, and how the operations of inversion and transposition can be extended to variables of this type. Galler and Perlis took up this topic again in their 1967 paper on the development of extensional features for Algol (see below).

Galler, B. A., A. J. Perlis, "A proposal for definitions in ALGOL," *CACM,* Vol. 10, No. 4, Apr. 1967, pp. 204–219.

A proposal for introducing methods of defining new data types and operators in ALGOL. Among the primitives added to ALGOL are means of finding the address of an element in storage. The details of the exposition are difficult to follow.

Galler, B. A., A. J. Perlis, *A View of Programming Languages,* Reading, Mass.: Addison-Wesley, 1970.

An approach to the study of programming languages by the means of Markov Algorithms. An unusual book, strongly oriented towards ALGOL-like languages, with a formal mathematical basis. There is a good chapter on data structures.

Gavrilov, M. A., A. D. Zakrevskii (eds.), *LYaPAS: A Programming Language for Logic and Coding Algorithms* (translated by Morton Nadler), ACM Monograph Series, New York: Academic Press, 1969.

Ghandour, Z., J. Mezei, "General arrays, operators and functions," *IBM Journal of Research and Development,* Vol. 17, No. 4, Jul. 1973, pp. 335–352.

General arrays are arrays whose components may be other arrays. A set of functions for constructing and manipulating such arrays is presented. These are defined in APL notation.

Ginsburg, S., S. A. Greibach, M. A. Harrison, "Stack automata and compiling," *JACM,* Vol. 14, No. 1, Jan. 1967, pp. 172–201.

Presents a mathematical model, the stack automaton, which embodies many of the features of modern compiling techniques. Useful description of a formal model of compilation.

Gower, J. C., "The handling of multiway tables on computers," *Computer Journal,* Vol. 4, No. 4, Jan. 1962, pp. 280–286.

Describes the processing of tables in terms of what is called *scanning.* Proposals for additions to Mercury Autocode are suggested. (Perhaps the origin of SEARCH in COBOL.)

Gray, J. C., "Compound data structure for computer aided design—a survey," *Proc. ACM Nat. Conference,* 1967, pp. 355–365.

Griswold, R. E., J. F. Poage, I. P. Polonsky, *The SNOBOL 4 Programming Language,* Englewood Cliffs, N.J.: Prentice-Hall, 1968.

Haley, A. C. D., "The KDF9 computer system," *Proc. AFIPS 22* (FJCC 1962), AFIPS Press, 1962, pp. 108–120.

Harary, F., R. Z. Norman, D. Cartwright, *Structural Models: An Introduction to the Theory of Directed Graphs,* New York: John Wiley, 1965.

A mathematical treatment of directed graphs ("digraphs"), a general form of structure which includes trees as a special case. This is primarily a mathematical work with illustrations from a wide field, including psychology, sociology, economics. No direct bearing on programming, but full of fascinating ideas and illustrations.

Hassitt, A., L. E. Lyon, "Efficient evaluation of array subscripts of arrays," *IBM Journal of R. & D.,* Vol. 16, No. 1, Jan. 1972, pp. 45–57.

In APL, a subscripted reference to an array, such as the form $A[I;J;K]$ is more complex than the corresponding references in FORTRAN or PL/I, since the subscripts I,J, and K may be scalars, vectors, or arrays. This paper contains a discussion of array handling in APL and indicated how efficient subscripts of a general form can be implemented on an interpreter.

Hauck, E. A., B. A. Dent, *The Burroughs' B6500/B7500 Stack Mechanism,* AFIPS Conference Proceedings, Vol. 32 (SJCC, 1968), Washington: Thompson Book Co., 1968, pp. 245–251.

Hellerman H., "Addressing multidimensional arrays," *CACM,* Vol. 5, No. 4, Apr. 1962, pp. 205–207.

This paper shows that the problem of mapping a dimensional space into the linear space of a machine is computationally equivalent to the conversion of a number from a fixed- to a mixed-radix number system.

Henhapl, W., "A storage model derived from axioms," *Technical Report,* TR 25.100, Vienna: IBM Laboratory, Sept. 1969.

Presents an implementable model for storage structure, storage mapping, and storage management and demonstrates that this model satisfies the storage axioms proposed in a formal definition (the ULD) of PL/I.

Hill, V., H. Langmaack, H. R. Schwarz, G. Seegmuller, *Efficient Handling of Subscripted Variables in ALGOL 60 Compilers,* Proc. Symbolic Languages in Data Processing, New York: Gordon and Breach, 1962, pp. 331–340.

Hoare, C. A. R., "Record handling," F. Genuys (ed.), *Programming Languages* (NATO Summer School, Villard-de-Lans), New York: Academic Press, 1967.

Hoare, C. A. R., "Notes on data structuring," (in) *Structured Programming,* APIC Studies in Data Processing, No. 8, New York: Academic Press, 1972.

An extensive article, providing an abstract theory of data types and data structuring. The paper concludes with a series of axioms for data types which might form the basis for program proofs.

Hoffman, S. A., "Data structures that generalize rectangular arrays," *Proc. SJCC,* Vol. 21, May 1962, pp. 325–333.

A generalization of arrays, and a means of specifying them by *descriptors* are presented. Reference expressions which allow these structures to be retrieved from storage and a storage mapping function are defined.

Holt, Anatol W., *et al.,* "Information System Theory Project, Final Report," *Technical Report,* RADC-TR-68-305, Clearinghouse AD 676972, Sept. 1968.

An important but difficult report on a project to clarify the precise description and efficient implementation of data structures. The project was one of the first to use a form of systems modeling and notation known as "Petri nets."

Iliffe, J. K., "The use of the Genie system in numerical calculation," (in) R. Goodman (ed.), *Annual Review in Automatic Programming, Vol. 2,* Pergamon Press, 1961, pp. 1–28.

The first, and one of the clearest, expositions of Iliffe's approach to system design.

... the use of a hierarchy of definition sets in Genie is its key feature, leading to the continuous evaluation principle, to the definition of *context,* and the debugging and symbolic correction schemes.

The paper includes a discussion of *codewords* as used in implementing arrays in the Genie system and subsequently expanded in *Basic Machine Principles.*

Iliffe, J. K., J. G. Jodeit, "A dynamic storage allocation scheme," *Computer Journal,* Vol. 5, No. 3, Oct. 1962, pp. 200–209.

An early description of a dynamic storage allocation system involving the use of codewords. The system described, implemented on the RICE University computer, allows generalized arrays to be defined and operated upon. An "array" includes program, vector, matrix, and more general structures. The use of codewords allows the distinction between compilation and interpretation to be less clearly embodied in the system design.

Iliffe, J. K., *Basic Machine Principles,* 2nd ed., London: Macdonald, 1972.

d'Imperio, M. E., "Data structures and their representation in storage," (in) *Annual Review in Automatic Programming, Vol. 5,* Halpern and Shaw (eds.), Elmsford, N.Y.: Pergamon Press, 1969.

Iverson, K. E., *A Programming Language,* New York: John Wiley, 1962.

Jodeit, J. G., "Storage organization in programming systems," *CACM,* Vol. 11, No. 11, Nov. 1968, pp. 741–746.

Johnson, L. R., "On operand structure, representation, storage, and search," *IBM Research Report,* RC-603, 1961.

Johnson, L. R., *System Structure in Data, Programs, and Computers,* Englewood Cliffs, N.J.: Prentice-Hall, 1970.

This presents an interesting description of many aspects of structure in computing. The chapters on data structures and tree structures are particularly valuable since Johnson worked on these with Iverson during the development of APL. Later chapters deal with task sequencing and language translation; they have interesting historical details but lack the technical depth of the earlier chapters.

Kain, R. Y., "Block structures, indirect addressing and garbage collection," *CACM*, Vol. 12, No. 7, Jul. 1969, pp. 395–398.

Kerr, R., G. M. Birtwistle, "SIMULA and application packages" (in) D. J. Evans (ed.), *SOFTWARE 71*, London, Transcripta Books, 1971.

Kilburn, T., D. J. Howarth, R. B. Payne, F. H. Sumner, "The Manchester University Atlas operating system. Part I: internal organization," *Computer Journal,* Vol. 4, No. 3, Oct. 1961, pp. 222–225.

Kilburn, T., D. B. G. Edwards, M. J. Lanigan, F. J. Sumner, "One-level storage system," *IEEE Trans. EC II,* Vol. 2, 1962, pp. 223–235, reproduced in: *Computer Structures—Readings and Examples,* G. G. Bell and A. Newell (eds.), New York: McGraw-Hill, 1971.

Knuth, D. E., *The Art of Computer Programming: Vol. 1, Fundamental Algorithms,* Reading, Mass.: Addison-Wesley, 1968.
> Chapter 2—Information Structures—is the size of a book in itself (237 pages) and contains extensive descriptions of lists, trees, multilinked structures, and dynamic storage allocation. There is valuable material on the implementation of data structures.

Lambird, R. J., "String enhancements to ANSI standard FORTRAN," *SIGPLAN Notices,* Vol. 6, No. 1, Jan. 1971, pp. 5–12; Vol. 6, No. 6, Jul. 1971, pp. 10–22; Vol. 6, No. 10, Nov. 1971, pp. 60–65.
> A well-written paper, explaining the reasons for adding string-handling facilities to FORTRAN and indicating some of the difficulties of achieving a consistent and satisfactory design.

Laurance, N., "A compiler language for data structures," *Proc. ACM 23rd Nat. Conference,* 1968, pp. 387–394.

Lawson, H. W., "PL/I list processing," *CACM,* Vol. 10, No. 6, June 1967, pp. 358–367.

Lukaszewicz, L., "EOL—a symbol manipulation language," *Comp. J.,* Vol. 10, May 1967, pp. 53–59.

Lynch, M. F., J. M. Harrison, W. G. Town, *Computer Handling of Chemical Structure Information,* London: Macdonald; New York: American Elsevier, 1971.
> The large amount of structural information handled by the chemical industry has fostered several advanced systems of data-structure handling. This monograph usefully summarizes this work.

MacLaren, M. D., "Data matching, data alignment, and structure mapping in PL/I," *SIGPLAN Notices,* Vol. 5, No. 12, Dec. 1970, pp. 30–43.
> This paper discusses the interaction between language features—in this case the design of the *record structure* in PL/I—and the resulting implementation standard. This is one of the few papers, apart from detailed compiler specifications, giving a general discussion of the decisions which need to be made in compiler implementation. Five algorithms for PL/I structure mapping are presented.

Madnick, S. E., "String processing techniques," *CACM,* Vol. 10, No. 7, July 1967, pp. 420–424.

Margolin, B. H., R. B. Parmelee, M. Schatzoff, "Analysis of free-storage algorithms," *IBM Systems Journal,* Vol. 10, No. 4, 1971, pp. 283–304.

Presents an algorithm for the management of free storage in a time-sharing system; this algorithm makes use of observed patterns of usage of different block sizes. Experiments showed a reduction of time spent in the supervisor mode by factors of 7 or 8 to 1.

Markov, A. A., *"The Theory of Algorithms,"* English translation published by Israel Program for Scientific Translations, Jerusalem, 1961.

Martin, R. S., J. H. Wilkinson, "Symmetric decomposition of positive definite band matrices," *Numerische Mathematik,* Vol. 7, 1965, pp. 355–361.

McCarthy, J., "Recursive functions of symbolic expressions and their computation by machine. Part I," *CACM,* Vol. 3, No. 4, Apr. 1960, pp. 184–195.

A famous paper which introduced the LISP programming system and, with it, many new and fundamental ideas in programming. (Part II of this paper has never appeared.)

McCarthy, J., "A basis for a mathematical theory of computation," (in) *Computer Programming and Formal Systems,* P. Braffort & D. Hirshberg (eds.), Amsterdam: North-Holland, 1963.

McCarthy, J., *et al., LISP 1.5 Programmer's Manual,* Cambridge, Mass.: M.I.T. Press, 1962.

Mealy, G. H., *Another look at data,* Proc. FJCC, Vol. 31, New York: Academic Press, Nov. 1967, pp. 525–534.

Milner, R., "String handling in ALGOL," *Computer Journal,* Vol. 10, No. 4, Feb. 1968, pp. 321–324.

Minker, Jack, "An overview of associative or content-addressable memory systems and a KWIC index to the literature: 1956–1970," *Computing Reviews,* Vol. 12, No. 10, Oct. 1971, pp. 453–504.

A review and an extensive bibliography (over 700 items). Many of the techniques involved are hardware techniques. In software, the work of Feldman and Rovner is specially cited in the review.

More, T., "Axioms and theorems for a theory of arrays," *IBM Journal of Research and Development,* Vol. 17, No. 2, Mar. 1973, pp. 135–175.

A theoretical treatment of arrays in which an axiomatic theory similar to that for sets is developed. APL is used as a starting point for the theory, and APL programs are used in checking the consistency of the axiomatic system.

Newell, A., F. M. Tonge, "An Introduction to Information Processing Language V," *CACM,* Vol. 3, No. 4, Apr. 1960, pp. 205–211.

Newell, A., *et al., Information-Processing-Language-V Manual,* Englewood Cliffs, N.J.: Prentice-Hall, 1965.

Perlis, A. J., C. Thornton, "Symbol manipulation by threaded lists," *CACM,* Vol. 3, No. 4, Apr. 1960, p. 195ff.

Phillips, J. R., H. C. Adams, "Dynamic partitioning for array languages," *CACM,* Vol. 15, No. 12, Dec. 1972, pp. 1023–1032.

Describes the techniques used in a language for array processing, UL/2. This language allows various partitions of rectangular arrays to be defined. The boundaries of these partitions need not be fixed but can be varied during the course of a computation. Array control information is held in the form of dynamic tree structures.

Pyle, I. C., "Character manipulation in FORTRAN," *CACM*, Vol. 5, No. 8, Aug. 1962, pp. 432-3.

Raphael, B., D. G. Bobrow, L. Feir, J. W. Young, "A brief survey of computer languages for symbolic and algebraic manipulation," D. G. Bobrow (ed.), *Symbol Manipulation Languages and Techniques*, Amsterdam: North-Holland, 1968.

A feature classification of 18 different languages for symbol manipulation.

Reinfelds, J., "A concept by concept description of the AMTRAN language," *SIGPLAN Notices*, Vol. 6, No. 11, Nov. 1971, pp. 32-59.

AMTRAN is a language intended for "scientists with some knowledge of numerical analysis or statistics, but no background in computer sciences." The basic data type is the *array* which may be created dynamically be concatenation. Greater emphasis than usual in mathematical languages is placed on two-dimensional layout.

Reynolds, J. C., "GEDANKEN—a simple, typeless language based on the principle of completeness and on the reference concept," *CACM*, Vol. 13, No. 5, May 1970, pp. 308-319.

In this (experimental) language, all compound data structures are treated as functions. The objection is that any computing process which accepts a particular data structure will accept any logically equivalent structure regardless of its internal representation.

Roberts, A. E., "A general formulation of storage allocation," *CACM*, Vol. 4, No. 10, Oct. 1961, pp. 419-420.

A brief formal statement of the problem of running large programs in a finite storage space. The paper is simply an exercise in formal description. No results are given.

Rohl, J. S., G. Cordingley, "List processing facilities in Atlas Autocode," *Computer Journal*, Vol. 13, No. 1, Feb. 1970, pp. 20-24.

The functions provided are: **head, tail, join,** predicates to test for **atom, number, empty, equal,** and some basic I/O for lists.

Rosenberg, A. L., "Addressable data graphs," *Technical Report RC3346*, IBM Reasearch, Yorktown Heights, May 1971.

Considers the class of data graphs implementable by relative addressing in terms of two equivalent uniformities, *rootedness* and *addressability*.

Rosenberg, A. L., "Data graphs and addressing schemes," *Journal of Computer and System Sciences*, Vol. 5, No. 3, June 1971, pp. 193-238.

A data graph is, roughly speaking, a data structure without the data elements. That is, it consists of the linkages in a data structure. This paper presents a model for data graphs which will enable a study of representation and accessing methods to be made. The paper discusses the conditions for relative addressing and relocatable data structures.

Ross, D. T., "Introduction to software engineering with the AED-O language," *Report ESL-R-405* M.I.T. DSR Project No. 71425, M.I.T., 1969.

A report on the AED-O language, developed by Ross as part of the Computer-Aided Design Project. The word *plex* is defined as the *amalgam* of data, structure and algorithm—it is one of Ross's valuable insights that these three aspects of computing are woven together inseparably.

AED provides a POINTER data type and a means of defining elements of lists containing many data types (called *beads*). There is a function, LOC, for obtaining the address of a variable, and a means of referencing data pointed at by a pointer variable: A(P). AED contained an early form of some of the ideas later incorporated in PL/I as pointers and based variables.

Sammet, J. E., *Programming Languages: History and Fundamentals*, Englewood Cliffs, N.J.: Prentice-Hall, 1969.

Satterthwait, A. C., "Programming languages for computational linguistics," (in) F. L. Alt, M. Rubinoff (eds.), *Advances in Computers, Vol. 7,* New York: Academic Press, 1966, pp. 209–238.

Discusses COMIT, SNOBOL, the Wayne Interpretive system, MIMIC and LRS. The most extensive treatment is given to COMIT—a complete program and sample results.

Sattley, K., "Allocation of storage for arrays in ALGOL 60," *CACM,* Vol. 4, No. 1, Jan. 1961, pp. 60–65.

One of three papers from an early American school of ALGOL implementors (the other papers are by Ingerman and by Feurzig and Irons). Discusses **own** arrays and the impact of recursive procedures. An early reference to the term "dope vector."

Schorr, H., W. M. Waite, "An efficient machine-independent procedure for garbage collection in various list structures," *CACM,* Vol. 10. No. 8, Aug. 1967, pp. 501–506.

Schwartz, J. T., "The SETL Language and Examples of its use," Courant Institute, New York University, 1973.

SETL is a programming language based on the mathematical theory of sets. The objective of the project, under development at the Courant Institute, New York University, is both to improve the expressive power of languages by appealing to well-established mathematical principles, and to employ the latest techniques of implementation and optimization to ensure adequate efficiency.

Shaw, C. J., "JOVIAL—A programming language for real-time command systems," R. Goodman (ed.), *Annual Review in Automatic Programming, Vol. 3,* 1963, pp. 53–119.

An important language, derived from the early ALGOL 60 design, widely used in military applications in the United States.

Shoffner, M. G., P. J. Brown, "A suggested method of making fuller use of strings in ALGOL 60," *CACM,* Vol. 6, No. 4, Apr. 1963, pp. 169–171.

Smith, J. W., "JOSS-II: Design Philosophy," *Annual Review in Automatic Programming Vol. 6,* Pergamon Press, 1970, pp. 183–256.

Standish, T. A., *A Data Definition Facility for Programming Languages,* Ph.D. Thesis, Carnegie Technical Report, 1967.

Strachey, C., "Towards a formal semantics," (in) *Proc. IFIP Working Conference on Formal Language Description,* North Holland, 1966.

Tou, J. T., P. Wegner (eds.), "Data Structures in Programming Languages," (Proceedings of a symposium, University of Florida, Feb. 1971, *ACM SIGPLAN Notices,* Vol. 6, No. 2, Feb. 1971.

This entire issue of *SIGPLAN Notices* is of the greatest importance to those concerned with programming languages and the theory of data structures. Papers by Wegner, Walk and Berry are of special interest.

Walk, K., "Modeling of storage properties of higher-level languages," (in) *SIGPLAN Notices,* Vol. 6, No. 2, Feb. 1971, pp. 146–170.

A comparative discussion of some high-level languages in terms of underlying storage models. A simple model, based on ALGOL 60, is introduced and shown to be inadequate for more complex languages. The relation of *independence* is introduced, and the basic operations on storage, allocation freeing, and assignment are defined.

Wegner, P., *Programming Languages, Information Structures, and Machine Organization,* New York: McGraw-Hill, 1968.

Wegner, P., "Data structure models for programming languages," (in) J. T. Tou, P. Wegner (eds.), "Data structures in Programming Languages," *ACM SIGPLAN Notices,* Vol. 6, No. 2, Feb. 1971, pp. 1–54.

A survey of data-structure models for programming languages. The approach is mathematically based but not excessively formal and there are valuable discussions on the importance of data structures and models of computations. The languages discussed include those, like PL/I, with an underlying storage concept and the problem of what Wegner calls the "dangling reference"—a pointer left referencing a location no longer occupied by the data.

Wegstein, J. H., W. W. Youden, "A string language for symbol manipulation based on ALGOL 60," *CACM,* Vol. 5, No. 2, Jan. 1962, pp. 54–61.

Weizenbaum, J., "Symmetric list processor," *CACM,* Vol. 6, No. 9, Sept. 1963, pp. 524–544.

An important paper describing a list processing language, SLIP, "embedded" in FORTRAN. SLIP is descended from earlier languages FLPL and IPL-V and uses "threaded" lists as advocated by Perlis, *et al.* (1960). A FORTRAN history of SLIP is included in the paper.

Weissman, C., *LISP 1.5 Primer,* Belmont, Calif.: Dickenson Publishing Company, 1967.

A good tutorial exposition of LISP. Without sacrificing mathematical exactness, this book takes the reader through the various functions of LISP, giving reasons for their introduction and graded examples in their use.

van Wijngaarden, A., B. J. Mallioux, J. E. L. Peck, C. H. A. Koster, "Report on the algorithmic language ALGOL 68," *Numer. Math.* Vol. 14, 1969, pp. 79–218.

ALGOL 68 contains extensive data-structuring facilities, including strings, arrays, and nonhomogeneous structures. It also contains methods by which the programmer can construct his own form of linked structures, based on the data type, **reference.** This is the reference manual for the language, and the reader is warned that it requires considerable effort to master.

Wilkes, M. V., "Lists and why they are useful," *Computer Journal,* Vol. 7, No. 4, Jan. 1965, pp. 278–281.

An expository paper on the underlying processes of a list processing system.

Williams, R., "A survey of data structures for computer graphics systems," *Computer Surveys,* Vol. 3, No. 1, Mar. 1971, pp. 1–21.

Willoughby, R. A., "A survey of sparse matrix technology," *IBM Research Report,* RC 3872, IBM Yorktown Heights, May 1972.

Windley, P. F., "Trees, forests, and rearranging," *Computer Journal,* Vol. 3, 1960, pp. 84–88.

Wirth, N., C. A. R. Hoare, "A contribution to the development of ALGOL," *CACM,* Vol. 9, No. 6, June 1966, pp. 413–432.

An important paper, containing a discussion of many of the principles of ALGOL and suggesting extensions and improvements. These have been implemented in the form of "ALGOL W." The extensions proposed include the data structure of type **record,** an access variable of type **reference,** and the concept of a **record class.**

Woodward, P. M., D. P. Jenkins, "Atoms and lists," *Computer Journal,* Vol. 4, No. 1, Apr. 1961, pp. 47–53.

An exposition of LISP, which helped to get list processing ideas known in a wider circle.

Woodward, P. M., "List programming," (in) L. Fox (ed.), *Advances in Programming and Nonnumerical Computation,* Elmsford, N.Y.: Pergamon Press, 1966.

Yershov, A. P., *Programming Programme for the BESM Computer,* Elmsford, N.Y.: Pergamon Press, 1959.

Early mention of the use of *stacks* in compilation.

Yershov, A. P., G. I. Kozhukhin, U. M. Voloskin, *Input Language for Automatic Programming Systems,* New York: Academic Press, 1963.

The title refers to a source language for BESM machines in the spirit of ALGOL. Additional features were added to make the language more attractive to mathematicians—these include array expressions and dynamic arrays whose bounds and **dimensions** can be changed during execution.

Yngve, V. H. (ed.), *COMIT Programmers' Reference Manual,* Cambridge, Mass.: M.I.T. Press, 1961.

Yngve, V. H., "COMIT," *CACM,* Vol. 6, No. 3, Mar. 1963, pp. 83–84.

A brief description, as part of a discussion on the documentation of programming languages. COMIT was designed specifically for linguistic research, and some of its ideas were later incorporated in SNOBOL.

Zienkiewicz, O. C., *The Finite Element Method in Structural and Continuous Mechanics*, New York: McGraw-Hill, 1967.

By splitting up continuous structures into "finite elements" matrix methods may be used for calculations that would otherwise require extensive analysis.

EXERCISES

8.1 Describe three uses for *stacks* in programming. Show how stacks may be implemented in languages with arrays but without stacks. What limitations may have to be imposed on the use of such stacks?

8.2 Examine a sample of programs using arrays and analyze the use of subscripts in array references. How many of these subscripts are:

- simple names,
- expressions which can be put in the FORTRAN form c∗v+k;
- more general expressions?

8.3 In a certain machine, the maximum number of elements in any dimension of an array is not allowed to exceed a certain size, N, this being the number which is conveniently representable in a certain field width on the machine.

Show how more than N elements can be contained in a structure by using a matrix, rather than a vector.

8.4 Show the correspondence between the elements of a vector and the corresponding elements of a matrix. Generalize this to show how an N-dimensional structure can be represented as an (N + 1)-dimensional structure.

8.5 In the proceedings of a conference on techniques for handling sparse matrices (Willoughby, 1969), Dr. W. Givens gave the following suggestions for hardware instructions which would help in matrix operations:

CLEAR TO ZERO   (given a first and last address)

LOAD NEXT NON–ZERO   (search for the next nonzero element and make its address available)

FIND THE LARGEST   (find the largest element in an array. or part of an array)

Show how each of these may be programmed in a high-level language.

8.6 Describe the differences

- in use
- in implementation

between the elements A[1], A[2], ... in the array A[1:10], and the elements A1, A2, ... in the structure:

1 A,
2 A1...   *A10*
2 A2...   *A10*
   etc   *A10*

8.7 Discuss the problems of allowing the valid subscripts of an array to take non-consecutive values, e.g., A(2), A(4), A(6), ... What applications would there be for this sort of array? What implementation problems would exist?

8.8 Describe the means of sharing storage in FORTRAN and in COBOL. What additional storage sharing methods were introduced in PL/I?

9
Expressions and Assignment

9.1 INTRODUCTION

To many people, the automatic translation of arithmetic expressions is one of the most impressive achievements of systems programming. The transformation of a complex formula of physics or engineering into a sequence of primitive machine instructions shows dramatically a computer's capability for the analysis and manipulation of symbols. Expression evaluation has also provided one of the most fruitful topics for research in programming.

Several of the earliest programming languages were able to evaluate mathematical expressions. In Europe, Ruthishauser (1952) and, in the United States, Laning and Zierler (1954) produced some of the first such systems. Later, in 1957, the evaluation of expressions was a prominent objective of FORTRAN, as shown in the derivation of its name from FORmula TRANslator (Backus, 1957). Other early systems including MATHMATIC, AUTOCODE, etc, also allowed the user to write expressions in mathematical notation.

In looking back at these pioneering efforts, we must remember that machines of that period were more primitive than those of today, and that the range of programming support then available was very limited. The ability to write programs or parts of programs directly in mathematical notation was a notable advance in technology and led to a mood of optimism regarding what was then called "Automatic Programming." (See, for example, Goodman, 1960. This describes an early conference in Brighton, England, where much of the discussion was devoted to high-level language translators, with a strong emphasis on formula translation.)

Although the mechanical translation of expressions into machine code relieves the programmer of much of the difficulty and tedium of coding, it hardly qualifies as a significant approach to automatic programming today. Most evidence on the actual use of programming languages shows that an "average" arithmetic expression is no more complex than

variable + constant.

(For examples, see the surveys on the use of high-level languages in Chapter 3.)

In a deeper sense, however, there is a close relationship between expressions and programs. To see this, we must consider expressions of a more general form than the familiar arithmetic expression. With this more general view, a complete program may be represented as an expression, in which operators include elements such as:

if

go to

assign

and delimiters include bracketing symbols such as:

begin . . . . . **end**

do . . . . **end**

This view has been developed in theoretical studies of programming based on Church's Lambda calculus, a mathematical formalism which was introduced as a means of studying the logical properties of functions and their evaluation. Perfectly general calculations can be expressed in the Lambda calculus—just as they can with a Turing machine. A *computation*, that is, the *execution* of a program, is represented by the evaluation of a lambda-expression (see references by Church and Landin in Chapter 5).

It must be emphasized that the relationship between expressions of the Lambda calculus and programs in most current programming languages is rather tenuous, although the concept is an illuminating one. The correspondence is closest in ALGOL (which formed the basis for Landin's work), though, even there, several statements (including assignment and the **go to**) cause difficulty.

Like other parts of programming languages, expressions have their own structure. Compared with most other parts of languages, this structure is simple and regular. It is recursive in nature—simple expressions may be combined into a more complex expression, which in turn may form the basis for still more complex expressions, and so on. Whatever the size of the expression, the rules of formation remain the same, giving the regularity of form which makes expressions amenable to mechanical processing.

In this chapter, we first consider simple expressions containing one operator and one operand, such as

$$A + B$$
$$T > Q$$

The syntax is simple, although there are several interesting semantic problems, which are discussed in the first part of the chapter. Later it is shown how simple expressions are combined to form general expressions, which may be of arbitrary complexity.

9.2 THE HISTORY OF ARITHMETIC OPERATIONS

From the volatile world of programming languages, the symbols used in mathematics have an appearance of great stability. However, although standard notations for elementary mathematical operations are now widely accepted, they took many centuries to evolve, and remnants of rival and outmoded notations still persist in text and reference books. An account of their history is given in a standard reference by Cajori (1928). (See especially Volume I for the history of operators for simple arithmetic notations. These operators are found in most programming languages.)

The following notes on the history of commonly used arithmetic symbols should give an idea of the length of time it has taken to develop some of our elementary mathematical notations, and perhaps temper the impatience of those involved in standardizing programming languages.

9.2.1 Addition and Subtraction

Early notations for addition include a slanting line / and the use of juxtaposition (that is, a + b was denoted by ab). The signs + and − came into use in the later part of the 15th century and were used in print by Widman in 1489, while other signs such as p and m were used in the 16th and 17th centuries. For a long time the sign ÷ was used to denote minus, mainly in German, Swiss and Dutch textbooks. This symbol appears frequently up to the 18th century.

Several writers have questioned the commonly accepted use of the signs + and − in a double sense, both to indicate the operations of addition and subtraction and to denote that a number is positive or negative. Among the proposed notations for denoting *signed numbers* mentioned by Cajori are the following:

a bar over the character: ā for minus a

inverting the letter: ɐ

⊢ for positive ⊣ for negative numbers

the *credit* and *debit* signs used in accounting

It is interesting to note that Iverson in APL uses a high-level sign to indicate a negative number:

$$\overline{1},\ \overline{2},\ \text{(etc.).}$$

9.2.2   Multiplication

The St. Andrew's cross ($\times$) was used in *Clavis mathematica* by W. Oughtred (1631). Cajori considers that Oughtred was also responsible for an earlier use (in the form of the letter X) in 1618. The use of the cross sign was closely bound up with the representation of *algorithms* for doing problems in proportion, and it is doubtful if these can be regarded as indicating the use of the sign for the operation of multiplication. Several other notations for multiplication were used, including a rectangle to denote the product of two factors separated by a comma.

$$\square 5 + 4 + 3,\ 7 - 3 : -10, \text{ est } 38$$

meaning,

$$(5 + 4 + 3) \times (7 - 3) - 10 = 38$$

(P. Herigone, *Cursus mathematici* (1644)—see Cajori, page 266).

A six-pointed star ($*$) was used by the Swiss, Johann Heinrich Rahn in *Teutsche Algebra* in 1659 and also by N. Mercator in *Logarithmotechnia* (1668), anticipating the sign used to denote multiplication in FORTRAN, COBOL, PL/I and other languages.

Leibnitz powerfully advocated the use of the dot for multiplication and this notation was widely adopted and is still common.

9.2.3   Division

There have been many notations for division. The most widely used sign today, $\div$, was introduced by Rahn, whose works were translated and published in England, where they were favorably received. The $\div$ sign was adopted in England and the United States, but not in other European countries, where the Leibnitz notation using the colon (:) was most common.

In 1923, the U.S. National Committee on Mathematical Requirements made the following recommendation (Cajori, page 275).

"Since neither $\div$ nor :, as signs of division, plays any part in business life, it seems proper to consider only the needs of algebra, and to make more use of the fractional form and (where the meaning is clear) of the symbol /, and to drop the symbol ÷ in writing algebraic expressions."

As we depart from simple operators to more specialized notations, their history becomes more complex and the patterns of usage less uniform. The fierce debate between Leibnitz and Newton on the notation for differentials shows how much heat can be generated by such arguments. Nearly every mathematical sign we use has a long history of experimentation and controversy, sometimes still in progress.

In programming, there are still many disputes over notations. Some apparent differences in language are simply differences in notation. On the other hand, some crucial differences between languages are obscured by similarities in notation.

One lesson to be learned from the history of mathematics seems to be that we should be cautious about notations which claim to be "natural" to mathematicians, or to any other class of people. No notations are truly natural, and few have attained the degree of universality that allows them to be accepted without question.

9.3　SIMPLE EXPRESSIONS

At first, we define an *expression* informally as an arrangement of references, operators, and brackets, obeying simple syntactic rules which insure that each operator has the appropriate number of operands.

A *reference* is a means of accessing a value, and the means of representing a reference include such forms as the literal, data name, function reference, etc.

Examples

```
10,X, Y(J), P —> T(3), x[a+1],
AMOUNT IN MASTER-RECORD
```

An *operator* is a value-returning function which may be represented by a simple typographic sign.

Examples

```
+, —, **
```

Brackets are typographic signs which mark the boundaries of expressions in character-string text.

Examples

( ) [ ] { }

An expression serves to denote a value and to indicate how it is to be computed. This distinguishes expressions from *statements,* which are usually commands to alter the state of a computation. Expressions may also affect the *program state* (in other words produce side-effects—see Chapter 12) but their main purpose is to define a sequence of operations for computing values.

A *simple expression* consists of two operands and an operator.

Examples

A + B

P > Q

All expressions can be built up from simple expressions of this form.

Operators may be placed next to their operands, their physical juxtaposition indicating the relationship of operator to operand. An operator with one operand (such as the logical operator **not**) is called *unary* or, since it is usually placed in front of the operand, *prefix*. An operator with two operands (such as the arithmetic operator **plus**) is called *binary*. Binary operators such as $+$, $-$, $>$, $<$, etc, which are placed between their two operands, are called *infix* operators.

In APL, the following terminology is used: *monadic,* for unary, *dyadic,* for binary.

In the following sections, we describe various kinds of operators which occur in programming languages. These operators illustrate several problems which arise in evaluating expressions. The problems are first discussed in the context of simple expressions. The extension to general expressions, containing more than one operator, is treated later in the chapter.

9.4   ARITHMETIC OPERATORS

We begin with the most familiar operators, those of common arithmetic. The arithmetic operators *plus, minus, multiply* and *divide* are represented in virtually all programming languages. Most languages also include *exponentiation* as an operator (expressed by $**$ in FORTRAN, COBOL and PL/I and an upward arrow: ↑ in ALGOL).

It might be thought that the design of arithmetic for programming languages would give comparatively few problems. Unfortunately, this is far from being the case. As we have seen in Chapter 7, the numbers we deal with in programming have finite sets of values, each set being distinguished by its *type*. The data types we meet in programming languages (which usually mirror the types available in machines) therefore do not coincide with the numbers of mathematics. This is the main cause of the frequent apparent anomalies that occur in most programming systems.

In elementary mathematics the operations of addition and multiplication are *commutative, associative* and *distributive*. These terms describe certain relationships between the operators and operands of an expression, independently of the actual form of the expression and the values of the data.

For any numbers *a*, *b* and *c*, we can illustrate these laws as follows:

	Addition	*Multiplication*
commutative law	$a + b = b + a$	$a \times b = b \times a$
associative law	$a+(b+c)=(a+b)+c$	$a \times(b \times c)=(a \times b)\times c$
distributive law for multiplication	$a \times(b+c) = a\times b + a\times c$	

The laws can be extended to larger expressions such as $a + b + c + d$, $(a + b)(c + d)(a - b)$, etc. and provide the basis for the methods of simplifying formulas we learn in elementary algebra.

One of the first surprises of computer arithmetic is to discover that the commutative, associative, and distributive laws do not apply as they do in mathematics. In floating-point arithmetic, automatic shifting and scaling may result in loss of accuracy, the magnitude of which may depend on the order of the operations. In fixed-point arithmetic, the magnitude of an intermediate result may exceed the storage space available for it. Sometimes such loss of accuracy can be reduced or eliminated by a rearrangement of the order of a computation.

Examples

In evaluating the expression

$a + b - c$

it may be more accurate to do the subtraction first.

$a - c + b$

For example, assuming left-to-right evaluation, $(99 + 1 - 98)$ needs three digits for its intermediate value, whereas $(99 - 98 + 1)$ needs only one.

In the example below, for simplicity, we use a restricted form of decimal floating-point in which

- an exponent has two digits
- a fraction has an integer and four decimal places.

In this system, 123.45 is represented as 1.2345E2 and 0.0012345 is represented as 1.2345E−3.

Now suppose that

$$a = 17298 \quad \text{i.e. } 1.7298E4$$
$$b = -17297 \text{ i.e. } -1.7297E4$$
$$c = 0.66 \quad \text{i.e. } 6.6E-1$$

Then

$$a + (b + c) = 1.7298E4 + (-1.7297E4 + 6.6E-1)$$
$$= 1.7298E4 + (-1.7297E4 + 0.000066E4)$$
$$= 1.7298E4 + (-1.7296E4)$$
$$= 0.0002E4$$
$$= 2.0000E0$$
$$(a + b) + c = (1.7298E4 - 1.7297E4) + 6.6E-1$$
$$= (0.0001E4) + 6.6E-1$$
$$= 1.0000E0 + 6.6E-1$$
$$= 1.0000E0 + 0.66E0$$
$$= 1.6600E0$$

The fact that the elementary laws of operator association are not followed makes it necessary for programming languages to be more explicit about the order of evaluation of unbracketed expressions than is usual in mathematics.

The three numeric data types of main interest in programming languages are *integers, floating-point* numbers, and *fixed-point* numbers. The arithmetic operations on these numbers are considered next.

9.5 FIXED-POINT OPERATORS

Fixed-point numbers are similar to integers in representing a set of values uniformly over a range. In contrast with integers, there are *two* distinguishing numeric quantities associated with each fixed-point value, a precision and a scale factor. The *precision* of a number is defined as the total number of digits needed for its representation; the *scale factor* as the number of digits needed for its fractional part. These two quantities make fixed-point arithmetic rather more complex than integer arithmetic.

At first we assume there is no upper limit to the size of number that can be represented. A scheme for adding or subtracting fixed-point numbers is shown in Fig. 9.1. The decimal (or binary) point is aligned and, in the result field, the number of digits each side of the point must be large enough to accommodate the larger of the fields of the two operands. To allow for a possible carry from the left-most place, the width of the result field must be one digit more than the extreme width of the two operands.

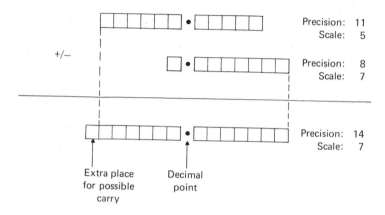

Fig. 9.1 Schematic diagram showing field sizes for accurate addition or subtraction. In the result field, the scale is the larger scale of the two operands. The precision is adjusted to allow a possible "carry" from the addition or subtraction operation.)

A multiplication scheme is shown in Fig. 9.2. Here, the total precision needed is the sum of the precisions of the operands; the scale factor, the sum of the two scale factors.

Now we consider a more realistic situation in which there is a limit to the maximum size of a fixed-point number. Each arithmetic operation may cause the result to "grow" and it is easy to construct quite modest expressions whose values will exceed apparently generous limits. In the following, we assume that the characteristics of the result of an expression are completely determined by the operands of the expression itself.

Suppose that N is the number of digits in the largest number which can be represented in the system. (It is more convenient to deal with the size of the field expressed as a certain number of digits than with the maximum absolute value, even though the value might be a more useful measure from a user's point of view.) We first consider the modified rules for fixed-point precision and scale factor when the maximum field width is N. Any

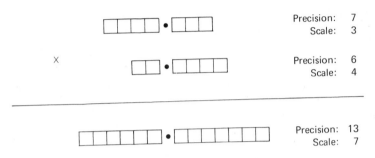

Fig. 9.2 Schematic diagram showing field sizes for accurate fixed-point multiplication. In the result field, the precision is the sum of the precisions of the two operands and the scale is the sum of their scales.

rule we may devise has to be such that the analysis needed to establish the number of shifts needed for decimal point alignment can be made *statically* by a compiler, from the declared precisions and scale factors. (Otherwise, we would merely duplicate the effect of floating-point arithmetic, in which shifting depends on the data values.)

An extreme view would be to disallow any computation whose result might potentially exceed N. Provided this was the case (and it could obviously be checked by a compiler) we would know that the result of $(A + B)$ could accurately be represented in the system.

This approach might be feasible for some computations, particularly for data-processing applications in which numeric values are updated by simple increments. However, as soon as we use operations which cause values to grow rapidly, such as multiplication or (more rapidly still) exponentiation, we can see that a practical solution cannot be found by constraining the values of the data or the operations that can be carried out. We must expect that the result of some expressions will exceed the required space and that possible truncation may occur—the task of the language designer is to find the most useful approach for controlling the loss of information this will entail.

We consider two approaches yielding maximum *significance* and maximum *accuracy*, respectively.

In the first, we would make sure that if truncation had to occur, it would involve loss of digits from the least significant end of the result only. To see the effect of this, we would take the ideal results given by Figs. 9.1 and 9.2 and select the N most significant (i.e., left-most) digits for preservation, truncating the extra digits where necessary from the right-hand end of the results.

In avoiding the loss of significant numbers, this scheme involves a potential loss of accuracy in all results. However, in using this approach we would lose the advantage of fixed-point working (its accuracy when the working space is adequate), without the advantages of floating-point flexibility.

The other approach, which places greater emphasis on the *accuracy* of the result, is to select the N least-significant digits in the result, truncating digits from the left-hand end of the result where necessary. (See Fig. 9.3.)

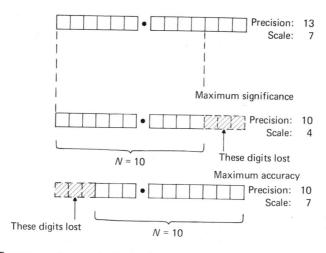

Fig. 9.3 Two truncation methods for finite fixed-point arithmetic. The true result of an arithmetic operation has a precision of 13 and scale of 7. Methods shown here are for a machine with a maximum word size of 10.

If we adopt the second approach, we have to decide what to do when a result does not fit into the result field. Since this is data dependent, it can only be detected during execution of a program. Detection is simple, however, since it merely implies the detection of a carry into the critical digit position.

We now consider a different approach, which makes use of information about the *target* of a given expression. Consider the statement:

```
C = A + B
```

or, in COBOL notation,

```
ADD A,B GIVING C.
```

It is obvious that the evaluation of $(A + B)$ may be influenced if the nature of the field C is known during evaluation. For example, in certain machines the addition may be carried out in the field C, avoiding the need to set up a separate working register.

This form of expression evaluation, which we may call "target-sensitive," is most suited to languages in which expressions only occur in certain contexts, such as in assignment statements. It is less appropriate for languages which allow expressions in any value-denoting position, for in some of these contexts the characteristics of a target may not be known.

It can be seen that unless a very unrelenting attitude towards field sizes is taken by a compiler when the source language is translated, the accuracy of fixed-point arithmetic cannot be guaranteed for all values of data and we are faced with detecting those cases in which information may be lost during the course of computation. Both COBOL and PL/I define means of detecting and optionally correcting data-dependent losses of accuracy.

9.6   FIXED-POINT ARITHMETIC IN COBOL AND PL/I

The rules of arithmetic are not completely specified in the ANSI COBOL Standard. However, COBOL is essentially a fixed-point language and is subject to the considerations reviewed above. The capability for writing arithmetic expressions in COBOL is comparatively limited and is mainly restricted to computational statements such as ADD, SUBTRACT, MULTIPLY, DIVIDE, and COMPUTE. In these statements, there is a well-defined target, which influences the computation.

In general, COBOL expression evaluation provides for maximum accuracy. There are two optional clauses which can be appended to any arithmetic statement—SIZE ERROR and ROUNDED. These specify actions to be carried out at execution time.

SIZE ERROR

This is the name of a condition which arises if the value of an operation cannot be stored in the field allocated for its target. In the case of ADD and SUBTRACT statements, the SIZE ERROR condition is only raised by the final answer; in the case of MULTIPLY and DIVIDE it is raised for intermediate results as well.

Suppose a SIZE ERROR option has been given and the size condition arises during a computation. Then, although the result may have been developed in the target variable, its value must be restored—this is one of the requirements of the SIZE ERROR condition. It does not apply if the clause is not used, in which cases unpredictable results may arise.

ROUNDED

The ROUNDED clause may be used on any arithmetic statement to ensure that the final result assigned to the target is rounded. Otherwise, results may be truncated, although the details of the method of truncation are not specified in the standard.

The treatment of expressions in PL/I is different, since each expression has an inherent type, including its precision and scale factor. This type is derived from the types of operands in the expression and does not depend, as in COBOL, on the type of a target for the expression.

A central factor in PL/I arithmetic is the value N, the number of digits in the largest conveniently representable number of the implementation. In practice, this is determined by the word size or register size of the machine on which it is implemented. The recognition of this number N overcomes one of the trickier parts of a language specification, particularly when the language is intended for a variety of machines. The variety of word sizes, number systems, rounding algorithms, etc., in different machines makes it difficult to achieve a uniform approach to arithmetic. Standard languages have often avoided this problem by leaving arithmetic essentially undefined. In order to solve at least part of this problem in PL/I, the word length of the machine has been brought into the language specification, making it possible to characterize an implementation of PL/I arithmetic by the single parameter N.

If we have two operands whose precisions and scale factors are $\{p_1, s_1\}$ and $\{p_2, s_2\}$ then the results are defined as follows:

Addition and subtraction

precision: $\min\{N, \max(p_1 - s_1, p_2 - s_2) + \max(s_1, s_2) + 1\}$

scale: $\max(s_1, s_2)$

Multiplication

precision: $\min(N, p_1 + p_2 + 1)$

scale: $s_1 + s_2$

Examining these results, we see that they provide the maximum accuracy results from Fig. 9.3. It will be seen that the precision for fixed-point multiplication is 1 greater than that suggested by the scheme illustrated. The extra digit is needed in PL/I arithmetic for the multiplication of COMPLEX fixed-point numbers, where there is a further addition which might bring a carry into the next position. Although not needed for REAL arithmetic, the extra precision is included for the sake of simplicity in the arithmetic rules.

As with COBOL, PL/I has means of detecting losses of accuracy when a result will not fit in the storage allocated for it. There are two PL/I *conditions* which may arise during expression evaluation.

FIXEDOVERFLOW

A condition which may arise during fixed-point arithmetic operations if the storage space (of length N digits) is exceeded. There is another condition, SIZE, which is raised by an assignment. Since expressions may be evaluated independently of assignment in PL/I, the two conditions are treated separately. SIZE ERROR in COBOL is an amalgam of FIXEDOVERFLOW and SIZE in PL/I.

ZERODIVIDE

This is treated as a separate condition from the overflow conditions, since it is possible to consider different corrective action if the condition arises. ZERODIVIDE does not distinguish between fixed- and floating-point numbers.

These are the standard rules for fixed arithmetic in PL/I. The language also includes a set of arithmetic built-in functions, which allow fixed-point arithmetic to be carried out to specified precision.

```
ADD(x,y,p,s)
MULTIPLY(x,y,p,s)
DIVIDE(x,y,p,s)
```

These evaluate the prescribed function on the first two arguments, according to the specified precision and scale (*p,s*). The use of these functions allows much greater flexibility than is possible with the standard operators. (Note that there is no SUBTRACT function. Subtraction is carried out by using a negative argument in the ADD function.)

Division

Special problems arise when we consider the operation of division applied to integers and fixed-point numbers. These arise from the nature of division itself, rather than from the fact that it is done on a computer.

For the expressions (a + b), (a − b), and (a × b), in which a and b are integers, the result is itself an integer. The precision needed to represent the result exactly, although greater than that of a or b, is bounded and can be predicted accurately from the precisions of a and b. This is clearly not the case with division. In general we cannot accurately represent the result of a division operation in a finite number of fractional digits—in mathematics we say that division is not *closed* in the field of integers or fixed-point numbers. The rules of fixed-point division are therefore always an interesting part of any language design.

FORTRAN expressions, with the exception of those involving exponentiation, are only defined for operands of the same type, in other words, between *real* and *real,* or *integer* and *integer* values. As might be expected, *real* division gives a *real* result. The rule for FORTRAN *integer* division is starkly simple—the result is the truncated integral value of the quotient. (See 7.1.1.3 of the FORTRAN standard, where this rule is given as part of the rule for assignment.)

Some simple examples show the effect:

$$2/1 \quad = 2$$
$$1/2 \quad = 0$$
$$5/3 \quad = 1$$
$$-3/5 \quad = 0$$
$$16/(-3) = -5$$

The rules for constructing expressions in ALGOL are more liberal than in FORTRAN and expressions of mixed types can be formed. In general, ALGOL follows the rule that results of operations between **integer** and **real** quantities are "promoted" to the type **real.** This approach is one way of obtaining accurate answers to integer divisions. By itself, it is not entirely satisfactory, however, since the **real** type of the result affects other operations in a general expression; this would make it impossible, for example, to carry out integer computations involving division. To meet this need, ALGOL has *two* division operations, represented by the signs / and ÷.

The / operator follows the promotion rule—it is valid for all four combinations of operator (**real/real, real/integer, integer/real, integer/integer**) and always yields a **real** result.

The ÷ operator can only be used for integer operands and yields an integer result, as in FORTRAN integer division. This is described in the ALGOL report (3.3.4.2) as follows.

$$a \div b = sign(a/b) \times entier(abs(a/b))$$

a neat use of the three recommended, noncomputational, standard functions of ALGOL. (The function *entier* is defined below in the section on conversions. The functions *sign* and *abs* respectively return the sign and absolute value of their operands.)

In PL/I, the rules for fixed-point division (which include integer division as a special case) have been one of the most troublesome areas in the design of the language. The rules have been frequently debated, and discussions continued during development of the standard. Let us briefly review some of the problems that arise.

When we allow a fixed-point result from a division operation, we have a range of possible choices in the accuracy with which to hold the result, in contrast with the choice available when only integer or floating-point results are allowed.

Take the simple case of integer division, say 2 divided by 3, and consider a system in which fixed-point numbers may be held to 6 numeric places. The question arises, where do we place the decimal point?

Looking at this operation in isolation, there is no difficulty. We get the greatest accuracy by placing the decimal point to the left of the result, giving six significant places of accuracy. However, problems arise when this result is combined with other numeric values in a larger expression, for example: 20 + (2/3). If we have already used the whole width of storage to hold the result of the division, there is no space for the integers 2 and 0—hence, some form of storage overflow takes place.

The rules for fixed-point division in PL/I are defined in terms of the precisions and scale factors of the two operands. If these are (p_1 , s_1) and (p_2 , s_2), then the precision and scale factor of the result are as follows.

precision : N

scale   : $N - p_1 + s_1 - s_2$

Thus the results of division are always promoted to the maximum precision for the implementation. In the case of integer division, in other words, when s_1 and s_2 are zero, the position of the decimal point in the result depends only on the precision of the first operand.

These rules for fixed-point division, forming part of standard PL/I, are a result of a compromise and have been selected from several possible division rules. They give useful answers in many cases, although there are several particular types of operand for which the results from applying the rules are anomalous. (These largely arise from the promotion of the result to maximum precision.)

Over the long period during which the rules have been debated and alternatives considered, it has been found impossible to derive rules which, while preserving the fixed-point nature of the result, do not give anomalous results in certain cases.

Exponentiation

Exponentiation is included as an operator in many languages, and, like division, it has its own special problems.

The most familiar use of exponentiation is that in which the exponent is an integer, when it may be expressed in terms of multiplication,

e.g., y^3 is equivalent to y × y × y

Integer exponents arise in simple formulas (areas, volumes, weights, etc.), in calculating sums of squares for statistical computations, in approximations to functions (curve fitting), and in many other applications.

An example of a noninteger exponent occurs in calculating the roots of numbers:

$x^{1/2}$ is equivalent to the square root of x,

$x^{1/3}$ is equivalent to the cube root of x, and so on.

Square root provides by far the most common example of the use of a nonintegral exponent, and is used, for example, in statistics, in the solution of differential equations, in problems of surveying, and in navigation.

In mathematics, exponentiation is defined for all real numbers, and also for complex numbers. In the case of nonintegral exponents, the relationship between exponentiation and multiplication breaks down and we have to define the function in a different way. The definition usually adopted is as follows

$$a^b \text{ is defined as } \mathbf{exp}\ (b\ \mathbf{log}\ a)$$

where **exp** and **log** are the exponential and natural logarithmic functions of mathematical analysis. This definition is valid for integer, real, and complex numbers. Since the functions **exp** and **log** are generally included as built-in functions, this formula suggests a technique for implementing the exponentiation operator for nonintegral exponents. However, this would be absurdly longwinded for the most commonly used cases of square and square root. Owing to the complexity of the algorithms needed for **exp** and **log**, the accuracy of the general formula would be inferior to that obtainable by more direct methods.

Here then we have a dilemma, similar to many others which arise in the design of programming languages. For symmetry and generality we may wish to allow the exponentiation operator to apply to operands of all types. For this, a general definition is available and could be used for its computation. However, the most frequent applications of exponentiation are for exponents of a very restricted class, for which direct methods of calculation are both more efficient and more accurate. Several issues are involved, including those of consistency, generality and implementation difficulty.

The problem may be partially solved by treating fractional exponents separately and in particular by providing a built-in function for square root: SQRT(x). There are many fast, accurate algorithms for square roots; and, by making this function accessible by name, the difficulties of recognizing this as a special case are avoided.

The following notes show some other aspects of treating exponentiation.

FORTRAN restricts the types of operand used in exponentiation. Only INTEGER**INTEGER and REAL**REAL or REAL**DOUBLE are allowed in FORTRAN.

ALGOL distinguishes between integer exponent and real exponents. For positive integer exponents, x^i is defined to be equivalent to x multiplied by itself i times, giving a result whose type is the same as x. This allows integer results for integers raised to an integral power, such as 7^4. However, the repeated multiplication rule does not apply if the exponent is negative, in which case another method of computation is necessary. Hence the type of a^i depends on the *value* of i, and this cannot in general be determined during compilation.†

PL/I also distinguishes between integer and noninteger exponents and allows a^i, where i is an integer, to be computed by repeated multiplication. Unlike ALGOL, it does not *require* interpretive evaluation of exponentiation.

Exponentiation is also extended to complex variables in PL/I.

Conversions

In everyday life, we are used to treating numeric items of data simply as numbers, without much thought of the *type* (integer, rational, irrational) to which they belong. In computing, matters are not so simple. The instruction sets of most machines have different operators for different classes of data—there will be an instruction for adding two binary numbers or two floating-point numbers, but not, generally speaking, for adding an integer to a floating-point number.

This difficulty can to some extent be avoided by restricting the types of data that can occur in expressions. However, it is usual in all languages to allow assignment between different types of numbers.

The same numeric value may be represented in several different data types—the mappings between the types are called *conversions*.‡ There are also mappings between internal and external formats of data, although these are sometimes not regarded as part of a language specification.

Since each data type determines a finite set of values, conversions could in principle be represented as tables with pairs of corresponding values. To see the problems of specifying data type conversions, consider the simple conversion table shown in Fig. 9.4. This shows part of a table of integers and fixed-point numbers of two very restricted types. The integers are all

---

†Since the type of such a factor cannot be deduced during compilation, this means that a general expression involving exponentiation must be *interpreted*. (See Grau, *et al.* (1967) page 34 for ways in which this is handled in many ALGOL compilers.)

‡FORTRAN restricts the word *conversion* to mappings between internal and external forms, and uses the term *altering* for transformations between internal forms.

COBOL uses *conversion* for mapping between internal representations and *editing* for internal-external mappings.

ALGOL uses the term *transfer function* for mappings between data representations.

positive and have two decimal digits; the fixed-point numbers are positive and have three digits precision, with a scale factor of one.

The two sets of values are of course very different in quantity—in this case, for each integer value, there are 10 fixed-point values. This disparity in density is typical of the various data types. (It is even more marked in mathematics, when for each integer there are an infinite number of rationals and for each rational an infinite number of irrationals.)

The manner of conversion from integer to fixed point is obvious—though it is not so obvious what to do in the opposite direction. One possibility would be to choose the nearest integer, involving some form of rounding. However, the usual conversion rule from fixed point to integer, as well as from floating point to integer, involves truncation rather than rounding.

In FORTRAN, conversions between INTEGER and REAL types are defined in terms of actions called *fix* and *float*. Fix is defined as follows.

> Fix means truncate any fractional part of the result and transform that value to the form of an integer datum. (FORTRAN standard, paragraph 7.1.1.3).

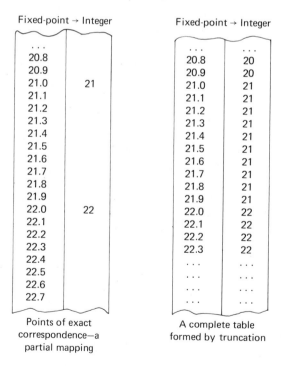

Fixed-point → Integer		Fixed-point → Integer	
. . .		. . .	. . .
20.8		20.8	20
20.9		20.9	20
21.0	21	21.0	21
21.1		21.1	21
21.2		21.2	21
21.3		21.3	21
21.4		21.4	21
21.5		21.5	21
21.6		21.6	21
21.7		21.7	21
21.8		21.8	21
21.9		21.9	21
22.0	22	22.0	22
22.1		22.1	22
22.2		22.2	22
22.3		22.3	22
22.4		. . .	. . .
22.5		. . .	. . .
22.6		. . .	. . .
22.7		. . .	. . .

Points of exact correspondence—a partial mapping

A complete table formed by truncation

Fig. 9.4 Fragment of a conversion table: fixed-point to integer

This seems to imply that conversion is effected by cutting off the fractional part of the physical representation of the number. Truncation is in fact the most convenient way of implementing conversion to integer type, and appears to be permitted by the FORTRAN standard. It produces strange results for certain internal representations of fractional numbers—for example in "twos-complement" representation a negative number is *increased* in size rather than decreased by simple truncation of its internal representation. This has led to the inclusion in the PL/I specification of the requirement that "truncation, if necessary, will be toward zero."

The ALGOL report describes the conversion from **real** to **integer** simply and elegantly in defining the transfer function *entier,* used as the basis of the ALGOL definition or real to integer assignment.

entier (E) "transfers" an expression of **real** type to one of **integer** type, and assigns to it the value which is the largest integer not greater than the value of E. (ALGOL report paragraph 3.2.5)

Target <base> and <scale>	Source <base> and <scale>			
	Binary fixed	Decimal fixed	Binary float	Decimal float
Binary fixed	$p''=p$ $q''=q$	$p''=\min(\text{ceil} (p*3.32)+1,N)$ $q''=\text{ceil}(q*3.32)$		
Decimal fixed	$p''=\min(\text{ceil} (p/3.32)+1,N)$ $q''=\text{ceil}(q/3.32)$	$p''=p$ $q''=q$		
Binary float	$p''=\min(p,N)$	$p''=\min(\text{ceil} (p*3.32),N)$	$p''=p$	$p''=\min(\text{ceil} (p*3.32),N)$
Decimal float	$p''=\min(\text{ceil} (p/3.32),N)$	$p''=\min(p,N)$	$p''=\min(\text{ceil} (p/3.32),N)$	$p''=p$

Note: Each table entry shows the <number-of-digits>, p', of the converted <precision>, and the <scale-factor>, q', of the converted <precision> as functions of the <number-of-digits>, p, and <scale-factor>, q, of the source <precision>. Those table entries left blank are for cases which never arise in the language definition. N is the maximum <number-of-digits> allowed for the target <base> and <scale>.

Fig. 9.5 Mapping functions for converting between decimal/binary and fixed/float in PL/I

(*Source:* ECMA/ANSI, BASIS/1-9)

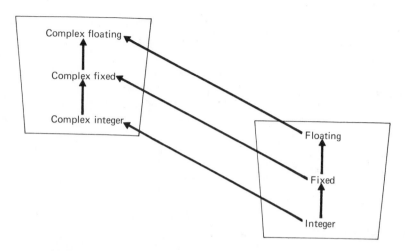

Fig. 9.6 A hierarchy of data types. The arrows indicate conversions which can be made without loss of accuracy. The increasing width of the boxes indicates field width, which must increase as conversions are made in the direction of the arrows.

In the foregoing, we have only considered the simplest of conversions between two simple types. As the number of data types increases, so does the number of conversions. The variety of conversions in COBOL, for which each different PICTURE in some sense represents a different type, is already very large. In the case of PL/I, in which there is a deliberate policy of defining all mappings between data types whenever they have a "reasonable" meaning, the number of potential conversions is so large that the "conversion package" becomes a significant part of any compiler.

Conversions have been illustrated in terms of a table of corresponding values. For a large set of data types this is obviously not an efficient way to implement conversions and an algorithmic method is called for. However, for *specifying* conversions it is usually clearest to use an approach based on mappings or relations—an example of a rather complex set of relations is given in Fig. 9.5, taken from the PL/I specifications.

In specifying a general set of conversion rules for a programming language, the designer has to establish, for each binary operation: op(x,y),

- the restrictions to be placed on the types of x and y;
- the *type* of the result, for each allowable pair of x-y types.

Each data type in a language represents a range of possible values, possibly related to the amount of storage used in the internal representation. We can arrange the various data types of a language in a hierarchy such that, in the "upward" direction of conversion, there is no loss of information. In general the higher a data type is on this graph, the more space it needs for its internal representation.

Figure 9.6 shows a hierarchy for numeric data, including complex numbers. To ensure that there is no information loss, the precisions of the various representations must be carefully designed. A hierarchy of this kind is the basis of many generalized expression-evaluation schemes. In any operation between data of different types, conversion of the "lower" type to the "higher" type is first carried out, so that the operation is carried out in the higher type. (See also Hext, 1967.)

9.7   OTHER TYPES OF OPERATOR

In elementary mathematics the notion of an expression or formula is normally restricted to those containing the arithmetic operators, $+$, $-$, $\times$, $\div$, and exponentiation. In programming languages, the term expression has a much wider context and we meet a number of other binary operators.

We discuss several operators which are found in programming languages. These may be classified into the following groups:

relational operators

logical operators

string operators

We also discuss another form of expression, the *conditional expression,* which appears in ALGOL 60 and which demonstrates a further example of the power of expressions.

9.7.1   Relational Operators

Mathematically, a *binary relation* is defined as a set of ordered pairs of elements from two sets.

As an example we may take the relation "greater than," expressed by the operator: $>$. An example of a simple expression involving this operator is

$$x > y$$

or, in words,

$$x \text{ is } greater \text{ } than \text{ } y.$$

For a given set of values of x and y, there is a set of ordered pairs for which this relation is true. If x and y are integers, the pairs (10,9), (7,0) are members of the set defined by this relation, while (3,4) and (12,12) are not.

Another way of looking at a binary relation is to say that the value of the *relational expression*

$$x > y$$

is either true or false, depending on the values of the operands x and y. This brings in the idea of an operator, acting on the two operands x and y, and has obvious similarities to the way in which arithmetic operators such as $+$ and $-$ behave.

A relational operator is an example of an operator which yields a result which is not in the domain of its operands.

The relational operators in FORTRAN, ALGOL, COBOL, and PL/I include the following.

equal, not equal, $(=, \neg =)$

greater, not greater, greater than or equal $(>, \neg >, >=)$

less, not less, less than or equal $(<, \neg <, <=)$

In FORTRAN and COBOL, these may be represented by

```
EQUAL, LESS THAN, ... etc. (COBOL)
.EQ. , .LT., ... etc. (FORTRAN)
```

These relational operators provide the basis for the conditional tests used in branching statements such as the IF statement.

9.7.1.1 Relations of more than two operands

Although we have illustrated two-valued or binary relations, a more general relation may have n operands. An example of a *ternary* (three-part) relation is:

$$X > Y > Z$$

Although this is notationally meaningful in mathematics, it either is illegal in programming (FORTRAN, COBOL, ALGOL) or may give an unexpected result (PL/I).

The mathematical meaning of the relation is that the triple (X, Y, Z) satisfies it, if X, Y, and Z are in descending order, according to some recognized ordering of the elements. To express the relation in FORTRAN or

ALGOL, it is necessary to write

$$(X \text{ .GT. } Y).\text{AND}.(Y.\text{GT}.Z) \text{ in FORTRAN}$$
$$(X>Y) \wedge (Y>Z) \qquad \text{in ALGOL}$$

Note, however, that these expressions involve two references to Y, instead of the single reference in the original expression. This might produce unintentional results if Y is a function with "side effects" (see Chapter 12). Note that it is syntactically correct to write

$$X>Y>Z$$

in PL/I, but the result is equivalent to

$$(X>Y)>Z.$$

The left-most relation is evaluated first, giving a truth value, expressed in PL/I as '0'B or '1'B. This result may be converted to numeric form in the next comparison if Z is numeric. Thus $3>2>0$ gives the correct value, '1'B, whereas $-7<-5<-3$ gives the value '0'B.

9.7.2   Logical Operators

The data type, *logical,* has the most restricted domain of values of all the types we consider—it consists simply of the two values: **true** and **false.**

A *logical operator* is a binary function, whose arguments are logical values and whose value is a logical value. Given any two values T_1, T_2 and a logical operator L, the result of the expression $T_1 \text{ L } T_2$ has the value **true** or **false.**

Owing to the restricted domain of logical values, it is possible to define the results of logical operations completely and compactly. One method frequently used is a "truth table." This is like a multiplication table, in that it shows the result of operations on all possible combinations of operands.

In addition to the *binary* logical operators, it is also important to consider the *unary* operator **not,** which has an important part in logical expressions. It results in a **true** value when applied to the value **false** and vice versa. See Fig. 9.7.

All languages include the binary logical operators **and** and **or,** with the truth tables shown in Fig. 9.8. The **or** function included in most languages is the "inclusive" **or,** which is true if either or both of the operands are **true.** (The "exclusive" **or** operator is included in some languages, such as LYaPAS, a language used for digital simulation. See Gavrilov and Zakrevskii, 1969.)

The **and** and **or** operators are present in FORTRAN, ALGOL, COBOL and PL/I and are also shown in Figure 9.8.

Truth table:

NOT	true	false
	false	true

ALGOL: ⌐

FORTRAN: .NOT.

COBOL: NOT

Note: The keyword NOT is also used to qualify some of the relational operators, e.g. NOT EQUAL. In the case of ambiguity, NOT is interpreted as a logical operator.

PL/I: ⌐

Fig. 9.7 The unary logical operation: NOT

∧ and	true	false
true	true	false
false	false	false

AND

∨ or	true	false
true	true	true
false	true	false

OR

Notation:

	AND	OR
ALGOL:	∧	∨
FORTRAN:	.AND.	.OR.
COBOL:	AND	OR
PL/I:	&	|

Fig. 9.8 Truth tables for the binary logical operators: AND and OR

ALGOL includes two additional logical operators:

$\equiv$ equivalent

$\supset$ implies

Although the terms used for these suggest a wider meaning, they are strictly logical operators, operating on logical values and defined by their truth tables.

It is possible to construct a wider set of logical functions, if we consider all the possible results of a binary operation. PL/I includes a "general" logical function, BOOL, which allows all combinations of operand and result to be specified. As indicated above, a logical function is completely defined by its truth table. The function BOOL has three arguments, the first two of which are the two operands, the third a 4-bit value defining the truth table. The reasons for including such a function and examples of its use are given in a paper by Foxley (1968).

9.7.3   String Operators

There is one indisputable candidate for a "universal" string operator, the *concatenation* operator. There are several notations for this, but we will use the keyword **cat** in the following examples.

The meaning of concatenation can be simply illustrated:

if S_1 is the string: ABC

   and S_2 is the string: XYZ

then S_1 **cat** S_2 is the string: $ABCXYZ$

The two operands are joined together (*catena* is a chain) to form a new string.

This operation has the following properties.

- It is *closed* in the domain of strings, i.e., the result of concatenating two strings is itself a string.

- It is *associative,* i.e.,

  A **cat** $(B$ **cat** $C) \equiv (A$ **cat** $B)$ **cat** C

  However, it is not *commutative,* i.e.,

  A **cat** B is *not* equivalent to B **cat** A

We can define a *null element* for the operation of concatenation, namely a "string" e such that

A **cat** e is equal to $A,$ for all A.

This element is called the *null string* or the *empty string* and plays much the same part in strings that *zero* plays in numbers.

However, in strings there is no "inverse" element. Given a string *S*, there is no "inverse string" *S'* for which:

$$S \textbf{ cat } S' = \text{the null string}$$

In some respects there is a parallel between the operation of concatenation in the field of strings and the operation of addition in the field of numbers. This is supported by the dictionary definition of "add"—the first definition in the Shorter Oxford English Dictionary is "to join or unite." However the absence of an inverse element severely weakens the case for regarding them as similar.

Similarly, although an equivalent operator to multiplication can be constructed by repeated concatenation, it is not possible to devise an equivalent to division. However, it is valuable to study string operations with similar technical concepts used for the study of arithmetic.

We next consider the relational operators for strings. These are used in constructing methods of searching and scanning strings and for sorting.

It is simple to define a relation of *equality* for single characters. This relation can be extended to strings containing more than one character, the condition for equality being that the strings

- have the same length;
- are equal, character by character.

It is less easy to define the relations *greater than* and *less than*. These relations are only defined for *ordered* sets, and we must therefore consider how an ordering can be associated with a set of strings.

We start by defining an ordering for individual characters. For many character sets, there is an accepted ordering based on established practice. For example, the sets of alphabetic and numeric characters are ordered conventionally: A, B, C, ... and 0, 1, 2, 3 ..., respectively. (Note that the ordering of concern is that of the graphic signs; for numbers, we naturally adopt the same ordering for these as for the *values* represented by the signs). Although these sets are "naturally" ordered, the total ordering of a complete character set, including special signs, punctuation signs, operators, etc., is not intrinsic and has to be specified. In setting up an ordering, the internal representations of the characters are usually taken into account.

An ordering of a character set $\{C_1\}$ is called a *collating sequence*. The ordering implied by a collating sequence enables the value of the relational expression $C(j) > C(k)$ to be defined for all values of j and k. In most languages, the collating sequence is not a part of the language specifications and cannot be modified or otherwise accessed from within the language.

A proposal for including such a specification was made by Shaw (1964). A similar proposal was included in the original specifications of PL/I (in the original SHARE report, see Appendix), but was later abandoned, because of extreme difficulties in defining its interaction with other elements of the language. The 1973 proposed revision of ANS COBOL includes a clause, the PROGRAM COLLATING SEQUENCE clause, which allows a collating sequence to be specified.

It is useful, in setting up searching and collating methods, to have a means of setting data fields to the highest or lowest values of the collating sequence. In COBOL, the figurative constants: HIGH-VALUE(S) and LOW-VALUES(S) provide a source of such characters, the length of the string being determined by context. In PL/I, the built-in functions HIGH(m) and LOW(m) return high and low level strings of length m.

Next consider the operators > and < as applied to strings of more than one character in length. The simplest case occurs when the two strings are of the same length. If A and B are the two strings to be compared and

$$A ::= a_1\, a_2\, a_3 \ldots \ldots a_n$$
$$B ::= b_1\, b_2\, b_3 \ldots \ldots b_n$$

to determine the ordering of A and B, we scan and compare the corresponding pairs of characters from left to right $a_1\, b_1$, $a_2\, b_2$, etc. We check for the first (i.e., left-most) pair, $(a_1,\, b_1)$ such that a_1 is not equal to b_1. It is this pair which determines the truth-value of the expression $(a > b)$.

If the two strings are unequal in length, it is usual to extend the shorter string to the length of the longer by "padding" with extra characters before making the comparison. In such situations, the high- or low-valued character strings obtained with HIGH or LOW can be used for padding to make sure that the appropriate collating sequences are preserved.

9.8 CONDITIONAL EXPRESSIONS

The *conditional expression,* a valuable innovation in language design, was first introduced in ALGOL 60. The ALGOL form of a conditional expression is syntactically similar to an **if** statement with both a **then** and an **else** part. However, it is not a statement, but a value-denoting construction; the words **then** and **else** are followed by expressions, rather than statements. The types of these expressions must be similar—they must both be arithmetic, both Boolean (logical), or both designational (label-valued). The *value* of the conditional expression is determined by evaluating the logical expression in the **if** clause and choosing the appropriate subsidiary expression. The whole construction, **if, then** and **else** parts, may be used in any syntactic position where a value is needed—typically in an expression or on the right-hand side of assignment statements.

Examples

$$y: = \text{ if } a > 0 \text{ then } 100 \text{ else } -100;$$
$$S: = \text{ if } (p > 5) \land (p < 9) \text{ then true else false;}$$

The syntax of conditional expressions allows a general expression to appear after the word **else**—this may itself be a conditional expression, so that a nest of conditions can be tested.

Example

The grade of a student is determined by his mark in a test. We can set the grade by means of the following assignment statement:

$$\text{grade}: = \text{ if mark} > 70 \text{ then } 1$$
$$\text{else if mark} > 60 \text{ then } 2$$
$$\text{else if mark} > 40 \text{ then } 3$$
$$\text{else if mark} > 25 \text{ then } 4$$
$$\text{else } 5;$$

If several conditions are to be tested in a nested conditional expression then, as the ALGOL report makes clear (see paragraph 3.3.3), the conditions are evaluated from left to right until one which has the value **true** is found. At this point, the value is assigned and no further conditions are tested.

Conditional expressions fill a gap in the value-denoting capabilities of programming languages. Conventional expressions (arithmetic, logical, string expressions) compute values from operands in the same domain. Thus, arithmetic expressions compute numbers from numbers, logical expressions compute truth-values from truth-values, and so on. Relational expressions compute truth-values from propositions or relations—these truth values may then be used in logical expressions, but the eventual outcome can only be a truth-value.

Conditional expressions allow general values (numbers, strings, truth-values, etc.) to be computed by means of propositions. There is no accepted mathematical notation for this, although the principle involved has wide-spread application in mathematics, particularly in defining the meaning to be given to primitive mathematical functions. (The origin of conditional expressions can be traced to a function called *conditional disjunction* first introduced by Church, 1948).

Conditional expressions were included in ALGOL as a result of the advocacy of McCarthy, expressed in a letter to the Editor of the *CACM*

(McCarthy, 1959) in which their advantages were closely reasoned.† The letter also contains a proposal for including recursive functions in ALGOL. This letter is an outstanding model of an effective language proposal—an eloquently and briefly argued case, with examples of the advantages and uses of the proposed extensions.

In spite of the experience with conditional expressions in ALGOL, they were not included in PL/I. In PL/I, logical values are represented by the bit values '0' B and '1' B. These may be used in arithmetic operations, in which they are converted to the numeric values 0 and 1. Any numeric value may therefore be multiplied by a logical value to give either *zero* or an *identity*—the value itself. Thus for example the conditional expression:

$$(\textbf{if } a > b \textbf{ then } 10 \textbf{ else } 20)$$

can be expressed in PL/I as

$$((a>b)*10+(\neg(a>b))*20)$$

(see Radin and Rogoway, 1965).

This approach to conditional expressions follows that of Iverson who used a similar illustration to explain why conditional expressions had been omitted from the design of APL. In several ways it is unfortunate that this point of view prevailed in the design of PL/I. In addition to their more natural, and therefore more easily understandable form, conditional expressions have several functional advantages over the use of characteristic bit-values.

First, they can be used to express conditional values of nonnumeric data; the use of multipliers is restricted to data with numeric significance.

Second, conditional expressions allow partially defined expressions to be specified. The rule for left-to-right evaluation allows conditional expressions to be written, some of whose result expressions may be undefined in certain cases. In the PL/I or APL case, *all* propositions and expressions must be evaluated each time the expression is evaluated. This difference also adversely affects the efficiency of the PL/I–APL approach, which in general requires an entire expression to be evaluated, whereas the ALGOL ap-

---

† In his papers, McCarthy used a rather more abstract representation for conditional expressions:

$$(p_1 \rightarrow e_1, p_2 \rightarrow e_2, \dots)$$

In this form, p_1, p_2, p_3, ... are a set of *propositions;* while e_1, e_2, e_3, ... are a set of *expressions.* The logical expression is evaluated from left to right until a *true* proposition is found—the corresponding expression, e, is then evaluated to give the result.

proach allows for branching out on the first **true** proposition. Finally, it is more convenient to write a *complete* test with conditional expressions, by using a final **else** clause whose value is the constant **true.** In PL/I and APL it is often necessary to construct a special "complement" relation to make sure of including all the tests not covered before.

The earlier ALGOL report leaves the type of a conditional arithmetic expression undefined. This means that in certain cases the code for such expressions would have to be interpretive. The ISO standard has modified this so that, where the type is not clear from declarations, it is taken to be **real.** (See ISO/TC 97, 1967.)

9.9 ARRAY EXPRESSIONS

In mathematics, arrays appear in the form of *vectors* (arrays of one dimension) and *matrices* (arrays of two dimensions). A familiar example of their use is in linear algebra, in which an array is formed from the coefficients of a set of linear equations. These represent transformations corresponding to uniform displacements, rotations, and magnifications of plane or solid bodies. Such transformations may be combined in various ways and follow laws similar to those of conventional arithmetic. A basic topic in the study of matrices is the development of matrix operations analogous to simple arithmetic operators—matrix (and vector) operations are defined corresponding to addition, subtraction, multiplication, and division. There are several programming packages in which matrices are a basic data structure and which provide built-in functions of operators for common matrix operations. (See Rice (1971) for a review of such packages.)

Another approach to array operations is that developed by Iverson (1962) in APL. Although the same operations $(+, -, \times, /)$ appear as in matrix arithmetic, the results of these operations are defined in a slightly different way. In APL, arrays are not matrices, but collections of elements of the same type, with prescribed operations and access functions. The array operations of APL arise from the recognition that, in computing, many applications are defined for sets of operands, and the corresponding programs consist of repetitions of elementary arithmetic processes. While the background of matrix operations is algebraic, that of APL is computational and algorithmic.

In the following section, we describe some of the simpler array operations which form the basis of APL. Several of these have also been incorporated in PL/I. At this stage, it is possible to treat the two languages as similar—later on, it will be clear that they differ quite radically in certain details.

9.10   ARRAY OPERATIONS

As in the case of general scalar expressions, array expressions can be broken down into simple array operations. In APL, array operations are generally represented as *operators*, whereas many corresponding PL/I operations are built-in *functions*. In contrast with other languages, APL has a large number of unary operators—and it is for these in particular that we normally find functions in other languages.

For operations involving two arrays, it is generally required that the two array operands obey certain constraints of size and structuring. In most cases the two arrays in a binary operation must have the same number of dimensions and the same number of elements. In certain cases, there may be an additional requirement for the upper and lower bounds of the arrays to be identical. Operands which satisfy these constraints are said to be *conformable* for the given operations.

We now describe some typical array operations. The results shown for PL/I are the "apparent" results from PL/I expressions. As we see below, these may be distorted when the operands and the target of the result share common elements.

9.11   BINARY OPERATORS GIVING ARRAY RESULTS

Arithmetic, relational and logical operators are defined for array operands, yielding array results. If we take any operator such as + (plus), then the result of $A + B$ is an array of the same size as A and B, the elements of which are formed by adding the corresponding elements in A and B. For the two operations + and −, this gives the same results as matrix addition and subtraction; but as can be seen from Fig. 9.9, other operations considerably differ from the rules of matrix arithmetic.

Basic binary operations are also defined between elements and arrays. In this case the element or scalar operand is treated as an array, and is conceptually expanded to the same size and structure as the array operand. Examples are shown in Fig. 9.10.

9.12   UNARY OPERATORS GIVING ARRAY RESULTS

Unary operators giving array results are shown in Fig. 9.11. Note that the trigonometric functions are unary functions in PL/I, but binary (dyadic) operator in APL. The APL operator '0', used for circular functions, has as its first argument an integer between $+7$ and -7, denoting the particular function (sine, cosine, arctan, etc.). This shows a limitation of the APL approach to operators; the use of single character operators has made it

$$A: \begin{bmatrix} 1 & 2 & 3 \\ 1 & 2 & 4 \end{bmatrix} \qquad B: \begin{bmatrix} 2 & 1 & -1 \\ 2 & -3 & 3 \end{bmatrix} \qquad C: \begin{bmatrix} 8 & 10 & 12 \\ 8 & 15 & 21 \end{bmatrix}$$

Arithmetic operators:

$$A + B: \begin{bmatrix} 3 & 3 & 2 \\ 3 & -1 & 7 \end{bmatrix} \qquad \text{(PL/I) } A*B: \begin{bmatrix} 2 & 2 & -3 \\ 2 & -6 & 12 \end{bmatrix}$$
$$\text{(APL) } A \times B:$$

Addition   Multiplication

Relational operators:

$$A > B: \begin{bmatrix} 0 & 1 & 1 \\ 0 & 1 & 1 \end{bmatrix} \qquad A = B: \begin{bmatrix} 0 & 0 & 0 \\ 0 & 0 & 0 \end{bmatrix}$$

Greater than   Equals

Other functions:

$$\text{(PL/I) } MAX(A,B): \begin{bmatrix} 2 & 2 & 3 \\ 2 & 2 & 4 \end{bmatrix}$$
$$\text{(APL) } A \lceil B:$$

Maximum

$$\text{(PL/I) } MOD(C,A): \begin{bmatrix} 0 & 0 & 0 \\ 0 & 1 & 1 \end{bmatrix}$$
$$\text{(APL) } A/C:$$

Residue

PL/I only:

$$A \| C: \begin{bmatrix} 18 & 210 & 312 \\ 18 & 215 & 421 \end{bmatrix}$$

Concatenation   Note: To avoid inclusion of blank
characters, the numbers must
be defined with $PICTURE$
specifications.

$$DIVIDE(C,A,3,2): \begin{bmatrix} 8.00 & 5.00 & 4.00 \\ 8.00 & 7.50 & 5.25 \end{bmatrix}$$

Fixed-point division (controlled precision)

APL only:

$$A \epsilon B: \begin{bmatrix} 1 & 1 & 1 \\ 1 & 1 & 0 \end{bmatrix}$$

Set membership

Fig. 9.9 Binary operators on arrays, giving array results

A, B, and *C* defined as in Figure 9.11.

Arithmetic operators:

$$A+10: \begin{bmatrix} 11 & 12 & 13 \\ 11 & 12 & 14 \end{bmatrix}$$

(PL/I) B**2: (APL) $B*2$:
$$\begin{bmatrix} 4 & 1 & 1 \\ 4 & 9 & 9 \end{bmatrix}$$

Addition   Exponentiation

Relational:

$$B=2: \begin{bmatrix} 1 & 0 & 0 \\ 1 & 0 & 0 \end{bmatrix}$$

$$C<15: \begin{bmatrix} 1 & 1 & 1 \\ 1 & 0 & 0 \end{bmatrix}$$

Fig. 9.10 Binary operators with scalar and array operands

necessary, even with the extensive character set of APL, to go outside the general scheme. The first operand of the circular functions is clearly not an operand in the normal sense, but may be regarded as a 'modifier' of the operator '0', so that effectively, there are 15 functions: 7O, 6O, . . . etc.

$$P: \begin{bmatrix} 1 & 2 \\ 3 & -4 \\ 0 & 5 \end{bmatrix}$$

$$Q: \begin{bmatrix} 4.75 & 1.675 \\ 3.92 & -8.325 \end{bmatrix}$$

$$R: \begin{bmatrix} 1+2I & 2-3I \\ 1-2I & 3+4I \end{bmatrix}$$

$$S: \begin{bmatrix} \text{'ABBCD'} \\ \text{'AXBB47'} \\ \text{'CAAX+5X'} \end{bmatrix}$$

Integer   Fraction   Complex   String

(PL/I) SIGN(P): (APL) $\times P$
$$\begin{bmatrix} 1 & 1 \\ 1 & -1 \\ 0 & 1 \end{bmatrix}$$

Sign

(PL/I) FLOOR(Q): (APL) $\lfloor Q$
$$\begin{bmatrix} 4 & 1 \\ 3 & -9 \end{bmatrix}$$

Floor

(PL/I) CEIL(Q): (APL) $\lceil Q$
$$\begin{bmatrix} 5 & 2 \\ 4 & -8 \end{bmatrix}$$

Ceiling

(PL/I) ABS(Q): (APL) $|Q$
$$\begin{bmatrix} 4.75 & 1.675 \\ 3.92 & 8.325 \end{bmatrix}$$

Absolute value

(PL/I) SUBSTR (S, 4, 1):
$$\begin{bmatrix} \text{'C'} \\ \text{'B'} \\ \text{'X'} \end{bmatrix}$$

Fig. 9.11 Unary array operators

9.13 GENERAL OPERATORS IN APL

Some APL operators will take a scalar and expand it to an array, others ("reduction" operators) carry out systematic operations on all elements of an array and produce a scalar result. There are permutation operators which rearrange the elements of an array, and selection operators which extract elements or subarrays from arrays.

Examples of these different classes of operator are as follows.

- **Index generator ι**

This has a scalar operand; its result is the vector of consecutive integers ranging from the system origin (0 or 1) to the specified integer.

Example

$$\iota 10 \; : \; 1 \; 2 \; 3 \; 4 \; 5 \; 6 \; 7 \; 8 \; 9 \; 10$$

This may be used for generating test data, for setting up iterative loops, for ordering elements of a set. It is an example of a "constructor" function (see Chapter 8).

- **Grade up $\uparrow$**

This operates on a vector operand A; the result is a vector of the same size as A giving the "index" of the corresponding element in A, in ascending order. Duplicate values of the elements in A are given different index values.

Examples

$$\uparrow 5 \; 1 \; 3 \; 6 \; 9 \; has \; the \; value: \; 2 \; 3 \; 1 \; 4 \; 5$$
$$\uparrow 2 \; 2 \; 4 \; 4 \; 1 \; 1 \; 6 \; has \; the \; value: \; 5 \; 6 \; 1 \; 2 \; 3 \; 4 \; 7$$

This is used for ordering and rearranging vectors.

- **Reduction /**

The reduction sign $(/)$ may be used with any arithmetic, relational, or other operator (let us call such an operator: p) to produce what is effectively a new operator $(/p)$. This composite operator can then be applied to any vector $\mathbf{V}$, with the result that p is effectively applied to the elements of $\mathbf{V}$. The operator $/p$ may be applied to the Kth row of a matrix by writing: $/p[K]$.

Example

1) The operator $/+$ sums the elements of a vector.

$$/+ \; 2 \; 4 \; 8 \; : \; 14$$

2) If *A* has the value: `1 2`
                               `5 7`
   then `/+[ 2]` *A* has the value: 12 (i.e., 5 + 7)

As we have seen, APL array operations provide a notation for expressing computations, especially repetitive computations, on structured sets of data. The remarkable compression of complicated algorithms into single APL statements, as shown by the following example, is made possible by the freedom to construct general expressions in which reduction, expansion, and selection operators can be used to convert intermediate results to a form suitable for the next operation. Using APL, it is often possible to avoid introducing auxiliary variables to act as counters, temporary stores, etc.,—in this respect, the language is truly "high-level" in providing freedom from attention to detail.

```
      ▽ Z←INV M;I;J
[ 1]    M←Q(1 0 +ρM)ρ(,QM),~J←1<ıI←1↑ρM
[ 2]    M←1Q(J,1)Q[1]M−(J×M[;1])∘.×M[1;]←M[1;]÷M[1;1]
[ 3]    →2×ı0≠I←I−1
[ 4]    Z←M[;ı1↑ρM]
      ▽
```

(*Source:* APL Users' Guide)

This program inverts the matrix M by Gauss-Jordan elimination. Line `[1]` creates an additional column for M; line `[2]`, which is executed at each iteration, performs an inversion.

The PL/I approach to array operations, as defined in the early versions of the language (i.e., up to and including the IBM Optimizer/Checker) differed considerably from that of APL.

Consider the following statement for setting the elements of an array *A* equal to zero, if their value is less than 100.

In APL the statement is:

```
A ← A × A > 100
```

In PL/I it is:

```
A = A * (A > 100);
```

The APL example, evaluated from right to left, proceeds in the following steps.

step 1: Evaluate *A* > 100. An array is formed whose elements are 0 or 1, according to the value of the corresponding element of *A*.

step 2: Apply the operator × (multiply). *A* is multiplied, element by element, by the array formed in step 1.

step 3: The array formed in step 2 replaces *A*.

In the IBM version of PL/I, the statement is first expanded into a loop. Conceptually, each assignment is executed separately, element by element.

$$A(1,1) = (A(1,1) * (A(1,1)>100);$$
$$A(1,2) = (A(1,2) * (A(1,2)>100);$$
$$\cdots$$

The comparison operations yield results '0'B or '1'B, and these are converted into numeric values 0 or 1 for the multiplication.

The different PL/I approach was chosen because of the wish to avoid having to create temporary storage for intermediate results in array expressions (all of them arrays, and possibly requiring extensive storage). In effect, the PL/I array facilities were defined as an extension of the looping capabilities.

The problem of extending the array capabilities of PL/I to match those of APL has been extensively discussed in the PL/I standards committees. One difficulty was the need to consider function references; in order to have "true" array expressions, it is essential to allow function references to return array values. This raises several problems both in definition and implementation. The problem of "interference" in PL/I, illustrates the differences between the two approaches.

Example

All elements of an array *M* are to be divided by the leading element. (This is a common requirement in matrix problems.)

The APL statement

$$M \leftarrow M \div M[1,1]$$

achieves this satisfactorily, but the similar PL/I statement:

$$M = M / M(1,1) \ ;$$

does not, since the first assignment in the expanded loop replaces *M*(1,1) by 1, so that in the remainder of the loop the other elements are unchanged. We have to write:

$$T = M(1,1) \ ;$$
$$M = M/T \quad ;$$

to get the required result.

The revised PL/I treatment of arrays, which more closely corresponds to the APL approach, is defined as part of the proposed PL/I standard (see the Appendix for references).

9.14   GENERAL EXPRESSIONS

We next see how the simple forms of expression we have discussed can be extended to more complex and powerful constructions.

The basic elements of a simple expression are *references, operators,* and *parentheses.* From a pair of references and an operator, we may construct a "simple expression," such as:

```
a + b
x ÷ g(t)
RATE * TIME
```

These may be used to denote values, just as *references* denote values.

The essence of the expression concept is that simple forms such as these may be used, as references are used, to build up further expressions.

Since we can write an expression in any position which requires a value-denoting object, we can write an expression in place of one of the references. The resulting expression in turn denotes a value, and may be used in any place which requires a value-denoting object... and so on.

In describing expressions, we are led naturally to recursive methods of description such as this. In all formal descriptions of expressions, we find recursive definitions—they involve "true" recursion, not introduced merely to express repetition. The expression is, in fact, one of the simplest examples of a recursive structure and it provides a natural place for the use of recursive procedures for recognition and translation.

Expressions provide a powerful and compact notation for complex algorithms. By using expressions we can avoid unnecessary decisions relating to storage allocation, type conversions and order of evaluation. We can see this by contrasting expressions written in a high-level language with corresponding instructions in machine language.

Example

1) In order to evaluate the expression $(a*b) + (c*d)$ in machine language, *two* temporary stores are needed.
2) In ALGOL, a two-way branch can be expressed by means of a single **go to** statement:

   go to (**if** $a>b$ **then** $L1$ **else** $L2$);

In machine language, *two* branch instructions have to be written.

In the syntax for expressions, it is possible to take any subexpression and enclose it in parentheses; it may then be used as an operand in further expressions.

Examples

```
(HIGH — LOW) * RATE
(a + b) * (a — b)
(L(I) — L(J))/2
(X — Y) + Z
```

In these examples, the *operands* corresponding to each operator are clearly defined by the parentheses.

The syntax of expressions does not require that all expressions should be fully parenthesized like this. However, in the process of compilation, a form equivalent to the parenthesized form must be developed, so that operands for each operator are precisely known.

In evaluating a fully parenthesized expression, the expressions in the innermost brackets are evaluated first—the expression is evaluated from the inside out. Parentheses may therefore be used to influence the order of evaluation of an expression. Even the fully parenthesized form does not completely specify the order of all operators, and a further decision must still be made by a compiler. For instance, in the second example, it is clear that both $(a + b)$ and $(a - b)$ must be evaluated before the multiplication, but it is not clear whether the addition or the subtraction should be done first.

9.14.1 Other Representations of Expressions

The fully parenthesized form is one of several equivalent ways of representing expressions. We also consider three other forms:

- functional form,
- tree form,
- parenthesis-free form

The functional form, like the parenthesized form, is found in current high-level languages. The other two forms are not generally available to users of a language, but are important in implementing compilers and their study provides an insight into the underlying structure of expressions.

9.14.1.1 Functional form

In functional form, each binary operator is expressed as a function, **f,** the operands appearing as the arguments of the function. Corresponding to infix operators such as +, *, we have functions:

add (x,y)

multiply (x,y)

Similarly, the unary operator (−) might be written

negative(x)

By writing operators in this way, we can see the relationship between arithmetic operators and the built-in or intrinsic functions of a programming language. In spite of their different notation, the trigonometric functions are just as much a part of a language as the operators + and −. We use functional notation for SINE, LOG, etc., because there is no other accepted mathematical notation; we also use it for SQRT which does have an accepted notation, because the usual square root sign is typographically unsuitable for a computer.

We may construct expressions in functional form in any language with sufficiently flexible capabilities for function definition. The list processing language LISP is strongly associated with the functional form, and in its original version allowed expressions to be constructed only in this way.

The order of evaluation of a functional expression is determined by the form of the function; the most-deeply nested functions are evaluated first. In other words, the arguments of a function must be evaluated before the function itself—an obvious requirement.

Expressions written in functional representation are easy to process, and their syntax can be simply and precisely defined. The disadvantages of using functional representation for programs are serious—the need to represent complicated algorithms by deeply nested, parenthesized structures leads to forms which are difficult both to write and to debug.

9.14.1.2   Tree form

Expressions can also be expressed as trees, in which the interior nodes represent functions and the terminal nodes represent variables. It is easy to see that the tree form is closely related to the functional form. The binary operator $\mathbf{f}(x,y)$, the basic unit of the functional form, can be represented by a simple tree as shown in Figure 9.12.

This tree represents the value obtained by applying the function **f** to the two arguments x and y. This simple tree can be used to denote a value in building up a larger tree, and so on, until finally a complete expression is represented.

The tree form is often used to illustrate the structural form of expressions; it has considerable intuitive appeal and the two-dimensional form

Fig. 9.12 A simple expression in tree form.

makes it easy to understand expressions that would otherwise be a mass of parentheses.

9.14.1.3 Parenthesis-free form (Polish notation)

In the parenthesized, functional, and tree forms of representing expressions, the relationships between functions and their arguments are denoted by parentheses or by the node/subnode relationship of the tree. In these representations, the form, and hence the meaning, of an expression can simply be discerned by the human eye. For a computer, limited to scanning the text character by character, they are not so suitable.

The parenthesis-free forms provide an alternative method of representing expressions. They were introduced by the Polish mathematician and logician, Lukasiewicz, who showed that, by writing operators in front of their operands instead of between them, the use of brackets was superfluous (Lukasiewicz, 1929). For example,

instead of $a + b$ we can write $+ab$,

instead of $a + b * c$ we can write $+a * bc$.

In most cases it is more convenient for a compiler to reverse the positions and place the operator *after* the operands, giving what is usually called *reverse* Polish notation. An expression of any complexity can be expressed in Polish notation without any need for brackets—the mapping from one form to the other can be achieved by a simple algorithm involving the use of a push-down stack. Once in reverse Polish notation, the expression may be directly evaluated by a computer (also with a stack).

The usefulness of Polish notation for expressions has made it a popular tool for compiler writing and many compilers now use reverse Polish notation as an internal representation of program text.

Early proposals by Hamblin for computer design were followed by at least two machine designs with built-in push-down stacks (the Burroughs B5000 and the English Electric KDF9), intended to be used both as a target for the translation of programs and for direct execution of the resulting code in Polish notation. See Hamblin (1962) for an account of various Polish notations and methods of translation from conventional mathematical notations.

Figure 9.13 shows the same expression expressed in the different forms discussed above.

Expression: $P*Q + (R-S)*T$

Fully bracketed form:

$$((P*Q) + ((R-S)*T))$$

Functional form:

$$ADD(MULT(P,Q),\ MULT(SUBTRACT(R,S),T))$$

Reverse Polish form:

$$PQ*RS-T*+$$

Tree form:

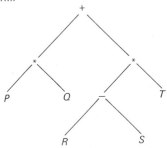

9.13 Four representations of the expression $P*Q + (R-S)*T$

9.14.2   Precedence of Operators

Consider the expression

$$L + M + N$$

This can be put into parenthesized form in two ways:

$$(L + M) + N,$$

in which the left-most addition is executed first;

$$L + (M + N),$$

in which the right-most addition is first.

Often, these two forms give identical results, but this is not always the case. The two methods of bracketing would certainly not be equivalent if we replaced the first plus sign by a multiply sign; compare the two versions of $L * M + N$:

$$(L * M) + N$$

and

$$L * (M + N)$$

It is clear that in general usage we do not treat all operators in the same way; some are more "binding" than others, so that most people, asked to evaluate

$$3 * 4 + 2$$

would give the answer 14 rather than 18. The relative binding strengths of operators establishes a sequence of operator *precedence*.

We first consider unbracketed expressions involving identical operators, such as:

$$a + b + c + d + \ldots$$
$$p * q * r * s * \ldots$$

These are usually evaluated in a single direction; the most commonly used direction being from left to right (ALGOL, COBOL), so that these expressions are equivalent to

$$(((a + b) + c) + d) \ldots$$
$$(((p * q) * r) * s) \ldots$$

FORTRAN allows the compiler to choose the most appropriate order of evaluation.

APL evaluates unbracketed statements from right to left.

PL/I evaluates all uniform expressions from left to right with the exception of exponentiation, which it evaluates from right to left. This gives the expression

$$a^{b^{c}}$$

which is expressed

a**b**c

and gives the value

a**(b**c),

following what was considered to be the more usual mathematical interpretation.

We next consider unbracketed expressions containing several types of operator. Two approaches have been used.

- a fixed order of precedence, based as far as possible on mathematical conventions

- no precedence between operators (i.e., all operators having the same precedence)—the order of evaluation being based on the order of operators in the text

Most programming languages use the first approach and define a fixed order of precedence. However, the lack of universally accepted precedence rules for all the operators used in programming has resulted in variations among programming languages, especially for the less commonly used operators such as relational and logical operators.

The following precedence for the common arithmetic operators is generally agreed:

exponentiation   *high*
multiplication, division
addition, subtraction   *low*

Examples

This precedence gives the following interpretations of fairly straightforward expressions, which will be seen to agree with the usual mathematical interpretations:

1) The expression, $a^2 + 4t$, which in programming language form is written

a**2 +4*t

is evaluated as follows

(a**2) + (4*t)

2) The expression, $\frac{1}{2}ax^3 - 4y$, which in programming language form may be written

a*x**3/2 − 4*y

is evaluated

$$((a*(x**3))/2) - (4*y)$$

Operator precedence is sometimes reflected in the formal syntax of languages by introducing into the syntax rules a series of intermediate forms. For example, in the FORTRAN specifications, no explicit operator precedence is given; instead, as the standard puts it "The rules for formation of expressions imply the binding strength of operators".

In FORTRAN and ALGOL, arithmetic expressions are constructed from the following elements:

primary:	a constant, a variable, or a parenthesized expression
factor:	a primary or a simple expression with exponentiation
term:	a factor or a simple expression with multiplication or division
simple arithmetic expression:	a term, or a simple expression with addition or subtraction

These forms are introduced to express the precedence of the arithmetic operators and to provide named units of text on which to base the semantic description of expression evaluation.

Figure 9.14 shows a table of precedence for FORTRAN, ALGOL, COBOL and PL/I. Note that there is general agreement among these languages on the precedence of arithmetic operators, but that there are differences for unary operators and some logical operators.

9.14.2.1 Equal-precedence operators—the APL approach

An alternative approach is adopted in APL, in which all operators have equal precedence. This is one of the more controversial features of APL; and the case for avoiding a hierarchy of operator precedence has been explained by Iverson (1966) (reference Appendix A to "Elementary Functions"). Briefly, Iverson argues that there is no universally established order of precedence of mathematical operators; that when asked to state how an unparenthesized mathematical expression is to be evaluated, even students of mathematics give a variety of answers. He concludes that the simplest way to avoid ambiguity in expressions is to evaluate them as they are written. Iverson makes the further claim that the left-to-right order of evaluation used by most languages for parenthesis-free expressions is less easy to understand and write than the right-to-left rule adopted in APL.

Exponentiation	↑			
Multiply, divide	× / ÷			
Add, subtract	+ −			
Relational	< ⩽ > ⩾ = ≠			
Not	¬			
And	∧			
Or	∨			
Implies	⊃			
Equivalent	≡			

ALGOL

Exponentiation	**		
Multiply, divide	* /		
Add, subtract	+ -		
Relational	.LT.	.LE.	.EQ.
	.NE.	.GT.	.GE.
Not	.NOT.		
And	.AND.		
Or	.OR.		

FORTRAN

Unary operators	+ -
Exponentiation	**
Multiply-divide	* /
Add, subtract	+ -
Relations	GREATER LESS EQUAL
Not	NOT
And	AND
Or	OR

COBOL

Exponentiation, unary operators	**	+ -
Multiply, divide	* /	
Add, subtract	+ -	
Concatenation	‖	
Relational	> >= ¬> = ¬= < <= ¬<	
And	&	
Or			

PL/I

Fig. 9.14 Tables of operator precedence

The APL rules for expressions can be simply stated:

- All operators have equal precedence.
- The order of evaluation of unparenthesized expressions is from right to left.
- The order of evaluation may be influenced by parentheses.

There is no doubt of the simplicity of these rules and the ability of most APL users to adapt to them without difficulty. The results they yield would be unfamiliar to most mathematicians unless they were familiar with the language. The right-to-left rule is an advantage in direct, interpretive implementation of APL.

In his advocacy of the APL rules, Iverson does not mention what is possibly the most telling argument in favor of "no precedence"—the fact that new operators can be introduced without changing the meaning of existing programs. APL has powerful function-definition capabilities and the absence of precedence rules means that new functions can be added to APL programs without the user having to be concerned with the precedence of the new operators.

9.15   EXPRESSIONS IN ALGOL, COBOL, AND PL/I

Nearly all high level languages include expressions of some degree of generality, allowing arbitrary numbers of operations and operands, and arbitrary nesting of subexpressions. In detail, however, there are several differences between the major languages.

9.16   FORTRAN EXPRESSIONS

As we have seen, FORTRAN originated with expression evaluation as a prominent objective of the language design. However, standard FORTRAN reflects its early beginnings by its constraints on the construction of arithmetic expressions. (Many FORTRAN compilers allow more general expressions than those defined by the ANSI standard.)

First, the operands in arithmetic expressions must all be of the same type—integer, real, double precision, or complex.†

Thus in order to add a single precision number S to a double precision number D, S must first be converted to double precision:

Example

FORTRAN coding to add a single precision number S to a double precision number D

```
        REAL S
        DOUBLE PRECISION D, TD
        . . .
        . . .
        TD = S
        D = D + TD
```

Second, the expressions used in subscripts, although they represent integer values, are not allowed to be general arithmetic expressions, but may

---

† There is one exception to this, namely that the exponentiation operator allows an integer exponent, whatever the type of the first operand.

only be of the restricted form:

$$c * v + k$$

where c and k are integer constants and v is an integer variable reference.

   This restriction makes it easier for a compiler to generate code for processing arrays—for example in DO-loops, which normally involve regular patterns of subscript evaluation. The simple linear subscript expression can be translated into increments of the subscript, involving only addition operations rather than multiplications. As in the previous example, more complex subscript expressions can be coded only by introducing temporary variables.

   The restrictions imposed by standard FORTRAN provide an interesting example of how a general form (the mathematical *expression*) has been tailored to an available technology—in this case the machine and compiling technology of the 1950's. The restrictions are irksome to those familiar with more general languages such as ALGOL or PL/I, and are not necessary for current medium and large systems. However, they still provide useful benefits to compiler writers for small machines.

9.17 ALGOL EXPRESSIONS

ALGOL has one of the most general treatments of expressions, allowing them to be written in any place where a value-denoting element is required. This includes the right-hand side of an assignment, the bounds in an array declaration, values in **for** list specifications, etc. The formal syntax of ALGOL distinguishes the following classes of expression:

arithmetic: giving **real** or **integer** results

Boolean: giving the results **true** or **false**

designational: giving a statement *label* result

In each of these, the type of the result can be determined from the syntax of the expression. The *conditional* expression has been described above and may return a value of any of these types.

9.18 COBOL EXPRESSIONS

Of the languages we discuss, COBOL has the least-developed facility for writing expressions. In contrast with ALGOL and PL/I, COBOL only allows expressions in a few clearly-defined places in a program. In most cases, value-denoting elements are restricted so that only simple references, or references with a constant increment or decrement, may be written.

The COMPUTE statement is most closely equivalent to the assignment statement found in other languages. Its general form is

```
COMPUTE identifier-1[ROUNDED] [,identifier-2[ROUNDED]]...
= arithmetic-expression[; ON SIZE ERROR imperative-statement]
```

This is the one COBOL statement which allows full formula translation. If it is necessary to use an expression in other contexts (e.g., as a subscript), the expression must be evaluated first and then assigned to an INDEX value.

Although the COMPUTE statement may be used for simple assignments such as

```
COMPUTE X = Y
COMPUTE RATE = RATE + 1
```

there are other COBOL statements which achieve these results more directly, and also form part of the expression-evaluating capabilities of COBOL. These are the statements

```
MOVE, ADD, SUBTRACT, MULTIPLY, and DIVIDE.
```

The MOVE statement copies data values from one record structure or element to another, or from a literal. The other statements carry out the simple arithmetic operations indicated, and are limited to a single type of binary operation, although there may be several operands.

Examples

The following examples of these statements are self-explanatory.

1) ADD 1 TO AMOUNT.
2) SUBTRACT DISCOUNT FROM PRICE-1, PRICE-2,
   PRICE-3.
3) DIVIDE N5 INTO TOTAL-AMOUNT GIVING RATE5
   ROUNDED REMAINDER R5.

In (1) we see how a variable may be incremented. The advantage of this form is seen more strikingly in (2) where the same amount is subtracted from three different elements. In (3) we see the use of the GIVING clause, which determines a result field. In this case we also see that the remainder of a division operation may be assigned to a nominated variable. In carrying out precise fixed-point arithmetic (for example in currency conversion or rate computation) it is important to have accurate control of the remainder from fixed-point divisions. COBOL allows the remainder to be made available as a direct result of the division operation—in other languages it may have to be computed by means of a separate operation.

9.19 PL/I EXPRESSIONS

One of the original objectives of PL/I was to associate an "official" meaning with any combination of symbols having a "reasonably sensible" meaning (Radin and Rogoway, 1965). This objective is exercised most fully in the PL/I treatment of expressions.

Unlike FORTRAN, ALGOL, and COBOL there is no classification of expressions (arithmetic expressions, logical expressions, etc.) There are just "expressions," in which all operators and operands of all "problem" data types (numbers and strings) may participate. The *types* of all expressions can be determined by inspection, an important factor in designing a compilable language.

The generality of expressions in PL/I is based on a much wider set of mappings or conversions between data types than is found in most languages. Examples of PL/I conversions between remote data types are as follows.

Numeric to Character String

This is fairly straightforward, since the external representation of any number is in the form of a character string. There remains the question of format; the standard format of what is known as "list-directed" I/O is used (see Chapter 11).

Character String to Numeric

This is more difficult and is a partial mapping, since some character strings (e.g., 'XYZ', '+ + +@') have no numeric counterpart. The conversion is defined as follows: if the character string is in the form of a number in list-directed form (input or output), then that is the result of the conversion. If not, the CONVERSION condition is raised when the code attempting the conversion is executed.

PL/I is one of the few compilable languages to include array expressions. Although the range of operators in PL/I is not as great as in APL, the facilities are in some ways more powerful, since they are extended to *structures* as well as arrays.

The ability to compile array expressions means that more efficient code can be generated; the interpreted expressions of APL are sometimes too inefficient for practical use.

Comparing the treatment of expressions in the four languages, it is now unnecessarily restrictive to adopt the constraints of FORTRAN or COBOL. This can be seen by the way in which these two languages have often been extended beyond the strict level of their standards by compiler writers. The generality of ALGOL and PL/I expressions can be useful in expressing complicated algorithms compactly and accurately. The conditional expression of ALGOL and the array expression of APL and PL/I are powerful extensions of the usual form of mathematical expression.

9.20 ASSIGNMENT

Assignment is an operation closely associated with the evaluation of expressions and is one of the most important in computing. Indeed, the chief object of many programs and subroutines is to assign values, either to variables or to an output device such as a printer, display unit, or transmission line. The importance of assignment is reflected in the high proportion of its use in typical programs (see Chapter 3).

Expressions were introduced in programming languages following a long history of development in mathematics and logic. Assignment brings a new aspect, that of storing values for subsequent use. To discuss its meaning, we need to consider how values of data are to be represented, and we may become involved with a discussion of the properties of computer storage. These are the aspects which mark the difference between programming languages and the otherwise similar fields of mathematics and logic.

To understand the operation of assignment, we need to distinguish between the *name* and the *value* of a variable. This crucial distinction can most easily be observed in the assignment statement, which gave the terms L-value (name) and R-value (value) used by Strachey, in a widely quoted paper (Strachey, 1956, reference in Chapter 5). L and R refer to the position of the variables in the most common way of writing the assignment statement. In most languages, "assign B to A" is written

$$A = B \qquad \text{(FORTRAN, PL/I)}$$
$$A := B; \quad \text{(ALGOL)}$$

However, assignment has produced the most diverse forms of notation of all basic operations, including a reversal of the order of writing the source and target of the assignment. For example, the same sense is given by

$$\text{MOVE B TO A} \quad \text{(COBOL)}$$
$$B \rightarrow A \qquad \text{(POP2)}$$

On the right-hand side of the statement (in its usual form) we have a value-denoting form, while on the left there is a name-denoting form. The meaning implied by the statement is more accurately conveyed by the expanded form:

"move the *value* of B to the variable whose *name* is A."

Assignment thus makes use of two basic accessing operations:

- given a location, retrieve a value;
- given a location and a value, set the contents of the location to the specified value.

In general, the operation of assignment applies to values rather than to storage representations. Hence the types of the two operands must be compatible so that there is a mapping between the data of the two types. These mappings are generally the same as those used for arithmetic operations, as described above.

9.20.1   Generalizations of Assignment

9.20.1.1   Multiple assignment

Several languages allow a value to be assigned to several variables by means of a single statement. Illustrations of such use include the initialization of variables and the transmission of the same value to the output fields of several different files.

Examples

COBOL

```
MOVE DAILY-RATE TO RATE IN OUTPUT-RECORD, RATE IN WEEKLY-LOG.
```

ALGOL

$$I := J := K := 1;$$

PL/I

```
I,J,K = 1;
```

Note the difference in notation between ALGOL and PL/I, made necessary by the lack of a separate assignment operator in PL/I. (In PL/I, the = sign is used to denote the relational operator, "is equal to," as well as the assignment statement.)

In general, the meaning of multiple assignment is defined as being equivalent to a sequence of simple assignment statements. The statement

```
A := B := C := D;
```

is defined as equivalent to

```
A := D;
B := D;
C := D;
```

This explication is adequate for many cases, but care has to be taken in cases where the assignment of a value to one of the target variables may affect values assigned to others.

For example, consider the fragment:

```
I := 1;
I := A[I] := A[I+1] := I+1;
```

One expansion of this multiple assignment might result in the following assignments:

```
I := 1;
I := 2;
A[2] := 3;
A[3] := 3;
```

However, this is *not* the meaning of this statement in ALGOL, or of its equivalent in COBOL or PL/I. In these languages, possible alterations to the subscripts or other accessing variables used in the targets are resolved by a ruling that all subscripts are evaluated before the assignment is carried out (more precisely, before the expression on the right-hand side is evaluated). Furthermore, multiple assignment is defined so that the value to be assigned, the right-hand side, need only be evaluated once and the result stored in a register or temporary store before assignment to the target variables.

The corrected version of the expansion for this example is therefore:

```
I := 1;
I := 2;
A[1] := 2;
A[2] := 2;
```

9.20.1.2 Data-structure assignment

In the same way that binary operators such as +, −, *, etc. have been extended to apply to array operands in APL and PL/I, the operation of assignment can be extended to apply to data structures rather than to elements. Array assignments are included in APL and PL/I; COBOL and PL/I allow assignment of record structures.

The purpose of data-structure assignment is broadly similar to that of other operations on data structures—to extend a basic operation to sets of elements rather than a single element. Many computing problems can be expressed in terms of structured sets of elements and repetitive operators on them. By extending elementary operations to such sets, simpler and sometimes more efficient programs can be written.

In all forms of data-structure assignments, there are constraints on the structuring of the variables, which must be *conformable* in the sense described above. As with binary operations, a scalar is conformable with any array (or any structure in PL/I), allowing all elements of an array to be set to a single value.

A = 0;	Initializes an array to zero.
TEXTOVERLAY = 'X';	This sets up a pattern for the printer to produce diagrams. TEXTOVERLAY is a DEFINED array of single characters which is to be printed.

Following the analogy with binary operations, the vector assignment statement

$$A = B;$$

is equivalent to a set of assignments

$$A(1) = B(1);$$
$$A(2) = B(2);$$
$$\cdots \qquad \cdots$$

of the elements in *A* and *B*.

This is the approach for array assignments in APL and PL/I. As discussed in the section on array expressions above, the meaning of an assignment statement in PL/I needs special consideration if the right-hand side is an array *expression* rather than an array variable. In such a case, the assignment is expanded to a sequence of assignment statements, in each of which the expression giving the value of the current element is evaluated. Therefore the statement:

$$A = B + C * D;$$

may be equivalent to the sequence of statements

```
A(1) = B(1) + C(1) * D(1);
A(2) = B(2) + C(2) * D(2);
...       ...        ...
```

In this form of the language, an array expression is only meaningful in association with an assignment statement. This is true of the IBM version of PL/I as currently implemented. However, in the proposed ECMA/ANSI standard for PL/I (see Appendix), this is changed so that an array expression yields a true array result, which is assigned element by element as before.

9.20.1.3 Corresponding (by name) assignment

In COBOL and PL/I there is a form of data-structure access in which the fields accessed depend on the *names* of the variables. The language forms in which this feature appears are

- the CORRESPONDING forms of the MOVE, ADD, and SUBTRACT statements in COBOL.

- the BY NAME option of the assignment statement in PL/I.

In data-processing applications, a program may process many types of record. Some of the fields of such records will serve a common purpose and be similarly named. The rules for naming fields in record structures allow duplicate names to be used, provided the fully qualified names of the fields are unique. The purpose of the *corresponding* or *by-name* feature is to simplify the processing of such fields.

Suppose we have two record structures, A and B, whose elements are respectively named

$$\{a_1, a_2, \ldots\} \text{ and } \{b_1, b_2, \ldots\}.$$

Then from the definition of data-structure operations given above, the result of a normal structure assignment of B to A is a set of assignments:

$$a_1 = b_1;$$
$$a_2 = b_2;$$
$$\ldots \quad \ldots$$

When the assignment is *corresponding* (or *by name*), a preliminary selection is made of those fields in A whose corresponding fields in B have the same name; only the corresponding elements are assigned. (The structures do not have to be conformable before this selection takes place.)

The assignment consists of two parts—the selection of matching elements, followed by the assignment itself. The new operation involved here is the "corresponding" selection, which could be regarded as a new access function, CORR(A,B), a selector of those elements of *B* whose names match those of *A*. The "corresponding" assignment can then be expressed in terms of a data structure assignment

$$A = C$$

where *C* is the result of applying the access function CORR(A,B) to the structure *B*.

As we have seen, this form of access is defined for MOVE and the simple arithmetic operations ADD and SUBTRACT in COBOL, while in PL/I it is generalized to the full assignment statement in which the right-hand side may be any structure expression. In both cases the language is defined so that the determination of matching names can be carried out by a compiler.

Example

With the following record definitions,

```
01 DAILY-OUTPUT.
    02 DAY-NO PICTURE 999.
    02 TYPE PICTURE X.
    02 OUTPUT-RATE PICTURE 999.

01 DEPARTMENT.
    02 DEPT-NO PICTURE AAA.
    02 BUDGET PICTURE 99999.
    02 MANPOWER.
        03 MALE PICTURE 999.
        03 FEMALE PICTURE 999.
    02 OUTPUT-RATE PICTURE 9999.
    ...
```

the following statement,

```
ADD DAILY-OUTPUT TO DEPARTMENT CORRESPONDING.
```

results in the following equivalent statement being executed.

```
ADD OUTPUT-RATE IN DAILY-OUTPUT TO
    OUTPUT-RATE IN DEPARTMENT.
```

BIBLIOGRAPHY

Anderson, J. P., A note on some compiling algorithms. *CACM*, Vol. 7, No. 3, Mar. 1964, pp. 149–150.

Considers two techniques for compilation, one based on an operand stack, the other based on the conversion of an expression into a tree.

Arden, B. W., B. A. Galler, R. M. Graham, "An algorithm for translating Boolean expressions," *JACM*, Vol. 9, No. 2, 1962, pp. 222–239.

Backus, J. W., *et al.*, "The FORTRAN automatic coding system," *Proc. WJCC*, Vol. II, 1957, pp. 188–193.

Benford, F., "The law of anomalous numbers," *Proc. Am. Phil. Soc.*, Vol. 78, 1938, pp. 551–572.

Bottenbruch, H., A. A. Grau, "On translation of Boolean expressions," *CACM*, Vol. 5, No. 7, 1962, pp. 384–386.

Brent, R. P., "On the precision attainable with various floating-point number systems," *Research Report RC 3751*, IBM Research, Yorktown Heights, Feb. 1972.

Brooker, R. A., "A programming package for generalized arithmetic," *CACM*, Vol. 7, No. 2, Feb. 1964, p. 119.

Burstall, R. M., "The semantics of assignment," *Machine Intelligence 2*, Elmsford, N.Y.: Pergamon Press, 1968, pp. 3–20.

Considers the semantics of programming languages from the point of view of Church's Lambda Calculus, and shows how various forms of assignment can be expressed in purely functional form.

Busam, V. A., D. E. Englund, "Optimization of expressions in FORTRAN," *CACM*, Vol. 12, No. 12, Dec. 1969, pp. 666–674.

Cajori, F., *A History of Mathematical Notations*, Vol. I, La Salle, Ill.: The Open Court Publishing Company, 1928.

This scholarly and readable book traces the history of the notations we now take for granted, but which took many years to reach their present state of stability. Vol. I includes most of the elementary notations found in programming languages; Vol. II discusses more advanced notations.

Chroust, G., "Comparative study of implementation of expressions," IBM Laboratory Vienna, *TR 25.112*, Mar. 1971.

This report examines methods for evaluating expressions, considering especially machine behavior during execution. Three machine parameters are considered: the choice of basic operations, order of evaluation, and the use of temporary stores. Conditions for the formal correctness of evaluation are considered.

Chroust, G., "Expression evaluation with minimum average working storage," *Information Processing Letters*, Vol. 1, No. 3, Feb. 1972, pp. 111–114.

Presents a method of evaluating expressions which minimizes the average use of registers (rather than the usual technique which minimizes the extreme use of registers). The technique is intended for use in multiprogramming situations.

Church, A., "Conditional disjunction as a primitive connective for the propositional calculus," *Portug. Math.*, Vol. 7, 1948, pp. 87–90.

Introduces a function [p,q,r] which has the value p or r according to whether q is *true* or *false* respectively.

Colin, A. J. T., "Note on coding reverse polish expressions for single-address computers with one accumulator," *Computer Journal*, Vol. 6, No. 1, 1965, pp. 67–68.

This paper describes a compilation technique (originally developed for an optimizing compiler for PL/I) in which an entire program is translated into the form of a tree. This form of the text allows interpretive code-generation, making use of a wider scope of information than is usually possible.

Denning, P. J., G. S. Graham, "A note on subexpression ordering in the execution of arithmetic expressions," *CACM*, Vol. 16, No. 11, Nov. 1973, pp. 700–702.

Discusses further results and counter-examples to the optimality of the solutions in Ramamoorthy and Gonzalez (1971).

Ershov, A. P., "On programming of arithmetic operations," *CACM*, Vol. 1, No. 8, 1959, pp. 3–6.

Forsythe, G. E., "What is a satisfactory quadratic equation solver?" in *Constructive Aspects of the Fundamental Theorem of Algebra*, Bruno Dejon, Peter Henrici (eds.), New York: Wiley-Interscience, 1969.

In a conference devoted to algorithms for finding the zeros of general polynomials, Forsythe amusingly points out the "near absence" of algorithms to solve quadratic equations in a satisfactory way. The problems are with round-off and with methods of dealing with underflow and overflow, for which he puts forward the suggestion that dynamic detection and possible correction should be incorporated in high-level languages.

Foxley, E., "Programming problems in mathematical logic," *BIT*, Vol. 8, 1968, pp. 104–121.

Considers the programming of purely logical problems in a high-level language like ALGOL. Discusses the advantages of including higher-order logical functions in programming languages.

Gavrilov, M. A., A. D. Zakrevskii (eds.), *LYaPAS: A Programming Language for Logic and Coding Algorithms. IEEE Transactions on Electronic Computers*, EC-15, No. 5, Oct. 1966; New York: Academic Press, 1969.

Goldberg, I. B., "27 bits are not enough for 8-digit accuracy," *CACM*, Vol. 10, No. 2, Feb. 1967, pp. 105–106.

Goodman, R. (ed.), *Annual Review in Automatic Programming*, Vol. I, Elmsford, N.Y.: Pergamon Press, 1960.

A collection of papers presented at a conference in Brighton, England, in 1969, in the "early days" of "automatic programming." Most of the topics presented concerned the design and implementation of high-level languages.

Gregory, R. T., "On the design of the arithmetic unit of a fixed-word-length computer from the standpoint of computational accuracy," *IEEE Transactions on Electronic Computers*, Apr. 1966, pp. 255–257.

This paper summarizes some of the results of Wilkinson (1963) pointing out the bad effects of certain choices in machine design for those concerned with scientific computation. Some machines, though inherently faster, have been effectively slower in achieving the accuracy of their forerunners, because the same computations have had to be done in double precision.

Hamblin, C. L., "Translation to and from Polish notation," *Computer Journal*, Vol. 5, No. 3, Oct. 1962, pp. 210–213.

This paper describes reverse and forward Polish notations for writing mathematical formulas without brackets and demonstrates the suitability of these notations for mechanical evaluation. Two subsidiary forms are defined, based on the order of evaluation of operations of the same precedence; these are "early-operator" and "late-operator" forms. Four techniques of translation are described, covering the major techniques used in compilers.

Hamming, R. W., W. L. Mammel, "A note on the location of the binary point in a computing machine," *IEEE Transactions on Electronic Computers,* EC-14, No. 2, Apr. 1965, pp. 260–261.

Considers the placing of the binary point before and after the first digit in computer representations of numbers. The authors conclude that for "human reasons" (i.e., close relationship with standard practice) it is better to have the point after the first digit for external representations.

Hext, J. B., "Compile-time type-matching," *Computer Journal,* Vol. 9, No. 4, Feb. 1967, pp. 365–369.

Points out that it is desirable to have the types of all operands (including temporaries) known during compilation, although this is impossible with some language designs. The types in some languages form a partially ordered set. A procedure is outlined for type determination and for inserting transfer functions in the code generated by a compiler.

Howell, K. M., "Multiple precision arithmetic techniques," *Computer Journal,* Vol. 9, No. 4, Feb. 1967, pp. 383–387.

Huskey, H.D., "Compiling techniques for algebraic expressions," *Computer Journal,* Vol. 4, No. 1, Apr. 1961, pp. 10–19.

Describes a single-pass method of translating algebraic formulas into machine language.

Huskey, H. D., W. H. Wattenburg, "A basic compiler for arithmetic expressions," *CACM,* Vol. 4, No. 1, 1961, pp. 3–9.

Huskey, H. D., W. H. Wattenburg, "Compiling techniques for Boolean expressions and conditional statements in ALGOL 60," *CACM,* Vol. 4, No. 1, 1961, pp. 70–75.

Iverson, K. E., *A Programming Language,* New York: John Wiley, 1962.

Iverson, K. E., *Elementary Functions: an Algorithmic Treatment,* SRA, 1966.

An APL approach to elementary mathematical functions. Appendix A contains an extensive discussion of the rules of expression evaluation in APL.

Kesner, O., "Floating-point arithmetic in COBOL," *CACM,* Vol. 5, No. 5, May 1962, pp. 269–271.

Knuth, D. E., *The Art of Computer Programming: Volume 2—Seminumerical Algorithms,* Reading, Mass.: Addison-Wesley, 1969.

This volume is essential reading for those who wish to study the arithmetic of computers from a programming point of view. There is extensive treatment of number systems, floating-point arithmetic, and rational arithmetic—less detail on fixed-point arithmetic.

Laning, J. H., W. Zierler, "A program for translation of mathematical equations for Whirlwind I," *MIT Engineering Memorandum,* E-364, Instrumentation Laboratory, Cambridge, Mass., 1954.

An early (1952-3) example of a system which accepted expressions written in mathematical notation.

Lukasiewicz, J., *Elementy Logiki Matematyczby* (Elements of mathematical logic), Warsaw, 1929.

Proposals for a notation to be used in logic. Origin of the Polish notation for expressions.

Matula, D. W., "Towards an abstract mathematical theory of floating-point arithmetic," *Proc. AFIPS Conf. SJCC,* Vol. 34, 1969, pp. 765-772, AFIPS Press, 1969.

Matula, D. W., "A formalization of floating-point numeric base conversion," *IEEE Trans. on Comp.,* C-19, 1970, pp. 681-692.

Matula, D. W., "Significant digits: numerical analysis or numerology?" *Proc. IFIP Congress,* 1971, TA-1, North-Holland, 1971, pp. 33-38.

A discussion of the basis of floating-point arithmetic. Among topics discussed are Benford's work on anomalous numbers (Benford, 1938), the relationship of significant digits to accuracy, the 'equivalent digit' formula often used (e.g., in the PL/I language specifications), and a discussion of truncation *vs.* rounding.

McCarthy, J., "Letter to the editor," *CACM,* Vol. 2, No. 8, Aug. 1959, pp. 2-3.

This letter proposes two additions to IAL, the language which later became ALGOL 60. The letter gives excellent justifications for two important innovations in ALGOL: conditional expressions and recursive functions.

McCarthy, J., "Recursive functions of symbolic expressions and their computation by machine. Part I," *CACM,* Vol. 3, No. 4, Apr. 1960, pp. 184-195.

Nakata, I., "On compiling algorithms for arithmetic expressions," *CACM,* Vol. 10, No. 8, 1967, pp. 492-494.

Ramamoorthy, C. V., M. J. Gonzalez, "Subexpression ordering in the execution of arithmetic expressions," *CACM,* Vol. 14, No. 7, July 1971, pp. 479-485.

Discusses the problem of optimizing the code for arithmetic expressions, particularly for machines with some degree of parallel operation.

Randell, B., L. J. Russell, "Single-scan techniques for the translation of arithmetic expressions in ALGOL 60," *JACM,* Vol. 11, No. 2, Apr. 1964, pp. 159-167.

Ravi, S., J. D. Ullman, "The generation of optimal code for arithmetic expressions," *JACM,* Vol. 17, No. 4, Oct. 1970, pp. 715-728.

Redziejowski, R. R., "On arithmetic expressions and trees," *CACM,* Vol. 12, No. 2, Feb. 1969, pp. 81-84.

Reitwiesner, G. V., "Binary arithmetic," (in) *Advances in Computers,* Vol. 1, pp. 284-289.

Rice, J. R. (ed.), *Mathematical Software,* New York: Academic Press, 1971.

Rutishauer, H., "Automatische rechenplanfertigung bei programmgesteuerten Rechenmaschinen," *Mitt. Inst. f. Angew. Math. Eth Zurich,* No. 3, 1952.

Samelson, K., F. L. Bauer, "Sequential formula translation," *CACM*, Vol. 3, No. 2, Feb. 1960, pp. 76–82.

A well-known paper describing how the compilation of languages can be effected using a "cellar" (i.e., a push-down store).

Schneider, V., "On the number of registers needed to evaluate arithmetic expressions," *BIT*, Vol. II, 1971, pp. 84–93.

This paper considers the number of storage registers needed to evaluate a compiled expression, assuming that no factoring or rearranging of the terms has been carried out. For nonparenthetical expressions, the number of registers is $N + 1$, where N is the number of operator procedure levels. If there are K levels of nested parentheses, this becomes: $(K + 1)*N + 1$.

Shaw, C. J., "On declaring arbitrarily coded alphabets," *CACM*, Vol. 7, No. 5, May 1964, pp. 288–290.

Sheridan, P. B., "The arithmetic translator-compiler of the IBM FORTRAN automatic coding system," *CACM*, Vol. 2, No. 2, Feb. 1959, pp. 9–21.

Stone, H. S., "One-pass compilation of arithmetic expressions for a parallel processor," *CACM*, Vol. 10, No. 4, Apr. 1967, pp. 220–223.

Tarski, A., "On the calculus of relations," *Journal of Symbolic Logic*, Vol. 6, No. 3, Sept. 1941, pp. 73–89.

An extended address on the history of the theory of relations. Tarski attributes the creation of the modern theory of relations to C. S. Pierce, whose work was extended and developed by E. Schroder.

Thacker, H. C., Jr., "Making special arithmetics available," (in) *Mathematical Software*, J. R. Rice (ed.), New York: Academic Press, 1971, pp. 113–119.

Presents the case for writing special arithmetic packages (e.g., multiple precision, integer arithmetic, rational arithmetic) in high-level languages.

van Wijngaarden, A., "Numerical analysis as an independent science," *BIT*, Vol. 6, No. 6, 1966, pp. 66–81.

Points out the differences between numerical analysis (particularly as employed on a digital computer) and classical mathematics. Introduces such terms as "imprecision," "incredulity," and "efficiency," commonly used in computing but unknown in mathematics.

Wilkinson, J. H., *Rounding Errors in Algebraic Processes*, London: HMSO, 1963; Englewood Cliffs, N.J.: Prentice-Hall, 1963.

A classic work by a famous numerical analyst.

Wood, D., "A proof of Hamblin's algorithm for translation of arithmetic expressions from infix to postfix form," *BIT*, Vol. 9, No. 1, 1969, pp. 59–68.

EXERCISES

9.1 The *residue* of an integer m, modulo n, is defined as the remainder when m is divided by n.

Write a program which reads in a sequence of integers and prints a corresponding sequence of residues, modulo N, in FORTRAN, ALGOL, COBOL, PL/I.

9.2 Consider the following fragment of program:

Y is assigned to X:

X is assigned to Y

Choose any language and construct a table of *types* for which these statements are valid. For which types is the value of Y unchanged?

9.3 Consider the same problem, but substitute input/output statements such as READ and WRITE for the assignment operation (i.e., the assignment is to take place to and from an auxiliary storage device).

9.4 What types may a, b, and c take for the following expressions to be valid in 1) ALGOL, 2) FORTRAN, 3) COBOL, 4) PL/I?

$a = b$

$a \wedge b$

$a > b$

$a > b \mid c$

$a < b < c$

9.5 In the expression

$(X+Y)*(X-Y),$

what is known about the order of execution of the addition and subtraction operations, according to the standard specifications of 1) ALGOL, 2) FORTRAN, 3) PL/I, 4) COBOL?

9.6 Write a program to discover which of the operations in 9.5 is carried out first.

9.7 In mathematics, x^2 can be expressed in the following equivalent ways.

$x**2$

$x*x$

$\exp(2 \log x)$

List as many ways as you can of expressing:

$x^3,$

the square root of x cubed.

Code these in PL/I, FORTRAN, or any other suitable language and compare the results for a range of values of x.

9.8 P. Naur proposed an "Environment Enquiry" for ALGOL 60, which has been incorporated in ALGOL 68. By this means, a programmer may obtain the value of certain implementation-defined quantities, such as the maximum size of an integer.

Write a program which will compute the maximum size of a FORTRAN or PL/I integer.

9.9 A polynomial expression such as: $ax^3 + bx^2 + cx + d$ can be evaluated in several different ways. Two of these are illustrated here.

$a*x**3 + b*x**2 + c*x + d$

$((a*x + b)*x + c)*x + d$ (Horner's method)

How many arithmetic operations are saved by the use of Horner's method

for a polynomial of 3rd degree

for a polynomial of nth degree?

What is the effect of using Horner's method on the accuracy of the result? (See Knuth (1969) Vol. 2, section 4.6.4.)

9.10 Write the following expressions in 1) FORTRAN or PL/I notation, 2) fully parenthesized form, 3) functional form, 4) reverse Polish, 5) tree form :—.

    a. $x^2 + 2axy - 7y^2$

    b. $(a+b)(3t^2 - \sin A)$

    c. $(a>b) \vee (c<d)$

9.11 Which of the following operations are 1) associative, 2) commutative?

    a. *a min b*   where *min* is the smaller of *a* or *b*

    b. *a mod b*   where *mod* gives the remainder when *a* is divided by *b*

    c. a *mean* b   where *mean* gives the average of a and b

9.12 Write conditional expressions whose operands and results are as follows.

operand	result
name of month (character string)	number of days (integer)
height of ground (integer)	color of map (character string)

9.13 a. State the advantages in implementing the statement

```
ADD 1 TO A     (COBOL)
```

rather than the statement:

```
A = A+1        (FORTRAN, ALGOL)
```

b. Extend this to a consideration of the COBOL form:

```
ADD 1 to A,B,C,D.
```

9.14 Given three integers, *a*, *b* and *c*, write an expression in 1) ALGOL and 2) PL/I, whose value is:

    a.   1 if *a, b,* and *c* are all equal

    b.   0 if *a, b,* and *c* are all different

    c. -1 if any two of them are equal.

10
Sequencing
and Control
Structures

10.1 INTRODUCTION

In this chapter we turn from the consideration of *data,* the raw material of computation, to that of *programs,* the means by which computations are carried out. In particular we consider the sequence in which the basic operations of a program are executed. In a program, operations are ordered in sequence of time, just as in a string or array the elements are ordered in storage or in some form of address space. The structure implied by this ordering is called the *control structure* of a program.

In the practical use of computers, it is essential to be able to execute each instruction more than once and perhaps many thousands of times. Executing the millions of instructions needed for a large computation would be unthinkable if each instruction had to be written out sequentially. The control structures of a programming language provide the means by which the reuse of program material can be accomplished. They include methods of branching and looping, and forms of controlled iteration in which sections of a program are executed many times while a specified variable is systematically incremented or decremented.

10.1.1 Basic Concepts

In the simplest form of control structure, statements are executed sequentially in the order in which they appear in a program. The "successor" of a statement is the statement which follows it in lexical order.

A sequence of statements may be written

$$S_1; \ S_2; \ldots S_n;$$

where the semicolon is the statement delimiter. We may regard the semi-colon or new-line as a *sequential operator,* so that $(S_i; \ S_j)$ means

do S_i
then do S_j

Note that in languages based on card format, there may be no specific character which acts as a statement delimiter and a new statement is indicated by a new line on the coding sheet.

Although the semicolon or new line may be the only sequential operator in certain kinds of command languages (such as the various "Job Control" languages), it is not adequate for application and programming languages, since it requires all program steps to be written out explicitly. We therefore need to introduce sequencing operators to allow conditional branching, looping, and other means of achieving multiple execution of statements. We may wish to replace the normal successor of a statement by some other statement (as in the **go to** statement) or by a rule for computing a successor statement (as in the **if, case, do,** and similar statements).

The widespread adoption of sequential execution of machine instructions may lead us to overlook the existence of alternative machine designs. In early machines using cyclic storage (e.g., mercury-delay lines), each machine instruction had to specify its successor—in effect, every instruction was a **go to.** This was the case in the first machine used by the author, the DEUCE machine,† in which each instruction had to contain the address of its successor—this consisted of a delay line address and a relative clock time when the instruction would appear.

In high-level programming languages, we tend to take it for granted that statements will be executed one after the other, as written. However, an example of a language in which each statement may be a branch is provided by SNOBOL (Griswold *et al.,* 1968).

A SNOBOL statement has the form:

label subject pattern = object go to

The action of a SNOBOL statement is to scan the specified string, looking for the nominated pattern. The **go to** part of the statement (which is

---

† The DEUCE machine was based on a machine called ACE, originally developed at the National Physical Laboratory, following a proposal by A. M. Turing. Turing's original paper has been republished, in a version edited by Davies (1972).

optional) consists of one of the following:

:(label)   ......   an unconditional branch

:S(label) ......   a branch to be taken when a matching pattern is found

:F(label) ......   a branch to be taken when a match is not found

Example

A section of SNOBOL coding is as follows: (page 59 of Griswold *et al.,* 1968)

```
LOOP    CARD = TRIM(INPUT)    :F(END)
        GT(SIZE(CARD),40)     :S(PRINT)
        BLANKS PADPAT         :F(ERROR)
        PUNCH = PAD CARD      :(LOOP)
PRINT   OUTPUT = CARD         :(LOOP)
        END
```

However, SNOBOL is unusual among programming languages, most of which are like most current machines based on the sequential execution of statements as written, except where the order of execution is altered by control statements.

Virtually all programming languages contain the following types of statement to control the sequence of operations in a program:

- the GO TO statement—for unconditional transfer,
- the IF statement—for conditional transfer,
- a looping statement—for controlled iteration.

These three statements are discussed in the first part of the chapter. Following this, more complex structures including those proposed for "structured programming" are discussed. Another type of sequence control is obtained by monitoring the program execution and branching when a certain *condition* arises. This method originated in hardware designs, but a language form of this has been incorporated in PL/I with the ON statement. Finally, the chapter contains a discussion of the parallel control of programs.

10.2 THE "GO TO" STATEMENT

The GO TO statement is the simplest example of a sequencing statement and appears in nearly all programming languages. The form of a GO TO statement is

GO TO statement-label

and its meaning is closely associated with the meaning given to a statement-label.

Statement labels are self-declaring—their appearance in a source program signifies both their existence and their meaning. In simple languages, that is languages without block structure or recursion, label values are equivalent to machine addresses; GO TO P can be realized as a branch instruction to the address of the statement at P. Even so, certain types of branching involve more complications than is the case with machine languages. For example, branching in and out of DO loops in FORTRAN is subject to a number of special restrictions because of the more complex environment during the execution of a high-level-language program. This environment includes the status and current values of those variables in the program which may be affected by a transfer of control.

This is seen in the case of block structured languages, in which the action of the GO TO statement may be even more complex. For a valid transfer to a point with label P, P must be "known" at the point of the GO TO statement. If P is not in the same block as the GO TO, it must be in one of the surrounding blocks; and execution of the GO TO will involve a transfer out of the block containing the GO TO. This form of GO TO is therefore similar to a block exit instruction and may involve considerable activity in the compiled code, such as the release of storage for variables local to the block.

The situation becomes even more involved in the case of the special form of procedure activation known as *recursion* (described in Chapter 12). In the use of recursion, a procedure block is entered more than once, for example by executing a statement 'call P' from within the procedure P itself. When a block has been entered recursively, each entry conceptually creates another set of local variables, including the label values local to the block. In some techniques for implementing recursion, a label value has two parts —one to identify the location of program code in the block, the other to represent the depth of recursion to which the label value corresponds.

10.2.1   Extended GO TO Statements

In many languages, including ALGOL, FORTRAN, COBOL and PL/I, there are additional forms of the GO TO statement which provide:

- the ability to branch to one of several predetermined labels, depending on the value of a certain variable (the multiway branch).

- the ability to set a GO TO statement so that it transfers to a specified point. This allows the user to set a return location at the end of a section of program being used as a subroutine.

FORTRAN

In FORTRAN, all statement labels are represented as integers as they were in several early symbolic programming languages. The multiway switch is provided by the computed GO TO statement which has the form

$$\text{GO TO } (L_1, L_2, \ldots L_n), i$$

where L_1, L_2, etc., are labels and i is an integer variable.

Example

$$\text{GO TO } (10, 30, 40, 10), \text{IVAL}$$

All possible branches must be listed. The current value of i determines which of the labels is used. The rules of FORTRAN do not state what happens if the value of i exceeds the number of labels in the list, except to specify that it is undefined. This error cannot be detected by a compiler, since i may be computed during the execution of the program. Some compilers (including those of IBM) have interpreted "i out of range" as a null statement. This interpretation is likely to be followed in the forthcoming ANSI standard.

Return from an internal subroutine may be accomplished by the assigned GO TO, whose syntax closely resembles the computed GO TO:

$$\text{GO TO } i, (L_1, L_2, \ldots L_n)$$

Example

$$\text{GO TO NEXT}, (10, 20, 30, 35)$$

In this case, i, instead of being used to index the list of labels, must itself have been given a label value (which must be one of those in the list) before execution of the statement. The variable i is set by a special form of the assignment statement:

$$\text{ASSIGN } k \text{ to } i$$

where k is an integer variable or constant whose value at the time of assignment is among the values used as a statement label. (Although the variable i may be used either for numeric integer values or for labels, these uses are mutually exclusive.)

Although the execution of the GO TO statement depends only on the value of i and not on the list of statement labels, the list is included in the GO TO statement because, in FORTRAN compilers, restricting the possible branch points from the GO TO statement to those in a specified list makes it easier to carry out the flow-analysis of the program, as needed in optimization.

ALGOL

In ALGOL, the **go to** statement is defined as follows:

<go to statement> :: = **go to** <designational expression>

A *designational expression* is a distinct form of expression whose purpose is to express a label value. Among its forms is the conditional expression described in Chapter 9, so that a possible form of **go to** is the following:

go to **if** $a > 10$ **then** $L17$ **else** $L18$;

This statement results in a transfer to label L17 or L18, depending on the value of a. It is easy to see how, by suitable nesting of the conditional expression, the effect of a multi-way branch can be programmed.

A more elaborate branching mechanism is provided by the ALGOL *switch*. A switch is an ALGOL data type, whose range of values must be specified in its declaration. A switch declaration, like any ALGOL declaration, appears at the head of a block, and consists of a *switch identifier*, which names the switch, and a *switch list*, a list of possible values of the switch.

Example

begin **integer** $A, B;$ **real** $X, Y;$
switch $SW: = L, M, N;$
. . . .

In this declaration, the switch SW can assume the values $L, M,$ and N.

Note that the switch list serves much the same purpose as the list of labels in the FORTRAN assigned GO TO statement. There is a difference, however, since in FORTRAN the list is appended to the GO TO statement, while in ALGOL the list is associated with the switch variable by declaration.

A **go to** statement can be written in the form

go to $SW[1]$;

which causes transfer to $L,$

go to $SW[2]$;

which refers to $M,$ and so on.

ALGOL switch declarations are not restricted to being simple labels—in fact, each member of the switch list may itself be a *designational expression,* which includes a simple label, a conditional expression yielding a label value or a subscripted switch identifier. The opportunities for obscure programming here are considerable and there are several difficulties in compiling a general form of such a statement. Consider, for example, the switch declaration

switch S: = **if** $x>1$ **then** $L1$ **else** $L2$, **if** $y<100$ **then** $L5$

else $L6$;

and a **go to** statement which refers to it:

go to $S[I]$;

Given that I has the value 1, which label is referred to?

Looking at the first designational expression, we see that it is the conditional expression

if $x>1$ **then** $L1$ **else** $L2$

It is obvious that in this case the meaning of the **go to** cannot be determined until execution time, when the current value of x is known. It would be possible to define the switch declaration so that all switch values were evaluated when the block is entered (this would be analogous to the rules for evaluating array bounds). However, the ALGOL specifications state that the switch values are established when the label is *used,* namely when the **go to** statement is executed. Interpretive code must therefore be present at execution time to evaluate the conditional expressions. (The rule is given in paragraph 5.3.4 of the ALGOL report (Naur, 1963).)

There are several anomalous situations which may arise from the use of switches—for example, x and y may not have been initialized when the **go to** statement is executed. Instead of treating this as an error, the ALGOL specifications state that in such cases the **go to** statement is to be regarded as a dummy statement, and no transfer is made (ALGOL report, 4.3.5). This makes testing of programs using switches very difficult.

A further problem can arise when one switch is defined in terms of other switches; this may lead to declarations which cannot be resolved because of circularity.

COBOL

In COBOL, statement labels are called *procedure-names* and refer to sections or paragraphs. COBOL procedure-names are used in the PERFORM statement, as well as in GO TO statements. They are written before the section or paragraph to which they refer, and paragraph names are followed by a period (.) and a space.

Example

```
FIRST-PART.    ADD 2 TO LIMIT.
...
SECOND PART.   IF LIMIT EQUAL 100 GO TO FIRST-PART.
```

Section names are followed by the key word SECTION and must be unique in a program. Paragraph names must be unique within a section but the same name may be used in different sections. A paragraph name may be qualified by a section name to remove ambiguity.

Example

```
READ-IN SECTION.
    PART-1. ...
    PART-2. ...
VALIDATION SECTION.
    PART-1. ...
    PART-2. ...
    PERFORM PART-1 IN READ-IN.
```

A multiway switch is provided by the following form of the GO TO statement.

```
GO TO procedure-name-1[,procedure-name-2]...
    DEPENDING ON identifier
```

This is like the computed GO TO in FORTRAN, the numeric value of the identifier determining which of the branches is to be taken. COBOL resembles ALGOL in regarding it as legal for the identifier to take a value outside the range of names in the list; as with ALGOL, the GO TO statement is then regarded as a null or dummy statement.

Subroutine return linkage can be provided by the ALTER statement. The form of this is:

```
ALTER procedure-name-1 TO PROCEED TO procedure-name-2
```

This is an unusual statement, both in its convoluted syntax and in its action.

Example

Suppose a COBOL program contains a section of code labeled COMMON-CODE and we wish to use this from several different points. At the end of COMMON-CODE we write a GO TO statement, GO TO RETURN, which will be used to branch back to the statement following the point of use. This return statement must be the sole statement in a labeled paragraph, as follows:

```
COMMON-CODE.
        text of common-code
        ...
L1.
        GO TO RETURN-POINT.
```

To set the return label and enter COMMON-CODE we write:

```
ALTER L1 TO PROCEED TO NEXT-SECTION.
GO TO COMMON-CODE.
NEXT-SECTION.
        next statement
```

The statement GO TO RETURN-POINT remains altered to GO TO NEXT-SECTION until another ALTER statement is executed.

Note that executing the ALTER statement effects a change in the program—this is unusual in high-level languages, which seldom allow a program to make changes to itself.

PL/I

PL/I has extended the label concepts of other languages, the most important new feature being the introduction of *label variables*. However, the treatment of PL/I *label constants* (these correspond to the "labels" of other languages) has also been developed and extended.

Any PL/I statement can be prefixed by a *label list,* a sequence of labels each followed by a colon (:). The label list serves to declare and initialize these label values, which are the label constants of the program (and are the potential values of the label variables).

Example

```
LABEL: X = X+1;
...
A: B: C: CALL SUB(1,5);
...
LOOP: DO WHILE(F); ... END;
```

A new feature introduced by PL/I is the ability to define *label arrays.*

Example

```
LAB(1):   X=X+1;
        ...
LAB(3):   IF T>0 THEN T=T-1;
        ...
LAB(12):
        ...
```

GO TO statements can be written:

```
GO TO LAB(3);
GO TO LAB(I+1);
```

A label array can be used to provide a multiway switch, the form: GO TO LAB(N) being similar to the computed GO TO of FORTRAN.

A PL/I *label variable* embodies a label value and has the full range of properties of other PL/I variables. Label values may be assigned to label variables, allowing complex sequencing to be set up with relatively low overheads.

Example

If a subroutine is labeled ROUTINE, it may be coded so that the last executed statement is:

```
GO TO LABVAR;
```

where LABVAR is a label variable.

```
        DECLARE LABVAR LABEL VARIABLE;
ROUTINE:
        code for the subroutine
        ...
        GO TO LABVAR;
```

To execute the subroutine, the return label is first set as follows:

```
        LABVAR=RETURN1;
        GO TO ROUTINE;
RETURN1:
        next statement.
```

As with any PL/I variable, label variables may have scope and storage attributes. They may be assigned, transmitted as arguments of procedures, and returned as values from function references. No arithmetic operations are defined for labels ($L + 1$ is *not* the label of the next statement), and the only comparison operations defined for labels are $=$ (equal) and $\neg =$ (not equal).

As with other forms of extended GO TO facilities, there are intrinsic problems with PL/I label variables. Among the more serious difficulties are the possible differences in scope between a label constant and a label variable. The assignment of a label value to a label variable may be perfectly valid when the assignment is made. However, when the time comes to use the label in a GO TO statement, it may no longer be valid (for example if the block to which the value refers has been terminated). These "dangling references," as they have been called (Wegner, 1971), are a penalty that is paid for the general referencing facilities provided by label variables.

10.2.2   Should the GO TO Statement Be Abolished?

For some time, the GO TO statement has been the subject of controversy, from both a theoretical and a practical point of view. Theoretically, it does not fit naturally among the other statements found in high-level languages.† The execution of a "program expression" (see Chapters 5 and 9) follows a hierarchic pattern, each unit returning a value to its neighbor above. In this model, the GO TO statement fits very uneasily, particularly in languages with block structure and recursion. Even in its simplest form, it suggests transfer to fixed, immutable text and leads to less readable and less reliable programs.

Until recently, programming errors were often regarded as inevitable. The little effort directed toward their elimination was devoted to better program documentation and the development of more elaborate and exhaustive test cases. However as the typical size of programming systems has increased, declining program reliability has led to a closer study of the use of the GO TO statement.

In 1965, Professor Dijkstra wrote his now famous letter to the editor of *CACM* proposing the abolition of the GO TO statement from programming languages. He discussed the anomalous theoretical position of the GO TO statement and attacked it on the grounds of poor readability and reliability. In later works on structured programming, Dijkstra clarified his arguments about the use of GO TO statements. (See Chapter 2 Bibliography.) His ideas have been tested by others in the field who have confirmed that the disciplined type of programming advocated by Dijkstra could produce substantial improvements in both economy and code reliability. In IBM, H. D. Mills (1971) applied Dijkstra's techniques to programming projects and measured the resulting program effectiveness. Mills' results show that the programming process can be considerably improved by strict adherence to the sequencing discipline implicit in the elimination of the GO TO statement.

Under Dijkstra's proposal, the GO TO statement would be eliminated from all high-level programming languages. All sequencing would then be specified by means of higher-level control statements such as IF, FOR and

---

†If we take a functional view of programming languages, the GO TO statement is not the only anomalous statement. The *assignment* statement, with its implication of assigning values to locations in storage, has a similarly uneasy fit with the Lambda calculus model of programming languages.

the CASE statements defined below. A set of basic control elements is shown in Fig. 10.1. However, there are certain situations in which the GO TO statement cannot be eliminated without severe technical difficulties or loss of function. Figure 10.2, shows program structures which cannot be expressed in terms of the basic control elements of Fig. 10.1. Such program structures require either the use of the GO TO statement or the introduction of control structures other than those in Fig. 10.1.

The case for abolishing the GO TO statement rests on the following view of programming. Given an overall task, the programmer breaks it down into a series of lesser tasks which are in turn broken down into still smaller

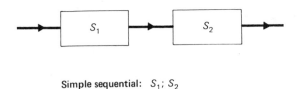

Simple sequential: $S_1; S_2$

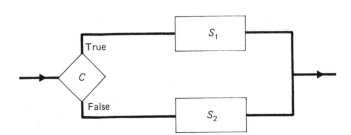

Conditional branch: if C then S_1 else S_2

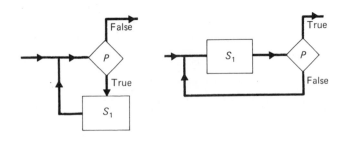

Loop: do S_1 while P do S until P

Fig. 10.1 Basic control elements

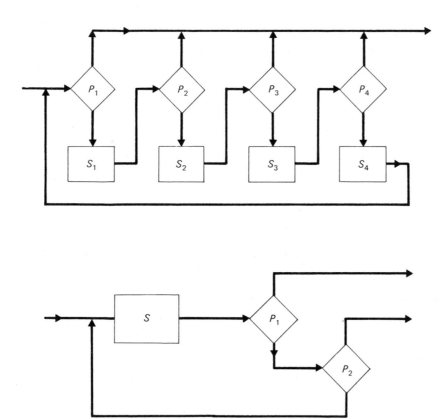

Fig. 10.2 Irreducible flowcharts. It is not possible to express these in terms of the basic control elements of Fig. 10.1 without duplicating some of the elements of the flow chart.

subtasks. At every level, the program's sequencing control must be such that, to perform each task, control returns to the point at which the command for carrying out that task is written. In this process, GO TO acts as an anarchist, respecting none of the hierarchic boundaries, but allowing control to be passed across these carefully structured levels. This may be seen particularly in the case of a GO TO statement which transfers control out of a deeply nested loop or block; the resulting upheaval is apparent in the large amount of code which has to be executed to implement such a transfer. The GO TO is at once too primitive—originating in the machine language BRANCH instruction—and too powerful—resulting in code of considerable complexity. Tracking the flow of a program which uses GO TO's and estimating the possible values of each known variable at each point may become an impossibly complex task.

Considerable interest has been taken in the theoretical conditions which would allow the removal of GO TO statements. Among the first to discuss this was van Wijngaarden (1966), who gave a method for defining the semantics of programming languages as well as a systematic procedure for removing GO TO statements from ALGOL programs. Knuth and Floyd (1970) discuss situations in which GO TO statements can be avoided. Ashcroft and Manna (1971) show how GO TO programs can be translated into programs containing DO-WHILE statements only. A paper by Martin (1973) considers the set of "primitive" control structures that might be used as the basis for programming languages. At a 1972 SIGPLAN meeting, practical aspects of programming using the GO TO statement were discussed.

Although there are advantages in reducing the use of the GO TO statement, its elimination from programming languages does not seem feasible unless compensating additions in the form of more powerful sequencing statements are made. The CASE statement (Wirth and Hoare, 1966), the use of decision tables to provide more complex sequencing primitives, and an EXIT from loops are among the alternatives which have been proposed to replace the GO TO function should it be eliminated.

10.3   THE "IF" STATEMENT

The IF statements of ALGOL, COBOL and PL/I all follow a similar form:

if condition **then** first-action **else** second-action

The structure of an IF statement differs from that of most other statements. Since the parts we have called "first-action" and "second-action" may themselves be statements, we see that an IF statement may contain another statement. This sometimes leads to problems in syntax design.

In the general form of the IF statement, the *condition* is any truth-valued quantity. This includes the following forms:

- **relational expression**

Examples

$a = b$	(ALGOL)
I.GT.J	(FORTRAN)
RATE–OF–DISCOUNT LESS THAN 5	(COBOL)
ERROR >= .001	(PL/I)

- **logical value** (ALGOL, FORTRAN)

ALGOL includes the data type **Boolean** and FORTRAN the type LOGICAL; in both cases their values may be *true* or *false*. Variables of these types may be used directly as conditions in IF statements.

Example (ALGOL)

begin Boolean $b1$;

  . . .

if $b1$ **then** $x:=0$

  else $x:=y+t$;

  . . .

- **bit-string value** (PL/I)

In PL/I, a BIT string of length 1 takes the place of a logical or Boolean variable.

Example

```
IF TRIGGER THEN CALL P;
IF SUBST (B,5,1) THEN GO TO J(N+1);
```

- **logical expression** (ALGOL, FORTRAN, COBOL, PL/I)

A logical expression may be constructed by linking together truth values with the logical operators, AND, OR, NOT etc.

Examples

$(a=b) \vee (a=c)$	(ALGOL)
`(I.GT.J).OR.(I.EQ.10)`	(FORTRAN)
`RATE-OF-DISCOUNT LESS THAN 5 AND`	(COBOL)
`    GREATER THAN 3`	
`(ERROR >=.001) & ¬TIME_EXPIRED`	(PL/I)

- **condition-name** (COBOL)

COBOL includes a special type of element called a *condition* which has a similar function to the logical variables of other languages. Each value associated with a condition is given a *condition-name,* and is distinguished by the special level number, 88. For an example, see Section 10.3.4.

The IF-THEN-ELSE construction allows two actions to be specified, one for a *true* value of the condition, the other for a *false* value. In some circumstances, it is only necessary to specify an action for the true condition, so that if the condition is false, the statement following the IF statement is executed. It is usual, in these circumstances, for the ELSE clause to be omitted, giving the simpler form: IF-THEN. This is the only form permitted by the FORTRAN logical IF.

Example

When the IF-THEN form is adequate, an error-testing statement could be

```
...
IF X=0 THEN CALL ERROR_HANDLER;
A=(T+B)/X;
...
```

The IF-THEN statement is less powerful than IF-THEN-ELSE, and may require extra condition testing to achieve the same effect as the IF-THEN-ELSE construction.

Example

In a language without the *else* clause:

```
IF(X=0) THEN L = 1;
        ELSE L = 2;
next statement
```

must be written

```
IF(X=0) THEN L = 1;
IF(X¬=0)THEN L = 2;
next statement
```

The IF-THEN-ELSE construction can be used to express the complete structure of a program without using GO TO statements. For an example of a program constructed in this form, see Algorithm 272, by M. D. MacLaren (1965). This algorithm has two main branches, one of which is entered after testing the value of one of its two parameters. The THEN clause, taken on the first entry to the procedure, has 31 statements. The ELSE clause, taken on subsequent entries, contains most of the remainder of the program and itself includes several IF and FOR statements. There is only one GO TO statement, which branches out of a loop to the statement following the end of the loop.

The two action statements following THEN and ELSE may themselves be IF statements, each with THEN and ELSE clauses. This form of construction is called a *nested* IF statement and may be used for multiway branches and other complex sequencing constructions.

10.3.1   The Problem of the "Dangling" ELSE

The nested form of **if** statement was included in a general form in ALGOL. The first ALGOL report (Naur, 1960) contained an ambiguity in the specification of the **if** statement. This came to be known as the problem of the 'dangling *else*' and has been the subject of several papers (Dahlstrand, 1961; Bottenbruck and Grau, 1961; Kaupe, 1963; Abrahams, 1966). The syntactic problems are not unique to ALGOL, but arise in any language with nested **if** statements.

Briefly, the problem arises when an **if** statement is nested within another **if** statement:

if C1 then if C2 then S1 else S2

In the original syntax it was not clear whether this was an **if-then** statement nested within an **if-then-else** statement

if C1 then [if C2 then S1] else S2

or *vice versa*

if C1 then [if C2 then S1 else S2]

It is easy to construct examples in which the two different interpretations give different results.

begin integer t,S; t: = 2; S: = 0; if t> 1 then if t>3 then S: = 1 else S: = 2;
X: . . .

When point X is reached, S has the value 0 under the first interpretation and 2 under the second interpretation.

The problem is a purely syntactic one for which Abrahams (1966) discusses several possible solutions.

- Revision of the syntax rules to exclude the ambiguous case

- The introduction of a requirement that every **if** statement have a corresponding **else** clause

- A means of pairing each **if** with its corresponding **else** (This may involve the use of alternative methods of syntactic description to those used in the ALGOL report.)

In the revised report on ALGOL (Naur, 1963), the first of these approaches was chosen, although, as Abrahams points out, the new rules also excluded some cases that were *not* ambiguous. COBOL and PL/I have each adopted a variant of the third approach.

The **if** and **else** symbols play the role of brackets in the parsing of complex **if** statements. In ALGOL 68, a departure from the traditional form of **if** statements has been made. The **if** statement is a fully bracketed structure, delimited by the symbols **if** and **fi**. (This is one of several cases in ALGOL 68 where the reverse form of a word is used to form a closing bracket.)

Example

$$\text{if } T > 10 \text{ then } A := \textit{next }(I); \ B := \textit{previous }(J)$$
$$\text{else } I := I+1; \ J := J-1 \text{ fi}$$

A similar form is used for conditional expressions:

$$K := 100 - \text{if } \textit{full} \text{ then } \textit{print } (\text{``}\textit{full}\text{''}); \ 0 \text{ else } x \text{ fi}$$

In this case, if the Boolean variable full is true, then K becomes 100 and the word "full" is printed; otherwise K is set to the value $100-x$.

10.3.2   The FORTRAN IF Statements

In FORTRAN, there are two IF statements, an *arithmetic* IF and a *logical* IF. The arithmetic IF is closely modeled on the testing instruction of the 704 computer. The statement tests an arithmetic value (represented by a FORTRAN expression) and branches one of *three* ways, depending on a positive, zero or negative value of the expression. This has some advantages when dealing with numeric conditions, and when originally proposed allowed easy code-generation for the 704 and similar machines. However, there are several disadvantages to this form of the IF statement now that its closeness to a particular machine architecture is no longer relevant.

The form of the arithmetic IF statement is

$$\text{IF (expression) } L_1, L_2, L_3$$

where

$$L_1, \ L_2, \ L_3$$

are integer labels.

Example

FORTRAN code for the error test shown above is as follows:

```
    IF (X) 10,20,10
 20 CALL ERR(N)
    GO TO 10
 10 A = (T+B)/X
```

This example shows how extra labels have to be introduced into the program to denote the two branches. It is obvious that in this form IF statements cannot be nested.

The FORTRAN logical IF statement, introduced with the later version of FORTRAN known as FORTRAN IV, has the form::

$$IF \ (e) \ S$$

where e is a logical expression and S is a statement.

A logical expression may be formed from one of the relational operators: .LT. (less than), .LE. (less than or equal to), etc. The previous example can thus be coded:

```
IF (X .EQ. 0) CALL ERR(N)
A = (T+B)/X
...
```

The absence of the ELSE clause makes it difficult to code certain types of complex decision. The statement S may not be a logical IF statement, nesting of logical IF statements is not possible either.

10.3.3 The ALGOL if Statement

As we have seen above, the ALGOL **if** statement allows full nesting of the **then** and **else** clauses. Since ALGOL also includes the *conditional expression*, whose value depends on the evaluation of a condition (see Chapter 9), the ALGOL facilities for conditional evaluation and discrimination are extremely powerful (Fig. 10.3).

```
procedure comp (V, X);  real array V;  integer array X;
begin real t;  integer i;
  if f(x⌊m⌋) × (if X[n−1, 1] ≠ 0 then f(x[X[n−1, 1]])
  else V[−1]) ≥ 0 then go to back;
  if (n=N) ∨ (n=1) then t : = V[n−1] + abs (f(x[m]))
  else t : = V[n−1] + 2 × abs (f(x[m]));
  if t > V[n] ∧ (n≠1 ⊇ X[n−1, 1] ≠ 0) then
  begin V[n] : = t;  i : = 1;
  for i : = i+1 while X[n−1, i−1] ≠ 0
  do X[n, i] : = X[n−1, i−1];  X[n, 1] : = m
  end;
back:  end comp;
```

Fig. 10.3 Example of the ALGOL **if** statement. This shows the complex type of branching possible with a fully nested form of the **if** statement. Note that in line 3 the condition part of the **if** statement is evaluated using a *conditional expression*, a type of expression not available in FORTRAN, COBOL, or PL/I. (See Lynch, 1965.)

10.3.4   The COBOL IF Statement

The most interesting feature of the COBOL IF statement is the variety of conditions that may be tested. In addition to the relational and logical expression found in other languages, COBOL allows two other types of condition, *class condition* and *condition-name.*

Class condition

The relationship of NUMERIC and ALPHABETIC with COBOL data types is described in Chapter 7. A class condition is an example of a *predicate,* a truth-valued function applied to a data-item, which in this case determines the *type* (i.e., a set of values) of an item.

Condition-name

The COBOL condition-name is a user-defined predicate. In this case, both the name of the condition and the set of values which determines its truth or falsity are defined by the program. A condition-name has the distinctive level number 88 and its associated values are specified in its declaration.

COBOL allows nested IF-THEN-ELSE statements, and there is a "null" action, specified by the phrase NEXT SENTENCE, which allows either the THEN or the ELSE part of the IF statement to be by-passed.

The sequencing of COBOL IF statements is such that the successor to a THEN clause is the next *sentence.* The ability to write a COBOL sentence containing several statements means that when a sequence of IF statements is linked to form a single sentence, these may be bypassed if the first condition is true. Compare the following two sections of coding:

Example 1:

```
IF QUALIFIED AND MOBILE MOVE NAME TO SHORT-LIST;
IF MARRIED ADD 1 TO M-COUNT;
ELSE ADD 1 TO UM-COUNT.
next sentence
   ...
```

Example 2:

```
IF QUALIFIED AND MOBILE MOVE NAME TO SHORT LIST.
IF MARRIED ADD 1 TO M-COUNT;
ELSE ADD 1 to UM-COUNT.
next sentence
   ...
```

The fact that Example 1 has a single sentence while Example 2 has two produces a completely different effect. See Fig. 10.4 for flowcharts of these statements.

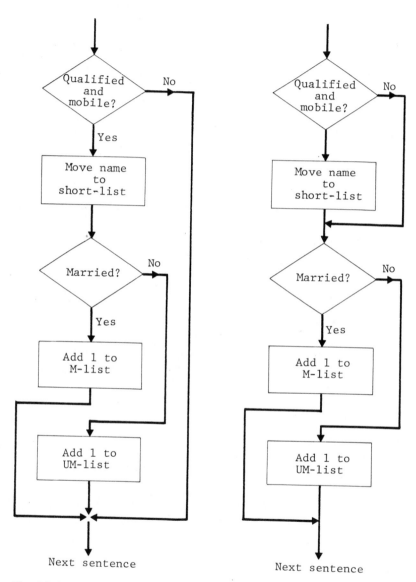

Fig. 10.4 Two examples of COBOL IF statement

10.3.5   The PL/I IF Statement

As with COBOL, the feature of interest is the variety of conditions that may be tested. PL/I does not have a logical or Boolean type and conditional testing is based on the bit string, "1"B and "0"B corresponding to the values *true* and *false*. The expression used to denote the condition in a PL/I statement must therefore be converted to a bit string of length 1.

In PL/I, the generality of conversion between data types means that nearly all problem data may be converted to bit-string type and it is therefore possible to use numeric and character-type string expressions in IF statements. This is in contrast with other languages in which only a restricted set of truth-valued expressions may be used.

Examples of special cases arising from the PL/I rules are as follows:

- **Bit-strings of length greater than 1**

  These are regarded as true if any one of the contained bits has the value 1.

- **Bit-strings of null length**

  These are regarded as false.

- **Arithmetic data** is converted to real, then to fixed-point binary, with precision $(p,0)$ according to its scale and precision. This is then interpreted as a bit-string of length p.

- **Character string data** may be converted to bit-string if it consists of the characters 0 and 1. Otherwise the CONVERSION condition is raised when the IF statement is executed.

Examples

```
IF A>B|C THEN...
IF X+5 THEN...
IF POINTERA = POINTERB & TEXT ¬= NULL THEN...
```

Either branch of an IF statement may contain a conditional statement. The problem of the dangling ELSE is dealt with, as in COBOL, by pairing the elements of the statement, so that each IF...THEN construction has a corresponding ELSE clause.

Example

```
IF T=0 THEN IF TRIGGER THEN CALL P; ELSE CALL Q;
```

In this example, P and Q are only called if $T=0$, since the ELSE clause belongs to the second IF statement.

To associate the calling of Q with non-zero values of T, we can introduce a *null* statement with an ELSE clause as follows:

```
IF T=0 THEN IF TRIGGER THEN CALL P; ELSE;
          ELSE CALL Q;
next statement;
```

If $T=0$, but TRIGGER has the value "0" B then the flow of control will pass to "next statement."

10.4   THE CASE STATEMENT

The ALGOL, COBOL, and PL/I IF statements provide for two-way branches and may only be used for coding multiway branches by including GO TO statements. A proposal was made by Wirth and Hoare (1966) for a statement called the **case** statement, which allows multiway branching similar to that provided by the IF statement. This statement was proposed as an extension to ALGOL 60, and was adopted (and extended) for the design of ALGOL 68. It has since been included in several languages designed for structured programming.

The syntax of the ALGOL **case** statement is as follows.

<case statement> ::= <case clause> **begin** <statement list> **end**

<case clause>   ::= **case** <integer expression> **of**

Example

```
case (t + 1) of
    begin
        n := n + 1;
        read (next);
        n := n−1
    end
```

When the **case** statement is executed, the value of $(t + 1)$ is used to select one of the subsequent statements. The effect of this is similar to that of a computed **go to,** except that the branch is made to a contained element rather than to a label. The entire selection of alternative actions is collected at one point, simplifying the checking of such constructions. Note that one of the statements to be selected could be a compound statement, that is a sequence of simple statements contained within **begin** ... **end** brackets. A flowchart of the **case** statement is given in Figure 10.5.

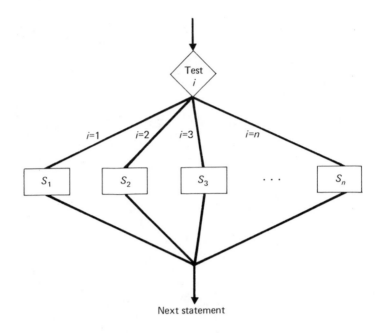

Next statement

case *i* of begin S_1; S_2; S_3; . . . S_n end

Fig. 10.5 Flow chart of the **case** statement

10.5   DECISION TABLES

Decision tables first appeared in connection with programming around 1957. Important early reports include that by Kavanagh (1960) describing work on TABSOL, a system developed by the General Electric Company. At about the same time, the CODASYL committee considered adding decision tables to the COBOL language: this work is represented by the DETAB-X and DETAB-65 languages (CODASYL 1962, SHARE 1966).

After a period of considerable enthusiasm in the early 1960's, interest in decision tables seemed to decline, although papers on the subject continued to be published. However, decision tables offer a more compact way of representing complex control structures than do conventional programming languages. In some applications, they are used as much for their convenience in documentation as for the production of programs.

A discussion of decision tables is made difficult by the absence of a standard notation and terminology. In the following, the terminology is based on that used in the survey and report published by the National

Computing Centre (NCC, 1970). This report contains a summary of the history and use of decision tables and an extensive annotated bibliography.

Basically, a decision table consists of *conditions* and *actions,* as in the IF-THEN statement:

IF condition THEN action

In decision tables, however, we are concerned with *sets* of conditions and *sets* of actions. The four basic parts of a decision table are shown in Fig. 10.6.

Condition statements	Condition entries
Action statements	Action entries

Fig. 10.6 Basic structure of a decision table

The *statements* (sometimes called the *stub* of the decision table) are descriptions of the conditions and actions, often expressed in natural language. The *entries* are indicators showing which conditions result in which actions.

In certain types of decision table, the statements fully describe the conditions and actions, and the entries consist of binary or ternary indicators (0 or 1, Y(es) or N(o)), together with hyphens or blanks to indicate "don't care." This form is called a *limited-entry* table. Alternatively, the entries may contain further information about the conditions or actions—it is then known as an *extended-entry* table. Any extended-entry table can be converted to a limited-entry table by expanding the number of entries. It is sometimes advantageous to do this, as limited-entry tables are easier to process than extended-entry tables. The two forms of table are shown in Figures 10.7 and 10.8.

In a limited-entry table in which there are N conditions, each of which may have a Yes or No outcome, there are 2^N entries in the table. A decision table in which all possible entries appear is called *complete*. A complete version of the condition portion of Fig. 10.7 is shown in Fig. 10.9.

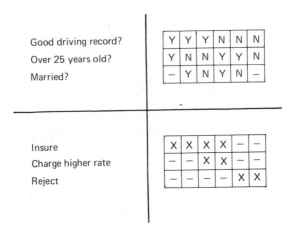

Good driving record?

Over 25 years old?

Married?

Y	Y	Y	N	N	N
Y	N	N	Y	Y	N
–	Y	N	Y	N	–

Insure

Charge higher rate

Reject

X	X	X	X	–	–
–	–	X	X	–	–
–	–	–	–	X	X

Fig. 10.7 A limited-entry table for motor insurance

Salaried employee?	N	N	N	Y
Hours worked	39 or less	Over 39, less than 45	45 or over	Any
Pay	Regular rate	Rate A	Rate B	Regular rate

Fig. 10.8 An extended-entry table for overtime rates

Good driving record?

Over 25 years old?

Married?

Y	Y	Y	Y	N	N	N	N
Y	Y	N	N	Y	Y	N	N
Y	N	Y	N	Y	N	Y	N

Fig. 10.9 A *complete* version of the conditions for the Table shown in Fig. 10.7

Over 65?	Y	N	N	N	N	N
Less than or equal to 65 and over 55?	N	Y	N	N	N	N
Less than or equal to 55 and over 45?	N	N	Y	N	N	N
Less than or equal to 45 and over 35?	N	N	N	Y	N	N
Less than or equal to 35 and over 25?	N	N	N	N	Y	N
Less than or equal to 25?	N	N	N	N	N	Y

Note: Only one Y may appear in a column.

Fig. 10.10 Conditions which are not independent

Sometimes, the conditions to be tested in a decision table are not independent, and the table cannot be made complete in this sense. This is illustrated in Fig. 10.10, in which the conditions are closely related to each other. The table shows the only valid entries for this particular set of conditions.

For the sake of brevity incomplete tables may also be used if the actions to be followed under several sets of circumstances may be grouped together in fewer than 2^N ways. A complete table and its reduced form are shown in Figs. 10.11 and 10.12, respectively.

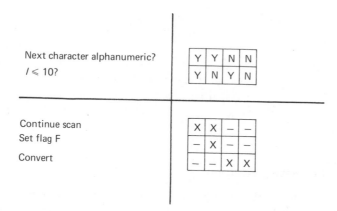

Next character alphanumeric?	Y	Y	N	N
$l \leqslant 10$?	Y	N	Y	N

Continue scan	X	X	—	—
Set flag F	—	X	—	—
Convert	—	—	X	X

Fig. 10.11 A *complete* decision table for editing

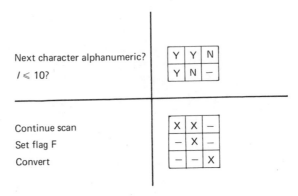

Fig. 10.12 A decision table for editing : reduced version

Next character alphanumeric?   Y   Y   Else

$I \leqslant 10$?   Y   N

Continue scan   X   X   —

Set flag F   —   X   —

Convert   —   —   X

Fig. 10.13 A decision table for editing using the ELSE rule

In cases where sets of actions can be grouped together, decision table size can also be reduced by means of an ELSE rule in the table. The ELSE column specifies the action to be taken for any condition not covered in the main body of the table. Fig. 10.13 presents an editing program using the ELSE rule.

10.5.1 Processing Decision Tables

Because of their format, decision tables need special methods of processing to produce running code. In many recently developed processors, the target language for translation is a high-level language such as COBOL or PL/I. By using such a language, many of the facilities needed by a decision table processor, such as dictionary construction, the generation of code for conditions and expressions, etc., can be taken over by the language compiler. Special tasks needed for decision-table processing include analysis of the table to determine errors in syntax, completeness, consistency, redundancy, etc.

There are two techniques commonly used to generate code from decision tables. One is the *rule-mask* technique, in which the table is examined at compile-time and a set of action masks constructed, one for each column of the table. Then, when the table is executed, the first step is to test all the conditions in the table and construct a selection mask. This is compared with the action masks to determine the outcome of the table. Rule mask techniques are described by Kirk (1965) and King (1966).

In the second technique, known as the *condition-tree* method, the decision table is converted to a sequence of conditional tests. Assuming the target language for the translator is a high-level language, these will be IF-THEN-ELSE statements. In the rule-mask method, all conditions must be tested before any actions can be executed; this obviously allows little scope for optimizing the evaluation of the conditions. However, in the condition-tree method, there is considerable freedom in choosing alternative coding for the IF-THEN-ELSE statements. See Reinwald and Soland (1966, 1967), Myers (1972).

To date, decision tables have not been included as an integral part of any *standard* programming language. In most cases, decision-table processors accept input of the tables as if they formed a self-contained language. Since in many cases the translating program acts as a preprocessor to a high-level language compiler, the statements of the "host" language are available to the programmer who uses the decision tables.

10.6 LOOPING STATEMENTS

The loop is the simplest way of using statements many times; it provides the means of programming *iterative* solutions, one of the commonest techniques used in programming. Looping is also valuable because data is frequently arranged in a regular pattern (for example in sequential files and arrays) for which looping is a natural method of processing. Another form of loop arises in certain kinds of systems programs—the so-called "wait" loop in which a program is held in a nonproductive loop, until some "event" such as an interrupt takes place.

Loops require a departure from regular sequential flow and can be programmed by means of the basic sequencing statements IF and GO TO. However, an important aspect of language design is the provision of statements designed specially to allow looping, such as the DO, FOR, and

PERFORM statements. These specialized looping statements not only make it easier for the programmer to set up the appropriate tests and controls for a loop, but also make it possible for a computer to produce the most efficient code.

In scientific computations, where some of the more complex looping structures are found, the innermost loops may be executed millions of times more frequently than the outer statements.

A loop involves repetitive execution of a sequence of statements. To specify a loop we have to describe:

- the *loop structure*—the specification of statements contained in the loop.

- the *loop control*—the means of controlling the iterations.

10.6.1 Loop Structure

Specifying the statements which form the body of a loop is largely a matter of establishing appropriate delimiters in the program text. In FORTRAN, ALGOL and PL/I, a loop statement (DO or FOR) is used at the head of the loop and forms one of the delimiters. The end of the loop is denoted by a terminating "bracket"—the END statement in PL/I, and the **end** bracket in ALGOL. In COBOL the unit of repetition is a *procedure*. The COBOL PERFORM statement allows a set of procedures to be specified as the contents of loop—unlike most other languages, these need not be contiguous sections of code.

It is important to allow nesting in loop specifications, so that loops can be defined inside other loops. An obvious example of the need for this is in *array processing*.

Example

To process all elements of a matrix, we need to process all rows (one loop), and each element within each row (another loop, nested within the first).

Typical code for processing an $M \times N$ matrix is as follows:

```
DO I = 1 TO M;     /* process a row        */
    DO J = 1 TO N; /* elements within a row */
        A(I,J) = some expression
    END;
END;
```

For efficiency, it is important that loops form contiguous sequences of program text and that multiple loops be "properly" nested, so that any inner loop lies *completely* within the bounds of any loop which contains it. This is not a logical requirement but simply one that makes it easier to develop efficient code. Given a suitable notation, there is no reason why the following loop structure should not be written:

```
repeat M times: [S1, S2, S3, S4]
```

where S1, S2, . . . , S4 are statements. As we see in Section 10.6.2.4, COBOL does in fact allow this construction.

Proper loop nesting allows program text to be compiled so that it is most efficient at the deepest level of nesting where the frequency of execution is highest. This is not possible when loops are constructed by means of statements such as IF and GO TO, where the natural looping of the program may be obscured and may only be detectable after considerable analysis by a compiler.

10.6.2 Loop Control

There are several important differences in methods of loop control treatment in various languages. The simplest form of looping statement is: "repeat *N* times" with a description of the statements to be repeated. This form is present in COBOL in the simple form of the PERFORM statement. In FORTRAN, ALGOL and PL/I, there is a more elaborate way of specifying iteration, requiring the introduction of a control variable which determines the behavior of the loop.

The control of looping statements may involve

- determining the number of iterations,
- determining some condition to be satisfied which will terminate the loop,
- providing a set of values to apply to successive iterations.

All loops require some form of test or discrimination to determine when the set of iterations is complete. A fundamental factor in the design of looping statements is the decision as to whether to make this test *before* or *after* each loop is entered.

FORTRAN is the only major language in which the test is made after execution of the loop. It follows that whenever a DO statement is reached in the course of execution of a FORTRAN program, the loop is executed at least once, whatever the values of the control variable and bounds.

Usually, as in ALGOL, COBOL and PL/I, the test is carried out before the loop is entered. This means that if the conditions are satisfied before the loop is encountered, the loop will not be entered at all but will be bypassed.

It is generally regarded as better programming practice to test before entering a loop rather than after. With this approach, it is easier to ensure that boundary conditions, particularly those occurring when one of the loop parameters becomes zero or negative, are correctly treated. This technique is sometimes known as that of "leading decisions" which might be summed up: "if there is to be a test, make it as soon as possible." (Iverson, 1962, p. 6.)

One way of controlling the number of iterations in a loop is to make it dependent on some *condition,* to be tested each time the loop is traversed. In ALGOL, COBOL and PL/I, loop specifications may include a *while* clause (the COBOL UNTIL clause) in which the condition has the same form as used in the IF statements of these languages.

The other form of loop control, the only one provided in FORTRAN, involves a *control variable* which is incremented each time the loop is executed. Loop specifications determine a sequence of values of the control variable, which may be used for systematic access to an array or to provide a set of values for a table. The specifications for a loop contain the following information:

- the name of the control variable: V,
- a starting value: S,
- an increment: E,
- a finishing value: F.

The iterations correspond to a sequence of values of V, starting at S, incrementing by E at each iteration. The sequence is

$$V = S, \ S+E, \ S+2E, \ S+3E, \ ...., \ F$$

The values of S, E, and F thus determine both the number of iterations in the loop and the values of the control variable V for each iteration.

In the specifications of the loop, V must be a numeric variable, generally an integer (required in FORTRAN), while S, E, and F may be constants, variables or, in ALGOL and PL/I, expressions.

We next come to another question to be decided in the design of loops.

- To what extent are V, S, E, and F accessible during or after the execution of the loop?

Examples of changes we might wish to make include the following:

- re-setting the value of V,
- changing the value of the increment E, or the finishing value F.

We may also wish to branch out of the loop and enter some code in which the most recently calculated value of V is important.

In deciding such questions, we need to consider the implementation of looping statements. In some machines, there is a "loop" instruction, which increments a counter then branches to a given location (the start of the loop) so long as the counter does not exceed an amount held in a specified location. Typically, the quantities on which the branch depends are held in machine registers or other special locations.

The use of a special machine instruction allows the most efficient execution of loops, since incrementing and testing are carried out in the course of executing the machine instruction. Since the loop parameters are usually held in registers, it follows that, during execution of the loop, they are not available in normal storage locations. In effect, the loop parameters are "frozen" when the loop is entered.

FORTRAN is most "protective" in its treatment of loop parameters and the FORTRAN DO loop was originally designed for efficient implementation using the branch and loop instructions of the IBM 704 machine. In these instructions (TXI and TXL), the values of the loop increments and limits were actually part of the instruction itself.

At the other extreme is ALGOL, in which all quantities involved in the **for** statement specification are accessible and may be altered during execution of the loop. In fact, the ALGOL loop is defined in the ALGOL report as equivalent to an **if-then** statement together with a **go to** statement. This makes it difficult to generate efficient code for ALGOL loops without extensive code analysis. PL/I more closely follows FORTRAN, as do many other languages (including ALGOL 68, which has moved away from the generality of ALGOL 60 loops).

In contrasting the two approaches typified by FORTRAN-PL/I and ALGOL-COBOL, we can see that, although the ALGOL-COBOL approach allows considerable flexibility, this could as well be obtained by **if** and **go to** statements. The FORTRAN-PL/I approach conveys important information to the compiler, allowing it to generate efficient code for the most usual cases.

A comparison of loop statements for FORTRAN, ALGOL, COBOL and PL/I is given in Table 10.1.

10.6.2.1　The FORTRAN DO statement

This is the simplest of looping statements, designed for easy code generation and optimization. Loop control is specified by a triplet of integers or integer variables, $\{m_1, m_2, m_3\}$, representing S, F, and E, which are frozen during execution of the loop. The increment m_3 may be omitted, in which case the value 1 is taken as a default.

TABLE 10.1 COMPARISON OF LOOPING STATEMENTS.

Name of statement	FORTRAN DO	ALGOL for	COBOL PERFORM	PL/I DO
Loop specifications	Bracket structure, end of loop is nominated in the DO statement	Single statement or compound statement (**begin** . . . **end**)	List of procedure names	Bracket structure, end of loop: END;
Position of test	Test is made after the loop	Test is made before the loop	Test is made before the loop	Test is made before the loop
Type of control variable	Integer variable	Variable of any type	Elementary item, numeric or index	Pseudo-variable or variable of any type. It must be numeric or string if **BY** and **TO** are used
Initial value	▪ Constant or integer variable ▪ Must be positive	Expression	▪ Literal or name of elementary item ▪ Must be positive	Expression
Increment	▪ Constant or integer variable. ▪ Must be positive ▪ May be omitted, default value is 1	Expression	▪ Literal or name of elementary item ▪ Must be positive	▪ Expression which can be converted to a numeric value ▪ May be omitted; the default value is 1

TABLE 10.1 (continued)

Name of statement	FORTRAN DO	ALGOL **for**	COBOL PERFORM	PL/I DO
Upper bound	▪ Constant or integer variable ▪ Must be positive	▪ Expression— must be specified if increment is given	▪ Literal or name of elementary ▪ Must be positive	▪ Expression which can be converted to a numeric value ▪ May be omitted
Can the loop parameters be accessed during execution of the loop?	No.	Yes. Will affect the behavior of the loop	Yes. Behavior of loop will not be affected	Yes. Behavior of loop will not be affected
Multiple specifications?	No	Yes	Yes	Yes

The statement is comparatively primitive when contrasted with looping statements in other languages, since there is no way of specifying a test by logical expression and no way of iterating for a *list* of values of the control variables. A control variable must always be introduced, even though it may never be needed. The loop parameters must all be integers or integer variables, so any *expressions* for starting, increment, or finishing values must be evaluated and assigned to temporary variables before the loop is started.

If there is a branch out of the DO loop before it is complete, the last assigned value of the control variable is preserved. However, when the DO loop ends "normally," with all iterations complete, the value of the control value is undefined. (In some implementations this value may be known and used; however it cannot be guaranteed in a "standard" FORTRAN compiler.)

A DO loop is headed by a DO statement, which has the form

$$\text{DO n i= } m_1, \ m_2, \ m_3$$

The end of the loop is a statement with label "n"—this "dummy" statement, introduced into FORTRAN for the purpose of terminating DO loops, is often coded as a CONTINUE statement.

Example

```
DO 9 I=1,N
IF (A(I) .LT. 0) GO TO 10
SUM = SUM + A(I)
9  CONTINUE
10 next statement
```

10.6.2.2   The ALGOL for statement

The ALGOL **for** statement represents the other extreme from the FORTRAN DO statement and allows full access to the loop parameters. The statement consists of a **for** clause followed by a *statement*. An ALGOL statement may be a compound statement—a sequence of simple statements delimited by **begin** and **end.** Looping over a sequence of statements may therefore be achieved by bracketing the sequence with **begin** and **end** symbols.

A **for** clause must include a control variable, even though this may not be needed in the calculation. This is the case even where the **while** clause is used. A list of control variable values may be given in the loop specification.

Examples

> **for** j := 1 **step** 1 **until** n **do begin** $A[j]$:= $A[j]+1$;
> $B[j]$:= **if** $j<t$ **then** 1 **else** 2; **end**

> **for** Q := $I,J,K,X\uparrow2$ **while** T, 1 **step** 3 **until** 27
> **do** T := $T+V[Q]$;

10.6.2.3   The PL/I DO statement

Although this uses the same keyword as FORTRAN, the detailed design of the statement differs from the FORTRAN DO statement. The main feature in which FORTRAN and PL/I statements are similar is in the protective treatment of the loop parameters during iteration.

The DO statement is a bracketing statement, one of the three PL/I statements which may be paired with an END statement (the others are PROCEDURE and BEGIN). In its simple form (i.e., without loop specifications), it acts as a statement bracket, in much the same way as **begin** and **end** act as brackets to form a compound statement in ALGOL. This form of bracket in PL/I does not have the scope properties of the BEGIN and END statement; as a scope-free bracket, the overheads of local storage allocation and interrupt handling are avoided. A common use for DO–END brackets in PL/I is for constructing compound statements, as sometimes needed for the IF statement.

$$DO \begin{Bmatrix} \text{pseudo-variable} \\ \text{variable} \end{Bmatrix} = \text{specification [,specification] } \ldots ;$$

where 'specification' is as follows:

$$\text{expression 1} \begin{bmatrix} \text{TO expression 2} & [\text{ BY expression 3]} \\ \text{BY expression 3} & [\text{ TO expression 2]} \end{bmatrix} [\text{ WHILE (expression 4)]}$$

Fig. 10.14 The PL/I DO statement

Example

```
IF TEST_DATA > 200
   THEN DO; DELTA=0; T=N+1; CALL ERROR('#104'); END;
   ELSE DO; DELTA=1; T=N-1; END;
   S1;
```

Here, the DO ... END statements are used to control the sequencing following the IF statement. Following execution of the CALL statement, the next statement to be executed is S1.

The full looping form of the DO statement is given in Fig. 10.14. Note that

- multiple specifications may be given, each one having an optional WHILE clause;
- the starting value, increment, and finishing value may be expressions;
- the increment and finishing value are optional; if a finishing value is given but no increment is, a default increment of 1 is taken.

Changes may be made to the increment, the finishing value, and the WHILE value during execution of the loop, but these changes have no effect on the behavior of the loop.

Examples

```
DO J=1 TO 10,10 TO 100 WHILE(EPS<T),
100 BY 5 WHILE(EPS<T*T);
...
loop
...
END;
DO SUBSTR(S,J,1) = 'A','B','C' ;
   J = J+5;
END;
DO WHILE(STATUS); CALL PROCESS ; END;
```

10.6.2.4 The COBOL PERFORM statement

The PERFORM statement in COBOL is more elaborate than the looping statements of other languages and fulfills other needs than just those of looping. As with other looping statements, there are two points of interest:

- specification of statements in the loop,
- loop control.

Loop specification—There are two forms of loop specification, each based on the COBOL units of program text, the *section* and the *paragraph,* identified by a COBOL *procedure-name.*

The first form is straightforward and consists of a single procedure-name:

```
PERFORM procedure-name-1
```

Example

```
PERFORM OUTPUT-ROUTINE.
PERFORM ERROR-CALCULATION.
```

The object of the iteration is the contiguous sequence of statements indicated by the procedure-name. In this case, OUTPUT-ROUTINE and ERROR-CALCULATION will be labels in the COBOL source program.

Unlike most other languages, the PERFORM statement, since it is not used as a header statement for the block of program text, allows remote looping. This means that the same section or paragraph can be executed with different control specifications from several points in the same program.

Example

Suppose we have prepared a short piece of COBOL code which prints a single line of information. This coding is collected in a paragraph or section called PRINT-LINE. It is used in a COBOL program which collects information from several sources, collates it, and computes various types of output. Then, at various points in the program, we can write

```
PERFORM  PRINT-LINE.
...
PERFORM  PRINT-LINE 4 TIMES.
...
PERFORM  PRINT-LINE UNTIL N>30.
```

The other form of loop specification is quite different and causes a large number of problems in the definition and implementation of COBOL. The loop specification may be written

```
procedure-name-1 THRU procedure-name-2
```

The instructions in the loop consist of the sequence of operations starting with the first statement in *procedure-name-1* and ending with the last statement in *procedure-name-2*. Between these, there may be any sequence of operations, including GO TO statements, PERFORM statements, ALTER statements, etc. There is no need for any particular physical relationship between the code in the two specified sections or paragraphs; it is simply the flow of control in the executed code which determines the contents of the loop.

There is one restriction in the form of loop which may be written—the logical sequence of any PERFORM statements contained within any other PERFORM statement must be strictly nested, that is, a "contained" PERFORM must be *completely* contained. This implies, for example, that a PERFORM loop must not be terminated from within another PERFORM loop.

Example

The following sequence is illegal.

```
        PERFORM A THRU D.
   A. —
   B. —
        PERFORM C THRU E.
   C. —
   D. —
   E. —
```

In this sequence, statement D is a terminal statement of the first loop, but an internal statement in C THRU E.

The reason for this rule can be seen when we consider the usual technique of implementing PERFORM. In the compiled code, a transfer instruction is placed after the last instruction in the code referred to by procedure-name-2. When the PERFORM statement is executed, this transfer instruction is set to refer to the instruction following the PERFORM. It is clear that only a single level of PERFORM can be active at any one time.

Loop control—Loop control in the PERFORM statement is expressed as follows.

```
        PERFORM procedure-name...
        VARYING identifier-1 FROM lower-limit BY increment
                    UNTIL condition
```

Both *lower-limit* and *increment* are literals or identifiers. The FROM and BY options are similar to those in other languages, but there is no provision for specifying an upper-limit, and the termination of the loop must be programmed by means of the UNTIL option.

Example

To increment a subscript from 0 to 2 until the upper bound is reached, we must write:

```
PERFORM MAIN-LOOP VARYING I FROM 0 BY 2 UNTIL I = 100.
```

The absence of the TO option makes it necessary to be very careful in coding the upper limit of the loop. In this example, for instance, it is essential that I passes through the exact value 100, otherwise the program will loop indefinitely.

A flowchart of the PERFORM statement, taken from the COBOL standard language specifications, is given in Fig. 10.15. Note that initialization of the control variable is done before the test, and that the control variable $V2$ is re-initialized before entry to the inner loop.

The PERFORM statement differs considerably from similar statements in other languages. Some of its advantages and disadvantages are as follows.

Advantages

■   It allows remote looping, so that the same sequence of code can be used from different locations. In other languages this is only achievable by means of *subprograms* or *subprocedures,* which are more elaborate and often involve greater overheads than PERFORM.

■   The simplest forms, such as

```
PERFORM ROUTINE-X 20 TIMES
```

are simpler than equivalent forms in other languages. There is no need to introduce a control variable unless one is needed.

Disadvantages

■   The complex form of loop specification makes it difficult, perhaps impossible, to perceive the structure of the program when reading and checking it.

■   The absence of a strictly nested bracket structure for loops makes it hard for a compiler to generate efficient code for loops. One of the advantages of loop structure is thereby lost.

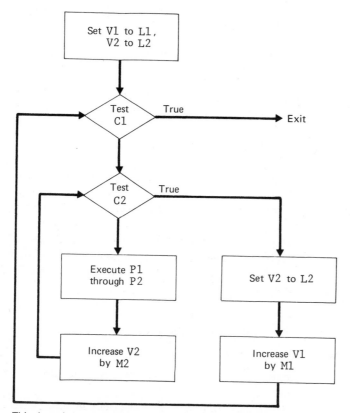

This chart shows the execution of the following statement:

```
PERFORM P1 THRU P2 VARYING V1 FROM L1 BY M1 UNTIL C1,
                   AFTER V2 FROM L2 BY M2 UNTIL C2.
```

Fig. 10.15 Flow chart of the COBOL PERFORM statement

10.7 CONDITION HANDLING

In the previous sections we have described methods of sequencing in which the programmer plans and codes each transfer of control taken by the program. We now consider another type of sequence control in which a program or part of a program is monitored throughout its execution. Transfer of control takes place when a particular set of circumstances occurs, causing what is known as an *interrupt*.

There are, in fact, two distinct types of interrupt. The more straightforward one, the one recognized in PL/I and COBOL, arises when control reaches a particular point of a program. Furthermore, this type of interrupt occurs as a result of actions in the program.

Other types of interrupt, sometimes called *asynchronous,* arise at unpredictable points in time, for reasons which may be quite unrelated to the execution of the program. An example of an asynchronous interrupt might be the pressing of an "attention" key to stop execution of a program, or an interrupt occurring at a particular point of time in the day to allow some critical section of a suite of programs to be entered. Asynchronous interrupts must be handled in so-called "real-time" applications, but cannot be treated by the condition handling facilities of PL/I or COBOL.

We first take a specific example from input-output, an important field for condition handling.

Consider the READ operation, used in accessing a sequential set of data.

The exact number of records in a given data set is not usually known, although it is clearly finite. Each READ operation is therefore in some sense tentative, since there may or may not be a record available for transmission.

The READ operation will normally be in a loop; and as soon as the end of the data set has been reached, it will be necessary to transfer control to another part of the program (for example to process the data).

In writing this program, we have to consider

- the nature of the special condition,
- the type of operation for which it may occur,
- the action to be taken when it does occur.

These are the elements from which the condition or interrupt handling language is composed.

We give the name *status-condition* to the set of circumstances we wish to detect in the execution of the program (the word *condition* is used in PL/I; however, this term has a different meaning in COBOL.)

Two different techniques are used in monitoring status-conditions.

- An action may be associated with a program or a specific part of a program.
- An action may be associated with a particular status-condition or set of status-conditions.

In COBOL, both techniques are used, while in PL/I only the second is used.

10.8   COBOL CONDITION HANDLING

The first technique is illustrated by the AT END phrase in COBOL. An example of its use is:

```
READ MASTER-INPUT FILE AT END GO TO PROCESS-ROUTINE.
```

Here, the action to be taken when *end-of-file* is detected is associated with a particular READ statement. An AT END phrase is written with each READ and in fact with all I/O statements processing sequential files. If another action is to be performed (say, when more than a certain number of records has been processed, or more than a certain number of errors has occurred), then another READ statement, with another AT END clause, is written. This approach binds together the operation, the condition, and the action

{ statement-S : status-condition-C : action-A }

The second approach is illustrated by the COBOL USE statement. A USE statement must appear at the head of the Procedure Division in a COBOL program. The fact that it is called the "declaratives" section indicates its nature. Like other COBOL declarations, it applies over the scope of the entire program.

Example

```
PROCEDURE DIVISION.
DECLARATIVES.
RECOVER-1 SECTION.
USE AFTER STANDARD ERROR PROCEDURE ON INPUT.
PART-1. MOVE FIELD-A to TEMP-A.
        PERFORM ERROR-REPORT.
PART-2. MOVE ST-NUMBER TO MESSAGE-AREA.
```

This example illustrates another aspect of status-conditions, the existence of *standard actions* to be taken in the absence of an action specified by the programmer. These are most clearly necessary in the case of error conditions which would inhibit normal continuation of the computation. Note that in COBOL the standard action is not replaced, but augmented. We shall see a further development of this concept in the interrupt-handling language for PL/I.

The USE statement can be seen as *binding* together a status condition and an action for the duration of a program:

{ program-P : status-condition-C : action-A }

10.9 PL/I CONDITION HANDLING

The condition-handling facilities of PL/I are considerably more extensive than those of other languages and are introduced in a rather different way.

The terminology used in PL/I is as follows:

condition—the status-conditions, recognized as part of the PL/I language.

enable (a condition)—an implied instruction to the compiler that it is to produce object code which detects the specified condition.

disable—the converse of enabling—the condition is not to be detected.

establish (an action)—the association of an action with a condition by means of the ON statement.

revert—the converse of establish, achieved by means of the REVERT statement.

signal (a condition)—creates the effect of a status-condition.

system-action—the action to be taken by the system if the programmer does not specify a particular action.

Twenty-one conditions are defined as part of the PL/I language. These are summarized in Table 10.2.

Some conditions are automatically detected by the hardware of current machines or by operating systems, while others need special detection by code inserted by a compiler. Since condition monitoring is done on a global basis in PL/I, it is necessary for the latter kind of condition to make special provision for code to be generated over those sections of a program where the conditions may arise. This leads to the principle of *enabling* in PL/I.

Enabling is a declarative action made by means of a *condition prefix,* which is a condition name, enclosed in parentheses and separated from the statement by a colon. Condition prefixes are placed before any statement labels. A condition prefix may be attached to any PL/I statement and its effect applies throughout that statement. When a condition prefix is attached to a PROCEDURE or BEGIN statement, its effect applies to all statements within the procedure or begin block.

The conditions which can be enabled by condition prefixes are as follows

```
CONVERSION
FIXEDOVERFLOW
OVERFLOW
SIZE
STRINGRANGE
STRINGSIZE
SUBSCRIPTRANGE
UNDERFLOW
ZERODIVIDE
```

These are the "prefixable" conditions of PL/I, and their inclusion in the language standard represents a measure of machine dependence, since

TABLE 10.2 SUMMARY OF PL/I CONDITIONS

Class	Name of condition	Description
Computational	CONVERSION	Invalid data in attempted mapping
	FIXEDOVERFLOW	Invalid result (fixed point)
	OVERFLOW	Invalid result (floating point)
	SIZE	Receiving field for numbers too small
	STRINGSIZE	Receiving field for strings too small
	UNDERFLOW	Invalid result (floating point)
	ZERODIVDE	Attempted division by zero
Input-Output	ENDFILE	Attempted access outside file limit
	ENDPAGE	Attempted access outside page limit
	KEY	Access error in RECORD I/O
	NAME	Access error in GET DATA
	RECORD	Wrong size of record
	TRANSMIT	Transmission error
	UNDEFINEDFILE	Access error for files
Program Checkout	STRINGRANGE	Invalid access to strings
	SUBSCRIPTRANGE	Invalid access to arrays
Storage Handling	AREA	Allocation space inadequate
	STORAGE	Total storage inadequate
System Action	ERROR	General error condition
	FINISH	Major task about to terminate
Programmer-Defined	CONDITION(ident)	Arbitrary, named condition

there is an implication that these particular conditions will *not* be detected by hardware.

Example

In the following procedure, all array references will be checked to see that the subscripts lie within their declared bounds.

```
(SUBSCRIPTRANGE): P: PROCEDURE;
                  DECLARE (A,B) (50,50) FLOAT;
                  ...
                  A(I,J)=B(I+R,J-R)+A(I+R,J-R);
                  ...
                  END P;
```

Disabling is also carried out by a prefix with a negative indicator, NO (e.g. NOSUBSCRIPTRANGE). The enabling/disabling status of a piece of code is determined when the program is written and compiled and cannot be altered dynamically.

The action to be taken depends on what is currently *established* by an ON unit. An action can be dynamically established for a given status condition by means of the ON statement. This has the form:

```
ON { condition-name } { on-unit }
```

where *condition-name* is a PL/I condition and *on-unit* is a single statement or block which specifies the action to be taken when the condition is detected.

Examples

```
ON ERROR PUT DATA;

ON ENDPAGE(REPORT)
    BEGIN;
        PAGES = PAGES + 1;
        PUT FILE(REPORT) EDIT (heading-data...)(F);
    END;
```

The action established by an ON statement is effective throughout the life of the block in which it is executed. This includes any blocks or procedures invoked by the given block. The action applies until it is overridden by another ON statement, revoked by the REVERT statement, or until flow of control leaves the block in which it was established.

Next we discuss the reasons behind the design of the ON statement and the consequences of its use on compilation and running code. First consider the *dynamic* nature of the ON statement. The action specified in an ON-unit can be changed during the course of a compilation by the execution of another ON statement for the same condition. The de-coupling of action from operation, the absence of binding between the two, allows greater flexibility of coding. The advantage of this can be seen in the conditions related to diagnostics and debugging—CHECK, SUBSCRIPTRANGE, etc. When some form of error is detected, the action for these conditions can be switched to provide monitoring and tracing with intermediate values and branches printed out. This print-out can be inhibited at other points in the program.

The fact that ON actions are inherited by called functions or procedures is referred to as the "descendance" of ON units. For the reason behind this, consider a programmer or group of programmers writing a large program.

The main program may contain error checks and recovery procedures to be handled by ON units which are written by the group controlling the project. When subprograms and procedures are written to perform work outside the scope of the main program, it is convenient to use the same diagnostic and testing modules. This is assured by the rules for inheriting ON units in these subsidiary functions and procedures. Programmers writing the main program can be sure that none of the subprograms will disturb the standard error detection and correction procedures they have established; while programmers writing subprograms do not have to write error procedures at all, but merely have to ensure that in the code they write the appropriate conditions are enabled.

10.9.1 A Model of the PL/I Condition-Handling Mechanism

To better understand the condition-handling mechanism, it is useful to have a model which represents the main features of the design.

We must conceive a set of procedures, one for each of the built-in conditions of PL/I. Strictly, we must consider these as procedure variables, since the values associated with the conditions may change during the course of a program.

At the beginning of a program, these procedure variables are initialized with a set of values corresponding to the system actions of each of the built-in prefixable conditions. (See page 402.) The PL/I specifications refer to these by the generic term: SYSTEM, but more accurately we should think, for example, of:

SYSTEM OVERFLOW—a procedure which issues a comment on the system output file and raises the ERROR condition.

SYSTEM STRINGSIZE—a procedure which issues a comment on the system output, truncates the string, and returns to the point of interrupt.

. . .

When an ON statement is specified, the ON unit becomes in effect a procedure with a hidden procedure-name. On execution of the ON statement, the hidden name of the procedure is *assigned* to the entry-variable corresponding to the specified condition. When a new block is entered, the whole list of procedure variables is copied to form a new list, the list for the previous block being saved as in a push-down list. On exit from the block, the previously saved list is restored.

When a status condition occurs, the effect can be simply described in terms of this model. The procedure variable corresponding to the specified condition is from the point where the condition arises.

10.10   A COMPARISON OF STATUS-CONDITION HANDLING IN COBOL AND PL/I

If we take localized condition handling as typical of COBOL and the ON statement as typical of PL/I, then apart from differences in the breadth of treatment, we can contrast the two approaches as follows:

10.10.1   Static Treatment of Status-Conditions (e.g., COBOL "AT END")

Advantages

- Simple to specify and implement.
- Efficient code may be generated for a single condition and action.

Disadvantages

- Inflexible—the action is fixed when the program is written.
- May be inefficient in source code—each processing statement must have an action specified.

10.10.2   Dynamic Treatment of Status-Conditions (e.g., PL/I ON statement)

Advantages

- Flexible and powerful—the lack of binding between action and operation allows dynamic modification of diagnostic and recovery actions.
- Separate modules can be developed separately and reliably.

Disadvantages

- The specification and understanding of ON-units presents some problems
- Inherited on-actions require extra coding and increase the overhead of block entry at execution time.

10.11   ASYNCHRONOUS PROCESSING

The control structures discussed above are based on a single thread of program control. As advances in engineering technology take single-stream logic design closer to its maximum speed, there is increasing interest in parallel systems. This parallelism can be exploited, in the design of operating systems, by allowing several *jobs* to run simultaneously. This form of parallelism need have no effect on the design of procedural languages, since parallel jobs may run independently of each other and programs can still be written in standard languages based on a single thread of actions.

Sometimes, however, it is desirable for an individual programmer to have sufficient control over the resources available in a system to initiate parallel processes—examples include the so-called "real-time" applications (airline reservations, process control, military command and control, etc.).

10.11.1   Primitive Operations for Parallel Processing

A number of proposals for languages to control parallel processes have been made (Gill, 1958; Conway, 1963; Anderson, 1965; Opler, 1965; Dennis and van Horn, 1966). The basic requirement is for a set of operations for:

- controlling parallel processes
- providing access to shared data
- providing protection from illegal access to private data

To begin with, a set of primitive instructions is described. This set is largely based on the paper by Dennis and van Horn (1966), which is itself based on that by Conway (1963) and Dijkstra (1965, 1968).

The **fork** command initiates a new stream of operations at a nominated point. For example, consider the sequence:

$$S1;$$
$$S2;$$
$$\textbf{fork } L;$$
$$S3;$$
$$. . .$$

After execution of the **fork** statement, there are two streams, one the sequence of statements starting at the label L, the other the continuing sequence: $S3$; $S4$; . . . .

Some means of continuing a process become necessary if and only if all processes of a given set have been terminated. The primitive operation proposed by Dennis and van Horn is an instruction of the form: **join** t,w. This decrements a given integer variable, t, and branches to w if t is zero. It is important that, during the execution of **join,** the value of t should be protected, so that no other process can access it.

Protection of data is obtained by the declaration: **private** x. Such data exists only so long as the process in which it is declared exists—after that, it is destroyed. At a **fork,** values of data declared private to the creating process are assigned as values of corresponding entities in the created process.

When data is shared by more than one processor, it is necessary to be able to protect this data while it is being updated to prevent other processes from accessing it. A proposed solution in the Dennis–van Horn paper is to associate a "lock bit" with each data object, this bit to be accessible to all processes accessing the data. Two commands operate on this: **lock** w and **unlock** w. These can be used to form a kind of bracket around the processing routines, within which w is inaccessible to other processes.

When a variable is locked, a process trying to access it enters a "wait" state. When several parallel processes, each sharing some common variable or machine resource, can be locked out because some *other* process has not completed, it is necessary to set up mechanisms to synchronize the two processes. The problem of designing such processes has been analyzed by Dijkstra, who put forward solutions to a range of problems including that of the "deadly embrace," in which a system is brought to a standstill by an interlocking set of mutually conflicting requirements. The solution adopted by Dijkstra is to introduce

- a new form of integer-valued variable called a *semaphore,*
- two primitive operations or semaphores, called P and V.

The P and V operators are defined as follows.

- $V(S)$; increases the value of the semaphore S by 1.
- $P(S)$: decreases the value of the semaphore S by 1, provided S is positive. If S is not greater than zero, the process in which P is executed **waits** until a V operation executed by some other process makes it so.

Each of these operators is defined as being indivisible—that is, no process can access the semaphore they refer to while the operations are in execution. This essential constraint makes it impossible to use an existing construction, such as: $S = S + 1$, in which there are two accesses to S. With this form, another process might gain access to S between the time it is accessed to form the value $S + 1$ and the time when the result is assigned to form the new value of S.

PL/I contains facilities for parallel processing in which the unit of parallel execution is the task, the activation of a PL/I procedure. The tasking facilities of PL/I are therefore most closely related to the procedure facilities, and are described separately in Chapter 12.

10.12 FURTHER READING

The separation of the control aspects of a programming language from its data-oriented aspects was advocated in a paper by Wilkes (1968). Control structures have been considered from a mathematical point of view by

Prosser (1959), Bohm and Jacopini (1966), and Scott (1970). A survey of control structures in programming languages, covering many of the topics in this chapter, is provided by Fisher (1972).

Of all control statements, most attention has been paid to the GO TO. Most of this stems from Dijkstra's famous letter advocating the elimination of the GO TO from programming languages (Dijkstra, 1968). Theoretical work throwing light on the GO TO statement has been done by van Wijngaarden (1966), Landin (1966), and Ashcroft and Manna (1971). The practical advantages of programming without the GO TO are discussed by Mills (1971) Knuth and Floyd (1970), and in papers presented at a SIGPLAN conference in 1972 (Leavenworth, 1972). A variety of additional control structures, which would allow the elimination of the GO TO, have been proposed. These include the CASE statement (Wirth and Hoare, 1966), improved looping capabilities (Wirth, 1971), a technique called "bounce-and-skip" (Nievergelt and Ireland, 1970) and a wide variety of control facilities found in the programming language, BLISS (Wulf, 1971; Wulf, Russell, and Haberman, 1972).

Much of the published work on the IF statement has been centered on the syntactic problems of the ELSE clause (Kaupe, 1963; Abrahams, 1966). The conditional part of the statement is discussed in Chapter 9.

Study of looping statements has mainly been directed to methods of generating optimal code, since loops account for a large proportion of the execution time of most programs. References to this work can be found in Chapter 5. Papers more closely related to theoretical aspects of looping and the design of languages include those by Schurmann (1964) and Galler and Perlis (1965).

Decision tables have been extensively covered in published papers. From a user's point of view, the NCC survey (NCC, 1970) is recommended—this contains an extensive annotated bibliography. Other papers are cited in the text.

The design of interrupt handling facilities in machines is discussed by Brooks (1962). The interrupt facilities of PL/I and techniques for implementing them are described in a paper by Noble (1968).

Several papers on parallel processing have been referred to in the chapter—perhaps the most useful for a general introduction are those by Gosden (1966), Dennis and van Horn (1966) and Habermann (1972). A number of papers have considered the uses of parallel processing in various fields—see, for example, Lehman (1966) and Miranker (1971).

An alternative to the inclusion of parallel processing primitives in programming languages is to design languages which involve fewer sequencing constraints—for examples of this approach, see the papers by Foster (1968) and Tesler and Enea (1968).

BIBLIOGRAPHY

Abrahams, P. W., "A final solution to the dangling **else** of ALGOL 60 and related languages," *CACM,* Vol. 9, No. 9, Sept. 1966, pp. 679–682.

Describes the problem of the ambiguity of the **if** statement as it originally arose in ALGOL and shows how it has been resolved in ALGOL and other languages. An alternative, less restrictive solution is proposed in which a distinction is drawn between "open" and "closed" statements. Syntax rules for these are given. **If** statements must be constructed so that **else** must always be preceded by a closed statement.

Anderson, J. P., "Program structures for parallel processing," *CACM,* Vol. 8, No. 12, Dec. 1965, pp. 786–788.

Describes 5 meta-commands

fork (label pair)
join (label list)
terminate (label list)
obtain (variable list)
release (variable list)

Ashcroft, E., Z. Manna, "The translation of GO TO programs to WHILE programs," *Proceedings IFIP Congress 71,* TA-2, pp. 147–152, North Holland, 1971.

In this paper it is shown that every "flowchart program" (i.e., a program written in a simple language involving assignments, test points, and GO TO statements) can be written without GO TO statements, but using WHILE statements. To transform such a program, it is necessary to introduce auxiliary variables to hold information about the status of the program.

Bernstein, A. J., "Analysis of programs for parallel processing," *IEEE Trans. on Electronic Computers,* Vol. EC 15, No. 5, Oct. 1966, pp. 757–763.

A set of conditions which determine whether or not two successive portions of a given program can be performed in parallel and still produce the same results.

Bohm, C., G. Jacopini, "Flow diagrams, Turing machines, and languages with only two formation rules," *CACM,* Vol. 9, No. 5, May 1966, pp. 366–371.

This paper discusses a simplified flowchart language in which the only control elements correspond to sequential operation, IF-THEN-ELSE, and the two looping statements DO-WHILE and DO-UNTIL. It is shown that some programs cannot be reduced to these simple operations without the introduction of a local store in the form of a push-down stack. A mathematical paper, important in the GO TO controversy. (See also Cooper, 1967.)

Brooks, F. P., "Instruction sequencing," (in) *Planning a Computer System—Project STRETCH,* W. Buchholz (ed.), New York: McGraw-Hill, 1962, pp. 133–149.

Discusses instruction sequencing at the hardware level. Four types of instruction sequencing for passing control from *sequence A* to a *sequence B* are defined.

- Normal sequencing—*A* keeps control
- Branching—*A* gives control to *B*

- Interruption—B takes control from A
- Executing—A lends control to B

These instructions have an effect on the design of programming languages. The discussion on interrupts is interesting in providing a parallel to the design of interrupts in a high-level language.

CODASYL Systems Development Group, "DETAB-X, preliminary specifications for a decision table structured language," Sept. 1962.

Conway, M. E., "A multiprocessor system design," *Proc. FJCC Conference 24,* 1963.
Contains descriptions of FORK and JOIN.

Cooper, D. C., "Bohm and Jacopini's reduction of flow charts," *Letter to the Editor, CACM,* Vol. 10, No. 8, Aug. 1967, pp. 463, 473.

Davies, D. W. (ed.), "A. M. Turing's original proposal for the development of an electronic computer," *Technical Report Com. Sci. 57,* National Physical Laboratory, Teddington, England, Apr. 1972.

Dennis, J. B., E. C. van Horn, "Programming semantics for multiprogrammed computations," *CACM,* Vol. 9, No. 3, Mar. 1966, pp. 143–155.
Contains basic functions for multiprogrammed systems based on project MAC. These include the concept of a process; the states of running, ready, and suspended; and a set of primitive operations, including FORK, JOIN, LOCK, UNLOCK, etc.

Dijkstra, E. W., "Cooperating sequential processes," (in) *Programming Languages (Proceedings of a NATO Conference),* F. Genuys (ed.), New York: Academic Press, 1968.
A tutorial exposition showing how processes acting concurrently and accessing the same data may become locked, unable to continue. Describes a solution, involving the introduction of semaphores.

Dijkstra, E. W., "GO TO statement considered harmful (letter to the editor)," *CACM,* Vol. 11, No. 3, 1968.
Letter advocating the abolition of the GO TO statement from programming languages.

Fisher, D. A., "A survey of control structures in programming languages," *SIGPLAN Notices,* Vol. 7, No. 11, Nov. 1972, pp. 1–13.
An excellent survey of control structures in existing languages and possible forms for future languages including those for parallel processing.

Foster, J. M., "Assertions: Programs written without specifying unnecessary order," (in) *Machine Intelligence 3,* D. Michie (ed.), Edinburgh: 1968, pp. 387–391.
This paper describes an experimental system which allows assertions to be made about the data in a program. Execution of the program involves a search for data which satisfies the assertions.

Galler, B. A., M. J. Fischer, "The iteration element," *CACM,* Vol. 8, No. 6, June 1965, p. 349.
Describes an extension to the programming language, MAD, which allows an iteration structure to appear within expressions.

Gill, S., "Parallel programming," *Computer Journal,* Vol. 1, No. 1, Apr. 1958, pp. 2–10.

This survey paper was the first paper to be published in the first volume of the *Computer Journal,* the main technical journal of the British Computer Society. It discusses aspects of parallel processing and illustrates the need for instructions to start a new branch, wait for completion of another branch, and terminate the current branch.

Gosden, J. A., "Explicit parallel processing description and control in programs for multi- and uniprocessor computers," *Proc. FJCC,* 1966, pp. 651–660.

A good review of parallel processing as it was in 1966. The point of view is that parallel processing should be specified by the programmer, and a review is made of several language proposals for parallel processing. There is a good bibliography.

Griswold, R. E., J. F. Poage, I. P. Polonsky, *The SNOBOL4 Language,* Englewood Cliffs, N.J.: Prentice-Hall, 1968.

Habermann, A. N., "Synchronization of Communicating Processes," *CACM,* Vol. 15, No. 3, Mar. 1972, pp. 171–176.

Hartmanis, J., "Further results on the structure of sequential machines," *JACM,* Vol. 10, No. 1, Jan. 1963, pp. 78–88.

Discusses the problem of constructing a sequential machine from two smaller machines connected in series or in parallel.

Karp, R. M., R. E. Miller, "Parallel program schemata," *Journal of Computer and System Sciences,* Vol. 3, No. 2, 1969, pp. 147–195.

Kaupe, A., "A note on the dangling **else** in ALGOL 60," *CACM,* Vol. 6, No. 8, Aug. 1963, pp. 460–462.

Kavanagh, T. F., "TABSOL, a fundamental concept for systems-oriented languages," *Proc. EJCC,* Vol. 18, 1960, pp. 117–127.

King, P. J. H., "Conversion of decision tables to computer programs by rule mask techniques," *CACM,* Vol. 9, No. 11, Nov. 1966, pp. 796–801.

Kirk, H. W., "Use of decision tables in computer programming," *CACM,* Vol. 8, No. 1, Jan. 1965, pp. 41–43.

Knuth, D. E., "The remaining trouble spots in ALGOL 60," *CACM,* Vol. 10, No. 10, Oct. 1967, pp. 611–618.

Knuth, D. E., R. W. Floyd, "Notes on avoiding GO TO statements," *Information Processing Letters,* Vol. 1, 1970, pp. 23–31.

Landin, P. J., "The next 700 programming languages," *CACM,* Vol. 9, No. 3, Mar. 1966, pp. 157–164.

Describes ISWIM, a family of languages directed towards expressions rather than statements. Shows how explicit sequencing, such as GO TO's, can be systematically removed from programs.

Leavenworth, B. M. (ed.), "Control structures in programming languages," *SIGPLAN Notices,* Vol. 7, No. 11, Nov. 1972.

This contains papers presented at a SIGPLAN meeting at which the question of programming without the GO TO statement was debated.

Lehman, M., "A survey of problems and preliminary results concerning parallel processing and parallel processors," *Proc. IEEE,* Vol. 54, 1966, pp. 1889–1901.

Lynch, W. C., "Recursive solution of a class of combinatorial problems, an example," *CACM,* Vol. 8, No. 10, Oct. 1965.

MacLaren, M. D., "Algorithm 272, Procedure for the normal distribution function," *CACM,* Vol. 8, No. 12, Dec. 1965, pp. 789–790.

Martin, J. J., "The 'natural' set of basic control structures," *SIGPLAN Notices,* Vol. 8, No. 12, Dec. 1973, pp. 5–14.
Discusses the suitability of control structures less restrictive than those proposed by Bohm and Jacopini (1966), for possible inclusion in programming languages without the GO TO.

Mills, H. D., "Top-down programming in large systems," (in) *Debugging Techniques in Large Systems,* Randall Rustin (ed.), Englewood Cliffs, N.J.: Prentice-Hall, 1971, pp. 41–55.
A description of structured programming, in the sense of Dijkstra (1969). The use of the GO TO statement is avoided and all sequencing is carried out by IF-THEN-ELSE, DO-WHILE and DO-UNTIL constructions.

Miranker, W. L., "A survey of parallelism in numerical analysis," *SIAM Review,* Vol. 13, No. 4, Oct. 1971, pp. 524–547.
This paper points out that many established numerical procedures are based on the assumption that the computer on which they are to be executed operates in a sequential fashion. A survey is made of procedures which do not require sequential operation; these include algorithms for optimization, root finding, the solution of differential equations and the solution of linear systems.

Myers, H. J., "Compiling optimized code from decision tables," *IBM Journal of Research and Development,* Vol. 16, No. 5, Sept. 1972, pp. 489–503.
Describes optimization methods which may be applied before, during, and after code generation.

Naur P. (ed.), "Report of the algorithmic language ALGOL 60," *CACM,* Vol. 3, 1960, pp. 299–314.
The original ALGOL report.

Naur, P. (ed.), "Revised report on the algorithmic language ALGOL 60," *CACM,* Vol. 6, No. 1, Jan. 1963, pp. 1–17.
The revised report and the basis for current standard ALGOL. Contains modifications to the **if** statement (removing the ambiguity of the dangling **else**), the **go to** and **switch** constructions, and the treatment of parameters.

NCC (authors: F. J. J. Johnston, J. C. Davis), "Decision tables in data processing," *The National Computing Centre,* (Science Associates/International Inc., New York) 1970.

An excellent brief summary of decision tables, their structure and use, and a survey of some available methods for processing them. The bibliography covers the history of decision tables from about 1957 onwards.

Nievergelt, J., M. I. Ireland, "Bounce-and-skip. A technique for directing the flow of control in programs," *Computer Journal*, Vol. 13, No. 3, Aug. 1970, pp. 261–262.

Describes a technique for directing the flow of control in block-structured languages, allowing the elimination of GO TO statements. Control is governed by the value of a condition variable which may be set by a TEST instruction. The current value of this variable may be used to control entry to, and exit from, all blocks.

Noble, J. M., "The control of exceptional conditions in PL/I object programs," *Proc. IFIP Congress 1968*, North Holland, 1971, pp. 565–571.

Opler, A., "Procedure-oriented language statements to facilitate parallel processing," *CACM*, Vol. 8, No. 5, May 1965, pp. 306–307.

The language proposals are: DO TOGETHER and HOLD.

Prosser, R. T., "Applications of Boolean matrices to the analysis of flow diagrams," *Proc. Eastern Joint Computer Conference, 1959*, pp. 133–138.

Reilly, E. D., F. D. Federighi, "On reversible subroutines and computers that run backwards," *CACM*, Vol. 8, No. 9, Sept. 1965, pp. 557–578.

Although written as a hardware proposal, this has interesting possibilities in high-level languages. Two instructions are discussed, an *execute* instruction and a *repeat* instruction that allows the repetition, either backwards or forwards, of a number of instructions varying some control instruction. The use of these instructions on certain regular types of processing such as matrix operations is discussed.

Reinwald, L. T., R. M. Soland, "Conversion of limited-entry decision tables to optimal computer programs, Part I: Minimum average processing time," *JACM*, Vol. 13, No. 3, Jul. 1966, pp. 339–358. "Part II: Minimum storage requirement," *JACM*, Vol. 14, No. 4, Oct. 1967, pp. 742–755.

A standard paper on the translation of decision tables into optimal programs, using the condition-tree method.

Schurmann, A., "The application of graphs to the analysis of distribution of loops in a program," *Information and Control*, Vol. 7, 1964, pp. 275–282.

Scott, D., "The lattice of flow diagrams," *Technical Monograph PRG-3*, Oxford University Computing Laboratory, 1970.

SHARE, "DETAB/65 pre-processor," *Program Package SDA 3396*, Jan. 1966.

Shedler, G. S., M. M. Lehman, "Evaluation of redundancy in a parallel algorithm," *IBM Systems Journal*, Vol. 6, No. 3, 1967, pp. 142–149.

Defines serial, latently parallel, and highly parallel algorithms. Discusses a root-finding algorithm in which redundant parallelism is introduced to make use of machine resources.

Silberg, B. (ed.), "Special issue on decision tables," *SIGPLAN Notices*, Vol. 6, No. 8, Sept. 1971.

This special issue includes an extensive bibliography and several papers on historically important techniques for decision table processing.

Tesler, L. G., H. J. Enea, "A language design for concurrent processes," *AFIPS Conference Proceedings,* Vol. 32, pp. 403–408, *SJCC,* 1968; Thompson Book, 1968.

Wegner, P., "Data structure models for programming languages in proceedings of a symposium of data structures in programming languages," *SIGPLAN Notices,* Vol. 6, No. 2, Feb. 1971, pp. 1–54.

Several models of data structure for high-level languages are considered. In discussing locator and label variables in languages like PL/I, the problem of dangling references is explained.

van Wijngaarden, A., "Recursive definition of syntax and semantics," (in) *Formal Language Description Languages for Computer Programming,* North Holland, 1966.

Describes a systematic procedure for reducing programs to the following simple elements: expressions, assignments, and procedure calls. In the course of this reduction, GO TO statements are eliminated.

Wilkes, M. V., "The outer and inner syntax of a programming language," *Computer Journal,* Vol. 11, No. 3, Nov. 1968, pp. 260–263.

The "outer" syntax of a language is concerned with organizing the pattern of a calculation and the flow of control. The "inner" syntax is concerned with the details of a calculation, and in particular with data operations. The paper uses ALGOL as an example and shows that the outer and inner syntaxes are almost disjoint. It is suggested that a clean separation of the two syntaxes would make it possible to extend a language by adding new data types and operations to the inner syntax, while preserving the form of the outer syntax.

Wirth, N., C. A. R. Hoare, "A contribution to the development of ALGOL," *CACM,* Vol. 9, No. 6, June 1966, pp. 413–432.

A set of proposed extensions to ALGOL 60, which were eventually implemented in the system known as ALGOL W. This paper contains a specification of the **case** statement, a generalization of **if-then-else** which provides a multiway branch.

Wirth, N., "The programming language PASCAL," *Acta Informatica,* Vol. 1, No. 1, 1971, pp. 35–63.

Wulf, W. S., "Programming without the GO TO," *Proc. IFIP Congress 1971,* North Holland, 1972, pp. 408–413.

Discusses the disadvantages of the GO TO statement and describes the control structure of the programming language, BLISS (Wulf *et al.,* 1972).

Wulf, W. S., D. B. Russell, A. D. Haberman, "BLISS: a language for systems programming," *CACM,* Vol. 14, No. 12, Dec. 1972, pp. 780–790.

A language designed for high efficiency and full access to hardware features, as needed in systems programming. Based (like LISP) on expressions, it has no GO TO, but includes a rich variety of sequence control primitives, including CASE and SELECT, 6 forms of loop, and 8 forms of exit mechanisms from local control environments.

EXERCISES

10.1 The labels of a FORTRAN program are: 10,20,30,40,50. *ISTMNT* is an integer variable.

    a) Describe the meaning of the following statements.

```
GO TO (10,30,40,10), ISTMNT
GO TO ISTMNT,(10,30,40,10)
```

    b) Which values of *ISTMNT* are valid for each of these statements?

    c) How may the values be assigned?

    d) Discuss the errors which may arise in each of these statements. Which of these errors can be detected when the FORTRAN program is compiled, and which can be detected only at execution time?

10.2 In COBOL, a paragraph of code named ROUTINE can be invoked by the following means:

    ▪ using a GO TO statement with an ALTER statement to set the return label,

    ▪ using the PERFORM statement.

    a) Write the necessary COBOL code to invoke ROUTINE by these two means.

    b) List the advantages and limitations of each approach.

10.3 a) Draw a flowchart of the following PL/I statement:

```
DO V1 = L1 BY M1  WHILE(¬C1),
   V2 = L2 BY M2  WHILE(¬C2);

   S1;
END;
```

    b) List the differences between this and the flowchart for the similar COBOL statement in Figure 10.7.

10.4 In PL/I (and ALGOL) it is possible to define a loop in which the control variable assumes a sequence of unrelated values.

```
DO I = 3,9,10,T+7;
   ...
END;
```

How can this be expressed in FORTRAN and in COBOL? The example in Fig. 10.4, Ex. 1, was programmed using two IF statements in a single COBOL sentence. Show how the same problem can be programmed using a nested IF statement.

10.5 Express the following FORTRAN statements in ALGOL, COBOL and PL/I notation:

```
IF (X+Y)  3,7,23
IF (A(2*X+10))  6,9,13
IF (T)  6,5,6
```

10.6 A program contains the following sequence of instructions

increment a counter N by 1

add the Nth element of TABLE to X

This sequence is to be executed many times. Show how a closed subroutine can be programmed incorporating this sequence of instructions, using the GO TO facilities of FORTRAN, ALGOL, COBOL and PL/I.

10.7 The loop control specification in DO and FOR statements may be regarded as *sequence-generating functions*, generating sequences of values of the control variable. Consider which of the following sequences can be generated by the loop-control mechanisms of ALGOL, FORTRAN, COBOL and PL/I:

a) arithmetic sequence (e.g., 2,4,6,8, . . .)

b) geometric sequence (e.g., 1,2,4,8,16, . . .)

c) Fibonacci sequence (e.g., 1,1,2,3,5,8,13, . . .)

d) a random sequence within a specified range.

10.8 The notation for declaring array bounds in ALGOL and PL/I is $N:M$, meaning that the array is to take the subscript values: $N, N+1, \ldots M-1, M$. Express this as a sequence-generating function.

10.9 Design a notation in which the subscript values of array declarations are expressed as sequence-generating functions.

10.10 The DO and FOR statements allow loops to be defined in terms of a sequence of regularly incremented values of a control variable. This allows all the elements of an array to be processed systematically, one after the other.

What alternative means are there for processing all elements of an array?

Are there corresponding techniques for processing all the elements of a record structure?

10.11 Write the decision tables given in Figs. 10.7 and 10.8 in terms of IF-THEN-ELSE statements.

Describe alternative ways in which these examples may be coded,

a) to optimize speed,

b) to optimize space.

11

Basic
Input-Output

11.1 INTRODUCTION

The work of many programmers, especially of those who deal with commercial data processing, is dominated by the problems of organizing, arranging, and transferring data from one medium or device to another. Many of these tasks are related to what is usually called *input–output* or I/O.

In spite of its importance, there are relatively few established concepts in I/O programming. Consider, for example, some of the words used in connection with I/O: *file, record, field, channel, key, block.* Each of these has several meanings outside programming. Looked at simply as a collection of English nouns, they have a remarkable degree of ambiguity. Even worse, from our point of view, is the lack of consistency with which they are used as technical terms in computing.

In its original sense, input–output was used to refer to the transmission of data between a computer system and its users. The importance of this is obvious—input is the data for a computation; output, the results which are sought. The meaning of the term has been distorted by its use to describe transmission of data between computers and large-scale storage devices. Techniques originally developed for transmitting data to human users have been adapted for transmitting to disks, drums, and other storage devices. This has influenced the development of I/O languages, and has incidentally resulted in such unconsciously humorous jargon as "reading from a drum," or "opening a disk."

The lack of an accepted conceptual basis for I/O is partly due to the enormous variety of available devices, many of which require special techniques of programming. With some devices, it is only possible to transmit a *sequence* of data in one direction; with others, sequential transmission is possible in two directions, forwards and backwards; in some, an access arm must be positioned over a track of a rotating surface before transmission can take place.

Furthermore, the configurations of typical computing systems have increased in size and complexity, as shown in Fig. 11.1. Growth in the complexity and variability of computing systems makes the design of I/O transmission statements more difficult and accentuates the *denotation* problem for I/O (the problem of referencing and accessing the large, changing population of data sets in a typical installation).

The origin of many I/O features in high-level languages can be traced to the design of input and output devices—card readers and punches, tape and disk units—and to techniques for the use of independent channels and buffers, etc.

The earliest machines for input and output were low-speed, sequential devices such as card and paper tape units, later to be followed by magnetic tape. Although early devices were slow, the maximum transmission rates became increasingly fast as magnetic tape came into wide use. To sustain these rates in running programs, it was necessary to adapt techniques of blocking and buffering. See Mock and Swift (1959), Ferguson (1960). Independent channels were introduced which could carry out a program of input-output actions independently of the arithmetic processing unit. Programming developments to improve system efficiency were introduced, including techniques for overlapping I/O transmission and CPU actions. These led to the development of programming systems or subsystems (sometimes given the name IOCS—Input Output Control System) to simplify the preparation of programs. Subsequently, the development of direct-access systems, based on disks and drums, changed many of the earlier approaches to I/O, as sequential methods originating from cards and tapes were replaced by "random" methods of access. Many of these developments have left their trace in the terminology and underlying concepts of high-level languages. See Bachman (1972) for an historical review of I/O systems, also Bartree (1966) and Weiss (1969) for descriptions of computer hardware.

Input-output languages are concerned with:

Denotation

A program must be able to refer to a variety of external objects: data, devices, networks, etc. The problem is to develop naming techniques precise enough to avoid ambiguity, yet flexible enough to allow programs to be transferred from one system to another with a minimum of recoding.

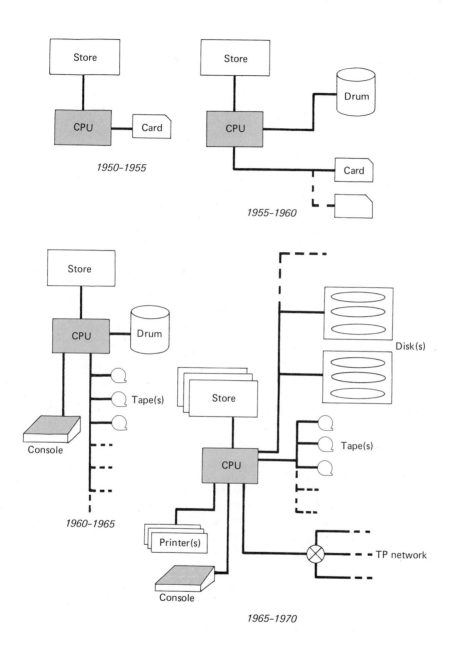

Fig. 11.1 Some typical system configurations: 1955–1970

Device independence

A programming language for general use must include statements which can be applied effectively to such inherently different hardware devices as

> reader, printer, punch;
>
> terminal;
>
> disk, drum.

Each of these classes of device may require different kinds of control at the machine-language level. Where possible, the programming language must allow programs to operate effectively, whatever type of actual device is used in the running system.

Efficiency

Data transmission rates for I/O devices range from one or two characters per second to hundreds of thousands of characters per second. The problem is to design I/O language which can keep a CPU efficiently employed while I/O is carried out at this range of speeds. Solutions have included methods of controlling the timing of operations (synchronization) and techniques for grouping I/O operations together (blocking and buffering).

Data independence

Since input-output is concerned with data in its external and internal forms, questions of data *representation* are obviously important. A wider goal includes that of making programs independent of the data *structures* they process. These two aspects are sometimes known as "physical" data independence and "logical" data independence. See Date, Heath, and Hopewell (1972).

Because of the variety of data representations and devices used for input-output, a technique frequently used is to interpose a *logical* interface between the programmer and the physical devices and media used in systems. In operating systems, there may be several "layers" of interface between the user and physical devices. A good account of this approach is given in Madnick (1969). In the programming languages we discuss, however, there is usually just one apparent level, embodied in the notion of a *file*. The use of files has allowed relatively simple I/O languages to be developed, in spite of the complexity and diversity of addressing methods of the actual devices used in a system.

11.2 FILES

Of all the terms used in data processing, the *file* is the most difficult to define satisfactorily. Two approaches are given below; first, a general and rather abstract definition, then the more specific meaning of the term as used in COBOL and PL/I.

In the IFIP vocabulary of terms used in computing (IFIP, 1968), a file is informally defined as an "organized collection of data elements." The elements of a file are data elements of various types, as described in Chapter 7. The *organization* of a file determines how the elements of a file may be accessed; it is a similar concept to that of the "structure" of a data structure.

A more precise and formal definition was developed by a SHARE committee (SHARE, 1959) and subsequently used by McGee (1959) in his paper, "Generalized File Processing." A file is defined as a set of triples:

$$\{e(i),p(j),v(i,j)\}$$

in which $e(i)$ represents an *entity*, $p(j)$ a *property* of an entity which may be assigned values, and $v(i,j)$ the *value* of the property $p(j)$ for the entity $e(i)$.

To illustrate the definition we take the information contained in a census of population. Suppose that for each of a set of towns we have information on the number of people in various age groups. Then the set of entities, $e(i)$, corresponds to the towns, the set of properties $p(j)$ to the various age ranges and the set $v(i,j)$ to the actual counts obtained by the census. Figure 11.2 shows some examples of data from a typical census, although its tabular arrangement does not imply that the information has to exist as an array. In fact, several different arrangements of this table could be made. The important factor is the set of *relationships* between towns, various age groups, and counts.

Other properties might also be considered as part of this file, such as occupations, salary ranges, etc. Each of these would imply further values of $v(i,j)$.

The foregoing definition of a file is abstract but general; however, to study files as embodied in most high-level languages we have to be concerned with details of implementation. In a programming language, the file referred to in a program should not need to be associated with a particular set of data at the time the program is written. References to files in a program (symbolic names such as MASTER-INPUT-FILE, OUTPUT-LIST, etc.) should be such that the meaning of the symbol—the actual data set—need not be decided when the program is written, and possibly not until it is executed. A file provides indirect access to data sets, just as a *variable* gives access to data representations. In both cases, the denotation of the symbolic name need not be established until the program is executed.

The ambiguity of earlier meanings of the term file led the designers of the IBM operating system, OS/360, to introduce the term *data set* (Clark, 1966). A data set is simply an organized collection of data; it corresponds closely to the general view of a file given above.

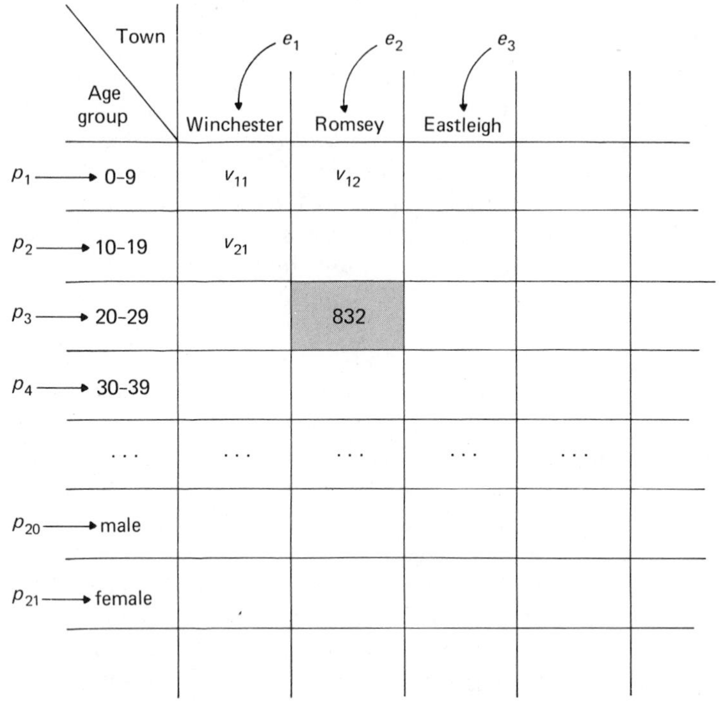

Town / Age group	Winchester	Romsey	Eastleigh		
	e_1	e_2	e_3		
p_1 → 0-9	v_{11}	v_{12}			
p_2 → 10-19	v_{21}				
p_3 → 20-29		832			
p_4 → 30-39					
...	...	...	...	...	
p_{20} → male					
p_{21} → female					

The census information for a part of the county of Hamsphire, England, can be regarded as a generalized *file*:
  The *entities* $\{e_i\}$ are towns in Hampshire.
  The *properties* $\{p_j\}$ are attributes of the population.
  The *values* $\{v_{ij}\}$ are the numbers of people in a given town who have the specified property.

Fig. 11.2 Census information as part of a generalized file

Meanwhile the term file has acquired a rather more specialized meaning in such languages as COBOL and PL/I. Before describing the file concepts of COBOL and PL/I, a number of factors regarding the physical representation of data sets are first discussed.

11.3 BLOCKS, RECORDS, AND FIELDS

In some media used for representing computer data, distinguishable physical boundaries exist which divide the data into groups. One obvious example is the physical boundary between the separate cards in a deck. Another is the block of information transmitted by a single hardware read or write instruction for a magnetic tape unit.

In the case of punched cards, the data of a program must be subdivided into units small enough to fit on single cards. However, in the case of magnetic tape, it may be better to collect data into larger units so that the overhead associated with reading and writing is spread over several items of information.

A unit of information to be processed by a program is called a *logical record.* These may be grouped together into physically distinct units called *blocks* (sometimes called *physical records*). A block is normally the unit of information transmitted by a single machine instruction.

For the most part, high-level programming languages are concerned with logical, rather than physical, records. However, the *blocking factor,* the number of logical records within a block, must somehow be known to the system; this information is needed to compute the size of the required buffer storage and to initiate execution of the detailed instructions needed to access individual records in the block.

Example

In COBOL, information about the number of records in a block may be specified as follows.

```
FILE SECTION.
FD INPUT-MASTER
     BLOCK CONTAINS 8 RECORDS
     ...
```

This form of specification fixes the block size at compile-time. A later form of binding is available in PL/I, where block size may be specified with an OPEN statement, so that it does not need to be fixed until the program is executed.

Since the unit of I/O processing in a high-level language is generally a logical record, there must be a means of defining the information contained in such a record. In COBOL, a logical record must be defined with level 1 in the Data Division of the program (see Chapter 8). In PL/I, any variable occupying "connected" storage may be transmitted as a logical record; this does not restrict the variable to being a level-1 structure.

To calculate the size of physical records, we must know the record length as well as the number of records in a block. In many cases, this can be computed by a compiler, but COBOL also provides a means of specification.

Example

```
FILE SECTION.
FD INPUT-MASTER
   BLOCK CONTAINS 8 RECORDS
   RECORD CONTAINS 80 CHARACTERS
   ...
```

Finally, we come to the basic components of all records and files, the elementary fields or data elements. These correspond to the basic items for which distinct data types are available—the integers, floating-point numbers, strings, etc., discussed in Chapter 7.

11.4   DATA SET LABELS

Some methods of storing data allow it to be moved about from one system to another. Examples include decks of cards, reels of tapes, disk packs, etc. In transferring data, there is the possibility that clerical or operator errors may cause the wrong data set to be associated with a given program. This danger is greatest when there are many data sets containing similar information—for example, when there is a routine daily or weekly run of a program. In commercial data processing the use of a wrong data set might cause catastrophic errors in the running of a business. It is just at this point, where the data is physically separated from the computer and may be subject to errors in handling, that this danger is most acute.

One means of reducing this danger is to include *labels* for the data sets. A data-set label contains information, in a prescribed format, describing the contents of the data set. The label itself is often included with the data set. This means that the data set becomes, in a sense, self-identifying, and this allows some of the difficulties caused by errors in denotation to be overcome.

Standard forms of data set labels have been agreed upon by several national and international bodies—these specify the layout and content of the labels and make it possible to define standard processing routines for creating, examining and updating labels.

11.5   DATA SET ORGANIZATION

The need for different types of file organization originally came from hardware considerations; there is obviously a considerable difference between the physical layout of data on a tape device, a terminal and a large scale memory. The organization of a data set is determined by the relationships between the elements of the set. In some cases, these determine the operations which may be carried out. For example, an instruction "get the next record" only has a meaning when the relation "next" is defined for the data set, that is if the data set has a defined order.

There are two kinds of data set organization—physical and logical. The physical organization of data on a storage device is obviously of concern to the system designer who must decide how to represent data elements, how to place the elements of data structures in storage, whether there is a need for internal pointers and, if so, whether they are to be embedded within the data, etc. To a large extent, high-level languages make it possible to avoid such decisions and write programs independently of the physical organization of the data.

It is much harder to eliminate the need for concern about the logical organization of data. Most current programming languages deal with data and data structures at a logical level. In many current operating systems, data sets are accessed by "access methods"—which are in effect methods of accessing logical data structures. A description of the background and objectives for the access methods in OS/360 is given by Clark (1966).

Although conceptually there are many possible data-set organizations, there are three which have a dominant position in current programming languages: *sequential, direct,* and *indexed.*

11.5.1 Sequential Organization

Much of the recorded data encountered in everyday life occurs in sequences, therefore sequentially organized data sets correspond to many natural patterns of information. Historically, this was the first type of organization to be developed and has always been the most important, since many I/O devices are only capable of accessing data sequentially (e.g., card readers and punches, tape devices, printers, etc.).

An input-output language for sequential data is simple to implement and to use, its chief defect being a certain lack of flexibility and its slow performance for problems in which access to data does not naturally occur in a sequential fashion. Because of its widespread use and suitability for many applications, and the fact that it illustrates many of the most important properties of all I/O methods, the discussion in this chapter deals mainly with sequential I/O.

11.5.2 Direct Organization

In direct organization, each access is expressed in terms of a record "address," rather than by reliance on the position of a "current" pointer to a record. Since each access depends only on an address and is independent of previous accesses, direct organization is used for random access to large data sets.

The term "direct access" is often used of disk and drum systems, but it should be noticed that core storage is also accessed by this means. Direct access is inefficient for devices which, because of their physical construction, present information serially. It is inherently impossible with certain kinds of device (e.g., card readers, terminals).

11.5.3 Indexed Organization

In this organization, data is logically arranged so that a certain distinguished field (a *key*) is arranged according to a regular pattern, generally in a sorted order. An *index* is constructed to indicate the position of the records in the data structure. Access to the data set is obtained by using a key as an argument to the access function. In some systems, there may be several sets of keys associated with the same data set. Access by more than one key is allowed in PL/I and in the latest ANSI COBOL standard.

A closely related organization is the *indexed sequential* organization, in which an index is constructed, but use may also be made of the sequential relationship between elements.

Example

An indexed sequential type of organization is used in several situations not connected with programming. For example, the use of multi-volume telephone directories, in which initial letters are printed on the back of the volumes, provides a simple illustration of an indexed sequential data structure. The volumes of some large directories, such as the London telephone directory, are marked by initial letters: A through H, I through N, O through R, S through Z. These letters serve as an index to locate a name approximately. When the correct volume of the directory has been obtained, a second level of index appears in the headings on each page. This is used to obtain a closer approximation to the entry; finally, sequential searching is used to locate the required entry.

In the main part of this chapter, we discuss statements and operators used for accessing sequentially organized data sets. Two aspects are examined: the processing of *records* and the processing of a *stream*. Many factors influencing the design of sequential I/O statements apply equally well to other organizations.

First, however, we discuss the file concepts of COBOL and PL/I, which illustrate how we may symbolically refer to the contents of data sets.

11.6 FILE CONCEPTS IN COBOL AND PL/I

In the following sections, the term "file" has a more limited meaning than before. We should, properly speaking, say 'PL/I File' or 'COBOL File', but will not make this distinction except where confusion might otherwise arise.

We take a file to mean the set of descriptive information used in accessing data sets in COBOL and PL/I. This information may include the organization of the data set, the record formats and means of data representation, the methods of labeling the data set, etc. It may also include the method of access to the file, such as whether it is to be processed sequentially, by means of an index, or by some other means.

During execution of a program, this descriptive information—the COBOL or PL/I file—may exist in several different states. At one point, it may simply have a name and a set of related attributes. At other points, when it has been "opened" there will generally be an associated data set; this association may be terminated by "closing" the file.

A file may first have to be "established" by declarative and procedural statements. Establishment includes declaration, selection, and opening. In this activity a number of properties or attributes may be associated with the file name and used to modify or control subsequent READ and WRITE statements.

Associated with each file are:

- a name (the name of the *file*, not necessarily the same as that of the data set),
- a set of attributes,
- the actual data being accessed—the data-set—or some means referencing it.

The similarity of this information (shown in Fig. 11.3) to that associated with a variable, as discussed in Chapter 7, will be apparent. The analogy, though useful in the study of I/O languages, cannot be taken too far, partly because the lifetime of a variable is limited to the period of time when the program defining it is in execution, whereas a data set may have an existence independent of the life of any program.

The introduction of files, with their associated attributes, has made it possible to design relatively simple READ and WRITE statements, in spite of the extreme complexity of I/O devices and systems. The complexity of the underlying system is reflected in the attributes associated with the file, while the READ and WRITE statements can remain relatively independent of the hardware.

We first consider the possible range of attributes of a file, how they are associated with a file name, and how they affect the execution of I/O statements. Considering COBOL first, there are three points at which attributes may be associated with a COBOL file:

- the ENVIRONMENT division—statically;
- the DATA division—statically;
- the OPEN statement of the PROCEDURE division—dynamically.

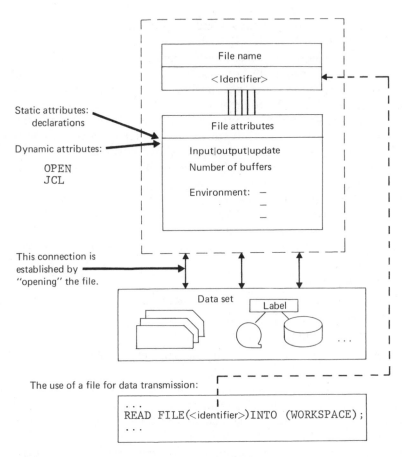

Fig. 11.3 The file concepts of PL/I and COBOL

From a conceptual point of view, it is irrelevant in which COBOL division the file declarations are given. Figure 11.4 shows an abstraction of the file attributes in a notation discussed in Chapter 5, which allows irrelevant syntactic considerations to be ignored. (Opportunity has been taken to remove one or two redundant specifications, such as those which are stated in the COBOL specifications to be "for documentation purposes only.")

Next, to compare COBOL and PL/I files, the same notation is used in Figure 11.5 to illustrate the sequential file attributes of PL/I.

The first impression, in comparing the two diagrams, is that COBOL file attributes are considerably more comprehensive than those of PL/I. This is indeed so, although we may notice that some attributes of a COBOL file

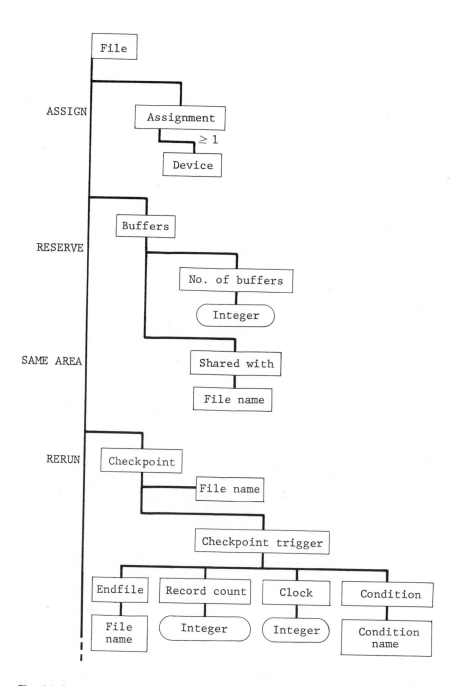

Fig. 11.4 Abstract syntax of COBOL sequential file attributes

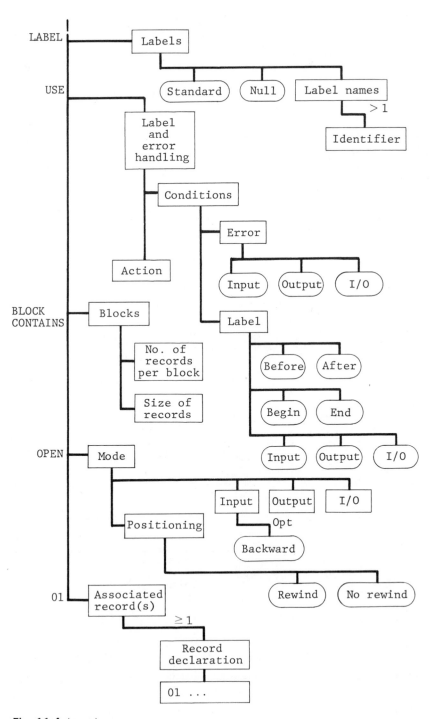

Fig. 11.4 (cont.)

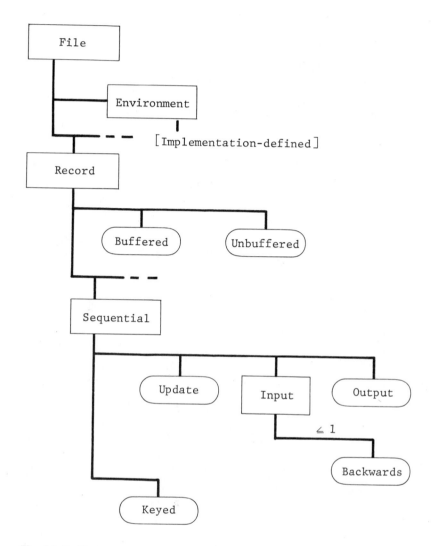

Fig. 11.5 Abstract syntax of PL/I sequential file attributes

are included in the ENVIRONMENT attribute of PL/I. Although the same term "environment" is used both in COBOL and PL/I, it is used in a different sense in the two languages.† COBOL first introduced the idea of

---

† Both COBOL and PL/I allow the user to *specify* an environment, although neither language has good facilities for the converse action of "interrogating" an environment. This useful facility was proposed by Naur (1964) for an extension to ALGOL.

an environment declaration. It was recognized that certain system parameters have to be specified in any program making extensive use of an operating system. COBOL includes such properties in the ENVIRONMENT DIVISION, expecting that changes will have to be made to these entries if the program is to run on another system. The exact form of declarations which may be made in a COBOL ENVIRONMENT DIVISION are a part of the COBOL language, although extensions are allowed for implementation-defined features. These may be given what are called "implementor-names."

In contrast, PL/I, treats the *contents* of the ENVIRONMENT attribute as "implementation defined," that is, not part of the language. Thus the set of keywords which may be written within the brackets following ENVIRONMENT may differ from one system to another.

There are also a number of minor differences between the two approaches of COBOL and PL/I, the following being the more significant:

11.6.1   Device Assignment

COBOL allows the specification of device assignment in the ENVIRONMENT division.

Example

```
SELECT TAX-SUMMARY ASSIGN TO UT-2400-S-TAXSUM
```

In this statement, TAX-SUMMARY is the name of a file, which is assigned to an external device, whose naming convention is established by the implementors. In this version, UT refers to the "utility" device-class (i.e., a mass-storage or tape device), 2400 is the number of a device, S means that it is sequentially organized, and TAXSUM is the name by which the data set is known outside the system. The name used in this example (UT-2400-S-TAXSUM) is an example of a COBOL *implementor-name,* which provides a means of adding implementation-defined features to a program.

There is no means of assigning data sets to devices in the PL/I language. However device assignment may be specified in the ENVIRONMENT option associated with a file. (This is the means of device assignment in the DOS/360 implementation of PL/I. Under OS/360, a system which allows later "binding" than DOS/360, device assignment is specified in the job control language.)

11.6.2   Buffer Assignment

Buffer assignment may be specified in the COBOL ENVIRONMENT DIVISION. In PL/I, buffer allocation may be specified in the ENVIRONMENT attribute.

Example

```
COBOL
        RESERVE 3 AREAS. . .
PL/I
        DECLARE  STOCK_RECORD CONSECUTIVE RECORD INPUT
                 ENV(RECSIZE(80) BUFFERS(3));
```

11.6.3   Checkpoint Specification

COBOL provides means of specifying "checkpoints" associated with a given file, by means of the RERUN statement. A checkpoint record is an instantaneous record or snapshot of the status of a program and the contents of its main storage sufficient to define the computation at a point in time. (It is equivalent to a machine *state* in the theory of computation.) Checkpoint records can be created and stored on a nominated device on the basis of the number of records processed on a given file. COBOL checkpoints are specified in the ENVIRONMENT division as part of the INPUT-OUTPUT section.

Example

```
ENVIRONMENT DIVISION.
.  .  .
INPUT-OUTPUT SECTION.
I-O-CONTROL.
.  .  .
RERUN ON MASTER-CHEKPT-1 EVERY 100 RECORDS OF ACCOUNT.
```

11.6.4   Associated Records

One of the main differences between COBOL and PL/I file declarations is in the association of record types with files. In COBOL, record types are associated with a file by including them with the file declaration.

Example

Suppose we have an output file for customer bills, and that there are three different types of print lines which are selected according to the data to be printed. A COBOL file declaration might be written:

```
FD  CUSTOMER-BILLS
    LABEL RECORDS ARE STANDARD
    DATA RECORDS ARE LINE-1, LINE-2, LINE-3.
01  LINE-1.
    02 OLD-BALANCE PICTURE $$,$$$.99.
    02 FILLER      PICTURE XXX.
    ...
```

```
01   LINE-2.
     02 AMOUNT-DUE  PICTURE $$,$$$.99.
     02 FILLER     PICTURE XXX.
     ...
01   LINE-3.
     02 ADDRESS  PICTURE X(30).
     ...
```

This specifies the record formats that will appear when the file CUS-TOMER-BILLS is created. As data is calculated, it is moved to LINE-1, LINE-2, or LINE-3, according to the data itself. The picture specifications associated with these record specifications ensure that appropriate editing takes place when the data is moved.

It might seem that, when a COBOL file is read, each record type is checked against the incoming data. However, this is not the case, and COBOL does not require the record types on a file to match those for which a declaration has been given. The record declarations are used:

- to establish the size of the input-output areas needed to process the data set—if several record formats are specified, as in the example above, the largest record size is used to establish the buffer size;

- to calculate the relative addresses of data items in the record.

In PL/I, there is no means of associating record types with a given file. Any independent variable occupying connected storage may be treated as a file record. This gives greater flexibility to the PL/I programmer; however, the advantage of the COBOL design is that a compiler is able to deduce the size of records on a file from the file specifications whereas in PL/I this information must be provided separately.

11.6.5   Open and Close

The names of these statements, traditional in most file-handling systems, have an almost Dickensian ring about them—we may imagine a dim, candlelit office, in the corner of which a clerk opens a huge ledger. ... OPEN and CLOSE were present in the early commercial languages FACT and COMMERCIAL TRANSLATOR, which provided many ideas later used in the design of COBOL. OPEN and CLOSE have not generally been included in scientifically oriented languages such as FORTRAN, nor are they included in the official proposals for input-output in ALGOL 60 (IFIP 1964). However, the design of these statements illustrates several important programming concepts, showing how various kinds of *binding* may be treated in programming languages. They are used both to provide extra function, and to improve the efficiency of implementation.

The PL/I OPEN statement, which allows any file attribute to be specified, acts as a dynamic file declaration and may be used to complete the specification of a file which has only been partly specified in a DECLARE statement. Taking the analogy between file and variable, OPEN and CLOSE in PL/I may be likened to the allocation and freeing of a variable.

Example

If it is known in advance how certain files are to be used, their attributes may be stated in declarations, allowing very simple OPEN statements. In PL/I, no OPEN statement is needed at all; and in the absence of explicit OPEN statements, files are implicitly opened when they are first used. In the following PL/I example, the required information on the files has been included in declarations. OPEN statements are therefore not required.

```
DECLARE
    (INA,INB,INC) FILE RECORD INPUT SEQUENTIAL
    ENVIRONMENT(FB RECSIZE(80) BLKSIZE(400)),
    (OUTA,OUTB,OUTC) FILE STREAM PRINT
    ENVIRONMENT(F RECSIZE(121));
...
READ FILE(INA) INTO (SCAN_POSITION);
...
PUT FILE(OUTC) (T(1),T(2),T(3))(FORMAT_C);
...
```

However, if complete file specifications cannot be fixed when a program is written, file attributes need not be set until that point in the program when the files are ready for use. In this case the required information may be specified on the OPEN statement.

```
DECLARE
    (MASTER1,MASTER2) FILE;
...
IF (TEST(I))
    THEN
        OPEN FILE(MASTER1)INPUT RECORD SEQUENTIAL
            ENVIRONMENT(F RECSIZE(80));
    ELSE
        OPEN FILE(MASTER1)INPUT RECORD SEQUENTIAL
            ENVIRONMENT(FB RECSIZE(80)
                        BLKSIZE(800));
...
```

Another important function of OPEN and CLOSE is to control the positioning of the implicit pointer associated with a sequential data set. PL/I and COBOL have means of specifying positioning at either end of the data set, repositioning at the beginning after reaching the end, and positioning at the end of an existing data set to allow new records to be added to the end.

Example

COBOL:

```
OPEN INPUT STOCK-RECORDS REVERSED.
```

PL/I:

```
OPEN FILE(PASS_TWO)RECORD INPUT BACKWARDS;
```

Some devices, such as card readers, are inherently incapable of backwards positioning. The validity of these language forms therefore depends on the device with which the file is associated.

Another purpose served by OPEN and CLOSE is to indicate when processing of data set labels is to be carried out. This may include checking the name on a tape reel, confirming its date of creation, establishing the user's right to access confidential data, etc. Once satisfactory processing of labels has been completed, the data set may be linked to the program for processing to begin.

Finally, the OPEN and CLOSE statements are important factors in the efficiency of implementing a language. A discussion of techniques used for implementing OPEN and CLOSE in operating systems is beyond the scope of this book, but an example is given in the paper by Clark (1966). This gives a flowchart of the OPEN macro in the IBM operating system OS/360; this macro is used for implementing OPEN statements in high-level languages in this system.

As shown in Clark's paper, a technique frequently used in implementing large operating systems is to break down the set of tasks needed for reading and writing data into smaller functions which can be coded in separate modules. Although the total space needed by all of these modules might exceed the main storage available, it is possible to load just the required modules dynamically as soon as the properties of the data set to be accessed are known. The process of loading these modules may take considerable time, since dynamic name links may have to be established. One of the purposes of the OPEN statement is to allow the programmer to give advance notice of the processing requirements of the program, so that loading of the necessary modules can take place. Similarly, the CLOSE statement allows space to be released for allocation to other modules, as soon as it is known that references to a particular file will no longer take place.

Are the OPEN and CLOSE statements needed in a high-level programming language? This question can be asked:

- because some high-level languages have been designed without including them;

- because, even in languages which include them, it is sometimes possible to avoid their use.

It is possible to design a system in which data sets are opened when the first I/O statement referring to them is executed. It is clearly undesirable to repeat an OPEN statement each time a file is accessed, since, apart from efficiency considerations, this may cause undesired repositioning of the pointer to the current record. Implicit closing presents more problems, since it is more difficult to detect that a program is *not* going to refer to a file.

In PL/I, if a file is not opened, the first READ or GET causes implicit opening. COBOL, however, is designed so that it is an error to attempt to read from an unopened file. This ensures that files can not be inadvertently accessed. COBOL files must also be explicitly closed, whereas PL/I files which are left open during the run of a program are automatically closed at the end of the program.

11.6.6   Summary of Differences Between COBOL and PL/I Files

The main differences between the COBOL and PL/I treatments of files are as follows.

- COBOL file attributes are more comprehensive than those of PL/I. Among the features included in COBOL are: label handling, checkpoint specifications, device assignment, block and record size. In PL/I, these are not part of the language, although such information may be included in the ENVIRONMENT attribute.

- PL/I file attributes can be more dynamically associated with a data set. File attributes in PL/I can be set either at compile time *or* at execution time; files can be used as arguments to procedures, or treated as variables. This variety of choices allows programs to be written which are less closely related to a specific file or data set.

11.7   TWO FORMS OF SEQUENTIAL INPUT-OUTPUT: STREAM AND RECORD

We now come to the statements which control input-output operations. For simplicity, we only deal with *sequential* I/O—omitting the techniques used for indexed and direct methods of access. Although this may seem to oversimplify the problems of I/O, the approach can be justified by observing that a high proportion of current I/O is sequential. Furthermore, the design of statements for sequential processing illustrates many of the principles on which more elaborate I/O is based.

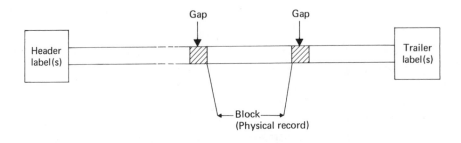

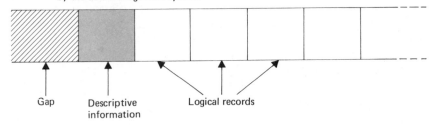

Each block is formed from a series of logical records.
A block may also contain descriptive information used
by the data-management system.

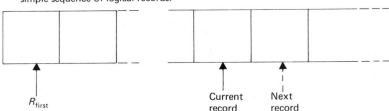

To the language user, the data set appears as a
simple sequence of logical records.

Fig. 11.6 A sequential data set

Figure 11.6 shows a typical layout of a *sequentially* organized data set.
In the following sections, we describe two essentially different forms of
sequential I/O—*record* and *stream*.

11.7.1   Record I/O

In *record* I/O, the unit of transmission is a record, the information contained
in a segment of contiguous storage. The editing functions which play such
a large part in stream I/O do not take place when record I/O is used. It

is typical in such programs to move data to an I/O area, described with a PICTURE specification. Editing can be carried out when the data is moved, rather than when I/O statements are executed—the picture specifications take the place of the format specifications of stream I/O.

11.7.2   Stream I/O

In *stream* I/O, data is represented externally as a sequence or stream of characters. In the program, it is specified by a data list, a list of data elements or structures. An important form of stream I/O is *formatted* I/O, in which a specification of the external data representation, a format, may be given. There are some forms of stream I/O in which a format is implicit and is supplied by the system.

These two forms of I/O, record and stream, correspond fairly closely to COBOL and FORTRAN I/O respectively. However, since neither form is, by itself, sufficiently flexible or powerful, each language contains what might be called a hybrid form of I/O, with leanings towards one of the basic forms. PL/I has facilities both for record and stream I/O, for each of which there are distinct file attributes and I/O statements.

11.7.3   Sequential Record I/O

Most sequentially organized data sets are stored in a physically sequential form; obvious examples include the storage of data on punched cards, tapes, and similar media. We should note, however, that the sequential *physical* placement of records is not essential; the critical requirement for sequential organization is that records of the data set are made available in a given sequence, so that it is meaningful to talk of the *next* record. In terms of the relations between elements of the data set, a sequential data set is one for which the successor relationship is valid. The actions involved in processing a sequential data set are shown in Fig. 11.7.

First, we must establish a connection between the file-name and the device on which the data set is stored. The device may have to be positioned so that the pointer to the current record is ready to access the first record in the set.

The main part of most sequential processing programs is a loop—the natural way of processing a sequential set is iterative. As each record is processed, two types of action may take place. The first is the movement of the conceptual pointer so that the next record is made available. The second is the transmission of a record between data set and store. The loop ends either when some condition has been established, for example, when a record being searched for has been found, or when the entire data set has been processed—the *end-file* condition.

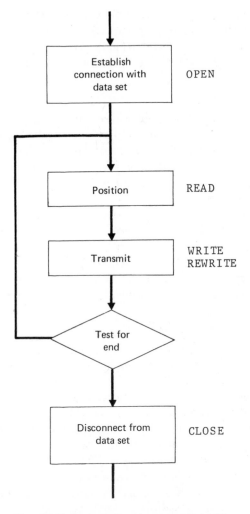

Fig. 11.7 Basic actions in sequential I/O

11.8   THE READ AND WRITE STATEMENTS

In accessing a data set sequentially, addressing is implicit rather than direct. As we have seen, access operations must include two components:

- a positioning operation which causes the next item in the data set to be accessed,
- a data transmission operation.

Some I/O statements both position and transmit; others may allow transmission without positioning, or positioning without transmission. As the data set is processed, a record is distinguished as the *current record*. We can imagine a hidden pointer, defined while a sequential file is open, identifying this record. The effect of a positioning statement is simply to change the position of this pointer.

PL/I allows positioning without transmission of data. For input (and update) files we may write

    READ FILE (filename) IGNORE (expression);

which allows records to be skipped on an INPUT or UPDATE file. The number of records skipped is determined by the value of the expression.

11.9   DATA TRANSMISSION IN RECORD I/O

As we have seen, the operand of a READ or WRITE statement in record I/O is a record structure, corresponding to a contiguous section of storage. The most important characteristic of record I/O is the transmission of storage representations of data values without conversion. It is the absence of data conversion in record I/O which explains its importance in data processing. In many cases a user may have to process large data sets on a regular daily, weekly, or monthly basis. A large commercial data set may contain millions of records; it is this scale of operations that makes the conversion of data from internal to external representation an extremely uneconomic proposition.

Although to the user of a programming language the apparent unit of transmission of READ and WRITE statements is a record structure, the actual unit is a *block* or *physical record*. Each block is generally read into or written from a storage buffer, a contiguous section of storage set aside by a compiler or operating system. Processing may be carried out

- in the buffer itself,
- by moving the data into a variable.

The term sometimes used for these in early I/O systems were *locate* mode and *move* mode respectively. These terms are sometimes still used.

11.9.1   Processing in the Buffer in COBOL and PL/I

Processing in the buffer is often the more efficient method, particularly when there are a relatively small number of accesses to the data in the program.

Example

Suppose we have a file, F, containing records described by a record description, R. The elements contained in R are $E1$, $E2$, $E3$, etc. In COBOL, the record R may be defined with the file F as follows:

```
FD   F
     BLOCK CONTAINS 6 RECORDS
     LABEL RECORDS ARE OMITTED
     DATA RECORD IS R.
01   R.
     02 E1 PICTURE ...
     02 E2 PICTURE ...
     02 E3 PICTURE ...
        ...
```

We can access the records of F by the following statements:

```
OPEN INPUT F.
READ F AT END GO TO SECTION-2.
```

Successive READ statements make the records of F available; for example when 3 READ statements have been executed, the current record is the third record in the data set, and references to $E1$, $E2$, etc. will access the appropriate elements of this record. The COBOL programmer does not have to be concerned with the physical location of the current record, which may be in a different position in storage after each READ statement. Details of blocking and buffering are also handled automatically by the system. As soon as the fourth READ statement is executed, the meanings of the names R, $E1$, $E2$, and $E3$ are changed, and the third record is no longer available. This means that any information in this record needed by the programmer must be copied while the record is still current.

In PL/I, file and record declarations are made separately.

Example

```
DECLARE F FILE RECORD ENVIRONMENT (...);
DECLARE 1 R BASED(P),
          2 E1 attributes,
          2 E2 attributes,
          2 E3 attributes,
             ...
```

The record R is now declared as a based variable, with an associated pointer, P. The accessing statements are:

```
OPEN FILE(F) INPUT;
READ FILE(F) SET(P);
```

When each READ statement is executed, the pointer, P, is set to point at the new current record. As before, the actual location of the record is of no concern to the programmer. The record and its elements may, as in COBOL, be accessed by the names R, $E1$, $E2$, etc. Since R has the BASED attribute, a reference to R is equivalent to a pointer qualified reference $P -> R$. Similarly, a reference to $E1$ is equivalent to $P -> E1$, etc.

The system actions corresponding to READ statements in COBOL and PL/I are almost identical; in both cases, a pointer is moved along an area of buffer storage as each READ statement is executed, changing the current meaning of the record and element names. The main difference between the two languages is that a pointer P is made explicitly available in PL/I, while this mechanism is hidden from the user in COBOL.

It might seem that the PL/I programmer, by saving the value of P, could gain access to previous records. However, this is not the case and valid accessing of R is only guaranteed for current settings of P. In COBOL, since only the field name can be used for accessing the data, only one version of the data (the current record) can be accessed at any one time.

For output, there is a sharper difference between COBOL and PL/I, particularly in the order in which the basic actions are executed. To illustrate this, assume there is an output record, S, with elements $H1,H2,H3$, so we can calculate the values of the elements in temporary variables $T1$, $T2$, ... etc. (WORKING STORAGE in COBOL) and are creating a new file, G.

In COBOL, we first open the file, which makes it possible to process the first record. Elements are moved from $T1$, $T2$ ... into $H1$, $H2$, etc. and records are transmitted to the data set by successive WRITE statements:

```
OPEN OUTPUT G.
...
(compute new values)
MOVE T1 TO H1, T2 TO H2, T3 TO H3,...
WRITE S.
```

In PL/I, the basic action for transmitting data from a buffer is the establishment of a pointer value for the record being transmitted. This is done with the LOCATE statement. There is no need to use a WRITE statement and data is automatically transmitted by the system when the buffer is full, or when the file is closed.

```
OPEN FILE(G) OUTPUT ENVIRONMENT (BUFFERED);
...
(compute new values)
LOCATE FILE(G) SET(P);
H1=T1; H2=T2; H3=T3;
```

Note that in COBOL, data is moved into the buffer first, after which the transmission statement is executed. In PL/I, addressability is first established, then assignment into the buffer is possible.

11.9.2   Move Mode Input-Output in COBOL and PL/I

As we have seen, when a record is read with locate-mode I/O, it is only addressable while it is current. In many applications, new data sets are created from existing ones, and data may have to be transferred from a record being accessed to a new record being created. Such data can be transferred by means of MOVE or assignment statements. However, both COBOL and PL/I include I/O statements which cause information to be moved out of the read-in buffer to a designated location.

We first consider the example as it might be expressed in COBOL.

With the same input file as before, suppose that G is an output file, with associated record S containing fields $H1$, $H2$, $H3$, etc.

The declaration might be

```
DATA DIVISION.
FILE SECTION.
FD G BLOCK CONTAINS 10 RECORDS.
    01 S.
        02 H1 PICTURE...
        02 H2 PICTURE...
        02 H3 PICTURE...
```

Then the transfer of data from the file F to record S can be accomplished as follows:

```
OPEN INPUT F.
OPEN OUTPUT G.
READ F RECORD INTO S AT END GO TO PHASE-3.
    ...
```

At this stage, the information contained in the input record R is now also in S, since the READ...INTO statement acts both as a READ and a MOVE. Following the READ statement, the next action in the program will typically be to move items of data into the new fields of the record, leaving the permanent information (names, addresses, headings, etc.) untouched.

There are similar statements for move-mode I/O in PL/I.

```
OPEN INPUT FILE(F), OUTPUT FILE(G);
READ FILE(F) INTO(S);
    ...
```

However, since there is no associated record with a PL/I file, there is only one copy of the record available at any one time, namely the record which has been moved into *S*. (It is not possible in PL/I to say: READ...INTO(var) SET(ptr), which would correspond to the COBOL statement.)

Corresponding to the READ...INTO statements, there are also WRITE...FROM statements in both COBOL and PL/I, which move data from a designated variable to an output data set.

11.10 INPUT-OUTPUT CONDITIONS AND ERRORS

It can be seen that techniques for accessing data sets, even by the simpler forms of sequential I/O statements, are more complex than the access methods for internal data structures described in Chapter 8. In certain cases, the fact that data sets have an independent existence, unrelated to a particular program, can lead to impossible access being attempted. Again, the data being read may have been prepared by different programs or different devices from those used for its access and the physical format of the data itself may be unsuitable. The mode of access may itself result in an undefined state—for example, getting the next record is impossible if the current record is the last one in the data set.

Any circumstance (or set of circumstances) which makes it impossible to complete a specified I/O operation is called an I/O *condition*. Included among such conditions are input-output *errors*, although it must be emphasized that all conditions are not errors—some are natural consequences of the method of programming. Some conditions, such as end-of-file, must be recognized because the logic of I/O programming depends on them, others, such as error conditions, because of their importance in establishing correct program behavior.

As we have seen, the normal method of processing sequential data sets is by means of statements which cause a current pointer to scan the ordered set of elements in the data set. Since the programmer has no means of knowing the number of records or elements in the data set, it is inevitable that, sooner or later, the current pointer will reach the boundary of the data set.

In COBOL I/O, statements referring to sequentially organized data sets may specify the action to be taken when a positioning condition arises; this is done by means of an AT END phrase attached to the READ and WRITE statements. In PL/I, the ENDFILE condition used with the ON statement provides the same effect; although the action specified relates to all I/O for a given file, rather than for a specific READ or WRITE statement.

Examples

Suppose that records in a file called DAILY-RATE are being examined to find the largest value of the item YIELD, which is stored in field MAX-YIELD. The whole data set is scanned and, at the end of the scan, control is transferred to a section called YIELD-REPORT.

COBOL

```
        OPEN INPUT DAILY-RATE.
READ-LOOP.
        READ DAILY-RATE AT END GO TO YIELD-REPORT.
        IF YIELD IS GREATER THAN MAX-YIELD
            MOVE YIELD TO MAX-YIELD.
        GO TO READ-LOOP.
YIELD-REPORT.
        . . .
```

PL/I

```
        OPEN FILE(DAILY_RATE) INPUT;
        ON ENDFILE(DAILY_RATE) GO TO YIELD_REPORT;
READ LOOP:
        READ FILE(DAILY_RATE) SET(P);
        IF YIELD > MAX_YIELD THEN MAX_YIELD=YIELD;
        GO TO READ_LOOP;
YIELD_REPORT:
```

Errors may also arise during transmission itself, caused by errors in data specifications, in the recorded form of data or in hardware in I/O devices. Some examples of errors and conditions which arise during data transmission are as follows:

11.10.1   Errors in Record Size

When data is being read, the size of record expected is specified by means of an FD entry in COBOL or a level-1 variable in PL/I. The record size is needed in the first instance to enable space to be allocated for a read-in area. If the records on the data set are larger than expected, it is clear that the results will be in error. In PL/I, this is called the RECORD condition.

11.10.2   Errors in Data Format

Format errors arise when there is some form of scanning and conversion of data, such as occurs in stream I/O. PL/I has two I/O conditions for this.

```
CONVERSION
NAME
```

The first applies to any form of data stream; the second is restricted to errors in data-directed input (see Section 11.17).

11.10.3   Errors in Hardware Devices

In certain situations, hardware malfunction may make it impossible for data to be transmitted correctly. Apart from signaling the error so that another part of the program can be entered, possible courses of action may be to note the current status of the machine and to record the error for subsequent analysis. In PL/I the TRANSMIT condition, and certain forms of the KEY condition, may be used to detect this form of error.

Another technique for specifying I/O conditions in COBOL is by means of the USE statement, which defines action to be taken throughout a program.

Example

```
DECLARATIVES.
ERROR-TREATMENT SECTION.
    USE AFTER STANDARD ERROR
        PROCEDURE ON FILE-1, FILE-2.
            - error treatment specified here -
    END DECLARATIVES.
```

If a large number of files is to be handled, or if there are a large number of alternating READ and WRITE statements, then it is rather heavy work to write the condition handling treatment with each statement. The USE statement allows condition handling to be specified on a global basis for a complete program. The action specified in a USE statement may be programmed to take place either before or after standard error procedures (standard for the compiler, not for COBOL, which does not specify any actions for error conditions). The USE statement is declarative and the actions, and the files with which the actions are specified, are fixed when the program is written.

The treatment of I/O conditions in PL/I differs from that in COBOL in the following ways:

- a larger number of I/O conditions are separately distinguished and named;

- for each condition, a standard system action is specified as part of the PL/I language;

- the specification of user action is more dynamic and flexible. It is executable, in contrast with the declarative nature of the COBOL treatment.

TABLE 11.1 Input-output conditions in PL/I

Condition name	When condition occurs
ENDFILE (file-ref)	On a GET or READ statement for a sequential file—if an attempt is made to read beyond the limits of the data set
ENDPAGE (file-ref)	On a PUT statement—when an attempt is made to print a line beyond the PAGESIZE setting
KEY (file-ref)	On any *keyed* I/O operation—if the key is invalid or cannot be found
NAME (file-ref)	On GET statements with data-directed input—if an identifier in the stream is not in the data list
RECORD (file-ref)	On a READ or REWRITE statement—if the actual record contains more (or less) data than the variable. May also be raised on the WRITE statement.
TRANSMIT (file-ref)	On any I/O operation—if there is a transmission error
UNDEFINEDFILE (file-ref)	On an OPEN statement—if the attempt to open a file is unsuccessful
CHECK (list of variable names)	On any I/O operation—when a variable in the list receives a new value

Note: In this table, "file-ref" includes any reference which denotes a file; it may include a file name, a file variable, or a function reference denoting a file value.

The input-output conditions defined in PL/I are shown in Table 11.1.

The technique for controlling the action to be taken when one of the conditions occurs is that used for all PL/I conditions, namely, the use of the ON statement (see Chapter 10). The PL/I ON statement, as it applies to I/O conditions, can be regarded as a generalization of the COBOL USE statement. The difference is that the action specified in an ON unit only applies after the ON statement has been executed and can be overridden by the execution of another ON statement. The action specified after a USE statement is fixed by compilation of the program and cannot be changed during execution of a program.

11.11 UPDATING A MASTER FILE

We now consider a typical data processing problem—that of updating the information in a business enterprise. Here we summarize the most commonly found features of sequential processing and introduce a further type of language statement—the REWRITE statement.

Programs for this type of application are perhaps the most common of all computer programs and in most cases they use sequentially organized

data. Variants of a related program are so common that it has been suggested that prototype programs might be written and applications generated
by the adjustment of a few key parameters (Petersen, 1971).

Critical information used in running a business is held in what is called
a master data set. Typical contents of such a data set might include:

- details of each part used or made in a manufacturing industry,
- information about each person employed in an organization,
- master copies of each policy issued by an insurance company.

Information such as this is vital to the running of a business. On-line
systems are used when it is important for data to be changed almost instan-
taneously; an example is an airline reservation system, in which bookings
are accepted, via terminals, in a random fashion.

In a batch system, it is common to store the master file as a sequentially
organized data set. This will be sorted on some key field in each record;
for example, the part number, the personnel number, or the policy number
in the examples quoted.

Changes to the data are collected in a batch, perhaps once a day or
once a week, to form the update run. Changes may arise for the following
reasons:

- stock levels of parts may have changed;
- employees may have joined, left, been transferred, promoted or been
  on a training course;
- policies may have been altered, claims made, new policies instated.

The changes are sorted in the same order as the master file and updating
of the master file is carried out as in the flow chart in Fig. 11.8.

Consider the master data set in an update problem. In an on-line system
this data set is a more or less permanent part of the system. It exists before
the updating transaction takes place, and persists afterwards. There is no
question of creating a new copy of the master data each time a transaction
is run. Hence in direct access systems we need statements which, having
accessed a record in the data set, can proceed to modify or delete it. This
presents many problems if the new data requires a different amount of
storage from the old.

With simpler sequential systems, working in batch mode, it is feasible
to create a new master data set each time updating is carried out. By creating
a new copy as the data is sequentially processed, the problems of adjusting
the storage space for changes in the size of records are avoided.

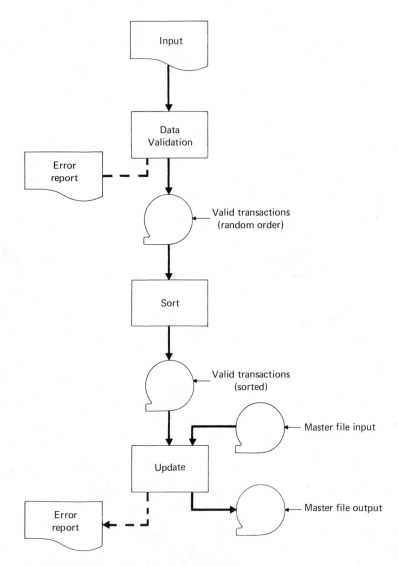

Fig. 11.8 Basic actions in sequential I/O

Both COBOL and PL/I have file attributes for files used in update programs (the terms used are I-O in COBOL, UPDATE in PL/I). These allow two-way transmission to the corresponding data sets (INPUT files only allow READ statements and OUTPUT files only allow WRITE statements). In COBOL, the I-O attribute may only be used for mass storage files (i.e., for data stored in a medium in which nonsequential access is possible), although this restriction does not apply to UPDATE files in PL/I.

PL/I and the most recent ANSI COBOL include an additional statement for updating files, the REWRITE statement. The effect of this is to transmit data to the record accessed previously by a READ statement; i.e., to the *current record,* without movement of the conceptual pointer. The file referenced in this statement must have been declared (or opened) with the UPDATE (PL/I) or I-O (COBOL) attribute.

11.12 SUMMARY—THE IMPORTANCE OF SEQUENTIAL PROCESSING

The update problem may be taken as typical of many commercial applications. First, we have a large set of data—generally much too large to get into the high-speed store of a computer. A primary concern of many commercial systems is to keep this set of data in an accurate and up-to-date state. It is often necessary to service queries on the data and to produce reports and statistics. However, the amount of computation on the data is often quite small.

The sorted order of the master records in the data set is simply a means of achieving efficient access, making use of the simplicity of the sequential access technique. A close relationship exists between sequential updating and *sorting.* The dominant position of sequential processing can be seen by estimates that sorting occupies up to 30% of the processing time of an average commercial data processing installation. Sequential record I/O is frequently used as a simple and efficient means of access to large collections of data. For the most part, the operations on the data are those of insertion, removal and update. In this form, the use of record I/O is closely related to the access functions of the data structures discussed in Chapter 8.

Further suggested reading on sequential file processing would include a general summary by Gildersleeve (1971) and several papers by Ghosh (1969). Other types of record handling are reviewed in two conference reports: IFIP (1969) and BCS (1970); and in papers by Chapin (1969), McGee (1969), and Senko (1969, 1970).

11.13 STREAM INPUT-OUTPUT

The term "stream," referring to a sequence of data transmitted by I/O statements, has been in use for some time; it seems to have originated in the input-output system used for the Atlas computer (Howarth *et al.,* 1962). The central idea is that input and output are to be regarded as consisting of a stream of characters, rather than records.

It is clear that stream I/O is sequential in nature. The sequence consists of data items, including variables and constants, expressed in external form as character strings.

In this chapter, we describe three kinds of stream I/O:

- I/O with programmer-defined format,
- I/O with implicit format,
- self-identifying data.

The first type, with formats explicitly defined by the programmer, was one of the first to be developed. It often requires considerable care on the part of the programmer, owing to the complexity of the notation needed for format description. To reduce this difficulty, the second type of I/O was introduced, in which standard formats are defined by the system, depending on the data types being transmitted; this is called *list-directed* input-output. Another form of stream I/O is that in which each data item is accompanied in the stream by some descriptive information—in the case we consider, by its name. This is called *data-directed* input-output.

Stream I/O was developed early in the history of programming languages. FORTRAN in particular included a powerful, though complex, form. At first, it was associated with scientific languages, because most scientific languages were originally implemented on binary, word-oriented machines. Users of such machines were forced to consider the external representation of data to a greater extent than those using commercial machines, many of which stored data in character form needing no conversion or editing for input or output.

For the most part, stream I/O has not been widely used for commercial data processing. Compared with record I/O, the stream I/O facilities available in many current languages are

- less flexible in their treatment of files,
- less efficient, due to conversion on input-output,
- lacking a simple relationship between I/O lists and data records.

However, elements of stream I/O techniques have found their way into commercial languages. For example, the Report Writing feature of COBOL contains many of the facilities for editing and formatting found in stream I/O languages.

11.13.1   Basic Elements of Stream I/O

As in record I/O, stream I/O statements have a keyword which distinguishes between input (READ or GET) and output (WRITE or PUT). In addition, the general form of a stream I/O statement contains two lists, a *data* list and a *format* list. These respectively describe the items to be transmitted and their external representation. The data list may contain

- variables,
- expressions (output only).

A format list contains

- field descriptors,
- control specifications.

A *field descriptor* specifies the external form of a data element in terms of a character string field. A *control specification* is a means of positioning a data element, inserting punctuation characters or creating new record boundaries.

For compactness, data and format lists are written in a form which allows repetitive specifications, looping, etc. The notations for expressing these repetitions are described below. The apparent similarity of FORTRAN and PL/I holds some dangers here, for, as explained below, there are some subtle differences in the control of I/O transmission between the two languages.

To explain the working of an I/O statement, we first expand the format and data lists into sequences of elementary items which are matched in pairs—this matching must also be carried out by an implementation during transmission of data.

- The data list is expanded to

  $\{e_1, e_2, e_3, \ldots e_n\}$

  where e_i is a data element.

- The format list is expanded to:

  $\{c_0, f_1, c_1, f_2, c_2, \ldots f_n, c_n\}$

  where c_i is a control format item and f_i is a field descriptor.

An I/O statement transmits elements according to this list, applying control actions between successive element transmissions according to the flowchart in Fig. 11.9.

The expanded data and format lists are shown as having the same number of elements. This is not required in writing an I/O statement. There is, however, a convention, both in FORTRAN and in PL/I, that when the two lists differ in length the data list controls the number of elements transmitted. If the format list is shorter than the data list, then the format list will be used again. In FORTRAN, if the format list is a simple list of format

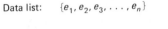

Data list: $\{e_1, e_2, e_3, \ldots, e_n\}$

Format list: $\{c_1, f_1, c_2, f_2, \ldots, c_n, f_n\}$

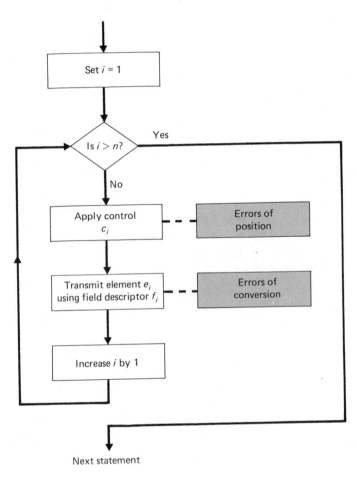

Next statement

Fig. 11.9 Format-controlled I/O

items (without brackets), then control will go back to the beginning of the list. If there are repeating groups in the format list, control will go back to the beginning of the most recently used group. In PL/I, control always goes back to the beginning of the format list. If, on the other hand, the format list is longer, its redundant items are ignored. (This applies both to PL/I and to FORTRAN.)

11.14   SPECIFICATION OF THE DATA LIST

We begin by considering the construction of the data list, the controlling factor in stream I/O statements. Any sequence of elements can be completely specified by writing out the names of the elements:

{element 1, element 2, ...}

This simple form, a list of references separated by commas, is used as a basis for constructing more elaborate forms of data list.

Examples

```
A,B,C
T(1),T(5),S(J-1)
'THE VALUE OF X = ' ,X
```

We next consider data structures. The convention is that a structure name in a data list indicates transmission of the whole structure, element by element. This is one of several points in the design of a programming language where an ordering of the elements in a data structure is implied. It is convenient to adopt the same ordering in all such circumstances, the most appropriate one being the storage ordering discussed in Chapter 8.

Examples

1) If P is a 5×5 matrix, then the appearance of the item

```
P
```

in a data list will result in the transmission of

$$P(1,1) \ P(1,2) \ P(1,3) \ ... \ P(5,5)$$

in PL/I and

$$P(1,1) \ P(2,1) \ P(3,1) \ ... \ P(5,5)$$

in FORTRAN.

2) If R is a PL/I structure with the following declaration:

```
1 R,
  2 S FIXED,
  2 T,
      3 T1 CHAR(6),
      3 T2 CHAR(4),
  2 U FLOAT;
```

then the appearance of the item

R

in a data list will result in the transmission of the elements

S, T1, T2, U

We next consider the problem of generalizing a simple list (i.e., a list of single elements) so that the programmer can define a sequence of arbitrarily repeating elements, retaining control over the generation of subsequences. Formally, this is closely related to problems of iteration control and syntax generation, and uses some of the same techniques, though in a less well-developed form. In the following discussion, we use a slightly abstract notation, which it is hoped is self-explanatory. The actual syntax used in FORTRAN, PL/I, etc., will be described later.

If L is a simple list,

$$L ::= a,b,c, \ldots$$

then the first facility required is a means of allowing elements of L to be lists. For this, we need a syntactic means of distinguishing the bounds of a sublist and for this purpose we can use parentheses without ambiguity.

If, in the list L, c is itself a list, $(x,y,z, \ldots)$, then L can be written:

$$L ::= a,b,(x,y,z, \ldots), \ldots$$

This facility for delimiting sublists is an essential requirement for applying control factors to data lists.

The first type of control to consider is how to specify repetitions of the sublist. The simplest case is repetition of a sublist an integral number of times. This could be represented by including a numeric factoring of the sublist as follows

$$L ::= a,b,\{n \text{ times}\}(x,y,z, \ldots), \ldots$$

(However, we shall see that this form is not allowed in data lists, although it is allowed in format lists.)

As in the case of statement iteration (i.e., the DO and **for** statements considered in Chapter 10), it may be convenient to introduce a *control variable,* which is incremented during repetitions of the sublist, and whose value is available during such expansion. A control variable is used in DO and **for** statements and may be similarly employed in data lists. To produce N versions of the sub-list: $(x,y,z, \ldots)$ we write:

$$\{i = 1 \text{ by } 1 \text{ to } n\}(x,y,z, \ldots)$$

Each time a new copy of the list is generated, a new value of i is established until the value n is reached. The current value of i may be used to select members of variables in the sublist; for example, i may be used as an array index so that the expansion of the list can be used to extract selected elements of an array.

Examples

$\{j=1 \text{ to } 100\}\{A(j)\}$

$\{d=3 \text{ by } 7 \text{ to } 365\}\{day(d)\}$

Finally, we may wish to omit certain elements in the list. If we think of the expansion activity just described as *conjunction,* the alternative action of *disjunction* may be expressed by a conditional form:

$$\{\text{if } p\}(x,y,z, \ldots)$$

where p is some predicate which must be *true* for the selection of the following item to occur.

Examples

$A,B,\{\text{if } test\}(C,D),\ E$

$P,Q,\{\text{if } B\}(R),\{\text{if}\neg B\}(S)$

The generation of sequences of items according to rules of conjunction and disjunction has been addressed in the theory of formal grammars. It is also related to the specification of statement-sequences in looping statements, and it is from the latter source that the language forms for data list construction in FORTRAN and PL/I have been derived. It is not possible simply to say "repeat n times"—an auxiliary variable must be introduced to control the number of repetitions. Only PL/I allows the disjunctive form, and, as with the DO statement, uses the clause:

$$\texttt{WHILE (expression)}$$

the expression being evaluated each time the generation of a list is repeated. For the item associated with this clause to be included, the value of the expression must equal '1'B when this point is encountered in the list.

11.14.1   PL/I Data Lists

A PL/I data list may be used in any of the three types of stream I/O.

EDIT (data list) . . . . edited I/O, requiring a *format* specification

LIST (data list) . . . . list I/O, a stream of elements with predetermined format

DATA (data list) . . . . data-directed I/O, self-identifying elements also with predetermined format

A PL/I data list is a sequence of list items separated by commas. The construction of a data list depends on its intended use. The critical factor is whether the list is to be used for input or for output. The difference between input and output lists is analogous to the different forms that may be written on the left- and right-hand sides of assignment statements. In the first case (*input* data list, left-hand side of assignment), the list specifies locations into which values are to be placed. The elements in the list must therefore only include *names* of elements or data structures. In the other case, (*output* data list, right-hand side of assignment), the list may contain any value-determining element. The choice for output lists is therefore wider and an output list may also include constants, function references, and any reference or expression which denotes a value. (As in Chapter 9, we say that input data lists contain *L*-values and output data lists, *R*-values).

Examples

An example of a PL/I data list is as follows:

        A(1),A(3),(A(I) DO I=6, 13, 14 BY 6 TO 30, 50)

This denotes the transmission of

        A(1),A(3),A(6),A(13),A(14),A(20),A(26),A(50)

The following example of a data list shows the use of a WHILE clause.

        (SUMN(I) DO I=1 TO N WHILE (I<F(X)))

11.14.2 The Implied DO of FORTRAN

The FORTRAN data list follows a similar pattern to that of PL/I, although the syntax is slightly simpler. A data list is constructed from simple lists and from "DO-implied" lists. The DO-implied list is similar to a repetitive specification, although the keyword DO is not used; the form

$$i = m_1, m_2, m_3$$

is used to denote looping in the list. Parentheses denote the scope of the loop. In this form, m_1 denotes the initial value of i, m_2 its final value, and m_3 is the increment applied to i for each repetition. If m_3 is omitted, a value of 1 is taken.

Examples

The following examples of FORTRAN data lists illustrate the implied DO of FORTRAN:

        A(I),I=1,50
        (TABLE(M,N),N=1,12),M=1,20,2)

11.14.3   Format Lists

In addition to a data list, the other major component of a stream I/O statement is a *format list* whose purpose is to indicate the external representation of data values.

In FORTRAN, a format list is specified in a distinct statement, separate from READ or WRITE statements. A FORMAT statement is given a label which is referenced in a READ or WRITE. A single format can therefore be used by several I/O statements.

Example

```
    WRITE (6,3) A,B,C
  3 FORMAT(F8.4,2E5.4)
```

In PL/I, a format list may also be separate, as in FORTRAN, or it may form a part of a stream I/O statement, in this case a GET or PUT, as in the more compact form

    GET FILE (file name) EDIT (data list) (format list);

Example

    GET FILE(INPUT_MASTER) EDIT(NO,RANGE,SIZE)(F10, A, E10.2);

A format list contains *format specifiers* to denote the data representation and may also contain *control specifiers* which determine the positioning of data items. As with data lists, format lists are composed of elementary items and repetitions of elementary items.

The technique for building a sequence of format items from a list of elementary items follows a principle similar to that used for data lists. As before, a list may contain a sublist as an element, the bounds of the sublist being denoted by parentheses. Repetition of items or sublists is achieved by means of a *repetition factor,* enclosed in parentheses, preceding the data item to be repeated. The use of a repetition factor avoids the need to introduce a control variable.

In FORTRAN the repetition factor, called a *group repeat count,* must be an integer constant. In PL/I the factor may be any expression, the result of which is converted to give an integer value. Nesting lists within lists allows a repeating structure to be built up containing many levels. Complex sequences of format and control elements can be constructed.

There is no WHILE clause in a format list, either in PL/I or in FORTRAN. However, a form of disjunction is available in PL/I; when a repetition factor is represented by an expression, and the evaluated expression yields a zero or negative value, the format item is skipped. Expressions denoting repetition factors are computed each time the corresponding format item is used, so very flexible treatment of formats is possible.

A general type of FORTRAN or PL/I, format specifier has the form

{type-descriptor} {field-width} {scaling-factor}

type-descriptor—a single letter which denotes the type of the external representation. This field must always be present; it controls conversions between internal and external representations.

field-width—denotes the number of characters used to represent the data on an external medium. Allowance must be made for signs, decimal points, etc.

scale-factor—controls the decimal-point position for numeric data.

The data stream is a sequence of characters representing data items. To position these items on the page of a report is therefore primarily a matter of inserting space characters in the stream; this is achieved by means of a spacing format item, X. FORTRAN also uses a control format item to establish the relationship between the data stream and records—the physical units of data transmission. The control character / (slash) indicates a record boundary in FORTRAN. (Originally / was used as a printer control character to indicate a skip to a new line). In PL/I, the transmission of data *records* is regarded as the province of RECORD I/O. However, the control format item, SKIP (expression) can be used in STREAM I/O to indicate a new line, or lines, in the data set.

The control formats in PL/I provide a set of editing facilities for preparing printed output—including reports, printed text, tables, graphs, etc.

A page is a set of n lines, each line containing m characters. The values of n and m may be associated with a file by means of the PAGESIZE and LINESIZE options. During data transmission with STREAM I/O, a conceptual pointer moves along the data stream as input or output takes place. The movement of this pointer can be controlled by the control formats which allow two types of positioning:

- *relative* positioning, relative to the current character;
- *absolute* positioning, related to the line, column or page associated with the file.

Relative positioning is achieved by means of the control formats:

X(expression)—giving relative character positioning,

SKIP[(expression)]—giving relative line positioning,

PAGE—giving relative page positioning.

Because of the nature of the hardware, all relative positioning on lines must be positive—it is not possible to backspace most printers! However, zero values for line positioning can be given, allowing overprinting of characters.

Absolute positioning is achieved by means of the control formats:

COLUMN(expression)—giving absolute character positioning,

LINE(expression)—giving absolute line positioning.

A column is the position of a character in a line—column 1 corresponds to the first character, column 2 to the second character, and so on.

As before, the current pointer can only move forward; hence absolute positioning on a line may cause the current pointer to move to a new page, and positioning on a column may cause it to move to a new line.

Example

If the line pointer is currently on line 20, then the control format, LINE(6), will move the pointer to line 6 of the next page.

11.14.4   Dynamic Formats in FORTRAN

After compilation, certain format specifications in FORTRAN may be held internally in literal form, that is, as strings of characters. During execution of a format-controlled READ or WRITE the compiled program scans the format specification, and in effect *interprets* the format, calling on necessary conversion and transmission routines. This makes it possible, in certain circumstances, to treat format specifications as data which can be changed during execution of the program. The programmer can, for example, read in format specifications along with the data they describe.

There are two techniques for making use of this aspect of FORTRAN formats:

- reading into a format with 'H' specification,
- using arrays as formats.

The first technique follows from the fact that data from an 'H' specification is associated with the format list rather than the data list.

Example

```
      X = 5.6
      WRITE (5,10) X
10    FORMAT(15HTHE ANSWER IS: ,F3.2)
```

When this is executed, the output is as follows.

THE ANSWER IS: 5.60

The first 15 characters come from the format statement, 10.
    If we now read using the same format,

READ (5,10) Y

the action has the opposite effect. We replace the contents of the Hollerith field in the format statement by the 15 characters which are read in at the beginning of the input text.
    A more powerful facility is provided by the ability to use arrays as format specifications. Thus we can say

READ(5,IFORM)

or

WRITE(6,OFORM)

where IFORM and OFORM are the names of arrays, containing literal representations of the appropriate format specifications. These arrays can be set up by one of two means:

- specification in a DATA statement,
- reading in, using the *A* format specification.

The format arrays must contain all the characters of a FORMAT statement, including parentheses. Since this data, essentially character string in nature, is stored in *A* format, and since the precise meaning of *A* format depends on the number of characters per word in the storage representation of the machine, there may be some difficulties in transferring such programs to other computers.

11.15 FORMATLESS I/O

Although the principle of format-directed I/O is simple, the need to construct a format specification for each data item using a fairly complex symbolic notation makes it difficult for the occasional programmer to use. The main concern of many users is with the content of the output, rather than with its form. It may be costly and of little advantage for results to be presented elegantly if the programmer's time, skill, or other resources must be used in the pursuit of such elegance.
    Hence there is need for a form of I/O in which the system, rather than the user, is responsible for laying out results on the printed page and pro-

ducing a standard format for each data variable. A similar requirement applies to computer input, where the user may be expected to prepare input data in a standard format which will accomodate most forms of data value. See Hassitt (1964, 1967) for proposals on simplified I/O for FORTRAN.

Clearly we cannot expect to eliminate the format statement without some reduction in flexibility. Let us first look at the functions carried out by programmer-defined formats. They include the specification of

- field widths,
- conversions,
- control of layout (positioning, spacing),
- inclusion of text (in the FORTRAN Hollerith field).

We can eliminate the need for explicit formats if we design

- standard external representations for all data types,
- standard print positions for output,
- standard input formats *or* a standard delimiter for the input stream.

These provisions form the basis of simplified I/O in several languages. We can study an example of formatless I/O in the list-directed input-output facilities of PL/I.

11.16   PL/I LIST-DIRECTED I/O

List-directed is the most suitable form of I/O for beginners, since it does not require the user to specify data formats. The basic syntax is

$$\{\texttt{GET or PUT}\} \quad \texttt{LIST}(\text{data list});$$

The keyword LIST distinguishes list-directed I/O from the other types of stream I/O, edit-directed (keyword: EDIT) and data-directed (keyword: DATA). The data list is of the same form as allowed in these other types of I/O.

In the design of list-directed I/O, a standard external representation is defined for all transmittable data types. (Basically these are restricted to numbers and strings. PL/I data classified as *control data,* such as label, files, tasks, events, etc., may not be transmitted by any form of stream I/O statement.) These representations are an important part of PL/I and are used in other places in the language where data must be printed or otherwise represented without a specified format (example: in converting numeric coded—i.e., nonPICTURE numbers—to character-strings).

For output, each data element is followed by at least one blank, the "built-in" delimiter for list-directed I/O. For PRINT files, there are a number of standard print columns (called *tabs*) on which, after insertion of the inter-element blank character, data items are aligned. The location of these tab positions is an implementation-defined property of the language. A given compiler may include means of adjusting the positions of the tabs.

Each PUT statement in list-directed I/O aligns the first item in the data list on the next available tab position (not on the next character, as in edit-directed I/O). There are three options, SKIP, PAGE and LINE, which can be written with a PUT statement and which modify the positioning action. These can only be used at the beginning of each transmission (i.e., once per PUT statement). They have the same effect (relative and absolute positioning) as the corresponding control-format items.

For list-directed input, it is not required that data should be in the same format as the output. Rather, a standard delimiter is chosen for each token in the input text (i.e., each contiguous string of data characters). One obvious delimiter for this purpose is the blank. However the use of the blank character causes difficulties in specifying null fields—we need a null field indicator to signify that no value is to be transmitted to the next data list element. Since it is obviously desirable to treat multiple blanks as equivalent to a single blank, the blank cannot be used as a null field indicator, therefore the comma is used instead.

Example

A data stream: 15,17,,20 with the statement

```
GET LIST (A,B,C,D);
```

will result in A, B and D being updated, while the value of C will remain unaltered.

The delimiter structure for PL/I list-directed input is as follows.

- Each pair of elements in the input stream is separated by at least one blank or comma.

- Multiple blanks are equivalent to a single blank.

- Each comma may be preceded or followed by one or more blanks.

- Null fields in the input stream are denoted by successive commas (or by commas interspersed with blanks).

11.17 I/O WITH SELF-IDENTIFYING DATA (DATA-DIRECTED I/O)

A further form of formatless stream I/O is that in which the data stream contains not only the value representations but also the *names* of the data items.

This form of I/O was included in the language, MAD, developed at the University of Michigan (reference: Arden *et al.,* 1964). The idea was further developed in PL/I and forms the part of stream I/O called *data-directed* I/O. Data-directed output is the easiest form of output if the user simply wants to obtain the values of certain variables, without having to be concerned with headings or other descriptive text. For input, the advantages are even greater. A simple GET statement can be written which will accept data values in any order—this is most difficult to achieve with other forms of stream input.

The data stream (originally called a "data set" in MAD) consists of names, *equals* signs, and value representations.†

Example

```
X = 10
M = 23E10
WORD = 'CAPABILITY'
```

The external form of the data, in which each element carries its own identification, allows the programmer to write an input statement without a data list. In effect, we can say at the beginning of a simple program, "read in the data for this problem."

Using data-directed I/O, this can be written simply

```
GET DATA;
```

On output, we normally want selected data only and the most usual form includes a data list.

```
PUT DATA(I, TABLE(3,*));
```

This will result in output of the name and value of I, followed by the elements of the third row of TABLE (the notation signifies a cross-section of TABLE—see Chapter 8).

PL/I also allows the special form:

```
PUT DATA;
```

in which all numeric and string data variables known at the point of the statement are transmitted. This is a valuable and powerful statement, and corresponds to a symbolic "dump" of the program. Because of the possibility

---

† This further use of the equals sign, added to its existing uses in programming as a relation and an assignment operator, is unfortunate. The colon sign ':' would have been preferable in this instance, conveying the implication of naming an item of data, just as a label names a statement.

that this statement will result in a very large volume of output, it must be used with discretion.

The details of the design and implementation of data-directed I/O present a number of problems. First, consider the input statement, GET DATA. When this statement is executed, the data stream is expected to contain a sequence of self-describing data elements such as the following:

$$A = 1.5 \quad X = 34E6 \quad S = \text{'J.JONES'} \quad etc.$$

Each data item must be delimited, and the set of elements to be read in with one GET statement must also be marked in some way. The convention adopted in PL/I is as follows:

blank(s) or comma . . . . . between items,

semicolon . . . . to terminate a list of items.

The items in an input data stream for a particular run of a program cannot be known when the program is compiled. How then does the executing code know where to assign and how to convert the values found when a GET statement is executed? The answer is that a symbol table, containing names, types, and locations must be present at execution time for programs which contain GET DATA statements. The symbol table is needed even when there is a data list on the GET statement, since the order of elements in the stream need not coincide with the order in the list.

Example

```
        GET DATA(A,B,C)
    Data stream:
        B = 917.5, A = '1101'B;...
```

In this example, no value for C appears in the stream. This is permissible, as the data list is a list of items which *may* appear in the stream. In implementation, the data list can be used to restrict the size of the symbol table needed at execution time.

Next we consider the following case:

```
        GET DATA(A,B,C);
    Data stream:
        B = 917.5, X = 236, A = '1101'B;
```

The presence of the item X in the stream is an error, since X is not in the data list. This error causes the NAME condition to occur. If no ON unit is established, the erroneous field will be ignored and skipped. However, it is possible to issue a diagnostic message by using the built-in function,

DATAFIELD, whose value in a NAME ON-unit is the entire erroneous field, less delimiter and surrounding blanks.

Example

```
ON NAME BEGIN;
            PUT FILE(DIAGNOSTIC)
                LIST('ERROR IN INPUT STREAM:'||DATAFIELD);
          END;
....
GET DATA(list);
....
```

11.18   STREAM I/O FOR INTERNAL TRANSMISSION

The stream I/O statements described above apply to the transmission of data between variables and "external" data. In PL/I, a useful extension to stream I/O is that for transmitting data from one variable to another, allowing the editing of internal data. This is achieved by replacing the FILE specification in a GET or PUT statement by the STRING option.

Examples

```
PUT LIST(NAME, CODENUMBER, SIZE) STRING(S4);
```

The data will be transmitted, suitably edited and delimited according to the rules of list-directed I/O, to the character string S4.

On input, it is possible to write a string expression, as follows:

```
GET EDIT(HEADING) STRING(TITLE||AUTHOR||DATE) R(FORMAT_1);
```

In this case, the source of the data will be the string formed by concatenating the variables TITLE, AUTHOR, and DATE. It is transmitted to a structure HEADING, according to the remote format specification FORMAT_1.

This facility allows the editing capability of stream I/O to be made available for use with internal character-string variables. It provides an alternative way of producing edited text which may be more efficient than using stream I/O. For example, in producing a report, the text of the report can first be assembled in a character-string variable, *S*, using the STRING option. The variable *S* can be transmitted using record I/O; since there are no conversions for this type of output, the WRITE statement will take less time than direct PUT statements from the original data.

11.19   REPORT WRITING

In rare cases, the result of running a program may be a single number, perhaps even a single bit (1—"the project cost is within the budget allowance," or 0—"the stock of half inch brass screws is below the critical level"). Most frequently, however, the output from a program is a complex set of information whose presentation in a comprehensible form is an important part of the programming process.

A *report* might be considered to be any form of readable output. However, it is usual to use the term "report-writing" for programs which produce printed output of a particular kind. Examples of output which might be considered a "report" include:

- financial accounts, company reports;
- tables, statistics, price lists, etc.;
- charts and diagrams.

It is usually required that such reports include:

- titles (main, section, and paragraph);
- headings and footings for each page;
- pagination;
- totals and subtotals of nominated fields (especially in statistical or financial reports).

The editing facilities available in many high-level languages may be used to produce reports. However, the production of reports by editing an output stream may be an unduly complex problem in coding. The programmer has to be concerned with page widths and depths, with positioning the "current line" on the printed page, with spaces needed for headings, with subroutines for forming totals and subtotals, etc. To simplify this process, report-writing languages and sublanguages have been introduced, which allow much of this detailed work to be done automatically by a compiling system.

Two approaches to report writing can be recognized. In the first, reports are treated as a special form of printed output produced by a general-purpose language system. New data types and processing options are introduced, while the string-handling features of the language can be used to prepare the output for printing. Report-writing elements are included in an elementary form in PL/I and more comprehensively in COBOL.

The second approach is to construct a language especially for producing reports. Several early languages were devised to produce formatted reports from existing files. See Sammet (1969) for examples. Later, more ambitious systems were produced such as RPG—a language for producing reports and for simple foms of data processing (IBM, 1969).

11.19.1   The Specification of a Report

The information needed to specify a report includes report *denotation* and *format* and the *implicit actions* (such as the calculation of subtotals, etc.) to be carried out during its production.

11.19.1.1   Denotation

A report, like a file, relates to information that is both inside and outside a computer. Much the same sort of problem arises as does with files—the report may be named, the relationship to existing files or data sets may need to be established, and perhaps the I/O device on which the report is to appear must be indicated.

11.19.1.2   Format

Information needed in specifying a report includes:

    page size—*width* (in numbers of character positions) and *depth* (in numbers of lines).

    headings and footings—*titles* at the beginning of a report, *page numbers* (with automatic incrementation), and running *headings* or *footings*. For reports which are to fit with preprinted forms, the headings may have to be printed within well-prescribed boundaries.

    totals—for many financial reports and standard commercial documents (invoices, bills of lading, etc).

11.19.2   The COBOL Report-Writer Feature

This forms a separate module of COBOL and includes a set of descriptive keywords for describing a report and three report-generating statements.

    First, the file to be used for the report is specified. As with all files, this is denoted by an FD (file definition) entry in the data division. A report file must be specially designated by the REPORT clause, which gives the names of the reports to appear. Thus a report file must be used for reports only, and the reports must be specified in advance.

    The format of a report is given in a special section of the data division, called the report section. The description of each report is headed by an entry

    RD   report-name

followed by three clauses which control the production of the report as a whole.

- **The CODE clause**—specifies an identifying character to be printed at the beginning of each line of the report (optional and usually only used when several reports appear on one file).
- **The PAGE-limit clause**—gives the overall size and structure of the report.
- **The CONTROL clause**—determines the internal structure of the report.

A report consists of a series of report groups, each containing one or more lines. The following special terminology is used in describing these groups.

DETAIL groups contain the main information of the report and are located by the GENERATE statement. The other types of groups are inserted automatically as the report is printed. They are classified as "headings" and "footings" and are created at certain points in the report, as determined either by the format of the report or by controls set to operate during its creation.

Groups depending on the format of the report are REPORT HEADING and REPORT FOOTING groups for titling the report and for summary information at the end, and PAGE HEADING and PAGE FOOTING groups for running heads on each page, page numbers, continuation signs, etc.

Control groups consist of CONTROL HEADING and CONTROL FOOTING groups. They are created automatically whenever one or more specified variables change value during the generation of the report—these variables must be specified in the CONTROL clause. The overall dimensions of a report, as set by the PAGE LIMITS clause, are in terms of the lines available on the printed page.

Example

The beginning of a report specification might be as follows:

```
REPORT SECTION.
RD EXPENDITURE-REPORT
    CONTROLS ARE FINAL YEAR MONTH
    PAGE LIMIT IS 55 LINES
    FIRST DETAIL 8
    LAST DETAIL 48
    FOOTING 52.
    . . .
    . . .
```

In this report, there will be a *control break* whenever a new value of year or month is encountered in the input data. This will allow annual and monthly totals to be accumulated and printed in CONTROL FOOTING groups.

The contents of a report are specified in declarations similar to those used for describing COBOL records. Each report group is given a level number 1. (Normally in COBOL, each printed line corresponds to a level-1 structure. Since a report group may contain several lines, a report line may therefore have level-2 or higher.)

In the description of a report group, attributes may be specified to control

- the position of data on the page,
- sources of data for the report,
- computations to be carried out during preparation of the report.

Each level-1 declaration must contain a type clause, indicating which type of report group is being specified.

Example

The title of a report may be specified as follows:

```
01  EXP-HEADING TYPE IS REPORT HEADING.
 02 LINE NUMBER IS 1
    COLUMN NUMBER IS 22
    PICTURE IS A(18)
    VALUE IS "EXPENDITURE REPORT".
 02 LINE NUMBER IS 4.
    03 COLUMN IS 25
       PICTURE IS A(3)
       VALUE IS "FOR".
    03 COLUMN IS 30
       PICTURE IS 9999
       SOURCE IS DATE-FIELD.
```

During production of a report, numeric quantities may be accumulated, to be printed out when control breaks occur.

Example

The detail line of an expenditure report may be specified as follows.

```
01  EXP-DETAIL TYPE IS DETAIL LINE NUMBER IS PLUS 1.
 02 COLUMN IS 2
    PICTURE IS 99 SOURCE IS DAY-NO.
```

```
02 COLUMN IS 15
   PICTURE IS A(10) SOURCE IS MONTH.
02 COLUMN IS 25
   PICTURE IS 9999 SOURCE IS YEAR.
02 COLUMN IS 35
   PICTURE IS ZZ9.99 SOURCE IS AMOUNT.
```

The quantities DAY-NO, YEAR and AMOUNT are assumed to be read in with the input data for the run. Then, with the control breaks specified above (YEAR and MONTH), it is possible to print out the monthly expenditure by defining a control footing as follows:

```
01  MONTHLY-CONTROL TYPE IS CONTROL FOOTING MONTH.
  02 LINE NUMBER IS PLUS 2.
     03 COLUMN 2 PICTURE X(9) VALUE "TOTAL FOR".
     03 COLUMN 15 PICTURE A(10) SOURCE MONTH.
     03 M-TOT COLUMN 35 PICTURE $$$$9.99 SUM AMOUNT.
```

By writing SUM, rather than SOURCE, it is possible to accumulate the purchase amounts until a control break occurs (in this case when a new month is encountered). It is reset to zero each time it is used, unless a RESET clause is specified. This allows the user to specify that resetting will only occur at a higher level of control.

Up to now, the only features that have been described have been the declarative parts of a report specification. So many of the details of report writing are contained in declarations that comparatively little needs to be written to produce the report. There are three report writing statements: INITIATE, GENERATE, and TERMINATE.

INITIATE and TERMINATE are something like OPEN and CLOSE. INITIATE prepares the system for report writing by resetting counters, setting up work spaces, etc., while TERMINATE ensures that all final footings have been created.

The GENERATE statement has the form

```
GENERATE identifier
```

where the identifier is the name of a DETAIL report group or an RD entry. As each specified group is generated, all the actions implicitly specified in the report declarations take place. These include testing of data values to initiate control breaks, stepping of LINE COUNTER and PAGE COUNTER registers, execution of routines specified in USE statements, etc.

The procedural statements needed to produce a report can be very simple. For example, to produce the expenditure report we may simply write:

```
      OPEN INPUT DATA-FILE OUTPUT REPORT-FILE.
      READ DATA-FILE AT END GO TO FINALLY.
      INITIATE EXPENDITURE-REPORT.
  DATA-LOOP.
      GENERATE EXP-DETAIL.
      READ DATA-FILE AT END GO TO FINALLY.
      GO TO DATA-LOOP.
  FINALLY.
      TERMINATE EXPENDITURE-REPORT.
      CLOSE DATA-FILE REPORT-FILE.
      STOP RUN.
```

BIBLIOGRAPHY

Arden, B. W., B. A. Galler, R. M. Graham, *The Michigan Algorithm Decoder,* Ann Arbor, Michigan, 1965.

Bachman, C. W., "The evolution of storage structures," *CACM,* Vol. 15, No. 7, Jul. 1972, pp. 628–634.

A valuable survey of the history of file concepts, from the earliest days when there was a 1 to 1 correspondence between "files" and storage devices to current data-base systems in which flexible, *n*-ary relationships must exist. The results are presented as "data diagrams," a useful graphical method of representation.

Bailey, M. J., M. P. Barnett, R. P. Futerelle, "Format-free input in FORTRAN," *CACM,* Vol. 6, No. 10, Oct. 1963, pp. 605–608.

Barron, D. W., J. N. Buxton, D. F. Hartly, E. Nixon, C. Strachey, "The main features of CPL," *Computer Journal,* Vol. 6, No. 2, 1963, pp. 134–142.

Input and output in CPL are defined in terms of *streams,* identified by integer constants. A stream is a sequence of items rather than of characters. CPL also has *files,* a form of data structure similar to a list.

Barron, D. W., A. G. Fraser, D. F. Hartley, B. Landy, R. M. Needham, "File handling at Cambridge University," *Proc. SJCC,* 1967, pp. 163–167; *AFIPS Conference Proceedings, Vol. 30,* AFIPS Press, 1967.

Bartree, T. C., *Digital Computer Fundamentals,* New York: McGraw-Hill, 1966.

See particularly Chapter 7, The memory elements, and Chapter 8, Input Output devices.

BCS, "Data organization for maintenance and access," Report of a two day conference at the University of Keele, The British Computer Society, 1970.

A useful collection of papers on data management and file design. The papers include both general reviews and detailed case studies as well as discussions of file handling packages. Additional papers by Stamper and Waters are referenced below.

British Standards Institute, "Magnetic tape labelling and file structure for data interchange," ES 4732: 1971.

Bryant, J. H., P. Semple, Jr., "GIS and file management," *Proc. of the National Conference of the ACM,* Sept. 1966, pp. 97–107.

Chapin, N., "Common file organization techniques compared," AFIPS conference proceedings 1969, *FJCC,* Vol. 35, pp. 413–422; AFIPS Press, 1969.

    This paper outlines the differences between sequential, direct, and indexed sequential file organizations. References give details of other comparisons.

Clark, W. A., "The functional structure of OS/360—Part III, Data management," *IBM Systems Journal,* Vol, 5, No. 1, 1966, pp. 30–51.

    This paper introduced the terms *data set* and *data management,* as defined for OS/360. The paper discusses methods of assuring device independence and the dynamic treatment of device dependence (e.g., OPEN processing).

CODASYL committee, "An information algebra—Phase I report of the Language Structure Group of the CODASYL Development Committee," *CACM,* Vol. 5, No. 4, Apr. 1962, pp. 190–204.

    An early attempt at defining a language for general data structures. The report was not well understood, since it was phrased in obscure jargon (glumps, bundles) and was technically too advanced for feasible implementation.

CODASYL committee, "Data Base Task Group Report to the Programming Language Committee," April 1971 Report, ACM, 1971.

Coffman, E. G., J. Bruno, "On file structuring for non-uniform access frequencies," *BIT,* Vol. 10, 1970, pp. 443–456.

Cooper, B. E., "Basic subroutine for the input of numbers, words and special characters," *Computer Journal,* Vol. 11, No. 2, Aug. 1968, pp. 157–159.

Daley, R. C., P. G. Neumann, "A general-purpose file system for secondary storage," *AFIPS Conference Proceedings,* Vol. 27, Part 1, pp. 213–229.

    Presents a hierarchical structure for files as developed for the MULTICS system.

Date, C. J., I. J. Heath, P. Hopewell, "A collection of papers on data independence," *Technical Report TR. 12.094,* IBM United Kingdom Laboratories, Mar. 1972.

    This includes three papers—the first two discuss logical data independence and physical data independence while the third defines certain restrictions that must be observed in accessing relational files.

Dowkart, A. J., *et al.,* "A methodology for comparison of generalized data management systems," *CFST1,* No. AD-811-682, Mar. 1967, p. 287.

Duncan, F. G., "Input and output for ALGOL 60 on KDF9," *Computer Journal,* Vol. 5, No. 4, Jan. 1963, pp. 341–344.

    An input-output scheme, within the strict spirit and letter of the ALGOL report, using *code procedures.* There are two kinds of procedure: those using a standard format; and those for which fine control over the appearance of the data is possible, using a "picture." If it is not possible to print the correct representation, *alarm* printing is used making the erroneous result obvious. Cf. Hoare (1963).

Dzubak, B. J., C. R. Warburton, "The organization of structured files," *CACM,* Vol. 8, No. 7, Jul. 1965, pp. 446–452.

Considers processing problems for data in the form of a connected graph. The example used is a "bill of materials." The paper shows graphs corresponding to a Bill of Materials "where used" list. Considers techniques for parts explosion and implosion, and various coding devices for trees and graphs.

Ferguson, D. E., "Input-output buffering and FORTRAN," *JACM,* Vol. 7, No. 1, Jan. 1960, pp. 1–9.

Fraser, A. G., "On the interface between computers and data communications systems," *CACM,* Vol. 15, No. 7, Jul. 1972, pp. 566–573.

A review of some problems of communicating with a communications system, including a discussion of a "standard interface."

Ghosh, S. P., M. E. Senko, "File organization: On the selection of random access index points for sequential files, *JACM,* Vol. 16, No. 4, Oct. 1969, pp. 569–579.

Examines an alternative to the indexed sequential method for accessing large sets of data. Instead of a hierarchy of indexes, data is located by means of linear interpretation on a set of key index points. In test cases, this technique resulted in better perfomance than the indexed sequential method.

Ghosh, S. P., "On the theory of consecutive storage of relevant records," *IBM Research Report RJ708,* 1970.

Ghosh, S. P., "File Organization: the consecutive retrieval property," *IBM Research Report RJ765,* 1970.

Ghosh, S. P., "File Organization: consecutive storage of relevant records on a drum type storage," *IBM Research Report RJ895,* Jul. 1971.

Gildersleeve, T. R., "Design of sequential file systems," New York: Wiley-Interscience, 1971.

A survey of problems which can be solved using sequential file processing and a discussion of techniques of efficient processing. The principles of this approach are carefully abstracted and this work is a good example of a generalized approach to input-output problems. The text is independent of the programming languages used—in fact, no coding examples are given.

Gotlieb, C. C., "General-purpose programming for business applications," in *Advances in Computers Vol. 1,* F. L. Alt (ed.), New York: Academic Press, 1960, pp. 1–42.

An early discussion of file handling; also an attempt to characterize "business" programming.

Gray, J. C., "Compound data structures for computer aided design; a survey," *Proceedings of 22nd National Conference ACM,* Publication P-67, New York: Academic Press, 1967, pp. 355–365.

Although this discusses data structures in the context of CAD, the results are of general interest. Discusses the languages CORAL, APL, ASP/ASP-7 and SLP and L[6].

Hamming, R. W., W. L. Mammel, "A note on the location of the binary point in a computing machine," *IEEE Transactions on Electronic Computers,* EC-14, No. 2, Apr. 1965, pp. 260–261.

Considers the placing of the binary point before and after the first digit in computer representations of numbers. The authors conclude that "for human reasons" (including close relationship with standard practice) it is preferable to have the point after the first digit in external representations.

Harrison, M. C., "File-handling within FORTRAN," *CACM,* Vol. 8, No. 8, Aug. 1965, pp. 514–515.

Describes a technique to define the handling of symbolic "files" on tapes by using FORTRAN. Three subroutines are defined: LOAD(NTAPE,TAPNAM), FILE(FILNAM,NTAPE,TABLE), FILEND(NTAPE,TABLE). These are essentially used for *positioning* the tape for subsequent READ, WRITE operations. Each tape comprises a number of *files,* interspersed with housekeeping information to help in locating the files. The technique allows tape programs to be written without knowledge of the *structure* of the files.

Hassitt, A., "Design and implementation of a general-purpose input routine," *CACM,* Vol. 7, No. 6, June 1964, pp. 350–355.

The author describes the advantages of list- and data-directed input and shows how these can be incorporated in a FORTRAN compiler.

Hassitt, A., "Data-directed input-output in FORTRAN," *CACM,* Vol. 10, No. 1, Jan. 1967, pp. 35–40.

Heath, I. J., "A semiformal description of Record I/O," *ECMA Working Papers,* ECMA/TC10/TG1/71/87, Aug. 1971.

One of the few formal descriptions of input-output, produced as part of the PL/I standardization program.

Hicks, H. T., "Using the COBOL Report Writer," *Datamation,* Vol. 18, No. 9, Sept. 1972, pp. 84–86.

A brief tutorial explaining the merits of this feature of COBOL.

Hoare, C. A. R., "The Elliott ALGOL Input/Output System," *Computer Journal,* Vol. 5, No. 4, Jan. 1963, pp. 345–347.

New statements were added to ALGOL, such as read and print. There are also format setting procedures. Cf. Duncan (1963).

Howarth, D. J., P. D. Jones, M. T. Wyled, "The Atlas scheduling system," *Computer Journal,* Vol. 5, No. 3, Oct. 1962, pp. 238–244.

IBM, "Card and disk system RPG II, fundamentals programmer's guide," *Form C21-7502,* 1969.

IFIP WG 2.1, "Report on input-output procedures for ALGOL 60," *CACM,* Vol. 7, No. 10, Oct. 1964, pp. 628–630.

Defines seven I/O "primitives" from which other I/O schemes can be derived. These primitives are to be expressed as ALGOL "code procedures"—machine language subroutines. The primitives are: insymbol, outsymbol, length, inreal, outreal, inarray, outarray.

IFIP/ICC, *Vocabulary of Information Processing,* Amsterdam: North Holland, 1968.

IFIP, "File organization," *Selected papers from FILE 68—an I.A.G. Conference,* Amsterdam: Swets & Zeitlinger N.V., 1969.

An interesting series of papers on file organizations for data-base and management-information systems. Includes theoretical approaches based on general systems theory (see Langefors, 1969) and descriptions of a number of actual systems.

Knuth, D. E. *et al.,* "A proposal for input-output conventions in ALGOL 60," *CACM,* Vol. 7, No. 5, May 1964, pp. 273-283.

An important proposal for adding extensive I/O capabilities to ALGOL 60. The proposals are essentially for 'stream' I/O, and include means for specifying format and layout. A data list is generated by a "list procedure," which is in fact a general method for generating lists of items. These proposals, though containing many interesting ideas, have generally proved too complex for implementation and the IFIP proposals (IFIP, 1964) have often been preferred in ALGOL implementations.

Knuth, D. E., *The Art of Computer Programming, Vol. 1: Fundamental Algorithms,* Reading, Mass.: Addison-Wesley, 1968.

See Section 1.4.4—Input and Output.

Langefors, B., "Elementary files and elementary file records in file organization," *IFIP,* 1969, pp. 89-96.

Defines:

1) *elementary message*—the smallest unit of *information* about a data item;

2) *elementary record*—the actual data;

3) elementary file records.

Lefkovitz, D., *File structures for on-line systems,* Spartan Books, Inc., 1969.

Madnick, S. E., "Design strategies for file systems: a working model," (in) *File Organization,* IFIP, 1969, pp. 117-136.

Presents a hierarchical model of a file system, with six levels: access methods, logical file system, basic file system, file-organization-strategy modules, device-strategy modules, and IOCS. This modular approach is intended to assist in designing file systems and to provide a structure for the comparison of existing systems.

Mandell, R. L., G. Estrin, J. Kunz, "The Record Format Language—A PL/I Extension for large files," (in) *File Organization,* IFIP, 1969, pp. 360-368.

McGee, W. C., "The formulation of data processing problems for computers," (in) *Advances in Computers,* F. L. Alt, N. Rubinoff (eds.), Vol. 4, New York: Academic Press, 1963.

Discusses attempts to construct a formalized theory of data processing. Describes early languages, FACT, Commercial Translator, etc., also the CODASYL Information Algebra. Includes a good review of the earlier literature.

McGee, W. C., "Generalized File Processing," (in) *Annual Review in Automatic Programming,* Vol. 5, No. 13, Elmsford, N.Y.: Pergamon Press, 1969, pp. 77-149.

This paper gives a general approach to input-output, treating *files* as examples of general information structures. As a preliminary to the main section of the paper, McGee gives a history of input-output development, starting with specialized systems for sorting and report writing, and leading to systems which support more general data-management facilities. McGee introduced the idea of a *schema,* a means of specifying the "structuring" of a file or data set independently of the values of the data elements within it. This term was subsequently taken up by the CODASYL group on Data Base and is an important part of the proposals for data-base extensions to COBOL (CODASYL 1971).

Merrett, T. H., "General programs for management systems," *Information Processing Letters,* Vol. 1, No. 1, 1971, pp. 17–20.

A "report writer" approach to file processing. A standard approach to sequential processing, allowing modification by parameters. (See also the paper by N. D. Peterson.)

Minker, J., J. Sable, "File organization and data management," *Annual Review of Information and Technology,* 1967, pp. 123–160.

Mock, O., C. J. Swift, "The SHARE 709 system: Programmed input-output buffering," *JACM,* Vol. 6, No. 2, Apr. 1959, pp. 145–151.

This system anticipated many later developments in operating system design. This is one of a series of short notes describing the principles of the system design.

Naur, P., "Environmental enquiries: machine dependent programming in common languages," *ALGOL Bulletin,* Vol. 18, Oct. 1964, pp. 26–28.

NCC, *Computer File Creation for Manufacturing Control,* Manchester, England: National Computer Center, 1968.

A short booklet (59 pages) outlining the design of files for a particular commercial application. Useful as a simple introduction to commercial data processing.

NCC, *Standard FORTRAN Programming Guide,* Manchester, England: National Computing Center, 1970.

Contains a very careful and precise description of standard FORTRAN, abstracted and interpreted from the ANSI standard. The section on formatted I/O is particularly helpful to anyone trying to understand the working of the FORTRAN system of format control.

Organick, E. I., *A MAD Primer,* Houston, Texas: University of Houston, 1964.

Perlis, A. J., "A format language," *CACM,* Vol. 7, No. 2, Feb. 1964, pp. 89–97.

Proposals for an output language for a printing device with an addressable buffer. An output specification has two parts, a *format* program and a *data* program.

Peterson, N. D., "A standard pattern for sequential-file maintenance," *COMPUTER* (IEEE), Vol. 4, No. 3, May/June 1971, pp. 5–9.

This paper presents a "prototype" for sequential-file maintenance. The author suggests that many applications can be coded by making simple modifications to this prototype.

Peterson, W. W., "Addressing for random access storage," *IBM Journal of Research and Development,* Vol. 1, No. 2, Apr. 1957, pp. 130–146.

A classic paper comparing the efficiencies of various types of search on random access devices.

Ranelletti, J. E., "Dynamic format specifications," *CACM,* Vol. 8, No. 8, Aug. 1965, pp. 508–510.

Defines the format specifications, ∗ and *T*. ∗ instructs the scanner to take the next *value* from the data list and is used for the repetitive factors, field width, and scaling, which may be read in dynamically. Similarly, *T* is used to read in type descriptions dynamically.

SHARE Committee on Theory of Information Handling, "General data files and processing operations," Report TIH-1,SSD-71,Item C-1663, 1959.

Senko, M. E., H. E. Meadow, *et al., File Design handbook,* Contract F30602-69-C-0100 (Rome Air Development Center), IBM San Jose Research Laboratory, IBM FSD, Gaithersburg, Nov. 1969.

A report of an extensive series of tests, on both simulation models and real configurations, of the relative performances of various file designs. The topics covered include basic descriptions of the hardware used in the tests, a description of the three access methods studied (sequential, direct, and indexed-sequential) and a discussion of space utilization on disk storage. The objective of the report was to provide the designer of a filing system with a set of guidelines based on firmly established test data.

Senko, M. E., "File organization and management information systems," (in) *Annual Review of Information Science and Technology,* Vol. 4, Chicago, 1970, pp. 111–143.

Smith, J. L., T. S. Holden, "Restart of an operating system having a permanent file structure," *Computer Journal,* Vol. 15, No. 1, Feb. 1972, pp. 25–31.

Although primarily concerned with the operational problems of recovery from failure, this paper contains much useful background information on file-system design.

Stamper, R. K., "Logical structures of files," (in) *BCS, Data Organization for Maintenance and Access,* 1970, pp. 28–54.

A good tutorial on general data structures. Discusses the distinction between data structures and storage structures, and between total and partial ordering of data elements. Emphasizes that data structures and their relations can be discussed separately from the programs that process them.

Waters, S. J., "Physical data structures," (in) *BCS, Data Organization for Maintenance and Access,* 1970, pp. 55–75.

A companion paper to that of Stamper (1970). A discussion of the physical representation of data, methods of access, and techniques of processing.

Waters, S. J., "Blocking sequentially processed magnetic files," *Computer Journal,* Vol. 14, No. 2, May 1971, pp. 109–112.

An algorithm for calculating block sizes for sequential files is proposed. This minimizes the "run time" of the program given various device characteristics, record lengths, number of buffers, etc.

Weiss, E. A., *Computer Fundamentals,* New York: McGraw-Hill Book Co., 1969.

Woodrum, L. J., "A model of floating buffering," *IBM Systems Journal,* Vol. 9, No. 2, 1970, pp. 118–144.

A description of buffering techniques. Compares *floating* buffers with *double* buffering. Includes a mathematical model of floating buffering.

EXERCISES

11.1 Consider the I/O statements in any program you are familiar with (especially consider the following types of program: file processing, scientific computation, a compiler).

    a. To what extent do the I/O statements in this program correspond to:

      true 'source-sink' I/O,

      I/O used for auxiliary storage?

    b. Outline a new version of the program in which the statements for 'storage' I/O are replaced by access functions to data structures.

11.2 The design of COBOL I/O is based on records rather than a formatted stream of items. How are the following needs met in COBOL?

    a. The printing of spaces between data items

    b. The printing of blank lines between sections of a report

    c. Looping through an output list, updating a control variable

    d. Changing the format used for interpreting input data, depending on the data being read.

11.3 List the differences between INPUT, OUTPUT, and UPDATE or I-O files. Since the statements that may be given for files with these attributes are restricted, discuss the suggestion that these attributes are logically redundant and could be eliminated from COBOL and PL/I.

11.4 Take a telephone directory and list the classes of information contained in it. Then consider the various types of search that are made on the directory by users and the telephone staff. Classify these searches into sequential, indexed-sequential, and direct.

11.5 Design a COBOL output procedure for printing the diagonal elements of a 10×10 table, together with identifying information. Compare this with an equivalent procedure in FORTRAN or PL/I stream I/O.

11.6 The records of a sequential file are similar to the characters of a string in forming an ordered set. To what extent does a sequential file have analagous facilities to the following string handling operators:

    a. concatenation,

    b. substring access to value (R-value),

    c. substring access to location (L-value),

    d. search (as provided by the INDEX function).

Show how these functions can be programmed in existing languages.

11.7 Give a list of statements which would be used in updating a sequentially organized master set of data. Explain why attributes like I-O or UPDATE, and statements like REWRITE, are not available with stream I/O.

11.8 A sequential file F is to be accessed using the statements OPEN, CLOSE, READ, and WRITE.

a. Write subroutines which access F as if it were an array, to produce the effect of the following statements:

```
A = F(I)
F(I) = A
```

b. List the similarities and dissimilarities between I/O statements such as READ/WRITE and the assignment statement.

c. Is this comparison affected by the difference between stream and record I/O?

11.9 Formatted stream I/O is controlled by both a data list and a format list, although the data list is the controlling factor in the transmission. Are there circumstances in which it would be preferable to have the format list, rather than the data list, control the data transmission?

11.10 In FORTRAN, a format specification must be written as a separate statement, distinct from the READ and WRITE statements. In PL/I, a format may either be written separately as in FORTRAN or be included as part of a GET or PUT statement. Discuss the relative advantages of these two approaches

a. from a user point of view,

b. from an implementation point of view.

11.11 A data stream consists of character strings delimited by an arbitrary character, c (this may be expressed as a literal or contained in a variable).

a. Design I/O statements which will read successive strings up to but not including the delimiter. Include specifications of a file, OPEN/CLOSE, and READ/WRITE statements, also any necessary treatment of errors or I/O conditions.

b. To what extent can this problem be programmed in FORTRAN, COBOL or PL/I? Can it be simulated with existing I/O statements or programmed as internal assignments?

11.12 An I/O statement containing a repetitive element in its data list is sometimes defined in terms of an iteration of a simpler statement. For example,

```
PUT ((A(I) DO I=1 TO N));
```

may be defined as equivalent to:

```
DO I=1 TO N;
    PUT(A(I));
END;
```

Discuss the circumstances when two statements such as these may *not* be equivalent.

11.13 A 3×3 table of integers with numbers of unknown size is to be printed. The numbers are to be printed as follows:

1	14	73
21	1040	91
4316	0	1001

Note that there should be a space of exactly 6 print positions between the figures in successive columns.

a. Discuss the problems involved in establishing the size of the numbers in this table and positioning the items.

b. Show how this problem may be programmed in existing languages.

12
Subroutines, Procedures, and Programs

12.1 INTRODUCTION

In this final chapter, we show how the elements of programming languages described in previous chapters—references, declarations, expressions, and various kinds of statements—are combined to construct *procedures* and *programs*. These two units play a central part in programming; the procedure as a unit of modularity in writing programs and in some cases as a unit of compilation, the program as a unit of execution. The design of syntax and semantics for procedures is perhaps the single most important activity in the development of programming languages.

In addition to their place at the head of the hierarchy of language elements introduced in Chapter 6, procedures are important for reasons of

- economy,
- protection,
- extensibility,
- modularity.

Economy

Procedures, in the form of subroutines and subprograms, allow the same piece of code to be used many times. This is important for economy in programming effort, and for making the most efficient use of storage space in the system.

Protection

Within each new procedure there may be

- a new level of naming,
- a new level of storage allocation,
- a localization of error treatment.

Each procedure provides a specialized environment within which new storage and values may be given to variables.

Extensibility

Procedures allow users to extend the capabilities of a language by augmenting the statements, built-in functions and operators which have been built in by the language designers.

Modularity

Procedures allow large programming tasks to be subdivided into smaller units, providing a basis for "modular programming," an important technique for constructing large and complex systems.

It is useful to distinguish two aspects of procedure structure, the *static* and the *dynamic*. Static structure is concerned with the form of the procedure as written by a programmer, with the components needed for procedure specification, and with methods of representation in the character set of a language. Dynamic structure is concerned with the behavior of a procedure when it is invoked. Static and dynamic structure respectively correspond to the *syntax* and *semantics* of procedures—one is concerned with how procedures are specified, the other with their behavior when they are executed.

We now consider the various parts of a procedure, as they appear in a typical programming language. First there is the sequence of instructions in the procedure, referred to as the procedure *body*. Although the same code may be used for many invocations, it may not behave identically on each occasion. One of the most useful properties of procedures is the capability for giving different treatment to each invocation by associating a different set of data with each call.

At this point, we come across a problem in terminology which must be discussed before coming to the details of procedure syntax. In different languages, various terms are used to describe the data used in communicating with procedures. Table 12.1 shows the terms used in FORTRAN, ALGOL and PL/I and is followed by a description and summary of the differences.

TABLE 12.1   Terminology Comparison

	FORTRAN	ALGOL	PL/I
Information *expected by* a procedure	dummy argument	formal parameter	parameter
Information *passed to* a procedure by a caller	argument	actual parameter	argument

- A *parameter* (called a dummy argument in FORTRAN, a formal parameter in ALGOL) is specified by the author of a procedure and indicates the information expected by the procedure. A parameter is a named item in the procedure which, on execution of the procedure, will correspond to some entity or value in the calling program. The name of a parameter is a "place-holder" for information which will become established when the procedure is invoked. Hence the terms "formal" and "dummy" used in ALGOL and FORTRAN.

- An *argument*† (actual parameter in ALGOL) is specified by the user of a procedure and indicates the information actually passed to the procedure when it is invoked.

12.2   SUBROUTINE AND FUNCTION PROCEDURES

There are two kinds of procedure which differ in the way in which their results are communicated to the caller. We give these the names "subroutine" and "function."

In a *subroutine* procedure, information may only be returned from a procedure by means of one of the parameters or by some variable shared between the caller and the procedure. A subroutine procedure is invoked by executing a statement, the most usual form being:

CALL procedure-name (argument-list)

Example

```
CALL PLOT(X+7, Y,T+K)
CALL REPORT_REVISION;
```

---

† A proverbial saying, generated during a heated discussion of this point of terminology: "Parameters are what you expect, arguments are what you get."

In ALGOL, the keyword CALL is not used and a procedure invocation is written

> *procedure-name (argument-list)*

as if there were a new statement in the language.

Example

> *rotate (A, theta);*
> *SMOOTH (T,(X + 7)/(Y−1));*

After execution of a subroutine procedure, control of the program normally resumes at the statement following the calling statement. (There are some cases when this normal sequencing is not followed—for example, when there is a branch out of the subroutine, or if there is an interrupt which causes control to leave the subroutine.)

The other type of procedure is a function procedure and this is invoked by evaluating a function reference, which has the form

> *procedure-name (argument-list)*

Invocation of a function results in the calculation of a value, and a function reference may appear wherever a value-denoting reference may appear.

Example

In the following assignment statements, UPDATE and product are function procedures.

```
NEW VALUE = UPDATE(FIELD,FILE_T);
range:= t+product(p+1) − product(g+1);
```

Subroutines and functions, are analogous to the language forms, *statements* and *expressions*. In spite of differences in the ways they are used, it is not necessary to have different syntax for the two forms. In both ALGOL and PL/I, the same code may be invoked either as a subroutine or as a function.

12.3 THE STATIC STRUCTURE OF PROCEDURES: THE SYNTAX OF PROCEDURE SPECIFICATION

A simplified diagram of procedure syntax showing components of its static structure is given in Fig. 12.1. This does not show the syntax of a particular language, but illustrates the components found in several widely used languages.

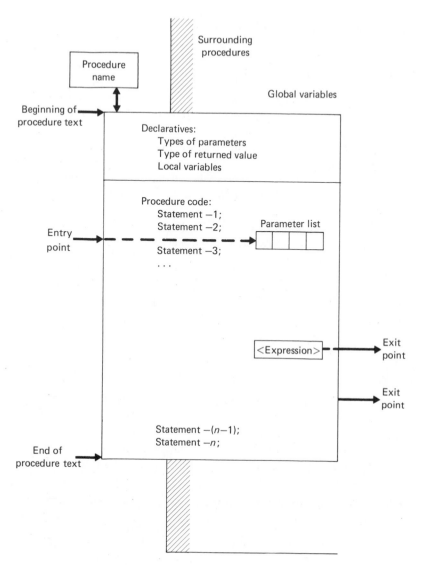

Fig. 12.1 The static structure of a procedure

A procedure specification is, in fact, a declaration of procedure structure. In writing such a specification, it is necessary to signify:

- the data passed to and from the procedure, i.e., parameters, the value or values returned (for function procedures), local and global data;

- the sequence of operations in the procedure; this includes entry and exit points for the code forming the procedure body.

12.3.1   Parameters

Procedure parameters are usually indicated at the head of a procedure declaration. The parameter names do not refer to *variables* in the usual sense of the term; rather, they are names used in the body of the procedure, which will be used to refer to the arguments of the procedure call when the procedure is invoked.

In compilable languages, the *number* of parameters is fixed when the procedure is compiled.† When it is called, the same number of arguments must be presented.

The types of parameters may also be specified in the procedure declaration. In ALGOL, this may be done in the *specification part* of the procedure.

Example

> **procedure** *section (f,a,b)*;
>> **real** *a,b*; **real procedure** *f*; ← specification part
>> **begin**
>> . . .   ← procedure body
>> **end**

In PL/I, parameters may be described in DECLARE statements, but only with *type* attributes—other attributes such as scope, initialization, storage class, etc., cannot be specified. The reason for this is that these other attributes relate to the allocation and storage of data as a variable, whereas, as noted above, a parameter is not a variable in its own right.

12.3.2   The Type of Value Returned by a Function Procedure

An additional specification is needed for function procedures, namely the type of the value returned when it is invoked. There are two points where this may be specified:

- in the function procedure specification itself,
- where the function is used.

---

† An arbitrary number of arguments can be used in some macro systems and command languages. The FORTRAN and PL/I functions MAX and MIN also accept any number of arguments.

In FORTRAN and ALGOL, the type of a function procedure is specified by including a type attribute with the heading of the procedure specification.

Example

FORTRAN

```
INTEGER FUNCTION TWIST (P,Q,R)
...
END
```

ALGOL

Boolean procedure *CHECK(R,S)*;

....

end

In FORTRAN, a function subroutine can be compiled independently. Its type can be determined either by the implicit type rules for FORTRAN (see Chapter 7) or by a FORTRAN type statement. For example, the function TWIST might be declared as follows in the program where it is used.

```
INTEGER  TWIST
```

In ALGOL such a declaration is not needed. It is not possible to compile parts of an ALGOL program separately, and the point at which a function procedure is used must lie within the scope of its declaration.

In PL/I, as in FORTRAN, a function procedure may be compiled separately. The RETURNS attribute can be used to specify the type of a function procedure, both in the heading of the procedure itself, and in a declaration at its point of use.

Example

If there is a PL/I procedure, CODELETTER, which produces a single character result, the heading of the procedure might be written

```
CODELETTER : PROCEDURE (P) RETURNS(CHARACTER(1));
...
END;
```

To ensure that this function is correctly specified at its point of use, its type is declared as follows.

```
DECLARE CODELETTER ENTRY RETURNS(CHARACTER(1));
```

Strictly speaking, such a declaration is only required if the full specification of the procedure is not "known" at the point of use, for example if the procedure CODELETTER is compiled independently.

12.3.3 Global Variables

Global variables are variables which are known outside the scope of a procedure as well as inside it. Changes made to such variables during execution of a procedure are preserved when the procedure terminates. In ALGOL and PL/I, data declared in a block surrounding a procedure is global to that procedure. In FORTRAN, COMMON data is global to all subprograms in a program. PL/I EXTERNAL data has a similar property.

Global variables can be used for communicating across the procedure interface. Compared with parameters, this can be a rather clumsy method of communication since each variable used must be updated before calling the procedure. There are advantages in that global data can often be more directly and efficiently accessed.

The use of global variables can lead to errors in programs, as pointed out in the paper by Wulf and Shaw (see reference in Chapter 6).

12.3.4 Entry and Exit Points

An *entry point* of a procedure is a point at which execution starts when the procedure is invoked. If there is only one entry point as with FORTRAN and ALGOL, it is natural to make it the first executable statement in the procedure body. In PL/I, it is possible to specify several entry points to the same body of code, by means of the ENTRY statement (see below).

When a procedure has been executed, control is normally returned to the point from which it was invoked. It is simplest to have the entry point at the beginning of the procedure code and the exit point at the end as follows:

$$
\text{entry} \longrightarrow \begin{bmatrix} S_1; \\ S_2; \\ S_3; \\ \ldots \\ \ldots \\ S_n \end{bmatrix} \longrightarrow \text{exit}
$$

In ALGOL a procedure body is often written as a *block* (i.e., a piece of code surrounded by **begin** and **end** brackets). Exit from such a block takes place for one of two possible reasons: 1) by flow of control reaching the last statement in the block, or 2) by transfer out of the block by means of a **go to** statement.

Several languages have means for defining more than one return point from a procedure. In FORTRAN and PL/I, the logical end of a subroutine is denoted by a RETURN statement, which returns control to the point of call. Any number of RETURN statements can be written in a procedure.

In the case of function procedures, FORTRAN and ALGOL require that an assignment be made to the symbolic name of the function before return is made; this is the method of transmitting a value back to the point of invocation.

Examples

A FORTRAN function, VAL, returns a value which depends on a test indicator, T. It has the value half X, twice X, or X, for negative, positive or zero values of T respectively. The variables X and T are in COMMON storage. The function may be written as follows:

```
      FUNCTION VAL
      COMMON X,T
      IF (T) 1, 2, 3
   1  VAL = X/2
      RETURN
   2  VAL = X
      RETURN
   3  VAL = X*2
      RETURN
      END
```

In PL/I, the means of returning a value is integrated with the sequencing statement. To terminate a PL/I function procedure, instead of assigning to the procedure name, an expression is written with the RETURN statement.

The previous example may be written in PL/I as follows, the variables X and T being declared in a block surrounding VAL.

```
      VAL: PROCEDURE;
              IF T < 0
                  THEN RETURN(X/2);
                  ELSE
                      IF T = 0
                          THEN RETURN(X);
                          ELSE RETURN(X*2);
          END;
```

12.3.5 The STOP Statement

The RETURN statement causes transfer back from a subprocedure to the calling procedure, returning control up one "level" of the calling hierarchy. In writing subprograms, it is sometimes important to be able to stop the run of a program without returning to the procedure from which the current procedure was called. Reasons for stopping a program may include exhaustion of available space or machine resources, unrecoverable error situations, etc.

FORTRAN and PL/I each have a STOP statement for this purpose, and COBOL has the statement STOP RUN. Execution of these statements stops the current program. In early systems, the computer literally stopped when these statements were executed, usually with some special pattern displayed on the console lights. In current operating systems, execution of a STOP or STOP RUN statement usually causes control to be returned to the point at which the program was initiated, normally the job level.

12.4 EXAMPLES OF PROCEDURE SYNTAX

In the following section, the syntax of procedures in FORTRAN, ALGOL and PL/I are contrasted.

12.4.1 FORTRAN

12.4.1.1 General syntax

FORTRAN distinguishes between *main programs* and *subprograms,* which may be separately compiled. There are two types of subprogram, for which the keywords SUBROUTINE and FUNCTION are used. The following statements may not be used within a function or subroutine: BLOCK DATA, SUBROUTINE, FUNCTION. It follows that FORTRAN procedure definitions cannot be nested inside other definitions.

12.4.1.2 Types of parameters (dummy arguments)

A parameter can be any type of data element, array, or external procedure. It is not specified in the 1966 FORTRAN standard whether dummy arguments may have type descriptors—this is one of the ambiguities to be clarified in a later version of the standard (see ANSI, 1971, reference in the Appendix).

12.4.1.3 Entry point

FORTRAN allows a single entry point, the first executable statement.

12.4.1.4 Exit point(s)

These are denoted by the RETURN statements, of which there must be at least one within each subroutine or function procedure. In addition, the STOP statement terminates the main program, and hence any procedure in which it is executed.

12.4.1.5 Type of value returned from function procedure

The type of a function may be: INTEGER, REAL, DOUBLE PRECISION, COMPLEX or LOGICAL. Type may be declared in the procedure heading or may be left unspecified, in which case an implicit type is determined from the form of the function name, using the same rules that apply for undeclared variables. Functions whose type is not specified but whose names begin with the letters *I, J, K, L, M* or *N* are given the type INTEGER; other unspecified functions are given the type REAL.

12.4.2 ALGOL

12.4.2.1 General syntax

The body of an ALGOL procedure is a statement, that is a single assignment, **if, go to** or **for,** or alternatively a compound statement or block.

ALGOL allows the definition of what are called "code" procedures (normally written in machine language) for functions which cannot be expressed in the ALGOL language. Code procedures were included as a means of extending the language, or, as in the case of I/O, for expressing facilities the ALGOL designers considered unsuitable for inclusion in the language itself.

In ALGOL the mode of transmission of arguments is denoted in the procedure specifications. All parameters are passed by name, except those that appear in the *value list* in the procedure heading (for a discussion of name and value parameters, see below).

12.4.2.2 Types of parameters (formal parameters)

The types of formal parameters may be denoted by one of 14 "specifiers": **real, integer, Boolean, array, real array, integer array, Boolean array, label, switch, procedure, real procedure, integer procedure, Boolean procedure, string.**

According to the ALGOL report, it is not necessary to specify the type of formal parameters called by name. This flexibility is obtained at some cost, for it means that code may have to be inserted to determine the type of an actual parameter corresponding to an unspecified name parameter.

In the following procedure containing the name parameters *a,b:*

> **procedure** *T* (*a,b*); **real** *a;*
> **begin**
> $a := b + 1;$
> . . .
> . . .

the actual parameter corresponding to *b* may be either **real** or **integer,** and code must be included to deal with both cases. In the IFIP subset of ALGOL, full specification of all formal parameters is required, simplifying the generation of code for the procedure interface.

12.4.2.3   Entry and exit points

ALGOL allows a single entry point, the first statement in the procedure body.

Execution of a procedure terminates when control reaches the last statement of the procedure body. A procedure may also be terminated by execution of a **go to** statement whose target is a label outside the procedure.

12.4.2.4   Type of value returned from a function procedure

The type of a function procedure must be specified in the procedure heading. The possible types are: **real, integer,** or **Boolean** and the values returned must be elements, not arrays.

12.4.3   PL/I

12.4.3.1   General syntax

In PL/I, functions and subroutines are represented with the same syntax and, as in ALGOL, procedure specifications can be nested to any depth. A procedure whose specification is not nested within another is called an *external* procedure. External procedures can be compiled independently.

PL/I recognizes two views of a procedure: that of its author and that of its user. PL/I allows both authors and users of procedures to specify the types of all data passed to and from the procedure. If these type specifications do not match, conversion routines are inserted in the object code. It is a principle of PL/I design that the need for such conversions can be detected by analysis of the program text, so that code can be generated as part of the compilation process.

12.4.3.2   Types of parameters

These may be of any PL/I data type and may be elements, arrays, or structures. They may be explicitly declared within the procedure, but if no explicit declarations are made, attributes are applied according to default rules. These rules are applied when the procedure is compiled, so that all parameters are fully specified at compile-time.

12.4.3.3 Entry points

There may be several entry points to a PL/I procedure, these being denoted by ENTRY statements. An ENTRY statement has a similar format to a procedure heading and may specify its own set of parameters. ENTRY statements are placed in the body of a procedure, at points where execution of the procedure is to start.

Example

A program is designed to produce reports, some being required weekly, others monthly. These reports have a similar format, except that the monthly report includes an extra summary section.

```
REPORT: PROCEDURE;
        ...
        declarations, etc.
        ...
MONTHLY_REPORT: ENTRY;
        ...
        code for monthly report
        ...
        GO TO COMMON;
WEEKLY_REPORT: ENTRY;
        ...
        code for weekly report
        ...
COMMON: common code used for both reports
        ...
        ...
        END;
```

12.4.3.4 Exit point

A procedure terminates on execution of a RETURN statement within the procedure. In the absence of an explicit RETURN statement, the terminating END statement of a procedure acts as a RETURN. Other statements which terminate a procedure are the EXIT and STOP statements, although these are defined in terms of task, rather than procedure, termination. The extended form: RETURN(expression) is used to specify the value returned by a function procedure.

As in ALGOL, a procedure may be terminated by the execution of a GO TO statement. Procedure termination may be very complex and difficult to debug if a label variable is used.

12.4.3.5   Type of value returned by a function procedure

The type of the value returned by a function can be specified by a RETURNS attribute forming part of the PROCEDURE statement. If the type is not explicitly specified, it will be determined according to default rules.

Variables of all types can be returned as function values. One important aspect in which PL/I differs from FORTRAN and ALGOL is that functions can return strings, arrays, or record structures. This capability was not available in the early versions of PL/I, but was added during the development of the standard. This addition to PL/I is important in establishing a uniform treatment for both variables and functions and allows function values to participate in array and structure expressions.

12.4.3.6   Local and global variables

Since procedure specifications may be nested inside other procedures, an internal procedure may have both local and global variables. In addition, variables with the EXTERNAL attribute are known throughout all external procedures forming a program.

12.4.3.7   Condition handling

The PL/I procedure is also a unit for the control of condition handling. The procedure is a unit of program over which the *enabling* (or disabling) of a condition is specified by means of a condition prefix. The scope of enablement or disablement is the procedure to which the prefix is attached.

12.5   THE DYNAMIC STRUCTURE OF PROCEDURES: THE SEMANTICS OF PROCEDURE INVOCATION

When a procedure is invoked, a complex sequence of actions is set into motion. These actions, which define the semantics or *dynamic structure* of procedures, are important because of the central position the procedure holds in programming languages.

The actions can be considered under two headings.

- flow of information
- flow of control

12.5.1   Information

- The arguments are prepared for passing to the procedure. In the case of passing by *value* (see below for a description), arguments in the form of expressions are evaluated before entry to the procedure.

- The arguments are associated with the parameters declared inside the procedure. During execution of the procedure, references to parameters may cause transfer of information to or from the procedure.

- As the procedure is entered, local data is made addressable. In block structured languages such as ALGOL or PL/I, data may be dynamically allocated on entry to the procedure.

- On completion of a function procedure, the value computed by the function is transmitted back to the point of call.

12.5.2   Control

- The address of the point of invocation is saved, so that execution can resume after the procedure is completed.

- Control is transferred to the entry point of the procedure.

- When the return point of the procedure is reached, control is transferred back to the address saved before the procedure was entered.

12.6   CALL BY NAME, CALL BY VALUE, AND CALL BY REFERENCE

One of the most important aspects of the dynamic structure of a procedure is the relationship set up between arguments and parameters when the procedure is invoked. Three techniques are commonly used in establishing this relationship; these are referred to as

- call by name,
- call by value,
- call by reference.†

12.6.1   Call by Name

The following model may provide help in understanding call by name. The program must be regarded as a structured text of characters including identifiers, operators, brackets, etc. This text provides the basis for the execution

---

† The first two terms are described in the ALGOL report (Naur *et al.*, 1963). The term "call by reference" was coined by Strachey.

model. As the program is executed, we must imagine a pointer scanning the program, statement by statement. When this pointer reaches a procedure invocation (i.e., a procedure call or function reference), the effect is as if the text at the point of invocation is replaced by a copy of the text of the procedure specification in which systematic changes have been made. The most important change is that each argument is moved into the procedure body as a character string, replacing all occurrences of the corresponding parameter. After the text of the procedure has been transformed, it is executed. The following shows how this model works, for a simple ALGOL program:

Example

A procedure P, has two formal parameters, L and M. The action of P is to increment a counter T by 1, then to add 10 to the value of M and assign the result to L. (The variable T is global to P; that is, it is declared in a procedure surrounding P.) Since there is no "value list" in the procedure specification, all parameters of the procedure are defined as being called by name.

$$\textbf{procedure } P(L,M); \textbf{ real } L,M;$$
$$\textbf{begin}$$
$$T := T+1;$$
$$L := M+10$$
$$\textbf{end}$$

A call of P, with arguments X and $Y+2$, is written:

$$\cdots$$
$$P(X, Y+2);$$
$$\cdots$$

In the model, the statement $P(X, Y+2)$ is replaced by a copy of the text of P, in which all occurrences of the *formal* parameters L and M are replaced by the *actual* parameters, X and $Y+2$. The modified text now has the form:

$$[T := T+1; \ X := Y+2+10]$$

Finally, this modified text is executed.

In some cases, further modifications to the text may be necessary. For instance, the arguments may have to be surrounded by brackets to achieve the intended result.

Example

If the second line of P contained a multiplication rather than an addition:

$$L := M \times 10$$

then the expanded version would be:

$$X := Y + 2 \times 10$$

Because of the higher precedence of multiplication compared with addition, the effect of this would be: $Y := Y + 20$. However, what is intended is:

$$X := (Y+2) \times 10$$

These additional brackets must be regarded as being added in the process of substitution.

Another difficulty arises if the symbolic names used for formal parameters are the same as those used for actual parameters. Although this is allowed in the syntax of ALGOL, if the substitution rules are followed literally there will be dual use of the same identifier in the translated code. To cover such cases, it is specified that parameter names must be made unambiguous by suitable systematic changes to the symbols.

Call by name provides a very powerful, and sometimes very complex, capability.

Suppose we invoke P with the following arguments:

$$P(X, \textbf{if } T < 5 \textbf{ then } Y + 2 \textbf{ else } Y)$$

The effect of the second argument is to reduce the increments applied to Y, once T has reached the value 5.

What will happen if this statement is executed when T has the value 4? Applying the rule outlined above, the conditional expression is copied in to replace the occurrence of M in the body of the procedure. The procedure body is now:

$$T := T + 1;$$

$$X := (\textbf{if } T < 5 \textbf{ then } Y + 2 \textbf{ else } Y) + 10:$$

This puts the test after the execution of the statement $T := T + 1$, so the effective value given to X is $Y + 10$, rather than $Y + 12$. The delayed evaluation of the expression in the body of the procedure text must be carefully considered in using such forms of argument.

To summarize, in call by name, each occurrence of the parameter name is conceptually replaced by the "form" of the argument—an exact copy of the text of the argument, subject to certain changes to avoid ambiguity. Each copy may produce a different answer when executed, depending on its position in the called procedure. A coding technique in which this is exploited is "Jensen's device" (see below).

The replacement method briefly described above is known as the "copy rule" and is described in the ALGOL report as follows.

> **4.7.3.2 Name replacement (call by name).** Any formal parameter not quoted in the value list is replaced, throughout the procedure body, by the corresponding actual parameter, after enclosing this latter in parentheses wherever syntactically possible. Possible conflicts between identifiers inserted through this process and other identifiers already present within the procedure body will be avoided by suitable systematic changes of the formal or local identifiers involved.

The copy rule, although useful as a descriptive model, does not provide a suitable method for implementing call by name—compilers do not have the procedure text available for copying nor could the copied text be directly executed even if it were available. In implementing call by name, it is usual to distinguish between calls in which the argument (actual parameter) is a single identifier (call by simple name) and those in which it is an expression. In the first case, it is sufficient to pass an address to the called procedure. However, in the case of an expression, the address passed to the called procedure may be that of a routine which will compute the value of the expression. Routines for such a purpose were given the name "thunks" by Ingerman and their use is described in Ingerman (1961), Irons and Feurzeig (1961), and Grau, Hill, and Langmaack (1967).

12.6.2 Call by Value

In call by name, account is taken of the form of procedure arguments. However, in many cases the action of a procedure is governed only by the *values* of the arguments. It is, of course, always possible to freeze the value of an expression by assigning it to a variable which is then passed to the procedure. However, this requires the introduction of a superfluous variable, and other effects may result from such an assignment.

ALGOL recognized the need for an alternative to passing arguments by name, and introduced the technique known as call by value which has the effect of fixing the argument values before the procedure is entered. Again, we quote the ALGOL report for a description:

> **4.7.3.1. Value assignment (call by value).** All formal parameters quoted in the value part of the procedure declaration heading are assigned the values of the corresponding actual parameters, these assignments being considered as being performed explicitly before entering the procedure body. The effect is as though an additional block embracing the proce-

dure body were created in which these assignments were made to variables local to this fictitious block with types as given in the corresponding specifications. As a consequence, variables called by value are to be considered as nonlocal to the body of the procedure, but local to the fictitious block.

Thus, to specify call by value in ALGOL, the programmer must write a list of the parameters to be treated in this way in the value list at the head of the procedure specification.

Example

> **real procedure** *interpolate* ($f,x,X1,X2,tolerance$);
> **value** $X1,X2,tolerance$;   ←the value list
> **real** $f,x,X1,X2,tolerance$; ←specification part
>> **begin**
>>   . . .
>>   procedure body
>>   . . .
>> **end**

In this procedure, $X1$, $X2$ and *tolerance* are value parameters and f and x are name parameters.

The effect of call by value is to transmit an R-value rather than an L-value, to use the terminology described in Chapter 9. Consequently, it is not possible to access the location of a value parameter from within the procedure. In particular, it is not possible to assign to a value parameter—a value parameter may only be on the right-hand side, never on the left-hand side, of an assignment statement in the body of the procedure.

12.6.3   Call by Reference

The third technique for passing arguments is call by reference (or call by address). In this, the calling program passes a reference to each argument; in an implementation, this will normally be a machine address. Call by reference is an important technique which combines some of the properties of both call by name and call by value.

When the arguments are simple variable names, the addresses of these variables are passed to the called procedure. If there is a subscripted argument, say $A(I, J)$, then the values of I and J are evaluated at the point of call, so that the location of the element is fixed before the called procedure is entered. From within the procedure, it is possible both to access the values of the arguments and (since their locations are available) to set them.

When the arguments are expressions, there are two possible interpretations of call by reference, which have different effects. The first is to pass a reference to some code which computes the expressions. This is the method of "thunks" described above, and reproduces the effect of call by name. The second method is to evaluate the expression outside the procedure and to pass an address where this computed value is to be found. This technique is frequently used in FORTRAN implementations and forms the basis for the method of passing arguments in PL/I.

In PL/I, variables are specially created to contain the values of expression arguments and are called "dummy variables." It is defined in PL/I that dummy variables are created

- for arguments of a procedure invocation which are expressions, constants, or function references;

- for arguments which do not "match" the expected parameters, and for which some form of conversion is therefore required.

Clearly, the circumstances governing the creation of dummy variables are important to the semantics of procedures. In effect, the creation of a dummy variable transforms a call by simple name into a call by value. Note that, in contrast with ALGOL, the choice of method, rather than being a fixed part of the procedure specifications, is controlled by the way in which the procedure is called.

The creation of dummy variables for constants removes one of the undesirable features of many FORTRAN implementations, in which it is possible to alter the values of constants by assigning to the corresponding parameters in the subprogram. Since FORTRAN constants are usually held in a constant pool for use by the whole program, it is possible in many FORTRAN compilers to change their values from within a subprogram. The creation of a dummy variable prevents this.

It can be seen that call by reference provides both the effect of call by value and the basic form of call by name in which a simple variable is passed (call by simple name). This flexibility led to call by reference being adopted as the only method of passing arguments in PL/I. Viewing the three methods, it is obvious that call by value is not sufficiently powerful to serve as the only method, since it does not allow parameters to be the target of assignments in the called procedure. Call by name is certainly powerful enough; the problem is that in its general form it causes difficulty in implementation. The adoption of call by reference as the only method of argument passing results in a possible deficiency in the language, that of passing an expression to a procedure. Although this cannot be directly expressed with call by reference, a similar effect can be achieved if the programming language allows procedure names to be passed as arguments. The required expression can then be represented as a procedure whose name is passed to the called procedure.

Example

In PL/I, to pass the expression $(x^2 + y^2)$ to a procedure called AREA, we can specify a procedure E:

```
E: PROCEDURE RETURNS(FLOAT);
   RETURN(X**2 + Y**2);
   END;
```

The procedure is invoked by writing CALL AREA(E).

Within the procedure AREA, E may appear in several value-denoting positions. When these are evaluated, the latest value of X and Y will be used.

12.7   FURTHER TOPICS

We next consider a number of topics related to the design and use of procedures. They illustrate the types of conflict which often arise in language design, between flexibility and freedom of expression, reliability and integrity of data, and efficiency of execution.

12.7.1   Built-In Functions

Most languages include a set of built-in functions which are a part of the language. In many respects, built-in functions are similar to the operators of a language. For example, we can look on exponentiation (e^x) and square root ($\sqrt{x}$) as unary (one-argument) operators on x. There is no essential difference between such operators and arithmetic operators such as $+, -, \times$ and $\div$. Syntactically, they are usually represented in programming languages in functional notation—we generally write SQRT(x) rather than $\sqrt{x}$. This is primarily because of the limited character sets in which programming languages have to be represented. (Even APL, which has gone further than most languages in developing operator notation, has had to introduce nonstandard notations for mathematical functions such as logarithm, sine, cosine, etc.)

The selection of a set of built-in functions is an important part of programming language design. Among the reasons for including a function as "built-in" are the following.

■   **Frequency of use**

This is the most strongly weighted reason. There is little published evidence on the frequency of such use; however, square root, sine, cosine, logarithm, and exponential are among the functions most widely used by engineers and scientists.

The introduction of "business" versions of small calculators indicates some possible standard functions for such users, including statistical functions, built-in calendar functions, etc.

- **Necessity for use**

Some functions, although their frequency of use may be low, provide information which it may be impossible to obtain by other means. Examples in PL/I include DIM (the number of dimensions of a PL/I array variable), COMPLETION (the completion status of an event variable), and the functions DATE and TIME.

- **Efficiency**

Many built-in functions, such as the trigonometric functions, sine, cosine, etc., can be computed with the arithmetic facilities found in most programming languages. However, the efficiency of execution would be much less than that obtainable from hand-coded or microcoded versions of the same functions.

- **Accuracy**

Some functions, although they can in principle be coded using the arithmetic facilities of a language, are so sensitive to errors in computation that accurate answers cannot be achieved. The arithmetic operators supplied as part of a high-level language are themselves the result of a compromise in matters of precision, rounding, etc. By coding functions in machine code, techniques may be used which are not available *via* the arithmetic facilities of the language.

Although most built-in functions are mathematical and computational, some are more closely related to the system. For example, Peter Naur (1964) recommended the inclusion of a class of "environment enquiries"—built-in functions by means of which a programmer could obtain information regarding the system on which a program is running. The functions suggested by Naur include those relating to data representation, storage capacity (or rather, remaining capacity), program check, and backing store. Environment enquiries are included in ALGOL 68 (van Wijngaarden *et al.,* 1969).

In most cases, built-in functions are computed by means of subroutines. In designing these, as much attention must be paid to their design reliability, accuracy, and speed as is paid to the hardware in the arithmetic units of a computer.

Virtually all mathematical functions can be expanded in the form of Taylor series, familiar to students of elementary analysis. However these expansions are not usually suitable for computation, since a large number of terms are usually needed for acceptable accuracy. An alternative technique is to represent the function, within a specified domain, in terms of what are known as Chebyshev polynomials (see Lanczos, 1956). These are polynomials which, for successively higher degrees, alternate in sign an increasing number of times within a specified domain. (This is usually restricted to the interval between 0 and 1.) It can be shown that any continuous function can be represented to an arbitrary degree of accuracy in terms of such polynomials. The advantage of expressing a function in terms of Chebyshev polynomials is that, for a given degree of polynomial, a function can be expressed to a greater degree of accuracy than with a Taylor series.

An extensive discussion of methods of computing mathematical functions is given in *Computer Approximations* by Hart, *et al.* (1968). This book reviews the most commonly used methods of computation, gives suitable driver subroutines, tables of coefficients, and estimates of accuracy for a wide range of commonly used mathematical functions. Chebyshev polynomials are described in Lanczos (1956) and Clenshaw (1962). See also Volder (1971) and Walther (1971) for a technique for computing mathematical functions particularly suited to small calculators.

Another important part of the design of built-in functions is to decide what action is to be taken when for some reason a result cannot be computed. This may arise either because the argument lies outside the domain in which the function is defined, or because some arithmetic condition such as overflow, underflow, zerodivide, etc. has occurred during execution of the subroutine. In many languages, this decision is left to the implementors of the language. Hill (1971) discusses the general problem for user-written functions and recommends the introduction of an extra parameter representing a label to be branched to in case of error. This only provides a partial solution to the problem of locating and recovering from errors in built-in functions, and requires a good deal of effort on the part of the user in setting up the code for the error labels. In PL/I, the ON statement can be used to monitor the computation of built-in functions and this provides a more general and flexible method of implementing Hill's suggestion.

12.7.1.1   Syntactic problems associated with built-in functions

The method of naming built-in functions must allow them to be recognized, without declaration, as a part of the language. The rules should allow functions like *sine, log, square root* to be recognized easily. The names must not conflict unduly with other names used for variables in the system. Finally, it is desirable that users should be able to replace the built-in functions of the language by their own versions of function procedures, coded with special attention to precision, speed, etc.

These requirements provide a rather difficult syntactic problem. One approach used in early systems was to establish a special naming convention, in which the set of possible names for special functions (called *system names*) would be distinguished by a special character not used in other names. However, in many current languages, the names of built-in functions follow the normal convention for constructing names in the language. In some cases, built-in function names are reserved words (i.e., they may not be used for other variables).

We have pointed out the similarity of built-in functions to the operators of a language. One advantage of operators, in most languages, is that they can accept operands (i.e., arguments) of different types. Thus the operator + (plus) is well-defined for different kinds of arithmetic operand—integers, floating-point numbers, fixed-point numbers, etc. This property has to be carried over to built-in functions, if they are to have the same flexibility as built-in operators. Furthermore, if user-defined function procedures are going to be allowed to replace the built-in functions, they must also have this capability. It is this reasoning which led to the introduction of the GENERIC attribute in PL/I.

12.7.2 The PL/I GENERIC Attribute

The operation represented by + in the expression $(A + B)$ has a different meaning if

> A is *fixed, B* is *float*
>
> A is *float, B* is *fixed*
>
> A is *float real, B* is *float complex*

and so on.

Similarly, the trigonometric functions, SIN, COS, TAN, etc., may be used with a variety of types of argument: *fixed, float, complex, array,* etc., and may have different meanings according to these different types. PL/I functions whose meaning depends on the types of their arguments are called *generic*—Strachey has used the term "polymorphic," perhaps an etymologically more appropriate word.

The GENERIC attribute of PL/I allows the construction of procedures with the generic property of the built-in functions and operators. Such procedures might be used to replace the existing built-in generic functions, or to allow extensions of the language according to similar principles.

In effect, a GENERIC entry name represents a set of procedures, each of which corresponds to a certain combination of argument types. The selection of the appropriate member of a GENERIC set is statically determinable from the types of the arguments used and may be carried out by a compiler.

The syntax of the GENERIC attribute is:

```
generic-attribute::=
 GENERIC(member-spec[,member-spec]...)
member-spec::=
 entry-expression WHEN({descriptor|*}
 [,{descriptor|*}]...)
```

An entry-expression is an entry constant, an entry name or a function returning an entry value. A descriptor is a set of attributes which controls generic selection. This set need not be complete and is not completed by defaults. Each descriptor corresponds to an argument position in a reference to a generic procedure. In interpreting a reference to a generic function, the choice of the appropriate member of the set is made by comparing the attributes of the arguments with the attributes in the descriptors. This comparison is made by taking each set of descriptors in turn, from left to right. An asterisk (*) denotes that selection is not to be made on the basis of a given argument. A member of the set of generic procedures is selected as soon as a set of descriptor attributes has been found which is a subset of the argument attributes. Conceptually, a generic reference is replaced by a reference to the selected member but with the original argument list. This equivalent reference determines how the arguments are converted to match the parameters.

12.7.3   Recursion

There are two senses in which the term *recursion* is commonly used in programming.

A recursive *definition* is one in which an object is defined in a way that involves some form of circularity. A familiar example is the definition of an expression, which states that an expression may itself contain an expression. Recursive definitions are also widely used in the ALGOL Report (see Appendix) to denote the arbitrary repetition of an element.

The recursive *use* of a procedure is a dynamic form of recursion. There are two forms, the first in which a procedure P calls itself (*direct* recursion), the second in which P calls another procedure which in turn calls P (*indirect* recursion).†

There is a close connection between recursive definitions and the use of recursion, since processing recursive structures is most naturally and efficiently accomplished by means of recursive procedures.

---

† Rutishauser (1963) points out that indirect recursion accounts for the majority of cases in which recursion is useful.

To some, recursion lies at the heart of computing. In his monograph, Barron (1968) suggests that recursion will eventually have as significant an effect on programming as did the invention of subroutines, since it provides an effective means of assembling large programs in a hierarchical manner.

Many of the types of examples which are normally used for illustrating recursion come from mathematics and from systems programming. There has been comparatively little development of recursive methods in commercial data processing. Although this may in part be due to the different nature of commercial problems, there is also a circular effect, the absence of recursion in COBOL and other commercial languages leading to the neglect of what might be an extremely useful technique. There is much scope for novel work here, for recursion can often provide advantages which are not always obvious. For an example, see Herz (1972).

Many program and data structures used in language systems are recursive in nature, and the use of recursion in compilers and operating systems arises naturally. An illustration of its value can be seen in the following example. Consider an elementary language consisting simply of a set of functions acting on prescribed arguments. In such a primitive language, recursion is needed to express the repeated application of functions an arbitrary number of times; it provides a similar facility to that provided by *iteration* in languages based on sequential flow and assignment.

Examples

Suppose we wish to express an integral power of a number in a primitive language containing only a multiplication function, **mult.** If the value of the exponent is known, a power can be represented by repeated application of **mult,** e.g., t^3 can be expressed functionally:

$$\textbf{mult } (t, \textbf{mult}(t,t))$$

However, it is not possible to represent a general function: t^n in this way, since, without knowledge of the value of n, it is not known how many applications of **mult,** and hence how many nested sets of brackets, are needed. This difficulty can be overcome by defining a recursive function, *power,* as follows:

$$power \ (t,n) ::= \textbf{ if } (n=1) \textbf{ then } t$$
$$\textbf{else}(\textbf{mult}(t,power(t,n-1)))$$

Recursion is a powerful primitive operator, one of a small number of basic operations which, in the mathematical theory of computability, can be proved adequate for computing any effectively computable function.

There are a number of mathematical functions which are conveniently defined recursively and which lend themselves to computation by recursive procedures. These include *factorial* (n) and *greatest common divisor* (m,n).

factorial(n)—the most commonly used illustration of recursion. For any positive integer, *n, factorial*(*n*) has the value

$$n.(n-1).(n-2) \ldots 3.2.1$$

and there is a relationship

$$factorial(n) = n.factorial(n-1).$$

The value of factorial(1) is 1 and the following ALGOL procedure computes *factorial*(*n*) for positive integral values of *n*.

> **integer procedure** *factorial*(*n*);
>
> **value** *n*; **integer** *n*;
>
> > *factorial* : = **if** *n* = 1 **then** 1 **else** *n* × *factorial*(*n*−1);

A corresponding program in PL/I would be

```
FACTORIAL: PROCEDURE (N) RECURSIVE;
           DECLARE N FIXED;
           IF N=0 THEN RETURN (1);
               ELSE RETURN(N*FACTORIAL(N-1));
           END;
```

Note that in PL/I the procedure has to be specified as RECURSIVE. This point is discussed further below.

Greatest common divisor—gcd (m,n)—(or highest common factor) of two integers *m* and *n* is the largest number which divides exactly into both *m* and *n*. An algorithm for *gcd* was among the earliest algorithms to be published and was given in Euclid's *Elements,* Book 7. The Euclidean algorithm can be informally described as follows.†

We first note that, since

$$gcd(m,n) = gcd(n,m)$$

it is possible, without loss of generality, to assume that $m \geq n$. The steps in the algorithm are as follows

1) Divide *m* by *n*, giving a remainder *r.*

2) If *r* = 0 (i.e., *m* is a multiple of *n*) then the value of the *gcd* is *n.*

3) Otherwise, replace (*m,n*) by (*n,r*) and return to step 1.

---

† For further discussion and analysis of Euclid's algorithm, see Knuth (1969) Vol. 2, Chapter 4. A generalization of the algorithm to compute the gcd of polynomials is discussed by Brown (1971).

An ALGOL procedure for this is as follows:

> **integer procedure** *gcd* (*m,n*);
>
> **value** *m,n;* **integer** *m,n;*
>
> *gcd:* = **if** *n>m* **then** *gcd* (*n,m*)
>
> > **else if** *m* = 0 **then** *n*
> >
> > **else** *gcd(n,remainder(m,n))*;

These two examples of algorithms are both very simple ones; more complex numeric problems which can be usefully solved by recursion include:

solution of polynomial equations,

methods of integration,

evaluation of functions defined by recurrence relations.

It is when we come to problems lying outside numerical analysis that recursion assumes its most significant role. Its scope of application includes the analysis of data structures, combinatorial problems, and syntax analysis. These arise in text processing, in language translation, and in many branches of systems programming.

As shown above, recursion can be used to represent an arbitrary number of applications of a function. An example of its use in symbol manipulation is in the evaluation of expressions.

A simple form of unbracketed expression such as

$$A + C - D * E$$

in which identifiers alternate with operators, can be evaluated without recursion, provided all operators have the same precedence. The method is to scan the string from left to right, building up the result in a single register or variable (call this : R). The next operator is then applied to the result R and the next operand. For example, the stages in the evaluation of the above expression are:

```
load A in R
add C to R
subtract D from R
multiply R by E
```

(Note that the absence of precedence rules gives an unfamiliar result; E multiplies the whole result, not just D).

Next consider expressions in which brackets or parentheses are used to group items together, such as

```
A + B * (C − D * E)
(L + M * (N − P)) / Q.
```

The method of evaluation is much the same as before, except that the "next operand" may now be either an identifier or a bracketed expression. The evaluation process recurses each time a left bracket is encountered, returning a value—the value of the operand—each time the corresponding right bracket is met.

The stages in evaluating the first expression are as follows, bearing in mind that unbracketed operations are evaluated from left to right:

```
load A in R
add B to R
multiply R by R'
              |
              | where R' is formed as follows:
              |
         load C in R'
         subtract D from R'
         multiply R' by E
```

The indentation shows where recursion takes place. In the section of the program in which the bracketed expression is being evaluated, the register R is replaced by another temporary register R', although the value of R must be preserved until the recursion ends.

Note that the result obtained from this evaluation is still not the normal result obtained from most programming languages. In most languages, multiplication has a higher "precedence" than addition and this affects the order of application of the operators. (See Chapter 9.)

Many structures encountered in systems programming are recursive in nature. Examples include:

arithmetic expressions,

block structure,

nested statements such as the *if* statement,

record structures.

Most list-processing languages have recursive data structures which are processed by means of functions. Recursion provides the means of achieving repetitive application of these functions. In these languages, operations like copying a list are most naturally achieved recursively. This may seem strange to those more familiar with the assignment operations of other languages. However, it should be remembered that a *list* is a more powerful type of data structure than the storage-based structures of many widely used languages. Copying a list is not the same type of operation as moving the contents of a segment of core storage, as in a group MOVE in COBOL. The operation of copying a list must reproduce the interrelationships between the elements of the structure, as well as the data contained within it.

Example

A list-processing function to copy a list is as follows:

> **list procedure** *copy* (*L*); **list** *L*;
>
> *copy* : = **if** *atom* (*L*) **then** *L*
>
>   **else** *cons*(*copy*(*head*(*L*))*copy*(*tail*(*L*)));

The function constructs a new list by extracting the head and tail of *L*, then extracting the head and tail of what remains, . . . , and so on, until an *atom* or element is found which is finally used in the constructed list (**if** *atom* (*L*) **then** *L*). The copy is built up by the use of the constructor function, *cons*.

    (The example is written in an ALGOL-like version of LISP, in which the LISP functions CAR and CDR are represented by the functions *head* and *tail*. See Woodward, 1966.)

12.7.3.1 The implementation of recursion

Although elegant and efficient techniques for implementing recursion have been developed (see for example Dijkstra, 1960) many compiler writers, when faced with small machines and large languages, have omitted recursion from the subsets they have chosen. For example, the official ISO subset of ALGOL (see Appendix) does not include recursion.

    As can be seen from the example on expression evaluation, when a function is entered recursively, it is necessary to preserve the "environment" of the previous evaluation. This means that new storage is needed for each level of recursion. In general, it is not known in advance how much storage will be needed, because this depends on the maximum depth of recursion. As the recursion "unwinds," this storage, incorporating results calculated in earlier stages, is released. Fortunately, the need for storage comes in a disciplined pattern; the first storage to be needed for a nest of recursions is the last to be released. The pattern of storage needs is matched by a *stack* method of storage allocation, and most methods of implementing recursion make use of a stack or push-down store at execution time.

A run-time stack may have to be supplemented by other mechanisms for recording the current status of the machine. For example, when a procedure is passed as an argument to a recursive procedure, the current depth of nesting must be recorded at the point of transmission.

It can be seen that the inclusion of recursion in a language may involve the introduction of mechanisms that would not otherwise be included. Thus there may be a difference in efficiency between the treatment needed for recursive procedures and the minimum treatment needed for nonrecursive procedures. Two ways of dealing with this have been followed.

- A compiler may analyze the flow of control in the program, testing for calls which may be recursive, and generating more efficient code when it can be shown that recursion is impossible. The analysis can be effected by means of a connection matrix as described by Warshall (1962). With this approach, it is difficult to produce optimum results in all cases, since it is sometimes not easy to determine when recursion cannot arise. These borderline cases will have recursive code generated for them.

- The language may have a rule requiring the user to state when a procedure may be called recursively. This approach was suggested by Strachey and Wilkes (1961). It is adopted in PL/I, where the option RECURSIVE must be specified with any procedure which is to be called recursively.

A more radical approach is to construct machines in such a way that the implementation of recursion is natural. Stack machines (Burroughs, 1961; Iliffe, 1972) simplify the implementation of recursion so that it is practicable for all procedures to be treated as recursive. This stack can be used for other purposes than recursion and can be incorporated as part of a high-level design for machines.

12.7.4   Side Effects

The main purpose of a function procedure is to compute a value, for use in an expression. During execution of a function procedure, however, there may be changes to data known outside the scope of the function itself. A function whose execution influences other data values is said to produce "side effects."

Example

A graph-plotting program plots the temperature of a furnace against time. Temperature readings are stored on a reel of tape on which they have been automatically recorded. After suitable initialization, the plotting program contains a loop:

```
DO T = T1 TO T2 WHILE (RANGE);
   XPLOT = T;
   YPLOT = READING;
   ...(code for plotting the graph)
   ...
END;
```

The function procedure READING may be written to obtain the next temperature from the tape, possibly testing for validity, converting the scale, correcting for instrument errors, etc.

```
READING:
        PROCEDURE RETURNS(FLOAT);
        DECLARE TEMP FLOAT;
        READ FILE (READINGS) INTO (TEMP);
        ...
        ..code for validating TEMP...
        ...
        RETURN(TEMP);
        END;
```

The function READING thus produces a side effect, since each time it is called the tape is advanced, producing a new value in the variable TEMP.

The previous example shows one of the most common types of side effect, in which I/O action in the function procedure alters the state of the machine. It is possible to have side effects without input-output, however.

Example

For the purpose of a survey it is necessary to choose towns in various regions of a country. Function procedures corresponding to each region, which return the name of a town, based on a selection technique which may be special to the region, are defined. When all towns in a region have been selected, a global variable is set to indicate that no more towns from that region are available.

The procedure for towns in the WEST might be as follows:

```
WEST: PROCEDURE RETURNS (CHAR(20));
        DECLARE W_COUNT FIXED INITIAL(N4);
        ...Code for selecting name...
        W_COUNT = W_COUNT - 1;
        IF W_COUNT <= 1 THEN W = '0'B;
        RETURN (NAME);
        END;
```

Here, W is a bit string of length 1 which is declared outside the procedure

WEST. It may be used to test whether there are any remaining towns for the survey:

```
DO I = 1 BY 1 WHILE (W);
   TABLE (I) = WEST;
END;
```

When the list of towns is exhausted, the function produces a side effect by setting the value of the global variable, *W*.

Side effects have to be considered in language design because of their influence on the meaning of a program. The point at issue is whether the behavior of a program with side-effects is well defined. For example consider the following pair of procedures:

```
N: PROCEDURE RETURNS(FIXED);
 DECLARE (S,T) FIXED STATIC EXTERNAL;
 T=T+1;
 RETURN (S*T);
 END;
M: PROCEDURE RETURNS(FIXED);
 DECLARE (S,T) FIXED STATIC EXTERNAL;
 S = S+1
 RETURN (S*T);
 END;
```

Each invocation of *M* and *N* will produce a new value. Furthermore, an invocation of *M* will affect subsequent values of *N,* and vice versa.

Now consider the values of expressions involving *M* and *N*. For example, consider:

```
(M+1) * (N+1)
M**2 + N**2
A(M)  + B(N)
```

where *A* and *B* are arrays.

It is clear from such examples that to define the values of expressions involving functions with side effects is much more difficult than when *M* and *N* are simple variables.

There are many other kinds of side effect, including those arising from the use of different names for the same data, sometimes called *aliasing*. Some of these cause difficulties in implementation, because the generation of even moderately efficient code in a compiler requires some simplification and commoning of references. Problems of compiler writing in the presence of side effects are described by Spillman (1971).

Some languages have rules to establish the meaning of programs with certain kinds of side effect. For example, in a statement of the form

$$A(L) = B(M) + C(N)$$

it may be defined as part of the language (as it is in COBOL and PL/I) that the values of L, M, and N are all established before the assignment is made. However, as soon as one such case is defined, it is often possible to construct others in which further ambiguity may arise. In spite of attempts to clarify the interpretation of side effects, it is seldom possible to include a full definition of all cases in which they may be used. From the user's point of view, it is best to avoid them, unless it can be made clear exactly when, and for what purpose, they are being employed.

12.7.5   Jensen's Device

This technique (originated by J. Jensen of Regnecentralen, Copehagen) makes use of the considerable power of call by name. To use the technique, a procedure is written with two or more *name* parameters. The body of the procedure is written in such a way that one or more of these parameters is updated during invocation of the procedure. In writing a procedure call, the arguments presented must be such that they are in some way interrelated—for example, by sharing a common variable. This is the variable which is updated during the procedure invocation. Because of the copying effect of call by name, changes in the updated parameter are reflected in changes in other parameters which depend upon it.

For example, consider the following procedure:

> **real procedure** *sum(start,increment,finish,term,variable)*;
>> **real** *term;*
>> **integer** *start, increment, finish, variable;*
>> **begin**
>>> **real** *s*;
>>> *s*: = 0;
>>> **for** *variable*: = *start* **step** *increment* **until** *finish*
>>>> **do** *s* : = *s* + *term*;
>>> *sum* : = *s*
>> **end** *sum*

If the procedure *sum* is invoked with simple arguments, such as

$$sum(1,2,10,X,Y);$$

it merely forms a multiple of the fourth argument—in this case, 5 times X, and the fifth argument Y is irrelevant. However, if the arguments presented to it are related as suggested above, a different kind of result follows. Consider the call

$$sum(2,2,100,A[x]/x,x);$$

If the rules of call by name are followed this will form the sum:

$$\frac{A[2]}{2} + \frac{A[4]}{4} + \frac{A[6]}{6} + \cdots \frac{A[100]}{100}$$

The power of Jensen's device is considerable and it is a technique that can be programmed in ALGOL 60, but not in most other languages. One of its disadvantages is that it is difficult to separate the design of the procedure body from that of the procedure call—each must be written with considerable care, since when using call by name a compiler is unable to detect errors in the same way as with more straightforward parameter mechanisms.

A discussion of Jensen's device, including further illustrations and an alternative proposal for treating array references, based on a lambda-calculus approach, is given in Rutishauser (1967).

12.7.6   Procedures as Data

In most programming languages, a careful distinction is made between data and programs. Data, in the form of variables, may be created, accessed, modified, and assigned. On the other hand, programs are treated as static objects, remaining essentially unchanged during a computation.

The situation is different with assembly languages, where it is possible to write programs which modify themselves during execution. Instructions may be altered or replaced, and new instructions may be created, in a way that is out of the question with most high-level languages. By such means, programs of great ingenuity and elegance can be constructed. The intuitive feeling of most programmers, namely that languages which allow instruction modification are inherently more powerful than those which do not, is discussed and confirmed in a paper by Elgot and Robinson (1964). It is therefore natural to consider extending the capability for modifying program text to high-level languages. The extent to which this is possible depends largely on the amount of compilation performed in a system and the extent to which programs are "bound" to the data they process.

An extensive capability for program modification is available in LISP (McCarthy *et al.,* 1962). The whole foundation of LISP is the construction of "functions" from "forms," and their subsequent evaluation. This provides great power but imposes an interpretive mode of execution on the system, with a resulting effect on efficiency. Later versions of LISP have moved away from this approach, allowing a greater degree of binding, and bringing LISP closer to more conventional languages.

Another means of constructing new functions from existing ones is provided by the ability to apply some but not all the arguments of a function.

For example, suppose we are given the "form" $Y**X$, which has two variables. Then, by giving X the value 2, we get a function in Y which might be called "square." If X has the value 3, we get the function "cube," and so on. The interactive language POP-2 (Burstall and Popplestone, 1971) allows functions to be defined in this way, by means of what is called *partial application*. This allows some of the formal parameters of a function to be made into what are called *frozen formals,* producing a new function with fewer parameters.

When treating programs as data, it is usual to represent a program or part of a program by a symbolic name. There is a problem in dealing with such names, since for a given program, there are two associated values: one the value of the text itself as a string, the other the value obtained by executing the program. The distinction between an evaluated and an unevaluated function is most important in languages which allow the manipulation of forms and expressions. For example in LISP, FUNCTION and QUOTE, which take a single expression as argument, denote that the expression is to be returned without evaluation.

When we come to compiled, rather than interpreted languages, the problems of manipulating programs as data become somewhat more difficult. If we are to maintain the compiling nature of the system, it is no longer possible to consider the direct execution of program text. Also, the binding carried out by a compiler reduces the flexibility of treatment that may be applied to procedure variables, compared with the treatment possible in interpretive languages such as LISP.

A facility for handling programs as data is provided by the ENTRY data type of PL/I. (The term ENTRY is used rather than PROCEDURE, because PL/I allows multiple entry points to a procedure. Each one of these entry points can be regarded as a distinct object.) Entry variables enjoy the full privileges of any "control" type of data, and can be assigned, compared ($=$ and $\neg =$), form a part of any data structure, and be a parameter or returned value from a function procedure.

Entry variables are declared with the attribute ENTRY, and to distinguish the declaration of a variable from that of a simple entry name (or entry constant) the keyword VARIABLE must also be written. The number of parameters expected and the type of each parameter may be specified, as well as the type of the value returned by a function.

Example

```
DECLARE P ENTRY VARIABLE(FLOAT,FLOAT,BIT(1)) RETURNS(FLOAT);
```

The full rules for declaring a PL/I entry variable are perhaps unduly complicated because of their interaction with the default and implicit rules of the language. The general principle is that code for invoking procedures by means of entry variables can be simply generated at compile time. Thus the entry constants that may be assigned to an entry variable must have a consistent set of parameters (i.e., same number of parameters and same types).

When entry variables are used, it is not necessary to fix the names of procedures to be invoked in a source program. The procedures may be represented by entry variables whose values may be dynamically assigned in the calling code. In spite of the considerable complexity of language and implementation introduced by entry variables, they provide considerable power and flexibility for writing interpreters and other programs whose flow of control depends on the data presented during a computation.

12.8 SUMMARY: ASPECTS OF PROCEDURE DESIGN

Procedure design is vital to any programming language, since the procedure is the most powerful tool for exploiting and extending the power of a language. However, there are many conflicting factors which makes such design an unusually difficult exercise in balance and judgment.

Looking first at the static structure, simplicity of procedure syntax can be achieved by 1) restricting the number of data types in the language, 2) allowing only a single point of entry to (and exit from) procedures, and 3) by restricting the largest unit of compilation and execution to a single procedure. These constraints reduce the declarative information needed with the procedure specifications. The syntax can be made simpler still if the language is *typeless,* so that no type declarations for arguments, parameters, function values, etc. have to be given.

The following factors tend to complicate the procedure syntax:

■   a large variety of data types in the language,

■   multiple entry and exit points,

■   "independent" compilation of procedures.

As more such features are added, the complexity of the design tends to be compounded. For example, the inclusion of a large number of data types may lead the language to adopt a "default" mechanism. When this is added to facilities for independent compilation, it adds further complexity to the rules for determining the types of arguments, parameters, and function procedures.

However, simplicity is not the only requirement for procedure design, and some of the features listed above, especially the facility for compiling procedures independently, contribute greatly to the convenience and effectiveness of programming in a given language.

Of the languages discussed above, ALGOL has the simplest procedure syntax. This simplicity is partly due to the lack of provision for independently compiled procedures. One aspect of ALGOL syntax that has caused some concern is the need to distinguish between name and value parameters in the *called* procedure, rather than in the calling code.

FORTRAN procedures also have a simple structure. Although FORTRAN allows separate compilation of subprograms, transfer of information across the program/subprogram boundary is considerably simplified by the FORTRAN approach to type matching and checking. Broadly speaking, FORTRAN does not require any checking of types to be made across such boundaries. Types must "match" for valid and predictable results, but FORTRAN compilers require the user to take responsibility for this matching of types. In this case, simplicity is achieved at considerable expense either in extra work on the part of the user or in diminished reliability.

PL/I has the most complex procedure syntax of the languages considered, since it incorporates all the facilities described above, plus a means of enabling the detection of ON conditions. As noted above, such a combination of features tends to produce more complexity than the sum of the parts. In compensation, PL/I offers considerable flexibility in procedure specification and use.

On the question of dynamic structure, one of the major points of difference among the three languages reviewed is in the method of passing arguments. Of the three types, call by value is only suitable for passing information into the procedure and does not allow new values to be returned from a procedure by means of its parameters. It is therefore not suitable as the *only* method of argument passing. Call by name is conceptually simple, though difficult to implement in its full generality. It is also unnecessarily inefficient when the objective is to pass the value of an expression; in this case, repeated evaluation of the expression is unnecessary and the alternative (assignment of the value to an auxiliary variable before passing) may be inconvenient. The third method of passing, by reference, has the merit that it can serve as the sole method of passing and can be implemented efficiently on most machines.

As the syntax of procedures is made more complex by including extra features and options, an increasing problem in implementation is faced. In some cases, the extra work of examining further alternatives and generating a greater variety of code types can be carried out at the time of compilation. Such increases need not have an unduly adverse effect on the efficiency of execution of a program, although it may considerably lengthen the time of compilation. However, some features of language design lead to code which must be executed when the program is run rather than when it is compiled. Examples include general call by name, dynamic data structures, and the passing down of ON condition handling. For features such as these, the behavior of a program might depend on the actual data encountered in a program, on the set of procedures already invoked, or on some similar characteristic which cannot be detected when the program is compiled.

In designing and implementing a language, the value of language features to the users of the system have to be weighed against any degradation in efficiency which might result from their use. If the procedure structure is too primitive, valuable advantages in convenience and economy of programming may be lost. If it is too complex, the complexity of code needed to implement the procedure interface may be such that procedures cannot be used with full freedom.

12.8.1 Other Forms of Procedure

The classical form of procedure described above, which forms a dominant feature of standard programming languages, evolved from the design of subroutines originally developed for early computing machines (see, for example, Wilkes, Wheeler, and Gill, 1957). However, this is not the only possible basis for the design of program modules.

Consider the sequence of actions which take place when a subroutine procedure is invoked (Fig. 12.2). For simplicity, we take a procedure, *P*, with a single entry point, a single exit point, and no internal branches.

In this form of call, the relationship between *M* and *P*, the calling procedure and the called procedure, is asymmetric. This lack of symmetry can be seen by considering the sequence in which the statements of *M* and *P* are executed. On transfer from *M* to *P* (the procedure **call**), the first statement in the body of *P* is always executed first. On transfer from *P* to *M*, (the **return**), *M* is resumed at the last point of control. During its execution, *P* remains in a subservient role relative to *M*.

Two other forms of procedure are considered below. The first, the *coroutine*, retains the sequential nature of operations, but as the name suggests has a more symmetric relationship between the calling and called code.

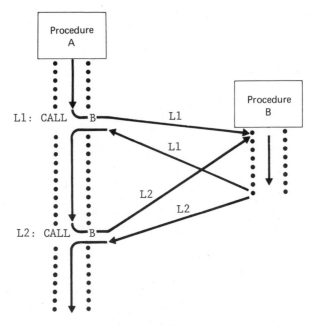

Fig. 12.2 Invoking a subroutine

The second form, the asynchronous or *task* procedure of PL/I, has the same hierarchic form as a subroutine; however operations in the called and calling procedures are no longer carried out in a single stream of sequential operations but may be executed in parallel instead.

12.8.2 Coroutines

The term *coroutine* was coined by M. E. Conway, whose paper is a good introduction to the subject. In coroutines, there is no master/slave relationship, as there is between a calling program and a subroutine or function. Only one coroutine procedure can be in execution at one time, but while it is active, it is in complete control. The control of sequencing in coroutines is shown in Fig. 12.3.

As each call is made, execution takes up from the last active point in the procedure; control passes like a thread, interleaved between the two sections of code. Since there is no sense in which a calling procedure is "higher" than the called, there is no "return" as there is with subroutines or functions and any coroutine can call another, provided its name is known at the point of invocation.

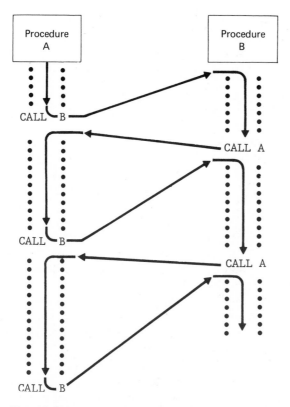

Fig. 12.3 Invoking a coroutine

An advantage of coroutines is that they make it easier for programs with complex sequencing logic to be written as separate modules. This is because the programmer does not have to establish all details of the sequencing structure in such a program.

Among the uses of coroutines are:

- processing data lists and format lists,
- constructing multi-pass processes,
- handling simulation problems.

Example

Suppose a *data list* consists of items A1, A2, ... and a *format list* consists of items F1, F2, ..., then an input statement can be subdivided into two processes. The first reads items of data, while the second converts this data according to the format list. The two processes can be written as two coroutines.

READ coroutine   CONVERT coroutine

```
READ A1          L: CONVERT A1
CALL CONVERT        CALL READ
READ A2             CONVERT A2
CALL CONVERT        CALL READ
...                 ...
...                 ...
READ An             CONVERT An
CALL CONVERT        CALL READ
GO TO NEXT          GO TO L
```

Note the simplicity and independence of each routine. The usual convention in I/O programming that the data list controls the items processed and the format list may be re-used (as discussed in Chapter 11) is handled by the GO TO statements at the end of each coroutine.

Although it is possible to develop new languages for representing coroutines, the facilities can also be provided by extending existing languages. Two capabilities are required, one to deal with the flow of control, the other with the methods of handling data.

Firstly, a method of sequencing is needed which allows control to be transferred to the point of a procedure that was most recently activated. This can be achieved by storing a current label with the procedure whenever any transfer is made. For this, some means of storing label values is needed. One method of doing so is by means of the label variable in PL/I.

The other need is for a means of communicating data between coroutines and for this purpose it is usual to use some form of global data. Fisher (1972) points out that ALGOL **own** variables provide the facility needed for coroutine communication, but in fact any form of global data which is preserved between calls will suffice. Thus, FORTRAN COMMON or PL/I STATIC EXTERNAL data can be used. There is perhaps some advantage to the ALGOL and PL/I approach, since the scope rules make the shared variables inaccessible except in the limited scope in which their names are known.

Gentleman (1971) gives an example of an extension to FORTRAN to allow the construction of coroutines.

12.8.3 PL/I Tasking

In the form of procedure activation known as a *task,* there is, as with subroutines and functions, a hierarchic relationship between the calling program and the called. However, instead of a single sequence of actions, the elementary operations in a set of tasks may be executed in parallel.

It is helpful to distinguish between the specification of a task as a sequence of program statements and its dynamic execution. The two aspects are illustrated in Fig. 12.4.

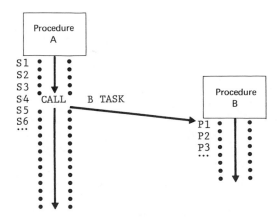

Fig. 12.4 Invoking a PL/I task

The actions of a task are represented by the statements in a procedure block, therefore, no unit smaller than a procedure can represent a PL/I task. A task is activated by the execution of a CALL statement. To distinguish this from a normal CALL statement, a *task option* must be included with the call; this is indicated by one or more of the following forms.

TASK   (task-name)

EVENT   (event-name)

PRIORITY(expression)

Any one of these, written with a CALL statement, indicates that a new task is to be started.

After execution of a tasking call, there are two streams of control: one for the calling program, which continues in execution, the other for the called procedure. Thus the CALL statement $S4$ in Fig. 12.4 has two successors, $S5$ and $P1$. The statements in the two tasks follow the normal rules of sequencing. It should be noted that although

$S1, S2, S3, S4, S5, \ldots .$

$P1, P2, P3, P4, P5, \ldots .$

each form a sequence, nothing can be said about the relative sequencing of the *S*-sequence and the *P*-sequence.

In Chapter 10, the major requirements for controlling parallel processes are summarized. Among the facilities needed are means for controlling the sequence of operations and for sharing and protecting data. We next relate these general requirements to the special case of the tasking facilities in PL/I.

As noted above, a PL/I task is started by the execution of a CALL statement with a task option. The variables nominated with a task option are used in controlling the execution of the task. In addition to starting a task, two key operations are terminating the task and synchronizing it with other activities in the system.

A task is initiated by execution of a procedure; it is ended on termination of the procedure, i.e., on execution of a RETURN statement returning control to the point of call. There is also a task terminating statement, EXIT, which terminates the current task. The STOP statement terminates the "major" task (i.e., the task initiated at the outset of the program) and hence all subsidiary tasks.

In many cases where parallel procedures are used, one procedure may process data provided by another procedure. To make sure that such data is available for processing, the parallel streams of actions may need to be synchronized during their execution. One or more of the tasks may be delayed until a certain condition has been fulfilled. For this, a *wait* state is introduced, a state of a procedure in which no action is currently taking place, although the procedure has not terminated. The key statement for task synchronization is the WAIT statement, which puts the "current" task (i.e., the task in which it is executed) into the wait state, until one or more nominated events are complete.

The WAIT statement refers to event variables; these are elementary items of control data introduced specifically for the control of task operations. A task waiting on a given event variable will remain in the wait state until the completion bit of the variable is set to '1'B. (This bit may be set by the system or by the program.)

Example

```
WAIT(EV)
```

This puts the current task into the wait state until *EV* is set to the value '1'B.

```
WAIT(EV1,EV2,EV3) (2)
```

This puts the current task into the wait state until any two of the three event variables are set to the value '1'B.

In a still more general form, an expression may be used:

```
WAIT(EVENTARRAY) (K)
```

This puts the current task into the wait state until K of the event variables in the array have been set to the value '1'B.

Data is shared between tasks by means of the parameter mechanism and by specifying it as global data to the called procedure. A certain measure of protection may also be obtained by means of the scope rules of procedures.

BIBLIOGRAPHY

Ayers, J. A., "Recursive programming in FORTRAN II," *CACM,* Vol. 6, No. 11, Nov. 1963, pp. 667–668.

Shows how the FORTRAN II compiler can be "tricked" into executing a recursive program. A call of a procedure by itself is achieved by passing a dummy move. The required pushdown store is achieved by auxiliary machine-language routines.

Barron, D. W., *Recursive Techniques in Programming,* London: Macdonald; New York: American Elsevier, 1968.

Brown, W. S., "On Euclid's algorithm and the computation of polynomial greatest common divisors," *JACM,* Vol. 18, No. 4, Oct. 1971, pp. 478–504.

Burstall, R. M., R. J. Popplestone, *POP-2 Reference Manual,* Edinburgh: Edinburgh University Press, 1971.

Clenshaw, C. W., *Chebyshev Series for Mathematical Functions—National Physical Laboratory Mathematical Tables, No. 5,* London: HMSO, 1962.

Conway, M. E., "Design of a separable transition-diagram compiler," *CACM,* Vol. 6, No. 7, July 1963, pp. 369–408.

The first available published article on coroutines, although the term appears to have been originally introduced by Conway in 1958.

Dahl, O. J., B. Myhrhang, K. Nygaard, *Simula 67, Common Base Language,* Publication No. S-2, Norwegian Computing Center, 1968.

Dijkstra, E. W., "Recursive programming," *Numerische Mathematik,* Vol. 2, No. 5, Oct. 1960, pp. 311–318.

Elgot, C. G., A. Robinson, "Random-access stored-program machines, an approach to programming languages," *JACM,* Vol. 11, No. 4, Oct. 1964, pp. 365–399.

A mathematical paper, in which a model for discussing computability, with a closer correspondence to "real" machines than, for example, the Turing machine, is derived. The effect of allowing instruction modification is shown to increase the power of a machine in certain circumstances.

Fisher, D. A., "A survey of control structures in programming languages," *SIGPLAN Notices,* Vol. 7, No. 11, Nov. 1972, pp. 1–13.

Gentleman, W. M., "A portable coroutine system," Information Processing 71, *Proc. IFIP Congress 71,* North Holland, 1972, pp. 419–424.

Describes extensions to FORTRAN which allow coroutines to be used. The paper contains an interesting discussion of the uses of coroutines.

Goldstein, A. J., "Recursive techniques in problem solving," *Proc. AFIPS 30,* SJCC, 1967, pp. 325–329.

Grau, A. A., "Recursive processes and ALGOL translation," *CACM,* Vol. 4, No. 1, 1961, pp. 10–15.

This describes a translation process related to that of Samelson and Bauer, 1960, (see reference in Chapter 9), but based on "tokens" or syntactic elements rather than single symbols. Grau points out that ALGOL has an elaborate bracket structure, while machine language is essentially bracket-free. One of the tasks of a translator is to decompose a bracketed structure into a bracket-free, sequential structure; as Grau points out, this is essentially a recursive process. (He claims that the other task of a translator, that of replacing the sequential form by target language, is "simple." This indicates a gulf between the two schools of compiler writing—the essentially theoretical, academic type such as Grau, and the "industrial" school, in which machine language generation occupies a much more dominant position than that of syntax analysis.)

Grau, A. A., U. Hill, H. Langmaack, *Translation of ALGOL 60,* New York: Springer-Verlag, 1967.

Hart, J. F., E. W. Cheney, C. L. Lawson, H. J. Maehly, C. K. Mesztenyi, J. R. Rice, H. G. Thacher, C. Witzgall, *Computer Approximations,* New York: John Wiley, 1968.

A reference work on methods of constructing computer approximations for mathematical functions—including square and cube roots, exponentials and hyperbolic functions, logarithms, direct and inverse trigonometric functions, gamma functions, error functions, Bessel functions, and elliptic functions. There is an extensive introduction to the methods used, and a valuable feature is the provision of several alternative versions giving different accuracies and ranges.

Herz, J. C., "Recursive computational procedure for two-dimensional stock cutting," *IBM Journal of Research and Development,* Vol. 16, No. 5, Sept. 1972, pp. 462–469.

The cutting-stock problem (which requires minimizing the loss of material in cutting a given rectangle of material into a set of smaller rectangles) has been tackled by iterative algorithms. This paper describes a recursive program which is faster than the iterative solution.

Hill, I. D., "Faults in functions, in ALGOL and FORTRAN," *Computer Journal,* Vol. 14, No. 3, Aug. 1971, pp. 315–316.

Discusses what action should be taken if the calculation of a value from a function procedure is either impossible or bound to be erroneous because of a faulty argument or other cause. The problem is to know what kind of value, if any, is to be returned to the point at which the function is used. Several alternatives are examined, the recommended method (suitable for ALGOL but not FORTRAN) being to give the function an extra parameter, a label, which is branched to if an error arises.

Hoare, C. A. R., "Procedures and parameters: an axiomatic approach," *Symposium on Semantics of Algorithmic Languages,* E. Engeler (ed.), Lecture notes in mathematics 188, New York: Springer-Verlag, 1971, pp. 102–116.

This discusses procedure specification and the rules of arguments and parameters from an axiomatic point of view. Proofs of several well-known techniques of parameter passing are indicated and proved valid provided the following restrictions are observed.

1) A distinction is made between (formal) parameters $\{x\}$ subject to assignment in a procedure and those $\{v\}$ which are not.

2) Let the arguments of a call which correspond to the parameters $\{x\}$ be $\{a\}$ and those corresponding to $\{v\}$ be $\{ev\}$.

3) Then the restriction is that all of $\{x\}$ are distinct, and none of $\{x\}$ appears in $\{ev\}$.

Iliffe, J. K., *Basic Machine Principles,* London: Macdonald; New York: American Elsevier, Second edition, 1972.

Ingerman, P. Z., "Thunks. A way of compiling procedure statements with some comments on procedure declarations," *CACM,* Vol. 4, No. 1, Jan. 1961, pp. 55–58.

Irons, E. T., W. Feurzeig, "Comments on the implementation of recursive procedures and blocks in ALGOL 60," *CACM,* Vol. 4, No. 1, Jan. 1961, pp. 65–69.

Johnston, J. B., "The contour model for block-structured process," *SIGPLAN Notices,* Vol. 6, No. 2, Feb. 1971, pp. 55–82.

The contour model is a theoretical and pedagogic model developed by Johnston for demonstrating the dynamic structure of languages, especially block structure languages such as ALGOL or PL/I. An abstract representation of an algorithm is distinguished and given separate treatment from a record of its execution, expressed as a series of snapshots or instantaneous pictures of the program state. These snapshots are represented in diagrams employing the notion of a *contour,* a boundary which corresponds to the block boundaries of the program. This notation was first presented at a SIGPLAN meeting in February 1971, in which several papers were presented showing the contour model applied to a number of machine and programming systems.

Kain, R. Y., "Block structures, indirect addressing, and garbage collection," *CACM,* Vol. 12, No. 7, July 1969, pp. 395–398.

Shows how the parameter mechanism is related to block structure. Shows the relationship between parameters and results, global variables, and local variables in the caller—called relationships.

Lanczos, C., *Applied Analysis,* Englewood Cliffs, N.J.: Prentice-Hall, 1956.

Includes a description of the use of Chebyshev polynomials.

Maynard, J., *Modular Programming,* London: Butterworth's, 1972.

McCarthy, J., *et al., LISP 1.5 Programmer's Manual,* Cambridge, Mass.: MIT Press, 1962.

McIlroy, M. D., "Mass produced software components," (in) *Software Engineering,* Naur and Randell (eds.), Brussels: Scientific Affairs Divison, NATO, 1969.

In this paper (abstracted), McIlroy outlines the justification of a software components industry, offering families of "routines" for any given job. The user would consult a catalogue of routines, offering various degrees of precision, robustness, time-space performance, and generality.

Morris, J. H., "Protection in programming languages," *CACM,* Vol. 16, No. 1, Jan. 1973, pp. 15–21.

Emphasizes the protective role played by procedures in programming languages.

Naur, P., "Environment enquiries—machine-dependent programming in common languages," *Algol Bulletin,* AB-18, Oct. 1964, pp. 26–33.

Rice, H. G., "Recursion and iteration," *CACM,* Vol. 8, No. 2, Feb. 1965, pp. 114–115.

Defines primitive recursive functions and comments on the wide range of such functions. An exception is Ackermann's function, which is recursive but not primitive recursive. Discusses Kleen's result that there is a general iterative process which can be used to evaluate recursively defined functions, even when they are not primitive recursive.

Rutishauser, H., "The use of recursive procedures in ALGOL 60," (in) *Annual Review in Automatic Programming,* R. Goodman (ed.), Vol. 3, Elmsford, N.Y.: Pergamon Press, 1963, pp. 43–51.

Describes indirect and direct recursivity, with two examples drawn from numerical methods, Romberg integration, and eigen-value determination. In the author's experience, most useful applications of recursion are of the indirect kind.

Rutishauser, H., *Description of ALGOL 60,* New York: Springer-Verlag, 1967.

A detailed description of ALGOL 60, by one of the original members of the ALGOL committee. Contains many interesting illustrations of the use of ALGOL and comments on the design of the language.

Spillman, T. C., "Exposing side-effects in a PL/I optimizing compiler," *Proc. IFIP Congress,* 1971.

The presence of side effects in programs makes it difficult to carry out certain optimizing transformations such as common subexpression elimination and code movement. PL/I has a number of features which allow the user to access data by alternative means. This paper considers ways of detecting such usage in order to carry out optimization. Among the PL/I language facilities discussed are: the DEFINED attribute, expressions involving pointers and offsets, assignments to label and entry variables, etc.

Strachey, C., M. V. Wilkes, "Some proposals for improving the efficiency of ALGOL 60," *CACM,* Vol. 4, No. 11, Nov. 1961, pp. 488–491.

Objections to *side effects* and unnecessary generality commonly found in programming languages are stated. The proposals to improve ALGOL include:

specification of *recursive* on procedures which may be called recursively;

introduction of a new entity called a *function* which is guaranteed to have no side effects;

addition of a method of calling procedures to be known as "call by simple name";

introduction of significant comments (hints to the compiler) in the form of a "note" statement.

Strong, H. R., "Translating recursion equations into flow charts," *Journal of Computer and System Sciences,* Vol. 5, No. 3, June 1971, pp. 254–285.

Strong, H. R., S. A. Walker, "Properties preserved under recursion removal," *SIGPLAN Notices,* Vol. 7, No. 1, Jan. 1972, pp. 97–103.

Recursion removal is the transformation of programs containing recursive calls by equivalent nonrecursive programs, generally by introducing some form of stack. Effectively, this is what must be done in implementing languages which allow recursion on conventional machines. This paper discusses the effect of this transformation on the properties of the program.

Volder, J. E., "The CORDIC trigonometric computing technique," *IRE Trans.,* Vol. EC-8, No. 3, Sept. 1959, pp. 330–334.

Refer also to the paper by Walther (1971).

Walther, J. S., "A unified algorithm for elementary functions," *AFIPS Proceedings,* Vol. 38, SJCC, 1971, pp. 379–385; AFIPS Press, 1971.

Describes a class of algorithms (originally devised by J. E. Volder, 1959) which can be unified to provide a single algorithm for computing a wide range of trigonometrical and other mathematical functions. The algorithm family has been used in small desk-top computers, where its simplicity and accuracy are an advantage.

Warshall, S., "A theorem on Boolean matrices," *JACM,* Vol. 9, No. 1, Jan. 1962, pp. 11–12.

van Wijngaarden, A., B. J. Mailloux, J. E. L. Peck, C. H. A. Koster, "Report on the algorithmic language ALGOL 68," *Numerische Mathematick,* Vol. 14, 1969, pp. 79–218.

Wilkes, M. V., D. J. Wheeler, S. Gill, *The Preparation of Programs for an Electronic Digital Computer* (Second edition), Reading, Mass.: Addison-Wesley, 1957.

Woodward, P. M., "List processing" (in) *Advances in Programming and Non-numerical Computation,* Elmsford, N.H.: Pergamon Press, 1966.

EXERCISES

12.1 The function procedure, BIGGEST, returns the value of the largest of the arguments presented to it. Discuss the problems of programming this function:

   a. when the types of the arguments may be mixed,

   b. when the number of arguments may differ for different calls of the function.

(These problems have had to be overcome in the MAX functions of FORTRAN and PL/I. A study of these functions and their implementation can form an introduction to this problem.)

12.2 One way of achieving the effect of a variable length argument in high-level languages is to pass the arguments as a data structure. You are asked to write a procedure whose first argument is a floating-point value of x, the next being the coefficients of an nth order polynomial in x. The procedure computes the value of the polynomial for the given value of x, returning the result as a floating-point number. Write this program when the set of coefficients are passed as a *vector* (FORTRAN, ALGOL, APL, . . .) or as a *stack* (PL/I, POP2, . . .).

12.3   Design two kinds of procedure declaration which make it clear whether the procedure is to be invoked as a subroutine or as a function and enable syntactic checking to be carried out to ensure that the .correct returning assignments are carried out.

How different from ALGOL or PL/I is this design, and what is gained or lost in the design?

12.4   A procedure is to be written which takes a table of 100 values and sorts them in ascending order. Show how this may be programmed

   a. if the table is passed as an argument to the procedure;

   b. if the table is treated as a global variable, shared between the calling and called procedures.

12.5 How would the above program be written if the table were to contain N values, where N is an arbitrary number?

12.6 Write a PL/I procedure for the GCD algorithm. (Hint: use the built-in function MOD.)

12.7 What advantages in implementation, if any, would there be if

   a. the depth of recursion in an ALGOL or PL/I compiler were limited to, say, 10?

   b. What limitations might be placed on the problems that could be solved with such a compiler?

12.8 Write a recursive procedure to convert an integer stored in binary form to decimal, removing leading zeros.

12.9 The following ALGOL program is designed to exchange the values of the two arguments x and y:

procedure *exchange* (x,y); **real** x,y;

  begin real k;

   $k := x$;

   $x := y$;

   $y := k$;

  end

Outline each step of the dynamic behavior of this program:

    a. for arguments A,B;

    b. for arguments X[I], I.

12.10 The following exercise is to be carried out on a "production" compiler to which you have access.

    a. Discover the minimum code involved in entry to a subroutine procedure call with two arguments (i.e., measure the time taken for a procedure with no body).

    b. Discover, or estimate, the *extra* overhead when there is an additional entry point.

    c. Compare this with twice the value obtained in the first paragraph.

    d. Establish some guidelines for saying when multiple entry points, rather than multiple copies of the same procedure, should be used.

12.11 The ALGOL procedures INCV and INCN each have a single formal parameter, passed by value and name respectively, and return the value of this parameter incremented by 1. Similarly, the procedures ADDV and ADDN return the value of the formal parameter, added to itself.

    The procedures are defined as follows:

> **real** a,b;
>
> **real procedure** $INCV(x)$; **value** x; **real** x;
>   **begin** $x := x + 1$; $INCN := x$ **end**
>
> **real procedure** $INCN(x)$; **real** x;
>   **begin** $x := x + 1$; $INCN := x$ **end**
>
> **real procedure** $ADDV(y)$; **value** y; **real** y;
> $ADDV := y+y$;
>
> **real procedure** $ADDN(y)$; **real** y;
> $ADDN := y+y$;

What is the value of a and b, after execution of the following statements?

    1. $a := 1$; $b := ADDV(INCV(a))$;

    2. $a := 1$; $b := ADDV(INCN(a))$;

    3. $a := 1$; $b := ADDN(INCV(a))$;

    4. $a := 1$; $b := ADDN(INCN(a))$;

(This example is due to Robert L. Weil, *CACM*, Vol. 8, No. 6, June 1965, p. 378).

12.12 In FORTRAN, the value returned from a function subprogram F must be assigned to F before a RETURN statement is executed. After the assignment statement has been executed, it is possible to extract the value of F for use in another statement:

```
F = A+1
...
T = F
...
RETURN
```

Describe what happens if a similar piece of code is executed in an ALGOL program.

12.13 Most scientifically oriented languages include the operator *exponentiation*, represented by ** or ↑. Explain why some of these languages also include the built-in function *square root*, although square root(x) can be written as: $x**0.5$.

Appendix

Throughout this book, examples have been given from commonly used programming languages, especially from FORTRAN, ALGOL 60, COBOL, and PL/I. This Appendix provides a brief summary of these languages, a history of their development and a list of references for further reading, including the full language specifications. Further references, including details of other languages discussed in the book, are included in the following general references:

T. E. Cheatham, Jr., "The recent evolution of programming languages," *Proceedings IFIP Congress 1971,* North Holland, 1972.

Infotech State of the Art Reports: No. 7, *High Level Languages* (1972); No. 19, *Commercial Language Systems* (1974), Maidenhead, England: Infotech Information Ltd.

S. Rosen (ed.), *Programming Systems and Languages,* 1965–1975, New York: McGraw-Hill, 1967.

J. E. Sammet, *Programming Languages: History and Fundamentals,* Englewood Cliffs, N.J.: Prentice-Hall, 1969.

J. E. Sammet, "Roster of programming languages," *Computing Reviews,* Vol. 15, No. 4, Apr. 1974, pp. 147–160.

D. Simpson (ed.), *High Level Programming Languages—The Way Ahead,* (British Computer Society conference proceedings), Manchester, England: NCC Publications, 1973.

FORTRAN

Although not the first "high-level" language to be developed, FORTRAN was the first to gain acceptance for regular use on routine programming tasks. It has been implemented on numerous machines and used for many types of application, not all of them scientific. The success of FORTRAN in such a wide field is something of a paradox, since it was originally developed for a specific machine, the IBM 704, and early versions of the language had a number of machine-dependent features—for example, tests of "sense switch," "divide check," etc.

The first version of FORTRAN was designed and implemented by the Programming Research Group of the Applied Science Division of IBM in New York around 1954–1955. The group was headed by John Backus, and the members of the working committee (listed in the first published reference manual) include R. J. Beeber, S. Best, R. Goldberg, H. L. Herrick, R. A. Hughes (University of California), L. B. Mitchell, R. A. Nelson, R. Nutt (United Aircraft Corporation), D. Sayre, P. B. Sheridan, H. Stern, and I. Ziller. The first FORTRAN compiler included extensive optimization, introduced to overcome the misgivings of many people about the use of a high-level language for routine processing. Although compilation time was slow, the acceptance of FORTRAN as an alternative to assembly-language coding owes a lot to the attention given to object-code efficiency in the first compiler.

In 1958 a revised version of FORTRAN, known as FORTRAN II, was issued, with a highly significant extension—the capability for defining subroutines and compiling them separately. This opened the way to a distinctive style of programming in which a main program embodies the major logic of the application while lower levels of detail are represented as a series of CALL statements to separately developed and separately compiled subprograms.

A later version of FORTRAN known as FORTRAN IV was issued as part of the IBSYS-IBJOB system on the IBM 7090/94. This contained a number of extensions including type statements, logical expressions in IF statements, and DATA and BLOCK DATA statements. At the same time, some of the machine-dependent features of FORTRAN II were removed. For various reasons FORTRAN IV did not completely supplant FORTRAN II and many programming groups continued using FORTRAN II for several years.

A major event in FORTRAN history was the development of a standard version of the language by the American Standards Association (now ANSI). This was the first time a programming language had been standardized and the process was lengthy and difficult. Work continued throughout the period from 1962 to 1966, and the committee defined two standards, one for

FORTRAN, the other for a subset language, Basic FORTRAN. The 1966 version of FORTRAN (ANS X3.9-1966) is the current standard FORTRAN and forms the basis of the discussions in this book. The specifications should be interpreted in the light of clarifications issued by the X3J3 Committee of ANSI, published in 1971.

The European standards body ECMA has also developed a FORTRAN standard between the two ANSI levels. The three levels (two ANSI, one ECMA) are recognized in the proposed ISO recommendation.

Work on a proposed revision to the FORTRAN standard continues in ANSI committee X3J3. Features under serious consideration for this are:

mixed-mode arithmetic,

generalized subscripts,

arrays of up to seven dimensions,

list-directed input-output,

character type data.

Summary of Standard FORTRAN

FORTRAN is a fixed-format language with no block structure. An executable program consists of a main program and any number of subprograms or external procedures.

Character set

26 alphabetic

10 numeric

11 others (blank $= + - * / ( ) , . \$$)

Declarations

Declarations are written in the form of specification statements which, in general, must precede the executable part of a program. In the absence of explicit declarations, implicit declarations are applied according to the first character of the name of the variable.

There are no reserved words in FORTRAN.

Data elements

Variables of the following types may be defined:

integer,

real,

double precision,

complex,

logical.

Literals, but not variables, of type "Hollerith" (i.e., character string) may be introduced.

Data-structures

Arrays of up to three dimensions may be defined; the lower bound of each dimension must be 1. In a FORTRAN main program, array bounds must be constants. In a subprogram, the bounds may be variable ("adjustable" in FORTRAN terminology), but in this case the array name and the variable names denoting the array bounds must be passed as arguments to the subprogram. FORTRAN defines the mapping of array elements onto a linearly addressed store and allows storage sharing by means of COMMON and EQUIVALENCE statements.

Operators and expressions

Arithmetic operators

$$+ \quad - \quad * \quad / \quad **$$

Relational operators

```
.LT. .LE. .EQ. .NE. .GT. .GE.
```

Logical operators

```
.AND. .OR. .NOT.
```

In general, arithmetic expressions must be constructed from operands of the same type, except that real and double-precision operands may be intermixed.

Statements

Executable statements

```
            assignment
            ASSIGN
            GO TO
            Arithmetic IF
            Logical     IF
            DO
            CONTINUE

            CALL
            RETURN
```

```
                    PAUSE
                    STOP

                    READ
                    WRITE
                    REWIND
                    BACKSPACE
                    ENDFILE
```

Non-executable statements

```
                    INTEGER
                    REAL
                    DOUBLE PRECISION
                    COMPLEX
                    LOGICAL

                    DIMENSION
                    COMMON
                    EQUIVALENCE
                    EXTERNAL
                    DATA

                    FORMAT

                    SUBROUTINE
                    FUNCTION
                    BLOCK DATA
```

FORTRAN BIBLIOGRAPHY

Historical

J. W. Backus, *et al.,* "The FORTRAN automatic coding system," *Proc. WJCC,* Vol. 11, 1957, pp. 188–198.

W. P. Heising, "History and summary of FORTRAN standardization development for the ASA," *CACM,* Vol. 7, No. 10, Oct. 1964, pp. 590–625.

Defining documents

ANS X3.9-1966, *American National Standard FORTRAN* and ANS X3.10-1966, *American National Standard Basic FORTRAN,* American National Standards Institute, 1966.

ANSI Committee X3J3, "Clarification of FORTRAN standards—second report," *CACM,* Vol. 14, No. 10, Oct. 1971, pp. 628–642.

ECMA-9, "ECMA Standard on FORTRAN," *ECMA,* Apr. 1965.

ISO Recommendation R1539 *Programming Language FORTRAN,* (First edition) ISO, Jul. 1972.

Related works

R. Bornat, Standard FORTRAN Programming Manual, (Second edition) Manchester, England: National Computing Centre, 1972.

ALGOL 60

In 1955, following a meeting in Darmstadt of the German Association for Applied Mathematics and Mechanics (GAMM), a committee to consider various aspects of communication among computer users was set up. Several subgroups to pursue development of formula translation and allied topics were subsequently set up. Meetings between these groups and various user organizations (USE, SHARE, DUO) and the Association for Computing Machinery (ACM) were later held in Los Angeles in May 1957 to examine ways of exchanging computer information. One aim of these meetings was to develop a single, universal computer language. Professor J. W. Carr, III, then president of the ACM, established an *ad hoc* committee to prepare a report on the development of such a language. The conclusions of this group and a similar GAMM committee contained many features in common and the two groups met jointly in Zurich during May and June of 1958 to prepare a consolidated proposal. This report was published in the *Communications of the ACM* in December 1958. The proposed language was then called IAL (International Algebraic Language), and subsequently became known as ALGOL (ALGOrithmic Language) 58.

The 1958 IAL report was informally written and imprecise in detail, but it created much interest and enthusiasm. The idea of developing a universal language for expressing mathematical computations was widely supported. In Europe, an ALGOL conference was held in Paris in November 1959 and seven representatives from Britain, Denmark, France, Germany, Holland, and Switzerland were selected to work on the language. In the United States, SHARE and USE formed ALGOL working groups and the Communications of the ACM published comments and proposals for the new language. Seven American representatives were selected to work with the European group. The two groups met in Paris in January 1960 to consider a draft report prepared by Peter Naur from the preliminary reports of several preparatory meetings. Several other proposals, including those by McCarthy, Green, Backus, and Perlis, were also considered at this meeting. The authors of the subsequent report, the first published version of ALGOL 60, were: J. W. Backus, F. L. Bauer, J. Green, C. Katz, J. McCarthy, P. Naur, A. J. Perlis, H. Rutishauser, K. Samelson, B. Vauquois, J. H. Wegstein, A. van Wijngaarden and M. Woodger. William Turanski, a member of the American group, was killed in an automobile accident just before the 1960 meeting and the final ALGOL report is dedicated to his memory.

The publication of the ALGOL 60 report was a notable event in programming language history. The language itself—compact and elegant—embodies ideas which have strongly influenced many subsequent languages. It was quickly established as a preeminent way of communicating and publishing algorithms; and important collections of ALGOL algorithms have been published in the *Communications of the ACM, Numerische Mathematik,* and the *Computer Journal.* It has also provided one of the most fertile grounds on which to base work in language theory and experiment, and many ALGOL-like languages have been developed for special purposes and to explore new ideas in language design.

Another important influence of the ALGOL report has been in the introduction of precise and formal methods of language description. The first ALGOL 60 report used a notation proposed by J. W. Backus and amended and extended by P. Naur. This notation, known as BNF (Backus-Naur form), has dominated the field of syntax definition ever since.

One of the simplifications adopted by the ALGOL designers was the omission of facilities for input-output, since they regarded this field as too undeveloped and too machine-dependent for inclusion in a "universal" language. Input-output was expected to be handled by "code procedures," i.e., procedures specifically written for each machine or system in machine language. This decision was much criticized and standard versions of ALGOL developed later include I/O facilities.

ALGOL 60 was adopted as an official language by IFIP and has been standardized by ECMA in Europe.

Summary of ALGOL 60

ALGOL 60 is a free-format language with block structure. A program consists of a single block or compound statement.

ALGOL programs can be represented in three forms: a *reference* language, the primary method of representation and the one from which the others derive: a *publication* language used for communicating programs between humans; and *hardware representations* which recognize the limitations of computing devices.

The following notes discuss ALGOL in terms of its reference language.

Basic symbols

> 52 letters   (upper and lower case)
>
> 10 digits
>
> 52 "delimiters"   (operators, brackets, and punctuation symbols, as well as words such as **for, begin, go to,** etc. These are regarded as single symbols in the reference language.)

Declarations

All variables must be declared—there are no defaults. Declarations of variables are written at the beginning of the block which defines their scope. Procedure declarations are headed by the **procedure** symbol and may be nested to an arbitrary depth.

Data elements

The following types of data element may be declared:

> **integer**
>
> **real**
>
> **Boolean**

Strings and labels, though not available as variables, may be used as actual parameters (i.e., arguments) of procedures.

Data structures

The primary data structure is the array, whose elements may be of type **integer, real,** or **Boolean.** Upper and lower bounds of arrays are not restricted in value and an array may have an arbitrary number of dimensions.

The **switch** is a vector of label values, but is not available as a variable.

Operators and expressions

Arithmetic operators

$$+ \ - \ \times \ / \ \div \ \uparrow$$

Relational operators

$$< \ \leqq \ = \ \geqq \ > \ \neq$$

Logical operators

$$\equiv \ \supset \ \vee \ \wedge \ \neg$$

Sequential operators

> **go to   if   then   else   for   do**

There are three types of expression:

arithmetic,

Boolean,

designational.

Each of these may include an **if** clause, allowing conditional evaluation of the returned value.

Statements

assignment

> **go to**
> **if**
> **for**

procedure (for activation of procedures)

dummy

ALGOL BIBLIOGRAPHY

Historical

J. W. Backus, "The syntax and semantics of the proposed International Algebraic Language of the Zurich ACM-GAMM Conference," *Proc. International Conf. Information Processing,* UNESCO, Paris, London: Butterworths, 1963.

P. Naur, (ed.), "Report on the algorithmic language ALGOL 60," *CACM,* Vol. 3, No.5, May 1960, pp. 299–314.

A. J. Perlis, K. Samelson (for the ACM-GAMM Committee), "Preliminary Report —International Algebraic Language," *CACM,* Vol. 1, No. 12, Dec. 1958, pp. 8–22.

Defining documents

ECMA-2 "Subset of ALGOL 60–ECMALGOL," *ECMA,* Apr. 1965.

ISO Recommendation R1538, *Programming Language ALGOL,* (First edition), ISO, Mar. 1972.

P. Naur, (ed.), "Revised report on the algorithmic language ALGOL 60," *CACM,* Vol. 6, No. 1, Jan. 1963, pp. 1–17; *The Computer Journal,* Vol. 5, 1963, pp. 349–367; *Numerische Mathematik,* Vol. 4, 1963, pp. 420–453.

COBOL

In May 1959 a meeting was held in Washington, sponsored by the U.S. Department of Defense, to consider the possibility of developing a common programming language for business applications. The meeting, which was attended by representatives of government and industry including several computer manufacturers, concluded that such a project was both feasible and desirable. It was at this meeting that there originated the body known as CODASYL (COnference On Data SYstems Languages) which is regarded as the sponsor of COBOL. In fact, CODASYL does not exist as an organization in the usual sense, although its committees and subcommittees work on a wide variety of topics related to data processing, not all of which are connected with COBOL.

Following the meeting, a Short Range Committee under the chairmanship of J. Wegstein (National Bureau of Standards) was set up to examine existing commercial languages and compilers and if necessary to develop a new language. Ideas and information were drawn from many sources, in particular from the FLOWMATIC System developed by Sperry-Rand, the Commercial Translator System designed by IBM, and the AIMACO System developed jointly by the Air Materiel Command and Sperry-Rand. It was decided to proceed with the development of a new language, and the name COBOL (COmmon Business Oriented Language) was adopted.

Interim reports were published in September and December 1959, following which revisions were placed in the hands of an editorial committee consisting of H. Bromberg and N. Discount (RCA), V. Reeves and J. Sammet (Sylvania), and W. Selden and G. Tierney (IBM). This work resulted in the publication of the first COBOL specifications in April 1960.

The publication of these specifications attracted considerable attention, since this was the first time that a group of industry and user representatives had collaborated on the development of such a complex entity as a programming language. The interest and sponsorship of U.S. government departments clearly lent considerable weight to the effort. Several other computer manufacturers and user representatives joined the committee; and a task group headed by J. L. Jones (Air Materiel Command) and G. M. Dillon (DuPont) produced an extensively revised report in June 1961.

Several aspects of the original proposals had been recognized as deficient; and an extended version of the 1961 specifications was produced in November 1962; this version included for the first time the Report Writer feature and the SORT verb.

The next version of COBOL was published in 1965 and contained several modifications and additions, including provision for I/O for mass storage and the inclusion of Table Handling (i.e., array handling).

Further versions of COBOL were published in 1968, 1969, 1970 and 1973, each containing further additions and clarifications. The medium for publishing proposals and additions to COBOL is the *COBOL Journal of Development*.

Standardization of COBOL began in January 1963 with an initial meeting of the X3.4.4 committee of the American Standards Association (now

ANSI). This group developed a standard by August 1966. For the purpose of the standard, and to facilitate subsetting of the language, COBOL was subdivided into a nucleus and eight functional processing modules:

Table handling,

Sequential access,

Random access,

Random processing,

Sort,

Report writer,

Segmentation,

Library.

Throughout this period of development the X3.4.4 group kept in close contact with various international bodies concerned with standardization. After extensive discussions and balloting, the standard was finally published in August 1968 as a U.S. Standard. One organizational change was made in the 1968 specifications, namely the removal of the *Random processing* module from the body of the report to an appendix.

Responsibility for revision of the 1968 standard was given to ANSI Technical Committee X3J4, which started work in 1969 and produced a draft proposal in June 1972. As before, there was close liaison with international bodies, notably ECMA Technical Committee TC6, and several ISO membership organizations. The proposed revision prepared by X3J4 was published in October 1973.

The revised specifications are, like the 1968 specifications, in the form of a nucleus and a set of modules, although these differ from those in the 1968 standard. There are now eleven modules as follows:

Table handling,

Sequential I-O,

Relative I-O,

Indexed I-O,

Sort–Merge,

Report writer,

Segmentation,

Library,

Debug,

Interprogram communication,

Communication.

Summary of Standard COBOL

A COBOL program is divided into four divisions: Identification, Environment, Data, and Procedure. Each division may be further subdivided into sections and paragraphs; in the Identification, Environment, and Data divisions, these are of predetermined structure. The Procedure Division may contain both declaratives and procedural statements. This division may be divided into segments, some of which may be dynamically overlaid during program execution. A program may call another program, although the effects of recursive calls are undefined.

Character set

26 alphabetic

10 numeric

15 other characters

Declarations

Data items, records, files, etc., must be explicitly declared. Such declarations should be complete since there is very little default facility in COBOL. Files are declared in the Environment Division, records and other data items in the Data Division. Declarative sections may also be included in the Procedure Division. Each declarative section contains code for handling error, exception, or debugging conditions.

The programmer must not use any of the COBOL reserved words for identifiers. (There are nearly 300 reserved words in the 1973 document.)

Data elements

Five categories of data may be defined:

alphabetic,

numeric,

alphanumeric,

alphanumeric edited,

numeric edited.

Data elements are defined with the PICTURE clause; the contents of the picture determine the category to which the item belongs.

Data structures

The most important basic data structure in COBOL is the record, which may be subdivided into group items and elementary items. Records may also contain arrays (which are called "tables") of up to three dimensions.

Arrays of records and records containing arrays may be specified. An array subscript must be an integer or simple variable name with an integer value. A special form of subscript called an "index," whose internal form is determined by the implementor of the language, may be used. Indexes may be used in simple expressions using the operators + and −.

Operators and expressions

Arithmetic operators

$$+ \ - \ * \ / \ **$$

Relational operators

```
GREATER  LESS  EQUAL
NOT GREATER  NOT LESS  NOT EQUAL
```

Logical operators

```
AND   OR   NOT
```

Statements

COBOL statements are formed from "verbs," each of which has a distinguishing keyword. The following classification of statements is given in the October 1973 version of the proposed ANSI standard. It will be seen that some verbs occur in more than one category, depending on the attached phrase.

Category	Verbs
Arithmetic	ADD
	COMPUTE
	DIVIDE
	INSPECT (TALLYING)
	MULTIPLY
	SUBTRACT
Compiler directing	COPY
	ENTER
	USE
Conditional	ADD (SIZE ERROR)
	CALL (OVERFLOW)
	COMPUTE (SIZE ERROR)
	DELETE (INVALID KEY)
	DIVIDE (SIZE ERROR)
	IF
	MULTIPLY (SIZE ERROR)

	READ (END or INVALID KEY)
	RECEIVE (NO DATA)
	RETURN (END)
	REWRITE (INVALID KEY)
	SEARCH
	START (INVALID KEY)
	STRING (OVERFLOW)
	SUBTRACT (SIZE ERROR)
	UNSTRING (OVERFLOW)
	WRITE (INVALID KEY or END-OF-PAGE)
Data movement	ACCEPT (DATE, DAY or TIME)
	ACCEPT MESSAGE COUNT
	INSPECT (REPLACING)
	MOVE
	STRING
	UNSTRING
Ending	STOP
Input-Output	ACCEPT (identifier)
	CLOSE
	DELETE
	DISABLE
	DISPLAY
	ENABLE
	OPEN
	READ
	RECEIVE
	REWRITE
	SEND
	START
	STOP (literal)
	WRITE
Inter-program communication	CALL
	CANCEL
Ordering	MERGE
	RELEASE
	RETURN
	SORT
Procedure branching	ALTER
	CALL
	EXIT
	GO TO
	PERFORM

Report writing	GENERATE
	INITIATE
	SUPPRESS
	TERMINATE
Table handling	SEARCH
	SET

COBOL BIBLIOGRAPHY

Historical

An official history of COBOL is given in the October 1973 ANSI document referenced below. The first widely available specifications of the full language were:

COBOL: Initial specifications for a Common Business Oriented Language, Dept. of Defense, U.S. Govt. Printing Office, April 1960.

COBOL-1961: Revised Specifications for a Common Business Oriented Language, Dept. of Defense, U.S. Govt. Printing Office, 1961.

Defining documents

ISO Recommendation R1989, *Programming Language COBOL,* First edition, ISO, August 1972.

Proposed Revision of American National Standard COBOL, ANSI (American National Standards Institute), 1973.

USA Standard COBOL, USAS X3.23-1968, USASI (United States of America Standards Institute), 1968.

PL/I

PL/I started life as a proposal, jointly prepared by a SHARE and IBM committee, for a language intended to provide a substantial advance on the facilities available in FORTRAN. Consolidated work on the proposal started in 1963 and the first published report was issued in March 1964 after only six months' work. The members of the group, known as the "3 x 3 committee" were B. Rosenblatt (Standard Oil of California, Chairman), H. S. Berg (Lockheed), J. L. Cox (Union Carbide), and G. Radin, C. W. Medlock, and B. Weitzenhoffer, all of IBM. Other contributors to this and the later report included T. Martin (Westinghouse), H. P. Rogoway (Hughes Dynamics), and L. Brown, J. Fabri and R. A. Larner of IBM.

Quite early in their work, the group decided that it was impossible to achieve their objectives if they had to produce a language operationally compatible with FORTRAN. The break with FORTRAN was made and the new language was designed with its own distinctive syntax and semantics.

After the March report, much further work was done, additional members of the group including M. D. McIlroy (Bell Telephone Labs) and R. C. Sheppard (Proctor and Gamble, representing GUIDE). A revised report was produced in June 1964. The pace of this work was undoubtedly hastened by the announcement in April 1964 of the IBM System/360, which was announced as providing four compilers for a "New Programming Language" or NPL. As it turned out, the National Physical Laboratory in Teddington, England, took exception to the use of the initials NPL, and the name of the language was shortly afterwards changed to MPPL and finally to PL/I. Responsibility for implementation, and later language, was assigned to the IBM United Kingdom Laboratory in Hursley, which has continued to hold the major responsibility for PL/I within IBM.

Although the 1964 reports of the SHARE committee include a number of concepts incorporated in PL/I, they now provide only an approximate impression of the final language. The reports were written in an informal, abbreviated style, leaving much to the interpretation of the reader. During the early stages of implementation and use of the language, many details had to be made more precise and substantial new sections were added. In the next few years, the language was revised in several areas, including input-output, fixed point arithmetic, the treatment of interrupts, tasking, generic procedures, and the control of default attributes. Major parts were added, including provisions for defining dynamic data structures (the BASED storage class, and the *locator* variables POINTER and OFFSET) and the *compile-time* facilities (proposed in only a limited form in the 1964 documents). Several new string handling primitives have been introduced and, in the proposed PL/I standard, the treatment of array and structure operations has been revised.

In the early stages, language specifications were issued by IBM in a series of documents, bearing the number C28-6571, which described the form of the language as implemented by IBM on System/360 machines. The need for separating the description of the language from its implementation had long been recognized and this led to the publication in March 1968 of a language specification, Y33-6003-0, "intended for the use of implementers and programming language designers concerned with language development and the study of languages." Later versions of this specification define the IBM version of PL/I.

Another important thread in the history of PL/I has been the development of a formal definition of the language. The difficulties of interpreting the original language specifications have been mentioned above: these remained, though to a lesser degree, with the "SRL" specifications. The Hursley group responsible for language and compiler definition resolved that a more technically sound definition was needed and had begun work in this direction in 1964 and 1965. For some time previously, the IBM Vienna Laboratory under H. Zemanek had achieved considerable eminence in methods of formal definition and had done preliminary work on the specification of PL/I syntax. A meeting was held in Hursley in October 1965 between the Vienna and Hursley groups and a plan was set up to produce a "universal language definition" (ULD) for PL/I. The starting point was to be the then current informal specifications to be known as ULD I. This was to be followed by a more rigorous semiformal definition to be produced at Hursley (ULD II) and finally by a completely formalized definition to be produced in Vienna (ULD III). Originally produced in 1968 and revised in 1969, this became *the* ULD for PL/I within IBM, providing a notable advance in rigor and completeness of language definition.

Work on standardizing PL/I began in 1965 and 1966 in the European standards body ECMA and the American Standards Association (now ANSI). When first discussed, the language was undergoing considerable revision and it was not clear that it was ready for standardization. However, in March 1968 IBM presented a document containing the language it considered firmly enough established to be considered. This document, called BASIS/1, became the working document for subsequent activity. The proposed standard for PL/I has been jointly developed by the ECMA and ANSI committees working in parallel, a noteworthy example of international cooperation. The work has involved the study and definition of the existing language, the design of revisions and extensions, and the development of a new notation for language definition, less formal than the Vienna ULD and intended for less specialized readers. Some major differences between the IBM version of PL/I and the proposed standard are as follows.

- The proposed standard does not include the preprocessor facilities.
- A new treatment of array operations has been introduced.
- A new version of the DEFAULT statement has been introduced.

In the following summary, (I) indicates features included in the IBM version of PL/I but not in the proposed ECMA/ANSI standard; (S) indicates features in the proposed standard but not in the IBM version.

Summary of PL/I

PL/I is a free-format language with block structure. A *program* consists of a set of external procedures, each of which consists of a single procedure block, within which other blocks may be nested.

Character set

26 alphabetic   (the IBM version of PL/I includes 3 extra "alphabetic extenders" #, @, and $)

10 numeric

19 special characters   (21 in the IBM version)

Declarations

Explicit declarations of variables are specified by means of DECLARE statements; these may appear at any point in the block which defines their scope. Procedure declarations are delimited by PROCEDURE and END statements and may be nested to an arbitrary depth. In addition to their type, variables may have other attributes, including scope (INTERNAL, EXTERNAL), storage class (AUTOMATIC, STATIC, CONTROLLED, and BASED), initialization (INITIAL), storage sharing (DEFINED). If attributes are omitted, default attributes may be applied as defined by the language. The application of default attributes may be controlled by the DEFAULT statement. If declarations are omitted, contextual declarations may be constructed by the compiler.

There are no reserved words in PL/I.

Data elements

Variables of the following types may be defined:

numeric, having (FIXED or FLOAT) scale, (BINARY or DECIMAL) base, and (REAL or COMPLEX) mode

CHARACTER string

BIT string

LABEL

ENTRY

FORMAT (S)

POINTER

OFFSET

AREA

FILE

TASK (I)

EVENT (I)

Additional type information may be conveyed by precision and scale specifications and by means of the PICTURE attribute.

Data structures

There are two built-in data structures, arrays and record structures, called simply "structures" in PL/I. Composite arrangements of these may be defined, e.g., structures containing arrays, and arrays containing structures. The language allows arbitrary numbers of dimensions and depths of nesting of these structures, although these will normally be restricted in an implementation. Upper and lower bounds of arrays may be denoted by variables. The storage class attributes STATIC, AUTOMATIC, CONTROLLED and BASED give control over the time when storage for data is allocated. In addition, pointers and offsets may be used for constructing linked data structures of arbitrary complexity.

Operators and expressions

Arithmetic operators

$$+ \quad - \quad * \quad / \quad **$$

String operator

|| (concatenation)

Relational operators

$$> \quad < \quad >= \quad <= \quad = \quad \neg=$$

Logical operators

$$\& \quad | \quad \neg$$

Expressions may be freely formed from operands and operators of a wide variety of types.

Statements

Structural Statements

```
PROCEDURE
ENTRY
BEGIN
DO
END
```

Declarative Statements

```
DECLARE
DEFAULT
FORMAT
```

Sequence control Statements

```
                    IF
                    GO TO

                    CALL
                    RETURN

                    STOP
                    EXIT    (I)

                    ON
                    REVERT
                    SIGNAL

                    WAIT
                    POST    (S)
                    CLEAR   (S)
```

null statement

Storage Statements

assignment
```
                    ALLOCATE
                    FREE
```

Input-Output

```
                    OPEN
                    CLOSE
```

Stream I/O

```
                    GET
                    PUT
```

Record I/O

```
                    READ
                    WRITE
                    REWRITE
                    DELETE
                    LOCATE
```

Preprocessor

```
%ACTIVATE    (I)
%assignment  (I)
%DEACTIVATE  (I)
%DECLARE   · (I)
%DO          (I)
%END         (I)
%GO TO       (I)
%IF          (I)
%INCLUDE     (I)
%null        (I)
%PROCEDURE   (I)
```

PL/I BIBLIOGRAPHY

Historical

SHARE Reports: *Report of the SHARE Advanced Language Committee,* March 1, 1964; *Report II of the SHARE Advanced Language Committee,* June 25, 1964.

G. Radin, H. P. Rogoway, "NPL: highlights of a new programming language," *CACM,* Vol. 8, No. 1, Jan. 1965, pp. 9–17.

Defining documents

The IBM version of the PL/I language is defined in:

GY33-6003-2 PL/I Language Specifications (IBM, June 1970).

The proposed ECMA/ANSI standard is contained in working documents issued by ECMA and ANSI. The latest version is BASIS/1–12 (July 1974).

Formal definition

The semiformal definition known internally as ULD II was produced in Hursley by a group including C. D. Allen, D. Beech, R. A. Larner, J. E. Nicholls, and R. Rowe. It was published in the following series of technical notes from the IBM Hursley Laboratory:

TN 3001 (Nov. 1966)   Concrete syntax of PL/I

TN 3002 (May 1967)   Abstract syntax of PL/I

TN 3003 (Oct. 1966)   A PL/I translater

TN 3004 (Nov. 1966)   An abstract interpreter of PL/I

The Vienna definition, embodying a complete formalization of PL/I syntax and semantics, was produced by a group including K. Alber, K.

Bandat, H. Bekic, G. Chroust, M. Fleck, H. Goldmann, V. Kudielka, P. Lauer, P. Lucas, E. Moser, P. Oliva, H. Stigleitner, G. Urschler, K. Walk, and G. Zeisel. The definition was published in the following series of IBM technical reports published by the IBM Vienna Laboratory.

TR 25.087   (June 1968) Method and notation for the formal definition of programming languages

TR 25.095   (June 1966) Formal definition of the PL/I compile time facilities

TR 25.096   (June 1969) Concrete syntax of PL/I

TR 25.097   (June 1969) Translation of PL/I into abstract text

TR 25.098   (June 1969) Abstract syntax and interpretation of PL/I

TR 25.099   (June 1969) Informal introduction to the abstract syntax and interpretation of PL/I

See also the following paper, which summarizes the work on the Vienna ULD:

P. Lucas, K. Walk, "On the formal description of PL/I," *Annual Review in Automatic Programming*, Vol. 6, Part 3, New York: Pergamon Press, 1970.

Related works

D. Beech, "A structural view of PL/I," *Computing Surveys*, Vol. 2, No. 1, Mar. 1970, pp. 33–64.

ABOUT THE AUTHOR

Mr. Nicholls is presently at the IBM Development Laboratory, Hursley, England. After graduating in mathematics at Hertford College, Oxford, he spent five years on production control at one of Tube Investments' steel works, where he was also involved in developing new methods of steel tube manufacture.

He first worked with computers when he joined the United Kingdom Atomic Energy Authority, Capenhurst, where he implemented an early DEUCE computer installation used for production control and large-scale plant simulation.

Mr. Nicholls joined IBM in 1961 to work on systems performance and took part in the design of a high-level language computer. Later he was involved with the early stages of the design of software for the System/360 series. In 1964 he began development of a PL/I compiler for a small machine and was then appointed Design Control manager for PL/I. In this capacity, he was responsible for the design of the internal structure and operating system requirements for PL/I compilers. This led to some of the early work on formal definition of PL/I. At this time, Mr. Nicholls was named Language Manager, in charge of language definition and development.

During 1968 and 1969, Mr. Nicholls was assigned to the IBM Research Laboratory, Yorktown Heights, where he took part in the initial stages of a new system design. As manager of an advanced systems group in Hursley, he has recently been responsible for developing new methods for producing interactive applications.

INDEX

Pages on which definitions appear are set in boldface type.